D0767911

HANDBOOK OF WRITING RESEARCH

HANDBOOK OF
Writing Research

edited by
CHARLES A. MACARTHUR,
STEVE GRAHAM, and JILL FITZGERALD

THE GUILFORD PRESS
New York   London

To Dorothy Hsiao, for her friendship, support, and love.
—C. A. M.

To Karen Harris—wife, colleague, and friend—everything I do is better because of you.
—S. G.

To my parents, Winifred May Fuller Fitzgerald and Robert Cornelius Fitzgerald,
for their unceasing support and love.
—J. F.

© 2006 The Guilford Press
A Division of Guilford Publications, Inc.
72 Spring Street, New York, NY 10012
www.guilford.com

Paperback edition 2008

Printed in the United States of America

This book is printed on acid-free paper.

Last digit is print number: 9 8 7 6 5 4 3 2

Library of Congress Cataloging-in-Publication Data
Handbook of writing research / edited by Charles A. MacArthur, Steve Graham, Jill Fitzgerald.
    p. cm.
   Includes bibliographical references and index.
   ISBN-10: 1-59385-750-0   ISBN-13: 978-1-59385-750-9 (trade paperback)
   ISBN-10: 1-59385-190-1   ISBN-13: 978-1-59385-190-3 (trade cloth)
   1. English language—Rhetoric—Study and teaching—Research—Handbooks, manuals, etc.
2. English language—Composition and exercises—Research—Handbooks, manuals, etc.
3. Report writing—Study and teaching—Research—Handbooks, manuals, etc. 4. Language arts—Research—Handbooks, manuals, etc. I. MacArthur, Charles A. II. Graham, Steven, 1950– III. Fitzgerald, Jill.
   PE1404.H358 2006
   808.'042'071—dc22
                                                                2005010766

About the Editors

Charles A. MacArthur, PhD, is Professor of Special Education in the School of Education at the University of Delaware. Dr. MacArthur's major research interests include understanding writing development and difficulties, designing instruction for struggling writers, applying technology to support reading and writing, and understanding learning processes in inclusive classrooms. He is currently principal investigator of a federally funded research project investigating instruction in decoding and spelling for adult basic education students. He is editor of the *Journal of Special Education.*

Steve Graham, EdD, is the Curry Ingram Professor in the Peabody College of Education and Human Development at Vanderbilt University. Dr. Graham's research has focused on identifying the factors that contribute to writing development and writing difficulties, developing and validating effective instructional procedures for struggling writers, and using technology to enhance writing performance. He is the former editor of *Contemporary Educational Psychology* and the current editor of *Exceptional Children.* He is also the author, with Karen R. Harris, of *Writing Better* (2005) and *Making the Writing Process Work* (1996), and, with H. Lee Swanson and Karen R. Harris, the coeditor of the *Handbook of Learning Disabilities* (2003).

Jill Fitzgerald, PhD, is Interim Dean and Professor of Literacy Studies at the University of North Carolina–Chapel Hill, where she has taught since 1979. Her primary research interests center on literacy issues for multilingual learners and early literacy development in relation to literacy instruction reform efforts. She has received the American Educational Research Association's Outstanding Review of Research Award and (with George Noblit) the International Reading Association's Dina Feitelson Award for Research. She currently serves on editorial boards for several research journals, including the *Journal of Educational Psychology, Reading Research Quarterly,* and *Contemporary Educational Psychology.*

Contributors

Robert D. Abbott, PhD, Department of Educational Psychology, University of Washington, Seattle, Washington

Dagmar Amtmann, PhD, Department of Rehabilitation Medicine, University of Washington, Seattle, Washington

Arnetha F. Ball, PhD, School of Education, Stanford University, Stanford, California

Richard Beach, PhD, College of Education, University of Minnesota, Minneapolis, Minnesota

Virginia W. Berninger, PhD, Department of Educational Psychology, University of Washington, Seattle, Washington

Pietro Boscolo, PhD, Department of Psychology, University of Padova, Padova, Italy

Jill Burstein, PhD, Educational Testing Service, Princeton, New Jersey

Julie Cheville, PhD, Graduate School of Education, Rutgers University, New Brunswick, New Jersey

Carol A. Donovan, PhD, Department of Special Education, University of Alabama, Tuscaloosa, Alabama

Kailonnie Dunsmore, PhD, School of Education, State University of New York at Albany, Albany, New York

Carol Sue Englert, PhD, Department of Counseling, Educational Psychology, and Special Education, Michigan State University, East Lansing, Michigan

Jill Fitzgerald, PhD, School of Education, University of North Carolina–Chapel Hill, Chapel Hill, North Carolina

Tom Friedrich, MA, Center for Writing, University of Minnesota, Minneapolis, Minnesota

Stephen J. Frost, PhD, Haskins Laboratories and Yale University School of Medicine, New Haven, Connecticut

David Galbraith, PhD, Department of Psychology, Staffordshire University, Stoke-on-Trent, Staffordshire, United Kingdom

Margie Gillis, PhD, Haskins Laboratories and Yale University School of Medicine, New Haven, Connecticut

Steve Graham, EdD, Department of Special Education, Vanderbilt University, Nashville, Tennessee

John R. Hayes, PhD, Department of Psychology, Carnegie Mellon University, Pittsburgh, Pennsylvania

Suzanne Hidi, PhD, Department of Curriculum, Teaching, and Learning, Ontario Institute for Studies in Education of the University of Toronto, Toronto, Ontario, Canada

George Hillocks, Jr., PhD, Department of Education and Department of English Literature and Language, University of Chicago, Chicago, Illinois

Ronald L. Honeycutt, PhD, Green Year-Round Elementary School, Raleigh, North Carolina

Brian Huot, PhD, Department of English, Kent State University, Kent, Ohio

Annette R. Jenner, PhD, Haskins Laboratories and Yale University School of Medicine, New Haven, Connecticut

Claudia Leacock, PhD, Educational Testing Service, Princeton, New Jersey

Charles A. MacArthur, PhD, School of Education, University of Delaware, Newark, Delaware

Troy V. Mariage, PhD, Department of Counseling, Educational Psychology, and Special Education, Michigan State University, East Lansing, Michigan

Deborah McCutchen, PhD, Department of Educational Psychology, University of Washington, Seattle, Washington

W. Einar Mencl, PhD, Haskins Laboratories and Yale University School of Medicine, New Haven, Connecticut

Dina Moore, PhD, Haskins Laboratories and Yale University School of Medicine, New Haven, Connecticut

Jeff Munson, PhD, Autism Research Center, University of Washington, Seattle, Washington

Michael Neal, PhD, Department of English, Clemson University, Clemson, South Carolina

George E. Newell, PhD, College of Education, The Ohio State University, Columbus, Ohio

Martin Nystrand, PhD, Department of English, University of Wisconsin–Madison, Madison, Wisconsin

Frank Pajares, PhD, Division of Educational Studies, Emory University, Atlanta, Georgia

Shelley Peterson, PhD, Department of Curriculum, Teaching, and Learning, Ontario Institute for Studies in Education of the University of Toronto, Toronto, Ontario, Canada

Paul Prior, PhD, Department of English and Center for Writing Studies, University of Illinois, Urbana, Illinois

Ruie J. Pritchard, PhD, Department of English Education, North Carolina State University, Raleigh, North Carolina

Kenneth R. Pugh, PhD, Haskins Laboratories and Yale University School of Medicine, New Haven, Connecticut

Gert Rijlaarsdam, PhD, Graduate School of Teaching and Learning, Utrecht University and University of Amsterdam, Amsterdam, The Netherlands

Rebecca Sandak, PhD, Haskins Laboratories and Yale University School of Medicine, New Haven, Connecticut

Ted J. M. Sanders, PhD, Utrecht Institute of Linguistics, Utrecht University, Utrecht, The Netherlands

Joost Schilperood, PhD, Faculty of Arts, Tilburg University, Tilburg, The Netherlands

Katherine Schultz, PhD, Graduate School of Education, University of Pennsylvania, Philadelphia, Pennsylvania

Timothy Shanahan, PhD, College of Education, University of Illinois at Chicago, Chicago, Illinois

Mark D. Shermis, PhD, Department of Educational and Psychological Studies, Florida International University, Miami, Florida

Michael W. Smith, PhD, College of Education, CITE Department, Temple University, Philadelphia, Pennsylvania

Laura B. Smolkin, EdD, Department of Elementary Education, University of Virginia, Charlottesville, Virginia

Liliana Tolchinsky, PhD, Department of General Linguistics, University of Barcelona, Barcelona, Spain

Mark Torrance, PhD, Department of Psychology, Staffordshire University, Stoke-on-Trent, Staffordshire, United Kingdom

Gary A. Troia, PhD, College of Education, University of Washington, Seattle, Washington

Gio Valiante, PhD, Department of Education, Rollins College, Winter Park, Florida

Huub van den Bergh, PhD, Utrecht Institute of Linguistics, Utrecht University, Utrecht, The Netherlands

William D. Winn, PhD, Department of Educational Psychology, University of Washington, Seattle, Washington

Contents

Introduction

Charles A. MacArthur, Steve Graham, *and* Jill Fitzgerald

The power of writing is richly captured in the famous quote: "The pen is mightier than the sword." Although most people recognize that writing is important, they are sometimes confused about the source of its power. With the coming of the atomic age, the quote acquired a new meaning for at least one young writer. He told his teacher that we now know what this saying actually means, that "the period about to end this sentence for just one thing has zillions of unexploded atoms."

Although writing is not really this explosive, it is one of humankind's most powerful tools. It lets us communicate with others who are removed by distance or time, allowing us to maintain personal links with family, friends, and colleagues. Writing connects more than just our immediate circle of associates and loved ones, however. It can foster and preserve a sense of heritage and purpose among larger groups of people. For instance, the Haida Indians in Canada recently transcribed their oral traditions in order to preserve their history, and books such as *Uncle Tom's Cabin* provided a catalyst for antislavery beliefs in 19th-century America (Swedlow, 1999). Writing also provides a flexible tool for persuading others. The first Athenian schools were founded in the fifth century B.C. to teach writing as a rhetorical tool for use in the public forum and law courts (Havelock, 1982). The persuasive power of writing is further demonstrated by pamphlets such as *Common Sense* by

Thomas Paine or Chairman Mao's *Little Red Book*, which influenced the course of history.

Writing's power further resides in its ability to convey knowledge and ideas (Graham, in press). Writing makes it possible to gather, preserve, and transmit information widely, with great detail and accuracy. As a result, writing is integrated into virtually all aspects of our society. Order is maintained through a series of written and codified laws. The administration of most social and political organizations depends upon memos, emails, written bylaws, and so forth. Job seekers must complete one or more written applications and are likely to use manuals and other print material to learn new occupational skills. Scientists and other academics share their findings and ideas in journals and on the web. Even everyday tasks such as cooking a microwave dinner or paying a bill involve following written directions.

Finally, writing provides an important means for personal self-expression. People use writing to explore who they are, to combat loneliness, to chronicle their experiences, and to create alternative realities. The power of writing is so strong that writing about one's feelings and experiences can be beneficial psychologically and physiologically, because it can reduce depression, lower blood pressure, and boost the immune system (Swedlow, 1999; Smyth, 1998).

Despite its importance, there is considerable concern about the writing capabilities of school-age children and youth. This distress was reflected in the 2003 report *The Neglected "R"* by the National Commission on Writing in America's Schools and Colleges. This report asserted that the writing of students in the United States "is not what it should be" (p. 7). This concern appears to be well founded, because findings from the National Assessment of Educational Progress indicated that three out of every four 4th-, 8th-, and 12th-grade students demonstrated only partial mastery of the writing skills and knowledge needed at their respective grade level (Greenwald, Persky, Campbell, & Mazzeo, 1999). The Commission's report provides a wake-up call to those who are interested in writing and its development. We wholeheartedly support the Commission's conclusion that writing needs to be at the forefront of current efforts to improve schools and the quality of education. If such efforts are to be maximized, however, they must draw upon what is known about writing, its development, and effective instruction for all children. In addition, we must apply new analytical tools and research methods to explore further each of these areas and examine the results of our endeavors.

Our overall purpose in this volume is to meet this challenge by bringing together critical reviews of the major theoretical, methodological, and instructional advances that have occurred over the last 15 years in the field of writing research, providing a 21st-century look at writing and writing research. A primary goal is to provide comprehensive coverage of what is known about writing development and instruction, and to point the way for future research. The volume focuses primarily on writing by school-age students rather than college students and adults. Although we have not been able to include all important programs of research, we believe that the volume broadly represents major lines of research on writing, including cognitive and sociocultural perspectives.

The 1970s and 1980s were times of great innovation in the field of writing research, as scholars first applied the theories and methods of cognitive psychology to the study of writing processes, and later used sociocultural theories to understand how the nature and development of writing are determined by social and cultural influences. The past 15 years have been a time for consolidation, extension, and, in some cases, attempted integration of research from wide-ranging[U1] perspectives. From a cognitive perspective, scholars have expanded and refined their theories in attempts to build more detailed models of writing processes related to models of other cognitive processes, including working memory, self-regulation, and reading. From a sociocultural perspective, scholars have likewise refined their theories of how writing develops through social interaction in discourse communities and have studied writing development in a wide variety of school and nonschool contexts. In this introduction, we preview the contents of the volume to aid readers in finding the chapters of most interest to them.

Theories and Models of Writing

The first section focuses on theoretical perspectives and models of writing. In Chapter 1, Martin Nystrand provides a historical perspective, tracing the development of research on writing as a cognitive and social process from the 1970s to the present, beginning with Emig's (1971) classic study of the writing processes of 12th-grade students. In Nystrand's account, the explosion of cognitive research in the 1970s was formed by intellectual currents, such as the growth of cognitive psychology and its application to language processes at institutions such as MIT, Harvard, and Carnegie Mellon, as well as by the development of a new model of English education focused on writing processes as represented by the Dartmouth Seminar of 1966. In addition, writing research was influenced by larger societal forces, such as the "literacy crisis" of the day, open admissions in urban public universities, and federal funding for educational research. The intellectual climate began to change in the 1980s as scholars in language and literacy challenged cognitive conceptions of language and insisted on the importance of social interaction and cultural context to an understanding of writing. In the "postmodern 1990s," the field became increasingly sociocultural as researchers focused on contexts for writing both in school and in a variety of nonschool settings.

John R. Hayes, in Chapter 2, discusses three particularly promising areas for future research. The first area, the role of working memory, is in the mainstream of research on cognitive models of writing. Hayes focuses particularly on research designed to test predictions made by Kellogg's (1999) model of working memory in writing. The second area, the impact of freewriting, originated in the instructional recommendations of Elbow (1973), but has led to research attempting to answer fundamental questions about cognitive processes. Finally, Hayes considers the potential of activity theory as a framework for understanding contextual factors in writing.

In Chapter 3, Gert Rijlaarsdam and Huub van den Bergh summarize the past decade of their research, which has focused on designing cognitive models that can explain individual variation in written products. They claim that it is essential to model cognitive processes dynamically by considering not only *which* processes (e.g., generating, rereading) occur but also *when* in the process they occur and in what order. Using such models with appropriate statistical analyses, they claim to be able to predict large proportions of the variance in the quality of products from writing process measures.

Paul Prior, in Chapter 4, provides a concise summary of the foundations of sociocultural theory in Marxism, pragmatics, and phenomenology, and discusses current writing research based on sociocultural frameworks. Sociocultural theories of writing use activity theory and view writing as a mode of social action rather than just a means of communication. Prior discusses three areas of sociocultural research on writing—analyses of relationships between orality and literacy, schooled literacy and its relationship to broader sociocultural practices, and studies of disciplinary writing and workplace writing in college and in the adult world.

In the final chapter in this first section, Mark Torrance and David Galbraith review theory and research on how the processing limitations of the human mind affect the complex set of cognitive processes required for writing. Their analysis goes beyond general capacity limitations of working memory to discuss specific constraints such as processing bottlenecks, the transient nature of short-term memory, and interactions between memory strategies and capacity. They also discuss research on methods of overcoming memory limitations by developing skills to automaticity, learning memory strategies, and using writing strategies that divide the overall task into manageable components.

Writing Development

The second section of this volume addresses developmental issues. Chapters in this section review research on the emergence of literacy in early childhood, development of knowledge and skills within a cognitive model, connections between brain research and cognitive research on writing, the development of motivation, the importance of self-efficacy, and developmental connections among oral language, reading, and writing. In Chapter 6, Liliana Tolchinsky reviews research on the development of understanding about writing in the preschool years prior to instruction. Children differentiate between writing and drawing before the age of 3 and, well before the development of the alphabetic principle, make distinctions about which letter strings are word-like and how different genres are formatted. Tolchinsky shows how, as in other areas of knowledge, children's errors in writing indicate not ignorance but a developing understanding based on reasoning.

In Chapter 7, Virginia W. Berninger and William D. Winn explore the implications of advancement in brain research, as well as writing technology for understanding writing and its development. They provide a brief primer on the brain and the use of neuroimaging, followed by a review of what has been learned about writing through the use of this technology. They then turn their attention to the potential of a different application of technology—the use of personal computers as a mechanism for transforming writing. They close their chapter by examining the need to integrate three perspectives that have played an important role in writing development: developmental neuropsychological, sociocultural, and learning science.

In Chapter 8, Deborah McCutchen extends the examination of children's and youth's writing development by reviewing empirical research on the cognitive processes involved in learning to write. She enriches this analysis by considering both social and instructional contexts that may support or thwart the development of sophisticated writing processes. She casts her analytical net broadly, examining the role of planning and other reflective processes; working and long-term memory; text generation and text production; as well as revision, critical reading, and problem solving in writing and writing development. She draws her chapter to a close by considering the paradox that less skilled writers sometimes generate text more fluently than do skilled writers.

Carol A. Donovan and Laura B. Smolkin (Chapter 9) focus on children's genre knowledge and how that knowledge is related to writing development. They ground their chapter in the belief that genre knowledge begins to develop prior to conventional writing abilities, and they describe three theories that frame the research on children's genre knowledge—the rhetorical, social, and cognitive-psychological/empirical traditions. Methodologies used in studies for their review are summarized in a taxonomy. The authors suggest that children's knowledge of micro- and macro-level features of typical school genres can be described as they develop over time, and that little is known about best ways to support young children's genre knowledge development.

The next two chapters deal with motivational issues. In Chapter 10, Suzanne Hidi and Pietro Boscolo take a broad look at theories of motivation and writing, beginning with theoretical research on interest. In their model, situational interest in a topic or activity develops through experience into enduring individual interest. In addition, they review theories of self-efficacy and self-regulation and discuss the motivational assumptions of social constructivist approaches to writing as a meaningful social activity. They attempt to integrate the various approaches and call for more research that combines the cognitive, affective, and social aspects of writing motivation.

Frank Pajares and Gio Valiante, in Chapter 11, focus more intensively on self-efficacy. They provide a concise summary of self-efficacy as part of social cognitive theory and offer an especially clear discussion of issues in measuring self-efficacy for writing. Their review of the research shows that self-efficacy is correlated with many measures of motivation and cognition and predicts signif-

icant variance in quality of writing even after taking into account prior writing achievement. They also review research on interventions that increase self-efficacy and discuss the educational implications.

Timothy Shanahan, in Chapter 12, pulls together a considerable body of research on the relationships among oral language, reading, and writing development. A basic theme in his chapter is that our older models of the development of the four language systems, which gave precedence to orality in the early years as an antecedent to print modalities, are no longer supported. Rather, although writing comes late in language learning, it has potential to be affected by the other modalities, and vice versa. He insightfully examines theory and research on how oral and written language are related, how reading and writing are interconnected, and how empirical study on cross-language relationships has changed over time.

Instructional Models and Approaches

The third section of this volume includes chapters on instructional models and approaches. In each chapter, the authors describe the theoretical basis for the instructional approach and review the evidence on the effects of the instructional intervention. In Chapter 13, Steve Graham presents a meta-analysis of 39 studies of cognitive strategy instruction in planning, revising, or editing. The overall effect sizes were large, maintained over time, and positive across achievement level, grade level, type of cognitive process, genres, and whether instruction was provided by researchers or teachers.

Carol Sue Englert, Troy V. Mariage, and Kailonnie Dunsmore (Chapter 14) thoughtfully explicate tenets of sociocultural theory in writing instruction research. Sociocultural theory helps us to understand how culturally and historically situated meanings are constructed, reconstructed, and changed through social mediation. The authors explicate three significant instructional tenets, or pedagogical principles, of sociocultural theory: Cognitive apprenticeships support novices, cultural tools and procedural facilitators are important supports for students in advance of expecting independent performance, and communities of practice are important for emphasizing knowledge construction and dissemination. Rather than learning about results of an exhaustive research review, readers encounter highlights of specific studies that illustrate and anchor the discussion of the three significant tenets.

In Chapter 15, we find Richard Beach and Tom Friedrich's examination of different strategies for written or oral responses to students' writing. They review different functions and purposes for response to writing, as well as research findings on the benefits of particular ways of responding. Effective feedback is significant because without it, many students do not engage in meaningful self-assessment and revision. Characteristics of effective feedback are delineated.

George E. Newell addresses the promises and challenges of empirical and theoretical studies of writing to learn in Chapter 16. He focuses especially on three general areas of research: how writing assignments can become ways of exploring and making sense of new ideas and experiences, how students may become more aware of a full range of conventions and genres, and how writing-to-learn approaches alter the roles of both teacher and student. He suggests that, to date, we have focused our research issues too narrowly on defining effective teaching and learning. Instead, he says, we need to address questions of how and why different kinds of curricular conversations in particular social contexts shape student learning.

In Chapter 17, Charles A. MacArthur reviews research on the impact of new technologies on writing and learning to write. He begins by considering the effects of technology on producing traditional linear texts, including word processing, computer support for writing and learning to write, and assistive technology for struggling writers. Then he considers the emerging research on composing hypermedia or hypertext and the effects of computer-mediated communication on writing. Noting the large gap between theoretical claims about the transformational effects of technology on writing and the empirical research, he calls for research to test these claims.

Although grammar instruction is a common staple of many writing programs, especially for older students, Michael W. Smith, Julie Cheville, and George Hillocks, Jr., in Chapter 18 conclude that teaching tradi-

tional school grammar (TSG) is ineffective. They argue that TSG does not provide an adequate description for the way language works, that students have difficulty learning it, and that teaching it has no impact on students' writing. While there are a number of alternative approaches to teaching grammar, they argue that there is no empirical evidence yet to support their effectiveness.

In the final chapter in this section (Chapter 19), Ruie J. Pritchard and Ronald L. Honeycutt examine the effectiveness of the popular process approach to writing instruction. They first consider how this approach to writing instruction has evolved over the years, noting that there are surprisingly different views on what this approach entails. They then review the literature to determine the effects of this approach on students' writing, as well as the impact of the National Writing Project Professional Development Model on writing practices and achievement.

Special Populations

The fourth section of this volume focuses attention on writing and special populations, including chapters on cultural diversity, gender, special education, and bilingual learners. In Chapter 20, Arnetha F. Ball advocates for cross-disciplinary approaches to the study of writing for students from culturally diverse backgrounds. She explicates ways in which theories that give prominence to the social context of writing have grounded most of the writing research on culturally diverse students. Next, she reviews the research according to three general factors that are addressed: the influence of teacher, classroom, and/or community contexts; the influence of students' culture or home discourse; and the effects of teaching strategies. She concludes with implications for teachers and for future researchers.

In the chapter on gender (Chapter 21), Shelley Peterson begins by noting two contrasting concerns motivating research on writing and gender: a concern with silencing of female voices and privileging of male writing styles versus a concern that the lower performance of males on formal writing assessments reflects stereotypes about masculinity. She reviews research on gender differences in written products on features such as characterization and theme, and both teacher and student perceptions of gender and writing competence. She then examines work on ideologies that shape girls' and boys' writing and looks at attempts to encourage students to write against traditional gender positions.

Students with learning disabilities have special difficulties in mastering reading and writing. In Chapter 22, Gary A. Troia reviews research on the characteristics of their writing and on successful interventions. The research documents the difficulties of these students with planning, revising, and text generation, and explores research showing that their problems with metacognition and motivation can be addressed with interventions that teach self-regulation. Based on the research, Troia proposes guidelines for the design of comprehensive writing programs for poor writers.

In Chapter 23, Jill Fitzgerald provides a compendium of 56 studies in the last 15 years on K–12 multilingual writing. She characterizes and critiques the methodologies used in the studies, then reports findings according to the types of questions addressed within age groups. Finally, she discusses the few dependable overarching conclusions that might be made from the collective studies and lays out significant needs for a future research agenda.

Research Methodology and Analytic Tools

The final section of the Handbook includes six chapters on research methodology and analytic tools. In Chapter 24, Katherine Schultz argues that qualitative research has produced critical understandings about writing. She supports her claim by tracing major conceptual advances in writing research and drawing on key studies to illustrate what the field has learned from this research. To the extent that writing occurs in particular social contexts that determine its meaning, qualitative methods are critical because of their focus on insiders' perspectives, emphasis on social and cultural context, tools for analyzing discourse, and the means to look across settings, including nonschool environments. Schultz illustrates the contributions of qualitative research by describing systematic programs of research on writing in primary classrooms in urban multiethnic schools, lit-

eracy practices in Mexican American communities, a large-scale longitudinal project in Great Britain, research on literacy and identity, and her own current work on how digital technologies shape writing.

Robert D. Abbott, Dagmar Amtmann, and Jeff Munson (Chapter 25) examine the use of statistical procedures in instructional field experiments and studies involving longitudinal data. They begin by considering the strengths of randomized field experiments in writing research and examining the statistical implications for power and type I error rates when such studies involve a small number of participants or are scaled-up across schools. Next, they focus on the design and statistical analysis involved in longitudinal approaches examining growth in writing. They concentrate on two approaches to analyzing longitudinal data: latent variable growth mixture modeling for change when measures are continuous, and latent transition analysis for change when measures of change are stages or categorical. To make these types of analyses more concrete, they illustrate their application with their own research on writing.

In Chapter 26, Ted J. M. Sanders and Joost Schilperoord shift the focus to a specific method they have developed for analyzing written products. They argue that the analysis of text structure provides a useful window for describing and understanding not only the written product but also the processes that the writer used to create the text. They contend that an analysis of the written product can yield identifiable traces of the cognitive actions employed during the construction of the text. They illustrate these claims by showing how their approach, procedures for incremental structure analysis, is applied and what it reveals about the cognitive actions of the author of the analyzed text.

Given the increasing emphasis on large-scale assessment of student writing, it is important to consider ways to increase the efficiency of those assessments, as well as their reliability and validity. In Chapter 27, Mark D. Shermis, Jill Burstein, and Claudia Leacock review work on the development and evaluation of automated essay scoring, or evaluation of essays by computers. They provide a basic explanation of how the systems work, review the evidence of reliability and validity, and describe the major systems in current use. In addition, they describe systems in development that can analyze the content of writing and provide evaluative feedback to students on specific aspects of the writing.

In Chapter 28, Brian Huot and Michael Neal offer a critique of current technologies for large-scale writing assessment, including indirect tests of writing, holistic scoring with rubrics, and computer-assisted scoring. They argue that developers of these methods of writing assessment have focused excessively on interrater reliability, without sufficient concern for the validity of the measures for particular purposes.

Finally, in Chapter 29, Kenneth R. Pugh, Stephen J. Frost, Rebecca Sandak, Margie Gillis, Dina Moore, Annette R. Jenner, and W. Einar Mencl examine the possible use of neuroimaging techniques in the area of writing. They consider the methodological and design challenges that must be addressed if neuroimaging is to be applied to the study of composition. Because little neuroimaging research has been conducted with writing, they draw upon neuroimaging research in spoken language and reading to develop a set of preliminary hypotheses about what might be anticipated as this methodology is applied more broadly to the area of writing.

References

Elbow, P. (1973). *Writing without teachers*. London: Oxford University Press.

Emig, J. (1971). *The composing processes of twelfth graders*. Urbana, IL: National Council of Teachers of English.

Graham, S. (in press). Writing. In P. Alexander & P. Winne (Eds.), *Handbook of educational psychology*. Mahwah, NJ: Erlbaum.

Greenwald, E. A., Persky, H. R., Campbell, J. R., & Mazzeo, J. (1999). NAEP 1998 Writing: Report card for the nation and states. Washington, DC: U.S. Department of Education.

Havelock, E. A. (1982). *The literate revolution in Greece and its cultural consequences*. Princeton, NJ: Princeton University Press.

Kellogg, R. T. (1999). Components of working memory in text production. In M. Torrance & G. C. Jeffery (Eds.), *The cognitive demands of writing: Processing capacity and working memory in text production* (pp. 42–61). Amsterdam: Amsterdam University Press

National Commission on Writing in America's Schools & Colleges. The need for a writing revolution. (2003). *The neglected "R."*: New York: College Entrance Examination Board.

Smyth, J. (1998). Written emotional expression: Effect sizes, outcome types, and moderating variables. *Journal of Consulting and Clinical Psychology, 66*, 174–184.

Swedlow, J. (1999). The power of writing. *National Geographic, 196*, 110–132.

Part I

THEORIES AND MODELS OF WRITING

Chapter 1

The Social and Historical Context for Writing Research

Martin Nystrand

The start of empirical research on writing in North America is typically benchmarked circa 1970, especially by the publication of Emig's *The Composing Processes of Twelfth Graders* in 1971 (Nystrand, Greene, & Wiemelt, 1993). This is not to say that no such studies had previously been conducted—Braddock, Lloyd-Jones, and Schoer, for example, reviewed such work in *Research in Written Composition* (1963)—but rather to note that such studies were isolated and unsupported by professional networks and support systems, including doctoral programs training writing researchers and overseeing dissertation studies, as well as refereed research journals and professional organization special interest groups devoted to such research. Cumulatively, these developments established Composition and Rhetoric as an academic discipline and research specialization in the 1980s.

With hindsight, we can see that the ideas about writing typically associated with the 1970s and 1980s were not altogether new. For example, articles about writing as a process had previously appeared as recently as Young and Becker (1965) and as early as 1912 in numerous articles in the *English Journal* (see Town, 1988), so Emig was not the first to conceptualize writing as a process. In addition, University of Chicago English professor Henry Sams promoted interest in invention in the 1940s. Yet his visionary efforts went nowhere amid the formalist

literary currents in his department. For invention to be put into play as a topic with currency in the field, it had to wait 35 years after Sams to be discovered once again and put on the map at the Conference on College Composition and Communication (the 4 Cs) and beyond, especially by Richard Young at Carnegie Mellon University in the 1970s and 1980s, when the cognitive science climate there was receptive to ideas about invention in terms of cognitive plans and goals. The influence of the Carnegie Mellon school of cognitive rhetoric, exemplified by the research of Flower and Hayes, ultimately derives from the currency it achieved within the 1970s and 1980s receptive contexts of the Conference on College Composition and Communication, the National Council of Teachers of English, new doctoral programs in departments of English, and federal research support, especially in the Center for the Study of Writing funded in 1985.

Many pioneering studies, like the researchers who conducted them, came from English education programs. Some of the most influential early writing researchers (e.g., James Britton and Nancy Martin in England), were English and language arts teachers who, despite their faculty and administrative associations with universities, had few if any graduate degrees. Both Britton and Martin were English Language Arts teachers at the United Kingdom's Harrow Weald school in the 1930s and 1940s before joining the English staff at the University of London's Institute of Education. Britton served there as department head from 1954 to 1969, followed by Martin, who chaired the department from 1970 to 1976. Some of the new voices were not even researchers; James Moffett (1968), for example, whose cognitive conception of writing figured prominently in the new discourse about writing, was an English and language arts teacher at Phillips Exeter Academy who eventually served on the faculties of Harvard University, the University of California at Berkeley, San Diego State University, and Middlebury College's Bread Loaf School of English.

The new discourse about writing sought to describe how ordinary students write, not to prescribe either how they should write or what their texts were to look like; notably, the scope of this new discourse was theoretical, not pedagogical, or not just pedagogical. Instruction was to be based not on the arbitrary rules and maxims of traditional school rhetorics; rather, it was to be informed by empirical findings and basic research, which was the mission of the National Institute of Education's new writing research program launched in the late 1970s and subsequently at the Center for the Study of Writing in 1985. The weakest writers came to be categorized in clinical fashion as Basic Writers (Shaughnessy, 1977), whose errors were approached not with worksheets and drills but rather with research agendas designed to uncover the history and logic of their writing strategies. Echoing psychologists all the way back to John Dewey (1884) and William James (1890), the new writing researchers posited the individual writer's mind as the seminal organizing principle of writing; they sought to explicate the cognitive structure of writing processes that transformed thought and agency into text. By the early 1980s, writing was commonly thought most fundamentally to be a dynamic, meaning-making process. This chapter examines the rise of empirical research on writing in the 1970s and 1980s that came about largely as a result of the confluence of two major and powerful forces: An academic formative context cultivating new ideas and methods, and a sociocultural receptive context transcending the university and serving to valorize and refract the ideas generated there.

The Formative Context

The Dartmouth Seminar

Between 1900 and about 1970, discourse about writing in the United States was mainly an instructional affair focused predominantly on prescriptive text features of model prose written by exemplary writers. Midcentury (and earlier) thinking about composition focused on model texts of the sort collected in countless Freshman English readers, and most ideas about writing by far concerned expository writing and reflected prescriptive grammar and "current traditional" rhetoric (Young, 1978). Five-paragraph themes, stipulating three main points regardless of topic or argument, constituted the focus of expository writing instruction in most secondary schools. Postsecondary writing instruction typically occurred exclusively in departments of English and focused on the humanities essay genre. The character of this instructional discourse was largely captured in formalist rules and maxims of the sort offered by Lucas (1955), Strunk and White (1959), and Warriner (1950).

This traditional conception of writing and writing instruction was sharply critiqued at the Anglo-American Conference on the Teaching of English, commonly called the Dartmouth Seminar, held at Dartmouth College in 1966. Britton, Moffett, and other members of the seminar, which included academics in English, linguistics, psychology, and education, as well as other researchers and schools people from both sides of the Atlantic, argued that school writing too often consisted of formulaic "dummy runs," and proposed an alternative structure emphasizing "personal growth" (Dixon, 1967). This new model viewed language—both writing and talking—as a cognitive and expressive process shaping and extending everyday experience by bringing it "into new relationships with old elements" (Dixon, 1967, p. 9). Drawing from philosophy (Ernst Cassirer, Suzanne Langer, and Michael Polanyi) and psychology (Jerome Bruner, George Kelly, Alexander Luria, Jean Piaget, and Lev Vygotsky), Britton subsequently elaborated this conception of language processes in *Language and Learning* (Britton, 1970). Borrowing from Piaget's model of cognitive development and Basil Bernstein's concepts of elaborated and restricted codes, Moffett spelled out a K–13 pedagogical sequence of writing development based on increasing levels of abstraction at which the experience is handled—what's happening? (record), what happened? (report), what happens? (generalization and analysis), and what may happen? (speculation)—subsequently published in *Teaching the Universe of Discourse* (Moffett, 1968). He argued that "the stuff to be conceived and verbalized is primarily the raw stuff of life, not language matters themselves" (p. 114).

This new model of English education sought to move the focus of curriculum and instruction away from traditional models of cultural heritage and skills. In their place, the reformers urged a bold and fundamental reconceptualization of instruction rooted in basic research about individual learning and processes of mind. Dixon (1967, p. 10) wrote:

> The question "What is English?" invites a different form of answer from, say, "What at our best are we doing in English classes?" If we wish to describe a process, composition for example, the first question will tend to suggest the finished product (the marks on the page even) rather than the activity of bringing together and composing the disorder of our experience. "What . . . doing" will suggest nominal forms of verbs (bringing, composing) and thus help to keep activities in mind.

Dartmouth seminar participants argued that effective reform required not new curricula or instructional techniques but rather a fundamental reconceptualization of the nature of English language education. Their thinking was motivated first by their belief that effective writing and reading instruction has less to do with teaching techniques and more with fundamental insights about language processes and learning. As Britton (1969) put it, "We teach and teach and they learn and learn: if they didn't, we wouldn't" (p. 81). To this end, the Dartmouth participants sought to downplay the concrete, "What is English?" outcomes of writing and reading, and instead foster the generative and active meaning-making processes of engaged writing and reading.

The Cognitive Revolution

Another source for the new discourse about writing, as well as both reading and learning,

was the Cambridge Cognitive Revolution at MIT and at Harvard University. Chomsky's seminal ideas on language as a rule-governed cognitive process (Chomsky, 1957, 1966, 1968) revolutionized linguistics, arguing that language performance (i.e., spoken utterances) transformed manifestations of underlying language competence. Because competence is innate, universal, and cognitive, he claimed, to study language was to investigate the structure of the mind, and linguistics was a branch of cognitive psychology. Inasmuch as Chomsky's structuralist arguments validated mind as a legitimate object of scientific inquiry, his work gave new energy to psychologists laboring under the behaviorist paradigm of B. F. Skinner. Harvard and MIT linguists and cognitive psychologists both, and sometimes together, in the "the heady psycholinguistic atmosphere of Cambridge, Massachusetts" (Smith, 1971, p. x) in a discipline called psycholinguistics, undertook many new programs of research, each aimed at deciphering and writing rules (grammars) structuring and underlying human behavior, including language.

Unsurprisingly, many of the key principles of this new Cartesian approach to language and human behavior—especially the premise that humans order experience by formulating mental representations (or schemas), enabling them to (1) organize their perceptions, understandings, and memories of the past; and (2) focus their expectations for the future—influenced doctoral students at Harvard, both in the Graduate School of Education and the Graduate School of Arts and Sciences, especially those who were writing dissertations in literacy, literacy instruction, and language development, including both writing and reading. Students from Harvard took courses with Chomsky at MIT, as well as with Jerry Fodor and Edward Klima, both professors of philosophy and psychology. At Harvard, faculty from MIT often attended a Tuesday Colloquium at Harvard sponsored by Miller and Bruner's Center for Cognitive Studies, part of the Social Relations Department.

During this time, a remarkable group of graduate students undertook research that eventually gained them considerable influence in their fields. These included Havard Graduate School of Education (HGSE) students Janet Emig, John Mellon, and Courtney Cazden. Cazden was a human development student working with cognitive psychologist Roger Brown; Charles Read was a doctoral student in linguistics; and Frank Smith was a doctoral student in psychology affiliated with the Center for Cognitive Studies (CCS), part of the Social Relations Department, where he worked with cognitive psychologists George Miller, Jerome Bruner, and Roger Brown.[1] Dartmouth Seminar participant Moffett was a research associate with HGSE. Cazden (1972, 1988) went on to become a noted expert on child language and classroom discourse. Emig (1971) and Moffett (1968), mentioned above, concerned themselves with cognitive conceptions of writing processes. Mellon (1969) devised an instructional method based on Chomsky's grammar called "transformational sentence-combining" for developing "syntactic fluency" (skill in manipulating syntax). Read (1971) uncovered the phonetic logic of preschool writers' "invented spelling" in work that served as an important precursor to subsequent studies of emergent literacy. And Smith (1971) developed a widely influential cognitive model of reading processes.

Ironically, not one of these students trained in the area of his or her eventual influence. Emig and Mellon studied in the English education program; there was no program at the time in writing research or composition studies. Read trained as a linguist, and Smith, a psychology student, took no courses in either education or reading; Moffett, as noted, was not even a student.

The Receptive Context

The Literacy Crisis

If empirical research on writing had important roots in the Cognitive Revolution of the 1960s and was launched circa 1970, its influence did not immediately take off until at least the mid-1970s. We get some sense of this in Figure 1.1 charting the citation record of Emig's *Composing Processes of Twelfth Graders* (taken from the Social Sciences Citation Index) between 1972 and 2003: Citations of Emig's study are rare we see, till the mid-1970s, when they roughly double and then increase steeply in the 1980s. The upturn reflects several developments at the time, both within and beyond academia. In the mid-1970s, two influential articles that

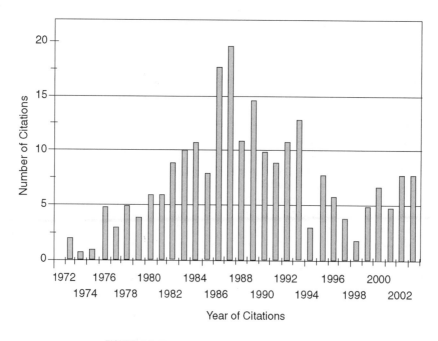

FIGURE 1.1. Emig (1971) citation: 1972–2003.

appeared in the popular press bemoaned a sharp decline in writing skills evident in America's colleges and universities, and heralded a literacy crisis in American schools. *Time*'s "Bonehead English"(Stone, 1974) attributed dramatic increases in remedial freshman composition classes to sharp increases in unprepared students. *Newsweek*'s December 8, 1975, cover story, "Why Johnny Can't Write" (Sheils, 1975), blamed the public schools for neglecting "the basics," noting a "displacement" of writing instruction by too many "creative" methods and "permissive" standards in too many "open" classrooms. For the public, both articles seemed to confirm the College Entrance Examination Board's 1973 report that SAT scores had fallen sharply. Clifton Fadiman, popular critic and longtime book reviewer for the *New Yorker*, blamed the "unshackled Sixties" (Fadiman & Howard, 1979, p. 10).

This was not the first literacy crisis in America, nor would it be the last. Indeed, periodic complaints about falling standards and declining writing and reading skills have been perennial in any industrialized nation where requirements for literacy continually change. Such claims are common during periods of demographic and class economic shifts, including our current globalizing society. Miller (1997) shows, for example, how the formation of college English in 18th-century Great Britain was driven by a rise in literacy, brought about by an expanding, upwardly mobile middle class with enough leisure time, interest, and money to take advantage of newly cheap print and strive to improve its social class status. It was at this time that college English was first taught, Miller shows, not as literature courses at elite universities such as Oxford or Cambridge, but in writing classes in the provincial colleges influenced and sometimes taught by rhetoricians such as Joseph Priestly, Alexander Bain, and Adam Smith.

Douglas (1976) documents the "creation of composition at Harvard" circa 1870, a result of its new president Charles William Eliot's transformation of Harvard from a small college for sons of landed gentry to a departmentalized modern university producing a demographically diverse meritocracy, or an "aristocracy of achievement," as Eliot put it. The new Harvard was to be for "students in all conditions of life," including poor students of "capacity and character" (Eliot, quoted in Douglas, 1976, p. 127), and its mission was to meet a need for correctness and clarity in written discourse posed by the demands of growing industrialization and the concomitant rise of a professional management class. Writing skill, understood as clarity, grammatical correctness, and preferred usage, became a social grace—a power button, as it were, a way of highlighting one's education, class affiliations, and upscale ambitions in an industrial economy.

A century later, in the 1970s, American colleges and universities oversaw even more dramatic and often violent demographic shifts. The Educational Opportunity Act of 1964, the Johnson administration's War on Poverty, and subsequent reauthorization of the Higher Education Act in 1968, including Upward Bound, Talent Search, and Special Services, sharply increased numbers of first-generation college students. William Angoff, director of the College Board Program for Educational Testing Service, attributed SAT declines publicized by *Time* and *Newsweek* to "the changing nature of the SAT population" (Angoff, 1975, p. 10). College campus Vietnam War protests exacerbated all these changes. Peter Hawkes (1996) documents how radical changes in writing instruction at Brooklyn College of the City University of New York (CUNY) were a direct response to the daily ferment of social and political change both on and off campus. Across America, student demonstrations, strikes, takeovers of campus buildings, smoke bombs, vandalism, and fires were persistent; police brutality against demonstrators was common. The demonstrations were largely about student draft deferments: Of Brooklyn College's 10,008 students in 1968, for example, only 119 were black, and 42 were Puerto Rican (Kihss, 1968, p. 48). Since few African Americans and Puerto Ricans qualified for student deferments, they were drafted in disproportionate numbers and sent to Vietnam to fight and often die.

In the fall of 1970, 6 months after four Kent State students were shot dead by National Guard troops, CUNY began its policy of open admissions 5 years ahead of its planned start in 1975; in the next 3 years, Brooklyn College's enrollments jumped from 14,000 to 34,000 students.[2] There, much to his surprise, it fell to Kenneth Bruffee, a young and new assistant professor of British Romantic literature, to design and direct a new freshman composition program. His radical reforms included extensive use of response groups in the new courses, as well as a establishing tutoring program located in a storefront facility near the campus subway exit staffed entirely by undergraduate students.

In Manhattan, at City College of New York, Mina Shaughnessy, a colleague of Bruffee, revolutionized writing instruction by making research into the "logic and history" of students' errors—not worksheet exercises in prescriptive grammar—an essential prerequisite to effective instruction (Shaughnessy, 1977). Like Britton and Martin in the United Kingdom, Shaughnessy had no graduate training for her work at City College. She had earned a BS degree in the Department of Radio/TV/Film at Northwestern University, with additional coursework in theology at Wheaton College (Illinois), followed by a Master's degree in English literature at Columbia University. These were her only academic credentials for her rapid rise through the CUNY system: In 1965, she served as the director of Search for Education, Elevation, and Knowledge (SEEK), an experimental undergraduate program designed to bring small groups of minorities into the CUNY system. SEEK became the immediate forerunner of the subsequent open admissions program, and in 1970, with the formal start of Open Admissions, Shaughnessy became director of City College's Basic Writing Program. Finally, from 1975 until her death in 1978, she served as dean of instructional resources for CUNY.[3] In her systematic examination of the errors in 2 million words of writing by 4,000 basic writers, Shaughnessy took cues from sociolinguist William Labov's (1972) *The Logic of Nonstandard English.* Shaughnessy's was a strong voice putting writing research front and center in efforts to improve writing instruction in the new discourse about writing that gained influence in the 1970s and 1980s.

Federally Funded Research and Development

Education reforms in Britain in the 1700s, at Harvard after the Civil War, and in American higher education in the 1970s clearly made writing instruction a key response to macro-demographic and class cultural shifts in the larger societies. These pedagogical innovations and reforms shaped ideas about writing, how it was taught, and particularly why it was taught. The reforms of the 1970s, however, brought into play substantial, unprecedented programs of federally funded basic empirical research and development (R&D) about all aspects of education on the part of the federal government.

During the early 1960s, the social sciences gained considerable influence in education research, and indeed education research, as measured by membership and papers presented at the American Education Research Association, did not fully take off till the social sciences came on board.[4] In 1963 Francis Keppel, who was dean of Harvard's Graduate School of Education, joined the Kennedy Administration as U.S. Commissioner of Education and continued on into the Johnson Administration. Keppel argued for education reform based on sophisticated programs of empirical research. "Education," he said, " is too important to be left solely to the educators" (Dershimer, 1976, p. 50):

> Our principal faults from the past are these: The most common form of educational research has been and is still the small, easily-mangaged project which focuses on miniature, obscure and non-controversial issues, which are seldom taken seriously by administrators or teachers. Education research has been and is still short of the best minds needed for the best possible results. Without the best of researchers, we have yet to show an innovative, creative vigor matching our counterparts in medicine, science, agriculture and industry. (Keppel, quoted in Dershimer, 1976, p. 60)

Keppel believed that education improvement was completely dependent on new research efforts undertaken independently of what he derisively called the professional "educationists," whom he regarded as "the foe" (Dershimer, 1976, p. 61) and whose bureaucratic concerns and myopic curriculum and instructional methods projects had clearly made a mess of the schools.[5] In the late 1950s and early 1960s, Keppel and many others found much to admire in the then-recent National Science Foundation (NSF)-funded physics instruction for high schools known as Physical Sciences Study Committee (PSSC)

Physics, a federal response to Russia's launch of Sputnik in 1957. Initial NSF funding totaled $445,000, increasing to $1.8 million by 1959. The director of this project was Jerrold Zacharias, an MIT physicist/scientist who had been at the Los Alamos Laboratory during the development of the atomic bomb in the 1940s. In 1960, Zacharias started Educational Services, Inc. (ESI), an education R&D facility concerned with all phases of education reform. Zaccharias was increasingly regarded by Keppel and the U.S. Office of Education as a "prototype of the caliber" of needed new scholars in education (Dershimer, 1976, p. 60). If the "educationists" represented the mediocre past in education, scientists and scholars like Zaccharias hopefully portended the future.

In 1963, Keppel was appointed U.S. Commissioner of Education, where he continued to expand the role of the federal government in education and favor well-funded research and development efforts. After the Kennedy assassination, federal investments in education were viewed as a critical part of Lyndon Johnson's War on Poverty. According to President Johnson, a former schoolteacher from Texas, education was "central to the purposes of this Administration, and at the core of all of our hopes for a Great Society" (Johnson, remarks to the White House Conference on Education, July 21, 1965, quoted in Dershimer, 1976, p. 69). In 1965 Keppel said, "The educator is the captain in a nationwide crusade to improve the quality of life; goals that seemed unreachable have become practical and close at hand" (p. 167). The new attitude was that the can-do nation that had built the bomb and was well on its way to the moon could surely end poverty and fix the schools. In 1964 the U.S. Office of Education funded four new federal R&D centers at Harvard,[6] Oregon, Pittsburgh,[7] and Wisconsin.[8] These were modeled after the Argonne Laboratories and the Brookhaven Laboratory, viewed by the President's Task Force on Education as "the great national laboratories of the Atomic Energy Commission" ("Report of the President's Task Force on Education," p. 34, quoted in Dershimer, 1976, p. 65). Each R&D center was predicated on "the view that education research would make a difference, that if you brought knowledge to bear on social problems it would improve them" (Ralph Tyler,

quoted in Dershimer, 1976, p. 65). The centers were budgeted to spend $300,000 to $1 million a year on long-term projects targeting significant, carefully defined educational problems[9]; each project, involving a team of empirical researchers and research assistants, was to conduct basic research culminating in the development of new curricula, instructional methods, and materials ready for implementation by teachers.[10] The research was to be conducted according to the highest scientific standards—"in its devotion to rigor, replicability, and presentation of data, as well as in its need for building a community of scholars to adjudicate disputes, relate the work to public needs and policies, and, of course, to garner the funds needed to conduct the research" (David Goslin, summarized by Kaestle, 1992, p. 57). In 1965 the Elementary and Secondary Education Act expanded the programs of the R&D centers and added six more, for a total of ten.

During the late 1960s, numerous American scholars sought to bring scientific methods to the professional community of the Conference on College Composition and Communication. Some of the earliest empirical research on writing dates from this time. Rohman and Wlecke (1964; Rohman, 1965) were the first writing researchers explicitly to conceptualize prewriting as a discrete stage in a process of composing unfolding over time. Richard Young and his colleagues elaborated a process-based tagmemic theory of rhetoric in numerous publications starting in 1965 (Young, 1968, 1969, 1978; Young & Becker, 1965; Young, Becker, & Pike, 1974). Rohman and Welke's work was sponsored by the U.S. Office of Education Cooperative Research. Young's studies were sponsored and funded by the then-new U. S. Office of Education-funded Center for Research on Language and Language Behavior at the University of Michigan.

In 1972 President Nixon and the 92nd Congress built on such initiatives by expanding and transforming the Cooperative Research Projects into the National Institute of Education (NIE) in 1972. In many ways, the new Center for the Study of Reading (CSR) at the University of Illinois at Champaign–Urbana, funded from 1976 to 1991, was the paradigm of such efforts, explicitly harnessing powerful new cognitive models of reading processes, along with innovative research methods, to the critical needs of schools to reverse declines in reading skills, particularly in inner cities. The CSR generated 750 technical reports, including work by Richard Anderson (1984) on schema theory, Meyer and McConkie (1973) on text structure analysis, Alan Collins and Tom Trabasso on inferential reasoning (Collins & Loftus, 1975; Trabasso & Van den Broek, 1985), Nancy Stein (1982) on story grammars, and Adams and Collins (1979) on comprehension models (see Pearson, 2001).

In 1977, preparing to launch a program of writing research, the NIE sponsored a conference on writing in June 1977 at NIE's Southwest Regional Laboratory (SWRL) in Los Alamitos, California. Speakers represented anthropology, psycho- and sociolinguistics, cognitive psychology, English education, English literature, and rhetoric, areas that would come to configure university faculty and programs that specialized in research on writing.

Among the first writing research sponsored by NIE was the cognitive work of Linda Flower and John R. Hayes at Carnegie Mellon University. Carnegie Mellon offered a timely context for the new empirical work on writing: The Department of English was chaired by Richard Young, an empirical researcher on tagmemics and invention (above). Hayes had been a fellow at Harvard's CCS, were he worked with Nobel Prize-winning psychologist Herb Simon on the cognition of problem solving (Hayes & Simon, 1975). Flower and Hayes (1980a, 1980b, 1981, 1984) developed a cognitive model of writing processes, identifying the components and organization of long-term memory, planning, reviewing, and translating thought into text. They derived their methodology of think-aloud protocols from Newell and Simon (1972).

In some ways, Flower and Hayes's research might seem to build on Emig's (1971) research: Common to both was a focus on cognitive writing/composing processes and the use of think-aloud protocols. But whereas Emig's case study work elaborated a conception of writing as a composing process, Flower and Hayes built a formal model delineating both the components and organization of writing processes; the two research initiatives drew from different sources. While Emig's study did not figure method-

ologically or conceptually into Flower and Hayes's work, it nonetheless shaped in departments of English a new climate that made those departments receptive to the work that Flower and Hayes did, laying the groundwork and opening a discursive space for sophisticated and rigorous empirical research in literary-oriented departments of English.

Other cognitive research on writing from the 1970s and early 1980s included Applebee's (1981) research on writing in the secondary school, Bissex's (1980) case study of her son's written language development, Bracewell, Fredericksen, and Fredericksen's (1982) study of writing and reading, Daiute's (1981) psycholinguistic study of the writing process, Faigley and Witte's (1981; Witte & Faigley, 1983) studies of revision, Kroll's (1978) study of egocentrism and audience awareness, and Bereiter and Scardamalia's (1987; Scardamalia, Bereiter, & Goelman, 1982) studies of writing processes.[11] By the early 1980s, writing was commonly thought most fundamentally to be a dynamic, meaning-making process, and had computers at that time had Windows desktops, the icon for a Composition Studies folder would surely have been Flower and Hayes's (1981) flowchart showing the underlying hierarchical organization of writing processes (see Figure 1.2).

The Social 1980s

As we have seen, Emig (1971) investigated writing as a cognitive composing process by interviewing Harvard professors about their writing styles and studying a few middle-class Chicago north-suburban 12th graders. Shaughnessy (1977) soon expanded the scope of the new discourse about writing by tracing the logic and history of errors in the writing of 4,000 New York City College basic writers, most of whom were first-generation college students. Showing that effective instruction of these writers required understanding the patterns and idiosyncrasies of the language of their speech communities, Shaughnessy inserted a clear social dimension into writing research and was the first composition scholar to claim that "writing is a social act" (p. 83). The power of this insight increased along with the increasing

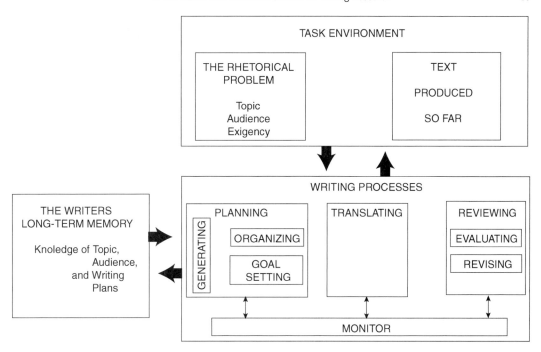

FIGURE 1.2. Cognitive process model of the writing processes (Flower & Hayes, 1981). Copyright 1981 by Lawrence Erlbaum Associates, Inc. Reprinted by permission.

diversity of postsecondary students as a result of open admissions and other new institutions that emerged in the late 1960s and early 1970s: By the late 1960s, a new community college opened every week (Graham, 1984, p. 223).

Writing researchers were not alone. During the 1970s, many important voices in linguistics began to challenge Chomsky's cognitive conception of language and his concepts of linguistic competence and native speaker. Reacting to Chomsky, Dell Hymes (1974) elaborated a concept of "communicative competence" within an "ethnography of communication," resituating syntax and autonomous language forms within the full set of "conventional resources" that speakers draw from to communicate within a given "speech community." Probing aspects of communicative competence, Sacks, Schegloff, and Jefferson (1974) wrote a grammar of situated—not universal—conversation moves. Chomsky (1957) had defined grammatical language as syntactic structures acceptable to "a native speaker." Noting the diversity of American native speakers of English, William Labov (1972) wrote a grammar for black English vernacular (BEV), in effect ask-

ing, "*Which* native speaker?" These many sociolinguistic studies added a social dimension to academic discourse about language and discourse.

By the 1980s, this new social perspective gathered momentum within writing studies. Challenging the Flower and Hayes (1981) cognitive model of writing processes, Nystrand (1982) argued that "the special relations that define written language functioning and promote its meaningful use . . . are wholly circumscribed by the systematic relations that obtain in the speech community of the writer" (p. 17). Bizzell (1982), also challenging Flower and Hayes's cognitive model, argued that "what's missing here is the connection to social context afforded by the recognition of the dialectical relationship between thought and language. . . . we can know nothing but what we have words for, if knowledge is what language makes of experience" (p. 223). Echoing Hymes, Faigley (1985) argued that "within a language community, people acquire specialized kinds of discourse competence that enable them to participate in specialized groups" (p. 238). Other research elucidating social dimensions of writing in the 1980s included

(1) Sommers's (1980) work treating revision in terms of writers' anticipation of discrepancies between readers' expectations and their own texts; (2) Heath's (1984), Scribner and Cole's (1981), and Smitherman's (1986) studies of the impact of individuals' membership in various discourse communities on their orientations toward writing and their abilities to meet the demands of typical school writing tasks; (3) Teale and Sulzby's (1986) research on emergent literacy and Dyson's (1983, 1984, 1988) studies of children's writing; (4) research of response groups in writing instruction (e.g., Gere & Stevens, 1985; for review, see DiPardo & Freedman, 1988; for a bibliographic review of the social constructionist philosophical foundations of this work, see Bruffee, 1984, 1986); and (5) Nystrand's (1986, 1989) reciprocity theory and his social-interactive model of writing.

The emerging focus on social aspects of writing, moreover, resulted from the very success of the writing process movement itself, which began to spread beyond departments of English as other departments and academic units incorporated more writing into their instruction. In discussions of academic writing, the premise that college writing was defined by the monistic Freshman English essay—Olson's (1977) autonomous text—began to give way to ideas about disciplinary writing in all its myriad and sundry genres across the curriculum. The resulting Writing Across the Curriculum (WAC) movement made problems of text, social context, and genre more salient and interesting to writing researchers, who, during the 1970s, had been interested in the composing process in some generic sense. Russell (1991) and Ackerman (1993) offered detailed accounts of the impact of WAC on the field's emerging interests in social aspects of writing.

Williams (1991) argued that the novice–expert distinctions that Flower and Hayes (1980a) make, for example, are not categorical but vary from field to field as individuals enter new disciplines. Writing differentiates not once and for all, Williams argued, as novice freshmen writers become expert senior essay writers, but rather repeatedly, each time individuals accommodate themselves to the modes of discourse characteristic of the new fields they choose to enter.

Odell and Goswami (1982) documented a comparable phenomenon in writing in nonacademic settings. Studies from the 1980s explicated (1) the role of context in writing (e.g., Brandt, 1986; Nystrand, 1983), (2) relationships of writing to reading (e.g., Bazerman, 1980; Bereiter & Scardamalia, 1984; Kucer, 1987; Nystrand, 1986; Tierney & LaZansky, 1980; Tierney, Leys, & Rogers, 1984), and (3) the relationship of writers to their discourse communities (e.g., Bizzell, 1982; Brodkey, 1987; Bruffee, 1986; Faigley, 1985). Research on writing and disciplinarity continued into the 1990s (e.g., Berkenkotter & Huckin, 1995; Geisler, 1994; Prior, 1998).

Cognitive models of writing had depicted writers as solitary individuals struggling mainly with their thoughts; audience was viewed, at most, as an ancillary element of the writing process. As writing research became more social in the 1980s, however, the relation of writers and their readers came to be an important research problem. Emig had had little to say about writers' readers; indeed, her conception of composing was one of language production rather than communication or a rhetorical act. For Emig, the writer's significant other was not a reader but a teacher; composing started with a "stimulus" (a school assignment) to which the writer "responded." In Flower and Hayes's (1981) model, audience became "a relevant constraint" on, but not a central element, in writing processes; it was part of the task environment. In another paper influential in the 1980s, David Olson (1977) had argued that because writers, unlike speakers, could not interact with their readers, writers' texts had to operate autonomously (by being completely explicit), with no reference to readers. Entire developmental theories of writing (e.g., Kroll, 1981) were based on the premise that learning to write required learning to produce "autonomous" texts that somehow had meaning only independently of writers' interaction with their readers.

In the 1980s, many of these ideas were challenged. Increasingly the nature of writing, like all language, was viewed as inherently social and interactive. Each act of writing began to be viewed as an episode of interaction, a dialogic utterance (cf. Voloshinov, 1973, p. 82), ideally exhibiting intertextuality (cf. Porter, 1986) within a particular scholarly community or discipline typified by particular premises, issues, and givens. For writing researchers, key questions now included the following: What determined the issues the writer examined? How much evidence was enough? Which evidence was essential? What was a suitable conclusion? To contend that it was the writer alone who determined each of these in accordance with his or her purpose did not adequately explain the principles involved in the behavior. Nor did postulating a black-box monitor as the key element of the composing process do more than beg questions about the organization of discourse. What criteria were relevant to the writer's making these evaluations? What principles shaped the writer's regulation of discourse? How did the character and possibilities of written text shape the writer's options? What principles governed the production of discourse? How were we to characterize these principles?

Finally, it is noteworthy that dramatic increases in the production of PhDs in Composition & Rhetoric during the 1980s fueled research into writing as a social process, especially as the new scholars investigated contexts beyond departments of English—not only in WAC programs but also in writing-intensive courses, writing tutorial centers, and writing and technology facilities. Between 1969 and 1979, programs increased from seven to 20; by 1993, there were 72, a tenfold increase (Figure 1.3). Inasmuch as the new researchers directed the new sites for writing in colleges and universities, they began to calibrate their ideas about writing in the context of the diverse and pluralistic universe of discourse characteristic of colleges and universities (see also Faigley, 1999).

The Postmodern 1990s

Empirical writing research by Britton, Emig, Shaughnessy, and others, we have seen, was initially fueled by efforts to understand the nature of writing as a prerequisite to improving instruction. In time, the Big Question, "What is writing?" began to take on a life of its own. Academics in psychology, linguistics, and anthropology pursued projects on writing. In 1984, a new refereed journal, *Written Communication,* offered the first

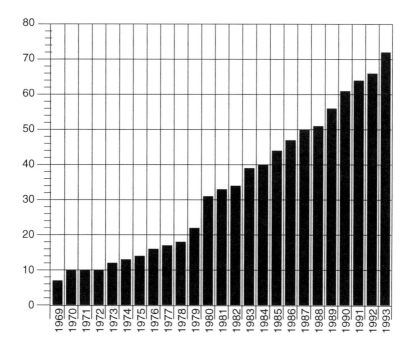

FIGURE 1.3. Cumulative increases in PhD programs in composition and rhetoric. From Brown, Meyer, and Enos (1994, p. 241). Copyright 1994 by Lawrence Erlbaum Associates, Inc. Reprinted by permission.

quarterly forum for reports of research about writing, with no requirement to include discussion of pedagogical implications and applications. During this period, *College Composition and Communication* made anonymous peer review standard procedure for assessing submissions. Special interest groups on writing research were established at the Conference on College Composition and Communication and the American Educational Research Association conventions.

In the 1990s, however, the Big Question, What is writing?, became less an exclusive focus as research became more sociocultural[12] and concerned more comprehensively with writing in all its situated contexts, especially beyond school: writing and technology in the workplace (e.g., Haas, 1996), writing and culture in communities and community centers (e.g., Brandt, 2001; Farr, 2000, forthcoming; Farr & Guerra, 1995; Fleming, in press; Flower, 1994, 1996; Freedman, 1994), writing and communication in industry (e.g., Barabas, 1990; Herndl, Fennell, & Miller, 1991), and investigations of writing in numerous other nonacademic settings (e.g., Bracewell & Breuleux, 1992; Duin & Hansen, 1996; McNamee, 1992; Palmer, 1992; Schriver, 1992); popular literacy (Trimbur, 2001), and the rhetoric of everyday life (Nystrand & Duffy, 2003). In addition, the spread of empirical research on writing beyond North America to Europe heightened the sociocultural variability in writing research (see Coppock, 1998), even if the character of much of this research is more cognitive than sociocultural: in Finland (Tynjälä, 2001); France (Allal, 2000; Allal, Chanquoy, & Largy, 2004; Espéret & Piolat, 1990), Italy (Boscolo, 1989; Boscolo & Mason, 2001), Norway (Berge, 2002; Dysthe, 2002; Evensen, 2002; Ongstad, 2002; Smidt, 2002), and Sweden (Karlsson, 2001). Current research on writing, reading, and literacy increasingly intersects with sociocultural, historical, political, disciplinary, institutional, and everyday contexts, especially in the material world beyond the academy—each situated and domain specific. As Andrea Lunsford (1990) puts it, we have become "a postmodern discipline, a postmodern profession" (p. 77), with more nuanced perspectives than all that have preceded.

Notes

1. John R. Hayes, who would 10 years later collaborate with Linda Flower to elaborate a cognitive model of writing processes (Flower & Hayes, 1981), was a researcher at the Center for Cognitive Studies at this time.
2. Bruffee (1984), cited in Hawkes (1996, p. 3).
3. Information about Mina Shaughnessy courtesy of Allen Streicker, Assistant Archivist, Northwestern University Archives.
4. AERA was founded in 1915 as the National Association of Directors of Educational Research to improve schools' efficiency; membership consisted of 8 men. In 1928, the name was changed to the American Educational Research Association, and by 1931 the organization had 329 members. Membership for the next three decades grew from 511 members in 1940 to 703 in 1950, and 1,774 members in 1960. In the 1960s, membership accelerated:

   1962: 2,210 members
   1964: 3,070 members
   1965: 3,789 members
   1966: 5,375 members
   1968: 8,350 members
   1970: 9,901 members

   By 1980, AERA had 12,737 members. See www.aera.net/divisions/h.
5. According to Keppel, "the state departments of education were the feeblest bunch of second-rate, or fifth-rate, educators who combined educational incompetence with bueaucratic immovability" (quoted in Graham, 1984, p. 63).
6. The Center for Study of the Individual and Cultural Differences in Education. Courtney Cazden was a project assistant in this new center.
7. The Learning Research and Development Center (LRDC), still in operation.
8. The Wisconsin Center for Education Research, still in operation.
9. According to the Research and Development Center Program Act of 1963, the centers were "to concentrate human and financial resources on a particular problem area in education over an extended period of time in an attempt to make significant contribution toward an understanding of, and an improvement of educational practice in, the problem area" (U.S. Department of Health, Education and Welfare, 1963, p. 27).
10. According to the request for proposals, "More specifically, the personnel of a center will

1. Conduct basic and applied research studies, both of the laboratory and field type.
2. Conduct development activities designed to translate systematically research findings into educational materials or procedures, and field test the developed products.
3. Demonstrate and disseminate information about the new programs or procedures which emerge from the research and development efforts. These activities may include demonstrations in a natural, or operational setting, the preparation of films, tapes, displays, publications, and lectures, and the participation in symposia and conferences.
4. Provide nationwide leadership in the chosen area (U.S. Department of Health, Education and Welfare, 1963, p. 27).

11. An important volume of cognitive papers on writing at this time was Gregg and Steinberg (1981). For reviews of cognitive research on writing, see Humes (1983), Kucer (1987), and Spivey (1990).
12. A Google search of "writing process" today (July 2004) brings up 610,000 Web pages, virtually all pedagogical, with no research citations, and aimed at teachers and students on preparing academic papers.

References

Ackerman, J. M. (1993). The promise of writing to learn. *Written Communication, 10,* 334–370.

Adams, M., & Collins, A. (1979). A schema-theoretic view of reading. In R. Freedle (Ed.), *Advances in Discourse Processes: Vol. 2. New directions in discourse processing* (pp. 1–22). Norwood, NJ: Ablex.

Allal, L. (2000). Metacognitive regulation of writing in the classroom. In A. Camps & M. Milian (Eds.), *Metalinguistic activity in learning to write* (pp. 145–166). Amsterdam: Amsterdam University Press.

Allal, L., Chanquoy, L., & Largy, P. (2004). *Studies in writing: Vol. 13. Revision: Cognitive and instructional processes.* New York: Kluwer.

Anderson, R. (1984). Role of the reader's schema in comprehension, learning, and memory. In R. C. Anderson, J. Osborne, and R. J. Tierney (Eds.), *Learning to read in American schools: Basal readers and content texts* (pp. 187–201). Hillsdale, NJ: Erlbaum.

Angoff, W. (1975). Why the SAT scores are going down. *English Journal, 64,* 10–11.

Applebee, A. N. (1981). *Writing in the secondary school* (NCTE Research Report No. 21). Urbana, IL: National Council of Teachers of English.

Barabas, C. (1990). *Technical writing in a corporate culture: A study of the nature of information.* Norwood, NJ: Ablex.

Bazerman, C. (1980). A relationship between reading and writing: The conversational model. *College English, 41,* 656–661.

Bereiter, C., & Scardamalia, M. (1984). Learning about writing from reading. *Written Communication, 1,* 163–188.

Bereiter, C., & Scardamalia, M. (1987). *The psychology of written composition.* Hillsdale, NJ: Erlbaum.

Berge, K. (2002). Hidden norms in assessment of students exam essays in Norwegian upper secondary schools. *Written Communication, 19,* 458–492.

Berkenkotter, C., & Huckin, T. (1995). *Genre knowledge in disciplinary communication: Cognition/culture/power.* Hillsdale, NJ: Erlbaum.

Bissex, G. (1980). *Gnys at wrk: A child learns to write and read.* Cambridge, MA: Harvard University Press.

Bizzell, P. (1982). Cognition, context, and certainty. *PRE/TEXT, 3,* 213–224.

Boscolo, P. (1989). When revising is restructuring: Strategies of text changing in elementary school children. In P. Boscolo (Ed.), *Writing: Trends in European research* (pp. 1–11). Padova, Italy: UPSEL Editore.

Boscolo, P., & Mason, L. (2001). Writing to learn, writing to transfer. In P. Tynjälä, L. Mason, & K. Lonka (Eds.), *Writing as a learning tool: Integrating theory and practice* (pp. 37–56). Dordrecht, The Netherlands: Kluwer.

Bracewell, R., & Breuleux, A. (1992, April). *Cognitive principles for the support of technical writing.* Paper presented at the 1992 Convention of the American Educational Research Association, San Francisco.

Bracewell, R., Fredericksen, C., & Fredericksen, J. (1982). Cognitive processes in composing and comprehending. *Educational Psychologist, 17,* 146–164.

Braddock, R., Lloyd-Jones, R., & Schoer, L. (1963). *Research in written composition.* Champaign, IL: National Council of Teachers of English.

Brandt, D. (1986). Text and context: How writers come to mean. In B. Couture (Ed.), *Functional approaches to writing: Research perspectives* (pp. 93–107). Norwood, NJ: Ablex.

Brandt, D. (2001). *Literacy in American lives.* New York: Cambridge University Press.

Britton, J. (1969). Talking to learn. In D. Barnes, J. Britton, & H. Rosen (Eds.), *Language, the learner, and the school* (pp. 79–115). Harmondsworth, UK: Penguin.

Britton, J. (1970). *Language and learning*. London: Allen Lane/Penguin Press.

Brodkey, L. (1987). *Academic writing as social practice*. Philadelphia: Temple University Press.

Brown, S., Meyer, P., & Enos, T. (1994). Doctoral programs in rhetoric and composition: A catalog of the profession. *Rhetoric Review, 12*, 240–251.

Bruffee, K. (1984). Collaborative learning and 'the conversation of mankind.' *College English, 46*, 635–652.

Bruffee, K. (1986). Social construction, language, and the authority of knowledge. *College English, 48*, 773–790.

Cazden, C. (1972). *Functions of language in the classroom*. New York: Teachers College Press.

Cazden, C. (1988). *Classroom discourse: The language of teaching and learning*. Portsmouth, NH: Heinemann.

Chomsky, N. (1957). *Syntactic structures*. The Hague: Mouton.

Chomsky, N. (1966). *Cartesian linguistics: A chapter in the history of rationalist thought*. New York: Harper & Row.

Chomsky, N. (1968). *Language and mind*. New York: Harcourt, Brace & World.

Collins, A., & Loftus, E. (1975). A spreading activation theory of semantic processing. *Psychological Review, 82*, 407–428.

Coppock, P. (Ed.). (1998). *The Semiotics of writing: Transdisciplinary perspectives ons the technology of writing*. Turnhout, Belgium: Brepols.

Daiute, C. (1981). Psycholinguistic foundations of the writing process. *Research in the Teaching of English, 15*, 5–22.

Dershimer, R. (1976). *The federal government and educational R&D*. Lexington, MA: Lexington Books.

Dewey, J. (1884). The new psychology. *Andover Review, 2*, 278–289.

DiPardo, A., & Freedman, S. (1988). Peer response groups in the writing classroom: Theoretical foundations and new directions. *Review of Educational Research, 58*, 119–149.

Dixon, J. (1967). *Growth through English*. Reading, UK: National Association for the Teaching of English.

Douglas, W. (1976). Rhetoric for the meritocracy: The creation of composition at Harvard. In R. Ohmann (Ed.), *English in America: A radical view of the profession* (pp. 97–132). New York: Oxford University Press.

Duin, A. H., & Hansen, C. J. (Eds.). (1996). *Nonacademic writing: Social theory and technology*. Mahwah, NJ: Erlbaum.

Dyson, A. H. (1983). The role of oral language in early writing processes. *Research in the Teaching of English, 17*, 1–30.

Dyson, A. H. (1984). Emerging alphabetic literacy in school contexts: Toward defining the gap between school curriculum and child mind. *Written Communication, 1*, 5–55.

Dyson, A. H. (1988). *Negotiating among multiple worlds: The space/time dimensions of young children's composing* (Technical Report No. 15). Berkeley, CA: National Research Center of Writing and Literacy.

Dysthe, O. (2002). Models and positions in text based supervision: An interview study with master degree students and supervisors. *Written Communication, 19*, 493–544.

Emig, J. (1971). *The composing processes of twelfth graders*. Urbana, IL: National Council of Teachers of English.

Espéret, E., & Piolat, A. (1990). Production: Planning and control. In G. Denhière & J. Rossi (Eds.), *Texts and text processing* (pp. 317–333). Amsterdam: North-Holland.

Evensen, L. (2002). Conventions from below: Negotiating interaction and culture in argumentative writing. *Written Communication, 19*, 382–413.

Fadiman, C., & Howard, J. (1979). *Empty pages: A search for writing competence in school and society*. Belmont, CA: Fearon Pitman.

Faigley, L. (1985). Nonacademic writing: The social perspective. In L. Odell & D. Goswami (Eds.), *Writing in nonacademic settings* (pp. 231–248). New York: Guilford Press.

Faigley, L. (1999). Veterans' stories on the porch. In M. Rosner, B. Boehm, & D. Journet (Eds.), *History, reflection and narrative: The professionalization of composition, 1963–1983* (pp. 22–37). Norwood, NJ: Ablex.

Faigley, L., & Witte, S. (1981). Analyzing revision. *College Composition and Communication, 32*, 400–414.

Farr, M. (2000). Literacy and religion: Reading, writing, and gender among Mexican women in Chicago. In P. Griffin, J. K. Peyton, W. Wolfram, & R. Fasold (Eds.), *Language in action: New studies of language in society*. Cresskill, NJ: Hampton Press.

Farr, M. *Rancheros in Chicagoacán: Ways of speaking and identity in a transnational Mexican community*.

Farr, M., & Guerra, J. (1995). Literacy in the community: A study of *Mexicano* families in Chicago (Discourse Processes Special issue). *Literacy Among Latinos, 19*, 7–19.

Fleming, D. (In press). *City of rhetoric: Making space for public life in American communities*. Albany, NY: SUNY Press.

Flower, L. (1994). *The construction of negotiated meaning A social cognitive theory of writing*. Carbondale: University of Southern Illinois Press.

Flower, L. (1996). Collaborative planning and community literacy: A window on the logic of learners. In L. Schauble & R. Glaser (Eds.), *Innovations in learning: New environments for education* (pp. 25–48). Mahwah, NJ: Erlbaum.

Flower, L., & Hayes, J. R. (1977). Problem-solving strategies and the writing process. *College English, 39,* 449–461.

Flower, L., & Hayes, J. R. (1980a). Identifying the organization of writing processes. In L. Gregg & E. Steinberg (Eds.), *Cognitive processes in writing* (pp. 3–30). Hillsdale, NJ: Erlbaum.

Flower, L., & Hayes, J. R. (1980b). The dynamics of composing: Making plans and juggling constraints. In L. Gregg & E. Steinberg (Eds.), *Cognitive processes in writing* (pp. 31–50). Hillsdale, NJ: Erlbaum.

Flower, L., & Hayes, J. R. (1981). A cognitive process theory of writing. *College Composition and Communication, 32,* 365–387.

Flower, L., & Hayes, J. R. (1984, January). Images, plans, and prose: The representation of meaning in writing. *Written Communication, 1,* 120–160.

Freedman, S. (1994). *Exchanging writing, exchanging cultures: Lessons in school reform from the United States and Great Britain.* Cambridge, MA: Harvard University Press.

Geisler, C. (1991). Toward a sociocognitive perspective on literacy: A study of an academic "conversation." In C. Bazerman & J. Paradis (Eds.), *Textual dynamics of the professions: Historical and contemporary studies of writing in professional communities* (pp. 171–190). Madison: University of Wisconsin Press.

Gere, A., & Stevens, R. (1985). The language of writing groups: How oral response shapes revision. In S. Freedman (Ed.), *The acquisition of written language: Revision and response* (pp. 85–105). Norwood, NJ: Ablex.

Graham, H. (1984). *The uncertain triumph: Federal education policy in the Kennedy and Johnson years.* Chapel Hill: University of North Carolina Press.

Gregg, L., & Steinberg, E. (Eds.). (1981). *Cognitive processes in writing.* Hillsdale, NJ: Erlbaum.

Haas, C. (1996). *Writing technology: Studies on the materiality of literacy.* Mahwah, NJ: Erlbaum.

Hawkes, P. (1996, October). *Open admissions and Vietnam protests: Tracing the politics of Kenneth Bruffee's collaborative learning.* Paper presented at Thomas R. Watson Conference, University of Louisville, Louisville, KY.

Hayes, J., & Simon, H. (1975). Understanding tasks stated in natural language. In D. Reddy (Ed.), *Speech recognition* (pp. 428–454). New York: Academic Press.

Heath, S. (1984). *Ways with words: Language, life, and work in communities and classrooms.* New York: Cambridge University Press.

Herndl, C., Fennell, B., & Miller, C. (1991). Understanding failures in organizational discourse. In C. Bazerman & J. Paradis (Eds.), *Textual dynamics of the professions: Historical and contemporary studies of writing in professional communities*

(pp. 279–305). Madison: University of Wisconsin Press.

Humes, A. (1983). Research on the composing process. *Review of Educational Research, 153,* 181–199.

Hymes, D. (1974). *Foundations in sociolinguistics.* Philadelphia: University of Philadelphia Press.

James, W. (1890). *Principles of psychology.* New York: Holt.

Kaestle, C. F. (1992). *Everybody's been to fourth grade: An oral history of federal R&D in education: A report to the National Research Council, Committee on the Federal Role in Education Research* (Research Report 92–1). Madison: Wisconsin Center for Education Research.

Karlsson, A. M. (2001). Analysing the multimodality of writing: A model and a method applied to personal homepages. In W. Vagle & K. Wikberg (Eds.), *New directions in Nordic text linguistics and discourse analysis: Methodological issues* (pp. 137–147). Proceedings from the NordText Symposium, University of Oslo, January 7–9, 2000. Oslo: Novus.

Keppel, F. (1965). The national commitment to education. *Phi Delta Kappan, 47,* 167–168.

Kihss, P. (1968, May 23). Brooklyn College defends actions. *New York Times,* p. 48.

Kroll, B. (1978). Cognitive egocentrism and the problem of audience awareness in written discourse. *Research in the Teaching of English, 56,* 269–281.

Kroll, B. (1981). Developmental relationships between speaking and writing. In B. Kroll & R. Vann (Eds.), *Exploring speaking–writing relationships: Connections and contrasts.* Urbana, IL: National Council of Teachers of English.

Kucer, S. (1987). The cognitive base of reading and writing. In J. R. Squire (Ed.), *The dynamics of langauge learning* (pp. 27–52). Urbana: National Conference on Research in English and ERIC Clearinghouse on Reading and Communication Skills.

Labov, W. (1972). The logic of nonstandard English. In W. Labov (Ed.), *Language in the inner city: Studies in the black English vernacular* (pp. 201–240). Philadelphia: University of Pennsylvania Press.

Lucas, F. (1955). *Style* (2nd ed.). London: Cassell.

Lunsford, A. (1990). Composing ourselves: Politics, commitment, and the teaching of writing. *College Composition and Communication, 41,* 77–86.

McNamee, G. D. (1992, April). *The voices of community change.* Paper presented at the Convention of the American Educational Research Association, San Francisco.

Mellon, J. C. (1969). *Transformational sentence-combining: A method for enhancing the development of syntactic fluency in English composition* (NCTE Research Report No. 10). Champaign, IL: National Council of Teachers of English.

Meyer, B. J. F., & McConkie, G. W. (1973). What is recalled after hearing a passage? *Journal of Educational Psychology, 65*, 109–117.

Miller, T. (1997). *The formation of college English: Rhetoric and belles lettres in the British cultural provinces*. Pittsburgh: University of Pittsburgh Press.

Moffett, J. (1968). *Teaching the universe of discourse*. Boston: Houghton Mifflin.

Newell, A., & Simon, H. (1972). *Human problem solving*. Englewood Cliffs, NJ: Prentice-Hall.

Nystrand, M. (1982). Rhetoric's audience and linguistics speech community: Implications for understanding writing, reading, and text. In *What writers know: The language, process, and structure of written discourse* (pp. 1–28). New York: Academic Press.

Nystrand, M. (1983). The role of context in written communication. *Nottingham Linguistic Circular, 12*, 55–65.

Nystrand, M. (1986). *The structure of written communication: Studies in reciprocity between writers and readers*. Orlando and London: Academic Press.

Nystrand, M. (1989). A social-interactive model of writing. *Written Communication, 6*, 66–85.

Nystrand, M., & Duffy, J. (2003). *Towards a rhetoric of everyday life: New directions in research on writing, text, and discourse*. Madison: University of Wisconsin Press.

Odell, L., & Goswami, D. (1982). Writing in a nonacademic setting. *Research in the Teaching of English, 16*, 201–223.

Olson, D. R. (1977). From utterance to text: The bias of language in speech and writing. *Harvard Educational Review, 47*, 257–281.

Ongstad, S. (2002). Triadic positioning(s) of early Norwegian research and development (R&D) on educational writing. *Written Communication, 19*, 345–381.

Palmer, J. (1992, April). *The rhetoric of negotiation: Professional writing at Apple Computer, Inc.* Paper presented at the Convention of the American Educational Research Association, San Francisco.

Pearson, P. D. (2001). *The Center for the Study of Reading's legacy*. Paper presented at the 2001 California Reading Conference. Available at www.ciera.org/library/presos/2001/pearson/01craper.pdf.

Porter, J. E. (1986). Intertextuality and the discourse community. *Rhetoric Review, 5*, 34–47.

Prior, P. (1998). *Writing/disciplinarity: A sociohistoric account of literate activity in the academy*. Mahwah, NJ: Erlbaum.

Read, C. (1971). *Children's categorization of speech sounds in English*. Urbana, IL: National Council of Teachers of English.

Rohman, D. G. (1965). Pre-writing: The stage of discovery in the writing process. *College Composition and Communication, 17*, 2–11.

Rohman, D. G., & Wlecke, A. O. (1964). *Pre-writing: The construction and application of models for concept formation in writing* (U.S. Office of Education Cooperative Research Project, No. 2174). East Lansing: Michigan State University.

Russell, D. (1991). *Writing in the academic disciplines*. Carbondale: Southern Illinois University Press.

Sacks, H., Schlegloff, E. A., & Jefferson, G. (1974). A simplest systematics for the organization of turn-taking in conversation. *Language, 50*, 696–735.

Scardamalia, M., Bereiter, C., & Goelman, H. (1982). The role of production factors in writing ability. In M. Nystrand (Ed.), *What writers know: The language, process, and structure of written discourse*. New York: Academic Press.

Schriver, K. (1992, April). *Collaboration in professional writing: The cognition of a social process*. Paper presented at the Convention of the American Educational Research Association, San Francisco.

Scribner, S., & Cole, M. (1981). *The psychology of literacy*. Cambridge, MA: Harvard University Press.

Shaughnessy, M. (1977). *Errors and expectations*. London: Oxford University Press.

Sheils, M. (1975, December 8). Why Johnny can't write. *Newsweek*, pp. 58–65.

Smidt, J. (2002). Composing oneself and the other: Changing positionings of teacher and students in secondary school writing. *Written Communication, 19*, 414–443.

Smith, F. (1971). *Understanding reading*. New York: Holt, Rinehart & Winston.

Smitherman, G. (1986). *Talkin' and testifyin': The language of black America*. Detroit: Wayne State University Press.

Sommers, N. (1980). Revision strategies of student writers and experience adult writers. *College Composition and Communication, 31*, 378–388.

Spivey, N. (1990). Transforming texts: Constructive processes in reading and writing. *Written Communication, 7*, 256–287.

Stein, N. (1981). The definition of story. *Journal of Pragmatics, 6*, 487–507.

Stone, M. (1974, November 11). Bonehead English. *Time*, p. 106.

Strunk, W., & White, E. B. (1959). *The elements of style*. New York: Macmillan.

Teale, W., & Sultzby, E. (Eds.). (1986). *Emergent literacy: Writing and reading*. Norwood, NJ: Ablex.

Tierney, R., & LaZansky, J. (1980). *The rights and responsibilities of readers and writers: A contractual agreement* (Education Report No. 15). Urbana: University of Illinois Center for the Study of Reading.

Tierney, R., Leys, M., & Rogers, T. (1984). *Comprehension, composition, and collaboration: Analysis of communicative influences in two classrooms.* Paper presented at the sixth annual Conference on Reading Research, Atlanta, GA.

Town, K. (1988). *The process approach: Early versions in the English Journal, 1912–1960.* Unpublished doctoral dissertation, Ohio State University, Columbus.

Trabasso, T., & Van den Broek. P. (1985). Causal thinking and the representation of narrative events. *Journal of Memory and Language, 24,* 612–630.

Trimbur, J. (2001). *Popular literacy: Studies in cultural practices and poetics.* Pittsburgh: University of Pittsburgh Press.

Tynjälä, P. 2001. Writing, learning and the development of expertise in higher education. In P. Tynjälä, L. Mason, & K. Lonka (Eds.), *Writing as a learning tool: Integrating theory and practice* (pp. 37–56). Dordrecht, The Netherlands: Kluwer.

U.S. Department of Health, Education and Welfare, Office of Education. (1963), *Cooperative research programs: Application instruction for research contracts.* Washington, DC: U.S. Government Printing Office.

Voloshinov, V. N. (1973). *Marxism and the philosophy of language* (L. Matejka & I. R. Titunik, Trans.). New York: Seminar Press.

Warriner, J. (1950). *English grammar and composition: Complete course.* New York: Harcourt Brace Jovanovich.

Williams, J. (1991). Rhetoric and informal reasoning: Disentangling some confounded effects in good reasoning and good writing. In J. Voss, D. Perkins, & J. Segal (Eds.), *Informal reasoning and education* (pp. 225–246). Hillsdale, NJ: Erlbaum.

Williams, J. (1991). Rhetoric and informal reasoning: Disentangling some confounded effects in good reasoning and good writing. In J. Voss (Ed.), *Informal reasoning and education.* Hillsdale, NJ: Erlbaum.

Witte, S. P., & Faigley, L. (1983). *Evaluating college writing programs* (Studies in Writing and Rhetoric No. 1). Carbondale: Southern Illinois University Press.

Young, R. (1968, September). Discovery procedures in tagmemic rhetoric: An exercise in problem solving (Studies in Language and Language Behavior, Progress Report No. Vll, U.S.O.E. Contract No. OEC-3-6-061784-0508). Ann Arbor: Center for Research on Language and Language Behavior, University of Michigan.

Young, R. (1969). Problems and the process of writing (*Studies in Language and Language Behavior*). Ann Arbor: Center for Research on Language and Language Behavior, University of Michigan. ERIC ED 029040.

Young, R. (1978). Paradigms and problems: Needed research in rhetorical invention. In C. Cooper & L. Odell (Eds.), *Research on composing: Points of departure* (pp. 29–47). Urbana, IL: National Council of Teachers of English, 1978.

Young, R., & Becker, A. (1965). Toward a modern theory of rhetoric: A tagmemic contribution. *Harvard Educational Review, 35,* 450–468.

Young, R., Becker, A., & Pike, K. (1974). *Rhetoric: Discovery and change.* New York: Harcourt, Brace & World.

Chapter 2

New Directions in Writing Theory

John R. Hayes

Over the last quarter of a century, writing researchers in Europe and America have been making fairly steady progress in improving our understanding of the cognitive and social processes involved in writing. New theoretical proposals have stimulated empirical studies, and new empirical findings have led to the reformulation and improvement of theories.

In this chapter, I have chosen to examine three quite different but interesting research initiatives that are shaping the evolution of writing theory today. I could have chosen many, but these are the three I found most intriguing:

- Research on the role of working memory in writing
- Studies of the efficacy of freewriting
- Proposals to use activity theory as a framework for understanding the context of writing

There is no underlying theme that unifies these three lines of research except for their potential for expanding our understanding of writing. Working memory is essential for the functioning of the cognitive processes involved in writing. Studies of freewriting may tell us how to use writing to improve thinking. Activity theory may help to make sense of the complex social and environmental factors that influence writing. These topics are being pursued by different research communities in different parts of the world. Research on working memory in writing is being carried out by psychologists in the United States, the United Kingdom, and France. Studies of freewriting, which started in English departments in the United States, are currently being carried out psychologists in the United Kingdom. Proposals for applying activity theory to writing are being most actively discussed in English departments in North America. What I present is a snapshot of these three lines of research, with some suggestions about where they may be heading.

Research on the Role of Working Memory in Writing

Anyone who has composed a brilliant sentence and then forgotten the end of it before it could be committed to paper has experienced one of the problems that limited memory creates for writers. In this section, I discuss research on the multiple roles that working memory can play in writing. Psychologists introduced the concept of working memory to describe the limitations that we experience in performing a variety of tasks that require memory. For example, we are very likely to run out of memory resources when we are asked to remember a list of 10 items or to multiply two three-digit numbers without the aid of pencil and paper.

Working memory is limited in the amount of material it can hold and in the length of time it can hold it. Understanding how different writing processes draw on the same limited working memory resources can help us understand how the processes may interfere with each other. For example, Chenoweth and Hayes (2001, p. 94) found that second-language learners were more skillful in editing their texts after they had composed them than while they were composing them. These researchers attributed the difference in editing skill to memory-based interference between the processes of composing and editing.

Baddeley and his colleagues (e.g., Baddeley & Hitch, 1974; Gathercole & Baddeley, 1993) have proposed a model of working memory that has separate stores for verbal and visual materials. The model consists of three parts: a phonological loop for storing verbal information, a visuospatial sketchpad for storing visual information, and a central executive that, among other functions, manages the other two parts.

The phonological loop consists of two parts. The first, called the *phonological short-term store*, represents verbal material in a phonological (auditory) code that decays within a few seconds. The second part is a subvocal, *articulatory rehearsal process* that refreshes the material in the short-term store. Engaging in articulatory rehearsal is experienced as speaking to oneself. Articulatory rehearsal has the effect of increasing the time that material can be maintained in the short-term store. For example, if you have looked up a phone number and want to remember it until you can dial it, you can repeat the number to yourself to keep it fresh in your mind. That is articulatory rehearsal.

It is possible to interfere with a person's articulatory rehearsal process in at least two ways: (1) by exposing the person to irrelevant speech, and (2) by articulatory suppression. Both of these methods for interfering with rehearsal were employed in a study of digit memory by Salame and Baddeley (1982). In this study, participants were shown lists of nine digits presented serially on a TV screen. Their task was to write down the digits immediately after they were presented.

In the irrelevant speech condition, one-syllable words or nonsense syllables were presented over a loud speaker during the visual presentation of the numbers. Participants were instructed to ignore the auditory input and to attend only to the visually presented digits. In the articulatory suppression condition, participants were asked to repeat the syllable *the* over and over during presentation of the digits.

Memory for digits was significantly reduced both by irrelevant speech (whether it consisted of meaningful words or nonsense syllables) and by articulatory suppression. However, the reduction caused by articulatory suppression was significantly greater than that caused by irrelevant speech. Furthermore, articulatory suppression and irrelevant speech together caused no more memory reduction than was caused by articulatory suppression alone. These results suggest that articulatory suppression is more effective in eliminating rehearsal than is exposure to irrelevant speech. Articulatory suppression may reduce memory for words by as much as 50% (Longoni, Richardson, & Aiello, 1993).

Ronald Kellogg (1988, 1990) is the researcher perhaps most responsible for promoting interest in the role of working memory in writing. He has carried out an extensive program of research on the cognitive resources demanded by the various cognitive processes involved in writing. In 1996, Kellogg and Hayes independently proposed that working memory be included as a central component in the modeling of writing. Kellogg's model, as slightly revised in 1999, is shown in Figure 2.1 and Hayes's model, in Figure 2.2. Both models include working memory and, in large part, both accept the description of working memory provided by Baddeley's model. However, the two models differ. Hayes's (1996) model represents working memory as a resource that is available to and presumably used by all of the writing processes. In contrast, Kellogg's model, both in the 1996 and the 1999 versions, makes specific predictions that particular writing processes draw on some of the components of working memory and not others. In particular, Kellogg (1999) asserts that translating and reading make use of verbal working memory but not spatial working memory, that editing and planning make use of spatial working memory but not verbal working memory, and that programming

	Working memory component		
Basic process	Spatial	Central executive	Verbal
Planning	X	X	
Translating		X	X
Programming		X*	
Executing			
Reading		X	X
Editing	X		

FIGURE 2.1. Kellogg's (1999) model of the role of working memory in writing. *For highly practiced motor skills, these demands are small if not negligible.

and executing motor movements (e.g., those used in typing or handwriting) use neither.

There is strong empirical support for the prediction that the phonological loop is involved in the process of formulating text. Levy and Marek (1999) have shown decrements in a sentence-writing task when participants were required to listen to irrelevant speech while performing the task. Chenoweth and Hayes (2003) asked adult writers to compose a sentence summarizing a wordless cartoon and found that articulatory suppression significantly slowed sentence production in this task. They also found that the pacing of the sentence production process was changed. Ordinarily, sentences are produced in parts. Each part is a short sequence

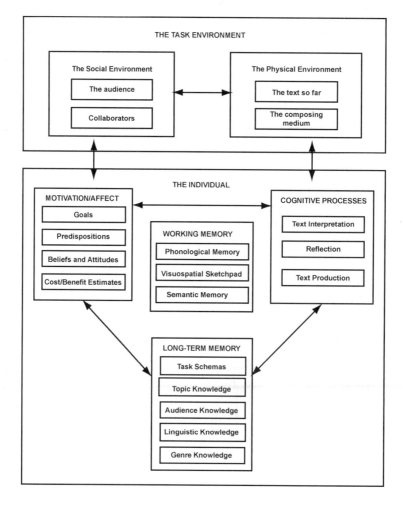

FIGURE 2.2. Hayes's (1996) framework for understanding cognition and affect in writing.

of words. The writer produces a sequence of words in rapid order, then pauses, produces another sequence, pauses, and so on. With articulatory suppression, the length of these parts was reduced to about 60% of the length observed without articulatory suppression.

Levy and Marek (1999) also provided empirical support for other aspects of Kellogg's (1996) model. In a series of experiments, these researchers compared the performance of writers who were exposed or not exposed to irrelevant speech on several writing tasks. In Experiment 1, Levy and Marek (1999) tested Kellogg's (1996) prediction that text production does not involve the phonological loop. They asked participants to transcribe text from one computer window to another. The researchers then compared the number of words typed and the number of words typed correctly by students exposed or not exposed to irrelevant speech. As Salame and Baddeley (1982) showed, irrelevant speech reduces verbal working memory capacity. Consistent with Kellogg's prediction, Levy and Marek (1999) found no significant differences between the groups on either measure.

In Experiment 2, Levy and Marek (1999) tested Kellogg's (1996) hypothesis that editing does not employ the phonological loop. They asked participants to detect spelling and grammatical errors in text and compared performance with and without irrelevant speech. They found no significant difference between these conditions. These results are at variance with Chenoweth and Hayes (2003), who found that articulatory suppression led to an increase in the number of uncorrected errors in the sentences that participants produced, suggesting a decrease in the effectiveness of the editing process under articulatory suppression.

Hayes and Chenoweth (forthcoming) have recently completed a study parallel to the Levy and Marek (1999) study but using articulatory suppression rather than irrelevant speech to interfere with verbal working memory. Participants were asked to transcribe texts from one window on a computer screen to another. In the articulatory suppression condition, the participants said "tap" in time to a metronome while transcribing the texts. In the control condition, they each tapped a foot in time to the metro-

nome. In contrast to Levy and Marek's results, Hayes and Chenoweth found that articulatory suppression significantly slowed typing rates (Control = 52.7 words/minute; Experimental = 44.5 words/minute) and increased the number of errors that appeared in the final texts (Control = 4.24/100 words; Experimental = 6.12/100 words).

In addition, keylog records allowed the researchers to identify typing errors that participants subsequently corrected, and thus did not appear in the final texts. The total number of errors (corrected and uncorrected) did not differ significantly between the "tap" and "no tap" conditions (even though the numbers of uncorrected errors did differ significantly). Thus, it appears that articulatory interference did not significantly influence the total error rate, but it did interfere with participants' ability to correct their errors. This result does not support Kellogg's (1999) prediction that editing does not rely on the phonological loop.

It seems likely that the differences in the results obtained by Levy and Marek (1999) and by Hayes and Chenoweth (forthcoming) are due to differences in the method of interfering with rehearsal. Salame and Baddeley's (1982) study indicated that articulatory suppression is substantially more effective in eliminating rehearsal than is exposure to irrelevant speech.

One might speculate that the slower typing rate Hayes and Chenoweth (forthcoming) observed in the articulatory suppression condition might be attributed to an increase in the amount of editing done by participants in that condition. However, participants in the articulatory suppression condition actually deleted about 15% less material than did participants in the control condition. This suggests that the reduced typing rate was not due to increased editing, but rather that articulatory suppression directly interfered with the process of text production, a result that appears to be inconsistent with Kellogg's (1999) prediction that text production does not rely on the phonological loop.

If typing does compete with the other writing processes for verbal working memory resources, then that suggests an interesting possibility. Since training in a skill typically reduces the working memory resources required by that skill, then it is possible that providing young students with training in typing could make it easier for them to learn other writing skills.

In any case, the empirical evidence relevant to Kellogg's (1999) hypotheses that editing and text production do not rely on verbal working memory is mixed. Further studies should be conducted to evaluate these hypotheses, as well as Kellogg's very interesting hypotheses that spatial working memory is involved in planning and editing. In whatever way the results turn out, Kellogg's model has served a very valuable role in stimulating new research.

Studies of the Efficacy of Freewriting

There is an ongoing debate about the best strategy for drafting texts. The most familiar advice to student writers is that they should first create an outline of the text in the form of an ordered list of topics and subtopics. After the outline has been created, the writer should use it to guide the production of formal sentences to be included in the final text. I call this strategy the *outline first* strategy. Of course, most teachers who advocate this strategy allow some flexibility. If difficulties arise, or new ideas are discovered, the outline can be modified. However, the thrust of the strategy is to make an outline and follow it while writing the text.

In his influential book *Writing without Teachers*, Peter Elbow (1973) famously criticized this drafting strategy in the following way:

> This idea of writing is backwards. That's why it causes so much trouble. Instead of a two-step transaction of meaning-into-language, think of writing as an organic, developmental process in which you start writing at the very beginning—before you know your meaning at all—and encourage your words gradually to change and evolve. Only at the end will you know what you want to say or the words you want to say it with. (p. 15)

In his critique, Elbow expresses what many writers have reported experiencing. Writing for them is not just putting down ideas already held. It also involves creating ideas during the process of writing. They experience writing as a discovery process (Murray, 1978) or, as Galbraith (1999) has

called it, "a knowledge-constituting process" (p. 137).

In *Writing without Teachers*, Elbow (1973) proposed an alternative to the outline first strategy that I call the *interactive* strategy. Rather than outlining what one plans to write and only then writing full sentences, Elbow recommends writing sentences right from the beginning. Writers are advised to plough ahead even if they are not sure of where they are going. Editing is to be left for last and should be avoided while the writer is producing text. To help writers acquire the skill of writing without editing, Elbow recommends that they do freewriting exercises for 10 minutes or so three times a week. In a freewriting exercise, writers write continuously, putting down anything that occurs to them, without editing and without looking back. As Elbow explains:

> The main thing about freewriting is that it is *nonediting*. It is an exercise in bringing together the process of producing words and putting them down on the page. Practiced regularly, it undoes the ingrained habit of editing at the same time you are trying to produce. It will make writing less blocked because words will come more easily. (p. 6)

In addition to reducing blocking, Elbow claims two other advantages for freewriting. First, he says that freewriting frees writers' normal ways of expressing themselves, their natural voices, which Elbow believes is important for effective writing: "The habit of compulsive, premature editing doesn't just make writing hard. It also makes writing dead. Your voice is damped out by all the interruptions, changes, and hesitations between the consciousness and the page" (p. 6).

Second, and in my opnion most interesting, Elbow claims that freewriting can help the writer to discover better ideas:

> [Freewriting is] also a way to produce bits of writing that are genuinely *better* than usual: less random, more coherent, more highly organized. (p. 8; emphasis in original)
>
> It boils down to something very simple. If you do freewriting regularly, much or most of it will be far inferior to what you can produce through care and rewriting. But the good bits will be much better than anything you can produce by any other method. (p. 9)

For Elbow, writing should proceed in a sequence of cycles, each of which consists of an episode of freewriting followed by editing. The function of editing is to select what is best in the last draft and to let it form a starting point for the next draft. As the writer moves from cycle to cycle, the meaning develops and changes. Carried out in this way, Elbow believes that

> writing is a way to end up thinking something you couldn't have started out thinking. Writing is, in fact, a transaction with words whereby you free yourself from what you presently think, feel, and perceive. You make available to yourself something better than what you'd be stuck with if you'd actually succeeded in making your meaning clear from the start. (p. 15)

These claims, if they were verified, would have very important implications for the study of writing and the practice of teaching writing. A writing strategy that stimulates better ideas could be important for everyone who writes. However, at the time Elbow made these claims, the empirical evidence supporting them, though fairly extensive, was anecdotal, consisting largely of self-reports by well-known writers (Murray, 1978). Since that time, a number of carefully designed studies have explored the effects of the outline first strategy, the interactive strategy, and other drafting strategies on the properties of the resulting texts.

In one of the earliest of these studies, Glynn, Britton, Muth, and Dogan (1982) compared four drafting strategies. Participants wrote a first draft either in (1) polished sentences, (2) complete but unpolished sentences, (3) organized notes, or (4) unorganized notes. They then edited their drafts to produce a final text. The authors found that the number of ideas that writers produced in their first drafts was least when they wrote polished sentences and most when they wrote unorganized notes.

An important series of studies by Kellogg (1988, 1990) provides further information about the impact of drafting strategies not only on the properties of the text produced, but also on the writing processes that produced them. In one experiment (Kellogg, 1988, Experiment 1), participants wrote a business letter under four drafting conditions

defined by the combination of two variables. I call these variables *draft quality* and *planning*. Draft quality was either rough or polished. In the rough condition, participants were told first to get their thoughts on paper without worrying about how well they were expressed, and then to edit later. In the polished condition, participants were directed to compose a polished draft with the chief aim of expressing their thoughts as well as possible from the beginning. Planning had two alterative values: outline or no outline. In the outline condition, participants were asked to spend 5–10 minutes writing an ordered list of points and subpoints. In the no-outline condition, participants began writing their letters without an outline.

During writing, participants were interrupted at frequent intervals and asked to report on the writing process they were engaged in at the moment: planning, translating, revising, or other. This innovative procedure allowed Kellogg (1988) to assess the impact of the experimental procedures on writing processes.

Kellogg found that participants in the outline condition wrote significantly longer essays, spent significantly more time writing (exclusive of planning time), and wrote letters that were rated significantly higher in idea development and in overall quality than did participants in the no-outline condition. There were no significant effects of the draft quality variable. Kellogg's other studies in this series (1988, Experiment 2; 1990) also indicate the superiority of the outline first strategy over other strategies.

Taken together, the studies of Glynn et al. (1982) and Kellogg (1988, 1990) seem to show that the outline first strategy, rather than being a problem, is actually beneficial for the kinds of assignments that students often have to do in school. However, this does not imply that Elbow's interactive strategy is not also useful. As Kellogg (1988) points out, it may be that this strategy is effective for some writers and for some kinds of texts, e.g. (literary texts).

In the early 1990s, Galbraith and his colleagues began a sequence of studies designed to explore further the effectiveness of the interactive strategy (Galbraith, 1992, 1996, 1999; Galbraith & Torrance, 2004). A first point made by these researchers is that the version of the interactive strategy implemented in the studies described earlier did not provide a strong test of the interactive drafting strategy as described by Elbow (1973). For example, in the interactive strategy, revision is separate from production, and should involve the extraction of ideas from a first draft to form a basis for a second draft rather than simply changing the first draft to improve its organization and expression. From Kellogg's (1988) writing process data, however, it is clear that his participants did not leave revision for last. Rather, production and editing were interleaved in all conditions. Furthermore, it is not clear from Kellogg's data what kinds of revisions the participants in the study were making. Thus, participants in Kellogg's no-outline condition may not have been, and probably were not, engaging in the interactive drafting strategy.

Second, Galbraith (1999) has provided a model in the spirit of neural network models to explain why writing might promote discovery of new knowledge. Unfortunately, the model is too complex to describe here. Let me just say that it provides a mechanism designed to explain how the act of composing a sentence might influence the writer's knowledge networks and thus set the conditions for the creation of new ideas. In particular, it suggests why this might be associated with the kind of unorganized initial draft advocated by proponents of the interactive strategy and why it might be inhibited by the kinds of explicit organization involved in outlining.

Third, Galbraith and his colleagues have carried out empirical studies designed to provide better assessment of the interactive strategy. For example, Galbraith and Torrance (2004) conducted a study parallel to the Kellogg study described earlier, but different from it in some important details. In the Galbraith and Torrance study, participants were given 20 minutes to produce a draft. Then they were given 5 minutes to summarize their main point; finally, they were given 20 minutes to revise their drafts. Thus, production and revision were clearly separated. For some participants, the first draft was available during revision; for others, it was not. These procedures were designed to provide a clear separation between production and revision, and to focus the

writers on using the main ideas in their drafts in creating the final texts.

Participants produced their drafts under four conditions defined by two variables: *draft quality* and *mode*. Draft quality was either unorganized or organized. In the unorganized condition, participants were instructed to think about the topic and to write down their thoughts as they unfolded, without worrying about how well organized or well expressed they were. In the organized condition, participants were instructed to aim for a well-organized article, with the structure of the final text, but without worrying about how well it was expressed. Notice that these conditions are similar to the draft quality condition in the Kellogg (1988) study except that they place emphasis on organization. The mode variable had two alternative values: sentences or notes. In the complete-sentences condition, participants were instructed to write the text in connected sentences. In the notes condition, participants were instructed to express their ideas in three- or four-word notes.

In contrast to previous studies, Galbraith and Torrance (2004) found that more ideas were produced in the complete-sentences conditions (both organized and unorganized) than in either of the notes conditions. This finding provides support for proponents of the interactive drafting strategy. However, as in the Kellogg study, higher quality final drafts were produced in the organized-notes condition than in the unorganized-sentences condition when the draft was available during revision, but that difference disappeared when the draft was not available. The authors interpreted this result to indicate that writers were revising in a manner more consistent with the interactive strategy when the draft was not present. Presumably, when the draft was absent, the writers were more likely to glean the best ideas rather than simply to do superficial editing.

Although this brief review mentions only a small part of what they have done, it is clear that Galbraith and his colleagues have pushed the debate forward on both the theoretical and empirical fronts. Where can we expect the discussion to go? I believe that there are two major directions in which we can expect progress. First, I expect that new studies will be developed that better match the conditions that Elbow specified for successful use of the interactive drafting strategy. Perhaps the most important omission of current studies is that the participants were not trained in interactive drafting. Clearly, Elbow believed that learning to write without editing was difficult and required practice. A better test of the interactive drafting strategy would involve participants who had been adequately trained in freewriting.

Second, I expect that researchers' interests will turn to the use of the interactive drafting strategy to improve the quality of ideas produced by professionals. For me, the most exciting claim that Elbow makes is that the interactive strategy can help writers to produce better ideas. The sensible place to test this claim would be with people who are in the business of producing ideas, such as scholars, scientists, and politicians. If it works for them, the social benefits could be considerable.

If it can be shown that the interactive strategy does promote the discovery of knowledge, then the question will be "How?" Is it tied to the physical production of sentences, or is the planning of formal sentences enough? This is a question that Elbow himself raised in *Writing without Teachers* (p. 51). Does discovery depend on tapping into the writer's latent disposition toward the topic, as Galbraith's model (1999) implies, or does it depend on the anticipation of audience response (e.g., "They won't believe that") or both? I foresee a lively and informative debate on these issues.

Using Activity Theory as a Framework for Understanding the Context of Writing

A number of researchers have been interested in exploring activity theory as a tool for understanding the complex relations of individual writing processes to the environmental context in which it occurs (Bazerman, 2003; Bracewell & Witte, 2003; Russell & Yanez, 2003; and many others). Before discussing this development, though, it will be helpful to think about the properties of a broad class of explanatory structures that are commonly called frameworks. I then use the discussion of frameworks as a starting place for the discussion of activity theory.

Frameworks: A Working Definition

Frameworks are representations designed to help us think about complex processes or situations. A simple framework may consist of nothing more than a brief list of elements or features. For example, the categories *prime, choice, select, standard,* and *utility* constitute a framework for judging and talking about meat quality.

More complex frameworks may also specify some or all of the relations among the elements. In some cases, these relations are designated simply as present or absent, and are represented diagrammatically by lines connecting the related elements. In other cases, the connections are characterized in more detail by using an arrow to indicate the direction of the relation or a label to indicate its type. Toulmin, Rieke, and Janik's (1979, p. 78) diagram of argument structure (shown in Figure 2.3) is an example of a framework that represents the direction of relations among its elements.

For this discussion, it is useful to distinguish between quantitative theories and frameworks (which, if sufficiently complex, might also be called qualitative theories). In a framework, all of the relations among the elements are specified qualitatively, that is, by stating their presence or absence, direction, type, or other qualitative features. By contrast, in quantitative theories, some or all of the elements and their relations are specified quantitatively, often by equations.

There are many ways in which frameworks can help us to think about complex situations. Here I list five, but the reader may be able to think of more.

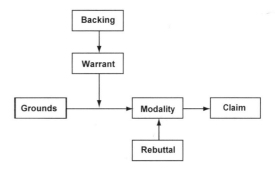

FIGURE 2.3. The Toulmin, Rieke, and Janik (1979) framework for describing argument.

FRAMEWORKS CAN AID MEMORY

Frameworks remind us of the elements and relations that are important for understanding a complex situation. For example, the journalists' five W's—who, where, when, what, why—constitute a framework that is intended to jog writers' memories when they create or edit a news story.

FRAMEWORKS CAN PROVIDE COMMON LANGUAGE

Frameworks provide labels that can facilitate discussion. The Toulmin et al. (1979) framework for argument has provided a common language for the discussion and analysis of arguments. Similarly, the Hayes and Flower model (1980) (see Figure 2.4) is a framework that has provided common language for discussing cognitive processes in writing.

FRAMEWORKS CAN FACILITATE ACQUIRING AND ORGANIZING KNOWLEDGE

If a person were to read a number of freshman argument papers, he or she might notice that many of them were not as convincing as they could be. However, without Toulmin's framework, the reader might not notice that a common feature of the less adequate papers was that they lacked rebuttals. Thus, frameworks can help us to notice commonalities in our environment. In the same way, frameworks can help us notice relations among items of knowledge already stored in

memory and thus provide an opportunity to reorganize that knowledge.

FRAMEWORKS CAN EMBODY EMPIRICAL PREDICTIONS

Because quantitative theories can be used to make very precise empirical predictions, many researchers value them more highly than frameworks. Indeed, it may be hard to see that frameworks have much value at all in this respect. However, we should recognize that most of the frameworks we encounter embody substantial empirical implications. The elements chosen for inclusion in the framework, and the relations among those elements, can provide a basis for important predictions.

The selection of elements by itself has empirical implications. For example, Hayes, Flower, Schriver, Stratman, and Carey (1987) proposed a framework for revision that included task definition as a major element. Building on this framework, Wallace and Hayes (1991) predicted and subsequently demonstrated that training in appropriate task definition significantly improved the revision performance of first-year college students. If we propose a framework in which we assert that certain relations among the elements are present and others are absent, we are making claims that may be empirically verifiable or not. If the framework asserts a relation between two elements, then we expect that changes in one will result in

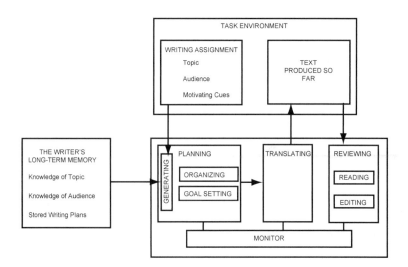

FIGURE 2.4. Hayes and Flower's (1980) process model of writing.

changes to the other. Kellogg's (1996) model, which postulates the presence of some and the absence of other relations between particular writing processes and particular working memory resources, is an excellent example of a framework that embodies strong empirical claims.

A FRAMEWORK CAN PROVIDE THE BASIS FOR A RESEARCH PROGRAM

A researcher may lay out a framework of elements and relations that he or she suspects is important for a topic, with the intention of using the framework as blueprint or guide for research to follow. The results of the research can then be used to revise or augment the framework. This was certainly the intention with which the Hayes and Flower (1980) model and the Hayes (1996) framework were proposed. These frameworks, as well as the models of Kellogg (1996), Levelt (1989), and Bereiter and Scardamalia (1987), have stimulated a quantity of research and produced results that could be used to modify and expand the original frameworks.

In summary, frameworks are useful because they help us to

- Organize our thinking by
  1. providing a common language for communication
  2. supplying cues to memory
- Acquire new knowledge by
  3. highlighting commonalities
  4. embodying predictions
  5. providing a basis for research programs

Activity Theory Applied to Writing

The previous description of frameworks was intended as a prologue to my discussion of activity theory and its relation to the study of writing. Activity theory is designed to describe purposeful actions that a person or a group of people undertakes by relating the actions to the environments in which they take place. The action and its environment are called an activity system. In what follows, I have drawn heavily on the very clear discussions of activity theory and its relation to writing by Russell and Yanez (2003). These authors use activity theory to understand the discontents of students in a large Midwestern university taking an Irish history course that involved writing.

Figure 2.5 shows a generic diagram of an activity system. It is a framework with seven elements, each of which is connected to every other element. Subject(s) refers to the people involved in the activity system. In the case that Russell and Yanez (2003) analyze, these are the teacher and the students in the course. Tools include the classroom, pen and paper, and word processors. Object/motive refers to the goals of the various participants, and division of labor describes the different roles that the teacher and students play in the activity system. Community refers to the social relations within the classroom and, presumably, to the broader community within which the classroom operates. Rules/norms are the formal and informal conventions governing writing in the activity system. The last element, outcome, refers to the changes that the activity system produces. In the case of a classroom, an important outcome would be learning.

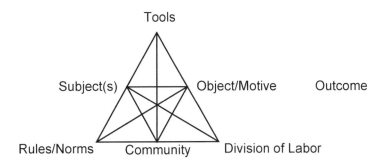

FIGURE 2.5. Russell and Yanez's (2003) generic activity system.

Russell and Yanez (2003) note that individuals are typically engaged in several activity systems at the same time. One of the students in the Irish history course, Beth, was involved in at least three activity systems that were relevant to the class. One was a journalism activity system. Beth, a journalism major, hoped to use the course to improve her ability to write news pieces. Another was an activity system that Beth learned in high school history class. In both the journalism and high school history classes, the norm was that students should write factual accounts of events. A third was the university activity system, where Beth's goal was to get a good grade and to graduate with a bachelor's degree.

In contrast to Beth, the most relevant activity system for the teacher was one related to academic (as opposed to high school) history. In academic history, the belief in factual accounts is considered naive. Rather, the norm for historians is to interpret critically various accounts of events to arrive at plausible (rather than true) interpretations.

These differences between the activity systems of Beth and her teacher led to conflicts. When she wrote short, factual paragraphs according to the norms of high school history and journalism, the teacher criticized her according to the norms of academic history, favoring long paragraphs that provide critical interpretation. Beth was frustrated, because she was engaging in familiar activity systems that she believed were appropriate, yet she was not getting the grades that she wanted as part of her university activity system. Only later in the course did she begin, with the help of her teacher, to recognize that the norms and goals of academic history could actually help her to evaluate news sources critically and therefore to write better news stories.

Russell and Yanez's (2003) analysis of this case provides a graceful example of how activity theory can be used to understand the context of writing events. Activity theory led to expectations (predictions, if you will) that might be stated as follows: If people acting together are experiencing conflicts, look for differences in the elements of the activity systems that they bring to the situation. Differences in the norms and goals of writing were identified in this case, and interviews suggested that the differences were at the root of the conflict. Furthermore, when Beth recognized that the goals of the two activity systems were actually not at odds, the conflict was ameliorated.

Of course, the analysis might not have turned our so neatly. Beth might have been perfectly attuned to the activity system of academic history but hated her teacher because he reminded her of her father. If this were the case, a different framework, perhaps a Freudian one, might have provided a more relevant analysis.

Thinking of activity theory as a framework, we can ask, "How well can it provide the five aids to thinking that we look for in a framework?" First, of course, activity theory can provide aid to memory. It can, in effect, say to us, "Hey, you forgot to take the impact of different writing tools into account." Second, it can provide common language, although, at the moment, that language may be in flux. Bracewell and Witte (2003), Spinuzzi (2003), and others have proposed additions and changes to the elements to adapt the theory to the special needs of particular topics. If specialization continues to occur, it is not clear how common the common language will be. Third, it can certainly provide an organizing scheme for knowledge. In parts of the Russell and Yanez (2003) article not reviewed earlier, the authors use activity theory to compare and contrast students' responses to the Irish history course. Fourth, activity theory does embody predictions. We saw this relatively informally in the Russell and Yanez (2003) analysis of the source of conflicts between student and teacher.

Bracewell and Witte (2003) have tested the predictive power of activity theory more formally. They collected transcripts of meetings of a group of engineers and city employees writing a "standards document" concerning municipal infrastructure. The authors predicted that topics specified as goals of a meeting would elicit more discussion than topics that were not marked as goals. This prediction was based on the reasonable inference from activity theory that goals drive activity. These researchers were able to provide statistically reliable evidence that three topics marked as goals were discussed more than two other topics not marked as goals.

These two examples provide suggestive but not strong evidence that activity theory can provide useful predictions for the study of writing. A critic might say that the amount of data analyzed in these studies is very small, or that many frameworks other than activity theory also emphasize the importance of goals. However, activity theory has not had much time to prove itself in the field of writing research. Presumably, much more data will be collected in the near future that can give us a better idea of how much predictive power activity theory can bring to the study of writing.

In my opinion, though, the future of activity theory will not depend on the empirical predictions that it provides. Activity theory is a fairly loose framework with relatively little empirical content, at least in the version we have discussed here. Rather, I believe that if activity theory is successful, it will be because it provides a basis for organizing programs of research. Judging by the large number of researchers interested in activity theory, I think there is a good possibility that it will provide a convenient framework for research programs, especially in the field of workplace literacy. Although short-lived enthusiasms have at times seemed endemic to English studies, I think there is a good chance that activity theory will have a lasting impact on literacy research.

In summary, the three research initiatives I have described here are just a small part of the total effort devoted to understanding the cognitive and social factors involved in writing. However, these three initiatives illustrate well the importance of making bold theoretical conjectures that go beyond what is known, as well as the critical evaluation of these conjectures on the basis of carefully collected empirical evidence. Together, theory and empirical evidence push forward our understanding of writing.

Acknowledgments

I wish to thank Karen Schriver of KSA Document Design and Research for invaluable help in the writing and preparation of this chapter and David Galbraith of Staffordshire University for insightful comments.

References

Baddeley, A. D., & Hitch, G. J. (1974). Working memory. In G. Bower (Ed.), *The psychology of learning and motivation* (Vol. 8, pp. 47–90). New York: Academic Press.

Bazerman, C. (2003). What is not institutionally visible does not count: The problem of making activity assessible, accountable, and plannable. In C. Bazerman & D. R. Russell (Eds.), *Writing selves/ writing societies: Research from activity perspectives* (pp. 428–453). Retrieved May 20, 2004, from wac.colostate.edu/books/selves_societies//.

Bereiter, C., & Scardamalia, M. (1987). *The psychology of written communication.* Hillsdale, NJ: Erlbaum.

Bracewell, R. J., & Witte, S. P. (2003). Tasks, ensembles, and activity. *Written Communication, 20,* 511–559.

Chenoweth, N. A., & Hayes, J. R. (2001). Fluency in writing: Generating text in L1 and L2. *Written Communication, 18,* 80–98.

Chenoweth, N. A., & Hayes, J. R. (2003). The inner voice in writing. *Written Communication, 20,* 99–118.

Elbow, P. (1973). *Writing without Teachers.* London: Oxford University Press.

Galbraith, D. (1992). Conditions for discovery through writing. *Instructional Science, 21,* 45–72.

Galbraith, D. (1996). Self-monitoring, discovery through writing and individual differences in drafting strategy. In G. Rijlaarsdam, H. van den Bergh, & M. Couzijn (Eds.), *Theories, models, and methodology in writing research* (pp. 121–141). Amsterdam: Amsterdam University Press.

Galbraith, D. (1999). Writing as a knowledge-constituting process. In M. Torrance & D. Galbraith (Eds.), *Studies in writing: Vol. 4. Knowing what to write: Conceptual processes in text production.* (pp. 137–157). Amsterdam: Amsterdam University Press.

Galbraith, D., & Torrance, M. (2004). Revision in the context of different drafting strategies. In L. Allal, L. Chanquoy, & P. Largy (Eds.), *Revision: Cognitive and instructional processes* (pp. 63–85). Dordrecht, The Netherlands: Kluwer.

Gathercole, S. E., & Baddeley, A. D. (1993). *Working memory and language.* Hove, UK: Erlbaum.

Glynn, S. M., Britton, B., Muth, D., & Dogan, N. (1982). Writing and revising persuasive documents: Cognitive demands. *Journal of Educational Psychology, 74,* 557–567.

Hayes, J. R. (1996). A new framework for understanding cognition and affect in writing. In C. M. Levy & S. Ransdell (Eds.), *The science of writing: Theories, methods, individual differences, and applications* (pp. 1–27). Mahwah, NJ: Erlbaum.

Hayes, J. R. & Chenoweth, N. A. (forthcoming).

Verbal working memory limits in a simple transcription task.

Hayes, J. R., & Flower, L. S. (1980). Identifying the organization of writing processes. In L. Gregg & E. Steinberg (Eds.), *Cognitive processes in writing: An interdisciplinary approach* (pp. 3–30). Hillsdale, NJ: Erlbaum.

Hayes, J. R., Flower, L., Schriver, K. A., Stratman, J., & Carey, L. (1987). Cognitive processes in revision. In S. Rosenberg (Ed.), *Advances in applied psycholinguistics: Vol. II. Reading, writing and language processing* (pp. 176–240). New York: Cambridge University Press.

Kellogg, R. T. (1988). Attentional overload and writing performance: Effects of rough draft and outline strategies. *Journal of Experimental Psychology: Learning, Memory, and Cognition, 14,* 355–365.

Kellogg, R. T. (1990). Effectiveness of prewriting strategies as a function of task demands. *American Journal of Psychology, 103,* 327–342.

Kellogg, R. T. (1996). A model of working memory in writing. In C. M. Levy & S. Ransdell (Eds.), *The science of writing: Theories, methods, individual differences, and applications* (pp. 57–71). Mahwah, NJ: Erlbaum.

Kellogg, R. T. (1999). Components of working memory in text production. In M. Torrance & G. C. Jeffery (Eds.), *The cognitive demands of writing: Processing capacity and working memory in text production* (pp. 42–61). Amsterdam: Amsterdam University Press.

Levelt, W. J. M. (1989). *Speaking: From intention to articulation.* Cambridge, MA: MIT Press.

Levy, C. M., & Marek, P. (1999). Testing components of Kellogg's multicomponent model of working memory in writing: The role of the pho-nological loop. In M. Torrance & G. C. Jeffery (Eds.), *The cognitive demands of writing: Processing capacity and working memory in text production* (pp. 25–41). Amsterdam: Amsterdam University Press.

Longoni, A. M., Richardson, A. T. E., & Aiello, A. (1993). Articulatory rehearsal and phonological storage in working memory. *Memory and Cognition, 21,* 11–22.

Murray, D. M. (1978). Internal revision: A process of discovery. In C. R. Cooper & L. Odell (Eds.), *Research on composing: Points of departure* (pp. 85–103). Urbana, IL: National Council of Teachers of English.

Russell, D. R., & Yanez, A. (2003). "Big picture people rarely become historians": Genre systems and the contradictions of general education. In C. Bazerman & D. R. Russell (Eds.), *Writing selves/writing societies: Research from activity perspectives* (pp. 331–362). Retrieved May 20, 2004, from wac.colostate.edu/books/selves_societies/

Salame, P., & Baddeley, A. D. (1982). Disruption of memory by unattended speech: Implications for the structure of working memory. *Journal of Verbal Learning and Verbal Behavior, 21,* 150–164.

Spinuzzi, C. (2003). Compound mediation in software development: Using genre ecologies to study textual artifacts. In C. Bazerman & D. R. Russell (Eds.), *Writing selves/writing societies: Research from activity perspectives* (pp. 97–124). Retrieved May 20, 2004, from wac.colostate.edu/books/selves_societies/

Toulmin, S., Rieke, R., & Janik, A. (1979). *An introduction to reasoning.* New York: Macmillan.

Wallace, D., & Hayes, J. R. (1991). Redefining revision for freshmen. *Research in the Teaching of English, 25*(1), 54–66.

Chapter 3

Writing Process Theory
A Functional Dynamic Approach

Gert Rijlaarsdam *and* Huub van den Bergh

In this chapter, we present key elements of a theory of writing processes based on our observations in the empirical studies we have conducted over the last 10 years. The theoretical framework rests upon two paradigms in cognitive psychology. One paradigm is the writing process model introduced by Hayes and Flower (1980; see also Hayes's 1996 revisions), which is assumed in this chapter as known. The second paradigm is parallel distributed processing (Rumelhart, McClelland, & the PDP Research Group, 1999). Connecting both paradigms, we propose a functional dynamic system as the basic structure of writing processes. The empirical data we present have three common features:

1. We adapted a weak novice–good novice paradigm. Much writing process research has been carried out using an expert novice paradigm. However, experts can be defined in different ways (Torrance, 1996). Experts may excel in some fields of writing because of their subject and/or genre knowledge. How experts became experts and the dimensions on which they differ from novices are not considered in most analyses. Hence, differences in writing processes between these extreme groups may have many causes. In order to circumvent this fallacy, just one group should be considered, whether (relatively) novices or experts (in one subject

area). In our studies, we investigate the writing process of writers about 15 years old and study the natural variance within this group.

2. Students in our studies wrote two argumentative, documented essays within a peer-audience-oriented contextual frame, while having access to documentation on the topic (clippings from newspapers and journals, tables and figures). Writing time varied from 60 to 103 minutes.

3. Students wrote under think-aloud conditions; protocols were fragmented into cognitive activities, and a jury evaluated the quality of the resulting text written by the student.

During our excursion to reach the final destination (the last section of the chapter), we visit six observation posts that serve as landmarks for a theory in development and can be considered as calibration points for a writing process theory. In the figure captions, we refer to the original studies.

Observation 1: What Constitutes a Writing Process?

To determine the constituting elements of writing processes, one may observe processes, and identify and categorize mental activities. One problem is how to define and se-

41

lect the mental activities. What should one distinguish; what should one leave out as irrelevant? Our solution was partly a functional approach—all process elements that together predict the resulting text quality were taken into account—and partly a theoretical one, as we started with a fine-grained scheme based on Hayes. This approach resulted in two findings:

1. The frequencies of eleven (broad) categories of cognitive activities explain 76% of the (true score) variance in product quality (Breetvelt, van den Bergh, & Rijlaarsdam, 1994, p. 116); categories were derived from the Hayes and Flower model (generating, translating, revising, etc.).

2. This result holds only when the factor time or "moment in the process" is included in the prediction. We distinguished three equal parts in the process. It turned out that none of the activities were effective during the whole process; some contributed during one or two phases in the same direction (positively or negatively), others, in reverse directions: positively in one phase, negatively in another (see Appendix 3.1).

3. We concluded that differences become apparent only when the moment activities are employed is taken into account. If the

moment an activity is employed is left out of the analysis, hardly any relation can be found between cognitive activities on one hand and text quality on the other. Therefore, the moment a cognitive activity takes place is crucial.

Observation 2: Dynamically Changing Patterns

As the text grows, the task situation changes. Writers adapt to these changes by carrying out different processes or cognitive activities, shown in Figure 3.1. The (mean) occurrence of two activities, reading the assignment and generating information, is plotted against the moment in the writing process. As time goes on or, more precisely, as the text grows, the probability of the occurrence of "reading the assignment" decreases. This activity, which is most likely to be observed at the beginning of the writing process, becomes increasingly unlikely toward the end. As is to be expected, at no time does the average writer engage in this activity as in the beginning of the writing process.

Generating information, however, shows a completely different course over the writing process. The mean probability of occurrence

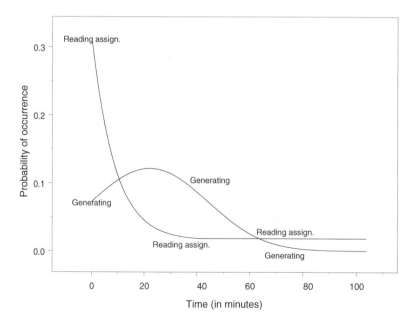

FIGURE 3.1. Mean changes in occurrence of "reading the assignment" and "generating" during the writing process. Data from Breetvelt, van den Bergh, and Rijlaarsdam (1996).

gradually increases from a low initial value to reach a peak (minute 20) from which it decreases to a very low level. Hence, in the beginning of the writing process, writers refrain from generating information and engage in other activities, such as "reading the assignment." These general patterns, observed with 15-year-olds, also occur with younger children. Van der Hoeven (1997) showed the same patterns for both activities in 11-year-olds.

Most cognitive activities studied thus far show a distinct pattern of occurrence during the writing process. The essential discovery is that each cognitive activity has a higher or lower probability of occurrence depending on the moment in the writing process: At different points in the writing, different cognitive activities dominate.

Observation 3: Dynamically Changing Relations between Processes and Text Quality

In Figure 3.2, we present the correlations between the frequencies of two cognitive activities ("reading the assignment" and "generating") and text quality at various moments during the writing process.

Reading the assignment is positively related to text quality only during the initial stages of the writing process. During later stages, the correlation between this activity and text quality decreases and soon becomes negative. Hence, students who (relatively) often consulted the assignment in the beginning, other things being equal, produced text of high quality. Conversely, writers who hardly consulted the assignment in the beginning wrote poor(er) texts. Writers who consulted the assignment frequently at the end of the writing process wrote poor texts, whereas writers who refrained from reading the assignment at the end of their writing process produced better texts.

The correlation between generating activities and text quality also changes during the writing process. It increases during the initial phases and reaches a maximum in the middle of the writing process, only to decrease during later stages.

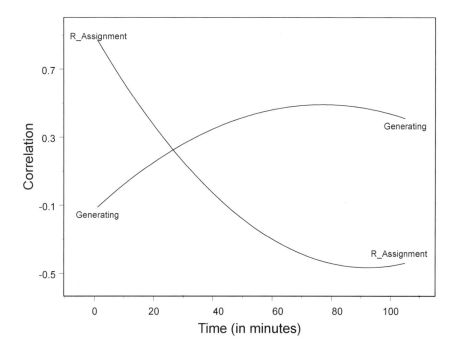

FIGURE 3.2. Correlations between the temporal distribution of two cognitive activities and text quality: "Reading the assignment" and text quality (R_Assignment), and "Generating" and text quality. Data from Breetvelt, van den Bergh, and Rijlaarsdam (1996).

Observation 4: Functional Alliances between Cognitive Activities

Form and function of cognitive activities need to be distinguished. The recursive nature of writing does not imply that an activity that occurs at occasion t has the same function in the writing process as the same activity at occasion t_x. It means, for instance, that revisions should be distinguished depending on the moment they are carried out. For instance, a writer with start-up troubles, beginning over and over again, might revise just as frequently as a writer who fluently produces a text and revises afterwards. These writers clearly write in different ways. We claim that the two types of revision in this example function differently.

To explore functional relations between cognitive activities, we connected cognitive activities to preceding activities. For this reason, we went looking for functional relations between several other cognitive and generating activities (van den Bergh & Rijlaarsdam, 1999). Here, we distinguish several types of

generating activities (Table 3.1). We based our typology of generating ideas on the cognitive activity that preceded the generating activity itself, if the preceding activity triggered the generation activity.

Figure 3.3 shows that five combinations of generating activities described in Table 3.1 have different patterns of distribution. This implies that the different combinations behave differently, which indicates a functional relationship. If the combinations were just random adjacent pairs, the distributions over the process would have overlapped. Therefore, making a distinction between the contexts that precede generating activities illuminates different processes in two respects. The mean number of generating *activities* linked to each combination is different, and the distribution of these combinations varies during the process.

This observation teaches us that, *in general*, we may predict that some combinations have a higher probability to occur at a certain moment in the process than others. This points to different functions of these pairs

TABLE 3.1. Some Examples of the Distinguished Types of Generating Activities Defined by Adjacent Pairs

Type of generating activity	Protocol fragment (some context; *adjacent pairs in italics*)
Assignment-driven generation	(Reading assignment:) "*. . . As adult who starts living alone, you can get a hard time. You must pass the time yourself. Social contacts were left at the parental home*" (Thinking:) "*no friends anymore*" (Writing down:) "no/less friends" (Thinking:) "eehm. . . ."
Rereading-text-driven generation	(Thinking:) ". . . ehm . . . /this is a citation or something/let me have a look/ citation of prof. X, and then . . . something written down/ *(Reads already written text:) "I state that/"* (Thinking:) "What then? Am I against the citation? Yes/. . . ."
Translation-driven generation	(Reading own text): "It is not good that human beings stay alone" (Writing:) "*I. . . . am*" (Thinking:) "I am disagreeing with this statement, I think/no, I don't agree/it's not good. . . . I have to think of something else"
Generation-driven generation	(Thinking:) ". . . should I continue that line of thinking/eeehhhmm/ something like . . ./or did I write first something . . . about . . . eeh . . . how people live nowadays. */I think/eeehh/ nowadays. . ./ yes, nowadays it is very normal that . . . people, eehh/no, nowadays they don't find it that strange*" (Writing:) "Nowadays, they don't find it that strange/ . . ."
Pause-related generation	(Silence, for at least 0.5 seconds) *Yes, I do agree with that point, I think nowadays people are too selfish.*

Note. Data from van den Bergh and Rijlaarsdam (1999).

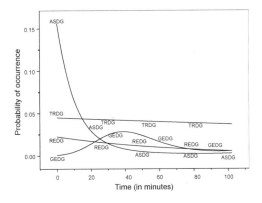
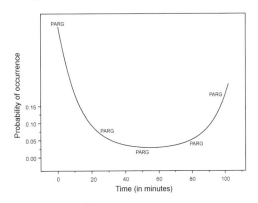

FIGURE 3.3. Changes in the mean probability of occurrence (y-axis) of assignment-driven generation (ASDG), rereading-text-driven generation (REDG), translation-driven-generation (TRDG), generation-driven generation (GEDG), and pause-felated generation (PARG). Data from van den Bergh and Rijlaarsdam (1999).

during the process. Note that we showed in Figure 3.3 the general pattern: Individual differences are large (van den Bergh & Rijlaarsdam, 1999, pp. 109–112). Individual differences are correlated with text quality: Some functional pairs are more effective in the beginning of the process; others, in a

later phase of the process (Figure 3.4). For instance, in Figure 3.4, it appears that the correlation between "translation-driven generation" (TRDG) and text quality is time dependent. The correlation is significant in the first quarter (negative) and after (about) 25 minutes, until (about) 75 minutes, when it is

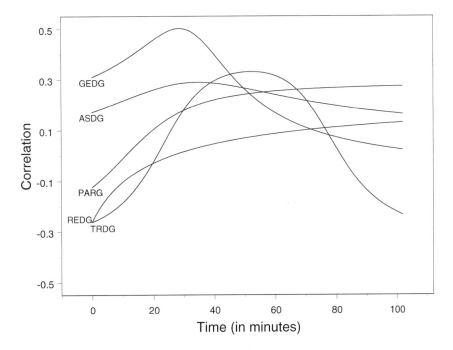

FIGURE 3.4. Correlation (y-axis) between occurrence of assignment-driven generation (ASDG), rereading-text-driven generation (REDG), translation-driven generation (TRDG), pause-related generation (PARG), generation-driven generation (GEDG), and text quality during writing (x-axis). Data from van den Bergh and Rijlaarsdam (1999).

positive. After (about) 85 minutes, it reaches significance again, but now it is negative: The more this activity occurs during the end of the process time, the weaker the text.

Please note that these changes in correlation between the occurrence of cognitive activities and text quality hold not only for "translation-driven-generation," but also for all other combinations; in all cases, the correlation with text quality is dependent on the moment in the writing process.

This observation leads one to reconsider the unit of analysis for theory building. When combinations of cognitive activities behave as functional relations, implying that the function of each activity varies according to the context, the preceding activity, then combinations rather than single activities should be considered as the unit of analysis.

Observation 5: Functional Compensatory Relations between Cognitive Activities

Observation 4 leads to the assumption that cognitive activities can fulfill different functions depending on the context in the process. The activity of "rereading already written text" is a good example to demonstrate this point. Rereading already written text functions within the reviewing component in the Hayes and Flower writing process model. In Hayes's revised model (1996), reading has a more central role in the writing process. Hayes distinguished several functions of reading during writing: "In addition to reading to evaluate, two other kinds of reading play an important role in writing: reading source texts and reading to define tasks" (1996, p. 18). However, Observation 4 pointed to the possible relation between "rereading already written text" and "generating ideas": a rather rare combination over the writing process (see Figure 3.3) but an effective combination when the writing process proceeds (see Figure 3.4). At least *some writers* seem to use rereading parts of their written text as input for new thoughts. This implies that rereading already written text and generating ideas must correlate. In this section, we explore this relation by reanalyzing the data reported in a former study (Breetvelt, van den Bergh, & Rijlaarsdam, 1996).

"Generating" has a rather low probability overall. It reaches a maximum of about .12 around 20 minutes after the start of the writing process and decreases slowly afterwards; that is, at around 20 minutes of writing, 12 out of 100 cognitive activities are "generating" activities (see Figure 3.1). The pattern for "rereading" is clearly different. The probability increases during the first 30 minutes, stays more or less constant for the next hour, then rises to a probability of about .30. When we relate the distribution of these processes to the quality of the written text, two clear pictures emerge (Breetvelt et al., 1996, p. 17). Writers who generated relatively often at the beginning wrote weak texts; writers who gradually increased the number of generating activities wrote the best texts.[1] For rereading the already written text, the correlation changes during the course of writing but is always positive. Note that these are the findings as long as we assume that these two processes are unrelated. However, it is tempting to hypothesize that rereading already written text can in some instances fulfill a supportive function for generating texts. Take, for example, the sequence in which the writer writes something down, rereads what he or she wrote, then generates another chunk of information. Indeed, if we account for rereading, the correlation between generating and text quality changes (Figure 3.5).

The correlation between generating and text quality changes dramatically if rereading is taken into account. It thus seems that the occurrence of rereading is related to the occurrence of generating. On the other hand (not shown in Figure 3.5), the correlation between rereading and text quality changes only marginally if we account for generating. This implies that generating does not have the same effect on rereading that rereading has on generating. Therefore, it is plausible that rereading serves generating in some writers, and that rereading has other functions, as well as serving as a tool for generating. In any case, the analysis shows that it is reasonable to map functional relations between cognitive activities.

This observation is a rather crucial indication that a univariate view on cognitive activities that play a role in a writing process limits the interpretation of the data and the building

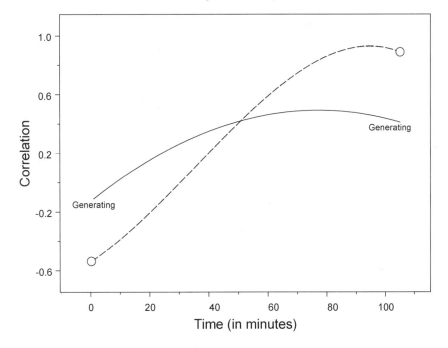

FIGURE 3.5. The changes in correlation (vertical axis) between generating and text quality in two conditions: raw correlation (solid line) and purified for rereading (dashed line). Reanalyzed data from Breetvelt, van den Bergh, and Rijlaarsdam (1996).

of a writing process theory. Such a view neglects the context in which cognitive activities do their work, or neglects the interdependency between activities, which can change during the process. From Figure 3.5, we learn that the effect of generating is larger when we correct for re-reading. However, the correction has a different effect in both halves of the process. We might interpret this observation as follows. Much generating in the beginning of the process is ineffective; those writers who generate much in the beginning, while leaning on rereading already written text as input for generating, appear to have written a poor text. In the second half of the process, generating contributes strongly to text quality. But those writers who use rereading already written text in the second half as input for generating profit more from this effect compared to writers who do not use rereading as input for writing. So the combination is inhibiting in the first half but facilitating in the second half: Functional relations appear to change over the process.

The observation points to individual differences in the way activities are functionally combined: Some writers make (relatively) more combinations of rereading already written text and generating of new information; other writers do not. It is difficult to interpret these different strategies. One possible interpretation is that writers with weak generation skills need the input of the already written text as a springboard for generating a new idea about which to write. This interpretation could be tested if data about the writers' generation skills were available, which is not the case. However, from another study, we got some indication that differences in processes are related to the quality of the skills involved in these processes. Van der Hoeven (1997), in her study on writing processes of 11-year-olds, measured revision skills with special, independent tasks. She observed that revision skill was positively related to most of the cognitive activities appearing in the writing-aloud protocols: structuring, writing (production of written text), rereading, evaluating, and transforming already written text. The higher the student's competence in evaluating already written text, the more instances of rereading, evaluating, and transforming were observed, and the better the resulting text. Interestingly, the competence of evaluating already written text was negatively related with the quality of text. Only by employing writing process activities of revision was this negative relation changed into a positive relation. This implies that the skill itself is not sufficient; writers have to apply the skill when they write.

Another important conclusion was that revision skill is related not only to the number of cognitive activities but, more importantly, also to their temporal distribution over the writing process as a whole. Participants with low revision skills generated fewer ideas in the beginning of the writing process compared to participants with relatively high revision skills scores. While the number of ideas gradually decreased in the high-revision skills group, this number increased in the low-revision skills group. Students high in revision skills reread, evaluated, and revised relatively little in the beginning and more toward the end of the writing process. These findings suggest that the quality of revision—revision skill—is related to the way the writer organizes the writing process, and thus affects the quality of the resulting text.

Observation 6: Individual Differences

Until now, we have shown general patterns of some cognitive activities and the relation of these patterns to the resulting text quality.

These patterns emerged from data on individual writers. We now turn to these individuals, to see in what respect they differ and how we can qualify these differences. Hence, Figure 3.5 in fact portrays the temporal distribution of two cognitive activities of nonexistent writers. In order to understand the writing process, we need to turn to individual writers and study the cognitive activities they carry out. Statistics allow for the estimation of individual patterns of occurrence of a cognitive activity (van den Bergh & Rijlaarsdam, 1996). In Figure 3.6, the differences in reading the assignment and generating between writers ($n = 36$) are presented. For each writer, the (estimated probability of) occurrence is plotted against the moment in the writing process.

Each line in Figure 3.6 represents one writer for either "reading the assignment" (right) or "generating" (left). The differences between writers appear to be relatively large. Some writers consult the assignment (relatively) frequently during the beginning and considerably less during later phases in the writing process. For other writers, an increase in the probability of occurrence of "reading the assignment" shows at the end of the writing. For yet another group of writers, the probability of observing this cognitive activity remains constant during the writing process.

The temporal distribution for generating shows that, for most students, there is an increase in generating activities during the beginning of the writing process, followed by a

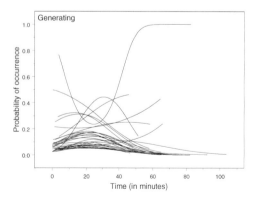

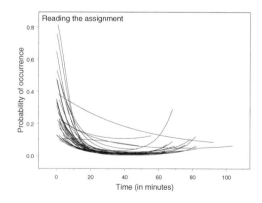

FIGURE 3.6. Changes in the probability of occurrence during the writing process for individual writers (left-hand panel, generating; right-hand panel, reading the assignment and documentation). Data from Breetvelt, van den Bergh, and Rijlaarsdam (1996).

decrease later on. In effect, most writers appear to follow the mean pattern. Nevertheless, there are clear exceptions, such as a student who generates much in the beginning and in the end but less in the middle stages, and students for whom the probability of generating continuously decreases.

The relation between both activities also differs between writers. For some writers there is a positive relation between "reading the assignment" and "generating," whereas for other writers, the relation between these two activities is negative. In fact, the correlation between the temporal order of both activities varies between writers from −.90 and .90. For some writers, we observed a negative correlation between these two activities, while for others, there is a strong positive correlation (see also Figure 3.3). Hence, some writers use the information in the assignment to generate new information to write about, whereas others do not need the information in the assignment to generate content information. Perhaps this difference in functional relation between these activities is mediated by topic knowledge; if one

knows enough about a topic, one does not need to consult the assignment to come up with ideas. However, if one does not know what to write, it seems a plausible strategy to see whether the assignment contains unused information.

To illustrate that the relation between cognitive activities can vary from writer to writer, we selected data from two writers. Figure 3.7 shows the (probability of) occurrence for "reading the assignment" and "generating." Two writers are singled out.

Remember that we have observed and discussed two essential differences between writers in temporal organization of cognitive activities thus far. First, these differences in temporal organization are related to differences in text quality (e.g., see Figure 3.2). Second, the differences in temporal organization of one activity are related to the temporal organization of other activities. Figure 3.7 plots the change in (probabilities of) occurrence for rereading and generating for two writers. It becomes clear that there is a huge difference in the temporal organization of both writers. Figure 3.7 shows that the re-

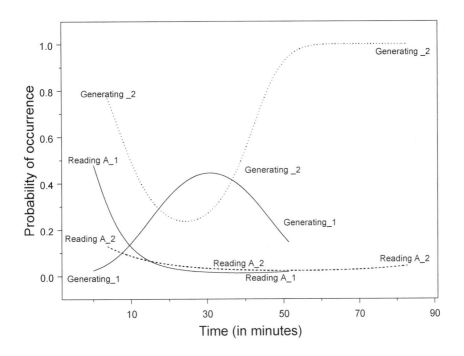

FIGURE 3.7. The temporal distribution over the writing process for two cognitive activities (reading the assignment and generating) of two writers. Data from Breetvelt, van den Bergh, and Rijlaarsdam (1996).

lation between the two activities differs for both writers. For the first writer, both activities are negatively correlated during the writing process ("reading the assignment" decreases as "generating" increases), whereas for the second writer, there is a positive relation between "reading the assignment" and "generating" (at least in the beginning of the writing process). These differences might be related to general procedural knowledge (cf. Alamargot & Chanquoy, 2001; van der Hoeven, 1997), but might also be a consequence of the specific task execution, because both determine the ongoing writing process.

Issues Related to an Empirically Based Writing Process Model

In this chapter, we have illustrated that with a limited set of cognitive activities and the factor time, much of the variance in text quality can be predicted. These activities are the building blocks for a writing process model. This model should predict how these building blocks are organized during a writing process: how individual activities have distinct temporal distributions, and the change of functional relations over time. This model should also predict how differences in cognitive and linguistic skills cause different processes. In a number of studies, we have tried to show empirical evidence for parts of the model presented earlier (e.g. Braaksma, Rijlaarsdam, van den Bergh, & Hout-Wolters, 2004; Breetvelt et al., 1994, 1996; Rijlaarsdam & van den Bergh, 1996, 1997; van den Bergh, Rijlaarsdam & Breetvelt, 1992, 1993; van den Bergh & Rijlaarsdam, 2001) or have shown the statistical model behind the analysis (e.g., van den Bergh & Rijlaarsdam, 1996; or more generally, Goldstein, 1995, especially Chapter 7). Nevertheless there remain several unresolved issues that touch upon the heart of the model.

One important issue to tackle is the *controlling system*: How does a cognitive system "know" which activity should follow a particular activity, and how does a system "know" that some combinations of activities must be frequent in a certain phase of the process? How do we specify the guide and control mechanisms, and the mechanisms that determine the employment of specific cognitive activities (Bruce, Collins, Rubin, & Genter, 1979; Fayol, 1994)? Traditionally, this task is reserved for the monitor. In the early Hayes and Flower model, a monitor was introduced as a check and balance system, and fed with blueprints of processes ("monitor configurations" or writer style; Hayes & Flower, 1980, p. 20). In his revised model, Hayes implemented "task schemas" that guide and control the process (Hayes, 1996, pp. 4 and 17). Also, the coordination of cognitive activities is an area of debate (Alamargot & Chanquoy, 2001). During the writing process, writers must continuously decide which activity to employ next. Will a writer generate new information, structure the information already available, or reread the text already written? Sometimes it is assumed that a next activity starts when the products previously processed are in accordance with the activities ensured by the component that follows (cf. Hayes, 1996). Hence, this controlling mechanism would hardly be costly in terms of cognitive resources. However, in think-aloud protocols, writers appear to instruct themselves from time to time (Breetvelt et al., 1994). Apparently, this monitoring activity, or the choice of activities to be employed, is at least partly under conscious control and therefore requires attention. This allows for the intrusion of general knowledge (topic knowledge or procedural knowledge) in the writing process. It is assumed that the sequence of activities is based partly on routine, and is therefore automatic and does not require conscious attention, yet it allows for an intrusion of other activities based on some evaluation of the product thus far. How do these routines work?

An interesting perspective on building a theory about processing routines is the parallel distributed processing model proposed and tested by Rumelhart et al. (1999). They propose a probabilistic system. Through experience during processing, connections between units are established. This probabilistic system of connection strengths between units develops over time. This system is not a stored task schema that must be retrieved: The patterns of activation or connection strengths are part of the cognitive units themselves. It seems likely that if the text grows (changes), the activated cognitive nodes change as well. By these changes, processes such as automatic spreading activation will activate other nodes (cf. Hinton & Anderson, 1981; Anderson, 1983; Rumelhart et al., 1999). Hence, the internal representation of the text changes with changes in the task situation. Writers react to these changes in terms of cognitive activities they employ.

A second issue is the *unit of observation.* In our illustrations, we started with cognitive activities as units and demonstrated that units can form functional pairs in which it is not the single cognitive activity that contributes to the quality of the resulting text, but a certain combination at a certain moment in the process. We need to identify larger functional units consisting of at least two related cognitive activities. Where does a functional unit start, and where does it end? And how does it relate (coordinated, superordinated-cause, subordinated-consequence) to the former and the following functional unit? In Table 3.1 we presented adjacent pairs, with some context. In some cases, it is apparent that the adjacent pair is part of a larger unit. The TRDG example, for instance, seems to be driven by another fragment, in which the writers rereads already written text. With cognitive activities as the building blocks of the writing process theory, we must now try to identify the generative syntax that accounts for the hierarchically related patterns of building blocks. Besides, the unit of analysis may be different for different writers. It is generally known that the size of units depends on the skill of an executor. Therefore, highly skilled writers may process larger units then lower skilled writers. Alternatively, skilled writers might show patterns of activities in their writing process (e.g., they have a pattern of generating, structuring, and formulating) (cf. van den Bergh, Herrlitz & Klein Gunnewiek, 1999; Dansac & Alamargot, 1999). Hence, relatively skilled writers might not operate solely on the level of individual activities; for these writers, specific combinations of activities are to be considered as one unit (cf. Kunst, 1978).

A third issue is that of the presumed *causal relation* between process and quality of the product. Earlier, a causal relation between distributional elements of an activity and quality of the resulting text has been suggested (at least). This conclusion seems obvious and is a crucial element in the theory thus far. It functions as an explanation of differences in processing, and pinpoints effective and less effective temporal patterns of a cognitive activity. However, from a methodological point of view, one could dispute the conclusion. In fact, a coincidence in time is observed. And although the temporal patterns are theoretically well founded, and the relations with text quality appear rather easy to interpret (it seems obvious that an activity like "reading the assignment" is especially correlated positively in the beginning of the writing process; see Figure 3.2), without proper experimental manipulation, causality cannot be proven.

A fourth issue concerns the *linearization* of the writing process. In think-aloud conditions, writers can only formulate one activity at a time. Therefore, according to the observations, writing is a linear process in which activities are ordered in time. In thinking on writing, and in many writing theories, this linearization is posed without questioning. Earlier, we did the same; however, there is hardly any reason why the writing process should be linear. In principle, not just aspects of a monitor are allowed to function next to other activities. Think, for instance, on the manifold, short, editing activities that appear to intrude into almost every string of activities. Also, activities seem to be strongly related. For instance, structuring can trigger the generation of new ideas; that is, during structuring, a new idea may pop up. In fact, this is a kind of parallel processing that we cannot do without, but it has received very little attention in writing research. The higher level units that appear to operate are, in fact, a kind of parallel processing in which several subprocesses are fused in to one.

We have not presented a complete theory on writing and writing processes. In fact, we do not have such a theory. Nevertheless, we have tried to sketch our way of thinking and make the skeleton of such a theory visible. It is clear, however, that we do not have definite answers; in some respects, we have just started to ask the right questions.

APPENDIX 3.1. Summary of Regression Weights per Writing Episode: The Relation between Occurrences of Cognitive Activities and the Quality of the Resulting Text

Cognitive activity	Writing process episode		
	1	2	3
Reading writing task and documentation	+	−	
Self-instructions			+
Goal setting	−	+	+
Generating ideas		+	
Structuring	−	+	
Meta comments		−	
Pausing		−	
Writing/text production			+
Rereading text			+
Evaluating text	+	−	
Revising text	−	−	

Note. +, positive relation; −, negative relation; blank, no significant relation. Adapted from Breetvelt, van den Berg, and Rijlaarsdam (1994). Copyright 1994 by Lawrence Erlbaum Associates. Adapted by permission.

Note

1. Note that if time were left out in our analyses, the net result would have been a correlation of about zero.

References

Alamargot, D., & Chanquoy, L. (2001). *Through the models of writing.* Dordrecht, The Netherlands: Kluwer.

Anderson, J. R. (1983). A spreading activation theory of memory. *Journal of Verbal Learning and Verbal Behavior, 22,* 261–295.

Braaksma, M., Rijlaarsdam, G., van den Bergh, H., & Hout Wolters, B. A. M. (2004). Observational learning and its effects on the orchestration of the writing process. *Cognition and Instruction, 22,* 1–36.

Breetvelt, I., van den Bergh, H., & Rijlaarsdam, G. (1994). Relations between writing processes and text quality: When and how? *Cognition and Instruction, 12*(2), 103–123.

Breetvelt, I., van den Bergh, H., & Rijlaarsdam, G. (1996). Rereading and generating and their relation to text quality: An application of multilevel analysis on writing process data. In G. Rijlaarsdam, H. van den Bergh, & M. Couzijn (Eds.), *Studies in writing: Vol. 1. Theories, models and methodology in writing research* (pp. 10–21). Amsterdam: Amsterdam University Press.

Bruce, B., Collins, A. M., Rubin, A. D., & Genter, D. (1979). A cognitive science approach to writing. In C. H. Fredericksen, M. F. Whiteman, & J. D. Dominic (Eds.), *Writing: The nature, development and teaching of written communication.* Hillsdale, NJ: Erlbaum.

Dansac, C., & Alamargot, D. (1999). Accessing referential information during text composition: When and why? In M. Torrance & D. Galbraith (Eds.), *Knowing what to write: Conceptual processes in text production* (pp. 79–98). Amsterdam: Amsterdam University Press.

Fayol, M. (1994). From declarative and procedural knowledge to the management of declarative and procedural knowledge. *European Journal of Psychology of Education, 6,* 99–117.

Goldstein, H. (1995). *Multilevel statistical models* (2nd ed.). London: Arnold.

Hayes, J. R. (1996). A new framework for understanding cognition and affect in writing. In C. M. Levy & S. Ransdell (Eds.), *The science of writing: Theories, methods, individual differences and applications* (pp. 1–27). Mahwah, NJ: Erbaum.

Hayes, J. R., & Flower, L. (1980). Identifying the organization of writing processes. In L. W. Gregg & E. R. Steinberg (Eds.), *Cognitive processes in writing: An interdisciplinary approach* (pp. 3–30). Hillsdale, NJ: Erlbaum.

Hinton, G. E., & Anderson, J. A. (Eds.). (1981). *Parallel models of associative memory.* Hillsdale, NJ: Erlbaum.

Kunst, H. (1978). *Cognitie van semantische systemen: Strategieën en interpretaties bij een structure of intellect vaardigheid* [Cognition of semantic systems: Strategies and interpretation of a structure of intellect skill]. Dissertation, University of Amsterdam, Amsterdam, The Netherlands.

Rijlaarsdam, G., & van den Bergh, H. (1996). Essentials for writing process studies: Many questions and some answers. In C. M. Levy & S. Ransdell

(Eds.), *The science of writing: Theories, methods, individual differences, and applications* (pp. 107–126). Mahwah, NJ: Erlbaum.

Rijlaarsdam, G., & van den Bergh, H. (1997). Cognitieve activiteiten tijdens het schrijfproces en hun relaties met tekstkwaliteit: Plannen en formuleren [Cognitive activities during the writing process and their relations with text quality: Planning and formulating]. In H. van den Bergh, D. Janssen, N. Bertens, & M. Damen (Eds.), *Taalgebruik ontrafeld* (pp. 275–284). Dordrecht, The Netherlands: Foris.

Rumelhart, D. E., & McClelland, J. L., & the PDP Research Group. (1999). *Parallel distributed processing: Explorations in the microstructure of cognition* (Vol. I). Cambridge, MA: MIT Press.

Torrance, M. (1996). Is writing expertise like other kinds of expertise? In G. Rijlaarsdam, H. van den Bergh, & M. Couzijn (Eds.), *Studies in writing: Vol. 1. Theories, models and methodology in writing research* (pp. 3–9). Amsterdam: Amsterdam University Press.

van den Bergh, H., & Rijlaarsdam, G. (1996). The dynamics of composing: Modeling writing process data. In C. M. Levy & S. Ransdell (Eds.), *The science of writing: Theories, methods, individual differences, and applications* (pp. 207–232). Mahwah, NJ: Erlbaum.

van den Bergh, H., & Rijlaarsdam, G. (1999). The dynamics of idea generation during writing: An online study. In M. Torrance & D. Galbraith (Eds.), *Studies in writing: Vol. 4. Knowing what to write: Cognitive perspectives on conceptual processes in text production* (pp. 99–120). Amsterdam: Amsterdam University Press.

van den Bergh, H., & Rijlaarsdam, G. (2001). Changes in cognitive activities during the writing process, and relations with text quality. *Educational Psychology, 21,* 373–385.

van den Bergh, H., Rijlaarsdam, G., & Breetvelt, I. (1992). Het stellen van doelen: Relaties met productkwaliteit [Formulating aims: Relations with text quality]. *Tijdschrift voor Taalbeheersing, 14,* 221–233.

van den Bergh, H., Rijlaarsdam, G., & Breetvelt, I. (1993). Revision processes and text quality: An empirical study. In G. Eigler & T. Jechle (Eds.), *Writing: Current trends in European research* (pp. 133–147). Freiburg: Hochschul Verlag.

van den Bergh, H., Herrlitz, W., & Klein Gunnewiek, L. (2000). Entwicklung von Fähigkeiten in einer Fremdsprache—vorsichtige Hypothesen. In G. Kischel & E. Gotsch (Eds.), *Wege zur Mehrsprachigkeit im Fernstudium* (pp. 115–138). Hagen: Fernuniversität.

van der Hoeven, J. (1997). *Children's composing: A study into the relationships between writing processes, text quality, and cognitive and linguistic skills.* Utrecht Studies in Language and Communication, Vol. 12. Amsterdam: Rodopi.

Chapter 4

A Sociocultural Theory of Writing

Paul Prior

The history of writing research and theory may be narrated in varied ways. Some reach back to the emergence of sophistic rhetoric among the ancient Greeks, whereas others point to the relatively recent development of focused research examining writing through psychological and anthropological methodologies. Emig's (1971) case studies of the writing processes of high school students, along with Britton, Burgess, Martin, McLeod, and Rosen's (1975) research on secondary students' (ages 11–18) writing in U.K. schools (which shifted attention from normative issues of how people *should* write to descriptive questions, such as how to classify writing), pointed a new generation of researchers to questions of writing as a form of activity. Research on writing processes in the United States initially settled on cognitive processing theory (i.e., Flower & Hayes, 1981); however, that paradigm was soon critiqued as too narrow in its understanding of context and was eclipsed by studies that attended to social, historical, and political contexts of writing. Since then, empirical research on writing has increasingly turned to sociocultural theories and methods emerging from psychology, anthropology, sociology, linguistics, and semiotics.

Since the 1970s, sociocultural studies of writing have been quite heterogeneous, including anthropological studies of literate practices in typical (i.e., non-Western, non-industrialized, or marginalized) anthro-

pological sites (e.g., Besnier, 1995; Heath, 1983; Ochs, 1988; Scollon & Scollon, 1981); cross-cultural psychological studies of the cognitive consequences of literacy (e.g., Scribner & Cole, 1981); examination of writing practices in scientific and other workplaces (e.g., Bazerman, 1988; Beaufort, 1999; Latour, 1999; Myers, 1990; Suchman, 2000; Swales, 1998); accounts of writing in relation to electronic media in schools and workplaces (e.g., Geisler, 2003; Hawisher & Selfe, 1999; Heath & Luff, 2000; Nardi, 1995); tracing of writing across home, community, and other settings (e.g., Brandt, 2001; Moll & Greenberg, 1990; Sheridan-Rabideau, 2001; Taylor & Dorsey-Gaines, 1988); and educational studies of writing in classrooms from kindergarten through graduate school (e.g., Casanave, 2002; Dias, Freedman, Medway, & Pare, 1999; Dyson, 1997; Gutierrez, Rymes, & Larson, 1995; Larson, 1999; Ivanic, 1998; Kamberelis, 2001; Lunsford, 2002; Michaels, 1987; Prior, 1998). Sociocultural theories represent the dominant paradigm for writing research today. This chapter is not intended as a comprehensive review of the literature; instead, it introduces the complex, interdisciplinary territory of sociocultural theory, explores some specific studies that illustrate how that theory has reshaped our understanding of writing, and, finally, considers future directions and challenges for sociocultural research on writing.

Key Tenets of Sociocultural Theory

Sociocultural theory rejects the notion that human action is governed by some Neoplatonic realm of rules, whether the linguistic rules of English, the communicative norms of some discourse community, or cognitive scripts for acting in a particular situation. Sociocultural theory argues that activity is *situated* in concrete interactions that are simultaneously *improvised* locally and *mediated* by prefabricated, historically provided tools and practices, which range from machines, made objects, semiotic means (e.g., languages, genres, iconographies), and institutions to structured environments, domesticated animals and plants, and, indeed, people themselves. Mediated activity involves *externalization* (speech, writing, the manipulation and construction of objects and devices) and *co-action* (with other people, artifacts, and elements of the social–material environment) as well as *internalization* (perception, learning). Objects come to embody human activity as they register its consequences. Texts are inscribed, tools are made, routes are worn in the land, buildings are constructed, and other species are domesticated (now genetically altered): Human activity makes worlds, leaving the traces of human projects object-ified in those worlds, and then inhabits those evolving worlds. Even a lone individual thinking is co-acting with other people through artifacts fabricated elsewhere, at other times, mostly by other people. I do not, for example, fully internalize the car and the road when I drive, the computer and its graphic software when I draw with them, or the other person when I converse with her. In each case, action and cognition are *distributed* so I must learn to act-with. Distributed activity inevitably crosses so many social and historical boundaries that activity, people, and artifacts are always heterogeneous (not pure or ideal). Thus, activity is also *laminated*, with multiple frames or fields coexisting, relatively foregrounded or backgrounded (see Goffman, 1974, 1981; Goodwin & Duranti, 1992; Prior, 1998; Prior & Shipka, 2003). In activity, people are not only *socialized* (brought into alignment with others) as they *appropriate* cultural resources but also *individuated* as their particular appropriations historically accumulate to form a particular

individual. Vygotsky (1987) argued that "the central tendency of the child's development is not a gradual socialization introduced from the outside, but a gradual individualization that emerges on the foundation of the child's internal socialization" (p. 259). In activity, *institutions* are made and remade, in part through making certain kinds of people who engage in certain kinds of practices for certain ends, in part through the production of object-ified worlds in which the institution becomes naturalized. However, the social world is also *personalized* as an individual's particular biographically formed stances, values, and practices are taken up by other people and to varying extents are embedded in cultural resources. Finally, activity involves signs-in-use (linguistic or nonlinguistic) that are concrete, historical, and dialogic, signs formed out of the materials at hand and in relation to historical chains of sign use.

Mapping Sociocultural Theory: A History of Three Entangled Traditions

Sociocultural theory has multiple, tangled histories that produce a complex interdisciplinary territory and diverse terminology. One central figure is Lev Vygotsky, who in the few short years of his active career in the Soviet Union before his death in 1934, produced a rich set of studies, theories, methods, and goals for research. Vygotsky (1978, 1987) proposed understanding human consciousness as sociohistorically produced, treated learning/development as a confluence of histories (phylogenesis, cultural genesis, and ontogenesis), and initiated research on the emergence of writing in childhood, as well as on ways that writing mediates problem solving and memory. Research that has continued the development of Vygotsky's ideas is sometimes simply referred to as *Vygotskian* or *neo-Vygotskian*. James Wertsch (1991), a leading Western proponent of Vygotsky's theories, prefers the term *sociocultural* to emphasize the importance of cultural mediation in human development. A. N. Leont'ev (1981), a colleague of Vygotsky's, often referred to *sociohistoric* theory to emphasize the importance of concrete histories—of the species, of cultural groups, of psychological systems. He named his own contribution to this line *activ-*

ity theory, arguing that durable, socially motivated activity is the appropriate unit of analysis for study of the affective and motivating spheres of consciousness that Vygotsky identified as fundamental in his last major work (*Thinking and Speech*). Yrjo Engestrom (1987, 1993), who is arguably the leading activity theorist in the world today, and Michael Cole (1996), who has been central to promoting the work of Vygotsky and Alexander Luria, Vygotsky's closest associate, prefer *cultural–historical activity theory* (CHAT) as the broad name and often specify the unit of analysis as *activity systems*. Drawing on sociohistoric theory in her cross-cultural studies of children's apprenticeship into thinking and action, Barbara Rogoff (1990) emphasizes the multichannel (verbal and nonverbal), *intersubjective* character of *guided participation* in cultural practices. Because of the emphasis on the mediated nature of cognition and action, many of these ideas are also discussed as examples of *distributed cognition* (e.g., Salomon, 1993) or of *functional systems* (e.g., Hutchins, 1995). Somewhat poetically, del Rio and Alvarez (1995) talk of functional systems as *architectures for mind and agency*.

Similar variations in emphasis and naming can be traced in other sociocultural traditions. Views of language (or, more generally, signs) as situated, dialogic, and indexical, developed by Voloshinov (1973, 1976) and then extended by Bakhtin (1981, 1986), are referred to as *dialogic* or *Bakhtinian*. For their anthropological study of apprenticeship, Lave and Wenger (1991) offer a theory of *situated learning* in *communities of practice*. To capture the structured improvisation of social life, Bourdieu (1977, 1990) offers key notions of *practice*, *habitus*, and *cultural capital*. Researchers routinely draw from diverse sociocultural traditions and figures. In developing his notion of *discourse genres* to address the tacit, embodied nature of communication, Hanks (1996) blends Silverstein's (1985) dialogic theory (which emphasizes functional and metapragmatic dimensions of communication) with Bourdieu's notions of practice and habitus. Holland, Lachicotte, Skinner, and Cain (1998) blend practice theory with Bakhtinian and Vygotskian work as they explore *self* and *identity* in *figured worlds*. At this point, readers may be wondering if there really is such a creature as sociocultural theory. There is.

Sociocultural theory has emerged out of three intensely interacting traditions: Marxism, pragmatics, and phenomenology. Each has fought against binaries: materialism versus idealism, nature versus humanity, the mind versus the body, the individual versus the collective. Marx's (Marx & Engels, 1976) "Theses on Feuerbach" rejected both idealism and materialism with its call to study "human sensuous activity, practice" (p. 6) and its assertion that people are not only materially produced but also produce themselves materially. References to this foundational text appear across practice-oriented approaches, at critical points, for example, in Bourdieu (1977), Leont'ev (1981), and Voloshinov (1976). Marx viewed society as built up from its concrete historical base and sought to replace cultural dogma with science:

> The social structure and the state are continuously evolving out of the life-process of definite individuals, however, of these individuals, not as they may appear in their own or other people's imagination, but as they *actually* are, i.e., as they act, produce materially, and hence as they work under definite material limits, presuppositions, and conditions independent of their will. (Marx & Engels, 1976, pp. 35–36; emphasis in original)

In developing his pragmatic account of education, Dewey (1916) described society as constantly rewoven in joint activity in specific environments, through which people come to form common understandings, aims, dispositions, and skills. Central to this reweaving is an environment, "every domesticated plant and animal, every tool, every utensil, every appliance, every manufactured article, every aesthetic decoration, every work of art," remade by human activity (p. 37). Dewey argues that this world of artifacts allows children to attain rapidly what humanity took ages to develop, that with such artifacts, "the dice have been loaded" (p. 37). Schutz's phenomenological sociology has been particularly influential for studies of practice, informing such key figures as Garfinkel (1967) and Goffman (1974). For Schutz (1967), the here-and-now is an improvisational achievement, but it does not stand alone: It is socially structured. Schutz describes a social world of layered zones: directly experienced intersubjective social reality, the world of contemporaries, and the worlds of predecessors and successors. The world of contemporaries is layered as well, including *people I am now in face-to-face interaction with, people I have met, people I know of but have not met, people I know of in an abstract way, collective entities* (e.g., the state), *objective configurations of meaning* (e.g., the grammar of English), and *artifacts* (pp. 180–181). Like Vygotsky and Dewey, Schutz views tools as carriers of social history: "A tool is a thing-in-order-to; it serves a purpose and for the sake of this purpose it was produced" (p. 201). Schutz and Luckmann (1973) state that subjective elements of knowledge are only taken into the social stock of knowledge by *objectivation*, "the embodiment of subjective processes in the objects and events of the everyday lifeworld" (p. 264).

The most prominent line of sociocultural theory is traced to calls in the 1920s by Vygotsky and Voloshinov for Marxist reconceptualizations of psychology and linguistics as disciplines whose proper object is the concrete historical activity of persons-in-societies. Vygotsky's (1978) fundamental question was how we become human through day-to-day engagements in the cultural practices of our communities and institutions. He argued that in such engagements we encounter, selectively appropriate, use, and refashion for others' use, material and semiotic resources that have been developed historically. Voloshinov (1973) critiqued theories of language, like those of Saussure, that assume some abstract system (of shared rules and a shared lexicon) governs performance. He argued that such systematization makes living languages dead, turning dynamic streams of socially charged discourse into abstract signals, emptied of all but a fixed denotative sense, uttered by no one, nowhere, at no time. Voloshinov's conclusion that language "is a purely historical phenomenon" (p. 82) explains why he and Bakhtin rejected the trope that language resides in some Neo-platonic realm of dictionaries, grammar books, and guides to social etiquette (whether located in society, the brain, or our genes).

Anthropology and sociology have distilled these traditions in theory and research on cultural practice. Hanks (1996) notes that much research in anthropological linguistics has been shaped by the Prague School's uptake of basic phenomenological tenets: that

language is only one mode of human communication, that use of language must be understood as historically specific (not a product of general systematic knowledge or rules), that meaning is intersubjectively arrived at by people drawing on linguistic and nonlinguistic experience, and that much of communication is tacit and silent. Bourdieu (1977, 1990) draws on phenomenology to emphasize the complex, improvised nature of individual perception and action, while at the same time displaying a Marxist attention to activity, the organization of work (formal and informal), and objectification (i.e., the historical accumulation of material, social, and cultural capital).

Marxism, pragmatics, and phenomenology have converged on key points. Each has sought to understand human activity through close attention to concrete, everyday practices/histories and has attended to ways that histories enter situations embedded in artifacts. Inverting the old social order, each has argued that human thought and action are not explicable in terms of abstract universals, not governed from above. Each sees the everyday world not as a pale shadow of the real and potent, but as a rich, historically continuous ground for human action. Each sees consciousness as a key term and seeks to wrest understanding from an ideological fog of political and religious dogma by focusing on the actual practices of people and attending to how people are socialized into cultural patterns of perception, thought, and action. Although variously mapped, the coalescence of a sociocultural approach encompassing these three traditions is apparent in a number of other overviews (see Bruner, 1996; Cole, 1996; Gee, 2000; Goodwin & Duranti, 1992; Hanks, 1996; Rogoff, 2003). In short, weaving together these three traditions should not be understood as a mark of eclecticism, but as a reflection of deep coherences in stance, as well as of intense historical dialogues among key figures across the traditions.

A Sociocultural Theory of Writing

Sociocultural approaches to writing reject the simple equation of writing with material texts or acts of inscription, seeing writing as chains of short- and long-term production, representation, reception, and distribution.

Writing involves dialogic processes of invention. Texts, as artifacts-in-activity, and the inscription of linguistic signs in some medium are parts of streams of mediated, distributed, and multimodal activity. Even a lone writer is using an array of sociohistorically provided resources (languages, genres, knowledge, motives, technologies of inscription and distribution) that extend beyond the moment of transcription and that cross modes and media (reading, writing, talk, visual representation, material objectification). Texts and moments of inscription are no more autonomous than the spray thrown up by the white water in a river, and like that spray, literate acts today are far downstream from their sociohistoric origins. Seeing writing as distributed and mediated means recognizing that all writing is collaborative, involving divisions of labor and forms of coauthorship. As in Schutz's (1967) account (discussed earlier) of the world of contemporaries, these divisions of labor may range from direct, face-to-face coproduction of texts to the provision of very anonymous resources (e.g., the word *text*). One important corollary of this view is the recognition that teachers in schools are always coauthors (often dominant ones) in students' writing as teachers take up many roles in the authorship function (deciding to write, setting deadlines, specifying style and topic, structuring the writing process, offering specific words and phrases). The fact that students are typically held fully accountable as authors is thus an interesting cultural practice (pointing to both power and the subject-producing dimensions of writing in school—the proleptic invitation to assume authorship and to accept its ideology). Contrary to prototypical images of writing and reading as private acts separated in space and time, sociocultural research has called attention to the many instances of face-to-face writing: cowriting of texts, writing on the chalkboard, graffiti, and so on. The role of such face-to-face writing and reading, mediated by talk, in children's early appropriations of literate practice remains to be explored.

Sociocultural theory argues for viewing writing as a mode of social action, not simply a means of communication. Writing participates in making particular kinds of people, institutions, and cultures, as well as indexing them. From Bazerman's (1988) studies of the slow historical formation of scientific report genres to Kamberelis's (1999) study of the ontogenetic emergence of genre in children's writing, North American genre theory (see Bazerman & Prior, 2005) illustrates this dual focus on situated meaning and social action. Miller (1984) and Bazerman (1988) took up Schutz's notion of typification to explore how genres work to order the world, to constitute persons and social formations, to typify both construals of what is going on and means of moving forward. Bazerman's framework also drew heavily on Bakhtin's (1986) discussion of speech genres as dialogic utterances and the Vygotskian understanding that mediational means (in this case, genres) produce people and culture. The next sections explore selected studies to give a flavor for the research program that has grown over the past three decades examining writing as a sociocultural practice. I have mapped these studies into three themes: redrawing the oral–literate divide, emerging schooled literacies, and writing in college and beyond. These three areas are offered as a tool, not as a rule, as neither mutually exclusive nor comprehensive. They are intended to give a feel for the range of ways that sociocultural theory has been taken up in specific studies of literate activity and for the picture of writing that has been emerging from such research.

Redrawing the Oral–Literate Divide

In early sociocultural studies of writing, Luria and Vygotsky looked developmentally at the emergence of writing, noting the intersections of drawing, scribbling, and writing, and the role of writing in remediating psychological systems having to do with memory and problem solving. Whereas Western rhetoric, following Plato, came to see writing as a rationale for ignoring the rhetorical canon of memory, Vygotsky identified writing as key to a revolutionary reorganization of memory, the externalization of memory in written texts being a prime example of mediated activity. Luria's (1976) studies in Uzbekistan in the 1930s informed cross-cultural psychology's studies, decades later, of literate/schooled and illiterate/unschooled minds in practice.

Scribner and Cole (1981) reported their complex series of ethnographic experiments with the Vai people of Liberia in the 1970s.

Their study of literacy, schooling, social contexts, and cognitive performance on a variety of tasks proved to be seminal in debates about the consequences of literacy, particularly alphabetic literacies, because they were able to take advantage of the natural laboratory of the Vai culture, where three dominant forms of literacy coexisted, each associated with different scripts, different modes of learning/instruction, different patterns of use, and different cultural significations. Vai literates used an indigenously developed syllabary that was taught and learned in everyday social relationships. Vai was used for diverse purposes, including letter writing, record keeping, literary and historical writing, religious practices, and representing foreign languages. It was socially limited (with fewer than 30% of adults able to read and write Vai), chirographic (handwritten), rarely used for government communication, and often known to individuals who had attended little or no Western schooling. Quranic literacy, in contrast, was learned formally (but not in Western schools) and emphasized rote memorization of the Quran in Arabic (a foreign language with an alphabetic script). While some used Arabic literacy for a wide range of activities, the dominant use was religious. Arabic script was typically encountered in print form in the Quran and other key Arabic texts. English (again, a foreign language with an alphabetic script) was learned in Western-style schools and used for a range of activities similar to Vai, except rarely to represent other languages. However, English was also used for government communication and appeared in a wide range of print texts and genres. Among the Vai, then, were individuals who had only one of these literacies along with those who were bi-, tri-, or multiliterates and others who were nonliterate; individuals who had attended Western and/or Quranic schools and those who had not; and individuals who were routinely involved in modern, urban activities and others who were traditional and rural. This diverse cultural landscape provided an opportunity to untangle the cognitive, behavioral, and ideological consequences of schooling, modern life, and literacy (in general or in the form of particular types of scripts).

Scribner and Cole (1981; Scribner, 1997) found that literacy did not have unique general consequences; instead, specific practices ("recurrent, goal-oriented sequences of activities") were associated with specific consequences, such as a certain kind of memorization (incremental) being associated with Quranic literacy; syllogistic reasoning, with English literacy; and certain kinds of verbal integration, with Vai. They concluded that the appropriate unit of analysis was not literacy, but *literate practices*, the "socially organized . . . use of a symbol system and a technology for producing and disseminating it," practices that involve "not simply knowing how to read and write in a particular script but applying that knowledge for specific purposes in specific contexts of use" (Scribner & Cole, p. 236). Extending the studies of Vygotsky and Luria, Scribner and Cole's work displays a basic sociocultural methodology (ethnography mixed with ethnographically informed tasks, analyzed quantitatively and qualitatively). Their study still stands as a clear argument for seeing literacy as situated, mediated sociocultural practices, as motivated and socially organized activity. It also set the agenda for subsequent research into literacy practices in a variety of specific sociocultural settings.

Besnier (1995) looked at literacy on Nukulaelae Atoll, home to about 350 Polynesians who were multilingual, had achieved close to universal but fairly basic literacy, and had near-universal but limited education (only 5% had attended secondary school). The Nukulaelae had a nonindigenous literacy, their script introduced by Western or Western-trained Samoan missionaries. For most Nukulaelae, literacy was used for interpersonal, personal, and familial purposes. Besnier's inventory of genres included letters, telegrams, invitations to feasts, sermons, lists (especially for record keeping), genealogies, minutes of meetings, song lyrics, names and slogans woven into mats for decoration, T-shirt illustrations, and graffiti. Besnier studied the Nukulaelae as a case of incipient literacy, literacy not widely and deeply woven into practices. He explored how the Nukulaelae adopted but also adapted literacy, how literacy altered but also accommodated earlier oral and nonverbal practices, and how literacy and orality continued to interact intensely. For example, Besnier analyzes ways that the sociocultural fact of separation—travel to other islands being a long-standing practice—and the uncharacteristically powerful expressions of emotion at departures were remediated in letter writing (both in affectively charged acts of writing the night before a ship visit and in the written expression of the letters). Here was a case in which written genres were markedly more emotional than oral. In addition to documenting processes of emergent literacy in this society, Besnier makes the broader point that literacy is wrapped up in multimodal semiotic practices in which cultural resources (texts, literate practices, identities, and ideologies) are creatively and improvisationally (re)worked in current activity.

In a more complex case, Kalman (1999) studied the mediated language practices of scribes and their clients at the Plaza de Santa Domingo in Mexico City. The scribes typed documents (e.g., contracts, tax forms, school assignments, love letters, petitions, letters of application), taking roles that ranged from pure typing through forms of joint composition, all the way to the role of primary composer (translating clients' purposes into language and form). Kalman details cases of clients, ranging from a homeless man seeking a letter to help him enter a shelter to an engineer getting a letter typed to accompany a set of technical drawings he was delivering to a firm. She explores complex negotiations over texts, genres, identities, contextualizations, and forms of participation in composing. In this particular cultural context, she was able to explore how oral practices of dictating and joint oral composition were negotiated, how talk and text interacted, and how social identities and literacies shaped participation. Kalman found that many clients with limited control over decoding and encoding written language displayed considerable familiarity with literate practices and that the scribes, though quite literate, were not guaranteed cultural respect or financial security because of that competence.

Sociocultural studies of transitions from orality to literacy (whether in individual ontogenesis or the cultural genesis of a particular group) have represented a central site for sociocultural inquiry into writing. These studies have highlighted more complex relations between orality and literacy than had been imagined, often tracing ways writing is drafted, negotiated, and received through talk as well as ways that talk (as in sermons) is partially prefabricated through writing. They have often focused on literacy practices in home and community rather than only at school or work. In short, studies in this area

have confirmed and extended Scribner and Cole's (1981) accounts of literate practice as the socially organized activity of production, distribution, reception, and use of texts tied to specific purposes in specific contexts.

Emerging Schooled Literacies

In modern societies, school has played a leading and very visible role in promoting literacy. It is widely seen as the site where children learn to read and write, and it emerged as a robust factor in cross-cultural studies of psychological functioning (Rogoff, 1981; Scribner, 1997). Yet as Heath's (1983) classic study of literacies in three U.S. communities showed, literate practices are first encountered in home and community, and the particular form of those practices can resonate or conflict with schooled literacies. Sociocultural studies of schooling, then, have sought to describe not only how writing is used and learned in school, but also how school writing is located in larger and deeper currents of sociocultural practice.

Continuing a series of studies of writing in elementary schools, Dyson (1997) draws on Bakhtin's and Vygotsky's theories to explore how children appropriate voices as they form imagined worlds through play, and how play and appropriation are central to the identities and social relations of the children. Following a class of students over 2 years (second to third grade), Dyson notes that, as composers, children "were not so much meaning makers as meaning negotiators, who adopt, resist, or stretch available words" (p. 4) and who in so doing work to alter the social and ideological "state of affairs" (Voloshinov, 1973) they have encountered. For example, Dyson traces the state of affairs in the third-grade class's Author's Theatre, where a student writes a text or script to be acted out, under his or her direction, with classmates. Author's Theatre texts routinely drew on media characters and plots. Dyson, for example, traces what happens as traditions of male superheroes and Greek (white) gods and goddesses (whose texts were not only being read but also watched on TV series, like *Hercules*) were reappropriated by an African American girl, Tina, who constructs a new superhero, Venus Tina. In text, talk, and drawings, Venus Tina is a strong black female who flies through the air on a magical (female) horse, rescuing children in trouble, transforming mean men into nice men, and making city parks safe and peaceful. Drawing, talking, writing, diverse words, images, and stories all come together in this tale. Writing here is a mode of participation in worlds of peer group, school, and society. Looking at ways that mass media shape children's early appropriations of literacy, Dyson emphasizes the active agency of children, seeing them as not simply being formed as cultural beings but as living culturally and engaging in critical appropriations and reconstructions of the cultural tools and artifacts they encounter.

Kamberelis (1999) offers detailed quantitative and interpretive analyses of children's (K–second grade) appropriations of three genres (narrative, scientific report, and poem). Analyzing a number of textual features, he found that these young writers had surer knowledge of narrative genres and, across genres, a better grasp of general features than microtextual features. He also noted the marked hybridity, especially the surprising blends of science and informational genres. In a detailed analysis of the talk and actions of two fourth graders as they dissect an owl pellet and then write up and present a report of their dissection, Kamberelis (2001) traces the hybridity of discourse practices. Analyzing genres, footings, and power relations, Kamberelis highlights a wide variety of voices, especially the use of unframed direct quotes ("Scalpel"; "Beam me up, Scotty") from the media. Kamberelis shows that this hybridity not only produced a written report that both the teacher and the other students found successful, but also shifted the politics of the classroom.

Moll has explored the intersections of biliterate–bicultural educational and social contexts from a Vygotskian perspective. Contesting cultural deficit accounts of Hispanic students, Moll and Greenberg (1990) identified diverse *funds of knowledge* in students' families and communities: knowledge of gardening, care of animals, car repair, music, building codes, religion, and so on. They note that these socially distributed funds are embedded in household and work activities, and that they involve specific literate and learning practices. Moll's research has extended to re-mediating school instruction by organizing study groups (teachers and researchers) that seek to understand students'

everyday funds of knowledge and then find ways to apply that understanding to redesign instruction (Moll & Whitmore, 1993). Moll (2000) has explored the emergence of biliteracy, seeking to describe the benefits it can confer in a public climate more likely to focus on students' deficits in the dominant code. He argues that writing is particularly valuable for children in creating imaginary worlds, worlds central to what he calls "the most important artifact created by children ... themselves, the formation of their personalities" (p. 262).

Through a close, situated analysis of classroom discourse, small-group talk, and texts, Lunsford (2002) studied a summer writing program for high school students (mainly rising seniors) at a major university. The program sought to help students learn sophisticated strategies for written arguments by teaching Toulmin's (1958) model (claim, evidence, warrant, qualifier) and the grammar of clarity (Williams, 1990), while offering rich support (lecture and small-group) for engagement with content and process. Lunsford analyzes the dialogic complexity of instructional terms even in this carefully theorized pedagogy. For example, students struggle to align Toulmin's notion of claims (in arguments) with the notion of points (which emphasized textual organization), both of which were being actively taught in the program, but also with other concepts (topic sentence, thesis) they had encountered in English classes. Managing such dialogic complexity was no trivial issue. Lunsford finds similar complexity in the reading of students' texts by peers and instructors, focusing particularly on the case of one student whose text acquired the reading that it was "contradictory," perhaps in part because of particular peer responses, as well as particular ways it took up the task. In general, Lunsford's analysis not only indicates the complexity of instruction in writing when seen as a practice, but also suggests how sociocultural analysis can identify processes that may promote or impede desired learning.

Sociocultural studies of school focus on close analysis of specific classroom practices; of the talk, reading, writing, observation, and action that make up literate practices; and of the specific kinds of collaborative work school sponsors. Whether understood in terms of Vygotsky's emphasis on how social interaction is transformatively internalized in development or Bourdieu's emphasis on the tacit accumulation of embodied *habitus*, it is the specific character and sense of classroom interaction that must be attended to in order to understand how learning happens (including failures to learn the official curriculum). As a site of writing development and use, school in these accounts emerges as a powerful force, but not an autonomous domain. Not only does writing in school happen in the context of broader literate practices in the home, community, and workplace, but also school itself is seen as a profoundly laminated institution, leading many sociocultural researchers to explore ways of taking advantage of such connections, especially for students whose everyday life-worlds are underrepresented in schooled practices.

Writing in College and Beyond: Disciplinary and Workplace Discourse Practices

Sociocultural studies of writing in college recapitulate many points made by sociocultural studies of writing in primary and secondary schools. There is the same need for close attention to classroom practices and the same sense that the classroom cannot be isolated. The writing that college, especially graduate, students do may be more involved and extended, and may have more stabilized external audiences; however, what is probably most distinct is the role of disciplinarity in college writing and the emerging blend of school and workplace. College writing emphasizes specialized forms of writing associated with disciplines and professions. Much of the research in this area has focused on genres as textual marks of disciplinarity.

Russell (1997) sketches interlocking *genre systems* (Bazerman, 1994, 2004) across interwoven activity systems (Engestrom, 1993) in college biology. The notion of genre systems points to ways that particular genres do not stand alone, but are linked in chains of production, distribution, and reception. A classroom includes the genres produced by the teacher (lecture, discussion, e-mail responses to students, blackboard notes, the syllabus, written assignments, responses written on or to student texts, course descriptions, grades), the genres produced by

the students (notes on class interactions, marking and notes on readings, e-mail questions or contacts with the instructor and/or other students, drafts of papers, final papers, etc.), disciplinary genres (articles, books, websites), and institutional genres (code of academic policies, registrar's records, stated requirements for major field, etc.). These genres coalesce into systems, with typified and dialogic chains (e.g., the teacher's assignment prompts the student to write a text, which occasions the teacher's response and a grade entered on a computer sheet sent to the registrar for inclusion in the official transcript). Each genre also stands in certain relations to genres in other settings. A lab report for a biology class is linked to the wider world of lab reports and other scientific genres. As the chain of genres grows, it implicates multiple activity systems. Russell (1997) notes that the activity system of the biology class is nested within the activity system of the university, both of which in turn are linked to a network of interested activity systems: corporations, government, advocacy groups, and so on. Russell concludes that "tracing the relation of a disciplinary or professional genre system to an educational genre system, through the boundary of a classroom genre system, a researcher, reformer, or participant can construct a model of ways classroom writing is linked to writing in wider social practices" (p. 546).

My own research has focused on writing and disciplinary enculturation, particularly in graduate programs. I began with basic questions about how writing tasks were assigned, completed, and responded to/graded in graduate classes (Prior, 1991). However, close analysis of these processes revealed surprising complexity and heterogeneity. Assignments were made, remade, and negotiated in various contexts. Students not only developed an evolving series of task representations but also took tasks up actively in terms of their own goals. Written texts were surprisingly diverse, yet were all read as versions of the task by the professor, who, not incidentally, often interpreted texts in light of his or her knowledge of, and past experiences with, the student. The challenge of understanding this complexity led me to explore dialogic theories of communication and activity theories of learning. In subsequent research (Prior, 1998), I traced how talk in a sociology seminar, responding to a student's dissertation prospectus, enacted a distributed revision process, how (in the same seminar) a series of written responses and revisions across two texts (a conference paper and preliminary examination) led to (tacitly) coauthored texts that blended internally persuasive and authoritative discourses (Bakhtin, 1981) for both the student and her professor, and how a student's paper for an American Studies seminar was linked to work in other seminars, to field research, and to experiences at home and in the community. Analysis of this last case led to research with undergraduates, graduate students, and professors to explore how writing is produced across a dispersed chain of events in varied settings. Prior and Shipka (2003) examine, for example, ways that writers, at all levels, actively selected and structured times and places for writing, chose ways of creating a particular attunement to the task (e.g., listening to certain music, drinking tea or coffee, finding a comfortable spot), sought out interactions with certain people (often friends or family not officially involved in the task) while perhaps avoiding others, and sometimes recruited earlier experiences and texts to the work at hand. As writers form and regulate worlds to regulate their own consciousness and actions, they do not just inhabit contexts, but actively produce "a lifeworld with a certain tone and feel, populated by certain people and their ideas, calibrated to a certain rhythm" (Prior & Shipka, 2003, pp. 230–231). These environment-selecting and -structuring practices highlight ways that individuals not only internalize social practices but also learn to produce them to shape their own and others' activity.

Sociocultural research on scientific and sociotechnical workplaces has highlighted complexly situated literate practices. Latour and Woolgar (1986) studied laboratory science from an anthropological, practice-oriented, pragmatic perspective. In place of abstract epistemological principles for validating knowledge, they identified a wide variety of concrete practices and artifacts as they followed scientific objects from being ambiguous phenomena (e.g., a series of spikes registered on a meter) at the laboratory bench to debatable scientific claims in technical articles, to accepted facts and ob-

jects to be traded. In particular, Latour and Woolgar traced cascading chains of inscriptions: bench notes, measurements, labels, printouts, drafts, published articles, grant applications, vitas, and so on. In a study of an early technology start-up company, Bazerman (1999) examines the *heterogeneous symbolic engineering* Thomas Edison engaged in at Menlo Park. He shows that making an electric light involved multiple activity systems, each with its own rhetorical situations and strategies. For example, securing patents from the U.S. government involved different kinds of work from that of securing city officials' permits for tearing up streets and laying down electrical wires or securing funding from investors to support the work of invention. Patents demanded detailed, dated, and witnessed laboratory notebooks, city permits involved expensive dinners and gifts of stock, and capitalists wanted assurance of near-term success (which for a period led Edison to fake demonstrations). Bazerman offers a stunningly complex view of the rhetorical and practical activity involved in moving from imagined invention to stabilized product. Heath and Luff (2000) analyze practices in new sociotechnical workplaces such as the operations center of the London Underground, where workers sit side by side at multimedia consoles, watching screens that bring representations of information from global networks, talking face-to-face, typing in information, and talking over phones or radios to others at distant sites. Their phenomenological analysis focuses, on the one hand, on the workers' carefully tuned attention to the gaze, bodily orientation, and quiet vocalizations (e.g., sighs) of other people—a communicative system for coordination that has deep roots in the evolutionary past of our species—and, on the other hand, on questions of how to read and act on complex computer-mediated visual displays of data.

Studies of writing in college and the workplace make clear the vast complexity of literate activity in our present society and the need for writers to continually learn new genres and textual practices. This research should inform writing instruction from kindergarten through college. For example, learning five-paragraph essay forms without learning how to analyze new genres and attune to new writing practices amounts to learning almost nothing of what will be needed as individuals follow their own sociohistoric trajectories.

Conclusion

At this point, it would be difficult to find situated studies of writing that do not at least gesture toward some sociocultural theory or cite the many writing researchers who have drawn on sociocultural theory and methodology in their own research. In general, sociocultural theory has become increasingly tightly knit as the phenomenological emphasis on making order in situated activity links up with the cultural–historical and pragmatic emphasis on the production of mediational means, artifacts, and people as a way of understanding how culture comes to be embodied in practice. Sociocultural theories of writing have found, however, that they cannot live easily within the borders of a folk notion of writing, so studies increasingly explore more semiotically rich units (I have proposed *literate activity*), in which an interest in writing leads to writing and reading, talk and listening, observation and action, and feeling and thinking in the world. Likewise, understanding what interests, constraints, and affordances have been built into our increasingly intelligent writing technologies calls for careful analysis of design practices, and writing with these technologies often segues seamlessly into multimedia practices that draw more on the language of film than print (Manovich, 2001). Sociocultural theories have also found that they cannot live easily in culturally bound spaces of writing (neither the lone writer in the garret nor the isolated classroom or workplace). Writing emerges out of far-flung historical networks, and the trajectories of a particular text trace delicate paths through overgrown sociohistoric landscapes. Finally, sociocultural research on writing has made it clear that much of the literate activity of writing is implicit and learned implicitly. If these discoveries are exciting, they are also disconcerting. Studies of writing face the need to trace and understand an increasingly complex semiotic phenomenon dispersed across widening spatiotemporal networks of activity and mediated by a growing array of tools. Moreover, writing is a phenomenon that

seems ever more connected to who we are and who we will become. These significant challenges for sociocultural inquiry are far from trivial, but reaching greater understanding of the ways writing technologies and practices have shaped, and are shaping, people and societies is also a task that holds great promise to mediate many of our future activities.

References

Bakhtin, M. M. (1981). *The dialogic imagination: Four essays by M. M. Bakhtin* (C. Emerson & M. Holquist, Trans.; M. Holquist, Ed.). Austin: University of Texas Press.

Bakhtin, M. (1986). *Speech genres and other late essays* (Vern W. McGee, Trans.). Austin: University of Texas Press.

Bazerman, C. (1988). *Shaping written knowledge: The genre and activity of the experimental article in science*. Madison: University of Wisconsin Press.

Bazerman, C. (1994). Systems of genres and the enactment of social intentions. In A. Freedman & P. Medway (Eds.), *Genre and the new rhetoric* (pp. 79–101). London: Taylor & Francis.

Bazerman, C. (1999). *The languages of Edison's light*. Cambridge, MA: MIT Press.

Bazerman, C. (2004). Speech acts, genres, and activity systems: How texts organize activity and people. In C. Bazerman & P. Prior (Eds.), *What writing does and how it does it: An introduction to analyzing texts and textual practices* (pp. 309–339). Mahwah, NJ: Erlbaum.

Bazerman, C., & Prior, P. (2005). Participating in emergent socio-literate worlds: Genre, disciplinarity, interdisciplinarity. In R. Beach, J. Green, M. Kamil, & T. Shanahan (Eds.), *Multidisciplinary perspectives on literacy research* (2nd ed.) Cresskill, NJ: Hampton Press.

Beaufort, A. (1999). *Writing in the real world: Making the transition from school to work*. New York: Teachers College Press.

Besnier, N. (1995). *Literacy, emotion, and authority: Reading and writing on a Polynesian atoll*. Cambridge, UK: Cambridge University Press.

Bourdieu, P. (1977). *Outline of a theory of practice* (R. Nice, Trans.). Cambridge, UK: Cambridge University Press.

Bourdieu, P. (1990). *The logic of practice* (R. Nice, Trans.). Stanford, CA: Stanford University Press.

Brandt, D. (2001). *Literacy in American lives*. Cambridge, UK: Cambridge University Press.

Britton, J., Burgess, T., Martin, N., McLeod, A., & Rosen, H. (1975). *The development of writing abilities (11–18)*. London: Macmillan.

Bruner, J. (1996). *The culture of education*. Cambridge, MA: Harvard University Press.

Casanave, C.P. (2002). *Writing games.* Mahwah, NJ: Erlbaum.

Cole, M. (1996). *Cultural psychology.* Cambridge, MA: Harvard University Press.

del Rio, P., & Alvarez, A. (1995). Tossing, praying, and reasoning: The changing architectures of mind and agency. In J. Wertsch, P. del Rio, & A. Alvarez (Eds.), *Sociocultural studies of mind* (pp. 215–247). Cambridge, UK: Cambridge University Press.

Dias, P., Freedman, A., Medway, P., & Pare, A. (1999). *Worlds apart: Acting and writing in academic and workplace contexts.* Mahwah, NJ: Erlbaum.

Dewey, J. (1916). *Democracy and education.* New York: Free Press.

Dyson, A. (1997). *Writing superheroes: Contemporary childhood, popular culture, and classroom literacy.* New York: Teachers College Press.

Emig, J. (1971). *The composing processes of twelfth graders.* Urbana, IL: National Council of Teachers of English.

Engestrom, Y. (1987). *Learning by expanding: An activity theoretical approach to developmental research.* Helsinki: Orienta-Konsultit.

Engestrom, Y. (1993). Developmental studies of work as a testbench of activity theory: The case of primary care medical practice. In S. Chaiklin & J. Lave (Eds.), *Understanding practice* (pp. 64–103). Cambridge, UK: Cambridge University Press.

Flower, L., & Hayes, J. (1981). A cognitive process theory of writing. *College Composition and Communication, 32,* 365–387.

Garfinkel, H. (1967). *Studies in ethnomethodology.* Engelwood Cliffs, NJ: Prentice-Hall.

Gee, J. (2000). The new literacy studies: From "socially situated" to the work of the social. In D. Barton, M. Hamilton, & R. Ivanic (Eds.), *Situated literacies: Reading and writing in context* (pp. 180–196). London: Routledge.

Geisler, C. (2003). When management becomes personal: An activity-theoretic analysis of Palm technologies. In C. Bazerman & D. Russell (Eds.), *Writing selves, writing societies: Research from activity perspectives* (pp. 125–158). Fort Collins, CO: WAC Clearinghouse and Mind, Culture, and Activity. Available online at wac.colostate.edu/books/selves_societies/

Goffman, E. (1981). *Forms of talk.* Philadelphia: University of Pennsylvania Press.

Goffman, E. (1974). *Frame analysis: An essay on the organization of experience.* Boston: Northeastern University Press.

Goodwin, C., & Duranti, A. (1992). Rethinking context: An introduction. In A. Duranti & C. Goodwin (Eds.), *Rethinking context: Language as an interactive phenomenon* (pp. 1–42). Cambridge, UK: Cambridge University Press.

Gutierrez, K., Rymes, B., & Larson, J. (1995). Script, counterscript, and underlife in the classroom: James Brown vs. *Brown v. Board of Education. Harvard Educational Review, 65,* 445–471.

Hanks, W. (1996). *Language and communicative practices.* Boulder, CO: Westview Press.

Hawisher, G., & Selfe, C. (1999). *Passions, pedagogies, and 21st century technologies.* Logan, UT and Urbana, IL: Utah State University Press and National Council of Teachers of English.

Heath, S. B. (1983). *Ways with words: Language, life, and work in communities and classrooms.* Cambridge, UK: Cambridge University Press.

Heath, C., & Luff, P. (2000). *Technology in action.* Cambridge, UK: Cambridge University Press.

Holland, D., Lachicotte, W., Skinner, D., & Cain, C. (1998). *Identity and agency in cultural worlds.* Cambridge, MA: Harvard University Press.

Hutchins, E. (1995). *Cognition in the wild.* Cambridge, MA: MIT Press.

Ivanic, R. (1998). *Writing and identity: The discoursal construction of identity in academic writing.* Amsterdam: John Benjamins.

Kalman, J. (1999). *Writing on the plaza: Mediated literacy practices among scribes and clients in Mexico City.* Cresskill, NJ: Hampton Press.

Kamberelis, G. (1999). Genre development and learning: Children writing stories, science reports, and poems. *Research in the Teaching of English, 33,* 403–460.

Kamberelis, G. (2001). Producing heteroglossic classroom (micro)cultures through hybrid discourse practice. *Linguistics and Education, 12,* 85–125.

Larson, J. (1999). Analyzing participation frameworks in kindergarten writing activity: The role of overhearers in learning to write. *Written Communication, 16,* 225–257.

Latour, B. (1999). *Pandora's hope: Essays on the reality of science studies.* Cambridge, MA: Harvard University Press.

Latour, B., & Woolgar, S. (1986). *Laboratory life.* Princeton, NJ: Princeton University Press.

Lave, J., & Wenger, E. (1991). *Situated learning.* Cambridge, UK: Cambridge University Press.

Leont'ev, A. N. (1981). *Problems of the development of mind.* Moscow: Progress.

Lunsford, K. (2002). Contextualizing Toulmin's model in the writing classroom: A case study. *Written Communication, 19,* 109–174.

Luria, A. R. (1976). *Cognitive development: Its cultural and social foundations* (M. Lopez-Morillas & L. Solotaroff, Trans.; M. Cole, Ed.). Cambridge, MA: Harvard University Press.

Manovich, L. (2001). *The language of new media.* Cambridge, MA: MIT Press.

Marx, K. & Engels, F. (1976). *Karl Marx and Frederick Engels: Collected works, Volume 5, 1845–47.* New York: International Publishers.

Michaels, S. (1987). Text and context: A new approach to the study of classroom writing. *Discourse Processes, 10,* 321–346.

Miller, C. (1984). Genre as social action. *Quarterly Journal of Speech*, 70, 151–167.

Moll, L. (2000). Inspired by Vygotsky: Ethnographic experiments in education. In C. Lee & P. Smagorinsky (Eds.), *Vygotskyan perspectives on literacy research: Constructing meaning through collaborative inquiry* (pp. 256–268). Cambridge, UK: Cambridge University Press.

Moll, L., & Greenberg, J. (1990). Creating zones of possibilities: Combining social contexts for instruction. In L. Moll (Ed.), *Vygotsky and education: Instructional implications and applications of sociohistorical psychology* (pp. 319–348). Cambridge, UK: Cambridge University Press.

Moll, L., & Whitmore, K. (1993). Vygotsky in classroom practice: Moving from individual transmission to social transaction. In E. Forman, N. Minick, & C.A. Stone (Eds.), *Contexts for learning: Sociocultural dynamics in children's development* (pp. 19–42). Oxford, UK: Oxford University Press.

Myers, G. (1990). *Writing biology: Texts in the social construction of scientific knowledge.* Madison: University of Wisconsin Press.

Nardi, B. (Ed.). (1995). *Context and consciousness: Activity theory and human–computer interaction.* Cambridge, MA: MIT Press.

Ochs, E. (1988). *Culture and language development: Language acquisition and language socialization in a Samoan village.* Cambridge, UK: Cambridge University Press.

Prior, P. (1991) Contextualizing writing and response in a graduate seminar. *Written Communication*, 8, 267–310.

Prior, P. (1998). *Writing/disciplinarity: A sociohistoric account of literate activity in the academy.* Mahwah, NJ: Erlbaum.

Prior, P., & Shipka, J. (2003). Chronotopic lamination: Tracing the contours of literate activity. In C. Bazerman & D. Russell (Eds.), *Writing selves, writing societies: Research from activity perspectives* (pp. 180–238). Fort Collins, CO: WAC Clearinghouse and Mind, Culture, and Activity. Available online at wac.colostate.edu/books/selves_societies/

Rogoff, B. (1981). Schooling and the development of cognitive skills. In H.C. Triandis & A. Heron (Eds.), *Handbook of cross-cultural psychology. Vol. 4: Developmental psychology* (pp. 233–294). Boston: Allyn & Bacon.

Rogoff, B. (1990). *Apprenticeship in thinking: Cognitive development in social context.* Oxford, UK: Oxford University Press.

Rogoff, B. (2003). *The cultural nature of human development.* Oxford, UK: Oxford University Press.

Russell, D. (1997). Rethinking genre in school and society: An activity theory analysis. *Written Communication*, 14, 504–554.

Salomon, G. (Ed.). (1993). *Distributed cognitions: Psychological and educational considerations.* Cambridge, UK: Cambridge University Press.

Schutz, A. (1967). *The phenomenology of the social world* (G. Walsh & F. Lehnert, Trans.) Evanston, IL: Northwestern University Press.

Schutz, A., & Luckmann, T. (1973). *The structures of the life-world* (R. M. Zaner & H. T. Engelhardt, Jr., Trans.). Evanston, IL: Northwestern University Press.

Scollon, R., & Scollon, S. (1981). *Narrative, literacy, and face in interethnic communication.* Norwood, NJ: Ablex.

Scribner, S. (1997). *Mind and social practice.* Cambridge, UK: Cambridge University Press

Scribner, S., & Cole, M. (1981). *The psychology of literacy.* Cambridge, MA: Harvard University Press.

Sheridan-Rabideau, M. (2001). The stuff that myths are made of: Myth building as social action. *Written Communication*, 18, 440–469.

Silverstein, M. (1985). The functional stratification of language and ontogenesis. In J. Wertsch (Ed.), *Culture, communication, and cognition: Vygotskian perspectives* (pp. 205–235). Cambridge, UK: Cambridge University Press.

Suchman, L. (2000). Making a case: "Knowledge" and "routine" in document production. In P. Luff, J. Hindmarsh, & C. Heath (Eds.), *Workplace studies: Recovering work practice and informing system design* (pp. 29–45). Cambridge, UK: Cambridge University Press.

Swales, J. (1998). *Other floors, other voices: A textography of a small university building.* Mahwah, NJ: Erlbaum.

Taylor, D., & Dorsey-Gaines, C. (1988). *Growing up literate: Learning from inner-city families.* Portsmouth, NH: Heinemann.

Toulmin, S. (1958). *The uses of argument.* Cambridge, UK: Cambridge University Press.

Voloshinov, V. (1973). *Marxism and the philosophy of language* (L. Matejka & I. Titunik, Trans.). Cambridge, MA: Harvard University Press.

Voloshinov, V. (1976). *Freudianism: A Marxist critique* (I. Titunik, Trans.; I. Titunik & N. Bruss, Eds.). New York: Academic Press.

Vygotsky, L. (1978). *Mind in society: The development of higher psychological processes* (M. Cole, V. John-Steiner, S. Scribner, & E. Souberman, Trans.). Cambridge, MA: Harvard University Press.

Vygotksy, L. (1987). *Problems of general psychology: The collected works of L. S. Vygotsky, Volume 1* (N. Minick, Trans.). New York: Plenum Press.

Wertsch, J. V. (1991). *Voices of the mind: A sociocultural approach to mediated action.* Cambridge, MA: Harvard University Press.

Williams, J. (1990). *Style: Toward clarity and grace.* Chicago: University of Chicago Press.

Chapter 5

The Processing Demands of Writing

Mark Torrance *and* David Galbraith

To facilitate the production of the text that you are now reading I (Torrance) am using a common word processing application running on a personal computer. As I write, the word processor is monitoring what I typed for spelling errors. If I asked it to, it would also check to see whether the text I produced is grammatical (according to its own, somewhat arcane, criteria). Elsewhere on the computer, an e-mail application is running, monitoring for incoming mail, as is bibliographic software that communicates with the word processor when I require it to do so. These are just the things I know about. In the background there appear to be a further 28 processes running, at least some of which are, I assume, essential to the effective working of the computer. Each of these is constantly either manipulating information or standing ready to do so. To accomplish all of this, each process draws, to varying degrees, on both the computer's random-access memory and its central processor. My current computer has plenty of RAM and a fast processor, and will multitask quite happily across all of these processes. This would definitely not have been true of the computer that I used 10 years ago. On that machine, running just two applications at once resulted in a radical reduction in performance and any further demands would make it grind to a halt.

There is, of course, another information-processing device involved in the production of this text. While I am writing, my mind is either simultaneously engaged in or rapidly switching between processes that perform all or most of the following functions: monitoring the thematic coherence of the text; searching for and retrieving relevant content; identifying lexical items associated with this content; formulating syntactic structure; inflecting words to give them the necessary morphology; monitoring for appropriate register; ensuring that intended new text is tied into the immediately preceding text in a way that maintains cohesion; formulating and executing motor plans for the key strokes that will form the text on the screen; establishing the extent to which the just-generated clause or sentence moves the text as a whole nearer to the intended goal; and revising goals in the light of new ideas cued by the just-produced text. These processes cannot all be performed simultaneously. Attempting to do so, as with a 10-year-old computer, would result in overload and writing would stop. The fact that I am writing this at all, therefore, is testament to the writing system's ability to coordinate and schedule a number of different processes within the limited processing resources afforded it by my mind.

Even with this coordination, the production of anything other than trivial text often comes close to crashing the system, as the following quote graphically describes:

> The initial gurgitation of material builds up a high pressure of nervous excitement leading to such physical symptoms as redness in the face,

headache, inability to sit down, lapses of concentration and extreme short temper, especially on interruption. Ordering the material presents agonising problems of rethinking. . . . problems of sequencing often lead to inability to write down a coherent sentence. The final process is well nigh unendurable. (anonymous writer quoted in Lowenthal & Wason, 1977, p. 781)

Or, as Flower and Hayes (1980, p. 33) put it:

The writer must exercise a number of skills and meet a number of demands—more or less all at once. As a dynamic process, writing is the act of dealing with an excessive number of simultaneous demands or constraints. Viewed this way, a writer in the act is a thinker on full-time cognitive overload.

This chapter explores current understanding of the ways in which the complex set of processes associated with the production of multisentence text are managed within the limitations imposed by structural features of the writer's mind. These processing limitations are inescapable and are therefore implicated in all theories that seek to explain text production in humans. This has been recognized by a number of researchers, with the result that there has been recent growth in writing research explicitly exploring working memory effects (see, e.g., overviews by Chanquoy & Alamargot, 2002; McCutchen, 1994, 1996). This chapter selectively reviews some of this research. Our aim is to paint a general picture of what is currently known about how processing limitations affect the functioning of the writing system and to tentatively suggest a framework for future research. In the first section, we explore the various ways in which text production might be resource-demanding. The set of phenomena sometimes attributed to a catchall "limited capacity working memory" have, we argue, several possible causes. These include, at least, effects associated with processing bottlenecks, with crosstalk among outputs, and with the transient nature of short-term memory. Our assumption is that theories that capture the complexity of the writing system need to be based in a sophisticated understanding of how that system might be constrained. In the light of this discussion, the second half of the chapter examines ways in which the cognitive demands of writing can be either adapted to or overcome.

Processing Constraints

Cognitive psychologists vary in how they account for limitations in the mind's capacity to process information. Two relatively distinct literatures have developed, each addressing different but complementary research questions. First, research exploring dual-task interference (e.g., Pashler, 1994a) starts from the observation that attempting to perform two tasks in close temporal proximity, even when these tasks are very simple, typically has a detrimental effect on performance on one or both tasks. Research in this area seeks to explain the (probably multiple) ways in which this interference might occur. Second, research exploring effects associated with the transient nature of short-term memory (STM) starts from the observation that there are severe limits to our ability to retain information in conscious awareness. The focus of this research is the set of mechanisms by which the mind is able to keep information available for immediate processing. An illustration of work in this area is recent debate about the role of Baddeley's "phonological loop" in memory for word lists (for example, Larsen & Baddeley, 2003, and subsequent commentary). Theory in both of these areas has been based on observation of people performing very simple tasks (pressing a key in response to a tone, recalling short lists of words) in controlled experimental conditions. The challenge for writing researchers is to explore how these basic processes constrain and are managed across the complex layers of information processing that comprise our ability to produce coherent text.

Dual-Task Interference

When our minds attempt to perform two cognitive tasks at the same time, this can sometimes result in degraded performance of one or both tasks: Trying simultaneously to read and hold a conversation is likely to result in either poor comprehension or poor communication, or both. In the context of written production, understanding the mechanisms underlying this phenomenon is important because there is potential during normal writing for the writing system to attempt to perform two tasks at once. It is also important because writing researchers have used experimental methods that deliberately seek to elicit dual-task effects.

Dual-task experimental methods involve participants performing a resource-demanding secondary task alongside producing text. Secondary tasks have taken a variety of forms, including monitoring characters or shapes displayed alongside text as it appears on the computer screen (Lea & Levy, 1999); responding to auditory reaction-time probes ("Press the button when you hear 'stop'"; e.g., Kellogg, 2001a); listening to unrelated speech or music (Levy & Marek, 1999; Ransdell & Gilroy, 2001); rapidly repeating a single syllable (Chenoweth & Hayes, 2003); or retaining in memory digits (Ransdell, Arecco, & Levy, 2001), words (Bourdin & Fayol, 2002), or shapes (Kellogg, 1999). Degraded writing performance is taken as indication that there is overlap between the cognitive resources required for performance of the secondary task and those required for writing. If, as Chenoweth and Hayes (2003) found, asking participants to repeat a single syllable while writing increases the number of grammatical and spelling errors that they make, then we might conclude that syllable repetition shares resources with the components of the writing system that are responsible for generating sentence and word structure. If the resource demands associated with syllable repetition are known, this then provides insight into the cognitive mechanisms associated with the primary (writing) task. Building up a picture of the resource demands of individual subprocesses should therefore allow conclusions to be drawn about which of these subprocesses compete for resources during text production.

Degraded performance on the secondary task can be interpreted in a similar way. In a series of studies, Kellogg and collaborators found that the time taken to respond to auditory probes that interrupt writing midflow is greater at some points in the writing process than at others (Kellogg, 1988, 1990, 2001a; Olive & Kellogg, 2002). They interpreted variations in reaction time in these studies as variation in the cognitive effort that the writer is devoting to the writing task at the time that the probe occurred.

CAPACITY EXPLANATIONS

A prerequisite for interpreting findings from research of this kind is an understanding of the ways in which performance of one task might interfere with the performance of an-
other. One possibility is that cognitive capacity is a fluid resource that is shared among some or all mental processes. Well-practiced components of the writing system—the motor planning necessary for keyboarding by a competent typist, for example—will run successfully while making very limited demands on cognitive capacity. Other components—those required to solve the "problems of sequencing" identified by the writer quoted in our introduction, for example—may make much higher demands. Performance on all tasks can proceed without detriment to any of them as long as total demand does not exceed available capacity. When it does, one or more tasks will be performed less well. For the frustrated writer we quoted earlier, organizing the text appeared to overload capacity, with detrimental affects for the formulation of syntactically correct sentences.

At its simplest, cognitive capacity can be thought of as a single resource that is shared across all currently running, resource-demanding processes (e.g., Kahneman, 1973). This has been the default assumption among writing researchers (e.g., Fayol, 1999; Kellogg, 1987; McCutchen, 1996; Olive & Kellogg, 2002; Swanson & Berninger, 1996b). Alternatively, capacity may be thought of as fractionated, with different resource pools being available to different tasks, depending on the particular representational code that a task manipulates (e.g., Caplan & Waters, 1999; Navon & Gopher, 1979). In an influential account, Baddeley (1986) has argued for distinct phonological and visuospatial resources. There is some evidence that this distinction holds true during text production. Kellogg and Catterton (1996, cited in Kellogg, 1999) asked participants to retain digits in memory (a phonological task) or shapes in memory (a visuospatial task) while composing sentences. Both spatial and digit preloads resulted in reduced sentence length and in increased production time compared to a no-preload control. Effects were greater, however, for digit preloads. Similarly Lea and Levy (1999), using a concurrent monitoring task, found greater detrimental effects on fluency (words transcribed per minute) with phonological monitoring compared with visuospatial monitoring.

If different resource pools exist, then it may be that different pools are drawn upon by different components of the writing system. Kellogg (1996, 1999) observed that planning—the processes by which writers decide content and structure for their text—is likely to involve proportionally less phonological and more visuospatial processing than realizing this content as full sentences: translating ideas into sentences must necessarily involve phonological encoding, whereas planning may be performed in part by manipulating preverbal codes. It is likely that these preverbal codes are in part spatial. The notes that writers' sometimes produce in advance of drafting full text often include boxes, arrows, tables, and other spatial features, and writers' talk about their text often includes spatial metaphors ("I think I'll put that section there"). Galbraith, Ford, Walker, and Ford (in press) present evidence suggesting that a secondary task designed to tap spatial but not visual resources during initial planning has no effect on participants' retrieval of relevant content. However, they found that this task reduced the extent to which ideas were reorganized during planning and that this was associated with a reduction in the quality and structural complexity of the text subsequently produced.

ALTERNATIVES TO CAPACITY EXPLANATIONS

Explanations for dual-task performance in terms of graded sharing of communal resources are seductively simple and all-embracing. If two tasks interfere, then they share resources; if not, then either they do not share resources (assuming multiple resource pools) or one or more of the tasks is automatic and therefore not resource-demanding. The capacity metaphor thus provides an easy explanation for, for example, developmental effects. Children necessarily devote a high proportion of available capacity to the orthographic processing necessary for the production of correctly spelled words and to the graphomotor processing associated with shaping letters on the page. Devoting resources to these low-level processes leaves less capacity for syntactic processing, content retrieval, rhetorical structuring, and so forth (e.g., Fayol, 1999). Hence, novice writers produce shorter and less complex sentences and texts compared with those of writers who have achieved greater levels of orthographic and graphomotor automaticity. Task effects can be explained in a similar way. Composing narratives

by hand interferes with performance on a secondary-probe response task to a substantially lesser extent than composing persuasive text using a word processor (Kellogg, 2001a). Kellogg explains this effect by arguing that writing by hand (a well-practiced motor skill) and composing narratives (a familiar genre) engage less cognitive capacity than keyboarding (a less well-practiced motor skill) and persuasive writing (a less well-practiced genre).

There are, however, problems here of both falsifiability and explanatory power: It is sometimes difficult to imagine patterns of data in research of this kind that could *not* be explained by some combination of capacity and automaticity effects. Some gains in explanatory power may be achieved by hypothesizing multiple resource types, in that this invites theorizing about the kinds of representations that are manipulated by different writing subprocesses. Arguably, however, this is at the cost of further reducing falsifiability (Christiansen & MacDonald, 1999). It is also not always clear what capacity explanations for dual-task effects tell us about underlying cognitive processes. Translating text into full sentences involves a complex set of interrelated mechanisms. Finding, for example, that probe reaction times are particularly slow when the writer's goal is to persuade suggests the need for detailed inquiry into the cognitive processes that are particular to persuasive writing. Arguably, capacity explanations in this and similar contexts, by accounting for behavior in terms of ubiquitous structures that operate independently of the writing process, tend to prematurely curtail this detailed investigation. Navon (1985) makes this point forcefully, arguing that advancing capacity allocation as an explanation for patterns of performance is like selling stones that, when added to water, make perfect soup, but only so long as they are combined with vegetables, meat, herbs, salt, pepper, and so forth

There are, however, alternative explanations for dual-task interference that do not invoke competition for limited capacity. One possibility is that the content of the output that results from performing one task interferes with the processing of another, a phenomenon sometimes described as crosstalk (Navon & Miller, 1987). The fact that monitoring letters presented to writers' peripheral vision slows written production (Lea & Levy, 1999) can be seen as evidence that phonological processing capacity is shared between letter monitoring and writing. Alternatively, it may be that outputs from the monitoring task—frequently changing phonemes—act as unwanted input to, and thus interfere with, writing subprocesses that take phonetic code as input, such as reading just-written text. Another possibility is that interference occurs as a result of competition, not for shared capacity but for one or more specific shared (or "bottleneck") mechanisms (Pashler, 1994a). The analogy here is of two road workers who share a single spade. This arrangement will result in a loss in productivity if, and only if, both of them want to dig a hole at the same time. If this situation occurs, then one worker will proceed with digging their hole at a normal pace, while the other waits, inactive, until the first worker has finished. Productivity losses as a result of letter monitoring may therefore occur because, on occasion, a low-level subcomponent of the writing process is temporarily halted because one or more of the mechanisms that it needs is being used to perform the letter-monitoring task.

It is probably the case that capacity, bottleneck, and crosstalk models provide equally good fits to much of the data that we discuss in this chapter (cf. Navon & Miller, 2002). A substantial advantage of crosstalk and bottleneck explanations of dual-task interference, however, is that they provide a framework for future inquiry. Bottleneck explanations, for example, necessarily hypothesize a specific mechanism that is required for the completion of both the writing and the secondary tasks. The theory ultimately stands or falls on whether or not this mechanism can be identified, and the inquiry involved in doing so will deepen understanding of how the writing system is organized.

Transient Memory

Young children, as they are developing the ability to construct more complex utterances, often run into the following problem. They start with the intention of expressing an important idea. Excitedly, they start speaking. At some point, they experience difficulty in retrieving the word needed to express a particular concept, or they identify the word but have difficultly retrieving its correct pronunciation. This results in delay, during which they might make several false starts, until finally, perhaps with prompting, they produce the desired word. There is then another pause, the child's face clouds, and they exclaim in annoyance, "Oh, now I've forgotten what I was trying to say."

Sentence production is typically theorized as a sequence of discrete processing stages from word retrieval through developing syntactic structure and retrieving phonology or orthography, to motor planning and execution. These processes, or their various constituent components, are capable of running in parallel. Thus, both in speech (Smith & Wheeldon, 1999) and in writing (Chanquoy, Foulin, & Fayol, 1990), people output the first words of a sentence while, behind the scenes, words for later parts of the sentence are still being retrieved. It is this cascading of processes that offers the potential for adult language production to be relatively free of pauses. If, however, one of the component processes is disrupted, then the smooth flow of information from process to process will be disrupted. The resulting delay may be sufficient for the writer's (or speaker's) message—the exact communicative intent of that specific sentence—to be lost from immediate awareness.

Problems resulting from the transience of STM are likely to multiply when a writing task requires the production of extended text. Sentences in coherent text do not simply communicate isolated packets of information. For the text to be successful, authors need to ensure that new sentences let readers associate the new content that this sentence expresses with their understanding of the text that they have already read. Achieving this coherence requires both that the new sentence makes local ties with the preceding one, and that it advances the message of the text as a whole. To make this possible, the author requires access not only to the content to be expressed but also to (some of) the content and surface structure of the preceding sentence, and to a higher level representation of the intended rhetorical structure for the completed text. To maintain fluency, this information needs to be accessed rapidly and relatively effortlessly, a requirement that is likely to tax substantially the mind's short-term storage capabilities.

EVALUATING TRANSIENT MEMORY EFFECTS

There are perhaps three different ways in which transient storage considerations might be implicated in accounts of writing competence (see for example, Swanson & Berninger 1996a). First, it may be that at some fundamental level, people vary in STM capacity, independent of the particular task that is being performed. Good STM ability will therefore lead to improved performance not just when writing but on all information-processing tasks that require temporary storage.

Second, it is possible that as writers become more experienced, they develop domain-specific memory-management strategies that allow them to make better use of the capacity that is available to them. If this is the case, then experienced writers may develop an ability to retain information while writing but not show related improvements in, for example, ability to retain digits in a simple memory task.

Third, writers may vary in the extent to which components of the writing system draw on or interfere with storage mechanisms. For example, it is probable that about-to-be-executed words are temporarily stored as a phonological code (which writers experience as hearing an inner voice; Chenoweth & Hayes, 2003; Witte, 1987). Getting this phonological representation onto the page requires retrieval of the spellings for its constituent words. Adult writers probably spell the vast majority of words without recourse to phonological (inner-voice/inner-ear) mechanisms. However, if the to-be-executed words include one or more with unfamiliar spellings, or if the writer suffers from a spelling-specific cognitive deficit, then attempting to retrieve a spelling may overwrite existing phonologically stored information, and the remainder of the to-be-written sentence will be lost or damaged. And because the message-level representation for the sentence will now have decayed, the writer will have to engage in some sort of strategic activity to re-create the lost content. It is likely, therefore, that the transience of STM will be less problematic if basic writing-specific abilities are well developed.

Writers may therefore vary in general STM capacity, in writing-specific memory management skills, and in the efficiency with which they execute components of the writing system. Each of these factors may affect writing performance, and it is worth exploring their relative importance. One way of determining general effects of STM independent of writing-specific effects is to examine developmental changes in the strength of the relationship between STM capacity and the quality of the written product. If practice results in better memory management or greater automaticity in some writing subprocesses, then, as writers mature, STM capacity should become less predictive of writing performance. In fourth- and sixth-grade students, Swanson and Berninger (1996a) found strong relationships between scores on a composite STM measure and both spelling and handwriting performance, and within this narrow range the relationship was largely independent of age. Across high school years, however, and with writing success measured just in terms of grammatical errors, there is some evidence of a marked decrease in the predictive power of STM. Daiute (1984) found that in eighth grade, 40% of the variance in number of errors was associated with variance in verbatim sentence memory. This reduced to just 1% for students in 12th grade.

Another way of teasing out "pure" STM effects is to contrast simple measures of short-term capacity with measures that require participants to retain information while simultaneously engaging in a processing task (Daneman & Carpenter, 1980). A simple measure of (phonological) STM capacity might involve participants recalling increasingly long lists of pronounceable nonsense syllables immediately after presentation, with their span recorded as the longest list that they can correctly recall. By contrast, a memory-plus-processing (or *complex span*) task (e.g., McCutchen, Covill, Hoyne, & Mildes, 1994; Ransdell & Levy, 1999; Swanson & Berninger, 1996a) might involve presenting participants with word lists of varying length. After presentation, they are required to write, for each word, a single sentence containing that word. A participant's "writing span" is the maximum number of sentences that can be produced in this way. (Ransdell and Levy found that this rarely exceeded four.) Complex span therefore represents a measure of STM performance within a specific processing context.

Complex span tasks have been used extensively in reading research and in that context appear to be better than simple span at predicting comprehension (Daneman & Merikle, 1996). Complex span performance in the context of writing has received much less attention. In college students, Ransdell and Levy (1999) found correlations between writing span and text quality ranging from .20 to .30, depending on the exact nature of the span task, and from .39 to .47 for correlations with rate of production. They did not, however, include a simple span measure in their analysis. Hoskyn and Swanson (2003), in a broad sample comprising adolescents, adults in their 30s, and elderly adults, found that a composite of several verbal complex span measures was much better than a simple digit span measure at predicting the structural complexity of participants' texts. In much younger children (grades 4 to 6), Berninger et al. (1994; Swanson & Berninger, 1996a) found correlations of .24 between writing quality and both an STM measure involving syllable recall and a complex span task involving listening to and then writing down sentences. They found that a composite of verbal and verbal–executive complex span measures contributed more to writing fluency (measured both in number of words and in number of clauses in completed texts) and text quality than did a composite of STM measures. However, STM capacity proved to be a better predictor of handwriting quality and spelling accuracy.

Interpreting findings in this area is complex, not least because there are multiple ways of operationalizing both writing span and writing performance. There does, however, seem to be good evidence to suggest that factors associated with the extent to which STM is used during writing are important in determining writing performance, independent of underlying STM capacity. Moreover, the fact that writing span tasks appear to contribute unique variance to performance, and that this effect remains even when other factors associated with verbal skill are controlled for, suggests that these effects are not simply due to varying efficiency of the writing system's component processes (Berninger et al., 1994). Research is needed that studies the full range of ages over which composition skills are likely to develop. However, existing findings suggest that part of developing writing expertise involves developing writing-specific memory management strategies.

Processing Constraints and the Writer

In summary, then, we have painted a picture of the writing system as a delicately balanced set of interrelated processes. These processes must be carefully scheduled if they are to receive and pass on information in a way that is fluent and uninterrupted. Failure in this scheduling can result in two processes competing for a single mechanism and/or in interference between process outputs. Because outputs from upstream processes are transient (their traces decay rapidly) any hiatus is likely to have substantial repercussions for the writing process as a whole. Activity to repair these negative effects—to reinstate the intended message, or to reconstruct a particular turn of phrase, for example—is likely to be a major feature of the production of anything other than the simplest of texts.

For most writers, and for most writing tasks, smooth flow is repeatedly interrupted. For example, production of the fourth and fifth sentences of the previous paragraph (which were composed using a keystroke logging program) involved a total of 60 pauses of 2 or more seconds. This was despite the writer experiencing "knowing what he wanted to say" before starting to write. To produce the final 429 characters in these sentences (in their first-draft version), over twice that amount of text was written and then deleted. There has been a tendency, based in Hayes and Flower's original conception of the writing process as being under strong executive control, to assume that this stop–start behavior results from writers moving deliberately and strategically through repeated plan–translate–revise cycles. Our impression, however, is that much of the minute-by-minute activity associated with getting ideas down on paper is not controlled in this way. Repeated hesitation, backtracking, and rewriting are at least in part a direct result of the need to repair problems that necessarily occur when complex information processing occurs within the constraints of limited cognitive resources. Writers do not calmly select different writing subprocesses as if they were tools to be used as and when needed. They are, in McCutchen's analogy, like a switchboard operator continually, and at times frantically, trying to coordinate and direct the inputs to and outputs from several component processes (McCutchen et al., 1994). How this coordination might be achieved is the focus of the remainder of this chapter.

Overcoming Processing Constraints

Developing writing maturity involves tailoring the writing system so as to minimize concurrent demands on the writer's cognitive resources. The discussion in the previous sections points toward three broad ways in which this might be achieved:

1. Subcomponent skills, and particularly low-level skills associated with transcription (handwriting or keyboarding) and spelling, can be practiced to the extent that they rarely invoke higher level processing mechanisms.
2. Writers may develop specific skills for maximizing the efficiency with which they use transient memory resources.
3. There are several strategic steps that writers can take—preplanning, making notes, rough drafting, and so forth—that serve to reduce the number of processes that have to be juggled during composition.

We briefly discuss each of these in the sections that follow.

Developing Automaticity in Low-Level Components

For present purposes, we think of a process as automatic if it occurs without voluntary control and interferes minimally with other processes. Pashler (1994b) observes that practice can lead to automaticity by streamlining the way in which a task is performed and thus decreasing the period for which potential bottleneck mechanisms are engaged. If, for example, spelling can be achieved without the writer actively invoking mechanisms for explicit retrieval from long-term memory (LTM)—if the writer can avoid having to stop and say "Now are there one or two *c*'s in *necessary?*" or avoid consciously computing subject–verb agreement errors (Fayol, Hupet, & Largy, 1999)—then this will leave these retrieval mechanisms free for exploring possible content.

Spelling and handwriting, the two low-level processes that are most obviously required in written production but not in speech, are obvious candidates for automati-

zation. Bourdin and Fayol, in a series of studies with varying age groups, explored differences in recall under spoken and written conditions (Bourdin, 1999; Bourdin & Fayol, 1994, 1996, 2002). These studies tend to confirm that when written production is less practiced, it interferes with conscious retrieval processes. In simple word-recall tasks, both second- and fourth-grade children recalled substantially fewer items when they were written than when they were spoken (Bourdin & Fayol, 1994). For adults, however, this effect was absent or even reversed, with slightly better recall with written responses. Predictably, adding composition demands by requiring that participants produce sentences containing the words to be recalled (a "sentence span" task) rather than recalling them in isolation also gave poorer written recall and better spoken recall in children. Again, this effect was not found in adults (Bourdin & Fayol, 1996). However, when the further demand that sentences need to be linked (a "text span" task) was added, and when the words presented were unrelated and so difficult to combine into a coherent text, adults then also performed less well in the written modality. This suggests that even when spelling and handwriting are very well practiced, they can still compete with higher level processes.

Of course Bourdin and Fayol's findings conflate spelling and handwriting effects. However, other research suggests that there is potential for interference between higher level processes and both spelling and handwriting (Fayol, 1999). Fayol and coworkers have found that spelling errors (specifically subject–verb agreement errors in French) increase in both children (Totereau, Thevenin, & Fayol, 1997) and adults (Fayol, Largy, & Lemaire, 1994) when combined with memory tasks. With more natural writing tasks, difficulty with spelling words appears to narrow the range of vocabulary that writers use. Wengelin (2005) found that her sample of adult dyslexic writers were more likely to pause midword and showed substantially lower lexical diversity than nondyslexic controls. These two phenomena appeared to be related, with a high proportion of the variance in lexical diversity predicted by the extent to which writers paused midword and the extent to which they engaged in concurrent editing. This suggests, perhaps, that spelling retrieval interferes with processes involved in lexical retrieval, and/or that midword pausing in itself results in the loss of lexical items that are awaiting transcription but are less common and therefore have a lower level of activation.

There appears also to be potential for interference between the graphical processing associated with transcription and higher-level writing processes, although the evidence here is less direct. Bourdin and Fayol (2000) found that in second-grade children, repetition of even a very simple graphic pattern while orally recalling word lists resulted in a 30% reduction in recall. If, as this suggests, very low-level graphomotor processes are capable of interfering with retrieval from LTM, then training specifically focused on improving children's handwriting should benefit not only handwriting neatness but also other aspects of text generation. This appears to be the case, at least in terms of the fluency with which text is produced (Berninger et al., 1997).

The findings summarized briefly here therefore suggest both that there is potential for conflict between low-level output processes (spelling and handwriting) and processes associated with generating and structuring content, and that with increased expertise in these low-level skills this conflict becomes less likely.

Efficient Memory Management

Part of becoming an efficient writer may involve development of specific ways either to maintain focus on currently important information or to use limited transient memory capacity to maximum effect. Although both of these possibilities have been mentioned in the writing research literature, neither has seen much direct research attention.

Several researchers have suggested that performance on complex span tasks may best be predicted by the extent to which participants are able to focus attention on currently important information and to suppress information that might interfere (e.g., Kane & Engle, 2003). Writers who are able to suppress, for example, tangential ideas that are activated through association with words currently being written, or who are able to ignore temporarily a poorly turned phrase, are more likely to get to the end of the sentence before their intended message decays. Ransdell and Levy argue that certain writers, identified by their high reading comprehension skill (Ransdell & Levy, 1999) or multilingualism (Ransdell, Arecco, & Levy, 2001), may be particularly good at suppressing irrelevant information. Furthermore, they suggest that skilled readers exhibit what they describe as "resource flexibility"—the ability to shift attention deliberately between potentially competing task demands. In their research, participants performed a written sentence span-task with instructions to maximize either memory performance or sentence quality. Skilled readers showed better recall when memory was emphasized and produced longer sentences when sentence quality was emphasized, suggesting an ability to shift processing priorities strategically. This effect was not present in participants with lower reading skill.

Another approach to memory management is to reduce the amount of information that needs to be held in STM. As discussed earlier, writers require access not only to a message-level representation of the sentence that is being produced but also, among other things, to more global representations that allow the writer to relate the content currently being transcribed to its wider context within the text. The more rapidly this information can be accessed during production, the less disruption its retrieval will cause. One mechanism by which rapid retrieval might be achieved involves structuring important information in LTM in such a way that it can be retrieved more or less effortlessly in response to specific cues in STM, an arrangement that Ericsson and Kintsch (1995) describe as long-term working memory (LTWM). Several authors have suggested that LTWM plays an important role in text production (e.g., Chanquoy & Alamargot, 2002; McCutchen, 2000), and it has been invoked as an explanation for reduced secondary-task interference in multilingual writers (Ransdell et al., 2001) and in writers with high domain knowledge (Kellogg, 2001b).

LTWM has intuitive appeal as a memory management strategy in writing. It clearly is not possible for writers to hold active in STM all of the information that they require to contextualize the sentence they are currently producing. So, while a sentence is being composed, writers need to be able to retrieve this information rapidly and effortlessly from LTM. For LTWM to fulfill this function, writers would need to develop specific schematic structures that allow chunking, labeling, storage, and subsequent retrieval of the information that they wish to communicate. Schemas representing typical text structures may serve this kind of memory-structuring function (e.g., Carey & Flower, 1989; Klein, 1999). As yet, however, little is known about how LTWM functions during writing.

Effects of Writing Strategy on Processing Demands

How writers choose to divide a writing task into subtasks, and how these subtasks are sequenced—their "writing strategy"—may have important consequences for accommodating writing within processing constraints. If, for example, content determination can be performed independently of sentence construction, or if sentence construction can be separated from transcription, then this removes the possibility that these processes might conflict.

Both outlining (producing structured notes) and rough drafting (producing full text, but with relaxed rhetorical constraints) are strategies that allow content planning to be conducted free of the demands of constructing well-formed and coherent text. There is consistent evidence that outlining does benefit writing (e.g., Kellogg, 1988, 1990), and some suggestion that certain forms of rough drafting may also be beneficial (Galbraith & Torrance, 2004). It is, however, unclear precisely how these strategies reduce processing constraints. In a series of experiments, Kellogg (1988) considered a number of possible explanations for the beneficial effects of outlining. The first was that storing the writer's plan externally frees space in working memory for other processes. However, Kellogg found that outlining was equally effective regardless of whether it was performed mentally or in external note form. Thus, although external storage may be important in other contexts (e.g., Benton, Kiewra, Whitfill, & Dennison, 1993), it cannot account for the beneficial effects in Kellogg's experiments. A second possibility is that separating planning content from translation (realizing planned content as full text) enables more cognitive effort

to be devoted to each process individually. Kellogg (1988) tested this by comparing performance on a secondary-probe reaction-time task administered while writers were producing the text itself, predicting that more cognitive effort (reflected in longer response times to the secondary task) would be devoted to translation in the outline conditions. He found no difference between conditions, which suggests that similar effort was devoted to translation in both cases. Taken together, these results suggest that the beneficial effect of outlining is not a consequence of more resources being available for individual processes. Kellogg concludes instead that the crucial effect of outlining is that it separates the planning and translation components of writing, enabling writers to organize their ideas more effectively prior to writing, and to focus their attention more exclusively on translating ideas into words during the production of the text itself. The effect, therefore, does not appear to be a consequence of reducing competition for a limited pool of resources, but rather of reducing interference between the processes, caused perhaps either by task switching or by conflict between outputs of the different processes.

Rough drafting, as a prewriting strategy, has been studied less frequently, and most research has reported no beneficial effects (e.g., Kellogg, 1988). There is a history, however, of writers espousing the benefits of producing a series of rough drafts as a strategy for generating content (e.g., Green & Wason, 1982). These accounts suggest that if rough drafting is effective, this is not so much because it separates planning content from translation, but, again, because it reduces interference between processes associated with exploring the intrinsic organization of a writer's topic knowledge and processes associated with satisfying rhetorical goals (Galbraith, 1999).

A less frequently used strategy, but one that is becoming increasingly practicable, is replacing manual transcription by speech input. As we discussed earlier, while transcription (graphomotor and spelling) expertise is poorly developed, there is potential for these processes to interfere with content determination. If, then, children were to write by dictation, we might expect gains not just in spelling accuracy but also in compositional quality. This appears to be the case: Children, and particularly children with learning disabilities, tend to create compositionally better texts when dictating than when writing by hand (De La Paz & Graham, 1997; Quinlan, 2004).

It is less clear, however, that experienced writers, who have gained automaticity in transcription, will benefit in the same way (Williams, Hartley, & Pittard, 2005). In a small study, Torrance and Baker (1998), compared probe response times for mature writers composing by hand, by keyboarding, and by speaking (using a human typist to permit perfect speech recognition). Contrary to expectations, they found that the speech-input condition interfered more with the probe-response task than both handwriting and keyboard-input word processing. One possible explanation for this finding is that the speech input gave an unfamiliar and unusually rapid tempo to the composition process. If writing involves a delicately balanced cascade of processes, some of which run in parallel, then changes in the pacing of transcription may disrupt this balance, at least until the writer has adapted to the new rhythm. Chanquoy, Foulin, and Fayol (1990) found that experienced writers, but not 8-year-olds, modify the rhythm of their writing process, increasing interclause pause lengths and decreasing intraclause transcription rate to accommodate conceptually more complex material. This suggests that pacing might be particularly important in the management of retrieval from LTM. There is some evidence to support this claim. As we noted earlier, although children recall better when speaking than when writing, the reverse appears to be true for adults (Bourdin & Fayol, 1994). Grabowski (2005) has replicated this effect and, based on the findings of a series of carefully controlled experiments, concludes that the benefits of recalling by writing may be rooted in the fact that writing forces a slower pace on the recall process.

The effect of writing strategy on writing process is therefore complex, and the efficacy of a particular strategy is likely to depend on more than just the extent to which it liberates processing capacity during translation. One final illustration of this comes from research exploring the ways in which reading back over just-written text affects the writing process. While producing full text, writers frequently pause and read over the one or two sentences that they have just written. This local reviewing does not, however, typically result in changes to the text. Rather, the sequencing of reading in relation to planning suggests that it serves to reinstate information about the content and/or linguistic form of immediately preceding sentences. Local reviewing may therefore serve to reduce demands on STM. This hypothesis is consistent with findings from a recent eye movement study that suggests that writers with low writing spans tend to read back more frequently than do high-span writers (Alamargot, Dansac, Ros, & Chuy, in press). However, Olive and Piolat (2002) found that preventing writers from reading back while producing short argumentative texts had no effect on either the quality of the finished text or the fluency with which it was produced. They also found that writers who were prevented from reading responded more rapidly to probes presented during subsequent transcription. This suggests that reinstating information about sentences just written and holding this in STM may interfere with production of the following sentence.

Conclusions

The idea that writing is a complex activity requiring the coordination of a variety of different cognitive processes and that the cognitive overload that this can induce is a fundamental problem in writing has been central to cognitive accounts of writing since their inception (e.g., Flower & Hayes, 1980). In their original form, these models characterized writing in terms of a small number of high-level processes, and subsequent research has typically employed a simple capacity model to explain how these processes compete for cognitive resources.

In this chapter, we have argued for a less strategic model of how different processes are coordinated, and for a more dynamic model of the writing process and its interaction with STM. First, we have suggested that once one focuses on the more implicit and less accessible processes involved in text production (as opposed to the relatively explicit and accessible processes involved in problem solving), the range of processes involved expands enormously, as does the number of ways these processes might interact. This changes the way we conceptualize the writing system. We have argued that writing research needs to take into account both these complexities and the contentious nature of dominant models of working memory. Second, we have attempted to demonstrate that although conflict among writing processes can often be explained in terms of competition for a common resource pool, other accounts tend to have more explanatory power. Alternatives include explanations in terms of competition among concurrent processes for shared cognitive mechanisms (with retrieval from LTM perhaps representing a particularly pervasive bottleneck), interference between the outputs of different processes, and problems associated with coordinating processes operating at different speeds. Third, consistent with most current accounts, we have suggested that working memory capacity is best viewed not as a fixed feature of individuals, but as dependent on task- and domain-specific memory management skills.

Finally, we have suggested that although some aspects of the writing process can be strategically controlled, others, such as the need to suppress irrelevant information or reread to refresh transient memory, arise as a consequence of a cycle of processing as it occurs online. In this context, writers have no option but to adapt as flexibly as they can. No matter how skilled we are at managing the writing process, there is an irreducible core of potential conflicts and writing will always be a struggle to reconcile competing demands. Writers—motivationally—have to accept this if they are to get the task done.

References

Alamargot, D., Dansac, C., Ros, C., & Chuy, M. (in press). Rédiger un texte procédural à partir de sources: Relations entre l'empan de production écrite et l'activité oculaire du scripteur [Composing a procedural text from sources: The relationship between written production span and the writer's eye movements]. In D. Alamargot, P. Terrier, & J. M. Cellier (Eds.), *Production, compréhension et usage des écrits techniques au travail* [Production, comprehension, and uses of technical writing in the work place]. Poitiers, France: Publications Octarés.

Baddeley, A. D. (1986). *Working memory*. Oxford, UK: Oxford University Press.

Benton, S. L., Kiewra, K. A., Whitfill, J. M., & Dennison, R. (1993). Encoding and external-storage effects on writing processes. *Journal of Educational Psychology, 85*(2), 267–280.

Berninger, V. W., Cartwright, A. C., Yates, C. M., Swanson, H. L., & Abbott, R. D. (1994). Developmental skills related to writing and reading acquisition in the intermediate grades—shared and unique functional-systems. *Reading and Writing, 6*(2), 161–196.

Berninger, V. W., Vaughan, K. B., Graham, S., Abbott, R. D., Abbott, S. P., Rogan, L. W., et al. (1997). Treatment of handwriting problems in beginning writers: Transfer from handwriting to composition. *Journal of Educational Psychology, 89*(4), 652–666.

Bourdin, B. (1999). Working memory and language production: Comparison of oral and written production in adults and children. *Annee Psychologique, 99*(1), 123–148.

Bourdin, B., & Fayol, M. (1994). Is written language production more difficult than oral language production—A working-memory approach. *International Journal of Psychology, 29*(5), 591–620.

Bourdin, B., & Fayol, M. (1996). Mode effects in a sentence production span task. *Cahiers De Psychologie Cognitive, 15*(3), 245–264.

Bourdin, B., & Fayol, M. (2000). Is graphic activity cognitively costly?: A developmental approach. *Reading and Writing, 13*, 183–196.

Bourdin, B., & Fayol, M. (2002). Even in adults, written production is still more costly than oral production. *International Journal of Psychology, 37*(4), 219–227.

Caplan, D., & Waters, G. S. (1999). Verbal working memory and sentence comprehension. *Behavioral and Brain Sciences, 22*(1), 77–94.

Carey, L. J., & Flower, L. (1989). *Foundations for creativity in the writing process: Rhetorical representations of ill-defined problems (Technical Report No. 32, June)*. Berkeley, CA: Center for the Study of Writing, University of California and Carnegie Mellon University.

Chanquoy, L., & Alamargot, D. (2002). Working memory and writing: Evolution of models and assessment of research. *Annee Psychologique, 102*(2), 363–398.

Chanquoy, L., Foulin, J.-N., & Fayol, M. (1990). Temporal management of short text writing by children and adults. *Cahiers de Psychologie Cognitive, 10*(5), 513–540.

Chenoweth, N. A., & Hayes, J. R. (2003). The inner voice in writing. *Written Communication, 20*(1), 99–118.

Christiansen, M. H., & MacDonald, M. C. (1999). Fractionated working memory: Even in pebbles, it's still a soup stone. *Behavioral and Brain Sciences, 22*(1), 97–98.

Daiute, C. (1984). Performance limits on writers. In R. Beach & L. S. Bridwell (Eds.), *New directions in composition research* (pp. 205–224). New York: Guilford Press.

Daneman, M., & Carpenter, P. A. (1980). Individual differences in working memory and reading. *Journal of Verbal Learning and Verbal Behavior, 19*, 450–466.

Daneman, M., & Merikle, P. M. (1996). Working memory and language comprehension: A meta-analysis. *Psychonomic Bulletin and Review, 3*(4), 422–433.

De La Paz, S., & Graham, S. (1997). Effects of dictation and advanced planning instruction on the composing of students with writing and learning problems. *Journal of Educational Psychology, 89*(2), 203–222.

Ericsson, K. A., & Kintsch, W. (1995). Long-term working memory. *Psychological Review, 102*, 211–245.

Fayol, M. (1999). From on-line management problems to strategies in written composition. In M. Torrance & G. Jeffery (Eds.), *The cognitive demands of writing: Processing capacity and working memory effects in text production* (pp. 15–23). Amsterdam: Amsterdam University Press.

Fayol, M., Hupet, M., & Largy, P. (1999). The acquisition of subject–verb agreement in written French: From novices to experts' errors. *Reading and Writing, 11*(2), 153–174.

Fayol, M., Largy, P., & Lemaire, P. (1994). Cognitive overload and orthographic errors—when cognitive overload enhances subject–verb agreement errors: A study in French written language. *Quarterly Journal of Experimental Psychology A: Human Experimental Psychology, 47*, 437–464.

Flower, L. S., & Hayes, J. R. (1980). The dynamics of composing: Making plans and juggling constraints. In L. W. Gregg & E. R. Steinberg (Eds.), *Cognitive processes in writing* (pp. 31–50). Hillsdale, NJ: Erlbaum.

Galbraith, D. (1999). Writing as a knowledge constituting process. In M. Torrance & D. Galbraith (Eds.), *Knowing what to write: Conceptual processes in text production* (pp. 139–160). Amsterdam: Amsterdam University Press.

Galbraith, D., Ford, S., Walker, G., & Ford, J. (in press). The contribution of different components of working memory to knowledge transformation during writing. *L1–Educational Studies in Language and Literature*.

Galbraith, D., & Torrance, M. (2004). Revision in the context of different drafting strategies. In L. Allal, L. Chanquoy, & P. Largy (Eds.), *Revision of written language: Cognitive and instructional processes* (pp. 63–86). Dordrecht, The Netherlands: Kluwer.

Grabowski, M. (2005). The writing superiority effect in the verbal recall of knowledge: Sources and determinants. In M. Torrance, D. Galbraith, & L.

van Waes (Eds.), *Writing and cognition: Research and applications*. Manuscript submitted for publication.

Green, D. W., & Wason, P. C. (1982). Notes on the psychology of writing. *Human Relations, 35*, 47–56.

Hoskyn, M., & Swanson, H. (2003). The relationship between working memory and writing in younger and older adults. *Reading and Writing, 16*, 759–784.

Kahneman, D. (1973). *Attention and effort*. Englewood Cliffs, NJ: Prentice-Hall.

Kane, M. J., & Engle, R. W. (2003). Working-memory capacity and the control of attention: The contributions of goal neglect, response competition, and task set to Stroop interference. *Journal of Experimental Psychology: General, 132*(1), 47–70.

Kellogg, R. (1988). Attentional overload and writing performance: Effects of rough draft and outline strategies. *Journal of Experimental Psychology: Learning, Memory and Cognition, 14*(2), 355–365.

Kellogg, R. (1999). The components of working memory in text production. In M. Torrance & G. Jeffery (Eds.), *The cognitive demands of writing: Processing capacity and working memory effects in text production* (pp. 43–62). Amsterdam: Amsterdam University Press.

Kellogg, R. T. (1987). Writing performance: Effects of cognitive strategies. *Written Communication, 4*, 269–298.

Kellogg, R. T. (1990). Effectiveness of prewriting strategies as a function of task demands. *American Journal of Psychology, 103*(3), 327–342.

Kellogg, R. T. (1996). A model of working memory in writing. In C. M. Levy & S. Ransdell (Eds.), *The science of writing: Theories, methods, individual differences, and applications* (pp. 57–71). Mahwah, NJ: Erlbaum.

Kellogg, R. T. (2001a). Competition for working memory among writing processes. *American Journal of Psychology, 114*(2), 175–191.

Kellogg, R. T. (2001b). Long-term working memory in text production. *Memory and Cognition, 29*(1), 43–52.

Klein, P. D. (1999). Reopening inquiry into cognitive processes in writing-to-learn. *Educational Psychology Review, 11*(3), 203–270.

Larsen, J., & Baddeley, A. (2003). Disruption of verbal STM by irrelevant speech, articulatory suppression, and manual tapping: Do they have a common source? *Quarterly Journal of Experimental Psychology A: Human Experimental Psychology, 56*(8), 1249–1268.

Lea, J., & Levy, C. M. (1999). Working memory as a resource in the writing process. In M. Torrance & G. Jeffery (Eds.), *The cognitive demands of writing: Processing capacity and working memory effects in text production* (pp. 63–82). Amsterdam: Amsterdam University Press.

Levy, C. M., & Marek, P. (1999). Testing components of Kellogg's multicomponent model of working memory in writing: The role of the phonological loop. In M. Torrance & G. Jeffery (Eds.), *The cognitive demands of writing: Processing capacity and working memory effects in text production* (pp. 25–41). Amsterdam: Amsterdam University Press.

Lowenthal, D., & Wason, P. C. (1977, June 24). Academics and their writing. *Times Literary Supplement*, p. 781.

McCutchen, D. (1994). The magical number three, plus or minus 2: Working memory in writing. In E. Butterfield (Ed.), *Advances in cognition and educational practice* (Vol. 2, pp. 1–30). Greenwich, CT: JAI Press.

McCutchen, D. (1996). A capacity theory of writing: Working memory in composition. *Educational Psychology Review, 8*(3), 299–325.

McCutchen, D. (2000). Knowledge, processing, and working memory: Implications for a theory of writing. *Educational Psychologist, 35*(1), 13–23.

McCutchen, D., Covill, A., Hoyne, S. H., & Mildes, K. (1994). Individual-differences in writing: Implications of translating fluency. *Journal of Educational Psychology, 86*(2), 256–266.

Navon, D. (1985). Resources—a theoretical soup stone. *Psychological Review, 91*, 216–234.

Navon, D., & Gopher, D. (1979). On the economy of the human processing system. *Psychological Review, 86*, 254–284.

Navon, D., & Miller, J. (1987). Role of outcome conflict in dual-task interference. *Journal of Experimental Psychology: Human Perception and Performance, 13*(3), 435–448.

Navon, D., & Miller, J. (2002). Queuing or sharing?: A critical evaluation of the single-bottleneck notion. *Cognitive Psychology, 44*(3), 193–251.

Olive, T., & Kellogg, R. T. (2002). Concurrent activation of high- and low-level production processes in written composition. *Memory and Cognition, 30*(4), 594–600.

Olive, T., & Piolat, A. (2002). Suppressing visual feedback in written composition: Effects on processing demands and coordination of the writing processes. *International Journal of Psychology, 37*(4), 209–218.

Pashler, H. (1994a). Dual-task interference in simple tasks: Data and theory. *Psychological Bulletin, 116*(2), 220–244.

Pashler, H. (1994b). Graded capacity-sharing in dual-task interference? *Journal of Experimental Psychology: Human Perception and Performance, 20*(2), 330–342.

Quinlan, T. (2004). Speech recognition technology and students with writing difficulties: Improving fluency. *Journal of Educational Psychology, 96*, 337–346.

Ransdell, S., Arecco, M. R., & Levy, C. M. (2001). Bilingual long-term working memory: The effects of working memory loads on writing quality and fluency. *Applied Psycholinguistics, 22*(1), 113–128.

Ransdell, S., & Levy, C. (1999). Writing reading and speaking memory spans and the importance of resource flexibility. In M. Torrance & G. Jeffery (Eds.), *The cognitive demands of writing: Processing capacity and working memory effects in text production*. Amsterdam: Amsterdam University Press.

Ransdell, S. E., & Gilroy, L. (2001). The effects of background music on word processed writing. *Computers in Human Behavior, 17*(2), 141–148.

Smith, M., & Wheeldon, L. (1999). High level processing scope in spoken sentence production. *Cognition, 73*(3), 205–246.

Swanson, H. L., & Berninger, V. W. (1996a). Individual differences in children's working memory and writing skill. *Journal of Experimental Child Psychology, 63*(2), 358–385.

Swanson, H. L., & Berninger, V. W. (1996b). Individual differences in children's writing: A function of working memory or reading or both processes? *Reading and Writing, 8*(4), 357–383.

Torrance, M., & Baker, A. (1998, July). *The processing demands of handwriting, word processing and speech-input word processing.* Paper presented at the European Writing Conference, Poitiers, France.

Totereau, C., Thevenin, M., & Fayol, M. (1997). The development of the understanding of number morphology in written French. In C. Perfetti, L. Rieben, & M. Fayol (Eds.), *Learning to spell* (pp. 97–114). Hillsdale, NJ: Erlbaum.

Wengelin, A. (2005). The word level focus in text production by adults with reading and writing difficulties. In D. Galbraith, M. Torrance, & L. van Waes (Eds.), *Writing and cognition: Research and applications.* Manuscript submitted for publication.

Williams, N., Hartley, P., & Pittard, V. (2005). Talking to write: Investigating the practical impact and theoretical implications of speech recognition (SR) software on academic writing tasks. In L. van Waes, M. Torrance & D. Galbraith (Eds.), *Writing and cognition: Research and applications.* Manuscript submitted for publication.

Witte, S. P. (1987). Pre-text and composing. *College Composition and Communication, 38*, 397–425.

Part II

WRITING DEVELOPMENT

Chapter 6

The Emergence of Writing

Liliana Tolchinsky

"Writing" is a polysemous word, with many different meanings. It can refer to the process of tracing letters on a surface, and also to the system of letters (i.e., to the abstract set of signs) used for recording a language, such as when we speak about *writing systems*. The term can also refer to the process of producing novels, poetry, scientific articles, newspaper reports, and other types of text. When someone replies to the question "What are you doing?" with "I'm writing," we assume that he or she is writing a novel and not simply a list of letters, although, in fact, either one could be the case. Yet another use of the term applies to the *language* used in writing. This is the sense that is implied when teachers complain about the way their students write, by which they usually mean that students are not producing the kind of constructions or vocabulary suitable for a written register. We can thus distinguish among writing (1) *as a notational system*, (2) *as a mode of production* (i.e., as a *process* of discourse production), and (3) *as a discourse style* or, more precisely, as a collection of *discourse styles* or genres (Ravid & Tolchinsky, 2002). Any of these aspects can be approached from a "*developmental* perspective," which considers how individuals learn the writing system used in their community, and how they come to understand the way writing works as a notational system for producing a diversity of discourse modes.

A developmental approach to writing is based on two main assumptions: First, children are sensitive to the presence and use of writing in their environment. Second, the ideas developed by children about writing and the different steps by which they come to understand how writing works cannot be equated with the way they happen to be taught to write.

Throughout the history of writing, "there was a constant concern for the structured transmission of the system from generation to generation and the method of instruction was passed along with the practical knowledge of the script" (Cooper, 1996, p. 37). Even among the earliest ancestors of our writing system, it was possible to find "writing manuals," which were lists of words (lexical lists) used to teach people how to write. It is no exaggeration to say that schooling and writing were born hand in hand (Halliday, 1987). However, noting that literacy in general, and writing in particular, are institutionally supported cultural practices or wondering about the possible relation between learning and instruction is one thing; another, very different thing is believing that what children know about writing is what they are institutionally taught. A developmental approach makes little sense for those who believe that learning is created by teaching.

From this perspective of literacy, even children who have not yet had formal instruction in how to read or write are asked to "read" or to "write," and their way of doing so can be observed and analyzed. The idea of observing the development of a certain capacity as early as possible was attempted by German psychologists in the 1930s (Hildreth, 1936) and applied more extensively by Luria and Vygotsky at about the same time (Luria, 1929/1978). From the 1970s on, this notion was developed by Ferreiro and her associates (e.g., Ferreiro, 1986, 1988; Ferreiro & Teberosky, 1979) in Spanish and subsequently applied in different languages and orthographies (e.g., Levin & Korat, 1993), and Sandbank, 2001, in Hebrew; Pontecorvo & Zuccchermaglio, 1988, in Italian; and Chan, 1998, in Chinese), with parallel enterprises in North America, Australia, and New Zealand. Although these various scholars differed widely in approach and motivation, all have actively contributed to our appreciation of the general domain of "preliterate children's conceptions on literacy"—or what Vygotsky called "the prehistory of written language." My first goal in this chapter is to review some of the findings concerning the development of the diverse aspects of writing.

From the onset, writing is not merely a tool for transmitting knowledge; it is also a source of knowledge; it is not only a problem space but also a resource for dealing with language and thought. Thus, my second goal is to show that the study of writing can be a window for the mind and an important source of insight into key issues in human development. Research on writing helps us to understand how children acquire and use this important tool for communication and learning. Furthermore, such research also reveals properties of our mental operations and can demonstrate the role of cultural artifacts in these operations.

Writing as a Mode of Production

The fundamental difference between production of speech, signing, reading, and writing is that only writing leaves visible traces. By looking at the traces, reading can be performed and the original piece of discourse can be reconstructed. The permanence of the traces as opposed to the ephemeral character of speech is an essential feature of writing.

Sound production begins spontaneously in young infants as babbling; so does graphic production. At 18 months, or even earlier, a child given a tool and a surface will produce graphic marks. The child will do that not for the sake of the activity, nor as a mere exercise, but for the traces. This was proved a long time ago, when children ranging in age from 15 to 38 months were studied in free play activities (Gibson & Levin, 1980). They were given a paper attached to a board and one of two tools, identical except that one left a trace, whereas the other did not. For all the subjects, elimination of the trace significantly reduced the graphic activity. Moreover, nontracing tools were rejected. While scribbling and afterwards, the infants pointed and named the products, but this behavior disappeared when no traces were left.

Similar precocity is shown for reading practices. Even infants are intelligent participants in book-reading activities. Children grasp the physical acts involved in reading—gazing, pointing, monitoring—but also become familiar with the typical language associated with books (Bus, van IJzendoorn, & Pellegrini, 1995; Snow & Ninio, 1986). Children from 8 to 18 months of age engaged in reading picture books progress from an attempt to eat the page to being able to participate fully in verbal dialogue while looking at the books. Book reading is, however, a cultural practice that is not democratically distributed. It greatly depends on the community's access to reading materials and on the adults in charge of making them available to children. Children raised in isolated communities with no experience with book-reading practices develop a representation of writing before developing a meaning for reading. For 3-year-olds in these communities, writing means the production of marks on paper, but reading has no definite meaning; it is confused with writing (Ferreiro, 1986). For example, children who had just jotted down some marks on a sheet of paper and were asked to read them back responded that they had already done so. Other children claimed that pencils were needed for reading. Such manifestations are not terminological issues; rather, they indicate that the nature of writing is understood at an earlier age because it leaves visible traces; it changes the object visibly, while reading does not.

Certainly, other graphic activities, such as drawing, leave visible traces. It is thus crucial to find out whether children make something different when writing or drawing. Levin and Bus (2003) analyzed the drawing and writing of 28- to 53-month old children, using tasks in which the children were asked to draw and write the same eight referents, in addition to writing their names. From the results, the authors concluded that children up to age 3 draw and write indistinguishable, nonrepresentational graphic products. However, the authors focused on only the products of drawing and writing. When the process of production is observed, a different picture emerges.

Even when their products are indistinguishable, however, 3- to 4-year-olds' motor plans can be clearly identified either for drawing or for writing. Brenneman, Massey, Machado, and Gelman (1996), who examined procedural competence through the analysis of children's videotaped action sequences, showed that children's action plans differ for writing and drawing. When drawing, children make wide, continuous, circular movements, whereas when writing, they lift their pencils off the page and interrupt their movements much more frequently; that is, although the graphic product does not look like writing to an external observer, children act differently when writing or drawing. The problem is that when the finished product is separated from the "writer" and the writing task, the traces "do not have meaning." Differentiation in action implies that 2- to 3-year-olds have implicit knowledge that drawing and writing are different activities even when they are unable to display these differences in their graphic products until a later age.

Because writing leaves traces, it is a very suitable mnemonic device. This basic feature enables planning, monitoring, revision, and editing in the process of composition. Writing makes it possible to reexamine whatever is expressed for further clarification or exploration.

Young children are also aware of the usefulness of such external memory strategies as note taking. When children were asked to suggest strategies to help them remember to perform a certain act (Kreutzer, Leonard, & Flavell, 1975), they were more likely to suggest external memory strategies (e.g., writing a note, asking someone to remind them) than internal memory strategies (e.g., rehearsal,

mental retracing). However, children do not take advantages of permanent tracing for mnemonics, planning, and editing until much later, and frequently only as a result of specific instruction.

Little research has been done on preschoolers' spontaneously resorting to writing to aid their own memory. In the pioneering study by Luria (1929/1978), children ages 3–5 years were given the task of remembering a certain number of sentences that exceeded their mechanical capacity to remember; once children realized that they were unable to remember the number of words given to them, the experimenter gave them each a sheet of paper and told them "to jot down" or to "write" the words he presented. According to the author, "in most cases the child was bewildered by our suggestion" (p. 149). Two reasons might be involved in children's bewilderment: that they did not know how to write, and that it did not occur to them that a way to remember is to jot down. In fact, Luria proceeded by pointing out to the children that writing is what adults usually do to help them remember. Only after the experimenter's instructions did children use writing to help them remember. Nevertheless, the younger children did not attempt to "read" what they had written when asked to recall the sentences. The kind of written displays these children produced (detailed in the next section) did not provide any clue for recalling the sentences, and the children were aware of this.

Attempts to modify a written product require a certain awareness on the part of the child that the interpretation of what has been jotted down depends on the graphic features of the product and not just the intention or willingness of the producer. This realization constitutes a developmental process. When children are required to read what they have just written, there is an interplay between what they have actually put on paper and what they wanted to write. Studies in which preschoolers and first graders have been asked to read back isolated words or texts they have just written have found that younger children repeat verbatim what they have been asked to write (Tolchinsky Landsmann, 1993) or what they wanted to write (Sandbank, 2001) irrespective of what was actually on the paper. Only with age did children attempt to modify the written texts and look for a correspondence between what they said and what was written.

A developmental process was also found when children were explicitly told and even encouraged to modify their texts. After having written a text read to them out of a book, preschoolers and first graders were asked to read back and correct what they had written in any way they liked (Sandbank, 2001). Although preschoolers were more concerned with graphic aspect of texts (e.g., the shape of the letters) and first graders, with graphophonemic correspondences and orthographic rules, both groups made modifications involving discourse level, that is, revision of the content and structure of texts. For example, one of the first graders wrote a list that was almost exclusively nouns written in a column (*Sweeties, Candies, Chocolates, on the roof was a chimney*). During the revision phase, however, he added an introductory phrase at the top of the text (*in the house there were*) and a conjunction (*and*) between the last noun and the short sentence to make the text more cohesive. Even children who were not writing conventionally were able to produce modifications at a discourse level. Young children, when asked to read and revise their texts, modified their texts in ways that more experienced writers do spontaneously.

An awareness of the basic feature of writing, that it leaves permanent traces, emerges spontaneously. But the perception of the enabling advantages of this feature for mnemonics, planning, and editing requires more developmental time and probably more experience with written language.

Writing as a Discourse Style

Unlike speech, the permanence of traces in writing enables a detachment in time and space between discourse products and discourse producers (Olson, 1997; Tolchinsky, 2003). As literate people, we have at our disposal pieces of discourse that were produced far away and a long time ago. These are encoded in the form of manuscripts, newspapers, books, and letters. Children growing up in a literate community are surrounded by these written products. To what extent are they aware that these material objects are carriers of discourse?

Texts are physical objects supporting discourse, and preschoolers have a notion of the type of discourse to be expected from certain types of physical supports. Therefore, if 4-to-5-year-olds are read a recipe from a storybook, or a typical fairytale from a newspaper, they might react with surprise and deny that these sorts of text are written there (Ferreiro & Teberosky, 1979). Preschoolers are also able to distinguish between different types of text. Hebrew-speaking 5-year-olds were asked to write a fairytale, *Ami ve'tami* ("Hansel and Gretel") and to describe the chocolate house in the tale. Their knowledge of phonographic conventions of written Hebrew was very poor; most of them could draw Hebrew letters, but they did not always know their phonic value. Nevertheless, their written outputs for narratives and for descriptions were very different. The narrative was written in long lines, one letter after the other, with hardly any internal spacing between them except for the names of the protagonists, which sometimes appeared with blanks on both sides. The description, on the other hand, looked very similar to a list of isolated words (Sandbank, 2001). Indeed, when asked to read what they had written, they interpreted the long lines as full utterances, parts of the tale.

When interpreting the description, however, they named the different elements in the house, saying that there were "chocolates, candies, and cookies." A similar graphic differentiation was found when researchers compared the way preschoolers wrote shopping lists and news, advertisements, and poetry (Pontecorvo & Zuccchermaglio, 1988; Tolchinsky Landsmann, 1993). Long before gaining a full command of the phonographic conventions of the written system, the graphic layout of children's text imitates the features of different genres.

Studies on young children's use of genre (Hudson & Shapiro, 1991; Pontecorvo & Morani, 1996; Sandbank, 2001) have revealed that children employ distinctly different forms to reflect different communicative purposes. The problem of placing information into a given genre is solved very early (Berman & Nir, 2004).

An interesting finding relative to young children's sensitivity to genre constraints is that this sensitivity prevented them from distinguishing between verbatim repetitions and paraphrases. Lee, Torrance, and Olson (2001) asked children to distinguish between a verbatim repetition and a close paraphrase of an utterance. The success rate was higher in nursery rhymes, which highlight surface form, than in narratives, where content takes precedence over form. With age, the effect of genre diminished and success became more consistent across tasks. The authors interpret this as requiring the ability to reflect on texts, as a consequence of literacy. In fact, this genre sensitivity on the part of young children is remarkable: They seem to realize that paraphrasing is quite acceptable in narratives but inappropriate in the case of poetry.

A common assumption about writing development is that it progresses, starting with sensitivity to letter–sound correspondences, then moving to form words and, subsequently, sentences, before finally reaching the level of extended discourse. But the research discussed in this chapter suggests that writing actually develops at many levels simultaneously. In addition, throughout this development, the knowledge acquired at each level constrains learning at all other levels. Children do not move unidirectionally from smaller to larger units. Rather, what children come to know about texts guides and constrains their knowledge of letters and words, and what they grasp about letter–sound correspondences guides and constrains their way of writing texts.

Writing as Notation

In our culture, the alphabet is the notation used in writing for encoding discourse. Thus, the development of writing as a notation reflects children's path in grasping the alphabetic principle.

As mentioned, Luria (1929/1978) and Vygotsky were among the first psychologists to undertake this endeavor. Their studies were carried out with Russian-speaking children just 10 years after the Soviet revolution. The time was ripe to demonstrate that the acquisition of cultural tools might lead to cognitive revolutions. They performed a surprisingly simple though daring test. They had 3-, 4-, and 5-year-olds listen to sentences. When they thought the children were unable to recall them, they instructed the

children to write the sentences down, *so that they could remember them better*. The request was strictly instrumental, because children had to write *so as to remember*. They found that regardless of the sentence, the youngest children produced similar "scrawls" for every word. This is why the children could not make use of their notes in recalling the sentences; their notes did not serve any mnemonic function. For this same reason, Luria described this written output as *undifferentiated–noninstrumental*.

Fifty years after Luria's pioneering experiments, a group of Argentinian psychologists made very similar findings, though guided by Piagetian rather than Vygotskian thinking (Ferreiro & Teberosky, 1979). Specifically, they worked with the belief that even when children have to incorporate conventional knowledge of a conventional kind derived from their membership in a social community (e.g., through language), they must make that knowledge their own and reconstruct it in their own terms. They believed that no knowledge begins from nothing, and all knowledge has a developmental story.

Many different tasks were used to explore this development. Children were asked to write words and sentences in the context of clinical interviews. But, in contrast with Luria, there was no functional aim to the request; children were not required to write for mnemonic or communicative purposes. It turned out that many of the young Argentinian native-Spanish speakers made similar "scrawls" regardless of the word or sentence they were asked to write. Ferreiro (Ferreiro & Teberosky, 1976) also termed this type of production "undifferentiated writing," because neither the child nor the adult could distinguish what had been written.

Nevertheless, children's writing displays the features of form common to writing in almost any language: linearity, presence of distinguishable units, regularity of blanks, and directionality (Gibson & Levin, 1980). By the age of 4, children's writing already appears as a linearly arranged string of distinctive marks separated by regular spacing. These findings are supported by numerous studies carried out in a variety of languages, including English, and seem to hold true independent of socioeconomic status or microcultural milieu (Bissex, 1980; Clay, 1982; Chan, 1998; Gibson & Levin, 1980;

Goodman, 1982; Harste, Woodward, & Burke, 1984). These studies demonstrate that the graphic pattern of writing is part of a child's mental space very early on. At age 4, writing has been internally grasped by the child as a particular activity that produces a specific formal output distinct from drawing, in that it is linear and discrete.

How do children interpret their own written words during the stage of *undifferentiated writing*? They behave as though the place where writing stands or the writer him- or herself, rather than any particular feature of the written display, determines the interpretation. Three- to 4-year-olds were shown pictures with a caption (e.g., a picture of a boat with the caption BOAT). Either as a result of their own guesswork or following a suggestion from an adult, children agreed that the word *boat* was written under the drawing of a boat. However, when the written word was "accidentally" moved to another picture, the reading of the word also changed (Bialystock, 1992; Ferreiro, 1988). So the same written word could come to mean *pipe*, under the drawing of a pipe. Apparently, they did not see the written word *boat* as being a representation of a boat, independent of the changes in contexts, referents, or conditions of productions.

Another typical behavior during the period of *undifferentiated writing* shows that children seem to believe that the writer determines the interpretation of what is written.

When asked to read back what they have written, children usually repeated verbatim the words they were asked to write, irrespective of the graphics they had produced.

One of the main contributions made by Ferreiro was her recognition of the formal work involved in early writing. She discovered that even children who do not know how to write conventionally hold certain criteria concerning the *distinctive features* that graphic displays must fulfill in order to be readable. In order for a string of letter-like forms to be readable, it must be of a limited number and have sufficient variety. These two constraints also regulate children's writing and seem to hold true across languages and scripts. A number of examples drawn from a study examining the development of word writing in Hebrew and Spanish (languages that use different scripts) serve to illustrate this claim. Participants were Spanish- and Hebrew-speaking preschool-age through second-grade children living in Barcelona and Tel Aviv (Tolchinsky & Teberosky, 1998).

We found that the written products of preschoolers, both in Spanish and in Hebrew, were constrained by the same formal features of number and variety. These initial similarities were followed by an increasing divergence as the distinctive features of the respective languages began to exert their influence. Figure 6.1 illustrates two series of written productions highlighting these initial

FIGURE 6.1. Written productions illustrating initial similarities in writing.

similarities. Those on the left were produced by an Israeli girl, Maya; those on the right were produced by a Spanish-speaking boy, Christopher, of the same age. The letters used by each child are the conventional letters of each script. In general, children do not invent forms for letters; rather, they use those provided by the environment. Yet in spite of the different letters, the written outputs reflect both formal constraints: (1) Every string should contain a similar amount of letters, and (2) adjacent letters should not be the same. The most striking observation was that children used the letters in their own names as a sort of repository of conventional letter shapes. Both the Israeli girl and the Spanish boy used the letters in their respective names when writing each word. It was rather shocking to find such an original solution appearing in two different scripts.

In all studies in the different languages explored, whenever a child is required to write his or her own name along with other words or sentences, the child's name always shows a higher level of development in any of the features being considered. If the study is concerned with superordinate features, they emerge earlier in children's own names. If conventional letters are the focus of study, it is also the first place where children use them (Chan, 1998; Ferreiro & Teberosky, 1979; Tolchinsky Landsmann & Levin, 1985).

Certainly, this might be related to the strong affective meaning we attach to our own names. But personal names also constitute the first clearly meaningful that text is resistant to being forgotten and unchanging in pronunciation. A 3- or 4-year-old who is told that a set of letters is his or her name, even circumstantially, will remember it when presented with the written name at a later date, whereas this is not usually the case for any other word (Tolchinsky Landsmann, 1993).

The rules that children impose on number and variety are not mere inventions, they reflect the actual distribution of word length and intraword variation found in real texts. English orthography also contains examples of this constraint. The only reason for repeating letters in the word *egg* is to fulfill the constraint that nouns, verbs, and adjectives must have at least three letters. In Spanish, no written word contains the same letter repeated more than twice in consecutive position, while in Hebrew, very few words contain the same letter repeated three times in consecutive position. But this use of formal constraints is not a direct application of social learning. It reflects an active selection because, although it is true that there are very few single-letter words, they are the most frequently used in any text.

As they explore the features of writing, the discovery that some features are distinctive helps children to organize their written materials. Under these self-imposed limitations on number and variety, children start using, time and again, the same forms in different combinations rather than creating new forms. This is one of the necessary conditions of a notation, but, more importantly, it facilitates the attribution of meaning to individual letters. Before the application of the two constraints, writing was a discontinuous, linear pattern. After their application, however, writing is made up of a small number of distinguishable and therefore manageable elements.

During the period in which children are engaged in exploring the formal features of writing, their behavior shows that they are aware that writing is *somehow* related to language. Three- to 4-year-olds, when required to read what they have written, will repeat verbatim the words they were asked to write. The occasion is created for a mapping of a verbal utterance onto a written display. Something said (a word, a sentence) is put into correspondence with a graphic pattern.

We must recall that children are at a stage in which reduction in number and variety of letters has already been established; therefore, they pronounce the utterance from a reduced number of written marks in front of them. And because the number of marks is reduced, parts of the utterance can be mapped more easily onto parts of the written display and, vice versa, parts of the written display can be mapped onto parts of the utterance.

When children turn to the letters and seek sound correspondences to guide their writing, they turn to a general model, a model suitable for every writing task, because every word and sentence has a phonic aspect. Children have discovered that the number and variety of graphic elements (letters) are related to the phonological aspect of words.

But how do children segment words so as to make these segments correspond to the graphic elements in the written string? On which "units" is the mapping based?

The Syllabic Hypothesis

According to Ferreiro (1988), once children have grasped the idea that writing is a representation of sound, they initially believe that each written mark roughly corresponds to a spoken syllable. Evidence for the syllabic hypothesis is provided by case and in-depth longitudinal studies of Argentine and Mexican children carried out by Ferreiro and her collaborators, by studies with Israeli children, and by further studies comparing Spanish- and Hebrew-speaking children (Tolchinsky & Teberosky, 1998).

It is not surprising that the syllable is the initial unit of correspondence. Since the earliest studies reported by Bruce in 1964, it has been established that when children are asked to break spoken words down into smaller parts, they tend to segment words into syllables before they segment into phonemes. Syllables are natural units of segmentation, because they have a phonetic substrate, whereas phonemes are linguistic constructs. Therefore, it is understandable that when children start segmenting words to map onto letters, they do so in terms of syllables.

Figure 6.2, which contains a number of examples of the "syllabic period" in two languages with different scripts, illustrates this period in the development of writing. The children were asked to write common nouns that form part of their typical out-of-school vocabulary and are similar in meaning and sound in the two languages. Two series of written productions can be seen for the same words. Those on the left were produced by a 5-year-old Hebrew-speaking girl, while those on the right were produced by a Spanish-speaking boy of the same age. The girl uses Hebrew letters and the boy, Roman letters. Nevertheless, the two sets of products are regulated by syllabic correspondence. We can prove this by repeating the word the children were asked to write and breaking it down into syllables (e.g., *sa-la-mi*). We see that the number of letters maps onto the number of syllables. Initially, the main concern within this age group is the correspondence between the *number* of syllables and the *number* of letters. When children are concerned mainly with quantitative correspondence, any letter will apparently do. At this point, a child's specific knowledge about letter names and their respective sound values plays an important role.

Two processes are active in this undertaking. On one hand, there is the analysis of the word, and on the other, the child's knowledge of the conventional sound value of the letters. At this point, a child's specific knowledge about letter names and their respective sound values plays an important role. It may

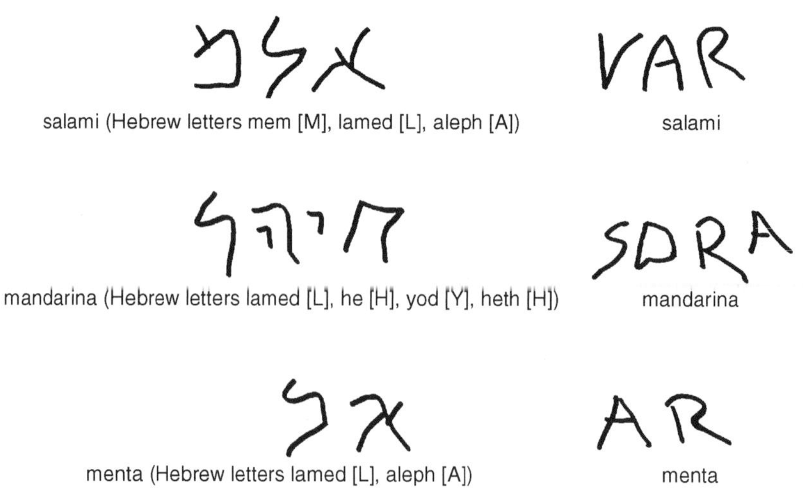

salami (Hebrew letters mem [M], lamed [L], aleph [A])

salami

mandarina (Hebrew letters lamed [L], he [H], yod [Y], heth [H])

mandarina

menta (Hebrew letters lamed [L], aleph [A])

menta

FIGURE 6.2. Examples of the "syllabic period."

be the case that some syllables—usually the initial one—are written with the corresponding conventional letters, while others are written with any letter some children may also identify one or more letters by their sound value and use them in a nonsystematic way when they recognize the presence of that sound in a word. For example, the Spanish boy whose writings appear in Figure 6.2 seems to have identified the letter *A*. He uses it in every word, but only one time instead of two in the first and second words (*salami* and *mandarina),* and not in the right place in the third word (*menta).* We may therefore find that some words have not yet been analyzed and are written with any letters; others have been partially analyzed, so that, since the child knew some letters, he or she used these; and still other words in which, by chance, the child knew all the letters. These various possibilities are typical of any process of transitional knowledge. Eventually, the two processes concur. Then, the written product will include a letter with its conventional sound value for each syllable.

There is no doubt that children's knowledge of letter names plays an important role in the acquisition of writing. Knowledge about letter names is one of the factors that influences writing development, but it does not operate identically in every language and script.

The syllabic hypothesis has not gone unchallenged. It has been called into question mainly by studies carried out in English (Kamii, Long, Manning, & Manning, 1993; Treiman, Tincoff, & Richmond-Welty, 1996), which suggest that children use alternative methods to understand the relation between written and spoken words.

One possibility is that the syllabic hypothesis is language-specific: a hypothesis that holds true for syllable-timed languages such as Spanish, Italian, and Chinese, but not English. This is highly probable, because segmentation strategies are influenced by the phonological structure of the language. Many more cross-linguistic studies are needed before we can reach a definitive answer.

The Alphabetic Principle

Children's discovery of links between letters and sound is a turning point in the conceptualization of writing. It means discovering a stable principle that is useful for representing any word. There is not a sudden shift from a stage in which words are regulated by syllabic correspondences to a stage in which words are regulated by alphabetic correspondences. Intermediate phases can be identified in which children produce syllabic–alphabetic mapping; that is, some syllables are fully represented, while others are not—for example, the word *gato (cat),* written GAO, where the first syllable is completely represented (*ga-,* written GA), but the second (*to)* is not. The transition is word-sensitive; certain words are regulated by alphabetic correspondences before others, depending on the structure of the word, the extent to which word components present any pronunciation difficulty, the way word components are represented orthographically, the child's previous knowledge of the word (i.e., whether this word is part of a child's inventory of well-written meaningful texts), and the child's previous knowledge of the letters used to represent the word.

With the discovery of the alphabetic principle, children find a stable frame of reference that is useful for representing any word. But it is in this transition to the alphabetic principle that the specific characteristics of the phonological and morphological structures of a language, and the way in which these characteristics are reflected in the script, play a crucial and distinctive role.

Learning Separation between Words

Developmental studies can disclose how children assimilate the convention of writing systems through their linguistic intuitions and, at the same time, how they must reformulate their intuitions to accommodate to the conventions of writing. The way children learn one of the main conventions of our writing system—that of graphic separation between words—illustrates these interactive processes between writing systems and users. If we ask 4- and 5-year-olds to write a story (rather than merely isolated words!), they will usually produce long strings of letters or letter-like elements with almost no graphic separation between them, in a form termed *scriptio continua*. This is true in English, and in

Hebrew as well. The question is how they move from this kind of writing to the conventional separation between words.

Words are relatively easy to define in the context of a particular writing system: one or more letters with blank spaces on both sides. But imagine for a moment that we want to explain what such graphic words correspond to in the sense of their corresponding linguistic units. This very much depends on the particular language. In English, as in other European languages, prepositions and articles are written as separate words, with blanks on both sides (*to the beach*), but in Hebrew, many prepositions, the definite article, and also some conjunctions are written as prefixes bound to the next word (e.g., *layam*). And even in Spanish and Italian, both Romance languages, the same elements *to* and *the* would be written separately in Spanish— *a la playa* (*to the beach*)—but all together— *alla spiaggia*—in Italian.

Another source of difficulty in establishing correlates between linguistic elements and written words beyond the limits of a particular language is that graphic words cover a range of units with different morphological status depending on a language. In Spanish, a graphic word may represent a single morpheme (e.g., *fin = end*), more than one morpheme (e.g., *cumpleaños = birthday*), or even an entire clause (e.g., *dámelo = give it to me*). There is no unique morpholexemic correlate to a graphic word outside the writing system of a particular language. So it is hard to see exactly what is meant by saying that words are separated by spaces, and it is even harder to imagine how this could be explained to a 6-year-old.

Besides, we cannot tell children to listen carefully to how we talk and then, whenever they hear a pause, to put a space, because in normal speech, people generally *do not* pause between words. Rather, in the course of speaking, words are typically grouped into prosodic units or intonational phrases that rarely coincide with what would constitute a grammatical "word" (Nespor & Vogel, 1986) and that, again, differ from one language to another. Thus, there is no simple physical basis in the input to cue children about how to isolate words (Tunmer, Bowey, & Grieve, 1983).

If children were "strict behaviorists," this would pose a serious problem, and segmen-

tation errors would pervade their output. Yet, although segmentation errors do occur in the very early stages of language acquisition (Peters, 1983), they are rare once children start using grammatical inflections and closed-class items more productively; that is, once young children are beyond the very initial stage of language acquisition and can consistently produce both content words (nouns, verbs) and function words (articles, conjunctions), there can be no question but that these are represented as *words* (Karmiloff-Smith, 1992).

Nonetheless, when preschool children are explicitly asked about what counts as a word, they will not consider each relevant item as belonging to the category of word. When asked directly if *table* is a word, they will agree; but when asked if *the* is a word, they typically answer in the negative. And even though 3-year-olds can correctly perceive, use, and combine words like *the*, when asked to count words in a sentence, they fail to count these as words.

Learning the conventional forms for separation between words constitutes a milestone in children's developing writing (as it was in the history of writing). Without such separation between words, texts are almost impossible to understand, whereas once words are written separately, even with gross mistakes in spelling, children's texts become far more legible.

Studies on the development of separation between words (Clemente, 1984; Ferreiro, Pontecorvo, Ribeiro Moreira, & Garcia Hidalgo, 1996) have shown that word class plays an important role in children's decisions about whether and where to make spaces. By and large, children tend to write proper nouns, nouns, and verbs with spaces between them, but they are less likely to separate articles from nouns or auxiliaries from main verbs; rather, they tend to attach these to one another in a kind of "hyposegmentation." In fact, this is a very reasonable assumption, since content words such as nouns and verbs typically have some delimited reference outside of any context, whereas function words or closed-class items can only be interpreted in relation to the other words with which they occur.

In the studies we undertook to examine the development of word separation in Spanish (Cintas, 2000; Tolchinsky & Cintas,

2001), we wanted to find out whether children would apply their implicit knowledge to such tasks, the kind they reveal when talking, or whether they would apply explicit notions of what counts as a word in order to decide where to put a space. The participants in the study were 5- to 8-year-old children, from preschool to third grade. They had to write two-word expressions and four-word sentences dictated to them and to rewrite a short fable read to them.

We found that when word classes are systematically controlled, children make distinctions inside the overall category of function words. Those that are used to modify nominals (e.g., determiners, personal pronouns) are written with spaces on both sides sooner than those that are part of verb groups. Proper nouns were conventionally separated with the highest frequency, followed by personal pronouns and adjectives, all of which are nominal categories, whereas verb clitics were the most frequently hyposegmented and least often conventionally separated, with adverbs lying between these two classes.

To illustrate this kind of selective "hyposegmentation," consider this excerpt from a text written by a first grader who was asked to rewrite a fable (Figure 6.3 and translation). The text—about a mule carrying gold

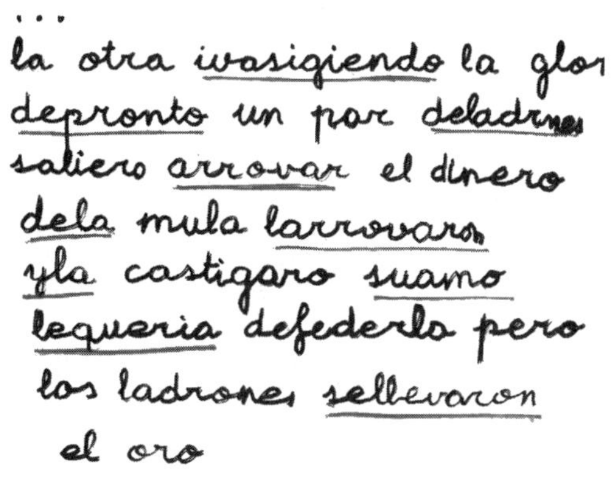

FIGURE 6.3. Example of lack of separation between words. Translation: "... the other *wasfollowing* the glory [= went after fame] *ofsudden* [= suddenly] a pair *ofrobbers* went *tosteal* the money *ofthemule* (they) *robbedit* and *punishedit itsowner wantedit todefend* [= wanted to defend it] but the thieves *se + took* [= for themselves] the gold."

stolen by two robbers—is written conventionally, though with some spelling mistakes. Underlined are the words she wrote together instead of separated. Auxiliaries are attached to main verbs; prepositions to other preposition, to nouns, and to verbs; and some conjunctions are attached to articles, as are possessive pronouns to nouns; that is, function words in general are hyposegmented more than content words. Yet children seem to make an even finer distinction than merely these two broad classes of words (open vs. closed). For example, the same form *la* is written separately when it functions as a determiner (*la otra = the other* [one]), but it is written together with the next word, when it functions as an indirect object clitic pronoun (*la robaron = it to steal = to steal it, la queria = it wanted to defend it = wanted to defend it*).

This is a clear instance of a kind of knowledge that is represented at various levels of accessibility. In speech, children segment and combine all kind of words, but their metalinguistic knowledge leads them to treat different classes of words differently. These same metalinguistic notions do motivate their decisions about where to put spaces when writing. The study further shows that children make subtle distinctions between syntactic categories and relations, and that they assume that the graphic separation between letters should reflect different syntactic relations between words.

In the domain of writing, as in other knowledge domains, children's errors do not simply indicate "ignorance"; rather, they reflect a different kind of reasoning. Certainly, in order to master the conventions of their system, children need to reformulate their original hypotheses. The question is: How can children come to reformulate this kind of linguistically motivated model of separation between words? I feel sure that they can do so by reading and writing texts of differing length and structure, texts that involve diverse classes of words in different syntactic contexts. It does not seem possible to grasp the conventions of a given writing system—Spanish or any other—by any form of explicit reasoning as to why spaces are obligatory in certain contexts. This kind of knowledge, I believe, can only be derived through actual use of and experience with writing.

Concluding Remarks

Children who grow up in a literate environment will not wait until the beginning of formal instruction to explore the features of writing. The graphic patterns of writing are part of their mental space from very early on—before the age of 3. At this initial stage, the meaning of the written pattern is determined by the place where it appears or by the child's intention as a writer, rather than by its features. Gradually, children become more selective as to what forms or combinations of forms are accepted as "writeable." Their writing becomes constrained by the same self-imposed criteria of number and variety. It is usually during this phase that children start looking for some correspondence between the length of words or phrases and the number of marks they put on paper. At the beginning, this correspondence is very global; if attempting to read, children will start saying a sentence, pointing at the beginning of what they have written, and will attempt to finish saying the sentence at the same time as their finger reaches the end of the written pattern. Slowly, however, they start looking for more articulated correspondences between parts of the utterance and elements in the written string. At this third stage, when children find a stable frame of reference that is useful for representing any word, they realize that number and variety of letters relate to the sound patterns of words. Finally, at a fourth stage, children discover the alphabetic principle, in which a letter represents each consonant and vowel in a word.

Throughout the development of writing, there are more opportunities for interaction and more developmental time, but the main source of this development is the act of writing, the interpretation and the uses of writing to which children are exposed. The conventions of writing—letter–sound correspondences, word separation—cannot be learned outside the written system. There is no way to acquire the conventions of a particular system except by discovering them in the system.

References

Berman, R. A., & Nir, B. (2004). Linguistic indicators of inter-genre differentiation in later language development. *Journal of Child Language, 31* 339–380.

Bialystok, E. (1992). Symbolic representation of letters and numbers. *Cognitive Development, 7,* 301–316.

Bissex, G. (1980). *GNYS AT WRK: A child learns to write and read.* Cambridge, MA: Harvard University Press.

Brennemann, K., Massey, C., Machado, S., & Gelman, R. (1996). Notating knowledge about words and objects: Pre-schoolers' plans differ for "writing" and "drawing." *Cognitive Development, 11,* 397–419.

Bus, A. G., & van IJzendoorn, M. H. (1988). Mother–child interactions, attachment, and emergent literacy: A cross-sectional study. *Child Development, 59,* 1262–1273.

Bus, A. G., van IJzendoorn, M. H., & Pellegrini, A. D. (1995). Joint book reading makes for success in learning to read: A meta-analysis on intergenerational analysis of literacy. *Review of Educational Research, 65,* 1–21.

Byrne, B., & Fielding-Barnsley, R. (1989). Phonemic awareness and letter knowledge in the child's acquisition of the alphabetic principle. *Journal of Educational Psychology, 81,* 313–321.

Chan, L. (1998). Children's understanding of the formal and functional characteristics of written Chinese. *Applied Psycholinguistics, 19,* 115–131.

Cintas, C. (2000). *La evolución de la separacion de palabras en el español escrito [The development of separation between words in written Spanish].* Unpublished dissertation, Universidad Autonoma de Madrid.

Clay, M. (1982). *What did I write: Beginning writing behaviour.* Exeter, NH: Heinemann.

Clemente, A. R. (1984). La segmentación de textos: El comportamiento evolutivo [Segmenting texts: The development behavior]. *Infancia y Aprendizaje, 26,* 77–86.

Cooper, J. (1996). Summerian and Akkadian. In P. Daniels & W. Bright (Eds.), *The world's writing systems* (pp. 37–40). New York: Oxford University Press.

Ferreiro, E. (1986). The interplay between information and assimilation in beginning literacy. In W. Teale & E. Sulzby (Eds.), *Emergent literacy: Writing and reading* (pp. 15–49). Norwood, NJ: Ablex.

Ferreiro, E. (1988). L'écriture avant la lettre. In H. Sinclair (Ed.), *La production de notations chez le jeune enfant: Langage, nombre, rythmes et melodies [The production of notations in young children: language, number, rhythms, and melodies]* (pp. 17–70). Paris: Presses Universitaires de France.

Ferreiro, E., Pontecorvo, C., Ribeiro Moreira, N., & Garcia Hidalgo, I. (1996). *Chapeuzino vermelho aprende a escrever [Little Red-hood learns how to write].* Sao Paulo: Atica.

Ferreiro, E., & Teberosky, A. (1979). *Los sistemas de escritura en el desarrollo del niño [Literacy before schooling]*. Mexico: Siglo XXI. Exeter, NH: Heineman.

Gibson, E., & Levin, H. (1980). *The psychology of reading*. Cambridge, MA: MIT Press.

Goodman, Y. (1982). El desarrollo de la escritura en niños muy pequeños [The development of writing in very small children]. In E. Ferreiro & M. Gómez Palacio (Eds.), *Nuevas perspectivas sobre los procesos de lectura y escritura [New perspectives on the process of reading and writing]* (pp. 107–128). Mexico City, Mexico: Siglo XXI.

Halliday, M. A. K. (1987). Language and the order of nature. In N. Fabb, D. Attridge, A. Durant, & C. MacCabe (Eds.), *The linguistic of writing* (pp. 135–154). New York: Methuen.

Harste, J. C., Woodward, V. A., & Burke, C. L. (1984). *Language stories and literacy lessons*. Porthmouth, NH: Heinemann.

Hildreth, G. (1936). Developmental sequences in name writing. *Child Development, 7*, 291–303.

Hudson, J. A., & Shapiro, L. R. (1991). From knowing to telling: Children's scripts, stories, and personal narratives. In A. McCabe & C. Peterson (Eds.), *Developing narrative structure* (pp. 89–136). Hillsdale, NJ: Erlbaum.

Kamii, C., Long, R., Manning, G., & Manning, M. (1993). Les conceptualisations du système alphabètique chez les jeunes enfants anglophones [The conceptualization of the alphabetic system in small English speaking children]. *Etudes de Lingüistique Appliquée, 91*, 34–47.

Karmiloff-Smith, A. (1992) *Beyond modularity*. Cambridge, MA: MIT Press.

Kreutzer, M. A., Leonard, C., & Flavell, J. H. (1975). An interview study of children's knowledge about memory. *Monographs for the Society for Research in Child Development, 401*(Serial No. 159), 1–58.

Lee, E., Torrance, N., & Olson, D. (2001). Young children and the say/mean distinction: Verbatim and paraphrasing recognition in narrative and nursery rhyme contexts. *Journal of Child Language 28*, 531–543.

Levin, I., & Bus, A. (2003). How is emergent writing based on drawing: Analyses of children's products and their sorting by children and mothers. *Developmental Psychology, 39*, 891–905.

Levin, I., & Korat, O. (1993). Sensitivity to phonological, morphological and semantic cues in early reading and writing in Hebrew. *Merrill–Palmer Quarterly, 392*, 233–251.

Liberman, I. Y., Shankweiler, D., & Liberman, A. M. (1992). The alphabetic principle and learning to read. In D. Shankweiler & I. Y. Liberman (Eds.), *Phonology and reading disability* (pp. 1–33). Ann Arbor: University of Michigan Press.

Luria, A. R. (1978). The development of writing in the child. In M. Cole (Ed.), *The selected writings of A. R. Luria*. New York: Sharpe. (Original work published 1929)

Nespor, M., & Vogel, I. (1986). *Prosodic phonology*. Dordrecht, The Netherlands: Foris.

Olson, D. R. (1996). Literate mentalities: Literacy consciousness of language, and modes of thought" In D. R. Olson (Ed.), *Modes of thought*, (pp. 141–151). Cambridge, UK: Cambridge University Press.

Peters, A. M. (1983). *The unit of language acquisition*. Cambridge, UK: Cambridge University Press.

Pontecorvo, C., & Morani, R. M. (1996). Looking for stylistic features in children's composing stories: Products and processes. In C. Pontecorvo, M. Orsolini, & L. Resnick (Eds.), *Early text construction in children* (pp. 229–258). Hillsdale, NJ: Erlbaum.

Pontecorvo, C., & Zucchermaglio, C. (1988). Modes of differentiation in children's writing construction. *European Journal of the Psychology of Education, 3*(4), 371–384.

Ravid, D., & Tolchinsky, L. (2002). Developing linguistic literacy: A comprehensive model. *Journal of Child Language, 29*, 417–447.

Sandbank, A. (2001). On the interplay of genre and writing conventions in early text writing. In L. Tolchinsky (Ed.), *Developmental aspects in learning to write* (pp. 55–74). Dordrecht, The Netherlands: Kluwer.

Snow, C., & Ninio, A. (1986). The contracts of literacy: What children learn from learning to read books. In W. Teale & E. Silzby (Eds.), *Emergent literacy: Writing and reading* (pp. 116–139). Norwood, NJ: Ablex.

Tolchinsky, L. (2003). *The cradle of culture and what children know about writing and numbers before being taught*. Mahwah, NJ: Erlbaum.

Tolchinsky, L., & Cintas, C. (2001). The development of graphic words in written Spanish: What can be learnt from counterexamples? In L. Tolchinsky (Ed.), *Developmental aspects in learning to write* (pp. 77–97). Amsterdam: Kluwer.

Tolchinsky, L., & Teberosky, A. (1998). The development of word segmentation and writing in two scripts. *Cognitive Development, 13*, 1–21.

Tolchinsky Landsmann, L. (1993). *El aprendizaje del lenguaje escrito [Learning written language]*. Barcelona: Anthropos.

Tolchinsky Landsmann, L., & Levin, I. (1985). Writing in preschoolers: An age related analysis. *Applied Psycholinguistics, 6*, 319–339.

Treiman, R., Tincoff, R., & Richmond-Welty, D. (1996). Letter names help children connect print and speech. *Developmental Psychology, 32*, 505–514.

Tunmer, W. E., Bowey, J. A., & Grieve, R. (1983). The development of young children's awareness of the word as a unit of spoken language. *Journal of Psycholinguistic Research 12*, 567–594.

Chapter 7

Implications of Advancements in Brain Research and Technology for Writing Development, Writing Instruction, and Educational Evolution

Virginia W. Berninger *and* William D. Winn

Two developments near the end of the 20th century altered the way researchers study writing and educators teach writing. The first development was the application of newly developed brain-imaging technologies to the study of the working brain in live human beings. The second development was the creation of affordable, user-friendly personal computers. Both of these scientific advances are leading to cultural evolution: Brain imaging is becoming a routine medical tool, and personal computers are in many homes and schools. In turn, the cultural evolution is leading to educational evolution as schools change educational practices to prepare students better for the emerging knowledge-based, global economy. We first review what has been learned from imaging studies about the brain basis for writing, and then discuss how integration of the developmental neuropsychological, sociocultural, and learning sciences perspectives may promote educational evolution. This integration incorporates distinctions between the internal and external environment but emphasizes that the writer's internal brain–mind and the external environment are a single interacting system. In this integration, we distinguish among the individual learner, the teacher's instructional behavior, and the in-

structional materials, tools, and curriculum (Figure 7.1); the brain's neuroanatomy, the brain's functions, and the observable behavior created by the brain for writing (Figure 7.2); and the multiple components of the internal functional writing system in the writer's mind (Figure 7.3).

Contribution of the Decade of the Brain to Writing

During the 1980s, technologies were developed that permitted researchers for the first time to scan the brains of *living* people while they performed mental tasks. The U.S. government committed substantial federal funding to support basic research on the human brain during the Decade of the Brain (1990–1999). The resulting knowledge explosion is changing our understanding of the developing and learning brain in profound ways. Previously, knowledge was limited to autopsy studies of individuals who lost specific brain functions due to disease or injury. Berninger and Richards (2002) reviewed findings from brain imaging about the reading brain, the writing brain, and the computing (math) brain, and related these to developmental and instructional research on

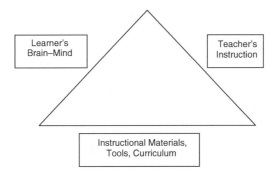

FIGURE 7.1. The learning triangle: Interactions among the learning writer, the writing teacher, and the instructional materials, tools, and curriculum for writing. Adapted from Berninger, Stage, Smith, and Hildebrand (2001).

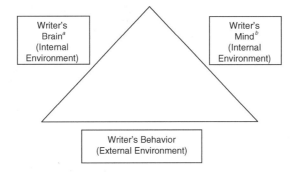

FIGURE 7.2. The brain–mind–behavior triangle. Based on Mesulam (1990). ^{a}Neuroanatomical structures at micro- and macro-level; ^{b}neural computations within and across brain regions.

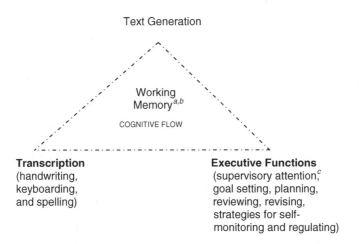

FIGURE 7.3. Triangle for the not-so-simple view of internal functional writing system. Modification of the simple view of writing in Berninger and Amtmann (2003). ^{a}Activates long-term memory during planning, composing, reviewing, and revising, and short-term memory during reviewing and revising output. ^{b}Components include (1) orthographic, phonological, and morphological storage units for verbal information, (2) a phonological loop for learning words and maintaining verbal information actively in working memory, and (3) executive supports that link verbal working memory with the general executive system (a distributed network of many executive functions) and with nonverbal working memory (which stores information in a visual–spatial sketchpad). ^{c}A complex system that regulates focused attention—selecting what is relevant and inhibiting what is not relevant, switching attention between mental sets, attention maintenance (staying on task), conscious attention (metalinguistic and metacognitive awareness), cognitive presence, and cognitive engagement.

97

reading, writing, and math. They also provided an introduction to basic principles in neural structure, brain function, brain development, and brain imaging technologies that allow educators and psychologists to read this rapidly growing imaging literature. This chapter provides an update on brain imaging studies related to writing processes. Readers unfamiliar with neuroanatomy can refer to figures in Chapters 3, 5, and 6 in Berninger and Richards (2002), which illustrate the brain location of specialized regions mentioned in this chapter. It is very surprising to many outside the field of education that preservice teachers are not required to take formal coursework about the brain, the organ of learning, by qualified instructors. Knowledge of this emerging research on the human brain may contribute to educational evolution by sensitizing teachers to the complexities of the organ that mediates teaching and learning, which are related but not in a direct way (see Figure 7.1 and Berninger & Richards, 2002).

The brain is an organ that allows an organism to (1) receive information from the external environment through the sensory input modalities and code that information internally; (2) compute new mental structures from the incoming sensory information, existing mental structures, and operations performed internally and externally; and (3) act upon the environment through the motor output systems. Nestled in the folds of human cortex are upward-extending bulges called gyri (plural for gyrus). The cerebral cortex is divided into four lobes (occipital, temporal, parietal, and frontal), and gyri with the same name occur on both the left and right side of the brain. Lobules are large gyri. Results of brain imaging studies are often reported in terms of specific gyri that are activated the most compared to other brain regions. Sometimes results are reported for sulci (plural for sulcus). In contrast to a gyrus, a sulcus is a downward-extending valley in the folds of cerebral cortex; sulci with the same name also occur on both sides of the brain. The structure of individual neurons (and presumably their computational properties) differs across the various gyri and sulci. Thus, each gyrus (and sulcus) may be a specialized computational mechanism. However, these computing mechanisms, which do not imply that the brain is merely a digital computer, do not operate in isolation from each other: Many mental functions are the result of a distributed network of computational mechanisms that communicate sequentially or simultaneously (thus, the "Talking Computers of Mind"; Berninger & Richards, 2002). That is why cutting-edge brain imaging studies report not only which brain regions are uniquely activated but also which specific brain regions are functionally connected (Cordes et al., 2000; Pugh et al., 2000).

The brain images, which show regions of significant brain activation in vivid color, are not photographs that directly capture regions of activation. The published images are the result of extensive data analyses that identify regions of significant activity relative to (1) neural noise in the whole brain and (2) control tasks. Results for functional imaging, in which participants perform target and control tasks while their brains are scanned, can only be interpreted in reference to those tasks, which share common processes but differ in a unique process that can be isolated when they are compared. Scanning the writing brain poses methodological challenges. For example, motor artifact is not a challenge for one kind of imaging that is invasive (radioactive substances are injected, so it can only be used with adults), but is for another kind that is not invasive and is safe to use with children. Real-world writing draws on many processes but imaging tasks have to be designed so that responses can be interpreted by comparing selected processes. Most (but not all) imaging of the writing brain has been done with normal adults who speak English, Japanese, Italian, German, or Finnish. More research is needed to evaluate whether results to date generalize to children as well adults, to those with specific writing disabilities as well as normal writers, and across languages. Mostly transcription processes have been studied, but a few studies have tackled elementary text-generation processes—word generation, with and without the constraints of sentence context (see Figure 7.3).

Writing Centers

Prior to the brain imaging studies in living people, three writing-specific brain regions were identified. In 1881 Exner observed that the posterior (rear) end of the middle frontal gyrus in the left frontal lobe was associated with writing function. Over a century later Anderson, Damasio, and Damasio (1990) proposed that Exner's area, as this first writing center is now called, may play a role in coactivation of movement sequences needed to generate letters. A second writing center was identified in the superior parietal lobule in the left parietal lobe (Basso, Taborelli, & Vignolo, 1978). Internal codes for letters may form in the left parietal lobe, whereas the graphomotor code for writing a letter in the external environment may be represented in the premotor region of the left frontal lobe (Brain, 1967), a third writing center. A graphomotor code requires the integration of two codes—orthographic for letter forms, and motor for hand output. Many mental processes require such cross-code integration.

Motor Codes

At one level of analysis, a writing brain expresses the internal language code in the external world through the grapho (hand)–motor system. This system may also be shared by the drawing brain that uses the hand to represent one's internal cognitions in the external world. The motor system controls not only execution of a motor act but also the planning for the execution of the motor act. One task used to study graphomotor planning requires an individual to tap the thumb with each finger in succession. This task activates the sensorimotor cortex, the cerebellum, and the supplementary motor area (Roberts, Dishrow, Roberts, & Rowley, 2000; Tegeler, Strother, Anderson, & Kim, 1999). The cerebellum plays a role in temporal coordination of separate processes, whereas the supplementary motor area provides a precise timing plan for organizing forthcoming motor sequences.

Orthographic Codes

In Garrett et al.'s (2000) study, detection (perception) of single letters, letter strings, and written word forms activated lower, posterior regions of the temporal and occipital lobes. When the task involved thinking about those letters rather than merely detecting them, the neural signature (pattern of brain activation) changed. Comparison of a

letter-matching judgment task and its control (a line judgment task) identified activation across a widely distributed network in the occipital lobe (both sides), temporal lobes (right side), parietal lobes (both sides), frontal lobes (both sides), and subcortical regions (both sides of the thalamus). Different patterns of neural activation involving different neural networks (and presumably different neural computations) were involved when the task was merely to detect the letters than when the task was to make judgments (decisions) about the commonalities in the letter patterns.

Cross-Code Integration

Many brain functions integrate internal codes. One study took advantage of properties of the Japanese orthography to compare copying orthographic symbols that could and could not be recoded phonologically (Matsuo, Kato, Tanaka, et al., 2001). Copying an orthographic symbol that could be phonologically coded uniquely activated only one region—the premotor area in the left frontal lobe. Copying an orthographic code that could not be phonologically recoded activated four regions—left premotor plus left parietal lobule (second writing center discussed earlier), occipital lobe (left), and posterior fusiform gryus (both sides). This pattern of results suggests that brain processing may be more efficient (less energy required to activate fewer regions) when cross-code integration is possible. Another study pointed to this same conclusion. Words with ideographic characters that could not be recoded phonologically showed greater activation than syllable characters that could be recoded phonologically. When the characters could not be phonologically recoded, three regions uniquely activated—Exner's area (the first writing center discussed earlier), fusiform gyrus, and posterior intraparietal sulcus (Matsuo, Kato, Ozawa, et al., 2001). Another study compared writing (which involves finger movement, language codes, and motor acts) and finger movements (which involve motor acts but not language [letters]). For this writing task, which isolates processes unique to writing rather than to motor processes alone, both of the writing centers discussed earlier activated—Exner's area and the left superior parietal lobule. In addition, regions in the occipital lobes (both sides), lingual and fusiform gyri (both sides), inferior temporal gyri (both sides), and superior cerebellum (both sides) activated (see Katanoda, Yoshikawa, & Sugishita, 2001).

Automatic versus Nonautomatic Processes in Motor Learning

Motor programs include both muscle-specific representations for ordering sequences of specific muscle movements and abstract motor plans that are not muscle-specific (Graham & Weintraub, 1996). When brain activation was compared before and after practice in moving a pen through novel mazes or square patterns, learning changed the pattern of activation in supplementary motor areas in the frontal lobe and the subcortical left cerebellum; and different circuits activated in the cerebellum during learning than after learning (Van Mier, Temple, Perlmutter, Raichle, & Petersen, 1998). Cerebellum activated during motor learning but basal ganglia activated only after motor skills were automatic (Mazziotta, Grafton, & Woods, 1991). When learning involved a visual–motor sequence, frontal areas activated more in early learning, and parietal areas activated more after practice (Sakai et al., 1998). Matsuo, Kato, Tanaka, et al. (2001) also compared nonautomatic (strategic) and automatic copying of orthographic symbols. On the one hand, nonautomatic copying uniquely activated the left superior parietal lobule (the second writing center discussed earlier), the left inferior prefrontal area, and the primary visual area in the occipital lobe (both sides). On the other hand, automatic copying uniquely activated the left premotor area (the third writing center discussed earlier), the inferior parietal lobule, the left occipital lobe, and the posterior fusiform gyrus (both sides). The only shared region for nonautomatic and automatic copying of orthographic codes was in the left occipital lobe. The contrasting patterns of activation showed that a different set of distributed neural processes is associated with nonautomatic (during learning) and automatic (after practice) integration of orthographic and motor codes for handwriting output.

Spelling

Brain imaging studies are isolating regions that process the phonological, orthographic, and morphological word forms involved in spelling. Rate of speech processing is related to normal spelling (Poldrack et al., 2001). Dyslexia, which impairs spelling, as well as reading, is related to problems in processing of the *phonological word form* but not in making auditory judgments about non-linguistic stimuli (tones) (e.g., Corina et al., 2001; Richards et al., 2000). The *orthographic word form* is sensitive to letter patterns rather than to visual features of individual letters (Cohen et al., 2002; Polk et al., 2002). The fusiform gyrus, which is a region involved in processing the orthographic word form (e.g., Dehaene, Le Clec'H, Poline, Bihan, & Cohen, 2002), responds to the written word form but not to numerical digits (Polk et al., 2002). Different brain regions activate for the *morphological word form* compared to the semantic meaning of words (Aylward et al., 2003; Richards, Aylward, et al., in press; Richards, Berninger, et al., 2005). The morphological, phonological, and orthographic word forms have unique as well as common neural signatures (patterns of activated regions) (Aylward et al., 2003, 2004; Crosson et al., 1999; Richards, Aylward, et al., in press; Richards, Berninger, et al., 2005). According to triple word form awareness and mapping theory (e.g., Berninger, Abbott, Billingsley, & Nagy, 2001; Berninger & Richards, 2002, Chapter 8), learning to spell (and read) requires becoming aware of each of the word forms—phonological, morphological, and orthographic and their parts—so the brain can compute mapping relationships among them. Early in spelling development, mapping relationships between phonemes (word parts in the phonological word form) and one- or two-letter spelling units (word parts in the orthographic word form) are most critical, but inflectional suffixes (morphological tense, number, and comparison markers) are also important (see Nagy, Osborn, Winsor, & O'Flahavan, 1994). Later in spelling development, mapping relationships among phonemes, morphemes (especially derivational suffixes marking part of speech, i.e., grammar function), and spelling units become critical (see Nagy et al., 1994). Although reading and spelling draw on the same three word forms, mapping processes for reading and spelling are not inverses or mirror images of each other (Read, 1981).

In Menon and Desmond's (2001) study of normal spelling, short sentences (familiar proverbs) were presented auditorially through speakers to both ears, and participants spelled dictated sentences by writing small letters on a 10 cm x 10 cm piece of paper on the right thigh. Spelling was compared to fixation only (a control that requires only focal visual attention). Spelling was associated with increased activation mostly in the left superior parietal lobe (the second writing center discussed earlier), but also to a lesser degree in the nearby left dorsal inferior parietal cortex. Activation was also observed in the left premotor cortex (the third writing center discussed earlier), sensorimotor cortex, and the supplementary motor cortex. Two research studies used the word completion paradigm in which a three-letter string (word stems for highly predictable words) is presented and the task is to complete it to spell a real word: (1) Ojemann et al. (1998) reported increased activation in left frontal and supplementary motor areas and right cerebellum, and decreased activation in right parietal regions and right insula; (2) Dhond, Buckner, Dale, Marinkovic, and Halgren (2001) identified temporal stages in the unfolding neural events, which proceeded from the back to the front of the brain, in normal spelling: The orthographic word form was initially processed in the visual association areas, but later multimodal coding (mapping) took place in Wernicke's area in the left temporal region and subsequently was completed in Broca's area in the left frontal region.

Word Generation

The verbal fluency task is used to study word generation without the constraints of sentence construction. A noun is presented auditorially, and the task is to generate a related verb—that is, to transform the word's part of speech. When word generation was compared to a motor-only control (bilateral tapping of each finger to thumb sequentially in response to an auditory tone), unique activa-

tion occurred in Wernicke's area (in left temporal lobe), Broca's area (in left frontal lobe), cingulate gyrus, and left dorsolateral prefrontal cortex (Holland et al., 2001). Another study of verbal fluency showed that the left inferior prefrontal cortex plays a role in goal-directed retrieval of semantic information from long-term memory and use of semantic information in working memory (Wagner, Paré-Blagoev, Clark, & Poldrack, 2001). Imaging techniques that are sensitive to the unfolding time sequence have shown that the left inferior frontal regions (Holland et al., 2001) may be involved in the first 30 seconds of the verbal fluency task, but left middle frontal regions (including the first writing center discussed earlier) may be involved in the next 30 seconds on the same task (Wood, Saling, Abbott, & Jackson, 2001).

The word generation task, which is used to study word generation with sentence context constraints, requires open-ended word production in final position to complete a seven-word sentence stem. Processes related to generating words for a particular sentence context were compared to one of two controls—either deciding which of two words completes the sentence stem or reading aloud the word in final position in a sentence stem (Kircher, Brammer, Andreu, Williams, & McGuire, 2001). For both controls, word generation resulted in unique brain activation in the left middle frontal gyrus (the first writing center discussed earlier), the anterior cingulate (part of the frontal attention system involved in conflict management), the precuneus (in back of the brain above the occipital cortex near the midline), and the right temporal cortex. When compared to the decision control, the greatest change in activation was found in several regions on the right—precuneus, anterior cingulate, posterior cerebellum, insula, lingual gyrus, and fusiform gyrus—and the middle and superior temporal gyri on both sides of the brain. When compared to the reading control, the greatest change in activation was found in the superior temporal gyrus (right), anterior cingulate, precuneus (left), left posterior cerebellum, left middle frontal gyrus (the first writing center discussed earlier), inferior parietal lobule (left), and frontal operculum (right). Overall there was greater activation on the right than on the left during the word generation task; the authors concluded that left neural circuitry may support language processes with more restricted semantic fields, whereas the right neural circuitry may support language processes with more open-ended linguistic context (multiple word meanings and multiple sentence interpretations).

Working Memory, Cross-Temporal Contingencies in Nonlinear, Multidimensional Time, and Automatic Processing

Middle frontal gyrus and superior parietal regions activate on language tasks that require children to hold phonological and orthographic word forms in working memory while processing word parts and making language judgments about them (Aylward et al., 2002). Thus, the first two writing centers (left middle frontal gyrus and left superior parietal regions) identified before the availability of *in vivo* brain imaging are associated with working memory function. Working memory in the internal environment (see interior of triangle in Figure 7.3) of the writer's brain/mind (see Figure 7.2) supports the writing process of text generation (see topmost vertex of triangle in Figure 7.3). Although traditional models of working memory have emphasized the spatial (capacity or span) dimension of working memory (e.g., McCutchen, 1996; Swanson & Berninger, 1996), recently there has been a growing recognition that the temporal dimension may be more fundamental to the function of working memory (Berninger, 1999; Fuster, 1997; Towse, 1998). In Fuster's (1997) pioneering research on nonhuman animal brains, the prefrontal cortex (a functionally defined region that overlaps with the structurally defined middle frontal gyrus) governs the temporal organization of many layers of cortex and subcortical regions to coordinate (1) short-term memory storage of incoming information from the environment, (2) long-term memory representations that are retrospective in time, and (3) mental set (anticipation) that prepares, through mechanisms involving forward time, the organism to act on the environment to achieve goals. The lateral (side) dorsal (top) prefrontal cortex (LDPFC), which makes and executes plans and has many connections to

parietal association cortex (Goldman-Rakic, Scalaidhe, & Chafee, 2000), plays a central role in the temporal coordination. The temporal coordination is achieved by complex, cross-temporal contingencies between (1) the posterior primary sensory cortex in the rear of the brain, which has bottom-up temporal flow of neural connectivity to manage direct contact with incoming information from the external world; and (2) the anterior primary motor cortex in the front of the brain, which has top-down temporal flow of neural connectivity to manage separate action domains (each with its feedback and feedforward mechanisms for specific sensory perception and motor acts) for operating on the external world. Anterior cingulate, which activates during the forward temporal contingencies involved in planning, manages conflicts in this complex temporal geometry. The LDPFC and the working memory circuits in the middle frontal gyrus may provide the brain's temporal mechanism for reconciling the past (travel back in time), the future (travel to future time), and the present (environmental update and current goal) for goal-directed behavior such as writing (see Berninger, 2004a).

Furthermore, in Fuster's (1997) model, frontal lobes have inhibitory mechanisms to protect the working brain from internal or external distraction. Acts that are well rehearsed until they are automatic are not stored in the frontal lobes. Thus, automatic acts may be protected from internal or external distraction because they are stored somewhere other than the frontal lobes and/or because they place fewer demands on frontal inhibitory processes for suppressing irrelevant information. The prefrontal cortex is involved in initial learning of procedural knowledge (novel structures of action) but not in performing well-rehearsed, automatic acts (automized structures of action). Seitz et al. (1997) have shown that controlled (strategic) processing of graphomotor stimuli and well-rehearsed acts with the same stimuli are housed in different parts of the neural architecture. The evolutionary advantage of automatization is that it reduces the temporal constraints on working memory and system management of the complex cross-temporal contingencies (Fuster, 1997) of the working brain (Luria, 1973). That is why automatizing low-level handwriting may free working memory for high-level composing goals by reducing the temporal constraints on it (the number of component processes that need to be orchestrated in real time) (Berninger, 1999).

Conclusions Based on the Brain Imaging Studies of Writing

Brain imaging of living people performing writing or writing-related tasks replicated evidence from autopsy studies that there are three writing centers in the brain—left middle frontal gyrus, left superior parietal lobule, and left premotor areas—but extended the prior findings by identifying additional activation in distributed computational networks, depending on the specific task studied. A growing body of brain imaging studies focus on units of language larger than the word (reviewed in Berninger, in 2004a; Berninger & Hooper, in press; Berninger & Richards, 2002), but discourse-level studies of the composing process had not been reported at the time of the current review. Brain imaging research will likely continue to add to our understanding of the writer's brain–mind (Figures 7.1, 7.2, and 7.3).

Computer-Mediated Cultural Transformation and Writing

Introduction of new technology has the potential to transform culture and the ways we think. For example, the invention of printing promoted the development of analytical skills at the expense of the rhetorical skills that enjoy an elevated status in oral traditions (Olson, 1991). The Reformation would not have succeeded without bibles printed in the vernacular, which gave ordinary (literate) citizens access to scripture directly, without the clergy acting as intermediaries and interpreters of holy texts. Neither the spread of scientific knowledge during the Renaissance and later nor the dissemination of technical information to the general population in travelogues and encyclopedias during the 18th-century Enlightenment would have been possible without the printed book. Computing may also be transforming the culture of literacy. Olson (1985) makes the case that because computers can only "understand" inputs that are completely unam-

biguous, teaching children to interact with computers leads to their developing more precision as they communicate. Salomon (1988) argues that the symbol systems and tools of computers can "become cognitive"; that is, they can be internalized by students and used for thinking, as can other cognitive processes be. Zellermayer, Salomon, Globerson, and Givon (1991) reported a significant increase in metacognitive writing-related activity by students after they had used an intelligent word processor that gave them real-time advice during composition. Ong (1982) credited new communication technologies with bringing us into a new oral tradition, a "second orality." The written language of e-mail and online chat is closer in form, usage, effect and context to spoken language than to written text.

The Decade of the Personal Computer

The 1990s could also be named the Decade of the Computer. Personal computers became widely available, and children born during this decade or thereafter will never know a world without personal computers (tools that require reading, writing, and reading–writing connections for many applications). Access to personal computers (monitors and keyboards) *may* alter the kinds of functional brain systems that are created to use computers for processing and producing written language (and other purposes). Functional brain systems are sets of component processes that are orchestrated to achieve specific goals (Luria, 1973). Liberman (1999) had the profound insight that language has no end organ and therefore teams with the sensory systems (ears and eyes) and the motor systems (mouth and hand) to interact with the external world. The Literacy Trek Project at the University of Washington is therefore studying how (1) the functional systems for Language by Ear (Listening), Language by Mouth (Speaking), Language by Eye (Reading), and Language by Hand (Writing) develop during the school-age years (Berninger, 2000); (2) these functional language systems are alike and different; (3) the functional language systems work together; (4) Language by Hand develops differently if the end organ is the keyboard versus the pen(cil); and (5) Cognition by Hand (external visual representations) and Language by Hand develop independently and in concert. Initial findings are that (1) the functional systems for listening, speaking, reading, and writing are distinct but moderately interrelated, and (2) the functional system for beginning writing may develop differently depending on whether the hand uses a pencil or a keyboard (Berninger et al., in press).

Cultural Evolution Affecting the Age at Which Writing Skills Are Taught and Practiced

The "process writing" movement not only transformed how writing is taught but also the age at which writing instruction is introduced. Before the 1980s writing instruction tended to be emphasized in the junior high and senior high years (Hillocks, 1986). Pioneering work of Graves (1983) in process writing and Clay (1982) in integrated reading–writing resulted in widespread introduction of writing to the first-grade classroom. Two decades later, writing is an integral part of most elementary classrooms, beginning in first grade and even kindergarten. Technological advances are leading to even earlier introduction of writing experience in homes and preschools. Because personal computers can be controlled through a mouse, even preliterate children, who have not mastered the alphabet sufficiently to use a keyboard, can use computers in meaningful, interactive ways. It is common in middle-class homes in the United States to observe children age 2 and above routinely using interactive computer programs with mouse access. Compact disc (CD) technology is also altering how parents and infants interact from birth onwards to facilitate language and cognitive development. Parents can interact with their infants and toddlers in reference to CD theater shows and concerts. Review of the CDs in the Baby Einstein Library (Baby Einstein Company, 2002) showed that the content provided rich audiovisual stimulation for right-hemisphere functions (music, real-world objects, visual shapes, colors, and poetry). This kind of stimulation is developmentally appropriate, since right side and posterior (back) brain structures myelinate earlier in development than do left side and anterior (frontal) brain structures; myelination supports more efficient neural transmission (see Chapter 4,

Berninger & Richards, 2002). This recent, widespread introduction of new technologies may alter the developmental timetables in which writing skills emerge, are scaffolded (guided by adults or technology), and are practiced. Although transcription skills (handwriting and spelling) are key to preventing future writing problems (Berninger & Amtmann, 2003), keyboarding is as essential as writing with pen(cil) in the 21st century.

Evolution Related to Changes in the Nature of Interactions between the Internal and External Environment

The effectiveness of computers as tools in literacy instruction has been reviewed elsewhere. Our focus in not on effectiveness but rather on how technology tools are transforming the writing process as the writer's internal mental world interacts with the external writing environment. For example, word processors may focus too much attention on the external technology environment, with the effect of drawing attention away from important internal metacognitive processes, such as planning and organizing in preparation for writing (Goldfine, 2001). Young writers may require special assistance for managing the attentional demands of interacting between internal and external environments during computer-assisted writing. Software prompts for spelling errors and unwieldy grammar alone may not be sufficient. Explicit instructional strategies for executive regulation of self-monitoring and repair may also be necessary (see Figure 7.3). Strategies need to be adapted to genre-specific writing. For example, the grammar checker in Microsoft Word's word processor was developed for writers of business English and may not be appropriate for teaching general composition (McGee & Ericsson, 2002). Some tools may constrain idea generation and elaboration. For example, Microsoft's PowerPoint® presentation program, which students are often encouraged to use in school writing, has been criticized for seriously constraining what can be said and for promoting appearance over content (Tufte, 2003). The format of Web pages—with many nonverbal representations (photographs, pictures drawn with graphic programs, diagrams, etc.), as well as verbal representations (written text)—may also transform the way minds interact with the external environment. A different kind of processing (hybrid nonverbal–verbal) may be needed for reading web pages than for reading long, complex text without any explicit nonverbal representations. This kind of processing for web reading may provide a necessary correction factor for the overly verbal bias of conventional schooling. The way information is structured in search engines on the Web may also transform the way internal cognitions are organized. Prior to the Web, library searches were biased to properties of external written language at the text level, which tends to be linear and sequential. However, search engines access on the basis of parallel semantic–conceptual maps, which do not encourage linear, sequential text required in writing for school assignments.

Radical "ConstructiVism" versus Piagetian "ConstructiONism"

Radical *constructivism* draws on ideas of European postmodern writers (Yeaman, Hlynka, Anderson, Damarin, & Muffoletto, 1996; Hlynka, 2004) and rejects both sociobiology (genetic influences) and behavioral theory (environmental determinants of learning and development) (Von Glasersfeld, 1984). Nevertheless, the influence of constructivism on educational research and practice has pushed the nature–nurture pendulum to the "nurture" side, but with a peculiar twist—only the importance of the environment has been recognized, not the importance of explicit, teacher-led instruction in the environment. Within the education community, constructivism has come to refer to the idea that people construct understanding of the world for themselves through mechanisms that build continuously from previous experiences stored in their individual intellectual "histories" (Maturana & Varela, 1992). The knowledge construction process is fueled by adaptation to the environment as an individual interacts with it, and because everyone's adaptations produce different histories, everyone's understanding is thus constructed and is different from everyone else's. Radical constructivists claim that because the world is not knowable in any objective way there is no objective reality for people to learn (Cunningham, 1992). Constructivism also has an anarchic dimension that renders it hostile to scientific inquiry, clear thinking, and rational action in education, or in any discipline (Dawkins, 1997; Sokal & Bricmont, 1998), but favorable to "politically correct" educational policies and actions that are not tested by science.

However, a less radical *constructionism* that emphasizes active interaction of the learner and the environment must be taken seriously (Harel & Papert, 1991). The goal remains the same—to help students construct understanding of the world but with guidance. As an intermediate step en route to constructing understanding, students now construct artifacts, which can be physical objects (Resnick 1996), computer programs (Papert, 1983), or computer models of natural processes (Barab et al., 2000). Physical objects and interactive computer programs exist in the external environment (not just as internal mental models), making it easier for students to experiment with external representations of ideas that are to be learned (i.e., represented internally). This argument can be extended to writing, which, by externalizing cognitions, makes it easier to reflect about those ideas and represent them more precisely in internal memory. According to Piaget (1970), who introduced "constructionism," cognition is not *pre*formed in the neurons of the newborn. The brain is not a passive organ that just waits for the correct environmental experiences to elicit its thinking and abilities. Rather, thinking develops as the neurons in the brain (the internal mental world) of the developing child interact with the external environment and *per*form. Initially, these interactions are with concrete objects in the external world (hence, the concrete operational stage of development). Eventually, the interactions are with internalized representations of those objects as abstract symbols (hence, the formal operational stage). Throughout development, new mental worlds in the inner environment are constructed as the child interacts with the external environment. Throughout development both biological (nature) and environmental (nurture) influences exert their effects. It is these nature–nurture interactions that are shortshrifted in contemporary educational theory, which influences thinking about writing development, writing instruction, and preparation of teachers for teaching writing.

Teachers cannot directly program students' brains, but explicit teacher modeling or cueing may affect the ease and quality of writing development. Research is needed to answer the following: Is occasional feedback from the teacher or peers (the teachable moment) in the writers' conference or author's chair sufficient, or does systematic, explicit instruction about the writing processes lead to higher writing achievement? Is meaning making sufficient, or are children most likely to construct meaningful written text for authentic communication goals if provided with systematic, explicit writing instruction? Explicit writing instruction should not be equated with rote drill (see Berninger et al., 2003) and may include the following: (1) *pairing stimuli close in time or space* (paired associate learning or fast mapping (which we use to teach alphabetic principle out of word context in the sound-to-letter[s] direction for spelling), (2) *teacher modeling* (which we use to teach transfer of automatic phoneme–spelling correspondences to spelling in word context), (3) *providing verbal and nonverbal cues and strategies* (which we use to teach self-regulated spelling during independent composing), (4) *teaching (1), (2), and (3) close in time* to overcome inefficiencies in temporally constrained verbal working memory (used in all our writing instruction; see Berninger & Abbott, 2003), and (5) explicit strategy instruction to develop self-regulation of the writer (Harris & Graham, 1996; Graham & Harris, 2003) using both computers (Graham & MacArthur, 1988) and pen(cil)s.

Integrating Three Perspectives in Creating Educational Evolution

Constructionism underlies the developmental neuropsychological perspective discussed first in this section. However, the sociocultural and learning sciences perspectives need to be integrated with that perspective and the traditional cognitive perspective (e.g., Alamargot & Chanquoy, 2001) to facilitate the kind of educational evolution that will prepare students best for 21st century literacy.

The Developmental Neuropsychological Perspective

NORMAL VARIATION

In any classroom, students exhibit considerable normal variation, which is individual differences due to biodiversity (Berninger & Richards, 2002). Although education is beginning to celebrate multicultural diversity (Banks & Banks, 1994, 1997, 1999), it has an enormous task ahead in developing constructive ways for both individuals and society to deal with genetically inherited predispositions *within* all cultural groups.

SYSTEMS APPROACH TO ASSESSMENT AND INSTRUCTION

Ongoing assessment of achievement is needed to make sure that these functional systems (sets of processes coordinated for a specific goal, such as writing) are developing in age-appropriate ways. When they are not, diagnostic assessment is needed to pinpoint which of the relevant processes in the learner's mind is interfering with normal development of a specific functional system; and those assessment findings should be translated into instructionally relevant intervention (Berninger, 2004b; Berninger, Dunn, & Alper, 2004). Instructional components should be packaged in real time in ways to maximize coordination of the components, so that the temporal limitations in working memory are overcome (e.g., by teaching all the components close in time in the same lesson; Berninger & Abbott, 2003; Berninger & Richards, 2002).

NATURE–NURTURE INTERACTIONS

Both genetic (e.g., Chapman et al., 2004) and brain influences (Berninger & Richards, 2002) constrain reading and spelling development, but the brain may normalize in response to explicit instructional interventions for reading (Aylward et al., 2003, 2004, Richards et al., 2000, 2002) and spelling (Richards, Aylward, et al., in press). Our functional magnetic resonance imaging (fMRI) evidence shows that good spellers are taught not born (Richards, Berninger, et al., 2005). The inner mental environment of the brain–mind and the external environment (where instructional cues are delivered) share bidirectional influences: The brain is a dependent as well as independent variable (Richards et al., 2000, 2002). The malleable brain responds to instruction.

OPTIMIZING THE LEARNING AND PERFORMANCE OF ALL STUDENTS

The idea that human intellect, learning, and behavior may be influenced to some degree by genes and brain has been taboo in most mainstream education and psychology for two and a half decades. Recently, some educational and cognitive psychologists are beginning to make a long-needed correction to this imbalance (Pinker, 2002; Winn, 2003a, 2003b). Pinker challenges a number of current popular beliefs about human nature, among them the idea that we are born with "blank slates" for minds, and presents a substantial body of scientific research that human nature is the result of not only environmental influence but also the interaction of the environment with dispositions inherited from our parents. Like Ryle (1949) before him, Pinker also challenges the myth of "the ghost in machine"—the idea that the mind is separate from and able to exist without the brain. To optimize the writing of all students, we need a multiconceptual triangulation that takes into account (1) learner differences (due to genetic and environmental influences), writing instruction, and instructional aids (Figure 7.1); (2) brain structures related to writing processes, computational mechanisms underlying writing processes, and observable writing behavior (Figure 7.2); and (3) all components of an internal functional writing system in the writer's brain (Figure 7.3).

The Sociocultural Perspective

Cognition develops through social interactions between adults and children, and develops optimally when instruction is aimed at the child's zone of proximal development—where there is cognitive challenge requiring an intellectual stretch but learning is within reach (Vygotsky, 1978). The teacher with a sociocultural orientation scaffolds (explicitly guides) the learning process (see Wong, 1998). Englert and colleagues (e.g., Englert, 1992; Englert, Raphael, Fear, & Anderson, 1988) introduced this important perspective to the field of writing and did not lose sight

of the important contribution of explicit teaching.

The Learning Sciences Perspective

VERBAL AND NONVERBAL SYMBOL SYSTEMS

Technology offers tools for teaching the nonverbal aspects of writing. Paivio's "dual coding" theory (Paivio, 1971; Clark & Paivio, 1991) proposed that humans possess both a verbal and a pictorial memory system, and that pictures are encoded in both systems, once as an iconic image and again as a verbal label, whereas words are encoded only once in the verbal system. Over 20 years of empirical evidence supports the dual coding of nonverbal information. However, the mechanisms that might account for how the visual and verbal systems interact to improve verbal learning or writing are not fully understood. Preliminary findings suggest that using graphic representations in problem solving involves fewer mental computations and places less demands on working memory (Winn, Li, & Schill, 1991).

EXTERNALIZING COGNITION IN LEARNING ENVIRONMENTS

Students write and draw to describe (or externalize or re-represent) their internal mental models (Scaife & Rogers, 1996). Once students can see their ideas expressed as objects before them, they can read and reread, think about them in novel ways, change them if necessary, and then reinternalize them as a mental model. The process is iterative as writers interact with their drawings and text. For example, software built for a course included a simple sketch tool that logged mouse movements (and other events) to replay in real time how a student drew a sketch—including false starts and changes not detectable in the final sketch alone (Tanimoto, Winn, & Akers, 2002). Results showed that once students' ideas became visible to them, they started experimenting with them in the external environment in ways they could not internally. In addition, when the temporal or spatial capabilities of internal working memory are exceeded, externalizing cognition through writing (language), or visual diagrams or pictures (nonverbal or combined verbal and nonverbal), may support internal working memory in a way that facilitates sustained problem solving until a goal is reached.

LEARNING BY INTERACTING WITH ENVIRONMENTS

The texts and sketches students produce when they externalize their thoughts change the learning environment, which now contains things that were not there before. These artifacts, which can be shared and discussed with others, are also part of the learning environment. Researchers in the learning sciences are becoming increasingly aware of the importance of the complete learning environment for understanding how students learn. Particularly important are the public actions students perform as they solve problems by externalizing their ideas. Recently, researchers have proposed two new ideas about the role of action and interaction with environments during learning (Barab, Evans, & Baeck, 2004; Jonassen, 2000; Leont'ev, 1978). The first idea is that cognition is not just a mental activity, but involves the mind interacting with the environment. The second idea is that if the bounds of cognition expand to include the body in an environment, then it is no longer possible to say with certainty whether an idea came from the environment, the student, or their interaction. To illustrate this point, Clark (1997, p. 163) invites us to imagine trying to catch a hamster with a pair of tongs. It is not possible to say whether the animal's attempts to evade capture cause us to wield the tongs as we do, or whether how we wield the tongs causes the animal's behavior. We are so tightly coupled to the environment that the idea of one action following or causing another is no longer tenable. As a result, the student and the learning environment comprise one single system rather than two interacting ones (Beer, 1995).

We propose that *the writing process is supported by a single system—the writer's internal brain–mind interacting with the external environment (including technology tools)*. Research with virtual reality technology, which uses head-mounted visual displays and a variety of gesture-based input devices to completely immerse students in environments created by a computer, illustrates this claim (Winn, 2003b). The student is tightly coupled to the environment by hardware that tracks the position and orientation of the head, hand, and sometimes other body parts, and uses the information to update instantaneously what the student sees, hears, and sometimes feels in the virtual world. The experience the student has is of being in a place rather than interacting with a computer. Virtual environments have proven effective and, in some cases, superior to desktop computer simulations when helping students learn in a variety of content domains (e.g., Barab et al., 2000; Dede, Salzman, Loftkin, & Ash, 1997; Hay et al., 2000; Winn, Windschitl, Fruland, & Lee, 2002). These mental worlds might be used effectively to support students' writing as writers access these mental worlds of their own construction. These mental worlds (virtual environments) are different from long-term memory stores. Students in virtual environments enjoy a heightened sense of "presence" (Witmer & Singer, 1998; Zeltzer, 1991), defined as the belief that one is actually in the virtual world rather than in the lab, or classroom with a helmet on one's head. Presence is positively correlated with enjoyment, engagement, and the amount students learn (Winn & Winschitl, 2001; Winn et al., 2002), and exhibits many of the properties Csikszentmihalyi (1990) has ascribed to the experience of "flow," which is complete engagement with a task such as writing. Kellogg (1994) described the self-reports of professional writers during "flow," when one loses sense of time and track of the external environment. This powerful affective experience, combined with the realism of experiences in virtual worlds, could well help students self-scaffold their own writing.

Implications for Writing Development and Instruction and Educational Evolution

Despite the predictable broad strokes of writing development (reviewed in Berninger & Abbott, 2001; Berninger & Richards, 2002), it is misleading to model a complex process such as writing on the basis of a simple comparison of novices and experts. The journey to skilled writing involves many small steps, false starts, plateaus, and regressions, along with some leaps forward and a few major developmental transitions along the way: The processes contributing to writing development cascade (overlap) and show developmental discontinuities. Contributing to these cascading and discontinuous processes are interactions among the internal structures and functions of the writer's brain, the external instruction, the external writing tools, and the external writing productions. Future research might address the interactions between internal working memory and external memory representations, rather than focusing exclusively on the inner workings of working memory. Instructional strategies can be designed that draw students' attention to both their internal mental environments and their external environments, with the latter used to scaffold the writing process. Instructional strategies should also emphasize the value of writing in externalizing cognition to overcome temporal and other limitations in internal working memory.

Grounding writing instruction on a greater understanding of nature–nurture interactions (a constructionist perspective) may also overcome the faulty premises of radical constructivism that underestimates the value and effectiveness of explicit instruction in writing. Improving teachers' knowledge of brain structures and functions involved in writing may increase their understanding of the complexity of the processes involved in learning to write. Improving teachers' understanding of normal variation (which is axiomatic in biology) may increase their tolerance of biological sources of diversity (individual differences in learners' brains) and willingness to individualize instruction. Vygotsky, who studied the role of social factors in cognitive development, encouraged his pupil Luria (1973) to pursue the biological factors in cognitive function. Future research on writing should acknowledge and investigate multiple sources of individual differences—biodiversity, as well as multicultural–social diversity. Currently there is a preoccupation with high-stakes standards and a mind-set that one benchmark will work for the population as a whole. This mind-set is at odds with what we know about biodiversity of the student body and the needs of society (see Chapter 12, Berninger & Richards, 2002). Students are poor writers for many different reasons. The rapid expansion of knowledge of brain processes in writing is leading to new approaches to brain-based, clinical assessment of writing

(Berninger, 2004b; Berninger et al., 2004). If educators are to optimize the achievement of all students, then we need a research-supported approach to assessment that meets the following criteria: (1) takes into account both developmental and individual differences; (2) generates individual profiles, with the strengths and weaknesses of every student; and (3) links evidence-based assessment findings with evidence-based effective intervention (Berninger et al., 2004). However, effective instruction will depend on the social context (sociocultural perspective) and the interactions between the internal and external enviornment (learning sciences perspective), as well as the writer's brain.

Conclusion

Advances in technology have led to a knowledge explosion about the brain and to rapid developments in the tools available to use in teaching writing. These technology-induced transformations will increasingly affect how educators do research and how education is practiced, especially in regard to writing. Those who train future teachers in the teaching of writing cannot ignore forever the biological influences on individual students who are learning to write, or the importance of explicit teaching in writing instruction.

Addresses and Acknowledgements

Preparation of this chapter was supported by Grant Nos. HD25858 and P50 33812 from the National Institute of Child Health and Human Development to Virginia W. Berninger and Grant Nos. REC-9873620 from the National Science Foundation and N00014-02-1-0502 from the Office of Naval Research to William D. Winn. The chapter reflects ongoing conversations and research collaboration between Berninger, who specializes in educational applications of developmental neuropsychology and cognitive neuroscience, and Winn, who specializes in educational applications of computer technology and virtual reality.

References

Alamargot, D., & Chanquoy, L. (2001). *Through the models of writing*. Dordrecht, The Netherlands: Kluwer.

Anderson, S., Damasio, A., & Damasio, H. (1990).

Troubled letters but not numbers: Domain specific cognitive impairments following focal damage in frontal cortex. *Brain, 113*, 749–760.

Aylward, E., Raskind, W., Richards, T., Berninger, V., & Eden, E. (2004, February). *Genetic, neurological, and instructional influences in the reading brain.* Symposium presented at the meeting of the American Association for the Advancement of Science, Seattle, WA.

Aylward, E., Richards, T., Berninger, V., Nagy, W., Field, K., Grimme, A., et al. (2003). Instructional treatment associated with changes in brain activation in children with dyslexia. *Neurology, 61,* 212–219.

Aylward, E., Richards, T., Berninger, V., Perrin, M., Field, K., Amie, B., et al. (2002). *Reliability of functional MRI activation over time.* Unpublished manuscript, University of Washington, Seattle.

Baby Einstein Company (2002). *Baby Shakespeare.* Lone Tree, CO: Author. (copyrighted Buena Vista Home Entertainment, Inc. at www.babyeinstein.com)

Banks, J., & Banks, C. (1994). *Cultural diversity and education: Foundations, curriculum, and teaching* (4th ed.). Boston: Allyn & Bacon.

Banks, J., & Banks, C. (1997). *Teaching strategies for ethnic studies* (6th ed.). Boston: Allyn & Bacon.

Banks, J., & Banks, C. (1999). *An introduction to multicultural education* (2nd ed.). Boston: Allyn & Bacon.

Barab, S., Evans, M. A., & Baek, E.-O. (2004). Activity theory. In D. Jonassen (Ed.), *Handbook of research on educational communication and technology* (2nd ed., pp. 199–214). Mahwah, NJ: Erlbaum.

Barab, S., Hay, K. E., Squire, K., Barnett, M., Schmidt, R., Karrigan, K., et al. (2000). The virtual solar system: Learning through a technology-rich, inquiry-based, participatory learning environment. *Journal of Science Education and Technology, 9*(1), 7–25.

Basso, A., Taborelli, A., & Vignolo, L. (1978). Dissociated disorders of speaking and writing in aphasia. *Journal of Neurology, Neurosurgery, and Psychiatry, 41,* 556–563.

Beer, R. D. (1995). Computation and dynamical languages for autonomous agents. In R. F. Port & T. Van Gelder (Eds.), *Mind as motion: Explorations in the dynamics of cognition* (pp. 121–147). Cambridge MA: MIT Press.

Berninger, V. (1999). Coordinating transcription and text generation in working memory during composing: Automatized and constructive processes. *Learning Disability Quarterly, 22,* 99–112.

Berninger, V. (2000). Development of language by hand and its connections to language by ear, mouth, and eye. *Topics in Language Disorders, 20,* 65–84.

Berninger, V. (2004a). The reading brain in children and youth: A systems approach. In B. Wong (Ed.), *Learning about learning disabilities* (3rd ed., pp. 90–119). San Diego: Academic Press.

Berninger, V. (2004b). Understanding the graphia in dysgraphia. In D. Dewey & D. Tupper (Eds.), *Developmental motor disorders: A neuropsychological perspective.* pp. 328–350 New York: Guilford Press.

Berninger, V., & Abbott, R. (2001). Developmental and individual variability in reading and writing acquisition: A developmental neuropsychological perspective. In D. Molfese & U. Kirk (Eds.), *Developmental variability in language and learning* (pp. 275–308). Hillsdale, NJ: Erlbaum.

Berninger, V., & Abbott, S. (2003). *PAL research-supported reading and writing lessons.* San Antonio, TX: Psychological Corporation.

Berninger, V., Abbott, R., Billingsley, F., & Nagy, W. (2001). Processes underlying timing and fluency: Efficiency, automaticity, coordination, and morphological awareness. In M. Wolf (Ed.), *Dyslexia, fluency, and the brain* (pp. 383–414). Extraordinary Brain Series. Baltimore: York Press.

Berninger, V., Abbott, R., Jones, J., Gould, L., Anderson-Youngstrom, M., Wolf, B., et al. (in press). Early development of language by hand: Composing, reading, listening, and speaking connections, three letter writing modes, and fast mapping in spelling. *Developmental Neuropsychology.*

Berninger, V., & Amtmann, D. (2003). Preventing written expression disabilities through early and continuing assessment and intervention for handwriting and/or spelling problems: Research into practice. In H. L. Swanson, K. R. Harris, & S. Graham (Eds.), *Handbook of learning disabilities* (pp. 345–363). New York: Guilford Press.

Berninger, V. , Dunn, A., & Alper, T. (2004). Integrated models of assessment for branching, instructional, and profile assessment. In A. Prifitera, D. Saklofske, L. Weiss, & E. Rolfhus (Eds.), *WISC-IV Clinical use and interpretation* (pp. 151–185). San Diego: Academic Press.

Berninger, V., & Hooper, S. (in press). A developmental neuropsychological perspective on writing disabilities in children and youth. In D. Molfese & V. Molfese (Eds.), *Handbook of child neuropsychology.* Mahwah, NJ: Erlbaum.

Berninger, V., Nagy, W., Carlisle, J., Thomson, J., Hoffer, D., Abbott, S., et al. (2003). Effective treatment for dyslexics in grades 4 to 6. In B. Foorman (Ed.), *Preventing and Remediating Reading Difficulties: Bringing Science to Scale* (pp. 382–417). Timonium, MD: York Press.

Berninger, V., & Richards, T. (2002). *Brain literacy for educators and psychologists.* New York: Academic Press.

Brain, L. (1967). *Speech disorders: Aphasia, apraxia, and agnosia.* London: Butterworth.

Chapman, N., Igo, R., Thomson, J., Matsushita, M., Brkanac, Z., Hotzman, T., et al. (2004). Linkage analyses of four regions previously implicated in dyslexia: Confirmation of a locus on chromosome 15q. *American Journal of Medical Genetics/Neuropsychiatric Genetics, 131B,* 67–75, and *American Journal of Medical Genetics* (Suppl. 03174) 9999:1.

Clark, A. (1997). *Being there: Putting brain, body and world together again.* Cambridge, MA: MIT Press.

Clark, J. M., & Paivio, A. (1991). Dual coding theory and education. *Educational Psychology Review, 3,* 149–210.

Clay, M. (1982). Research update: Learning and teaching writing: A developmental perspective. *Language Arts, 59,* 65–70.

Cohen, L., Lehéricy, S., Chhochon, F., Lemer, C., Rivaud, S., & Dehaene, S. (2002). Language-specific tuning of visual cortex?: Functional properties of the Visual Word Form area. *Brain, 125,* 1054–1069.

Cordes, D., Haughton, V., Arfanakis, K., Wendt, G., Turski, P., Moritz, C., et al. (2000). Mapping functionally related regions of brain with functional connectivity MRI (fcMRI). *American Journal of Neuroradiology, 21,* 1636–1644.

Corina, D., Richards, T., Serafini, S., Richards, A., Steury, K., Abbott, R., et al. (2001). fMRI auditory language differences between dyslexic and able reading children. *NeuroReport, 12,* 1195–1201.

Crosson, B., Rao, S., Woodley, S., Rosen, A., Bobholz, J., Mayer, A., et al. (1999). Mapping of semantic, phonological, and orthographic verbal working memory in normal adults with functional magnetic resonance imaging. *Neuropsychology, 13,* 171–187.

Csikszentmihalyi, M. (1990). *Flow: The psychology of optimal performance.* New York: Harper & Row.

Cunningham, D. (1992). Assessing constructions and constructing assessments: A dialog. In T. M. Duffy & D. H. Jonassen (Eds.), *Constructivism and the technology of instruction: A conversation* (pp. 35–44). Hillsdale NJ: Erlbaum.

Dawkins, R. (1997). *Unweaving the rainbow: Science, delusion and the appetite for wonder.* Boston: Houghton Mifflin.

Dede, C., Salzman, M., Loftin, R. B., & Ash, K. (1997). Using virtual reality technology to convey abstract scientific concepts. In M. J. Jacobson & R. B. Kozma (Eds.), *Learning the sciences of the 21st century: research, design and implementing advanced technology learning environments* (pp. 361–413). Mahwah, NJ: Erlbaum.

Dehaene, S., Le Clec'H, G., Poline, J.-B., Bihan, D., & Cohen, L. (2002). The visual word form area: A prelexical representation of visual words in the fusiform gyrus. *Brain Imaging, 13,* 321–325.

Dhond, R., Buckner, R., Dale, A., Marinkovic, K., & Halgren, E. (2001). Spatiotemporal maps of brain activity underlying word generation and their modification during repetition priming. *Journal of Neuroscience, 21,* 3564–3571.

Englert, C. S. (1992). Writing instruction from a sociocultural perspective: The holistic, dialogue, and social enterprise of writing. *Journal of Learning Disabilities, 25,* 153–172.

Englert, S., Raphael, T., Fear, K., & Anderson, L. (1988). Students' metacognitive knowledge about how to write informational tests. *Learning Disability Quarterly, 11,* 18–46.

Exner, S. (1881). *Untersuchungen über die Lokalisation der Funktionen in der Grossshirnrinde des Menschen.* Vienna: Wilhelm Braumuller.

Fuster, J. (1997). *The prefrontal cortex: Anatomy, physiology, and neuropsychology of the frontal lobe* (3rd ed.). New York: Raven Press.

Garrett, A., Flowers, D. L., Absher, J., Fahey, R., Gage, H., Keyes, J., et al. (2000). Cortical activity related to accuracy of letter recognition. *NeuroImage, 11,* 111–123.

Goldfine, R. (2001). Making word processing more effective in the composition classroom. *Teaching English in the Two-Year College, 28,* 307–315.

Goldman-Rakic, P., Scalaidhe, S., & Chafee, M. (2000). Domain specificity in cognitive systems. In M. S. Gazzaniga (Ed.), *The new cognitive Neurosciences* (pp. 733–742). Cambridge, MA: MIT Press.

Graham, S., & Harris, K. R. (2003). Students with learning disabilities and the process of writing: A meta-analysis of SRSD studies. In H. L. Swanson, K. R. Harris, & S. Graham (Eds.), *Handbook of learning disabilities* (pp. 323–344). New York: Guilford Press.

Graham, S., & MacArthur, C. (1988). Improving learning disabled students' skills at revising essays produced on a word processor: Self-instructional strategy training. *Journal of Special Education, 22,* 133–152.

Graham, S., & Weintraub, N. (1996). A review of handwriting research: Progress and prospects from 1980 to 1994. *Educational Psychology Review, 8,* 7–87.

Graves, D. (1983). *Writing: Teachers and children at work.* Exeter, NH: Heinemann.

Harel, I., & Papert, S. (1991). *Constructionism.* Norwood, NJ: Ablex.

Harris, K., & Graham, S. (1996). *Making the writing process work: Strategies for composition and self-regulation.* Cambridge, MA: Brookline.

Hay, K. E., Crozier, J., Barnett, M., Allison, D., Bashaw, M., Hoos, B., & Perkins, L. (2000,

April). Virtual gorilla modeling project: Middle school students constructing virtual models for learning. In B. Fishman & S. O'Connor-DivelBliss (Eds.) *Proceedings of the Fourth International Conference on the Learning Sciences* (pp. 212–213). Mahwah, NJ: Erlbaum.

Hillocks, G. (1986). *Research on written composition: New directions for teaching.* Urbana, IL: National Conference on Research in English.

Hlynka, D. (2004). Postmodernism in educational technology: Update: 1996–present. In D. Jonassen (Ed.), *Handbook of research on educational communication and technology* (2nd ed., pp. 243–246). Mahwah, NJ: Erlbaum.

Holland, S., Plante, E., Byars, A., Strawsburg, R., Schmithorst, V., & Ball, W. (2001). Normal fMRI brain activation patterns in children performing a verb generation task. *NeuroImage, 14,* 837–843.

Jonassen, D. H. (2000). Revising activity theory as a framework for designing student-centered learning environments. In D. Jonassen & S. Land (Eds.), *Theoretical foundations of learning environments* (pp. 89–122) Mahwah, NJ: Erlbaum.

Katanoda, K., Yashikawa, K., & Sugishita, M. (2001). A functional MRI study on the neural substrates for writing. *Human Brain Mapping, 13,* 34–42.

Kellogg, R. (1994). *The psychology of writing.* New York: Oxford University Press.

Kircher, T., Brammer, M., Andreu, N., Williams, S., & McGuire, P. (2001). Engagement of right temporal cortex during processing of linguistic context. *Neuropsychologia, 39,* 798–809.

Liberman, A. (1999). The reading researcher and the reading teacher need the right theory of speech. *Scientific Studies of Reading, 3,* 95–111.

Leont'ev, A. N. (1978). *Activity, consciousness and personality.* Englewood Cliffs, NJ: Prentice-Hall.

Luria, A. R. (1973). *The working brain.* New York: Basic Books.

Matsuo, K., Kato, C., Ozawa, F., Takehara, Y., Isoda, H., Isogai, S., et al. (2001). Ideographic characters call for extra processing to correspond with phonemes. *NeuroReport, 12,* 2227–2230.

Matsuo, K., Kato, C., Tanaka, S., Sugio, T., Matsuzawa, M., Inui, T., et al. (2001). Visual language and handwriting movement: Functional magnetic resonance imaging at 3 tesla during generation of ideographic characters. *Brain Research Bulletin, 55,* 549–554

Maturana, H., & Varela, F. (1992). *The tree of knowledge: The biological roots of human understanding* (rev. ed.). Boston: Shambhala.

Mazziotta, J., Grafton, S., & Woods, R. (1991). The human motor system studied with PET measurements of cerebral blood flow: Topography and motor learning. In N. Lassen, D. Ingvar, M. Raichle, & L. Friberg (Eds.), *Brain work and mental activity: Alfred Benzon Symposium, 31,* 280–290.

McCutchen, D. (1996). A capacity theory of writing: Working memory in composition. *Educational Psychology Review, 8,* 299–325.

McGee, T., & Ericsson, P. (2002). The politics of the program: MS WORD as the invisible grammarian. *Computers and Composition, 19,* 453–470.

Menon, V., & Desmond, J. (2001). Left superior parietal cortex involvement in writing: Integrating fMRI with lesion evidence. *Cognitive Brain Research, 12,* 337–340.

Mesulam, M. (1990). Large-scale neurocognitive networks and distributed processing for attention, language, and memory. *Annals of Neurology, 28,* 597–613.

Nagy, W., Osborn, J., Winsor, P., & O'Flahavan, J. (1994). Structural analysis: Some guidelines for instruction. In F. Lehr, & J. Osburn (Eds.), *Reading, language, and literacy* (pp. 45–58). Hillsdale, NJ: Erlbaum.

Ojemann, J., Buckner, R., Akbudak, E., Snyder, A., Olinger, J., McKinstry, R., et al. (1998). Functional MRI studies of word-stem completion: Reliablity across laboratories and comparison to blood flow imaging with PET. *Human Brain Mapping, 6,* 203–215.

Olson, D. (1985). Computers as tools of the intellect. *Educational Researcher,* 14(5), 5–8.

Olson, D. (1991). Literacy and objectivity: The rise of modern science. In D. Olson & N. Torrance (Eds.), *Literacy and orality* (pp. 149–164). New York: Cambridge University Press.

Ong, W. (1982). *Orality and literacy: The technologizing of the word.* London: Methuen.

Papert, S. (1983). *Mindstorm: Children, computers and powerful ideas.* New York: Basic Books.

Paivio, A. (1971). *Imagery and verbal processes.* New York: Holt, Rinehart & Winston.

Piaget, J. (1970). Piaget's theory. In P. H. Mussen (Ed.), *Carmichael's manual of child psychology* (Vol. 1, 3rd ed., pp. 703–732). New York: Wiley.

Pinker, S. (2002). *The blank slate: The modern denial of human nature.* New York: Viking.

Poldrack, R., Temple, E., Protopapas, A., Nagarajan, S., Tallal, P., Merzenich, M., et al. (2001). Relations between the neural bases of dynamic auditory processing and phonological processing: Evidence from fMRI. *Journal of Cognitive Neuroscience, 13,* 687–697.

Polk, T., Stallup, M., Aguirre, G., Alsop, D., Esposito, M., Detre, J., et al. (2002). Neural specialization for letter recognition. *Journal of Cognitive Neuroscience, 14,* 145–159.

Pugh, K., Mencl, W., Shaywitz, B., Shaywitz, S., Fullbright, R., Constable, R., et al. (2000). The angular gyrus in developmental dyslexia: Task-specific differences in functional connectivity within posterior cortex. *Psychological Science, 11*, 51–56.

Read, C. (1981). Writing is not the inverse of reading for young children. In C. Frederickson & J. Domminick (Eds.), *Writing: The nature, development, and teaching of written communication* (Vol. 2, pp. 105–117). Hillsdale, NJ: Erlbaum.

Resnick, M. (1996). Beyond the centralized mindset. *Journal of the Learning Sciences, 5*, 1–22.

Richards, T., Aylward, E., Raskind, W., Abbott, R., Field, K., Parsons, A., et al. (in press). Converging evidence for triple word form theory in child dyslexics. *Developmental Neuropsychology.*

Richards, T., Berninger, V., Nagy, W., Parsons, A., Field, K., & Richards, A. (2005). Brain activation during language task contrasts in children with and without dyslexia: Inferring mapping processes and assessing response to spelling instruction. *Educational and Child Psychology, 22*(2), 62–80.

Richards, T., Berninger, V., Aylward, E., Richards, A., Thomson, J., Nagy, W., et al. (2002). Reproducibility of proton MR spectroscopic imaging: Comparison of dyslexic and normal reading children and effects of treatment on brain lactate levels during language tasks. *American Journal of Neuroradiology. 23*, 1678–1685.

Richards, T., Corina, D., Serafini, S., Steury, K., Dager, S., Marro, K., et al. (2000). Effects of phonologically-driven treatment for dyslexia on lactate levels as measured by proton MRSI. *American Journal of Radiology, 21*, 916–922.

Roberts, T., Disbrow, E., Roberts, H., & Rowley, H. (2000). Quantification and reproducibility of tracking cortical extent of activation by use of functional MR imaging and magnetoencephalography. *American Journal of Neuroradiology, 21*, 1377–1387.

Ryle, G. (1949). *The concept of mind*. London: Hutchinson.

Sakai, K., Hikosaka, O., Miyauchi, S., Takino, R., Sasaki, Y., & Putz, B. (1998). Transition of brain activations from frontal to parietal areas in visuomotor sequence learning. *Journal of Neuroscience, 18*, 1827–1840.

Salomon, G. (1988). Artifical intelligence in reverse: Computer tools that become cognitive. *Journal of Educational Computing Research, 4*, 123–140.

Scaife, M., & Rogers, Y. (1996). External cognition: How do graphical representations work? *International Journal of Human–Computer Studies, 45*, 185–213.

Seitz, R., Canavan, A., Yaguez, L., Herzog, H., Tellman, L., Knorr, U., et al. (1997). Representations of graphomotor trajectories in the human parietal cortex: Evidence for controlled processing and automatic performance. *European Journal of Neuroscience, 9*, 378–389.

Sokal, A., & Bricmont, J. (1998). *Fashionable nonsense: Postmodern intellectuals' abuse of science.* New York: Picador.

Swanson, H. L., & Berninger, V. (1996). Individual differences in children's working memory and writing skills. *Journal of Experimental Child Psychology, 63*, 358–385.

Tanimoto, S., Winn, W.D., & Akers, D. (2002). A system that supports using student-drawn diagrams to assess comprehension of mathematical formulas. *Lecture Notes in Computer Science 2317*, 100–102.

Tegeler, C., Strother, S., Anderson, J., & Kim, S.-G. (1999). Reproducibility of BOLD-based functional MRI obtained at 4 T. *Human Brain Mapping, 7*, 267–283.

Towse, J. (1998). On random generation and the central executive of working memory. *British Journal of Psychology, 89*, 77–101.

Tufte, E. (2003) *The cognitive style of PowerPoint.* Cheshire, CT: Graphics Press.

Van Mier, H., Temple, L., Perlmutter, J., Raichle, M., & Petersen, S. (1998). Changes in brain activity during motor learning measured with PET: Effects of hand performance and practice. *Journal of Neurophysiology, 80*, 2177–2199.

Von Glasersfeld, E. (1984). An introduction to radical constructivism. In P. Watzlawick (Ed.), *The invented reality*. New York: Norton. (Originally published in P. Watzlawick (Ed.), *Die Erfundene Wirklichkeit*. Munich: Piper [Author's translation]. Also available at www.umass.edu/srri/vonglasersfeld/onlinepapers/

Vygotsky, L. (1978). *Mind and society*. Cambridge, MA: Harvard University Press.

Wagner, Q., Paré-Blagoev, E. J., Clark, J., & Poldrack, R. (2001). Recovering meaning: Left prefrontal cortex guides controlled semantic retrieval. *Neuron, 31*, 329–338.

Winn, W. D. (2003a). Beyond constructivism: A return to science based research and practice in educational technology. *Educational Technology, 43*(6), 5–14.

Winn, W. D. (2003b). Learning in artificial environments: Embodiment, embeddedness and dynamic adaptation. *Technology, Instruction, Cognition and Learning, 1*, 87–114.

Winn, W. D., Li, T.-Z., & Schill, D. E. (1991). Diagrams as aids to problem solving: Their role in facilitating search and computation. *Educational Technology Research and Development, 39*, 17–29.

Winn, W. D., & Windschitl, M. (2001). Learning in artificial environments. *Cybernetics and Human Knowing, 8*(3), 5–23.

Winn, W. D., Windschitl, M., Fruland, R., & Lee, Y. L. (2002). When does immersion in a virtual environment help students construct understanding? In P. Bell, R. Stevens, & T. Satwitz (Eds.), *Keeping learning complex: The proceedings of the fifth International Conference of the Learning Sciences (ICLS)*. Mawah, NJ: Erlbaum.

Witmer, B. G., & Singer, M. J. (1998). Measuring presence in virtual environments: A presence questionnaire. *Presence: Teleoperators and Virtual Environments, 7,* 225–240.

Wong, B. Y. L. (1998). Analyses of instrinsic and extrinsic problems in use of the scaffolding metaphor in learning disabilities intervention research: An introduction. *Journal of Learning Disabilities, 31,* 340–343.

Wood, A., Saling, M., Abbott, D., & Jackson, G. (2001). A neurocognitive account of frontal lobe involvement in orthographic lexical retrieval: An fMRI study. *NeuroImage, 14,* 162–169.

Yeaman, A., Hlynka, D., Anderson, J.H., Damarin, S., & Muffoletto, R. (1996). Postmodern and poststructural theory. In D. Jonassen (Ed.), *Handbook of research on educational communication and technology* (pp. 253–295). Mahwah, NJ: Erlbaum.

Zellermayer, M., Salomon, G., Globerson, T., & Givon, H. (1991). Enhancing writing-related cognitions through a computerized writing partner. *American Educational Research Journal, 28,* 373–391.

Zeltzer, D. (1991). Autonomy, interaction and presence. *Presence: Teleoperators and Virtual Environments, 1,* 127–132.

Chapter 8

Cognitive Factors in the Development of Children's Writing

Deborah McCutchen

As a communicative act, writing is undeniably a social event between the writer and audience. In addition, writing is also a cognitive act, one often accomplished by an individual writer whose audience is only as immediately present as the writer's imagination, knowledge, and experiences allow. As a cognitive psychologist, my perspectives on the development of writing are grounded in the cognitive paradigm; however, the research on children's writing extends far beyond that single paradigm (see the other chapters in this volume). In this chapter, I review empirical research on the cognitive processes involved in the development of children's writing, together with some discussion of the social and instructional contexts that may support or thwart the development of sophisticated writing processes.

Seminal Models of Writing Processes

The field's growing recognition of the importance of the broader contexts of writing is reflected in Hayes's (1996) revision of the seminal model of composing that he and Flower proposed over 25 years ago (Hayes & Flower, 1980). In his revised model, Hayes (1996) supplemented descriptions of cognitive processes with broader discussions of context, motivation, affect, and memory.

The three major cognitive processes described originally by Hayes and Flower (1980)—planning, translating, and reviewing—were retained in the 1996 model but were substantially reconceptualized. Planning was subsumed under the broader label *reflection*, which encompasses problem solving (including planning), decision making, and inferencing. Translating was retitled *text production* and has been elaborated considerably by Chenoweth and Hayes (2001). The original reviewing process has been expanded to include *text interpretation*, as well as embedded reflection and text production, all under the control of a revision-specific task schema (see also Hayes, 2004). These elaborated cognitive processes are attributed to the individual, as are affective components (e.g., goals, predispositions, beliefs), and knowledge from the writer's long-term memory (e.g., knowledge of topic, genre, audience) and working memory.

External to the individual, according to Hayes (1996), is the task environment, comprising both the social and physical environment. The social environment includes the audience, collaborators, and I suggest, in the case of student writers, the instructional context. The physical environment includes the developing text and the composing medium.

The revised model proposed by Hayes (1996) remains designed to account for expert writing. Children's writing processes do not typically reflect all the components of expert performance, and influential in the study of children's writing has been an alternative model offered by Bereiter and Scardamalia (1987). Rather than modeling children's writing as a deficient version of expert writing, Bereiter and Scardamalia proposed an alternative model to explain how writing might be accomplished (by children or adults) without many of the sophisticated strategies described by Hayes. Bereiter and Scardamalia characterized such writing as "knowledge telling." To generate text, writers probe memory with a cue derived either from the writing assignment's topic (e.g., "Something I know about football is . . .") or genre (e.g., "Once upon a time . . ."), and as related knowledge is scanned in the memory network, content for the text is retrieved.

Although knowledge telling is frequently cited as a model of children's writing, Bereiter and Scardamalia (1987) argued that knowledge telling cannot necessarily be distinguished from more strategic processes on the basis of text quality alone. Skilled writers, they argued, may engage in knowledge telling and still produce a quality text (e.g., when writing about familiar material in a well-rehearsed context; see Torrance, 1996), and experts and novices alike may struggle with a writing task, with the result sometimes being an ill-structured text.

I have previously characterized knowledge telling as a potentially adaptive response to the heavy processing demands that writing can impose on novice writers (McCutchen, 2000), and I make a similar argument in the following pages. However, Goldman (1995), among others, has argued that knowledge telling is an equally adaptive response to the instructional and social contexts in which children frequently find themselves. In many classrooms, children often write to an audience of one—the teacher—on a topic defined by the teacher, for a reason specified by the teacher. In such situations, children have few opportunities to develop their own goals and little invitation to do anything other than report their existing knowledge. When put in similar situations, expert writers often balk (Freedman, 1984). In more supportive and authentic situations, children can display more sophisticated skills (Cameron & Moshenko, 1996; Cameron, Hunt, & Linton,

1996; Graves, 1983; Scardamalia, Bereiter, & Lamon, 1994).

Planning and Other Reflective Processes

Planning figured prominently in early versions of the Hayes and Flower model (1980; Flower & Hayes, 1981, 1984). According to Hayes and Flower (1980), planning entails setting goals, generating content, and organizing that content in terms of the developing text. Plans can be general or more local, and they can be made prior to writing or evolve during writing (Galbraith, 1996; Gould, 1980). Planning is downplayed considerably in Hayes's (1996) model; in fact, after a review of planning research, Hayes and Nash (1996) concluded that planning is not the sine qua non of writing expertise, as had sometimes been suggested. Although it is true that skilled writers generally spend more time planning than less-skilled writers (Bereiter & Scardamalia, 1987; Flower & Hayes, 1981), skilled writers also spend more time generating and revising their texts. Thus, Hayes and Nash (1996) argued, it is not the *proportion* of writing time spent planning that distinguishes experts from novices, but overall time on task. Planning is simply one thing, among many, that experts do more than novices.

Clearly, all writers, including children, engage in some planning. A key difference between most children and experts is the nature of their planning, specifically, whether planning is devoted to generating content or to developing other sorts of goals. Expert writers can be quite articulate about the various aspects of their planning. Experts formulate goals for their texts (e.g., to reach a given audience, to present a particular persona) and then develop plans to achieve those goals (e.g., to adopt a particular genre or rhetorical stance, to include or avoid specific vocabulary). Consider, for example, the protocol of a professional sports writer as he prepared his responses to readers' letters for his weekly newspaper column (in McCutchen, 1988):

I try to read them [the readers' letters] and react to them in a way that is entertaining. And I will not be deadly serious about it unless I feel that it is demanded by the subject matter. . . . And I try to avoid being jargonistic or requiring expertise for a reader to understand the answers, because I believe that this is a pretty good way to bring a lot of nontraditional sports readers into the section. So I don't want to alienate them by writing in a way which requires them to know—presupposes that they know a lot of things. (p. 309)

After articulating his plan (which involved audience and tone, as well as rhetorical purpose), the writer then used it to regulate his writing, including his choice of specific words much later in the writing session.

Young children's protocols, in contrast, typically reveal little explicit conceptual planning, especially in advance of writing. Analyses of prewriting pauses reveal that children often begin writing within a minute of receiving a writing task, and they are often incredulous when told that some writers spend 15 minutes or more before they write (Bereiter & Scardamalia, 1987). In a study with sixth-grade writers, Cameron and Moshenko (1996) reported that, on average, students spent slightly over 2 minutes planning before beginning to write. However, students' prewriting planning was quite variable, with the standard deviation exceeding a minute and a half.

Whereas expert writers take a writing assignment and develop a plan to make it their own (e.g., Flower & Hayes, 1980; Freedman, 1984), children frequently seem to use the assignment itself as a plan—a plan focused largely on retrieving relevant content from memory. The protocols produced by young writers frequently consist of children saying aloud the words as they write (Bereiter & Scardamalia, 1987; McCutchen, 1988). The question is always, however, whether children are not able to plan or are simply not able to articulate their plans as well as expert writers. Indeed, when the contexts are meaningful, even young children show signs of planning for a specific audience as they adapt the (sometimes oral) texts they produce for audiences who are physically present or absent (Cameron & Wang, 1999; Littleton, 1998), or who vary in age or setting (Lee, Karmiloff-Smith, Cameron, & Dodsworth, 1998).

Typically, however, protocols produced by children as they write often are dominated by content generation. Still, amid the content

generation we can sometimes see glimpses of emerging online attention to audience and text coherence, as in the following excerpt from the protocol of a 10-year-old spontaneously editing her developing text about roller skating (in McCutchen, 1988):

Hold it, no, "*the* wheels." I'm going to put "*the* wheels," not just "wheels" 'cause they won't know where the wheels—well, "*the* wheels." (p. 315; emphasis in original)

Although not as articulate as the sports columnist, this young writer was clearly thinking about her audience, wondering whether "they," her readers, would know which wheels she was describing. Unlike the sports editor, this young writer's plans for an audience were not separate goals that she set in advance and worked toward; rather, issues of audience surfaced momentarily as she wrestled with content. Bereiter and Scardamalia (1987) analyzed protocols from children at age 10, 12, 16, and 18, and reported that approximately 90% of the statements produced by the two youngest groups involved either (1) generation of content or (2) explicit dictation or rereading. Content generation was the predominant form of planning across all the age groups (see also Langer, 1986), and even for the oldest age group, content generation comprised nearly half of the protocols (Bereiter & Scardamalia, 1987). With increasing age, children tend to plan more in advance of writing and include more conceptual (i.e., noncontent) planning into their writing activity, and both variables have been linked to the sophistication of the main point in the resulting text (Bereiter, Burtis, & Scardamalia, 1988).

Even when explicitly asked to plan in advance, young children often have difficulty separating planning from writing (but see Cameron & Moshenko, 1996). When asked to make notes in advance of writing, the 10-year-olds described by Bereiter and Scardamalia (1987) typically wrote what amounted to a first draft of the composition itself, whereas older children (ages 12 and 14) produced ideas that they later expanded into text. Comparisons between the children's "notes" and "texts" indicated that one third of the notes generated by the 10-year-olds received only minor changes as they were turned into text. In contrast, 12-

and 14-year-old children made substantial changes to virtually all their notes. Similar developmental differences in planning were reported by Langer (1986). In addition, when evaluating paraphrases of main points taken from their texts, older children were far more likely than younger children to refer to their original intentions, that is, to their plans (Bereiter et al., 1988).

The children observed by Bereiter and Scardamalia (1987) had difficulty not only with planning beyond content, but also with distinguishing the planning activities of others. After viewing a videotape of a writer planning aloud, adults were able to identify distinct planning concerns (e.g., general goals, audience, content, organization), but children were far less successful in making distinctions (Bereiter & Scardamalia, 1987). Furthermore, the developmental trend in distinguishing planning activities mirrored the developmental trend in children's own ability to plan: Ten-year-olds correctly identified far fewer of the planning activities than did 12- and 14-year-olds. Thus, young children's planning is dominated by content generation, and planning and text generation are tightly intertwined. Around age 12, children may begin to distinguish between plans and text; however, their plans are still dominated by content generation. Conceptual planning remains relatively rare, even in late adolescence; and instructional attempts to improve children's texts by increasing their conceptual planning often meet with limited success (e.g., Bereiter & Scardamalia, 1987) unless accompanied by considerable instructional support (e.g., Cameron & Moshenko, 1996; De La Paz & Graham, 2002; Page-Voth & Graham, 1999).

Text Production

Chenoweth and Hayes (2001) elaborated the translating component described originally by Hayes and Flower (1980; Kaufer, Hayes, & Flower, 1986), proposing a detailed model of written language production in which a task schema directs cognitive processes. Those cognitive processes generate prelinguistic ideas, translate those ideas into language (often with considerable revision), and transcribe the language into written form. Other writing researchers have made similar distinctions between text generation and transcription (Berninger & Swanson, 1994). It is assumed that text generation shares many cognitive components with oral language generation, such as content selection, lexical retrieval, syntactic formulation, and so on (e.g., de Beaugrande, 1984; McCutchen, Covill, Hoyne, & Mildes, 1994). Transcription, in contrast, entails the cognitive and physical acts of forming written (as opposed to spoken) representations of text.

Although component processes can be distinguished conceptually, protocols of skilled writers indicate there is often considerable interplay among text production processes. Prelinguistic ideas may be abandoned when appropriate language is difficult to generate (McCutchen, 1988), and new ideas may be prompted by the act of generating text (Galbraith, 1996). Even skilled writers make frequent revisions in word choice and grammatical structure in the course of translating ideas into language (Chenoweth & Hayes, 2001; Kaufer et al., 1986; McCutchen, 1988). In addition, text production draws on resources from long-term memory and working memory. Children's text production is sensitive to development across multiple levels of the model, from task schema to cognitive processes, to memory resources.

Task Schema

According to Bereiter and Scardamalia (1987), children may approach the writing task with a task schema that differs from that of expert writers, resulting in different control processes overseeing text generation. Because children's initial experiences with discourse are largely conversational, their schema for text generation may be shaped by oral schemas. Prominent in conversational schemas is the concept of turn taking (i.e., making room for and taking cues from the conversational partner). In contrast, text generation during writing often must operate without the interactive prompts provided by conversational partners. Bereiter and Scardamalia (1987) suggested that when children transfer oral, conversational schemas to the generation of written text, they frequently write only a single conversational turn, with the resulting texts being short and incomplete. This suggestion has garnered empirical support from studies showing that children write longer texts, and texts of higher quality, when they are provided with a "conversational" partner during writing (Daiute, 1986; Daiute & Dalton, 1993) or even simple prompts to say more (Bereiter & Scardamalia, 1987). Indeed, effective writing instruction for young children frequently incorporates active collaboration and peer response (Boscolo & Ascorti, 2004; Calkins, 1986; Cameron et al., 1996; Graves, 1983), thereby emphasizing the implicit dialogue between writer and reader.

Cognitive Processes

SPELLING

The model of text production proposed by Chenoweth and Hayes (2001) did not distinguish spelling from other aspects of transcription, but for children, spelling represents a considerable challenge (Berninger et al., 1997, 2002). The costs associated with poor spelling skills extend beyond the readability of the text, because dysfluent word retrieval processes can compete with other writing processes for limited resources. Evidence for such competition among processes comes from a study by Graham, Harris and Chorzempa (2002), documenting that spelling instruction improved children's writing fluency, at least in the short term.

Spelling difficulties arise in English (for adults, as well as children) because of variable mapping of the more than 40 phonemes of English onto the alphabet of only 26 letters. While the mapping problem is not unique to English or to the Roman alphabet (e.g., Harris & Hatano, 1999), orthographic rules in English are complex (Venezky, 1970). Many researchers have observed patterns in the growth of children's spelling (e.g., Bissex, 1980; Chomsky, 1970; Henderson & Beers, 1980; Read, 1981; Treiman, 1993; Varnhagen, 1995), leading to various stage models of the development of spelling.

Gentry's (1982) well-known stage model of children's spelling of English (see also Ehri, 1992) described five stages extending through the early elementary years. The initial stage of spelling, the *precommunicative stage*, involves the child's first use of alphabetic symbols to represent language. As the label implies, spelling during the precommunicative stage is often unreadable, be-

cause the symbols bear little relationship to the sounds of the words being represented. Because children are not yet mapping individual letters to sounds, they may confuse the number of letters in a word with quantifiable aspects of the referent, such as size or number, writing longer letter strings to represent larger objects. Such a referential strategy has been observed in children learning to spell across a variety of languages (Ferreiro & Teberosky, 1982; Share & Levin, 1999). Phonological strategies begin to emerge in the *semiphonetic stage*, as the child begins to use letters to represent some, but not necessarily all, sounds within words. During the semiphonetic stage, children may use the names of letters to represent entire words, as in the classic example from Bissex (1980), RUDF (i.e., "Are you deaf?"). When they do attempt to represent individual sounds within words, children seem differentially sensitive to vowel and consonant distributions across words. Children learning English are more likely to include letters representing initial and final consonants than other sounds within words (Ehri, 1986), and vowel spellings are generally more difficult (Treiman, 1993; Varnhagen, Boechler, & Steffler, 1999). A similar tendency for consonants to be more fully represented than vowels (specifically, vowel diacritics) was observed in children learning to spell Hebrew (Share & Levin, 1999), but the opposite pattern was reported for Spanish and Italian (Ferreiro & Teberosky, 1982; Pontecovo & Zucchermaglio, 1990). More complete representations of the phonological structure of words are represented in children's spelling during the *phonetic stage*, but often with unconventional orthography (e.g., EGL for *eagle*). As children move into the *transitional stage*, and finally to *conventional spelling*, they observe more orthographic conventions.

For languages such as English, in which spelling does not map transparently onto phonology (Venezky, 1970), the later stages of spelling development are linked to children's growing awareness of orthography (Varnhagen, 1995) and how it reflects word meaning, as well as sound (Ehri, 1992; Carlisle, 1988). Evidence from English (Griffith, 1991; Treiman, 1993), Hebrew (Share & Levin, 1999), French (Pacton & Fayol, 2003), and Greek (Bryant, Nunes, & Aidinis, 1999) indicates that children become aware of phonological aspects of spelling before morphological aspects. Furthermore, children's written narratives document that they generally gain control over the spelling of English inflections earlier than the spelling of most derivational morphemes (Carlisle, 1996; Green et al., 2003).

Despite controversies about specific stages and strategies, a general picture emerges from the research on children's spelling. After an initial period of "play" with letter-like symbols, children's early spelling attempts are supported by their awareness of phonological information, followed by increasingly sophisticated awareness of the relationships among phonology, orthography, and morphology.

HANDWRITTEN TRANSCRIPTION

As described by Berninger and Swanson (1994), spelling is subsumed under the process of transcription, together with other cognitive and motor demands of handwriting. Like spelling skill, control of handwriting increases with age (Berninger & Graham, 1998; Berninger & Swanson, 1994). Clearly, the motor and cognitive aspects of handwritten transcription require effort on the part of very young children, and considerable research has examined the extent to which other aspects of writing are compromised by the effort required by transcription. Given the limited resources of working memory (Baddeley, 1998), fluent transcription is important if higher level aspects of writing are to have the resources needed to develop and function well (Dellerman, Coirier, & Marchand, 1996; McCutchen, 2000). A key question in the development of children's writing skill has been how the two core processes of text production—transcription and text generation—compete for cognitive resources as children's writing skills develop.

Transcription has been shown to interfere with text generation and other writing processes. Bereiter, Fine, and Gartshore (1979, reported in Bereiter & Scardamalia, 1987) periodically interrupted children as they were writing and were thus able to compare what children said they were about to write with what they actually wrote. Bereiter et al. estimated that the resource cost imposed by transcription resulted in loss of content from

perhaps one of every 10 phrases written by young children.

Berninger and Swanson (1994) found that transcription-related measures (i.e., retrieving letters from memory and writing them) were particularly strong predictors of writing quality for children just learning to write but diminished in importance as other components of writing emerged. Examining a wide range of component processes, Berninger and Swanson found that transcription measures accounted for more unique variance in composition quality in their primary grade sample than in their intermediate grade or junior high sample. Furthermore, improving handwriting fluency among young children has led to general improvements in the fluency of their text generation (Berninger et al., 1997, 2002; Graham, Harris, & Fink, 2000).

Other researchers have examined transcription costs by comparing written texts to dictated texts. The logic behind such comparisons is that if rhetorical constraints are held constant, any differences between written and spoken texts can be attributed to the added demands of transcription during writing. Cleanly separating production demands from rhetorical constraints (and, thus, transcription from text generation and other aspects of writing) is not always straightforward, but some findings emerge consistently from comparisons of oral and written production.

Children's written texts are typically shorter than their dictated texts (Bereiter & Scardamalia, 1987; Hidi & Hildyard, 1983; McCutchen, 1987), while differences favoring dictation are not as consistent for adults (Gould, 1980; Grabowski, Vorwerg, & Rummer, 1994; Reece & Cumming, 1996). Differences between children's writing and dictation might have a variety of sources, and Bereiter and Scardamalia (1987) reported a study designed to disentangle several competing explanations (specifically, time and interference). They asked children to produce texts in three conditions: (1) writing, (2) regular dictation, and (3) slow dictation (i.e., a dictation rate indexed to the child's own writing rate). Although dictation produced longer texts, quality ratings showed little difference across conditions. However, following simple prompts to produce more, children's written texts were rated higher in quality than those produced in either of the dictation conditions. Bereiter and Scardamalia concluded that the brevity of children's written texts is a primary factor contributing to the perception that children often speak better than they write. They argued that by age 10 (the age of their youngest subjects), the processing cost associated with transcription is largely offset by other affordances of writing; however, the same may not be true for younger writers (King & Rental, 1981).

Reece and Cumming (1996) argued that once transcription reaches minimal levels of fluency, part of the advantage of writing over conventional dictation results from the availability of a visible, developing text. Like Bereiter and Scardamalia (1987), Reece and Cumming (1996) found that texts written by 10- to 12-year-old children were shorter but higher quality than texts dictated in the conventional manner. However, when they had children dictate texts and simultaneously transcribed those texts on a computer screen in a simulated speech recognition condition, they found that quality ratings were higher than for handwritten texts. Thus, comparisons between writing and traditional dictation may have been confounded by the absence of the visible text.

Resource demands of transcription were also examined in a series of experiments by Bourdin and Fayol (1994), who varied response modality (spoken vs. written) in a serial recall task. Bourdin and Fayol found that recall was significantly poorer in the written condition for children but not for adults. They reasoned that transcription processes of children are still relatively inefficient and draw on resources that could otherwise be devoted to the recall task. Bourdin and Fayol were able to interrupt adults' overlearned, highly fluent transcription processes by requiring them to write in cursive uppercase letters, with the result that adults then showed poorer recall when writing than when speaking. In similar experiments, the task changed from serial recall to text recall (Bourdin, Fayol, & Darciaux, 1996) and text generation (Olive & Kellogg, 2002), with the consistent finding that transcription imposed higher resource costs for children than for adults. Thus, the process costs of transcrip-

tion are relatively high for very young writers, but as handwriting processes become fluent, text generation and other writing processes become less limited by transcription.

For children with writing disabilities, however, transcription demands can be a persistent problem. Graham (1990) replicated Bereiter and Scardamalia's (1987) procedures with children with learning disabilities and found quite different results. For children with learning disabilities, the resource demands imposed by transcription resulted in written essays that were consistently shorter and lower in quality than dictated essays, even after prompts to say more. Quinlan (2004) found quality differences in narratives written by fluent and less-fluent adolescents (not all of whom had formal diagnoses of learning disabilities), but those differences decreased substantially when adolescents composed using commercial speech recognition software.

Thus, for typically achieving children in the early stages in writing acquisition (generally grade 3 and below) and for children with learning disabilities, transcription processes may not be fluent, thereby limiting text generation. After grade 4 or so, the transcription processes of typically achieving children develop sufficient fluency, reducing demands on working memory. However, transcription may never become so automatic that it requires no resources. Indeed, transcription (spelling and handwriting) contributes significantly to writing skill across elementary school and into junior high school (Berninger & Swanson, 1994; Graham, Berninger, Abbott, Abbott, & Whitaker, 1997), and resource costs are still associated with translating processes (transcription plus text generation), even for adults (Kellogg, 2001).

TEXT GENERATION

Text generation, according to Berninger and Swanson (1994; also Chenoweth & Hayes, 2001), is the mental production of a linguistic message, distinct from transcription of that message into written text. Like speech, text generation involves turning ideas into words, sentences, and larger units of discourse within working memory. As in speech, pauses in the stream of language generated during writing are influenced by syntactic junctures such as paragraph, sentence, and clause boundaries (Chanquoy, Foulin, & Fayol, 1996), as well as by the text genre (Matsuhashi, 1981). The translation of ideas into language may be more or less difficult depending on the coded representation of the ideas themselves and on aspects of the target language. If ideas are coded in nonverbal modes (Flower & Hayes, 1984), or if ideas are being coded into the writer's non-native language (Chenoweth & Hayes, 2001), generating text can be more difficult.

There are several lines of research documenting developmental and individual differences in the fluency of children's text generation. Text length is often used as an index of production fluency, and older children typically write longer texts than younger children (e.g., Berninger & Swanson, 1994; Loban, 1976). Similarly, texts written by children with learning disabilities are shorter than those by their typically developing peers (Graham, 1990). McCutchen et al. (1994) observed that older children generated individual sentences more fluently than did younger children, but at all grade levels, skilled writers were more fluent than less skilled writers. In addition, skilled writers were faster accessing even individual words. Even for high school students, the ability to generate language efficiently is a key predictor of writing quality (Dellerman et al., 1996).

Text coherence is another index of text production that has been used frequently to study the development of writing skill. Derived from work by Halliday and Hasan (1976), coherence analysis examines the linguistic connections within texts (e.g., lexical repetitions, referential ties), as well as more global text coherence. A well-documented finding in such research is that older children write more coherent texts than do younger children (Cox, Shanahan, & Tinzmann, 1991; McCutchen, 1986, 1987; Wright & Rosenberg, 1993).

Working Memory Resources

Fluent text production is important because, during complex tasks such as writing, cognitive processes compete for limited resources within working memory. Inefficient processes at one level can consume resources that might otherwise be devoted to higher level processes such as planning and revising (Marchand, Coirier, & Dellerman, 1996; McCutchen, 2000). Working memory has been related to text generation in a number of tasks. Bereiter and Scardamalia (1987) presented children with chunks of related information and found that the number of informational chunks children coordinated within a single sentence was related to how well they defended a thesis in an expository writing task. Bereiter and Scardamalia attributed the relationship to the working memory resources that each child had available during the two text-generation tasks. Dellerman et al. (1996) found that a similar coordination task predicted writing skill even in high school students. Similarly, Tetroe (1984; reported in Bereiter & Scardamalia, 1987) linked working memory and text generation at the discourse level. Tetroe asked children to write stories that were to end with specific sentences, and she varied the number of constraints imposed by the ending sentences. Tetroe independently assessed children's working memory spans and found a marked decrease in children's ability to honor the ending-sentence constraints as the number of constraints exceeded their memory spans. Thus, children's text generation—at both the sentence and the discourse level—is constrained by available working memory resources.

Working memory constraints may also make it difficult for writers to avoid (and later correct) certain grammatical errors. For example, subject–verb agreement and certain syntactic structures become more difficult to coordinate as more words intervene between the key constituents. Daiute (1984) found negative correlations between short-term memory capacity and the frequency of errors in students' texts. In addition, Fayol, Largy, and Lemaire (1994) were able experimentally to induce agreement errors by increasing writers' memory load. Thus, text production fluency is important not only in its own right but also because of its implications for working memory resources. Working memory demands imposed by text-production processes (transcription and text generation) early in writing acquisition may contribute to the rarity of planning and revising in young children's writing, and increase children's reliance on strategies such as knowledge telling.

Long-Term Memory Resources

For all writers, knowledge stored in long-term memory is critical during writing. For children, many of whom rely on the knowledge-telling strategy, knowledge of topic and genre can be especially helpful. During knowledge telling, topic and genre cues are used to generate memory probes, enabling young writers to produce better texts when they are more familiar with a topic, because the memory network accessed by probes is more interconnected. Similarly, young writers should produce better texts when they are more familiar with a genre, because memory probes will be more systematically related. Differences in text quality due to increased knowledge have been observed for both familiar topics (DeGroff, 1987; Langer, 1984; McCutchen, 1986) and the familiar narrative genre (Cox et al., 1991; Hidi & Hildyard, 1983). However, the narrative advantage may be most pronounced for younger children (Langer, 1985) and in oral as opposed to written productions (McCutchen, 1987). Even knowledge telling can produce relatively coherent texts when its associative search processes operate on a rich and well-structured knowledge base, or when prompted by a well-learned schema for a particular genre.

Thus, more recent studies of writing have augmented Hayes and Flower's (1980; Kaufer et al., 1986) original view of translating, distinguishing transcription from text generation, and adding the notion of a task schema. Because of the relatively early acquisition of fluency in transcription processes (age 10 or so for typically developing children), it is understandable that transcription was not included in Hayes and Flower's model of expert writing. However, to explain either developmental or individual differences in the acquisition of writing, both transcription and text generation must be considered (Berninger & Swanson, 1994; Chenoweth & Hayes, 2001; Graham, 1990). Although inefficient transcription processes may strain cognitive resources, this should not be taken as a recommendation to teach spelling and handwriting isolated from other aspects of writing. An appropriate task schema is likely developed only in the context of composing extended text, so meaningful composition tasks are critical (e.g., De La Paz & Graham, 2002).

Revision

Hayes (1996, 2004) elaborated the original description of the revision process offered by Hayes and Flower (1980). He proposed that revision, like language generation, is guided by an overall task schema, and influenced by working memory and long-term memory resources. The task schema directs multiple cognitive processes, which include critical reading, problem solving, and text production. Revision thus involves schema-guided reading, text evaluation, and rewriting when necessary. Children's revision can be examined in relation to each aspect of Hayes's elaborated model.

Task Schema

Wallace and Hayes (1991; Wallace et al., 1996) provided evidence supporting the existence of a revision task schema. Most writers (adults, as well as children) seem to operate under a revision schema focused on surface features of the text, rather than the conceptual level, and thereby spend most revision effort on surface features of the text (e.g., Butterfield, Hacker, & Plumb, 1994; Chanquoy, 2001; Faigley & Witte, 1981; Fitzgerald, 1987; McCutchen, Francis, & Kerr, 1997). With very brief instruction, Wallace and Hayes (1991; Wallace et al., 1996) were able to reorient college writers to revise for meaning. Their instruction was so brief (8 minutes) that Wallace and colleagues argued they could not have taught students revision processes per se; rather, they argued, they simply altered the students' revision schema by directing students' attention to meaning over mechanical features of texts (see also Graham, MacArthur, & Schwartz, 1995).

Critical Reading Processes

With increasing age and writing skill, writers are more likely to revise for meaning

(Butterfield et al., 1994; Faigley & Witte, 1981). McCutchen et al. (1997) argued that some of this development is related to writers' ability to read texts critically. In that study, we listened as middle school students worked collaboratively to revise texts within which we had created logical inconsistencies by rearranging sentences, and we found that skilled and less-skilled writers employed markedly different reading strategies. Skilled revisers developed a macrostructure of the text they were revising (see Kintsch, 1998) and considered the entire text as they worked, whereas less-skilled revisers did not. For example, even during their initial reading of the texts, skilled writers readily recognized sentences that were out of place, and they revised accordingly. The following exchange is typical of the strategy skilled writers used as they worked in pairs to revise a text describing the voyage of Christopher Columbus:

STUDENT 1: Wait—that should be somewhere on the top. Maybe after (reads) "However, Columbus also believed that the world was round. Many people laughed at this idea. They thought the world was flat." (Inserts and reads) "Columbus hoped to prove his theory, so he would sail west in order to reach the East. "

STUDENT 2: Yeah. That would work. Put that up there.

In contrast, we observed that less-skilled writers used a more local, sentence-by-sentence strategy that interfered with their ability to consider the text's larger meaning. The following excerpt depicts a less-skilled writer revising the same Columbus text, examining and commenting on each sentence individually, attending to spelling errors, but completely missing the incongruous mention of the sailors' threatened mutiny (in McCutchen et al., 1997):

STUDENT 3: (Reads) "Christopher Columbus was determined to find an all water route to the East Indies." That's good. (Reads) "Discovering this could bring him fame and fortune. However, however, Columbus also believed that the world was round." OK. (Reads) "Many people"— geez! (corrects spelling, reads) "laughed at this idea. They thought the world was

flat." Next, that's good. (Reads) "But still the sailors threatened to take over and turn back." That's good. (p. 673)

We concluded, like Hayes (1996, 2004), that sophisticated revision may depend on sophisticated reading strategies (see also Beal, 1996). Additional evidence comes from instructional studies. For example, when instructed in ways to monitor their text comprehension during revision, children as young as age 9 revised more effectively (Beal, Garrod, & Bonitatibus, 1990; see also Englert, Hiebert, & Stewart, 1988).

Problem Solving

To solve a problem with an existing text, the writer must recognize the problem and then take appropriate steps to correct it. Such problem solving involves comparing a representation of the *actual* text to a representation of the *intended* text, noting discrepancies and initiating changes to bring the actual text more in line with the intended text (Bereiter & Scardamalia, 1987; Flower, Hayes, Carey, Shriver, & Stratman, 1986). Several processes in this sequence can be problematic for young children, the first being the representation of the intended text. As mentioned previously, younger children are less likely to engage in much planning; thus, they have fewer specified "intentions," and their memory representations of the intended text are often vague (Bereiter et al., 1988).

Second, young children may have difficulty differentiating their interpretations from the actual text. Older children are better able than younger children to distinguish inferred from explicit text information (Beal, 1990a, 1990b, 1996) and to revise problematic texts by adding information to support necessary inferences (Beal, 1990b). Thus, children's difficulty forming an accurate representation of the text can inhibit their ability to revise effectively.

Third, children may have difficulty generating alternative language to correct a problem, even once they detect it. Beal (1990a) reported that younger children had more difficulty than older children in diagnosing and correcting text problems, even when the problems were pointed out to them. Bereiter and Scardamalia (1987) reported similar developmental trends in children's ability both to detect problems in texts and to accurately diagnose the source of those problems. Moreover, they observed that children were more likely to identify a text problem than to diagnose the problem adequately and correct it.

If the role of the task schema is simply to direct cognitive process, alterations in the task schema should have little effect without adequate operation of revision-related cognitive processes. Indeed, Wallace et al. (1996) found that their brief schema-directed instruction did not increase meaning-based revision among struggling college writers. Again, all levels of component writing processes need to function in concert for effective writing to result.

Memory Resources

TOPIC KNOWLEDGE

At least some of children's revision difficulties may result from knowledge and strategies that they bring (or *do not* bring) to the revision task. McCutchen et al. (1997) examined how students' memory resources affected their revision success. In that study, we asked students to revise two texts, one about Christopher Columbus (a familiar topic) and another about Margaret Mead (an unfamiliar topic). We found that children, as well as adults, were more likely to correct meaning-related problems in the Columbus text than in the Mead text. Thus, topic knowledge helped writers recognize and resolve inconsistencies between the actual and the intended text when they brought that topic knowledge to bear during revision (see also Butterfield et al., 1994; DeGroff, 1987).

WORKING MEMORY

Multiple aspects of the revision process may be constrained by available working memory resources. Piolat, Roussey, Olive, and Amada (2004) found that among college students, those with larger working memory spans were more successful than students with smaller spans in correcting spelling errors. Also, using a variant of the dual task paradigm, they documented that the critical reading involved during revision was more effortful than reading merely to understand.

AUDIENCE AWARENESS

Another memory resource that can influence children's revision is knowledge of audience. Although children sometimes show implicit audience awareness during text generation (Cameron et al., 1996, Cameron & Wang, 1999; Lee et al., 1998; Littleton, 1998), children often have difficulty being critical readers of their own texts, missing errors in their texts that they readily see in texts by others (Bartlett, 1982). However, when working face-to-face with a reader (even another child), young writers have been found to revise more effectively (Boscolo & Ascorti, 2004; Daiute, 1986; Daiute & Dalton, 1993); so the challenge seems to be helping children internalize a representation of the reader.

Holliway and McCutchen (2004) provided young writers with firsthand experience of the potential difficulty readers might have with their texts. We asked children to describe abstract figures, and independent readers then tried to choose the described figure from among a set of similar figures. We found no effect of simply telling children how successfully readers could use their texts to identify the figures. However, after children took their reader's role and matched text descriptions to figures themselves, they revised more effectively.

Thus, children can experience difficulty with all levels of the revision process as described by Hayes (1996, 2004). Like many writers, children seem to employ a schema for revision that focuses on surface and mechanical revisions rather than revisions of text meaning, and that tendency may be even stronger when children have inadequate topic knowledge. Children may develop inadequate representations of the intended text because of minimal planning, and problematic representations of the actual text because of unsophisticated reading strategies. As a result, they may have additional trouble distinguishing the actual from the intended text, as well as difficulty internalizing their audience. To be maximally effective, instruction will likely need to address multiple aspects of the revision process (MacArthur, Graham, & Harris, 2004).

A Paradox in the Development of Writing Skill

Throughout this chapter and elsewhere (McCutchen, 2000), I have made the general claim that more fluent text-production processes free working memory resources, allowing the writer to move beyond knowledge telling and engage in higher level processes, such as planning and reviewing. Given this view of increasing fluency as writing skill develops, we are led to something of a paradox when we examine writers at work: Less-skilled writers sometimes generate text more fluently than do skilled writers. Children's protocols consist primarily of their saying words as they put them to paper (Bereiter & Scardamalia, 1987), whereas skilled writers frequently wrestle with phrasings (Chenoweth & Hayes, 2001; McCutchen, 1988, 2000).

The solution to this apparent paradox becomes evident when we consider the tasks that writers set for themselves. Whereas text generation is the primary task of many young writers, the sports columnist quoted early in this chapter (like most expert writers) imposed task constraints reflecting his sense of genre, audience, style, and topic that complicated his writing task considerably. Still, such complications did not exceed his working memory capacity, because he possessed two crucial components of writing expertise—fluent text-production processes (text generation and transcription) and extensive writing-relevant knowledge. Expert writers are thereby able to transcend the limits of working memory, as traditionally defined (Baddeley, 1998) and capitalize on resources from long-term memory (see Kintsch, 1998). The result is not necessarily an effortless writing process for the expert, but it is an effective one that yields high-quality text.

Without such fluent processing and extensive writing-relevant knowledge, novice writers remain limited by working memory capacity, and within such constraints, writing strategies such as knowledge telling may serve an adaptive function. Many current models of writing instruction are geared (implicitly or explicitly) toward helping students manage the resource demands of writing *and* move beyond knowledge telling. Effective instruction can lessen resource demands by explicitly scaffolding components of the writing process (e.g., De La Paz & Graham, 2002; MacArthur et al., 2004), or by distributing components of the task across time or across members of the classroom community (e.g., Boscolo & Ascorti, 2004; Calkins, 1986; Graves, 1983). However, without such external supports, a beginning writer may resort to knowledge telling just to cope with resource demands, and nonoptimal variants of writing processes may persist. In order to articulate a complete model of writing acquisition—one that will be useful in future refinements of instructional practice, researchers need to pay increased attention to how component writing processes, as well as memory resources, are employed by developing writers.

Acknowledgments

Preparation of this chapter and collection of some data reported herein were supported by Grant No. P50 HD-33812 from the National Institute of Child Health and Human Development.

References

Baddeley, A. D. (1998). *Human memory: Theory and practice.* New York: Allyn & Bacon.

Bartlett, E. J. (1982). Learning to revise: Some component processes. In M. Nystrand (Ed.), *What writers know: The language, process, and structure of written texts* (pp. 345–363). New York: Academic Press.

Beal, C. R. (1990a). Development of knowledge about the role of inference in text comprehension. *Child Development, 61*, 247–258.

Beal, C. R. (1990b). Development of text evaluation and revision skills. *Child Development, 61*, 1011–1023.

Beal, C. R. (1996). The role of comprehension monitoring in children's revision. *Educational Psychology Review, 8*, 219–238.

Beal, C. R., Garrod, A. C., & Bonitatibus, G. J. (1990). Fostering children's revision skills through training in comprehension monitoring. *Journal of Educational Psychology, 82*, 275–280.

Bereiter, C., Burtis, B. J., & Scardamalia, M. (1988). Cognitive operations in constructing main points in written composition. *Journal of Memory and Language, 27*, 261–278.

Bereiter, C., Fine, J., & Gartshore, S. (1979, April).

An exploratory study of micro-planning in writing. Paper presented at the meeting of the American Educational Research Association, San Francisco, CA.

Bereiter, C., & Scardamalia, M. (1987). *The psychology of written composition*. Hillsdale, NJ: Erlbaum.

Berninger, V., & Graham, S. (1998). Language by hand: A synthesis of a decade of research on handwriting. *Handwriting Review, 12*, 11–25.

Berninger, V. W., & Swanson, H. L. (1994). Modifying Hayes and Flower's model of skilled writing to explain beginning and developing writing. In J. S. Carlson (Series Ed.) & E. C. Butterfield (Vol. Ed.), *Advances in cognition and educational practice: Vol. 2. Children's writing: Toward a process theory of the development of skilled writing* (pp. 57–81). Greenwich, CT: JAI Press.

Berninger, V. W., Vaughan, K. B., Abbott, R. D., Abbott, S. P., Rogan, L. W., Brooks, A., et al. (1997). Treatment of handwriting problems in beginning writers: Transfer from handwriting to composition. *Journal of Educational Psychology, 89*, 652–666.

Berninger, V. W., Vaughan, K. B., Abbott, R. D., Begay, K., Coleman, K. B., Curtin, G., et al. (2002). Teaching spelling and composition alone and together: Implications for the simple view of writing. *Journal of Educational Psychology, 94*, 291–304.

Bissex, G. L. (1980). *GNYS AT WRK: A child learns to read and write*. Cambridge, MA: Harvard University Press.

Boscolo, P., & Ascorti, K. (2004). Effects of collaborative revision on children's ability to write understandable narrative texts. In L. Allal, L. Chanquoy, & P. Largy (Eds.), *Studies in writing: Vol. 13. Revision: Cognitive and instructional processes* (pp. 157–172). Norwell, MA: Kluwer.

Bourdin, B., & Fayol, M. (1994). Is written language production more difficult than oral language production: A working memory approach. *International Journal of Psychology, 29*, 591–620.

Bourdin, B., Fayol, M., & Darciaux, S. (1996). The comparison of oral and written modes on adults' and children's narrative recall. In G. Rijlaarsdam, H. van den Bergh, & M. Couzijn (Eds.), *Theories, models, and methodology in writing research* (pp. 159–169). Amsterdam: Amsterdam University Press.

Bryant, P., Nunes, T., & Aidinis, A. (1999). Different morphemes, same spelling problems: Cross-linguistic developmental studies. In M. Harris & G. Hatano (Eds.), *Learning to read and write: A cross-linguistic perspective* (pp. 112–133). New York: Cambridge University Press.

Butterfield, E. C., Hacker, D. J., & Plumb, C. (1994). Topic knowldge, linguistic knowledge, and revision skill as determinants of text revision. In J. S. Carlson (Series Ed.) & E. C. Butterfield (Vol. Ed.), *Advances in cognition and educational practice: Vol. 2. Children's writing: Toward a process theory of the development of skilled writing* (pp. 83–141). Greenwich, CT: JAI Press.

Calkins, L. M. (1986). *The art of teaching writing*. Portsmouth, NH: Heinemann.

Cameron, C. A., Hunt, A. K., & Linton, M. (1996). Written expression in the primary classroom: Children write in social time. *Educational Psychology Review, 8*, 125–150.

Cameron, C. A., & Moshenko, B. (1996). Elicitation of knowledge transformational reports while children write narratives. *Canadian Journal of Behavioural Science, 28*, 271–280.

Cameron, C. A., & Wang, M. (1999). Frog, where are you?: Children's narrative expression over the phone. *Discourse Processes, 28*, 217–236.

Carlisle, J. F. (1988). Knowledge of derivational morphology and spelling ability in fourth, sixth, and eighth graders. *Applied Psycholinguistics, 9*, 247–266.

Carlisle, J. F. (1996). An exploratory study of morphological errors in children's written stories. *Reading and Writing: An Interdisciplinary Journal, 8*, 61–72.

Chanquoy, L. (2001). How to make it easier for children to revise their writing: A study of text revision from 3rd to 5th grades. *British Journal of Educational Psychology, 71*, 15–41.

Chanquoy, L., Foulin, J. N., & Fayol, M. (1996). Writing in adults: A real-time approach. In G. Rijlaarsdam, H. van den Bergh, & M. Couzijn (Eds.), *Theories, models, and methodology in writing research* (pp. 36–43). Amsterdam: Amsterdam University Press.

Chenoweth, N. A., & Hayes, J. R. (2001). Fluency in writing: Generating text in L1 and L2. *Written Communication, 18*, 80–98.

Chomsky, C. (1970). Reading, writing, and phonology. *Harvard Educational Review, 40*, 287–309.

Cox, B. E., Shanahan, T., & Tinzmann, M. B. (1991). Children's knowledge of organization, cohesion, and voice in written exposition. *Research in the Teaching of English, 25*, 179–218.

Daiute, C. A. (1984). Performance limits on writers. In R. Beach & L. S. Bridwell (Eds.), *New directions in composition research* (pp. 205–224). New York: Guilford Press.

Daiute, C. A. (1986). Do 1 and 1 make 2?: Patterns of influence by collaborative authors. *Written Communication, 3*, 382–408.

Daiute, C., & Dalton, B. (1993). Collaboration between children learning to write: Can novices be masters? *Cognition and Instruction, 10*, 281–333.

de Beaugrande, R. (1984). *Text production: Toward a science of composition*. Norwood, NJ: Ablex.

De La Paz, S., & Graham, S. (2002). Explicitly teaching strategies, skills, and knowledge: Writing instruction in middle school classrooms. *Journal of Educational Psychology. 94*, 687–698.

DeGroff, L. C. (1987). The influence of prior knowledge on writing, conferencing, and revising. *Elementary School Journal, 88*, 105–116.

Dellerman, P. Coirier, P., & Marchand, E. (1996). Planning and expertise in argumentative composition. In G. Rijlaarsdam, H. van den Bergh, & M. Couzijn (Eds.), *Theories, models, and methodology in writing research* (pp. 182–195). Amsterdam: Amsterdam University Press.

Ehri, L. C. (1986). Sources of difficulty in learning to spell and read. In M. L. Wolraich & D. Routh (Eds.), *Advances in developmental and behavioral pediatrics* (Vol. 7, pp. 121–195). Greenwich, CT: JAI Press.

Ehri, L. C. (1992). Review and commentary: Stages of spelling development. In S. Templeton & D. R. Bear (Eds.), *Development of orthographic knowledge and the foundations of literacy: A memorial festschrift for Edmund H. Henderson* (pp. 307–332). Hillsdale, NJ: Erlbaum.

Englert, C. S., Hiebert, E. H., & Stewart, S. R. (1988). Detecting and correcting inconsistencies in the monitoring of expository prose. *Journal of Educational Research, 81*, 221–227.

Faigley, L., & Witte, S. (1981). Analyzing revision. *College Composition and Communication, 32*, 400–414.

Fayol, M., Largy, P., & Lemaire, P. (1994). Cognitive overload and orthographic errors: When cognitive overload enhances subject–verb agreement errors, a study in French written language. *Quarterly Journal of Experimental Psychology, 47*, 437–464.

Ferreiro, E., & Teberosky, A. (1982). *Literacy before schooling*. Exeter, NH: Heinemann.

Fitzgerald, J. (1987). Research on revision in writing. *Review of Educational Research, 57*, 481–506.

Flower, L., & Hayes, J. R. (1980). The dynamics of composing: Making plans and juggling constraints. In L. W. Gregg & E. R. Steinberg (Eds.), *Cognitive processes in writing* (pp. 31–50). Hillsdale, NJ: Erlbaum.

Flower, L., & Hayes, J. R. (1981). The pregnant pause: An inquiry into the nature of planning. *Research in the Teaching of English, 15*, 229–248.

Flower, L., & Hayes, J. R. (1984). Images, plans, and prose: The representation of meaning in writing. *Written Communication, 1*, 120–160.

Flower, L., Hayes, J. R., Carey, L. J., Shriver, K., & Stratman, J. (1986). Detection, diagnosis, and the strategies of revision. *College Composition and Communication, 37*, 16–55.

Freedman, S. W. (1984). The registers of student and professional expository writing: Influences on teacher responses. In R. Beach & L. S. Bridwell (Eds.), *New directions in composition research* (pp. 334–347). New York: Guilford Press.

Galbraith, D. (1996). Self-monitoring, discovery through writing and individual differences in drafting strategy. In G. Rijlaarsdam, H. van den Bergh, & M. Couzijn (Eds.), *Theories, models, and methodology in writing research* (pp. 121–141). Amsterdam: Amsterdam University Press.

Gentry, J. R. (1982). An analysis of developmental spelling in *GNYS AT WRK. Reading Teacher, 36*, 192–200.

Goldman, S. R. (1995). Writing as a tool for thinking and reasoning. *Issues in Education: Contributions from Educational Psychology, 1*, 199–204.

Gould, J. D. (1980). Experiments on composing letters: Some facts, some myths, and some observations. In L. W. Gregg & E. R. Steinberg (Eds.), *Cognitive processes in writing* (pp. 97–127). Hillsdale, NJ: Erlbaum.

Grabowski, J., Vorwerg, C., & Rummer, R. (1994). Writing as a tool for control of episodic representation. In G. Eigler & T. Jechle (Eds.), *Writing: Current trends in European research* (pp. 55–68). Freburg, Germany: HochschulVerlag.

Graham, S. (1990). The role of production factors in learning disabled students' compositions. *Journal of Educational Psychology, 82*, 781–791.

Graham, S., Berninger, V., Abbott, R., Abbott, S., & Whitaker, D. (1997). The role of mechanics in composing of elementary school students: A new methodological approach. *Journal of Educational Psychology, 89*, 170–182.

Graham, S., Harris, K. R., & Fink, B. (2000). Is handwriting causally related to learning to write?: Treatment of handwriting problems in beginning writers. *Journal of Educational Psychology, 92*, 620–633.

Graham, S., Harris, K. R., & Chorzempa, B. F. (2002). Contribution of spelling instruction to the spelling, writing, and reading of poor readers. *Journal of Educational Psychology, 94*, 669–686.

Graham, S., MacArthur, C., & Schwartz, S. (1995). Effects of goal setting and procedural facilitation on the revising behavior and writing performance of students with writing and learning problems. *Journal of Educational Psychology, 87*, 230–240.

Graves, D. H. (1983). *Writing: Teachers and children at work*. Exeter, NH: Heinemann.

Green, L. B., McCutchen, D., Schwiebert, C., Quinlan, T., Eva-Wood, A., & Juelis, J. (2003). Morphological development in children's writing. *Journal of Educational Psychology, 95*, 752–761.

Griffith, P. L. (1991). Phonemic awareness helps first graders invent spellings and third graders remember correct spellings. *Journal of Reading Behavior, 23*, 215–233.

Halliday, M. A. K., & Hasan, R. (1976). *Cohesion in English*. London: Longman.

Harris, M., & Hatano, G. (1999). *Learning to read and write: A cross-linguistic perspective*. New York: Cambridge University Press.

Hayes, J. R. (1996). A new framework for understanding cognition and affect in writing. In M. C. Levy & S. Ransdell (Eds.), *The science of writing* (pp. 1–27). Mahwah, NJ: Erlbaum.

Hayes, J. R. (2004). What triggers revision? In L. Allal, L. Chanquoy, & P. Largy (Eds.), *Studies in writing: Vol. 13. Revision: Cognitive and instructional processes* (pp. 9–20). Norwell, MA: Kluwer.

Hayes, J. R., & Flower, L. S. (1980). Identifying the organization of writing processes. In L. W. Gregg & E. R. Steinberg (Eds.), *Cognitive processes in writing* (pp. 3–30). Hillsdale, NJ: Erlbaum.

Hayes, J. R., & Nash, J. G. (1996). On the nature of planning in writing. In M. C. Levy & S. Ransdell (Eds.), *The science of writing* (pp. 29–55). Mahwah, NJ: Erlbaum.

Henderson, E. H., & Beers, J. W. (Eds.). (1980). *Developmental and cognitive aspects of learning to spell: A reflection of word knowledge.* Newark, DE: International Reading Association.

Hidi, S., & Hildyard, A. (1983). The comparison of oral and written productions of two discourse types. *Discourse Processes, 6,* 91–105.

Holliway, D. R., & McCutchen, D. (2004). Audience perspective in young writers' composing and revising: Reading as the reader. In L. Allal, L. Chanquoy, & P. Largy (Eds.), *Studies in writing: Vol. 13. Revision: Cognitive and instructional processes* (pp. 87–101). Norwell, MA: Kluwer.

Kaufer, D. S., Hayes, J. R., & Flower, L. (1986). Composing written sentences. *Research in the Teaching of English, 20,* 121–140.

Kellogg, R. T. (2001). Long-term working memory in text production. *Memory and Cognition, 29,* 43–52.

King, M., & Rental, V. (1981). Research update: Conveying meaning in written texts. *Language Arts, 58,* 721–728.

Kintsch, W. (1998). *Comprehension: A paradigm for cognition.* New York: Cambridge University Press.

Langer, J. A. (1984). The effects of available information on responses to school writing tasks. *Research in the Teaching of English, 18,* 27–44.

Langer, J. A. (1985). Children's sense of genre: A study of performance on parallel reading and writing tasks. *Written Communication, 2,* 157–187.

Langer, J. A. (1986). *Children reading and writing: Structures and strategies.* Norwood, NJ: Ablex.

Lee, K., Karmiloff-Smith, A., Cameron, C. A., & Dodsworth, P. (1998). Notational adaptation in children. *Canadian Journal of Behavioural Science, 30,* 159–171.

Littleton, E. B. (1998). Emerging cognitive skills for writing: Sensitivity to audience presence in five-through nine-year-olds' speech. *Cognition and Instruction, 16,* 399–430.

Loban, W. (1976). *Language development: Kindergarten through grade twelve* (Research Report No. 18). Urbana, IL: National Council of Teachers of English.

MacArthur, C. A., Graham, S., & Harris, K. R. (2004). Insights from instructional research on revision with struggling writers. In L. Allal, L. Chanquoy, & P. Largy (Eds.), *Studies in writing: Vol. 13. Revision: Cognitive and instructional processes* (pp. 125–137). Norwell, MA: Kluwer.

Marchand, E., Coirier, P., & Dellerman, P. (1996). Textualization and polyphony in argumentative composition. In G. Rijlaarsdam, H. van den Bergh, & M. Couzijn (Eds.), *Theories, models, and methodology in writing research* (pp. 366–380). Amsterdam: Amsterdam University Press.

Matsuhashi, A. (1981). Pausing and planning: The tempo of written discourse production. *Research in the Teaching of English, 15,* 113–134.

McCutchen, D. (1986). Domain knowledge and linguistic knowledge in the development of writing ability. *Journal of Memory and Language, 25,* 431–444.

McCutchen, D. (1987). Children's discourse skill: Form and modality requirements of schooled writing. *Discourse Processes, 10,* 267–286.

McCutchen, D. (1988). "Functional automaticity" in children's writing: A problem of metacognitive control. *Written Communication, 5,* 306–324.

McCutchen, D. (2000). Knowledge acquisition, processing efficiency, and working memory: Implications for a theory of writing. *Educational Psychologist, 35,* 13–23.

McCutchen, D., Covill, A., Hoyne, S. H., & Mildes, K. (1994). Individual differences in writing: Implications of translating fluency. *Journal of Educational Psychology, 86,* 256–266.

McCutchen, D., Francis, M., & Kerr, S. (1997). Revising for meaning: Effects of knowledge and strategy. *Journal of Educational Psychology, 89,* 667–676.

Olive, T., & Kellogg, R. T. (2002). Concurrent activation of high- and low-level production processing in written composition. *Memory and Cognition, 30,* 594–600.

Pacton, S., & Fayol, M. (2003). How do French children use morphosyntactic information when they spell adverbs and present participles? *Scientific Studies of Reading, 7,* 273–287.

Page-Voth, V., & Graham, S. (1999). Effects of goal setting and strategy use on the writing performance of and self-efficacy of students with writing and learning problems. *Journal of Educational Psychology, 91,* 230–240.

Piolat, A., Roussey, J-Y., Olive, T., & Amada, M. (2004). Processing time and cogntive effort in revision: Effects of error type and of working memory capacity. In L. Allal, L. Chanquoy, & P. Largy (Eds.), *Studies in writing: Vol. 13. Revision: Cognitive and instructional processes* (pp. 21–38). Norwell, MA: Kluwer.

Pontecovo, C., & Zuccliermaglio, C. (1990). A passage to literacy: Learning in a social context. In Y. M. Goodman (Ed.), *How children construct lit-*

eracy (pp. 50–98). Newark, DE: International Reading Association.

Quinlan, T. (2004). Speech recognition technology and students with writing difficulties: Improving fluency. *Journal of Educational Psychology, 96,* 337–346.

Read, C. (1981). Writing is not the inverse of reading for young children. In C. H. Frederiksen & J. F. Dominic (Eds.), *Writing: The nature, development, and teaching of written communication* (pp. 105–118). Hillsdale, NJ: Erlbaum.

Reece, J. E., & Cumming, G. (1996). Evaluating speech-based composition methods: Planning, dictation, and the listening word processor. In M. C. Levy & S. Randsell (Eds.), *The science of writing* (pp. 361–380). Mahwah, NJ: Erlbaum.

Scardamalia, M., Bereiter, C., & Lamon, M. (1994). The CSILE Project: Trying to bring the classroom into World 3. In K. McGilly (Ed.), *Classroom lessons: Integrating cognitive theory and classroom practice* (pp. 201–228). Cambridge, MA: Bradford/MIT Press.

Share, D., & Levin, I. (1999). Learning to read and write in Hebrew. In M. Harris & G. Hatano (Eds.), *Learning to read and write: A cross-linguistic perspective* (pp. 89–111). New York: Cambridge University Press.

Tetroe, J. (1984, April). *Information processing demand of plot construction in story writing.* Paper presented at the meeting of the American Educational Research Association, New Orleans, LA.

Torrance, M. (1996). Strategies for familiar writing tasks: Case studies of undergraduates writing essays. In G. Rijlaarsdam, H. van den Bergh, & M. Couzijn (Eds.), *Theories, models, and methodology in writing research* (pp. 283–298). Amsterdam: Amsterdam University Press.

Treiman, R. (1993). *Beginning to spell.* New York: Oxford University Press.

Varnhagen, C. K. (1995). Children's spelling strategies. In V. W. Berninger (Ed.), *The varieties of orthographic knowledge: II. Relations to phonology, reading, and writing* (pp. 251–290). Dordrecht, The Netherlands: Kluwer.

Varnhagen, C. K., Boechler, P. M., & Steffler, D. J. (1999). Phonological and orthographic influences on children's vowel spelling. *Scientific Studies of Reading, 3,* 363–379.

Venezky, R. (1970). *The structure of English orthography.* The Hague: Mouton.

Wallace, D. L., & Hayes, J. R. (1991). Redefining revision for freshmen. *Research in the Teaching of English, 25,* 54–66.

Wallace, D. L., Hayes, J. R., Hatch, J. A., Miller, W., Moser, G., & Silk, C. M. (1996). Better revision in 8 minutes? Prompting first-year college writers to revise more globally. *Journal of Educational Psychology, 88,* 682–688.

Wright, R. E., & Rosenberg, S. (1993). Knowledge of text coherence and expository writing: A developmental study. *Journal of Educational Psychology, 85,* 152–158.

Chapter 9

Children's Understanding of Genre and Writing Development

Carol A. Donovan *and* Laura B. Smolkin

Children, like adults, write for a range of purposes (Bissex, 1980; Chapman, 1994, 1995; Dyson, 1999; Graves, 1975; Newkirk, 1987, 1989; Zecker, 1999). An important part of "doing school" is mastering the most frequently appearing generic forms (Cope & Kalantzis, 1993; Martin, 1989; Martin & Rothery, 1986). In children's everyday lives in schools, two genres receive the most attention: stories and informational texts (Kress, 1982, but see Dixon, 1987, for a different view). Stories expand from the folktale prominent in the preschool set to high fantasy and science fiction for gifted upper elementary students. Informational texts expand from concept books to picture information books, to science and social studies textbooks (with the occasional enlightened teacher using authentic materials and magazine articles).

In this chapter we have attempted to provide a comprehensive review of the literature on children's understandings of genre as related to writing development. We believe genre knowledge develops prior to conventional writing abilities and include studies of children's pretend readings, dictations, and oral readings of early writing attempts to provide the broadest description of children's genre knowledge and writing development. We begin by examining the theoretical models framing research in this area, and continue with the methodologies employed for collecting and analyzing data. We move next to the general questions that have been asked, then to the major findings to date in this emergent field of research. Finally, we consider implications for instruction and the important research still needed.

Theoretical Frameworks and Reviews of Relevant Research Used to Investigate Children's Genre Knowledge

Theoretical frameworks in studies of children's genre knowledge and writing development appear to be influenced by three major traditions. The rhetorical tradition examines the structure of language with intent to provide descriptive models. The social tradition acknowledges a shared structure of language, repeatedly pointing to the fact that language is never a solitary pursuit. The cognitive-psychological tradition centers itself in examinations of practical experiences to learn how individuals and/or groups make sense of their various language encounters. Generally, studies from this third tradition ground themselves not in a theoretical frame but in the review of related research. We have organized our review of framing sections by the tradition invoked, and present the major figures of the tradition cited by researchers of genre knowledge development.

131

The Rhetorical Tradition

Rhetorical studies have a long history. In a sense, work here began with Aristotle's examination of features and functions of tragedy, comedy, dithyrambic poetry, and phallic songs. According to Britton, Burgess, Martin, McLeod, and Rosen (1975), this classificatory work reemerged in 1776 with Campbell's four oratorical goals, then moved closer to still utilized classification systems in the mid-1800s with Bain's five categories: description, narration, exposition, oratory, and poetry. More modern work in this area continues to view the text as an object; structuralists of various stripes look for the patterns within texts. King and Rentel (1984) call upon Propp, Favat, Todorov, and Levi-Strauss in their theoretical framing.

To the degree that identified texts' structural components are highlighted, it may be possible to include work deriving from Sydney School here as well, despite the social aspects of the system. When, for example, Pappas (1991, 1993), Duke and Kays (1998), Kamberelis (1998, 1999; Kamberelis & Bovino, 1999), Donovan (2001), and Donovan and Smolkin (2002) rely upon text characteristics identified by Hasan (1984) or Martin and Rothery (1980, 1981), they incorporate theories of structure into their work.

Social Traditions

To our way of thinking, attention to the social aspect of texts first arose during the Soviet era. Bahktin's work in particular has been featured in a number of genre development studies' frameworks, including those of Chapman (1994, 1995), Kamberelis (1999), and Elster and Hanauer (2002). This socially informed text *Weltanschauung* is equally evident in Rosenblatt's (1938) highlighting of readers' receptions of text. We also include the work of various functional linguists, our reasoning being that these individuals have examined the text within the context, describing the relationships between systems that make meaning possible. So, when King and Rentel (1984), Langer (1986), and Pappas (1991) cite Halliday's work on learning about meaning making, they, too, are addressing the social aspects of texts. Or when Schnoor (2004) considers Rosenblatt's work

on response, she, too, frames her study within this social tradition.

Here, too, though far more data-based than the theoretical works noted earlier, we include the work of particular sociolinguists. For us, Labov and Waletzky's (1967) work on the structure of oral narrative is linked to Bakhtin's notions of primary oral genres. This particular study has highlighted story structure for many who have written about genre knowledge, including Martin and Rothery (1980), Hasan (1984), Stein and Glenn (1979), and Langer (1986).

Much of the work calling upon this tradition incorporates many of Berkenkotter and Huckin's (1993) theoretical principles, seeing genres and knowledge thereof as dynamic and situated, recognizing form and content, dualities of structure, and community ownership. Dyson's work (e.g., 1983, 1999) in particular follows this tradition.

The Cognitive-Psychological/Empirical Tradition

In many senses, genre-related work in this tradition actually originates with the work of Bartlett (1932), who, through his memory experiments, first established the psychological reality of story structures. Stein's work with numerous colleagues (e.g., Stein & Albro, 1997; Stein & Glenn, 1979; Stein & Policastro, 1984) all originates from this cognitive tradition of individuals and their abilities to complete various cognitive tasks. In making use of various Piagetian notions, Britton et al.'s (1975) framework attends to this tradition. Langer (1986), too, relies heavily upon cognitive-psychological research as she recalls work completed by Bereiter and Scardemalia, Flavell, and Markman in her opening materials. Duke and Kays (1998), opening with references to Hidi and Hildyard, situate their work within this tradition as well.

Methods Utilized to Study Children's Genre Knowledge

Data Collection Methods

In our review of the literature for this chapter, we noted that, with the exception of work done for special education students (e.g., Graham & Harris, 1993; Troia & Graham, 2002), there were very few quasi-experimental studies involving control groups and outcome measures. Most work has been descriptive and/or qualitative in nature. Given that, we have decided to focus on the nature of the tasks presented. The tasks are important because they let us know the purpose for the writing and the nature of scaffolding provided by either the teacher or the researcher, or by the conditions in which the text was produced. Here, we are using our taxonomy of scaffolded tasks (Donovan & Smolkin, 2002) to present a brief overview of the data collection methods utilized in studies of genre knowledge development.

METHODS USING TASKS OF UNKNOWN SCAFFOLDING

In studies placed in this category, the conditions under which children produced texts are unknown. In some studies, for example, genre and discourse-related issues have been noted by researchers investigating classroom discourse (e.g., Cazden, 1988; Heath, 1983), the writing process (e.g., Calkins, 1986; Graves, 1975), and early writing (e.g., Clay, 1975; Dyson, 1983, 1999; King & Rentel, 1984; Kroll, 1991).

Other studies of genre knowledge development have been based on the examination of students' writing produced in the classroom as part of instruction. For example, Britton and his colleagues (1975) requested students' writing samples from teachers in British secondary schools, along with a description of the assignment for which they were produced. Sowers (1985), Newkirk (1987), Chapman (1994, 1995), and Rothery (1984) examined primary-grade children's writing. Though function might be inferred (Chapman, 1994), without knowing the history of the task or desire that prompted the writing, knowledge of possible support that was provided remains unavailable to readers of these studies.

METHODS USING TASKS PROVIDING NO SCAFFOLDING

Studies of students' self-generated, self-selected writing (e.g., Bissex, 1980; Kroll, 1991) fall into this category. Bissex (1980) examined the form and function of her son Paul's self-generated writing from 5 to 7 years of age but does not supply sufficient information to make generalizations about any specific ways in which Paul's family scaffolded his compositions.

METHODS USING TASKS OF VARYING LEVELS OF SCAFFOLDING

When specific tasks are used to collect data about children's genre knowledge, there is no question about the purpose for the texts' production. Different tasks support children's ability to demonstrate their genre knowledge to greater and lesser degrees. These tasks, used to explore children's genre knowledge, can be arranged along a continuum of support, described below.

Prompted for a Specific Genre. At the lowest level of support are tasks that prompt children to produce the genre requested. Several studies have requested that children compose original texts and produce them either orally, as in Applebee's (1978) "Tell me a story," through dictation (King & Rentel, 1984), or in their own writing (e.g., Donovan, 2001; Harste, Woodward, & Burke, 1984; Kamberelis, 1999; King & Rentel, 1984; Langer, 1985, 1986; Sulzby, Barnhart, & Hieshema, 1989).

Prompted for a Specific Genre with Support. More scaffolding is provided when children do not have to generate or formulate all of the ideas but must still hold them in memory while composing the text. These include tasks such as recounting past experiences (e.g., Purcell-Gates, 1988), recalling and writing familiar texts (Kamberelis & Bovino, 1999), and completing a story following a stem such as Stein and Albro's (1997) "Once there was a fox. . . . " Such prompts activate children's story schema by introducing the formulaic beginning and common antagonist.

Instructed to Produce Recurring Text. Highly contextualized and routinely produced texts such as learning logs and daily journals provide even greater scaffolding (e.g., Wollman-Bonilla, 2000). Children have the support of the long-term context that has shaped and provided guidance in the production of certain texts at particular times.

Instructed to Produce Unknown Text with Visible Support. Tasks at this level provide visual or text support related to completing the task. Having a visual or text support at hand, even if it is not familiar, provides additional and continuous support for task completion. Such tasks include pretend readings of unfamiliar, wordless, and occasionally text-masked books (Bamberg, 1985; Berman & Slobin, 1994; Duke & Kays, 1998; Purcell-Gates, 1988), construction of expository text (Boscolo, 1996), as well as interviews in which children have their self-produced texts available during discussion (Donovan & Smolkin, 2002; Kamberelis & Bovino, 1999).

Instructed to Reproduce a Known Text. Scaffolding is increased yet again by asking children to reproduce a known text. Visible and familiar picture support is provided throughout the task at this level. Tasks include taking a turn to pretend to read a book that was just read aloud (King & Rentel, 1984; Pappas, 1991, 1993; Pappas & Brown, 1987), and pretending to read a familiar storybook (e.g., Sulzby, 1985).

Instructed to Produce Text with Instruction Provided. The highest level of support with written texts is direct instruction with revision. This category includes the use of text structure supports such as teaching story grammar (e.g., Baumann & Bergeron, 1993; Fitzgerald & Teasley, 1986; Gordon & Braun, 1985) or expository text structures (e.g., Gordon, 1990; Raphael & Kirschner, 1985; Wray & Lewis, 1995). Also included is the teaching of general planning strategies that are applied to writing of different genres (e.g., Troia & Graham, 2002). The highest possible level of scaffolding a writing-related task could provide is demonstrated by Englert and her colleagues' (1991) study in which they modeled and supported children's use of strategies for planning, organizing, drafting, editing, and revising their compositions in two specific genres.

METHODS USING MULTIPLE TASKS AND VARYING LEVELS OF SCAFFOLDING

Some studies have included multiple tasks in order to get multiple perspectives of children's knowledge (e.g., Cox & Sulzby, 1984; Donovan & Smolkin, 2002; Harste et al., 1984; Kamberelis & Bovino, 1999; King & Rentel, 1984; Langer, 1985, 1986; Purcell-Gates, 1988; Sulzby et al., 1989). Kamberelis and Bovino (1999), for example, asked kindergarten, first-grade, and second-grade chil-

dren to produce both a story or informational text based on a familiar book of that genre and an original story or information text.

Data Analysis Methods

Much of the research on children's genre knowledge has focused on micro-level aspects such as linguistic features (i.e., specifics of word usage, vocabulary, tense, and cohesion) that are consistent in, and often specific to, different genres (Boscolo, 1996; Cox, 1991; Hicks, 1990; Kamberelis, 1999; Pappas, 1991, 1993; Pappas & Brown, 1987; Purcell-Gates, 1988; Schnoor, 2004). Additional focus has been on more macro-level features, the inclusion of specific elements that make up the "grammars" of a genre (e.g., Englert, Stewart, & Hiebert, 1988; Fitzgerald & Teasley, 1986; Gordon, 1990; Hasan, 1984; Pappas, Keifer, & Levstick, 1999; Stein & Glenn, 1979; Troia & Graham, 2002). Researchers have also employed the global structure of content relationships, generally displayed through visual diagrams, and building on Meyer's (1975) work on how texts are structured (Chapman, 1994; Donovan, 2001; Donovan & Smolkin, 2002; Langer, 1985, 1986; Newkirk, 1987). And some research has applied analytic scales to consider additional factors such as quality and creativity (e.g., Fitzgerald & Teasley, 1986).

MICRO-LEVEL FEATURE ANALYSIS

Researchers (Christie, 1986; Cox, 1991; Kamberelis, 1999; Martin, 1984; Martin & Rothery, 1986; Pappas, 1991, 1993; Pappas & Brown, 1987; Pappas et al., 1999; Rothery, 1984, 1989) working from Halliday's Systemic Functional Linguistic tradition have considered children's understandings of the linguistic features and lexicogrammar of both story and informational genres. Researchers in this, as well as other, traditions (oral storytelling, pretend reading, readings of emergent writing, early writing, elementary school writing) have examined what young children know about the micro-level features of both story (e.g., Applebee, 1978; Kamberelis, 1999; Pappas & Brown, 1987; Purcell-Gates, 1988; Stein & Glenn, 1979; Sulzby, 1985) and informational genres

(Cox, 1991; Duke & Kays, 1998; Kamberelis, 1999; Newkirk, 1987; Pappas, 1991; Wollman-Bonilla, 2000).

MACRO-LEVEL FEATURE ANALYSIS

We have known a great deal about the macro-level structure of stories for quite some time (Bartlett, 1932; Hasan, 1984; Labov & Waletsky, 1967; Mandler & Johnson, 1977; Propp, 1968; Rumelhart, 1975; Stein & Glenn, 1979). The structure of informational texts (e.g., Martin, 1989; Meyer, 1975), a less developed area, continues to be examined. The general nature of a text, according to Hasan (1984), is the overall structure, or grammar, of the message form particular to specific genres. (global elements). These grammars, or genre elements, are important, because they provide information about the stories (Hasan, 1984) and the information books (Pappas et al., 1999), typically written for children, that are abundant in the schools and to which children from mainstream homes have most likely been exposed. The specific elements of science genres (Martin & Veel, 1995; Unsworth, 1998, 2001), including their visual components (Kress & van Leeuwen, 1996; van Leeuwen, 2000), as well as the features in children's science compositions (Wollman-Bonilla, 2000), have also been considered.

ANALYSIS OF ADDITIONAL FEATURES

Some studies have utilized analytic scales to assess children's story (e.g., Fitzgerald & Teasley, 1986; Troia & Graham, 2002) and informational writing (e.g., Troia & Graham, 2002). Troia and Graham, for example, considered length plus overall quality of stories and essays produced by fourth and fifth graders. Quality for stories was the sum of the scores for organization of story elements and appeal, which examined stylistic elements. Quality for essays was determined by length plus overall quality, which was the sum of the scores for macro-level organization and clarity. In a similar manner, Fitzgerald and Teasley (1986) assessed fourth graders' stories. However, they used different criteria to determine quality and examined additional features: coherence, temporal and causal links, and creativity.

Major Questions Regarding Genre and Writing Development

In this section, we present what appear to us to be the three major research questions addressed by research on children's understandings of genre and the relationship between that understanding and writing development. Although issues of genre have been discussed in other research on children's writing (e.g., Dyson, 1999; Graves, 1975; Leung, 2001), we are restricting our review to questions arising from studies specifically examining children's genre knowledge.

What Is the Nature of Children's Genre Knowledge and Their Developing Understanding of Genre Features?

The most frequently asked question in this evolving area of children's genre knowledge is "What is the nature of children's genre knowledge and their developing control/understanding of genre features?" This question about story knowledge has been asked by many researchers from many disciplines (e.g., Applebee, 1978; Chapman, 1994, 1995; Donovan, 2001; Donovan & Smolkin, 2002; Kamberelis, 1999; Kamberelis & Bovino, 1999; King & Rentel, 1984; Langer, 1986; Pappas, 1993; Pappas & Brown, 1987; Stein & Albro, 1997; Stein & Glenn, 1979; Stein & Policastro, 1984; Sulzby, 1985). It has also been asked about information genres by fewer but ever-growing numbers of researchers, including Chapman (1994, 1995), Donovan (2001), Donovan and Smolkin (2002), Duke and Kays (1998), Kamberelis (1999), Kamberelis and Bovino (1999), Langer (1985, 1986), Newkirk (1987), Pappas (1991, 1993), and Tower (2002, 2003). And, although the question does not appear in the genres typically explored by those influenced by systemic functional linguists, a few studies have also considered children's developing understandings of poetry (e.g., Kamberelis, 1999; Schnoor, 2004).

In What Ways Do Different Tasks and Other Methodological Choices Reveal Differences in Children's Genre Knowledge?

Our second question considers the role of research tasks in uncovering children's genre knowledge, under the assumption that different tasks require different levels of cognitive ability. As Englert et al. (1988) suggested, "The facilitative effects for different text structures cannot be assumed for different tasks, presentation modes, or response modes" (p. 144). Troia and Graham (2002) reinforced this point; their instructional study found no transfer from story writing to persuasive essay writing. Thus, the accumulation of information from studies using both similar and different tasks is crucial to generating theory about genre knowledge development. As noted earlier, some studies have included multiple tasks in order to get multiple perspectives of children's knowledge (e.g., Cox & Sulzby, 1984; Donovan & Smolkin, 2002; Harste et al., 1984; Kamberelis & Bovino, 1999; King & Rentel, 1984; Langer, 1985, 1986; Purcell-Gates, 1988; Sulzby et al., 1989). Use of multiple tasks provides insight into children's more and less secure concepts about genre. And, in a sense, these multiple tasks help prevent a slide down the slippery slope that considers component functions as separate rather than linked (Smagorinsky, 1995).

Also part of methodological choice is whether to link what children can produce (implicit knowledge) with what they are able to articulate (explicit knowledge). While the majority of studies reviewed herein have focused on children's implicit knowledge, information collected across a variety of tasks that require different levels of explicit control can provide both insights into the range of elementary school children's implicit and explicit knowledge of the two major genres important to school success and clues about possible instructional supports. This relationship of implicit and explicit knowledge has so far been investigated in only a small number of studies (Donovan & Smolkin, 2002; Kamberelis, 1999; Smolkin & Donovan, 2004), with researchers using a range of tasks, including explicit explanation of genre features.

How Can We Best Support
Young Children's Genre Knowledge
and Writing Development in Different Genres?

An important but similarly underrepresented area is research exploring how best to support children's genre knowledge development. Relatively fewer published data-based studies have addressed the issue of providing elementary school children experiences with or explicit instruction in specific genres (Duke & Kays, 1998; Fitzgerald & Teasley, 1986); fewer still have addressed actual instructional support in writing in different genres (e.g., Gordon, 1990; Lewis, Wray, & Rospigliosi, 1994; Troia & Graham, 2002).

Major Findings of Research on Children's Genre Knowledge and Writing Development

Children's Genre Knowledge and Their Developing Awareness of Genre Features

CHILDREN HAVE DIFFERENTIAL EXPERIENCE AND EXPOSURE TO A VARIETY OF GENRES

A number of studies have documented children's exposure and experience with reading and writing different genres in their homes (e.g., Pellegrini, 1991; Purcell-Gates, 1996; Taylor & Dorsey-Gaines, 1988; Teale, 1986). Other studies have looked at genre experiences in schools (Caswell & Duke, 1998; Chapman, 1994, 1995; Duke, 2000; Pappas, 1993; Smolkin & Donovan, 2001; Smolkin, Donovan, & Lomax, 2000), considered the impact of experience with multiple genres on children's preference for informational texts (Caswell & Duke, 1998; Horowitz & Freeman, 1995; Smolkin et al., 2000), and examined genre knowledge (Duke & Kays, 1998; Pappas, 1991). Although this research has not been conducted in ways that allow claims of causality, it does suggest that increased exposure to a particular genre is linked to increased genre knowledge.

GENRE KNOWLEDGE IS EMERGENT

Research has shown even very young children use oral language for different purposes (e.g., Halliday, 1975), demonstrate an emerging awareness of the different genres of written language (Christie, 1984; Kroll, 1991; Newkirk, 1989; Pappas, 1991, 1993; Pappas & Brown, 1987; Pontecorvo, 1997; Purcell-Gates, 1988; Zecker, 1999), and write using approximations of appropriate written language genres based on the purpose for their compositions (Bissex, 1980; Chapman, 1994; Harste et al., 1984). Research has indicated that by kindergarten, for many children, the foundation of written genre knowledge is established, apparent in their scribbles and other unconventionally written and abbreviated texts produced (e.g., Donovan, 2001; Donovan & Smolkin, 2002; Kamberelis, 1999; Kamberelis & Bovino, 1999; Newkirk, 1987; Pappas, 1993; Sulzby, 1985). These studies complement the pretend reading studies that have shown kindergarten and younger children using appropriate language registers for "reading" a storybook (Pappas, 1991, 1993; Pappas & Brown, 1987; Purcell-Gates, 1988; Sulzby, 1985), and "reading" an information book (Duke & Kays, 1998; Pappas, 1991, 1993). This fits with Kress's (1994) perspective that writing development necessarily includes genre knowledge, because specific purposes for writing must take on specific language structures. Thus, he believes that children's knowledge of genre is as important as their developing control of the conventions of spelling and punctuation.

MICRO-LEVEL FEATURES IN CHILDREN'S GENRE KNOWLEDGE AND WRITING

Researchers (Christie, 1986; Kamberelis, 1999; Martin, 1984; Martin & Rothery, 1986; Pappas, 1991, 1993; Pappas & Brown 1987; Pappas et al., 1999; Rothery, 1984, 1989), working from Halliday's systemic functional linguistic tradition have provided insights into children's understandings of the linguistic features and lexicogrammar of both story and informational genres. Researchers in this tradition and others (oral storytelling, pretend reading, readings of emergent writing, and early writing) have demonstrated that young children know micro-level features of story (Donovan, 1997; Kamberelis, 1999; Pappas, 1993; Pappas & Brown, 1987; Purcell-Gates, 1988; Sulzby, 1985) and informational genres (Cox, 1991; Duke & Kays, 1998; Kamberelis, 1999, Kamberelis & Bovino, 1999; Newkirk, 1987; Pappas, 1991, 1993; Wollman-Bonilla, 2000). They have also documented that micro-level knowledge of a variety of written genres develops early and becomes more complex with age (e.g., Applebee, 1978; Kamberelis, 1999; Langer, 1986; Stein & Albro, 1997) and increased experience with specific genres (Duke & Kays, 1998; Pappas, 1993). Although aware-

ness of the need to use a variety of genres in the elementary grades has risen because of this growing body of knowledge, this micro-level work has to date provided teachers with little concrete information on guiding their students' writing development.

MACRO-LEVEL FEATURES IN CHILDREN'S GENRE KNOWLEDGE AND WRITING

Children have also demonstrated knowledge of macro-level features in stories they have produced orally (e.g., Hasan, 1984; Stein & Albro, 1997; Stein & Glenn, 1979), in pretend reading studies of stories and informational genres (Pappas, 1991, 1993), and in their written texts (Chapman, 1994; Donovan, 2001; Donovan & Smolkin, 2002; Kamberelis, 1999; Kamberelis & Bovino, 1999; Langer, 1986; Newkirk, 1987; Wollman-Bonilla, 2000). Increased facility with macro-level features in a variety of literacy-related areas has been demonstrated in a number of studies (see Grabe, 2002, for a review).

CHILDREN'S APPROXIMATIONS TOWARD MATURE FORMS PROCEED THROUGH INTERMEDIATE FORMS

Various researchers have sought to create continua that might enable teachers to assess a child's current abilities, in order to determine appropriate instruction. To this end, they have worked to describe what Newkirk (1987) terms the intermediate forms, stages, or levels of production between the beginnings of writing and the mature forms. Rothery (1984), for example, described a "developmental genre typology" she and her colleague Martin had created. Like Britton and colleagues (1975), they described writing as emerging from an initial starting place, in this case, the "observation comment," into two separate paths, one expository and the other narrative. They suggested that the move to expository writing should be no more difficult than narrative (story) if models are provided. Still, neither this typology nor that of Britton et al., however helpful for thinking of the general nature of development, provide sufficient information and detail on the transitional forms to guide instruction.

In a study of third-, sixth-, and ninth-graders' reading and writing of stories and reports, Langer (1986), working from Meyer's (1975) prose analysis system, found that by third grade, children had well-developed understandings of both story structure and reports that served them in reading and writing of those texts. However, even though children in this study had a good foundation in the production of stories and informational texts (knowledge of story was greater), the instruction they received between third and ninth grades did not seem to provide the support necessary for substantial growth in complexity of their compositions in either genre. From this work, Langer (1992) created a continuum for children's report writing that began with "simple description" and ultimately built to "point of view with defense." She did not create a story writing continuum.

Newkirk (1987), then Chapman (1994, 1995), then Donovan (2001) and Donovan and Smolkin (2002) followed Langer's (1986, 1992) work on macro-level organization of texts, also using visual diagrams to show the relationships between content in both stories and information texts. In addition to providing more evidence that primary-grade children could write non-narrative texts (Chapman, 1994; Donovan, 2001; Donovan & Smolkin, 2002), these studies provided rich descriptions of young children's non-narrative texts, as well as additional insights about developing transitional forms in different genres.

Methodological Choices Impact Findings

Studies utilizing multiple methods generally have found that children usually demonstrate greater ability with the more highly supportive tasks (Donovan & Smolkin, 2002; Harste et al., 1984; Kamberelis & Bovino, 1999; King & Rentel, 1984). King and Rentel (1984) examined first and second-graders' dictated and written original stories, as well as a pretend reading of a fairytale just read aloud. These tasks demonstrated the difficulty the written task can impose on production, because the pretend readings were more complex than the dictated stories, which in turn were more complex than the children's written stories. Kamberelis and Bovino (1999) found, with few exceptions, that children produced more complex stories and informational texts in

response to their more highly scaffolded task (write a familiar text) than for the less scaffolded task (write an original text). Based on these findings, they suggest that "relying on cultural artifacts as scaffolds seemed to index and activate textual, intertextual, and contextual knowledge about particular discursive fields that children possessed even if they could not analyze, verbalize, or critique such knowledge" (p. 163).

In our own work with multiple tasks (Donovan & Smolkin, 2002), we found instances in which (1) scaffolding helped and enabled more sophisticated products, (2) scaffolding concealed abilities and actually seemed to constrain student production, and (3) children called upon their own forms of scaffolding. Children could produce organizationally more sophisticated story texts during the more highly scaffolded task of pretend reading than they could during the less scaffolded task of writing from prompts. They found support for their written compositions in text they already knew, utilizing intertextual connections (e.g., Cairney, 1990) to scaffold their writing, which, as for students in Kamberelis and Bovino's (1999) study, led to more sophisticated texts. However, in our "pretend readings" of an information book task, the text we selected provided such a simplistic version of an information book that upper elementary school children did their pretend reading in a similar simplistic manner, thus demonstrating less of their generic knowledge than was demonstrated through less scaffolded tasks. Clearly, then, tasks can constrain a display of abilities.

Supporting Young Children's Genre Knowledge Development and Writing Development in Different Genres

In 1986 Fitzgerald and Teasley remarked that there were few studies of the effect of instruction on narrative writing. In some ways, some 18 years later, that picture is little changed. Though there has been an ever-increasing amount of qualitative or descriptive research considering young children's abilities and knowledge with different genres, there are to date relatively few published quasi-experimental or experimental studies (including control groups and pretest–posttest measures) on the impact of genre instruction on elementary school children's writing in a range of genres. And we could find only one study (Troia & Graham, 2002) in which one instructional approach to supporting children's development in a particular genre was contrasted with another approach. Given these caveats, we present what we have been able to learn about instruction, writing, and genre knowledge.

STUDIES INVOLVING REPEATED EXPOSURE TO A SPECIFIC GENRE

Data from the research indicate that as few as three rereadings of a particular book can support children's use of specific story (Pappas & Brown, 1987; Pappas, 1993) and information (Pappas, 1991, 1993) genre features, and that continued exposure likely contributes to increases across several months (Duke & Kays, 1998).

STUDIES INVOLVING INSTRUCTION

The handful of instructional studies examining the impact of explicit teaching of genre features on elementary school children's writing abilities has focused primarily on teaching children the text structure of story (e.g., Fitzgerald & Teasley, 1986), exposition (Englert et al., 1988; Lewis et al., 1994), or poetry (Schnoor, 2004). Other studies have attended to the procedural knowledge of composition by providing explicit instruction in strategies for different components of the writing process (e.g., Englert et al., 1991; Gordon, 1990; Troia & Graham, 2002) and examining the impact of that instruction on children's abilities to compose different genre.

Findings in these studies indicate that direct teaching of narrative story structure, expository text structures, and poetry was responsible for children's improved understandings of, and abilities, in those genres. Schnoor (2004), for example, had teachers present various subgenres of poetry to 3- and 4-year-old preschoolers. She found age-related differences in the ability to both recall the poems and discuss the generic elements of the poetry. Likewise, the studies of explicit instruction in strategies for composing different types of texts found that students with the instruction outperformed control students.

Implications for Practice and Further Research on Genre Knowledge Development and Writing Development in Different Genres

We know that genre knowledge is emergent and that increased experiences with a particular genre are likely linked to children's increased knowledge of that genre. We have learned about the micro- and macro-level features of typical school genres and about the intermediate forms of children's developing notions of genre. We understand that methodological choices impact the results of studies in this area. And, finally, we know that we have a lot to learn about how best to support young children's genre knowledge development and writing development in different genres. Below, we consider the implications of the research reviewed for future studies and classroom practice.

Exposure to a Variety of Genres

The studies we reviewed for this chapter suggest that early and continued experience with different genres provides a foundation of knowledge about those genres from which children draw when reading, writing, and discussing different genres. Therefore, it seems logical that providing children with greater exposure to, and meaningful experiences with, reading and writing a range of important genres in their earliest schooling experiences, and throughout elementary school, would be beneficial. However, additional research is needed to determine which genres are best introduced when, how much exposure is optimal, and what meaningful experiences are best. More research on the development of genre knowledge would support our understanding of these issues as well.

Development of Genre Knowledge

Several developmental continua could help teachers who seek to scaffold their students' abilities in story and information report writing (Chapman, 1994; Donovan, 2001; Langer, 1992; Newkirk, 1987). These continua, with these emphases on intermediate forms, could potentially serve as a basis for scaffolding student writing. However, we need to know more about how children's genre knowledge/writing develops over time for a range of genres in a variety of settings, and for students with differential levels of school-like literacy experiences. Very young children's genre knowledge/writing development from a range of sociocultural backgrounds will need to be part of these long-term investigations to answer questions about the beginnings of this developmental progression. Importantly, this will provide a better understanding of the types of support leading to greatest facility with complex genre forms.

Supporting Genre Knowledge Development in Classrooms

Data from the research indicate that a few rereadings of a particular book can support children's use of genre features (e.g., Pappas, 1991), and that continued exposure likely contributes to even greater facility with those elements (Duke & Kays, 1998). Yet there remain few published instructional studies of practices designed to support genre knowledge. Future studies will need to contain not only rich descriptions of teachers' approaches to writing instruction in various genres but also measures that clearly report children's growth.

The Importance of Teacher Knowledge

As more and more research points to the need for children to know about and experience a range of genres, it becomes more important for teachers to know the features to which they must draw their students' attention. Teacher knowledge of genre is undoubtedly a variable of great importance when considering how best to support children's growing control of genres for reading and writing. We do not, however, have research that connects teachers' genre knowledge with their ability to support student development in this area. We need research that examines the impact of professional development on teachers' instruction and ability to scaffold, and to provide appropriate experiences for children.

As work proceeds in the areas we have described, we will learn more about children's earliest differentiation of generic types, about the nature of exposures to differing genres, and about instruction that supports children's successful growth in written communications. We look forward to this expanded knowledge base.

References

Applebee, A. (1978). *The child's concept of story: Ages 2 to 17.* Chicago: University of Chicago Press.

Bamberg, M. (1985). *Form and function in the construction of narratives: Developmental perspectives.* Unpublished doctoral dissertation, University of California, Berkeley.

Bartlett, F. (1932). *Remembering: A study in experimental and social psychology.* New York: Cambridge University Press.

Baumann, J. F., & Bergeron, B. S. (1993). Story map instruction using children's literature: Effects on first graders' comprehension of central narrative elements. *Journal of Reading Behavior, 25,* 407–437.

Berman, R. A., & Slobin, D. I. (1994). *Relating events in narrative: A crosslinguistic developmental study.* Hillsdale, NJ: Erlbaum.

Berkenkotter, C., & Huckin, T. (1993). Rethinking genre from a sociocognitive perspective. *Written Communication, 10,* 475–509.

Bissex, G. L. (1980). *GNYS AT WRK: A child learns to write and read.* Cambridge, MA: Harvard University Press.

Boscolo, P. (1996). The use of information in expository text writing. In C. Pontecorvo, M. Orsolini, B. Burge, & L. B. Resnick (Eds.), *Children's early text construction* (pp. 209–227). Mahwah, NJ: Erlbaum.

Britton, J., Burgess, T., Martin, N., McLeod, A., & Rosen, H. (1975). *The development of writing abilities* (11–18). London: Macmillan.

Cairney, T. H. (1990). Intertextuality: Infectious echoes from the past. *Reading Teacher, 43,* 478–485.

Calkins, L. M. (1986). *The art of teaching writing.* Portsmouth, NH: Heinemann.

Caswell, L. J., & Duke, N. K. (1998). Non-narrative as a catalyst for literacy development. *Language Arts, 75,* 108–117.

Cazden, C. (1988). *Classroom discourse: The language of teaching and learning.* Portsmouth, NH: Heinemann.

Chapman, M. L. (1994). The emergence of genres: Some findings from an examination of first grade writing. *Written Communication, 11,* 348–380.

Chapman, M. L. (1995). The sociocognitive construction of written genres in first grade. *Research in the Teaching of English, 29,* 164–192.

Christie, F. (1984). Varieties of written discourses. In *Children writing: Reader* (pp. 11–51). Geelong, Australia: Deakin University Press.

Christie, F. (1986). Writing in schools: Generic structure as ways of meaning. In B. Couture (Ed.), *Functional approaches to writing: Research perspectives* (pp. 221–240). Norwood, NJ: Ablex.

Clay, M. M. (1975). *What did I write?: Beginning writing behavior.* Portsmouth, NH: Heinemann.

Cope, B., & Kalantzis, M. (1993). *The powers of literacy: A genre approach to teaching writing.* Pittsburgh: University of Pittsburgh Press.

Cox, B., & Sulzby, E. (1984). Children's use of reference in told, dictated, and handwritten stories. *Research in the Teaching of English, 18,* 345–366.

Cox, B. E. (1991). Children's knowledge of organization, cohesion, and voice in written exposition. *Research in the Teaching of English, 25,* 179–218.

Dixon, J. (1987). The question of genres. In I. Reid (Ed.), *The place of genres in learning: Current debates* (pp. 9–21). Geelong, Australia: Deakin University Press.

Donovan, C. A. (2001). Children's development and control of written story and informational genres: Insights from one elementary school. *Research in the Teaching of English, 35,* 452–497.

Donovan, C. A., & Smolkin, L. B. (2002). Children's genre knowledge: An examination of K–5 students' performance on multiple tasks providing differing levels of scaffolding. *Reading Research Quarterly, 37,* 428–465.

Duke, N. K. (2000). 3.6 minutes per day: The scarcity of informational texts in first grade. *Reading Research Quarterly, 35,* 202–224.

Duke, N. K., & Kays, J. (1998). "Can I say 'once upon a time'?": Kindergarten children developing knowledge of information book language. *Early Childhood Research Quarterly, 13,* 295–318.

Dyson, A. H. (1983). The role of oral language in early writing processes. *Research in the Teaching of English, 17,* 1–30.

Dyson, A. H. (1999). Coach Bombay's kids learn to write: Children's appropriation of media material for school literacy. *Research in the Teaching of English, 33,* 367–402.

Elster, C. A., & Hanauer, D. I. (2002). Voicing texts, voices around texts: Reading poems in elementary school classrooms. *Research in the Teaching of English, 37,* 89–134.

Englert, C. S., Raphael, T., Anderson, L., Anthony, H., Stevens, D., & Fear, K. (1991). Making strategies and self-talk visible: Cognitive strategy instruction in writing in regular and special education classrooms. *American Educational Research Journal, 28,* 337–373.

Englert, C. S., Stewart, S. R., & Hiebert, E. H. (1988). Young writers' use of text structure in expository text generation. *Journal of Educational Psychology, 80,* 143–151.

Fitzgerald, J., & Teasley, A. B. (1986). Enhancing children's writing through instruction in narrative structure. *Journal of Educational Psychology, 78,* 424–432.

Gordon, C. J. (1990). A study of students' text structure revisions. *English Quarterly, 23,* 7–30.

Gordon, C. J., & Braun, C. (1985). Metacognitive processes: Reading and writing narrative discourse. In D. L. Forrest-Pressley, G. E. MacKinnon, & G. Waller (Eds.), *Metacognition, cognition, and human performance* (pp. 1–75). New York: Academic Press.

Grabe, W. (2002). Narrative and expository macrogenres. In A. M. Johns (Ed.), *Genre in the classroom: Multiple perspectives* (pp. 249–267). Mahwah, NJ: Erlbaum.

Graham, S., & Harris, K. R. (1993). Self-regulated strategy development: Helping students with learning problems develop as writers. *Elementary School Journal, 94,* 169–182.

Graves, D. H. (1975). An examination of the writing processes of seven year old children. *Research in the Teaching of English, 9,* 227–241.

Halliday, M. A. K. (1975). *Learning how to mean: Explorations in the functions of language.* London: Edward Arnold.

Harste, J. C., Woodward, V. A., & Burke, C. L. (1984). *Language stories and literacy lessons.* Portsmouth, NH: Heinemann.

Hasan, R. (1984). The nursery tale as a genre. *Nottingham Linguistic Circular, 13,* 71–102.

Heath, S. B. (1983). *Ways with words: Language, life, and work in communities and classrooms.* New York: Cambridge University Press.

Hicks, D. (1990). Narrative skills and genre knowledge: Ways of telling in the primary grades. *Applied Psycholinguistics, 11,* 83–104.

Horowitz, R., & Freeman, S. (1995). Robots versus spaceships: The role of discussion in kindergartners' and second graders' preferences for science text. *Reading Teacher, 49*(1), 30–40.

Kamberelis, G. (1998). Relationships between children's literacy diets and genre development: You write what you read. *Literacy Teaching and Learning, 3,* 7–53.

Kamberelis, G. (1999). Genre development and learning: Children writing stories, science reports, and poems. *Research in the Teaching of English, 33,* 403–463.

Kamberelis, G., & Bovino, T. D. (1999). Cultural artifacts as scaffolds for genre development. *Reading Research Quarterly, 34,* 138–170.

King, M., & Rentel, V. (1984). Transition to writing. In F. Christie (Ed.), *Children writing: Reader* (pp. 57–64). Geelong, Australia: Deakin University Press.

Kress, G. (1982). *Learning to write.* New York: Routledge.

Kress, G. (1994). *Learning to write* (2nd ed.). New York: Routledge.

Kress, G., & van Leeuwen, T. (1996). *Reading images: The grammar of visual design.* London: Routledge.

Kroll, L. R. (1991, August). *Meaning making: Longitudinal aspects of learning to write.* Paper presented at the Annual Meeting of the American Psychological Association, San Francisco, CA.

(ERIC Document Reproduction Service No. ED 340 043)

Labov, W., & Waletzky, J. (1967). Narrative analysis. In J. Helm (Ed.), *Essays on the verbal and visual arts* (pp. 12–44). Seattle: University of Washington Press.

Langer, J. A. (1985). Children's sense of genre: A study of performance on parallel reading and writing tasks. *Written Communication, 2,* 157–187.

Langer, J. A. (1986). *Children reading and writing: Structures and strategies.* Norwood, NJ: Ablex.

Langer, J.A. (1992). Reading, writing, and genre development: Making connections. In M.A. Doyle & J. Irwin (Eds.), *Reading and writing connections* (pp. 32–54), Newark, DE: International Reading Association.

Leung, C. (2001). A cognitive anthropological perspective on first-graders' classifications of picture storybooks. *Reading Psychology, 22,* 17–40.

Lewis, M., Wray, D., & Rospigliosi, P. (1994). . . . And I want it in your own words. *Reading Teacher, 47,* 528–536.

Mandler, J. M., & Johnson, N. S. (1977). Remembrance of things parsed: Story structure and recall. *Cognitive Psychology, 9,* 111–151.

Martin, J., & Rothery, J. (1980). *Writing Project Report No. 1.* Sydney: Department of Linguistics, University of Sydney.

Martin, J., & Rothery, J. (1981). *Writing Project Report No. 2.* Sydney, Australia: Department of Linguistics, University of Sydney.

Martin, J. R. (1984). Language, register and genre. In F. Christie (Ed.), *Children writing: Reader* (pp. 21–30). Geelong, Australia: Deakin University Press.

Martin, J. R. (1989). *Factual writing: Exploring and challenging social reality.* Oxford, UK: Oxford University Press.

Martin, J. R., & Rothery, J. (1986). What a functional approach to the writing task can show teachers about "good writing." In B. Couture (Ed.), *Functional approaches to writing: Research perspectives* (pp. 241–265). Norwood, NJ: Ablex.

Martin, J. R., & Veel, R. (Eds.). (1995). *Reading science.* London: Routledge.

Meyer, B. J. F. (1975). *The organization of prose and its effects on memory.* Amsterdam: North-Holland.

Newkirk, T. (1987). The non-narrative writing of young children. *Research in the Teaching of English, 21,* 121–44.

Newkirk, T. (1989). *More than stories: The range of children's writing.* Portsmouth, NH: Heinemann.

Pappas, C. C. (1991). Young children's strategies in learning the "book language" of information books. *Discourse Processes, 14,* 203–222.

Pappas, C. C. (1993). Is narrative "primary"?: Some insights from kindergartners' pretend readings of stories and information books. *Journal of Reading Behavior, 24,* 97–129.

Pappas, C. C., & Brown, A. (1987). Young children learning story discourse: Three case studies. *Elementary School Journal, 87,* 455–466.

Pappas, C. C., Keifer, B. Z., & Levstick, L. S. (1999). *An integrated language perspective in the elementary school* (2nd ed.). New York: Longman.

Pellegrini, A. D. (1991). A critique of the concept of at risk as applied to emergent literacy. *Language Arts, 68,* 380–385.

Pontecorvo, C. (Ed.). (1997). *Writing development: An interdisciplinary view.* Philadelphia: John Benjamin.

Propp, V. (1968). *Morphology of the folktale* (L. Scott, Trans.). Austin: University of Texas Press.

Purcell-Gates, V. (1988). Lexical and syntactic knowledge of written narrative held by well-read-to kindergartners and second graders. *Research in the Teaching of English, 22,* 128–160.

Purcell-Gates, V. (1996). Stories, coupons, and the *TV guide*: Relationships between home literacy experiences and emergent literacy knowledge. *Reading Research Quarterly, 31,* 406–428.

Raphael, T. E., & Kirschner, B. W. (1985). *The effects of instruction in comparison/contrast text structure on sixth-grade students' reading comprehension and writing products* (Research Series No. 161). East Lansing: Michigan State University, Institute for Research on Teaching.

Rosenblatt, L. (1938). *Literature as exploration.* New York: Appleton–Century.

Rothery, J. (1984). The development of genres: Primary to junior secondary school. In F. Christie (Ed.), *Children writing: Reader* (pp. 67–114). Geelong, Australia: Deakin University Press.

Rothery, J. (1989). Learning about language. In R. Hasan & J. R. Martin (Eds.), *Language development: Learning language, learning culture* (pp. 199–256). Norwood, NJ: Ablex.

Rumelhart, D. (1975). Notes on a schema for stories. In D. Bobrow & A. Collins (Eds.), *Representation and understandings* (pp. 211–236). New York: Academic Press.

Schnoor, D. J. (2004). *"Sing it, um, say it, um, read it again!": Poetry and preschool children's meaning-making responses.* Unpublished doctoral dissertation, University of Virginia, Charlottesville.

Smagorinsky, P. (1995). The social construction of data: Methodological problems of investigating learning in the zone of proximal development. *Review of Educational Research, 65,* 191–212.

Smolkin, L. B., & Donovan, C. A. (2001). Comprehension acquisition and information book read alouds in a first grade classroom. *Elementary School Journal, 102,* 97–122.

Smolkin, L. B., & Donovan, C. A. (2004). Developing a conscious understanding of genre: The relationship between implicit and explicit knowledge during the five-to-seven shift. *National Reading Conference Yearbook, 53,* 385–399.

Smolkin, L. B., Donovan, C. A., & Lomax, R. G. (2000). Is narrative primary?: Well, it depends . . . . *National Reading Conference Yearbook, 49,* 511–520.

Sowers, S. (1985). The story and the all-about book. In J. Hansen, T. Newkirk, & D. Graves (Eds.), *Breaking ground* (pp. 73–82). Portsmouth, NH: Heinemann.

Stein, N. L., & Albro, E. R. (1997). Building complexity and coherence: Children's use of goal-structured knowledge in telling stories. In M. Bamberg (Ed.), *Narrative development: Six approaches* (pp. 5–44). Mahwah, NJ: Erlbaum.

Stein, N. L., & Glenn, C. G. (1979). An analysis of story comprehension in elementary children. In R. Freedle (Eds.), *New directions in discourse processing* (pp. 53–120). Hillsdale, NJ: Erlbaum.

Stein, N. L., & Policastro, M. (1984). The concept of a story: A comparison between children's and teachers' perspectives. In H. Mandl, N. L. Stein, & T. Trabasso (Eds.), *Learning and comprehension of text* (pp. 113–155). Hillsdale, NJ: Erlbaum.

Sulzby, E. (1985). Children's emergent reading of favorite storybooks: A developmental study. *Reading Research Quarterly, 20,* 458–481.

Sulzby, E., Barnhart, J., & Hieshima, J. (1989). Forms of writing and rereading: A preliminary report. In J. Mason (Ed.), *Reading and writing connections* (pp. 31–61). Needham Heights, MA: Allyn & Bacon.

Taylor, D., & Dorsey-Gaines, C. (1988). *Growing up literate: Learning from inner-city families.* Portsmouth, NH: Heinemann.

Teale, W. H. (1986). Home background and young children's literacy development. In W. H. Teale & E. Sulzby (Eds.), *Emergent literacy: Writing and reading* (pp. 173–206). Norwood: Ablex.

Tower, C. (2002). "It's a snake, you guys!": The power of text characteristics on children's responses to information books. *Research in the Teaching of English, 37,* 55–88.

Tower, C. (2003). Genre development and elementary students' informational writing; A review of the literature. *Reading Research and Instruction, 42*(4), 14–39.

Troia, G. A., & Graham, S. (2002). The effectiveness of a highly explicit, teacher-directed strategy instruction routine: Changing the writing performance of students with learning disabilities. *Journal of Learning Disabilities, 35,* 290–305.

Unsworth, L. (1998). "Sound" explanations in school science: A functional linguistic perspective on effective apprenticing texts. *Linguistics and Education, 9,* 199–226.

Unsworth, L. (2001). *Teaching multiliteracies across the curriculum: Changing contexts of text and image in classroom practice.* Philadelphia: Open University Press.

van Leeuwen, T. (2000). It was just like magic: A multimodal analysis of children's writing. *Linguistics and Education, 10,* 273–305.

Wollman-Bonilla, J. (2000). Teaching science writing to first graders: Genre learning and recontextualization. *Research in the Teaching of English, 35,* 35–65.

Wray, D., & Lewis, M. (1995). Extending interactions with nonfiction texts: An EXIT into understanding. *Reading, 29*(1), 2–9.

Zecker, L. B. (1999). Different texts, different emergent writing forms. *Language Arts, 76,* 483–90.

Chapter 10

Motivation and Writing

Suzanne Hidi *and* Pietro Boscolo

The psychological conceptualization of motivation to write has developed relatively recently and has continued to change under the influence of the various motivational theories and theoretical views of writing that have developed over the past two and a half decades. In this chapter, we introduce these developments in chronological order and describe them in greater depth.

Psychological research on writing started officially at the end of the 1970s, when a few cognitively oriented scholars "discovered" writing—particularly expository writing—as an ability to be investigated in terms of information-processing and problem-solving strategies. Interestingly, there were a few early psychological studies on a motivational aspect of writing, writing apprehension (Daly & Miller, 1975a, 1975b). The increasing interest in the cognitive aspects of writing, however, may have constrained the development of studies on writing apprehension, which continued in the 1980s only as an isolated line of research. Due to the focus on cognition, the motivational and affective dimension of writing tended to be neglected or ignored by writing researchers in the 1980s (e.g., Boscolo, 1995; Hayes, 1996; Hidi, 1990). The most important early cognitive model of writing processes (Hayes & Flower, 1980) included motivation only as an element of the writing-task environment, such as the "motivating cues" of the teacher's stern expression that make a stu-

dent understand that a task is to be taken seriously (p. 12). Developmental studies have also focused on the cognitive aspects of writing. For instance, in Bereiter and Scardamalia's (1987) seminal book on written composition, there was no reference to motivation to write. In spite of some isolated voices in the 1980s arguing for the need for researchers to take into account the writer's needs, attitudes, beliefs, and intentions (e.g., Beach & Bridwell, 1984), on the whole, the cognitive approach contributed only in an essentially implicit way to the investigation of motivational and affective aspects of writing. By underlining the complexity and difficulty of the writing process, as well as its metacognitive dimensions, cognitive researchers prepared the way for subsequent studies on writing self-efficacy and self-regulation. The impressive development of motivational research during the 1980s had an impact on writing research only toward the end of the decade, when interest researchers on the one hand, and self-efficacy researchers on the other, demonstrated that writing is a complex activity involving not only cognitive and metacognitive processes but also affective components. The integration of metacognitive and affective aspects of writing was further investigated in studies on self-regulation and on its motivational implications. The outcome of these developments led to a new conceptualization of the writing process, as demonstrated by Hayes's (1996) revised model, in which motivational variables have a more important role.

In the 1980s, the social-constructivist approach to literacy and literacy learning developed under the influence of Vygotsky's legacy and cultural studies of language and cognition. In this approach, writing is viewed as a cultural practice rather than as a cognitive ability; thus, it provides a perspective that is quite different in theory and method from more traditional research on writing motivation. However, as we see later, some social constructivism aspects have high motivational potentials, such as an emphasis on writing in natural settings, collaborative writing, and the dialogical dimension of written communication. According to this approach, motivation to write is not a "variable" of writing tasks assigned to students in school or in psychological studies, but is deeply rooted in the contexts in which writing is a meaningful, authentic activity.

Recently, Bruning and Horn (2000) argued that nurturing students' positive beliefs about writing, fostering authentic writing goals and contexts, providing students with a supportive context for writing, and creating a positive emotional classroom environment are the conditions that determine students' motivation to write. Theirs is an integrated view in which students' beliefs about writing interact with instructional and environmental factors. We are also concerned with such conditions; however, we titled this chapter "Motivation and Writing" instead of "Motivation to Write," because our aim was not to only to identify the conditions that can contribute to developing students' motivation to write but also to present the state of the art on this topic, including the relationships between writing research on the one hand, and motivational research on the other.

Writing as a Motivational Problem

Given the unique problems related to writing motivation (Hidi, Berndorff, & Ainley, 2002), it is intriguing that relatively few research studies have been conducted in the area. As Nolen (2003) noted, writers, in contrast to readers, produce/create texts rather than simply consume them. Thus, readers can be motivated by the material to persist in

reading, and they can select ideas provided by the author of the text to store and to link with already stored information, creating unique associations. Similarly, science and math problems provide information with which students can interact. Writers, on the other hand, have to produce texts often with only minimal environmental/curricular input. For example, when given a topic to write about, the ideas and text generated require a knowledge base on which the individual can draw. In addition to the difficulty created by knowledge factors that are prerequisites for writing, the complexity of the task; the solitary nature of the activity, with no immediate feedback; and the effort needed to persist in the task are other aspects of writing that can adversely affect writers' motivation (Zimmerman & Risemberg, 1997).

Researchers have focused on understanding these motivational problems from the theoretical perspectives of interest, self-efficacy, self-regulation, and the social and cultural nature of writing. These perspectives form the headings for the remainder of this chapter.

Interest and Writing

Interest has been defined as a motivational variable, as well as a psychological state that occurs during interactions between persons and their environment, and is characterized by increased attention, concentration, and affect. In addition, the term *interest* also refers to a relatively enduring predisposition to engage with particular content, such as objects, events, and ideas. In contrast to cognitively driven motivational theories, in interest theory, interest is always considered to have both an affective and cognitive component. The assumption that affect is an inherent component of interest, and that it has a biological foundation are critical features that set it apart from other motivational constructs (Hidi, 2003). Thus, experiencing interest involves positive affect from the outset of experience that can be assumed to be combined or integrated with cognition as it develops (Hidi & Renninger, 2004; Krapp, 2000, 2003; Renninger, 2003). Another general characteristic of interest is its content or object-specificity. Rather than being globally interested, individuals have interest in some activity, subject, topic, task, or even text segments (Alexander & Murphy, 1998).

Research has demonstrated that interest is one of the motivational variables that has a powerful positive effect on individuals' cognitive performance and affective experience (for reviews, see Hidi, Renninger, & Krapp, 2004; Hoffman, Krapp, Renninger, & Baumert, 1998; Renninger, Hidi, & Krapp, 1992; Schiefele, 1998). Although the positive influence of interest on academic writing has been well established across individuals and knowledge domains, research has been equivocal on how interest can best be utilized to improve writing performance. These equivocal findings may be due to researchers' failure to distinguish between various forms and phases of interest development (Hidi & Renninger, in press).

Recognizing that there have been two distinct ways in which the role of interest in learning has been investigated, Hidi and colleagues (e.g., Hidi, 1990; Hidi & Anderson, 1992; Hidi & Baird, 1988) argued that these two categories corresponded to the two different ways in which the psychological state of interest can be generated in people. Situational interest is evoked rather suddenly by something in the environment that focuses attention and represents an affective reaction that may or may not have a long-term effect on individuals' knowledge and value systems (see also Murphy & Alexander, 2000). The second category, individual interest, has a dual meaning. It refers to both a psychological state and a relatively enduring predisposition to attend to events and objects, as well as to reengage in activities (for reviews, see Krapp, 2000; Renninger, 2000). This predisposition develops slowly, tends to be long-lasting, and is associated with increased knowledge and value (Renninger, 1992, 2000).

Early on, researchers recognized that although there are differences between situational and individual interest, they are not dichotomous phenomena; they overlap in several areas (for a more complete review, see Hidi & Harackiewicz, 2000; Hidi, 2000, 2001). In addition, researchers have suggested that there is a developmental thread between environmentally triggered experiences of interested engagements that produce the psychological state of interest and the development of individual interest as a predis-

position (Hidi & Anderson, 1992; Hidi & Renninger, in press; Krapp, 2002; Renninger, 2000; Silvia, 2001). More specifically, Hidi and Renninger (in press) argued that interest development involves four phases. According to the model, in the first phase, situational interest for a particular content is triggered. If the triggered situational interest is sustained, the second phase, referred to as maintained situational interest, evolves. In the third phase, this type of interest shifts into an emerging individual interest, in which knowledge is accruing, fueled by individuals' "curiosity questions" about the content of their interest (Renninger, 2000), and increased effort to self-regulate and identify with the content of their interest (Hannover, 1998; Krapp, 2000, 2003; Todt & Schreiber, 1998). In the fourth and final phase, referred to as a well-developed individual interest, the person has increased ability to self-regulate, a widening knowledge base, and increased value for the content. The relevance of these four developmental phases to writing is discussed further below.

In addition to situational and individual interest, in some investigations, researchers have focused on the effect of topic interest on academic performance. The definition of topic interest has been unclear. In early studies, some researchers (e.g., Hidi & McLaren, 1991) considered topic interest to be a form of situational interest. In subsequent studies, topic interest has been viewed as a form of individual interest (e.g., Benton, Corkill, Sharp, Downey, & Khramtsova, 1995; Schiefele, 1996; Schiefele & Krapp, 1996). More recently, researchers have pointed out that topic interest may be closely linked to individual interest in some cases and to situational interest in others (Hidi, 2001), and Ainley, Hidi, and Berndorff (2002) have empirically demonstrated that both situational and individual interest can contribute to topic interest.

The evaluation of the role of writers' interest in topics is complicated not only by the various ways in which topic interest has been conceptualized but also by how it has been measured. In the first set of studies that investigated the influence of topic on writing performance, Hidi and McLaren (1991) asked sixth-grade students to write on high- and low-interest topics. These selections were based on writers' previous ratings of the interestingness of various topics. Whereas the data indicated that students' motivation to write increased if they were given topics of interest, this motivation did not necessarily result in improved writing performance. Analysis of the data suggested that knowledge factors play a major role in the quality of the writing that students produce (Boscolo & Mason, 2000; Tobias, 1994). For example, young children may be fascinated by the topic of space travel; however, those who have not accumulated knowledge on the topic cannot adequately write about it. The authors concluded that individuals may have problems writing even on highly interesting topics, if they do not have sufficient content knowledge. On the other hand, Renninger, Ewen, and Lasher (2002) reported that if a topic identified as an individual interest (i.e., topics for which an individual had increased knowledge and value) was inserted in a passage, then 11-year-old students tended to write longer reconstructive recalls and attended better to the meaning of the text. It should be noted that in Hidi and McLaren's previoiusly mentioned studies, only triggered and/or maintained situational interest was measured, whereas Renninger et al. (2002) identified emergent and/or well-developed individual interest.

In their study on interest, knowledge, and narrative writing, Benton et al. (1995) used a different form of interest measure. Whereas Renninger et al. (2002) considered stored knowledge to be a component of individual interest, Benton et al. (1995) treated interest and knowledge as separate measures. Ninth graders and undergraduate college students wrote a story about baseball. After the students finished their compositions, their knowledge of and interest in the topic were evaluated. The interest measure included a 7-point scale of students' interest in baseball and five questions regarding their experiences playing or watching baseball. On the basis of the interest measure, participants were placed in high- and low-interest groups. The findings indicated that although knowledge and interest were positively correlated, there were differences in the ways in which they affected writing performance. For example, although both individual interest and topic knowledge influence the planning process, only knowledge predicts the interestingness of the produced text. It is important to

note that the authors of this study evaluated individual interest by giving only one topic (baseball) to students to establish which individuals had high and low levels of individual interest in it. This type of rating does not separate those students who have well-developed individual interest from the ones who have maintained situational interest or emerging individual interest. Renninger et al. (2002) used more relative measures to identify different levels of individual interest. Participants in their study filled out a questionnaire that asked them about their knowledge of, feelings about, and actual activity with 40 different activities previously identified as being of potential interest for that age group and population of students.

In a follow-up study, Albin, Benton, and Khramtsova (1996) investigated how individual differences in undergraduate students' interest in two topics (baseball and soccer) were related to narrative writing. The results indicated that interest in baseball was significantly related to writing measures, such as producing topic-relevant ideas controlling for gender, discourse, and topic knowledge. In addition, students wrote more topic-relevant information on the relatively high-interest topic (baseball) than on the relatively low-interest topic (soccer).

So far we have been considering how the level of interest in the content that one writes about influences the quality of writing production. However, there is another way in which interest in writing varies among individuals. In recent years, a number scholars have underlined the importance of writing as an interesting activity (Boscolo & Cisotto, 1997; Lipstein & Renninger, in press; Nolen, 2003, in press). Boscolo and Cisotto (1997) argued that whereas interest in a topic may facilitate and energize writing, topic interest does not guarantee interest in writing as an activity. Thus, topic interest may be a necessary condition for interest in writing, but it is not a sufficient one. Similarly, Nolen (2003, in press) suggests that motivation for writing may come from an individual's interest in a topic or it may be related to experiences of creative endeavours that are accompanied by positive emotions, such as sense of accomplishment at being able to communicate one's thoughts and feelings. She emphasizes that her research does not view reading and writing activities simply as means to an end (i.e., as tools to be used in learning activities). Rather, she is concerned with how reading and writing could become interesting activities for the learner. This view of writing characterizes the social-constructivist approach to literacy learning, which is addressed later in this chapter.

In a longitudinal study using qualitative methods, Nolen (2003) examined the developmental path of writing and reading that leads from situational to individual interest. Children in grades 1–3 and their teachers were observed regularly in their classrooms and interviewed annually about reading and writing. In addition, observational field notes on literacy activities provided extra information on classroom context and student development. The results of the study showed that in both reading and writing, there was developmental progress from situational to more long-term individual interest.

Lipstein and Renninger (in press) investigated 12- to 15-year-old students' interest in writing and examined the relations between students' interest and their competence, effort, feelings of self-efficacy, and goals. They also suggested conditions that need to be in place to support students to write effectively. In their investigation, Lipstein and Renninger utilized the four-phase model of interest development (Hidi & Renninger, in press) in explaining students' responses to questionnaires and interviews. The researchers found that all students, regardless of their phase of interest, had developed a sense of what writing involves and recognized the importance of self-expression. The findings, however, showed differences between students in various phases of interest development. For example, student goals, perceptions of the effort that writing tasks require, and circumstances that can make writing a positive experience varied across different phases of interest development. Students with low levels of interest in writing aimed at getting the task done (i.e., finishing the task as soon as possible). Students with maintained situational interest for writing expressed an interest in doing things well, as defined by their teachers, and in getting good grades. Students with individual interest in writing also wanted to do well, but their standards seemed to have been more self-defined, such as feeling good about their writing. Students' willingness to put effort in the writing tasks similarly varied across the different phases of interest development. Interestingly, both students with low interest in writing and those with individual interest reported putting lots of effort in their writing tasks, but for different reasons. Low interest seems to have coincided with lack of both procedural and discourse knowledge, resulting in a slow and onerous procedure. In the case of students with individual interest in writing, the researchers speculated that these types of writers may launch into writing without clear planning, and thus require more time to structure and organize their abundant ideas. An alternative explanation is that writers with individual writing interest have expanded discourse and procedural knowledge related to writing, and are willing to invest considerable effort to develop their texts for others. Students with maintained situational interest did not feel that they expended great effort on writing.

Students in various phases of interest development also differed in how much they liked writing and felt self-efficacious. Low interest in writing coincided with considering writing boring and painful. Students with individual interest in writing talked about how much they liked to write and considered it "a real fun thing to do." Students in these two groups displayed strong negative and positive feelings, respectively. In contrast, students with maintained situational interest did not express strong affect. Descriptions of self-efficacy—a topic to which we now turn—positively correlated with interest development.

Self-Efficacy and Writing

Self-efficacy is a cognitive construct that represents individuals' beliefs and personal judgements about their ability to perform at a certain level and affects choice of activities, effort, and performance (Bandura, 1986, 1997; Pajares, 1996; Schunk & Swartz, 1993; Zimmerman, 1989, 2000a). Self-efficacious individuals are more willing to participate, to work harder, and to persist longer in tasks and have less adverse reactions when encountering difficulties than do those who doubt their capabilities. Self-efficacy was also found to be predictive of the challenge level of academic tasks students choose to perform (e.g., Bandura & Schunk, 1981), and students' effort, as measured by their rate of performance and expenditure of energy (e.g., Multon, Brown, & Lent, 1991). Self-efficacy theory, like other cognitively oriented motivational theories, considers affect as an outcome of cognitive processing (Meyer & Turner, 2002). For example, increased self-efficacy has been shown to result in less stress and anxiety.

Self-efficacy for writing refers to individuals' perceptions of their ability to produce certain types of texts (Pajares & Johnson, 1994; Pajares & Valiante, 1997; Schunk & Swartz, 1993; Zimmerman & Bandura, 1994). Positive associations between self-efficacy for writing and writing outcomes have been demonstrated in many investigations over the last 20 years. For example, Schunk and Swartz (1993) investigated the relationship between fourth and fifth graders' writing self-efficacy and writing skills, and reported that self-efficacy was highly predictive of both writing skill and strategy use. They summarized the findings as follows: "Learners who feel competent about writing should be more likely to choose to write, expend effort, and persist at writing tasks than students who doubt their capabilities" (p. 338). An additional result of this study was that a process goal and progress feedback given to students enhanced the transfer of writing strategy use, skill, and self-efficacy. Other researchers demonstrated that writing self-efficacy of older students was predictive of their intrinsic motivation to write and of self-regulatory processes involved in high or adequate levels of writing (see Zimmerman & Risemberg, 1997, for a review of the literature), and that adults' self-efficacy for writing predicted their writing performance (McCarthy, Meier, & Rinderer, 1985; Pajares & Johnson, 1996; Shell, Murphy, & Bruning, 1989).

Self-efficacy information is acquired from an individual's own performance, including physiological indices, as well as feedback from others. One important issue is how accurate students' judgement is regarding their self-efficacy. Graham and Harris (1989) reported that learning disabled students showed unrealistically high self-efficacy judgements of their capabilities for creative writing. In addition, they demonstrated that

self-instructional strategy training of learning disabled fifth and sixth grade students produced meaningful and lasting improvements in their composition skills and significantly increased their self-efficacy. Graham and Harris concluded that to accurately evaluate one's capabilities is an important metacognitive skill, and that young children and problem learners have difficulties in assessing their problems and performance.

Self-Efficacy and Interest

Research on interest and self-efficacy developed independently, although some researchers argued that increased self-efficacy results in increased interest (e.g., Bandura & Schunk, 1981; Zimmerman & Kitsantas, 1999). Hidi et al. (2002) argued that interest is not simply an outcome of self-efficacy, but that the two variables are closely associated and may reciprocally influence each other's development. On the theoretical level, both interest and self-efficacy are content/domain specific (Bandura, 1986; Krapp, Hidi, & Renninger, 1992; Pajares & Johnson, 1994; Renninger, 2000); therefore, in any given area, the two variables must be related to the same knowledge base, and their development should be interrelated. At the empirical level, Hidi et al. (2002) demonstrated that interest and self-efficacy are closely associated. They investigated 180 sixth graders' argument writing and examined whether writing self-efficacy and liking are general or genre-specific, and whether these variables are related to general interest in writing. The results showed that students' liking and self-efficacy were genre-specific. For example, students' liking and self-efficacy for writing stories were different from those for summaries. In addition, there was a positive association between genre-specific liking and self-efficacy and general interest in writing.

From a developmental perspective, interest and self-efficacy may have a reciprocal relation. On one hand, self-efficacy theory postulates that when individuals receive feedback, either from others or from their own activity, this information can show that they are competent and able to continue to learn, thus strengthening their self-efficacy (Bandura, 1986). Engaging in and continuing to work with interesting activities may provide additional information that may contribute to increasing self-efficacy. Research findings demonstrated that when students are engaging in an activity with interest, they tend to be focused, effortful, persistent, and to experience positive emotions (Ainley et al., 2002; Renninger, 2000). With such engagements, one would expect improved performance and corresponding increases in self-efficacy. On the other hand, the literature suggests that self-efficacious individuals perceive themselves as being capable of dealing with a given task, and are motivated to engage in that task. These individuals also exhibit increased effort, persistence, and positive emotional reactions (Bandura, 1997; Zimmerman, 2000a). Thus, when individuals are self-efficacious about a task, this may impact positively on their interest, even in the case of tasks that they initially may have seen as boring.

Self-Regulation of Writing

Writing is a particularly demanding activity, because various cognitive, metacognitive, and linguistic processes must be coordinated. A student who is assigned a writing task has to make decisions not only about what and how to write, but also about the use of time, the selection of sources to gain information, the strategies to be adopted, and so on. In summary, writing requires self-regulation. The cognitive models of writing cited at the beginning of this chapter include metacognitive and executive control components, such as the planning phase and the monitor function in Hayes and Flower's (1980) model, and text interpretation and reflection in Hayes's (1996) revised model. Self-regulation, however, is by no means only a cognitive and metacognitive matter. Although various definitions of self-regulation have been given according to different theoretical perspectives (see Zimmerman, 2000b; Zimmerman & Schunk, 2001, for a review), all agree that self-regulated students are not only metacognitively and behaviorally active, but also motivationally active in attaining their learning goals. With regard to writing, self-regulation refers to self-initiated thoughts, feelings, and actions that writers use to attain various literary goals, which include improving their writing skills and en-

hance the quality of the text they create (Zimmerman & Risemberg, 1997). A self-regulated writer is one who can successfully manage the complexity of writing. High competence in the use of strategies is likely to make a writer feel more efficacious. High self-efficacy, in turn, activates a writer's self-satisfaction and may stimulate his or her interest in the writing task and writing in general (Graham & Harris, 2000). In the 1990s, Graham, Harris, and colleagues (e.g., Graham, Harris, & Troia, 2000; Harris, & Graham, 1996; Harris, Graham, Mason, & Saddler, 2002) designed a writing program called Self-Regulated Strategy Development (SRSD), that aimed at helping students, particularly those struggling with writing, become self-regulated and goal-oriented writers, under the assumption that a self-regulated writer is also one who "wants" to write.

Although self-regulation is a major area in motivational research, empirical studies on the relationships between the use of self-regulatory strategies in specific domains and other motivational variables are not numerous. Zimmerman and his coworkers (Zimmerman & Kitsantas, 1999, 2002; Zimmerman & Risemberg, 1997) have analyzed self-regulation of writing according to Bandura's (1986) social-cognitive model. In an essentially descriptive conceptualization, they view self-regulation as involving three elements: the person, the behavior, and the environment. Behavioral self-regulation implies an individual's observation of his or her behavior and its modification to reach a goal or hold an achievement standard. Environmental self-regulation takes into account the feedback coming to the individual from his or her environment. Finally, internal self-regulation regards an individual's use of his or her affective states (e.g., anxiety control) and cognitive processes (e.g., the use of memory strategies).

This triadic view allowed Zimmerman and Risemberg (1997) to identify, on the basis of famous writers' experiences, 10 types of writing self-regulatory activites, grouped according to the three elements listed earlier. A writer regulates his or her *environment*, for instance, by choosing, adapting, or modifying a suitable writing environment (e.g., a quiet and silent place); controls his or her *behavior* (e.g., by taking into account how much he or she has written in a certain time, or by using verbalization to facilitate idea generation); and practices an *internal control* over his or her activity (e.g., by allotting time to be assigned to writing, or by setting specific objectives for the writing task).

The strategies of a self-regulated writer can also be described, with more emphasis on motivational and affective aspects, in the frameworks of recursive models of writing (Zimmerman & Kitsantas, 1999, in press). Hayes and Flower (1980) provided such a model. They disntinguished three recursive phases of the writing process: planning, translation, and revision. A similar model is Rohman's (1965), that includes forethought, performance, and self-reflection phases. The various postulated phases of writing provide a framework in which self-regulation strategies and the related affective states as well as motivational processes can be described. For instance, in the forethought or planning phase of writing, the cognitive and metacognitive processes related to a writer's reflection on what and how to write are also connected to his or her motivation and goals. More specifically, in this phase, the writer can deal with his or her self-efficacy beliefs ("Am I able to manage this writing task?"), expectations regarding the outcome ("Will I write a good text?"), interest ("Do I like carrying out this writing task? Is writing interesting to me?"), mastery goals ("Through writing, I elaborate my thoughts about the topic") and performance goals ("I want to write the best essay in my class").

In addition, Zimmerman and Kitsantas's (1999) analysis goes beyond a descriptive classification of self-regulatory strategies as it focuses on the developmental sequence of writing self-regulation. In this sequence are four progressive levels. The first level of regulation is observation, in which the learner gets information from watching a model, such as a teacher who shows how to combine several simple sentences into a complex one. The second level of regulation is emulation; that is, the student learns to enact the model's (e.g., the teacher's), performance. In other words, at this level, the student tries to compose a sentence autonomously based on the model's performance. In the third level of regulation, self-control, the learner is able to use a particular strategy as planned and self-monitors the process. Primary sources of motivation at this level are the learner's self-

satisfaction reactions stemming from awareness of matching or surpassing the model. In the fourth level, self-regulation, students learn to adapt their performance to different internal and external conditions. Primary sources of motivation at the self-regulation level are high self-efficacy and interest in writing. A basic aspect of self-regulation is the ability to shift from processes (the steps through which a skill is achieved at a proficiency level) to outcome goals that is, to the target that a writer wants to achieve (e.g., writing a summary without exceeding a certain number of words). A novice writer takes the advantage by using a strategy until he or she is able to master it: His or her objective—and that of his or her teacher—is to learn a process well (process goal). However, when the writing process becomes automatic, the student can pose another type of objective (i.e., outcome goal) and check by him- or herself the quality of the performance. For a novice writer, the process goal precedes the outcome goal, because, as a novice, he or she needs to learn through a guide and cannot learn from his or her errors. Moreover, those errors might produce frustration, which is particularly damaging during an initial learning phase.

The relationships between the self-control and self-regulation levels and their motivational correlates have been analyzed in a study on the acquisition of a writing revision skill (Zimmerman & Kitsantas, 2002). Female high school students were assigned a writing task that consisted of combining a series of simple sentences into a single, nonredundant sentence. Participants were divided into several groups according to three conditions: process goal, outcome goal, and shifting goal. Girls in the outcome goal condition had to rewrite simple sentences into a complete sentence using the minimal number of words; that is, focus was on the target, not on the procedure. Girls in the process goal condition were told they should concentrate on properly following the steps to carry out the task. Girls in the shifting goal condition were told to concentrate on the procedure, but after 15 minutes, when they achieved automaticity, they had to rewrite the sentences using the minimal number of words. The results showed that girls who shifted to outcome goal (from self-control to self-regulation level) performed best in the writing task. They also displayed the highest self-efficacy beliefs, were most self-satisfied, and reported to be interested in the writing task. In contrast, when participants focused on the outcome and neglected the process, they tended to attribute their errors to low ability and were less satisfied with their performance. This more negative attitude to writing was reflected in lower self-efficacy and reduced interest in acquiring the writing skill.

In a subsequent study, Zimmerman and Kitsantas (2002) investigated the relationship between the first (observation) and second (emulation) levels, namely, the influences of modelling and social feedback on the acquisition of a writing revision skill. The study aimed to demonstrate the dependence between the two levels and, more specifically, how the type of observational learning influences subsequent learning and attitude toward writing skill during emulative practice. The same writing revision task as in the 1999 study was employed. College students were assigned to one of six conditions: mastery modeling, coping modeling, and no modeling, each with and without social feedback. Students in the mastery modeling condition observed the experimenter showing how to use the revision strategy (observation level) without any error, whereas students in the coping model condition observed the experimenter who modeled the strategy, including making and correcting errors, as well as gradually reducing them. Students in the no-modeling condition were shown the training problems on an overhead projection screen and told to study them for a subsequent similar task. After the observation phase, all students had to solve 12 practice problems (emulation level). In the social feedback condition, students received positive feedback from the experimenter about their performance, whereas in the no-social-feedback condition, they received no feedback. Before the practice phase, all participants were asked to indicate their perceptions of self-efficacy for solving the problems. After the practice phase, they were posttested for self-efficacy, writing skill attributions, self-satisfaction, and interest.

Students' writing skills in the coping modeling group surpassed those in the mastery modeling group, who surpassed those in the no-modeling control group. Unexpectedly, there was no significant difference in self-efficacy beliefs of students before the emulation phase, in that all the modeling groups showed high levels of self-efficacy. However, during practice, self-efficacy beliefs were modified according to the outcomes. Students in the coping modeling conditions displayed a smaller decline in self-efficacy during posttesting than students in the mastery modeling groups, and both groups displayed a smaller decline than the no-modeling group. Students in the coping modeling group displayed higher levels of self-satisfaction and interest than those in the mastery modeling group.

Zimmerman and Kitsantas's (1999, 2002) studies made an important contribution to research on motivation and writing; they demonstrated that teaching students self-regulatory strategies, even at the early phases of self-regulation development, can contribute to improving not only students' writing performance but also their attitude to writing, including self-efficacy.

Writing as a Meaningful Activity

The cognitively oriented research on writing has underlined the active role of the writer as an individual engaged in the complex processes of writing, from planning to revision. Emphasis on the writer as an active processor had a strong, albeit implicit, motivational implication: A strategic writer, one who can competently manage the difficulties of writing, has positive self-efficacy beliefs, is satisfied with his or her writing performance, and is likely to engage more willingly in new writing tasks. In contrast, poor writers are more likely to have low self-efficacy beliefs and feel anxiety, or apprehension, relative to writing.

The view of writing that essentially focuses on rather solitary cognitive processes and language use has been contrasted over the past two decades with the development of the social constructivist approach to literacy and literacy learning. This approach emphasizes that people carry out literate practices—reading, writing, and also oral activities focusing on written language, such as commenting on or discussing what has been read and written—in contexts from which those practices and activities take their functions and meanings. In this framework, there are no "general" abilities of reading and writing; rather, there are various readings and writings related to the social and cultural contexts in which they are practiced, such as school, workplace, and everyday life. Thus, literacy events are more than individual acts of meaning making and language use. The meaning and language that are built and used are framed by the social identity of the individual and the social context in which literate practices are carried out (Kucer, 2001). In the same perspective, literacy learning is not simply learning to read and write, but is a pattern of practices through which students construct meanings.

In general, the social-constructivist approach assumes that the processes of classroom discourse are motivating in that they are processes of meaning making (e.g., Englert, 1992; Gambrell & Morrow, 1996; Hiebert, 1994; Nelson & Calfee, 1998). By participating in classroom activities, a student learns the functions of reading, writing, and the other literate practices, and comes to construe what it means to be literate (Nolen, 2001, in press). Oldfather and Dahl (1994), who have criticized "externally" stimulated motivation by teachers, proposed a concept of motivation as emerging from the intrinsic value of literate activities, that is, from the social-cognitive and affective processes that children experience in the social construction of meaning.

According to this approach, reading and writing are closely related practices, and motivational aspects are usually viewed in relation to literacy learning. However, over the past two decades, the social-constructivist idea that writing is a meaninful activity, rather than a process, has been adopted by several researchers in their conceptualization of motivation to write. Whereas, in the cognitive approach, motivation to write is nourished and sustained by the writer's cognitive resources, in the social-constructivist approach, writing is viewed as a meaningful activity that can provide its own motivation. Writing is meaningful for students when it is aimed at expressing and communicating thoughts and feelings related to classroom activities and personal experiences. These various functions of writing are integrated in the view of writing as a social activity, which shows affective, as well as cognitive advantages associated with collaboration in a community of learners and writers. Classroom collaboration is the condition for creating a community of discourse practices through

which students can discover their identities as learners (e.g., Daiute, 1989; Higgins, Flower, & Petraglia, 1992; McLane, 1990; Morrow & Sharkey, 1993; Oldfather & Dahl, 1994).

However, meaningfulness depends not only on the relevance of the activities that require and justify writing, but also on the close link between writing and other school activities and disciplines. Although occasions to write in school tend to be closely related to the teaching of language skills, writing can be used for many objectives and in various subjects, such as science, social studies, and mathematics, that is, across the curriculum (Petraglia, 1995). In the last two decades, the Bakhtinian concept of genre as a typified response to situations that are construed socioculturally as recurrent, has contrasted the idea of text types as fixed and "general" models for writing instruction (Bakhtin, 1986; Berkenkotter & Huckin, 1993; Freedman, 1995; Dias, Freedman, Medway, & Paré, 1999). According to this view, there are as many text "types" as there are recurring situations, in and out of school, where writing is required to express, elaborate, and communicate feelings and ideas, information and events, rules and instructions.

The close connection between writing and other school disciplines has been emphasized in a few recent studies on writing-to-learn, that is, on the role of writing as a tool in the learning of various school subjects. This research topic has been thoroughly investigated over the past two decades (for reviews, see Klein, 1999; Tynjälä, Mason, & Lonka, 2001) although its motivational aspects usually have been neglected. Mason and Boscolo (2000) conducted an intervention study with elementary school children aimed at producing conceptual change in the study of science. One of the hypotheses of the study, in which students were intensively engaged in writing while learning science, was that writing in the science class would contribute to changing students' attitude toward writing; that is, engaging learners in various writing activities (note taking, commenting on experiments, expressing doubts, synthesizing, etc.) would also increase both their interest in writing those specific text types, and their perception of writing usefulness. The results showed that writing helped bring about conceptual change, with positive effects on students perceived usefulness of writing.

However, no difference emerged relative to interest in writing the specific text types presented in the study.

In another intervention study on the teaching of literature to ninth graders, Boscolo and Carotti (2003) found a positive effect of the use of writing on students' understanding and response to literature, but only a partial effect on their motivation. In this study, writing was also extensively used as a tool for making students understand literature in greater depth and to help them express their feelings and emotions. Whereas students' perceptions of the usefulness of writing activities increased, no significant increase in their interest in writing activities was found after the intervention.

There seem to be two possible explanations for these results. First, as argued in this chapter, school writing experience is often not attractive to students, who may come to view writing as both a difficult academic activity and a threatening one, due to teachers' evaluations. If so, an intervention aimed at stimulating students' interest in writing activity may not be sufficient to produce a change in attitude, although it may contribute to making students perceive writing as more useful. Thus, perception of usefulness may be an aspect of motivational change, a step prior to, or even independent of, individual interest development. The second possible reason for the lack of expected influence of the intervention on interest regards measures. Whereas no effect emerged when interest in writing was measured through self-report questionnaires, analysis of students' freely written comments at the end of the intervention gave different results, in that those assigned to the writing condition expressed their satisfaction with their writing experiences in the learning of various subject matters. These results suggest that a major problem in research on interest in school activities may be represented by the validity of its assessment, usually limited to self-reports, as suggested previously in this chapter.

Conclusion

In this chapter, we have presented state-of-the-art research on the topics of motivation and writing. Regarding motivation, the most important finding that emerged from our analyses is that the critical motivational variables involved in writing may be more interrelated than previously recognized. The results of studies on interest, self-efficacy, and self-regulation show that there are close relationships between the energizing and self-representational aspects of these motivational variables: Usually, an interested writer is also a self-efficacious and self-regulated one, whereas the mastery of cognitive and linguistic tools that characterizes an expert writer is likely to improve or sustain his or her positive motivational attitude toward writing. However, in some areas, there is a need for further investigations of how these variables develop. For example, the relationship between cognitive and affective aspects of writing is addressed differently by interest and self-efficacy researchers, and an integration between the two perspectives would be beneficial to the field. Because interest researchers tend to focus on the positive affect experienced by interested writers, and self-efficacy researchers, on self-efficacious writers' reduction of anxiety and stress, there is also a need to revisit the positive and negative affective components of writing.

From the perspective of writing research, the view of writing as a meaningful activity in a community of literacy learners has provided relevant contributions to investigations of interest in writing, but some questions related to this approach require further research. One question regards the motivational correlates (interest, self-efficacy, self-regulation) of the social construction of meaning that characterizes literate practices according to the social-constructivist approach, and particularly the conditions under which the meaningfulness of the writing experience can really be motivating for students. Another question regards emphasis on the social aspects of writing and its relationship to the somewhat contradictory view of writing as a solitary endeavor. Writing researchers should not forget that in most school situations, a writer can usually rely on very few resources besides him- or herself. In conclusion, although a certain level of integration has been reached in some areas of research in motivation and writing, more investigations are needed on the relationship among the cognitive and affective components of writing and the "motivating" features of instructional contexts.

References

Ainley, M., Hidi, D., & Berndorff, D. (2002). Interest, learning, and the psychological processes that mediate their relationship. *Journal of Educational Psychology, 94,* 1–17.

Albin, M. L., Benton, S. L., & Khramtsova, I. (1996). Individual differences in interest and narrative writing. *Contemporary Educational Psychology, 21,* 305–324.

Alexander, P. A., & Murphy, P. K. (1998). Profiling the differences in students' knowledge, interest, and strategic processing. *Journal of Educational Psychology, 90,* 435–447.

Bakhtin, M. M. (1986). *Speech genres and other late essays.* Austin: University of TexasPress.

Bandura, A. (1986). *Social foundations of thought and action: A social-cognitive theory.* Englewood Cliffs, NJ: Prentice-Hall.

Bandura, A. (1997). *Self-efficacy: The exercise of control.* New York: Freeman.

Bandura, A., & Schunk, D. H. (1981). Cultivating competence, self-efficacy, and intrinsic interest through proximal self-motivation. *Journal of Personality and Social Psychology, 41,* 586–598.

Beach, R., & Bridwell, L. S. (Eds.). (1984). *New directions in composition research.* New York: Guilford Press.

Benton, S. L., Corkill, A. J., Sharp, J. M., Downey, R. G., & Khramtsova, I. (1995), Knowledge, interest and narrative writing. *Journal of Educational Psychology, 87,* 66–79.

Bereiter, C., & Scardamalia, M. (1987). *The psychology of written composition.* Hillsdale, NJ: Erlbaum.

Berkenkotter, C., & Huckin, T. N. (1993). Rethinking genre from a socio-cognitive perspective. *Written Communication, 10,* 475–509.

Boscolo, P. (1995). The cognitive approach to writing and writing instruction: A contribution to a critical appraisal. *Cahiers de Psychologie Cognitive, 14,* 343–366.

Boscolo, P., & Carotti, L. (2003). Does writing contribute to improving high school students' approach to literature? *L1—Educational Studies in Language and Literature, 3,* 197–224.

Boscolo, P., & Cisotto, L. (1997, August). *Making writing interesting in elementary school.* Paper presented at the seventh biannual meeting of the European Association for Research on Learning and Instruction, Athens, Greece.

Boscolo, P., & Mason, L. (2000, September). *Free recall writing: The role of prior knowledge and interest.* Paper presented at the Writing Conference 2000, Verona, Italy.

Bruning, R., & Horn, C. (2000). Developing motivation to write. *Educational Psychologist, 35,* 25–37.

Daiute, C. (1989). Play as thought: Thinking strategies of young writers. *Harvard Educational Review, 59,* 1–23.

Daly, J. A., & Miller, M. D. (1975a). The development of a measure of writing apprehension. *Research in the Teaching of English, 9,* 242–249.

Daly, J. A., & Miller, M. D. (1975b). Further studies in writing apprehension: SAT scores, success expectations, willingness to take advanced courses and se differences. *Research in the Teaching of English, 9,* 250–256.

Dias, P., Freedman, A., Medway, P., & Paré, A. (1999). *Worlds apart: Acting and writing in academic workplaces contexts.* Mahwah, NJ: Erlbaum.

Englert, C. S. (1992). Writing instruction from a sociocultural perspective: The holistic, dialogic, and social enterprise of writing. *Journal of Learning Disabilities, 25,* 153–172.

Freedman, A. (1995). The what, where, when, why, and how of classroom genres. In J. Petraglia (Ed.), *Reconceiving writing, rethinking writing instruction* (pp. 121–144). Mahwah, NJ: Erlbaum.

Gambrell, L. B., & Morrow, L. M. (1996). Creating motivating contexts for literacy learning. In L. Baker, P. Afflerbach, & D. Reinking (Eds.), *Developing engaged readers in school and home communities* (pp. 115–136). Mahwah, NJ: Erlbaum.

Graham, S., & Harris, K. R. (1989). Improving learning disabled students' skills at composing essays: Self-instructional strategy training. *Exceptional Children, 56,* 201–214.

Graham, S., & Harris, K. R. (2000). The role of self-regulation and transcription skills in writing and writing development. *Educational Psychologist, 35,* 3–12.

Graham, S., Harris, K. R., & Troia, G. A. (2000). Self-regulated strategy development revisited: Teaching writing strategies to struggling writers. *Topics in Language Disorders, 20,* 1–14.

Hannover, B. (1998). The development of self-concepts and interests. In L. Hoffman, A. Krapp, K. A. Renninger, & J. Baumert (Eds.), *Interest and learning* (pp. 105–125). Kiel, Germany: IPN.

Harris, K. R., & Graham, S. (1996). *Making the writing process work: Strategies for composition and self-regulation.* Cambridge, MA: Brookline.

Harris, K. R., Graham, S., Mason, L. H., & Saddler, B. (2002). Developing self-regulated writers. *Theory into Practice, 41,* 110–115.

Hayes, J. R. (1996). A new framework for understanding cognition and affect in writing. In C. M. Levy & S. Ransdell (Eds.), *The science of writing* (pp. 1–27). Mahwah, NJ: Erlbaum.

Hayes, J. R., & Flower, L. S. (1980). Identifying the organization of writing processes. In L. Gregg & E. R. Steinberg (Eds.), *Cognitive processes in writing* (pp. 3–30). Hillsdale, NJ: Erlbaum.

Hidi, S. (1990). Interest and its contribution as a mental resource for learning. *Review of Educational Research, 60,* 549–571.

Hidi, S. (2000). An interest researcher's perspective:

The effects of extrinsic and intrinsic factors on motivation. In C. Sansone & J. M. Harackiewicz (Eds.), *Intrinsic and extrinsic motivation* (pp. 309–339). San Diego: Academic Press.

Hidi, S. (2001). Interest, reading, and learning: Theoretical and practical considerations. *Educational Psychology Review, 13*, 191–208.

Hidi, S. (2003, August). *Interest: A motivational variable with a difference.* Presentation at the 10th biannual meeting of the European Association for Research in Learning and Instruction, Padua, Italy.

Hidi, S., & Anderson, V. (1992). Situational interest and its impact on reading and expository writing. In K. A. Renninger, S. Hidi, & A. Krapp (Eds.), *The role of interest in learning and development* (pp. 215–238). Hillsdale, NJ: Erlbaum.

Hidi, S., & Baird, W. (1988). Strategies for increasing text-based interest and students' recall of expository texts. *Reading Research Quarterly, 23*, 465–483.

Hidi, S., Berndorff, D., & Ainley, M. (2002). Children's argument writing, interest and self-efficacy: An intervention study. *Learning and Instruction, 12*, 429–446.

Hidi, S., & Harackiewicz, J. (2000). Motivating the academically unmotivated: A critical issue for the 21st century. *Review of Educational Research, 70*, 151–179.

Hidi, S., & McLaren, J. (1991). Motivational factors in writing: The role of topic interestingness. *European Journal of Psychology of Education, 6*, 187–197.

Hidi, S., & Renninger, K. A. (in press). The four-phase model of interest development. *Educational Psychologist.*

Hidi, S., Renninger, K. A., & Krapp, A. (2004). Interest, a motivational variable that combines affective and cognitive functioning. In D. Y. Dai & R. J. Sternberg (Eds.), *Motivation, emotion, and cognition: Integrative perspectives on intellectual functioning and development* (pp. 89–115). Mahwah, NJ: Erlbaum.

Hiebert, E. H. (1994). Becoming literate through authentic tasks: Evidence and adptations. In R. B. Ruddell, M. R. Ruddell, & H. Singer (Eds.), *Theoretical models and processes of reading* (4th ed., pp. 391–413). Newark, DE: International Reading Association.

Higgins, L., Flower, L., & Petraglia, J. (1992). Planning text together. *Written Comunication, 9*, 48–84.

Hoffman, L., Krapp, A., Renninger, K. A., & Baumert, J. (Eds.). (1998). *Interest and learning.* Kiel, Germany: IPN.

Klein, P. D. (1999). Re-opening inquiry into cognitive processes in writing-to-learn. *Educational Psychology Review, 11*, 203–270.

Krapp, A. (2000). Interest and human development during adolescence: An educational-psychological approach. In J. Heckhausen (Ed.), *Motivational psychology of human development* (pp. 109–128). London: Elsevier.

Krapp, A. (2002). Structural and dynamics aspects of interest development: Theoretical considerations from an ontogenetic perspective. *Learning and Instruction, 12*, 383–409.

Krapp, A. (2003). Interest and human development: An educational-psychological perspective. In L. Smith, C. Rogers, & P. Tomlinson (Eds.), *Development and motivation: Joint perspectives* (pp. 57–84). *British Journal of Educational Psychology Monographs, 2* (Series II).

Krapp, A., Hidi, S., & Renninger, K. A. (1992). Interest, learning and development. In K. A. Renninger, S. Hidi, & A. Krapp (Eds.), *The role of interest in learning and development* (pp. 3–25). Hillsdale, NJ: Erlbaum.

Kucer, S. B. (2001). *Dimensions of literacy.* Mahwah, NJ: Erlbaum.

Lipstein, R., & Renninger, K. A. (in press). "Putting things into words": 12–15 year-old students' interest for writing. In S. Hidi & P. Boscolo (Eds.), *Motivation and writing: Research and school practice.* Oxford, UK: Elsevier.

McCarthy, P., Meier, S., & Rinderer, R. (1985). Self-efficacy and writing: A different view of self-evaluation. *College Composition and Communication, 36*, 465–471.

McLane, J. B. (1990). Writing as a social process. In L. C. Moll (Ed.), *Vygotsky and education* (pp. 304–318). Cambridge, UK: Cambridge University Press.

Mason, L., & Boscolo, P. (2000). Writing and conceptual change: What changes? *Instructional Science, 28*, 199–226.

Meyer, D. K., & Turner, J. C. (2002). Discovering emotion in classroom motivation research. *Educational Psychologist, 37*, 107–114.

Morrow, L. M., & Sharkey, E. A. (1993). Motivating independent reading and writing in the primary grades through social cooperative literacy experiences. *Reading Teacher, 47*, 162–165.

Multon, K. D., Brown, S. D., & Lent, R. W. (1991). Relation of self-efficacy beliefs to academic outcomes: A meta-analytic investigation. *Journal of Counseling Psychology, 18*, 30–38.

Murphy, P. K., & Alexander, P. A. (2000). A motivated exploration of motivation terminology. *Contemporary Educational Psychology, 25*, 3–53.

Nelson, N., & Calfee, R. C. (1998). The reading–writing connection viewed historically. In N. Nelson & R. C. Calfee (Eds.), *The reading–writing connection: The Ninety-seventh yearbook of the National Society for the Study of Eucation, Part 2* (pp. 1–51). Chicago: University of Chicago Press.

Nolen, S. B. (2001). Constructing literacy in the kindergarten: Task structure, collaboration and motivation. *Cognition and Instruction, 19*, 95–142.

Nolen, S. B. (2003, August). *The development of in-*

terest and motivation to read and write. Paper presented at the 10th biannual meeting of the European Association for Research on Learning and Instruction, Padova, Italy.

Nolen, S. B. (in press). The role of literate communities in the development of children's interest in writing. In S. Hidi & P. Boscolo (Eds.), *Motivation and writing: Research and school practice.* Oxford, UK: Elsevier.

Oldfather, P., & Dahl, K. (1994). Toward a social constructivist reconceptualization of intrinsic motivation for literacy learning. *Journal of Reading Behavior, 26,* 139–158.

Pajares, F. (1996). Self-efficacy beliefs in academic settings. *Review of Educational Research, 66,* 543–578.

Pajares, F., & Johnson, M. J. (1994). Confidence and competence in writing: The role of writing self-efficacy, outcome expectancy, and apprehension. *Research in the Teaching of English, 28,* 313–331.

Pajares, F., & Valiante, G. (1997). The predictive and mediational role of the writing self-efficacy beliefs of upper elementary students. *Journal of Educational Research, 90,* 353–360.

Petraglia, J. (Ed.) (1995). *Reconceiving writing, rethinking writing instruction.* Mahwah, NJ: Erlbaum.

Renninger, K. A. (1992). Individual interest and development: Implications for theory and practice. In K. A. Renninger, S. Hidi, & A. Krapp (Eds.), *The role of interest in learning and development* (pp. 361–395). Hillsdale, NJ: Erlbaum.

Renninger, K. A. (2000). Individual interest and its implications for understanding intrinsic motivation. In C. Sansone & J. M. Harackiewicz (Eds.), *Intrinsic and extrinsic motivation* (pp. 373–404). San Diego: Academic Press.

Renninger, K. A. (2003). Effort and interest. In J. Guthrie (Gen. Ed.), *The encyclopedia of education* (2nd ed., pp. 704–709). New York: Macmillan.

Renninger, K. A., Ewen, L., & Lasher, A. K. (2002). Individual interest as context in expository text and mathematical word problems. *Learning and Instruction, 12,* 467–491.

Renninger, K. A., Hidi, S., & Krapp, A. (1992). *The role of interest in learning and development.* Hillsdale, NJ: Erlbaum.

Rohman, G. (1965). Pre-writing: The stage of discovery in the writing process. *College Composition and Communication, 16,* 106–112.

Schiefele, U. (1996). Topic interest, text representation, and quality of experience. *Contemporary Educational Psychology, 12,* 3–18.

Schiefele, U. (1998). Individual interest and learning—what we know and what we don't know. In L. Hoffman, A. Krapp, K. A. Renninger, & J. Baumert (Eds.), *Interest and learning* (pp. 91–104). Kiel, Germany: IPN.

Schiefele, U., & Krapp, A. (1996). Topic interest and free recall of expository text. *Learning and Individual Differences, 8,* 141–160.

Schunk, D. H., & Swartz, C. W. (1993). Goals and progress feedback: Effects on self-efficacy and writing achievement. *Contemporary Educational Psychology, 18,* 337–354.

Shell, D. F., Murphy, C. C., & Bruning, R. H. (1989). Self-efficacy and outcome expectancy mechanisms in reading and writing achievement. *Journal of Educational Psychology, 81,* 91–100.

Silvia, P. J. (2001). Interest and interests: The psychology of constructive capriciousness. *Review of General Psychology, 5,* 270–290.

Tobias S. (1994). Interest, prior knowledge, and learning. *Review of Educational Research, 64,* 37–54.

Todt, E., & Schreiber, S. (1998). Development of interests. In L. Hoffman, A. Krapp, K. A. Renninger, & J. Baumert (Eds.), *Interest and learning* (pp. 25–40). Kiel, Germany: IPN.

Tynjälä, P., Mason, L., & Lonka, K. (2001). *Writing as a learning tool.* Dordrecht, The Netherlands: Kluwer.

Zimmerman, B. J. (1989). A social-cognitive view of self-regulated academic learning. *Journal of Educational Psychology, 81,* 329–339.

Zimmerman, B. J. (2000a). Self-efficacy: An essential motive to learn. *Contemporary Educational Psychology, 25,* 82–91.

Zimmerman, B. J. (2000b). Attainment of self-regulation: A social cognitive perspective. In M. Boekaerts, P. Pintrich, & M. Zeidner (Eds.), *Self-regulation: Theory, research, and applications* (pp. 13–39). Orlando, FL: Academic Press.

Zimmerman, B. J., & Bandura, A. (1994). Impact of self-regulatory influences on writing course attainment. *American Educational Research Journal, 31,* 845–862.

Zimmerman, B. J., & Kitsantas, A. (1999). Acquiring writing revision skill: Shifting from process to outcome self-regulatory goals. *Journal of Educational Psychology, 91,* 1–10.

Zimmerman, B. J., & Kitsantas, A. (2002). Acquiring writing revision proficiency through observation and emulation. *Journal of Educational Psychology, 94,* 660–668.

Zimmerman, B. J., & Kitsantas, A. (in press). A writer's discipline: The development of self-regulatory skill. In S. Hidi & P. Boscolo (Eds.), *Motivation and writing: Research and school practice.* Oxford, UK: Elsevier.

Zimmerman, B. J., & Risemberg, R. (1997). Become a self-regulated writer: A social cognitive perspective. *Contemporary Educational Psychology, 22,* 73–101.

Zimmerman, B. J., & Schunk, D. H. (Eds.) (2001). *Self-regulated learning and academic achievement. Theoretical perspectives.* Mahwah, NJ: Erlbaum.

Chapter 11

Self-Efficacy Beliefs and Motivation in Writing Development

Frank Pajares *and* Gio Valiante

Researchers who have investigated the field of composition have historically focused on the skills and abilities that writers bring to this critical craft, as well as the instructional practices that teachers use to increase the skills and foster the abilities of their students. These efforts have primarily been aimed at understanding the thought processes underlying the compositions of students. As Hull and Rose (1989) observed, however, the more that was learned about the relationship between students' cognitive abilities and the manner in which they engaged text, the more complex the relationship seemed to be. One effort to address this complexity has focused on the self-beliefs that underlie student motivation in writing. Findings from this avenue of inquiry have led researchers to suggest that students' beliefs about their own writing processes and competence are instrumental to their ultimate success as writers.

Author Erica Jong is credited with the insightful aphorism, "How can I know what I think unless I see what I write." Writing is not only a process of making meaning but also an activity through which individuals engage in self-understanding. Consequently, it is not surprising that researchers in the field of composition should find themselves exploring students' self-processes. After all, it is through introspection and self-reflection that meaning is constructed. The assumption

that self-knowledge is inextricably connected to human competencies is now so taken for granted that it is a central tenet of most modern theories and views of human cognition, motivation, and behavior. Similarly, the idea that students' self-beliefs play a critical role in their academic success is so widely accepted that self-constructs are a regular staple in studies of academic competence in all areas. This focus on students' self-beliefs as a principal component of academic motivation is grounded on the taken-for-granted assumption that the beliefs that students create, develop, and hold to be true about themselves are vital forces in their success or failure in school.

In this chapter, we examine the contribution made by research on motivation and self-beliefs about writing to the study of writing in academic settings. We focus on students' self-perceptions of their own writing competence, or writing *self-efficacy* beliefs. First we provide a brief overview of the self-efficacy component of social cognitive theory, followed by a description of the manner in which these beliefs are typically operationalized and assessed. This is followed by a synthesis of research findings that address the relationship between writing self-efficacy, other motivation constructs related to writing, and writing outcomes in academic settings. These findings demonstrate that students' confidence in their writing capabilities influences their writing motivation, as well as various writing outcomes in school. We close by offering some academic implications and strategies that may help guide future research in the area of writing motivation.

Overview of Self-Efficacy Beliefs

When Bandura (1986) put forth a social cognitive theory of human functioning, educators found in it a view of academic development in which students are seen as proactively engaged in their own learning. Key to this sense of agency is the fact that what students think, believe, and feel powerfully affects their success or failure in their academic endeavors. Standing at the very core of social cognitive theory are self-efficacy beliefs, which in the context of schooling can be defined as students' judgments "of their capabilities to organize and execute the courses of action required to attain designated types of performances" (Bandura, 1986, p. 391). From this social cognitive perspective, self-efficacy beliefs provide the foundation for academic motivation and successful accomplishment, because when students believe that their actions can produce the outcomes they desire, they have the incentive to act and persevere in the face of difficulties.

According to Bandura (1997), students' academic accomplishments can often be better predicted by their self-efficacy beliefs than by their previous attainments, knowledge, or skills. It goes without saying of course that no amount of confidence can produce success when requisite skills and knowledge are absent. But it bears noting that self-efficacy beliefs are themselves critical determinants of how well knowledge and skill are acquired in the first place. The contention that self-efficacy beliefs are a critical ingredient in human functioning is consistent with the view of many theorists and philosophers who have argued that the potent affective, evaluative, and episodic nature of beliefs makes them a filter through which new phenomena are interpreted.

The self-perceptions that students come to hold about their capabilities influence the choices they make and the courses of action they pursue. Students tend to select tasks and activities in which they feel competent and confident and to avoid those in which they do not, for unless they believe that their actions will have the desired consequences, they have little incentive to engage in those actions. How far will an interest in journalism take a student who feels hopeless as a writer? Whatever factors operate to influence behavior, they are rooted in the core belief that one has the capability to accomplish that behavior.

Self-efficacy beliefs also help determine how much effort students will expend on an activity, how long they will persevere when confronting obstacles, and how resilient they will be in the face of adversity. In general, the higher a student's sense of efficacy, the greater will be the effort, persistence, and resilience. Students with a strong sense of personal competence in an academic task will approach difficult tasks as challenges to be mastered rather than as threats to be avoided. They have greater intrinsic interest and deep engrossment in activities, set themselves challenging goals and maintain strong commitment to them, and heighten and sustain their efforts in the face of failure. Moreover, they more quickly recover their sense of efficacy after failures or setbacks, and attribute failure to insufficient effort or deficient knowledge and skills that are acquirable.

Finally, self-efficacy beliefs also influence thought patterns and emotional reactions. Students with low self-efficacy may believe that things are tougher than they really are, a belief that fosters anxiety, stress, and a narrow vision of how best to solve a problem. One can well understand how such affective reactions can powerfully influence the level of accomplishment that one ultimately achieves. This function of self-efficacy can also create the type of self-fulfilling prophecy in which one may accomplish what one believes one can accomplish; that is, the perseverance associated with high self-efficacy is likely to lead to increased performance that in turn raises one's sense of efficacy and spirit. Conversely, the giving-in associated with low self-efficacy helps ensure the very failure that further lowers confidence and morale.

Students form their self-efficacy beliefs by interpreting information primarily from four sources. The most influential source is the interpreted result of previous performance, or mastery experience. Students engage in activities, interpret the results of their actions, use these interpretations to develop beliefs about their capability to engage in subsequent tasks or activities, and act in concert with the beliefs created. Typically, outcomes interpreted as successful raise self-efficacy; those interpreted as failures lower it. Students also form their self-efficacy beliefs through the vicarious experience of observing others perform tasks. This source of information is weaker than mastery experience in helping to create self-efficacy beliefs, but when students are uncertain about their own abilities, or when they have limited prior experience, they become more sensitive to it. A significant model in a student's life can help instill self-beliefs that will influence the course and direction that life will take.

Students also create and develop self-efficacy beliefs as a result of the social persuasions they receive from others. These persuasions can involve exposure to the verbal judgments that others provide. Naturally, teachers play an important part in the development of an individual's self-beliefs. Effective persuaders must cultivate students' beliefs in their own capabilities while at the same time ensuring that the envisioned success is attainable. And, just as positive persuasions may work to encourage and empower, negative persuasions can work to defeat and weaken self-efficacy beliefs. In fact, it is usually easier to weaken self-efficacy beliefs through negative appraisals than to strengthen such beliefs through positive encouragement.

Finally, somatic and emotional states such as anxiety, stress, arousal, and mood also provide information about efficacy beliefs. Students can gauge their degree of confidence by the emotional state they experience as they contemplate an action. Strong emotional reactions to an academic task provide cues about the anticipated success or failure of the outcome. When students experience negative thoughts and fears about their capabilities, those affective reactions can themselves lower self-efficacy perceptions and trigger additional stress and agitation that help ensure the inadequate performance they fear.

Self-efficacy has generated a great deal of research in education. In general, researchers have established that students' self-efficacy beliefs are highly predictive of academic outcomes across domains. These findings prompted Graham and Weiner (1996) to conclude that self-efficacy beliefs have been stronger predictors of academic and behavioral performances than have other self-beliefs. In fact, "efficacy beliefs have been related to the acquisition of new skills and to the performance of previously learned skills at a level of specificity not found in any of the other motivation conceptions that include an expectancy construct" (p. 75). The Roman poet Virgil observed that "they are able who think they are able." The French novelist Alexandre Dumas wrote that when people doubt themselves, they make their own failure certain by themselves being the first to be convinced of it. There is now ample evidence to suggest that Virgil and Dumas were absolutely correct. In the area of writing, recent efforts have shed light on the influence of self-efficacy beliefs on various writing outcomes.

Assessing Writing Self-Efficacy

Self-efficacy beliefs vary in level, strength, and generality, and researchers assessing self-efficacy in the area of writing do well to consider each dimension when constructing a writing self-efficacy instrument (see Bandura, 2001). Let us assume, for example, that a researcher wishes to assess students' self-efficacy to write an essay. First, there are different levels of task demands that the researcher may tap. These can range from the lower level of writing a simple sentence with proper punctuation to the more challenging level of organizing sentences into a paragraph so as to clearly express an idea. Students are asked to rate the strength of their belief in their capability to perform each of the levels identified. The self-efficacy scale would thus provide multiple items of varying difficulty that collectively assess the domain of essay writing at a particular academic level. Items should of course be prototypical of essay writing rather than minutely specific features of writing (e.g., confidence to form letters), and they should be worded in terms of *can*, a judgment of capability, rather than of *will*, a statement of intention (e.g., "How confident are you that you can write a strong paragraph that has a good topic sentence or main idea?"). Finally, self-efficacy instruments should always be administered prior to the outcomes with which they will be compared and in as close temporal proximity as possible.

Writing self-efficacy will also differ in generality across the full spectrum of writing. Students do not typically judge themselves equally efficacious across all types of language arts activities or even across all types of writing. Because a student's self-beliefs will best predict the performances that most closely correspond with such beliefs, belief and outcome assessed should carefully correspond. Hence, if students have been asked to provide judgments of efficacy to write an expository essay, these judgments should be compared with scores that represent their skill in writing the type of essay about which they provided their judgments. It is unwarranted to use these judgments to predict performances related, for example, to writing poetry or short stories, or to grades in language arts that have been obtained from scores on activities that are only partly related, or even unrelated, to writing. Criteria for scoring the essay should be based on the content of the items presented in the efficacy instrument on which the students made their judgments.

Three ways of measuring writing self-efficacy have predominated. The first involves assessing students' confidence that they possess particular writing *skills*. Items can assess students' confidence in their ability to successfully perform grammar, usage, composition, and mechanical writing skills, such as correctly punctuating a one-page passage or organizing sentences into a paragraph so as to clearly express a theme (see McCarthy, Meier, & Rinderer, 1985; Meier, McCarthy, & Schmeck, 1984; Pajares & Johnson, 1994, 1996; Shell, Colvin, & Bruning, 1995; Shell, Murphy, & Bruning, 1989). Items can also assess students' confidence in their ability to display skills related to writing a story—skills such as telling about the main character's feelings or about the setting (Graham & Harris, 1989a). In some instruments, skills assessed are those identified by language arts teachers as appropriate to their students' writing level (Pajares, Miller, & Johnson, 1999; Pajares & Valiante, 1997, 1999, 2001). A second way of measuring writing self-efficacy involves assessing the confidence that students have to complete writing *tasks* such as writing a term paper, authoring

a short fiction story, or writing a letter to a friend (Pajares & Johnson, 1994; Shell et al., 1989, 1995). Reliability for items in these scales has ranged from .85 for elementary school samples to .95 for older students.

It bears reemphasizing that research questions should always be formulated with an eye toward enhancing the correspondence between self-efficacy and performance assessment, for the relationship between belief and performance will be stronger when self-efficacy assessed matches the outcome of interest. In one study, researchers asked students to provide two types of efficacy judgments—confidence in the skills required to compose an essay and confidence to perform various writing-related tasks (Pajares & Johnson, 1994). The skills self-efficacy measure predicted students' skill in composing essays whereas the tasks self-efficacy measure did not. Of course, composite scores from reliable, multiscale self-efficacy instruments can provide teachers and counselors with information regarding students' general writing confidence, and results may be useful in studies of complex writing-related outcomes that do not easily lend themselves to analyses that ensure correspondence between belief and outcome.

When completing self-efficacy scales, students provide their judgments either along a Likert-scale continuum or by filling in any number from 0 to 100 as a measure of their self-efficacy for each skill or task. Self-efficacy scales with a 0–100 response format have been found to be psychometrically stronger than those with traditional Likert formats (see Pajares, Hartley, & Valiante, 2001). This is consistent with Bandura's (1997) caution that "including too few steps loses differentiating information because people who use the same response category would differ if intermediate steps were included" (p. 44). Since neither a Likert-type scale nor a 0–100 scale is more difficult or longer than the other, using a format that adds predictive utility is warranted.

In some studies, the writing outcome of interest is students' grades in language arts classes rather than scores on a particular writing task. Consequently, a third method of measuring students' writing self-efficacy beliefs is to use items asking students to provide a rating of their confidence that they can earn either an A, B, C, or D in their language arts class. These confidence judgments are then compared with actual grades obtained (e.g., Pajares, Britner, & Valiante, 2000). Reliability indexes have ranged from .86 to .89 with samples of middle school students.

Ultimately, to gauge the appropriateness and adequacy of a self-efficacy measure, researchers must make a theoretically informed and empirically sound judgment reflecting an understanding of both the domain under investigation and its different features, as well as of the types of capabilities the domain requires and the range of situations in which these capabilities might be applied. These understandings can then be used to evaluate an efficacy measure by the level of specificity of its items, the range of task demands that it includes, and the correspondence between the beliefs that are tapped and the outcome that is measured.

Writing Self-Efficacy and Writing Outcomes

Researchers have consistently reported that writing self-efficacy beliefs correlate with the writing performances that correspond to those beliefs. Early self-efficacy studies were conducted with college undergraduates. Typically, performance assessments consisted of essay scores provided by English professors or researchers trained in holistic scoring. Beta coefficients on regression models in which self-efficacy beliefs predicted these essay scores ranged from .32 to .42 (e.g., McCarthy et al., 1985; Meier et al., 1984; Shell et al., 1989). Writing self-efficacy also correlated with variables such as writing anxiety, grade goals, depth of processing, and expected outcomes. Another consistent finding was that writing apprehension did not predict writing performance in regression models that included self-efficacy.

Recent findings support these results (e.g., Pajares et al., 1999; Pajares & Johnson, 1996; Pajares & Valiante, 1999; Rankin, Bruning, & Timme, 1994; Schunk & Swartz, 1993; Shell et al., 1995; Wachholz & Etheridge, 1996; Zimmerman & Bandura, 1994; also see Bruning & Horn, 2000). Regression analyses have been accompanied by path analyses that provide information about direct and indirect effects of belief on performance. In general, results reveal that writing self-efficacy makes an independent contribution to the prediction of writing outcomes. This is the case even when powerful covariates such as writing aptitude or previous writing performance are included in statistical models. Effect sizes between writing self-efficacy and writing outcomes in models that control for previous performance assessments have ranged from 0.19 to 0.40. Writing self-efficacy is also associated with motivation variables such as writing apprehension, perceived value of writing, self-efficacy for self-regulation, writing self-concept, and achievement goal orientations in writing, and it mediates the effect of gender and preperformance on writing performance (see, for example, Graham & Harris, 1989a, 1989b; Pajares et al., 1999; Pajares & Valiante, 1997; Schunk, 2003; Zimmerman & Bandura, 1994).

Writing Self-Efficacy and Writing Motivation

Motivation constructs other than self-efficacy have been prominent in studies of writing. *Writing apprehension* was first used by Daly and Miller (1975) to describe a form of writing anxiety that correlated with SAT verbal scores, perceived likelihood of success in writing, and willingness to take writing courses. Recently, researchers have reported that, although writing apprehension typically correlates negatively with writing performances, when self-efficacy beliefs are controlled, the relationship of apprehension is vastly reduced and even nullified (Pajares et al., 1999; Pajares & Valiante, 1997, 1999). These findings are consistent with the contention of social cognitive theorists that anxiety is mediated by self-efficacy beliefs. In other words, writing apprehension is largely a result of the confidence with which a student approaches a writing task or activity. Similar findings have been reported by researchers exploring the role of anxiety in mathematics (e.g., Hackett & Betz, 1989). If self-efficacy beliefs are a cause of physiological reactions such as writing apprehension, interventions designed to improve writing by decreasing anxiety may be useful to the degree that they increase students' confidence in their writing ability.

The *value* that students ascribe to writing has also been included in studies of writing, and results have shown that, as with writing apprehension, the influence of perceived value on writing outcomes is nullified when self-efficacy beliefs are included in the statistical models (Pajares et al., 1999; Pajares & Valiante, 1997, 1999; Shell et al., 1989). Expectancy–value theorists have argued that self-efficacy and valued outcomes codetermine the tasks in which individuals will engage and the success they will experience (Wigfield & Eccles, 1992). They have also suggested, however, that value beliefs may well develop from competence assessments (Linnenbrink & Pintrich, 2003). According to self-efficacy theorists, self-efficacy judgments determine the value that people place on tasks and activities. Students who expect success in an academic activity tend to value that activity. There may in fact be a developmental component at work in this process, such that value and self-efficacy beliefs are unrelated for younger children but become more closely related as students get older and come to value those skills and activities at which they excel (Wigfield, 1994).

Students' *self-efficacy for self-regulation*—the confidence to use self-regulated learning strategies—is also related to writing competence (Harris & Graham, 1992; Schunk & Zimmerman, 1994; Zimmerman, Bandura, & Martinez-Pons, 1992; Zimmerman & Martinez-Pons, 1990; also see Zimmerman & Risemberg, 1997). Self-regulated learning strategies include planning and organizing writing assignments, finishing writing tasks in a timely fashion, or using the library to gather information for writing projects. Students develop beliefs about their academic capabilities as a result of how successful they perceive their self-regulatory strategies to be (Bandura & Schunk, 1981). Consequently, students' perceived self-regulatory skills predict the confidence with which they face academic tasks. Confidence in self-regulatory strategies has also been linked to greater strategy use, higher intrinsic motivation, and more adaptive attributions (Pintrich & De Groot, 1990; also see Schunk & Zimmerman, 1994; Zimmerman & Kitsantas, 1999).

Self-efficacy and writing competence increase when students are provided with *process goals* (i.e., specific strategies they can use to improve their writing), as well as regular feedback regarding how well they are using such strategies (Graham & MacArthur, 1988; Graham, MacArthur, Schwartz, &

Page-Voth, 1992; Schunk & Swartz, 1993). When process goals are linked with feedback, writing competence improves even more, and strategy use increases (Schunk & Swartz, 1993). Instruction in self-regulatory strategies increases both writing skills and self-efficacy. For example, when learning disabled students are taught self-instructional strategies for writing stories and essays, their writing skills, revision skills, and writing self-efficacy increase. These strategies include setting goals, self-recording progress, using mnemonic strategies, learning revision strategies, using self-instructions for strategy induction, and self-evaluating progress (Graham et al., 1992; Graham & Harris, 1989a, 1989b; Graham & MacArthur, 1988; also see Gersten & Baker, 2001).

Academic *self-concept* beliefs are widely acknowledged to influence academic outcomes across domains (Pajares & Schunk, 2005; Skaalvik, 1997). Self-concept beliefs differ from self-efficacy beliefs. In studies of academic motivation, self-concept is typically measured at a domain level of specificity whereas self-efficacy is more typically assessed at a skills- or task-specific level. Self-concept also includes judgments of self-worth. A writing self-concept item such as "Writing makes me feel inadequate" differs in tone and substance from a self-efficacy item that may ask, "How sure are you that you can correctly spell all words in a one-page story or composition?" The two constructs need not be related. Some students may feel confident about their writing but may not feel the corresponding positive feelings of self-worth, in part because they take no pride in their writing accomplishments (for a discussion of this issue, see Pajares, 1996, 1997; Pajares & Schunk, 2001, 2005). Writing self-concept—the judgments of self-worth associated with one's self-perception as a writer—is not prominent in the motivation literature, but verbal self-concept has been a focus of numerous studies. Researchers have reported significant relationships between verbal self-concept and academic outcomes such as reading (Skaalvik, 1997). They have also reported modest but significant gender differences in verbal self-concepts favoring girls (Marsh, 1989), and these differences may exist even at very early ages (Crain, 1996). Studies in which writing self-concept and skills-specific writing self-efficacy are included as predictors of skills-specific writing performance (such as skills required to write an essay) reveal that writing self-efficacy beliefs are significant predictors, whereas writing self-concept beliefs are not (Pajares et al., 1999).

Achievement goal orientations, the reasons that students have for doing their academic work, are prominent in studies of academic motivation. Researchers describe these goals in terms of task, performance–approach, or performance–avoid orientations. Task goals represent students' concern with mastering material and learning as an end in itself; performance–approach goals represent students' concern with wanting to do well so as to display their ability; performance–avoid goals represent students' concern with wanting to do well so as to avoid showing a lack of ability. Holding task goals in writing is positively related to writing self-efficacy, whereas holding performance–avoid goals is negatively related (Pajares et al., 2000). Performance–approach goals seem to be positively related to writing self-efficacy for boys, but they are unrelated for girls.

When several of these constructs are included in a study of writing competence, findings tend to support the contentions of social cognitive theory as regards the predictive role of self-efficacy. For example, Shell et al. (1989) reported a significant correlation between students' writing skills self-efficacy and their holistic scores on an essay, but they found no significant correlations between the perceived value of writing and essay scores. In a number of studies, self-efficacy, self-concept, perceived value, apprehension, self-efficacy for self-regulation, and previous writing performances correlated with the writing competence of students from elementary school to college, but multiple regression and path analyses revealed that only self-efficacy and preperformance assessments, such as writing aptitude, were significant predictors (Pajares et al., 1999, 2000; Pajares & Johnson, 1996; Pajares & Valiante, 1997, 1999, 2001).

The Role of Gender

Students' writing performances, motivation, and self-efficacy beliefs have been found to differ as a function of gender. Typically, researchers have found that girls report stronger confidence in their writing capabilities than do boys, at least through middle school (Eccles et al., 1989; Pajares et al., 1999; Pajares & Valiante, 1997, 2001; Pajares, Valiante, & Cheong, in press; Wifgield, Eccles, MacIver, Reuman, & Midgley, 1991). These differences may begin at early ages (see Crain, 1996; Eccles, Wigfield, Harold, & Blumenfeld, 1993), and it is possible that they may diminish, or even reverse, as students get older. Pajares and Johnson (1996) reported that, at grade 9, boys held stronger writing self-efficacy than did girls. This reversal is not unusual, given that researchers have often reported that girls experience a drop in their academic motivation and self-perceptions of competence as they reach high school (Bruning & Horn, 2000; Phillips & Zimmerman, 1990), perhaps because they begin to encounter classroom structures that emphasize a masculine form of discourse (Cleary, 1996). It seems likely, however, that gender differences in writing self-efficacy may in part be a function of previous success with writing. Differences favoring girls are typically rendered nonsignificant when previous achievement is controlled (Pajares et al., 1999; Pajares & Valiante, 1999).

Although girls typically score better than do boys on writing performance indexes and are rated better writers by their teachers, they do not display the corresponding stronger confidence in their writing capabilities. This phenomenon may be due to the manner in which boys and girls report their self-efficacy beliefs. Recall that self-efficacy is typically assessed by asking students to report the strength of their confidence that they possess various writing skills, can accomplish different writing tasks, or can earn particular grades on writing assignments or classes. Group differences in the average level of confidence reported are interpreted as gender differences in self-efficacy. However, researchers have suggested that boys tend to be more self-congratulatory in their responses to these sorts of instruments, whereas girls tend to be more modest (Wigfield, Eccles, & Pintrich, 1996). Noddings (1996) contended that boys and girls may well use a different "metric" when providing confidence judgments, adding that these sorts of ratings may represent more of a promise to girls than they do to boys. If this is the case, actual differences in confidence may be masked or accentuated by such a response bias.

Comparisons with peers are important determinants of self-efficacy beliefs (Bandura, 1997; Schunk, 1995). To investigate whether the manner in which students compare themselves as writers can inform the phenomenon just described, Pajares and Valiante (1999) asked middle school boys and girls not only to provide writing self-efficacy judgments in the traditional manner (confidence in possessing specific writing skills) but also to make comparative judgments regarding their writing ability versus that of other boys and girls. The aim was to discover whether gender differences in writing self-efficacy were congruent with gender differences in ability comparisons. Consistent with previous findings, results revealed that girls outperformed boys in writing but that girls and boys reported equal writing self-efficacy. When students were asked whether they were better writers than their peers, however, girls expressed that they were better writers than were boys in their class or in their school. These findings have been obtained both at the elementary and middle school levels (Pajares et al., 1999; Pajares & Valiante, 1999). It is evident that, regardless of the ratings that boys and girls provide on writing self-efficacy measures, girls consider themselves better writers than the boys. When gauging their ability relative to the task, boys report higher levels of self-efficacy; when gauging their ability relative to one another, boys and girls agree that girls are better writers. If researchers are to continue to explore gender differences in self-beliefs, they will need to address that issue with questions that will provide these sorts of insights (also see Schwarz, 1999).

Many gender differences in social, personality, and academic variables have been found to be a function of gender orientation—the stereotypical beliefs about gender that students hold—rather than of gender (Eisenberg, Martin, & Fabes, 1996; Hackett, 1985; Harter, Waters, & Whitesell, 1997). For example, gender differences in moral voice and empathy disappear when gender stereotypical beliefs are controlled (Harter et al., 1997). Eccles's (1987) model of educa-

tional and occupational choice posits that cultural milieu factors such as students' gender role stereotypes are partly responsible for differences in course and career selection, and in confidence beliefs and perceived value of tasks and activities. Most research related to this hypothesis has been conducted in the area of mathematics and science, where researchers report that girls enroll in fewer mathematics and science classes in part because they sex-type mathematics as a male domain.

To determine whether gender differences in writing motivation and achievement are a function of gender-stereotypical beliefs rather than of gender, researchers have asked middle school students to report how strongly they identified with characteristics stereotypically associated with males or females in American society (Pajares & Valiante, 2001, 2002). Results revealed that significant gender differences in writing self-efficacy, writing self-concept, self-efficacy for self-regulation, task goal orientation in writing, perceived value of writing, and writing achievement were all rendered nonsignificant when gender-orientation beliefs were controlled. Instead, femininity was associated with writing self-efficacy. These findings have been obtained at each level of schooling from grades 4 to 11 (Pajares et al., in press).

Social cognitive theory does not endow gender or gender self-beliefs with motivating properties, but fields in the areas of mathematics, science, and technology are typically viewed by students as being male-dominated (see Eisenberg et al., 1996). In these fields, a masculine gender orientation is associated with confidence and achievement because students have the notion that success in these areas is a masculine imperative (Eccles, 1987; Hackett, 1985). Language arts in school is typically associated with a feminine gender orientation in part because writing is viewed by most students, particularly younger students, as being a feminine activity. As a consequence, a feminine orientation is associated with motivational beliefs related to success in writing. One challenge before language arts educators is to alter students' views of writing so that it is perceived as relevant and valuable both to girls and boys. A challenge for all educators, and for the broader culture, is to continue to expound and model gender self-beliefs that encompass both the feminine expressiveness and the masculine instrumentality that are critical to a balanced self-view.

Developmental Influence on Writing Self-Efficacy

Some researchers have investigated the development of writing self-efficacy beliefs, particularly from elementary school to grade 10. In one study, students' self-efficacy to accomplish writing tasks increased as they progressed from grade 4 to grade 10 (Shell et al., 1995). This is an intuitive finding. Older students are more capable than are younger students of accomplishing the writing tasks on which their self-efficacy is based. There were no differences, however, between students in grades 4, 7, and 10 in their confidence that they possessed various grammar, usage, and composition skills. Since, again, older students are in better possession of those skills, one wonders why their confidence in their skills did not increase proportionately. Other researchers have reported that students in the first year of middle school report stronger confidence in their writing skills than do students in grades 7 and 8 (Pajares & Valiante, 1999), again in the face of older students having greater writing competence. This pattern of decreasing confidence in language arts skills is consistent with findings from expectancy–value researchers who have reported that students' self-concepts of ability in English decrease from the start of grade 6 to the end of grade 7 (Wigfield et al., 1991).

In an effort to provide a developmental perspective of students' writing motivation and self-efficacy beliefs, Pajares et al. (in press) used data obtained from cohort groups of 1,266 students from grades 4 to 11 (each grade was represented). The researchers sought to determine whether the strength of students' writing self-efficacy beliefs changes as students progress from elementary to high school and to analyze whether the changes in writing self-efficacy across school levels differ as a function of key competence and motivation indexes in writing. Writing self-efficacy beliefs diminished as students moved from elementary school to middle school and then remained at that level during high school. The researchers conjectured that it is possible that confidence

in writing skills is not well nurtured as students progress through school, even in the face of the skills themselves being developed (see Cleary, 1996; Phillips & Zimmerman, 1990). If this is indeed the case, this is particularly unfortunate because the vast majority of students begin school believing that they can write (Calkins, 1983). As various researchers have documented, middle school seems to be the critical juncture at which academic motivation decreases.

Self-efficacy is not the only motivational belief that decreases as students progress through school. Pajares and Cheong (2003) reported that task goal orientation also decreases as students progress from elementary school to high school. However, students with higher writing self-efficacy, writing self-concept, self-efficacy for self-regulation, perceived value of writing, and writing aptitude had higher task goals at each level of schooling.

Educational Implications

It has now been over 25 years since Bandura (1977) first introduced the construct of self-efficacy. Since that time, it has become a staple in studies of academic motivation and achievement. Over two decades of research on the influence of self-efficacy beliefs in academic functioning have confirmed Bandura's claim that self-efficacy beliefs play an influential role in the choices that students make, the effort and perseverance they exert, and the level of success they attain. Consequently, an important pedagogical implication to emerge from these findings is that teachers do well to take seriously their share of responsibility in nurturing the self-efficacy beliefs of their pupils, for it is clear that these beliefs can have beneficial or destructive influences. Parents, teachers, schools, and all who play a role in the lives of youth are responsible for helping students develop their competence *and* confidence as they progress through school.

As children strive to exercise control over their surroundings, their first transactions are mediated by adults who can either empower them with self-assurance or diminish their fledgling self-beliefs. Young children are not proficient at making accurate self-appraisals, and so they must rely on the judgments of others to create their own judgments of confidence and of self-worth. Teachers who provide children with challenging tasks and meaningful activities that can be mastered, who chaperone these efforts with support and encouragement, and who believe in their students and convey this belief help ensure that their students will develop a robust sense of confidence (see Mills & Clyde, 1991).

Walker (2003) outlined a number of ways in which teachers can help students cultivate their sense of writing efficacy. One way is to give students greater autonomy in the writing choices and goals that form their instruction. When students are able to select some of their own writing topics and assignments, interest and personal investment are heightened. Collaborative writing groups and discussion also foster self-efficacy and motivation. Students must also be helped to develop the strategic self-regulated learning strategies that lead to improved self-monitoring (see Schunk, 2003; Zimmerman, 2002). Self-efficacy and self-regulation are kissing cousins, and one cannot easily be developed without the other. When students learn appropriate methods with which to regulate their own learning, these metacognitive skills help them to monitor their understanding, self-evaluate their strengths and weaknesses, engage self-corrective actions, and make appropriate choices.

When classroom structures are individualized and instruction is tailored to students' academic capabilities, social comparisons are minimized, and students are more likely to gauge their academic progress according to their own standards rather than compare it to the progress of their classmates. To some degree, students will inevitably evaluate themselves in relation to their classmates regardless of what a teacher does to minimize or counter these comparisons. In individualized learning settings, however, students can more easily select the peers with whom to compare themselves. Individualized structures that lower the competitive orientation of a classroom and school are more likely than traditional, competitive structures to increase self-efficacy and academic motivation (Schunk, 1995).

If there is one finding that is incontrovertible in education and in psychology, it is that children learn from the actions of models. Schunk and his colleagues have demonstrated that different modeling practices can differently affect self-beliefs (see Schunk, 2003). For example, when peer models make errors, engage in coping behaviors in front of students, and verbalize emotive statements reflecting low confidence and achievement, low-achieving students perceive the models as more similar to themselves and experience greater achievement and self-efficacy. It is of course also important for teachers to engage in effective modeling practices and to select peers for classroom models judiciously so as to ensure that students view themselves as comparable in learning ability to the models. Students who model excellence can imbue other students with the belief that they too can achieve that excellence.

Self-efficacy and other motivation beliefs ultimately become habits of thinking that are developed like any habit of conduct, and teachers are influential in helping students to develop the self-belief habits that will serve them throughout their lives. Teachers should of course endeavor to prevent students from developing negative self-conceptions in the first place. Given the academic failure that some students experience, this is a challenging task. Nonetheless, students should be able to face difficulties, or even fail, without losing the drive and motivation required to try again and to improve. When students have little confidence in their capabilities, a sense of pessimism and "negative thinking" can pervade their academic endeavors (see Scheier & Carver, 1993). Students with positive expectations that result from a strong sense of confidence approach tasks with optimism and continue to strive in the face of difficulty; those with low confidence and few expectations for success are more likely to withdraw their effort and give up on their goals.

Some self-efficacy researchers have suggested that teachers should pay as much attention to students' perceptions of competence as to actual competence, for it is the perceptions that may more accurately predict students' motivation and future academic choices (Hackett & Betz, 1989). Assessing their students' self-efficacy beliefs can provide teachers with important insights. For example, researchers have demonstrated that self-efficacy beliefs strongly influence the choice of majors and career decisions of college students (Hackett, 1995). In many cases, unwarranted low confidence, rather than lack of capability, is responsible for maladaptive academic behaviors, avoidance of courses and careers, and diminishing school interest and achievement. Teachers and parents will readily attest to the fact that there are situations in which inaccurate self-beliefs, rather than a weak knowledge base or inadequate skills, are responsible for students shortchanging themselves academically. In these cases, identifying, challenging, and altering inaccurate judgments are essential to academic success and adaptive functioning.

There are also ways of maintaining a joint focus on the development of mastery and buttressing the self-beliefs that accompany it. Writing programs such as the Writers' Workshop endeavor to build students' writing self-efficacy in the belief that confidence is essential to skill improvement (e.g., Atwell, 1987; Calkins, 1994). Attention to children's self-efficacy beliefs is made an explicit feature of teacher education in such programs, and preservice teachers are taught to assess both competence and the beliefs that accompany competence as part of writing evaluations. In addition, students' own self-evaluations include self-reflection geared to understanding the affective and motivational self-beliefs that are an essential part of writing. McLeod (1987) rightly observed that because writing is as much an emotional as a cognitive activity, affective components strongly influence all phases of the writing process. She urged researchers to explore affective measures with an eye toward developing a "theory of affect" to help students understand how these affective processes may inform their writing. It seems clear that students' writing self-efficacy beliefs should play a prominent role in such a theory.

References

Atwell, N. (1987). *In the middle.* Portsmouth, NH: Boynton/Cook-Heinemann.

Bandura, A. (1977). Self-efficacy: Toward a unifying theory of behavioral change. *Psychological Review, 84,* 191–215.

Bandura, A. (1986). *Social foundations of thought and action: A social cognitive theory.* Englewood Cliffs, NJ: Prentice-Hall.

Bandura, A. (1997). *Self-efficacy: The exercise of control.* New York: Freeman.

Bandura, A. (2001). *Guide for constructing self-efficacy scales—revised.* Available from Frank Pajares, Division of Educational Studies, Emory University, Atlanta, GA, 30322.

Bandura, A., & Schunk, D. H. (1981). Cultivating competence, self-efficacy, and intrinsic interest through proximal self-motivation. *Journal of Personality and Social Psychology, 41,* 586–598.

Bruning, R., & Horn, C. (2000). Developing motivation to write. *Educational Psychologist, 35,* 25–38.

Calkins, L. (1983). *Lessons from a child: On the teaching and learning of writing.* Exeter, NH: Heinemann.

Calkins, L. (1994). *The art of teaching writing.* Portsmouth, NH: Heinemann.

Cleary, L. M. (1996). I think I know what my teachers want now: Gender and writing motivation. *English Journal, 85*(1), 50–57.

Crain, R. M. (1996). The influence of age, race, and gender on child and adolescent multidimensional self-concept. In B. A. Bracken (Ed.), *Handbook of self-concept: Development, social, and clinical considerations* (pp. 395–420). New York: Wiley.

Daly, J. A., & Miller, M. D. (1975). The empirical development of an instrument to measure writing apprehension. *Research in the Teaching of English, 9,* 272–289.

Eccles, J. S. (1987). Gender roles and women's achievement-related decisions. *Psychology of Women Quarterly, 11,* 135–172.

Eccles, J. S., Wigfield, A., Flanagan, C., Miller, C., Reuman, D., & Yee, D. (1989). Self-concepts, domain values, and self-esteem: Relations and changes at early adolescence. *Journal of Personality, 57,* 283–310.

Eccles, J. S., Wigfield, A., Harold, R. D., & Blumenfeld, P. B. (1993). Age and gender differences in children's achievement self-perceptions during the elementary school years. *Child Development, 64,* 830–847.

Eisenberg, N., Martin, C. L., & Fabes, R. A. (1996). Gender development and gender effects. In D. C. Berliner & R. C. Calfee (Eds.), *Handbook of educational psychology* (pp. 358–396). New York: Simon & Schuster/Macmillan.

Gersten, R., & Baker, S. (2001). Teaching expressive writing to students with learning disabilities: A meta-analysis. *Elementary School Journal, 101,* 251-272.

Graham, S., & Harris, K. R. (1989a). Components analysis of cognitive strategy instruction: Effects on learning disabled students' compositions and self-efficacy. *Journal of Educational Psychology, 81,* 353–361.

Graham, S., & Harris, K. R. (1989b). Improving learning disabled students' skills at composing essays: Self-instructional strategy training. *Exceptional Children, 56,* 201–214.

Graham, S., & MacArthur, C. (1988). Improving learning disabled students' skills at revising essays produced on a word processor: Self-instructional strategy training. *Journal of Special Education, 22,* 133–152.

Graham, S., MacArthur, C., Schwartz. S., & Page-Voth, V. (1992). Improving the compositions of students with learning disabilities using a strategy involving product and process goal setting. *Exceptional Children, 58,* 322–334.

Graham, S., & Weiner, B. (1996). Theories and principles of motivation. In D. C. Berliner & R. C. Calfee (Eds.), *Handbook of educational psychology* (pp. 63–84). New York: Simon & Schuster/ Macmillan.

Hackett, G. (1985). The role of mathematics self-efficacy in the choice of math-related majors of college women and men: A path analysis. *Journal of Counseling Psychology, 32,* 47–56.

Hackett, G. (1995). Self-efficacy in career choice and development. In A. Bandura (Ed.), *Self-efficacy in changing societies* (pp. 232–258). New York: Cambridge University Press.

Hackett, G., & Betz, N. E. (1989). An exploration of the mathematics self-efficacy/mathematics performance correspondence. *Journal for Research in Mathematics Education, 20,* 261–273.

Harris, K., & Graham, S. (1992). Self-regulated strategy development: A part of the writing process. In M. Pressley, K. Harris, & J. Guthrie (Eds.), *Promoting academic competence and literacy in school* (pp. 277–309). San Diego: Academic Press.

Harter, S., Waters, P., & Whitesell, N. (1997). Lack of voice as a manifestation of false self-behavior among adolescents: The school setting as a stage upon which the drama of authenticity is enacted. *Educational Psychologist, 32,* 153–173.

Hull, G., & Rose, M. (1989). Rethinking remediation: Toward a social-cognitive understanding of problematic reading and writing. *Written Communication, 6,* 139–154.

Linnenbrink, E. A., & Pintrich, P. R. (2003). The role of self-efficacy beliefs in student engagement and learning in the classroom. *Reading and Writing Quarterly, 19,* 119–137.

Marsh, H. W. (1989). Age and sex effects in multiple dimensions of self-concept: Preadolescence to adulthood. *Journal of Educational Psychology, 81,* 417–430.

McCarthy, P., Meier, S., & Rinderer, R. (1985). Self-efficacy and writing. *College Composition and Communication, 36,* 465–471.

McLeod, S. (1987). Some thoughts about feelings: The affective domain and the writing process. *College Composition and Communication, 38,* 426–435.

Meier, S., McCarthy, P. R., & Schmeck, R. R. (1984). Validity of self-efficacy as a predictor of writing performance. *Cognitive Therapy and Research, 8,* 107–120.

Mills, H., & Clyde, J. A. (1991). Children's success as

readers and writers: It's the teacher's beliefs that make the difference. *Young Children, 46*(2), 54–59.

Noddings, N. (1996, April). *Current directions in self research: Self-concept, self-efficacy, and possible selves.* Symposium presented at the meeting of the American Educational Research Association, New York, NY.

Pajares, F. (1996). Self-efficacy beliefs in academic settings. *Review of Educational Research, 66,* 543–578.

Pajares, F. (1997). Current directions in self-efficacy research. In M. Maehr & P. R. Pintrich (Eds.), *Advances in motivation and achievement* (Vol. 10, pp. 1–49). Greenwich, CT: JAI Press.

Pajares, F., Britner, S. L., & Valiante, G. (2000). Writing and science achievement goals of middle school students. *Contemporary Educational Psychology, 25,* 406–422.

Pajares, F., & Cheong, Y. F. (2003). Achievement goal orientations in writing: A developmental perspective. *International Journal of Educational Research, 39,* 437–455.

Pajares, F., & Johnson, M. J. (1994). Confidence and competence in writing: The role of writing self-efficacy, outcome expectancy, and apprehension. *Research in the Teaching of English, 28,* 313–331.

Pajares, F., & Johnson, M. J. (1996). Self-efficacy beliefs in the writing of high school students: A path analysis. *Psychology in the Schools, 33,* 163–175.

Pajares, F., Hartley, J., & Valiante, G. (2001). Response format in writing self-efficacy assessment: Greater discrimination increases prediction. *Measurement and Evaluation in Counseling and Development, 33,* 214–221.

Pajares, F., Miller, M. D., & Johnson, M. J. (1999). Gender differences in writing self-beliefs of elementary school students. *Journal of Educational Psychology, 91,* 50–61.

Pajares, F., & Schunk, D. H. (2001). Self-beliefs and school success: Self-efficacy, self-concept, and school achievement. In R. J. Riding & S. G. Rayner (Eds.), *International perspectives on individual differences: Vol 2. Self-perception* (pp. 239–266). London: Ablex.

Pajares, F., & Schunk, D. H. (2005). Self-efficacy and self-concept beliefs: Jointly contributing to the quality of human life. In H. Marsh, R. Craven, & D. McInerney (Eds.), *International advances in self research* (Vol. 2, pp. 95–121). Greenwich, CT: Information Age.

Pajares, F., & Valiante, G. (1997). Influence of writing self-efficacy beliefs on the writing performance of upper elementary students. *Journal of Educational Research, 90,* 353–360.

Pajares, F., & Valiante, G. (1999). Grade level and gender differences in the writing self-beliefs of middle school students. *Contemporary Educational Psychology, 24,* 390–405.

Pajares, F., & Valiante, G. (2001). Gender differences in writing motivation and achievement of middle school students: A function of gender orientation? *Contemporary Educational Psychology, 20*, 366–381.

Pajares, F. & Valiante, G. (2002). Students' confidence in their self-regulated learning strategies: A developmental perspective. *Psychologia, 45*, 211–221.

Pajares, F., Valiante, G., & Cheong, Y. F. (in press). Writing self-efficacy and its relation to gender, writing motivation, and writing competence: A developmental perspective. In S. Hidi & P. Boscolo (Eds.), *Motivation and writing: Research and school practice*. Dordrecht, The Netherlands: Kluwer.

Phillips, D. A., & Zimmerman, B. J. (1990). The developmental course of perceived competence and incompetence among competent children. In R. J. Sternberg & J. Kolligian (Eds.), *Competence considered* (pp. 41–67). New Haven, CT: Yale University Press.

Pintrich, P. R., & De Groot, E. V. (1990). Motivational and self-regulated learning components of classroom academic performance. *Journal of Educational Psychology, 82*, 33–40.

Rankin, J. L., Bruning, R. H., & Timme, V. L. (1994). The development of beliefs about spelling and their relationship to spelling performance. *Applied Cognitive Psychology, 8*, 213–232.

Scheier, M. F., & Carver, C. S. (1993). On the power of positive thinking: The benefits of being optimistic. *Current Directions in Psychological Science, 2*, 26–39.

Schunk, D. H. (1995). Self-efficacy and education and instruction. In J. E. Maddux (Ed.), *Self-efficacy, adaptation, and adjustment: Theory, research, and applications* (pp. 281–303). New York: Plenum Press.

Schunk, D. H. (2003). Self-efficacy for reading and writing: Influence of modeling, goal setting, and self-evaluation. *Reading and Writing Quarterly, 19*, 159–172.

Schunk, D. H., & Swartz, C. W. (1993). Goals and progress feedback: Effects on self-efficacy and writing achievement. *Contemporary Educational Psychology, 18*, 337–354.

Schunk, D. H., & Zimmerman, B. (Eds.). (1994). *Self-regulation of learning and performance: Issues and educational applications*. Hillsdale, NJ: Erlbaum.

Schwarz, N. (1999). Self-reports: How the questions shape the answers. *American Psychologist, 54*, 93–105.

Shell, D. F., Colvin, C., & Bruning, R. H. (1995). Self-efficacy, attributions, and outcome expectancy mechanisms in reading and writing achievement: Grade-level and achievement-level differences. *Journal of Educational Psychology, 87*, 386–398.

Shell, D. F., Murphy, C. C., & Bruning, R. H. (1989).

Self-efficacy and outcome expectancy mechanisms in reading and writing achievement. *Journal of Educational Psychology, 81*, 91–100.

Skaalvik, E. (1997). Issues in research on self-concept. In M. Maehr & P. R. Pintrich (Eds.), *Advances in motivation and achievement* (Vol. 10, pp. 51–97). Greenwich, CT: JAI Press.

Wachholz, P. B., & Etheridge, C. P. (1996). Writing self-efficacy beliefs of high- and low-apprehensive writers. *Journal of Developmental Education, 19*, 16–24.

Walker, B. J. (2003). The cultivation of student self-efficacy in reading and writing. *Reading and Writing Quarterly, 19*, 173–187.

Wigfield, A. (1994). The role of children's achievement values in the self-regulation of their learning outcomes. In D. H. Schunk & B. J. Zimmerman (Eds.), *Self-regulation of learning and performance: Issues and educational applications* (pp. 101–124). Hillsdale, NJ: Erlbaum.

Wigfield, A., & Eccles, J. (1992). The development of achievement task values: A theoretical analysis. *Developmental Review, 12*, 265–310.

Wigfield, A., Eccles, J. S., & Pintrich, P. R. (1996). Development between the ages of 11 and 25. In D. C. Berliner & R. C. Calfee (Eds.), *Handbook of educational psychology* (pp. 148–185). New York: Simon & Schuster/Macmillan.

Wigfield, A., Eccles, J., MacIver, D., Reuman, D., & Midgley, C. (1991). Transitions at early adolescence: Changes in children's domain-specific self-perceptions and general self-esteem across the transition to junior high school. *Developmental Psychology, 27*, 552–565.

Zimmerman, B. J. (2002). Becoming a self-regulated learner: An overview. *Theory into practice, 41*, 64–70.

Zimmerman, B. J., & Bandura, A. (1994). Impact of self-regulatory influences on writing course attainment. *American Education Research Journal, 31*, 845–862.

Zimmerman, B. J., Bandura, A., & Martinez-Pons, M. (1992). Self-motivation for academic attainments: The role of self-efficacy beliefs and personal goal setting. *American Educational Research Journal, 29*, 663–676.

Zimmerman, B. J., & Kitsantas, A. (1999). Acquiring writing revision skill: Shifting from process to outcome self-regulatory goals. *Journal of Educational Psychology, 91*, 241–250.

Zimmerman, B. J., & Martinez-Pons, M. (1990). Student differences in self-regulated learning: Relating grade, sex, and giftedness to self-efficacy and strategy use. *Journal of Educational Psychology, 82*, 51–59.

Zimmerman, B. J., & Risemberg, R. (1997). Becoming a self-regulated writer: A social cognitive perspective. *Contemporary Educational Psychology, 22*, 73–101.

Chapter 12

Relations among Oral Language, Reading, and Writing Development

Timothy Shanahan

Historically, reading and writing (literacy) have been thought of as secondary form of language—highly dependent upon the more primary oral forms (listening and speaking) (Berninger, 2000). This view makes sense in terms of the ontogeny of language (Hauser, 1996), because it is well documented that some societies have never developed literacy, but oral language is inescapable. Moreover, there are societies in which reading has been prevalent, but writing has been much less available (Spufford, 1979). Archeological accounts suggest that written language developed later in human history than oral language (Schmant-Besserat, 1993), and that same pattern is *generally* true for individual development as well: Most children begin speaking around the age of 12–18 months, while written language rarely appears before 36 months, and 60–84 months is more characteristic for the onset of beginning reading (Wood, 1981).

Within this general schema, the receptive forms of language (listening and reading) are posited as being more basic than the productive forms (reading and writing), with relatively earlier onsets for listening and reading, and with more formative roles to play in overall language learning. This formativeness has its basis in the fact that language is a social activity; thus, while language learning can be characterized as a form of invention

(see, e.g., Read, 1975), this is not a strictly accurate description of construction because of the requirement that language learning entail mastering a *shared and existing* system of language. This in no way challenges the idea that certain aspects of the language learning process may be "hardwired" into human cognition (Lenneberg, 1967), because even within that theory, it takes language input to make the language learning mechanism go—which is why children in France learn French and children in China learn Chinese (much to the relief of their parents).

The four language systems (speaking, listening, reading, writing) develop in "overlapping and parallel waves rather than in discrete, sequential stages" (Berninger, 2000, p. 66). What this means is that, though writing comes late in the language learning arc (Vygotsky, 1978) or takes longer to accomplish "full" development than the other language systems, it has the potential to be affected by oral language and reading, and likewise can influence the development of those systems, though it is less likely to affect them than to be affected by them. Understanding how the different language systems are correlated with each other can reveal the degree to which progress in writing may be determined by oral language and reading development, which students will likely do best in writing, and why writers err in particular ways. This review examines the theory and empirical research into how oral language (speaking and listening) is related to literacy (reading, writing, and spelling), how the components of literacy, particularly reading and writing, are interconnected, and the changing nature of the empirical study of cross-language relationships.

How Writing Is Related to Oral Language Development

Writing instruction is usually not introduced until students enter school, around age 5, although certain writing behaviors—such as marking—can begin quite early (Hildreth, 1936), and nascent forms of true written composition often begin to appear prior to schooling (Bissex, 1980; Harste, Woodward, & Burke, 1984). But even when early writing does take place, oral language development is already far in advance of written forms.

Given this, it seems likely that oral language development could be a valuable foundation for writing. Young writers would likely rely on their oral knowledge of many aspects of language, including phonological awareness, lexicon, morphemes, syntactic structures, discourse organization or structure, and pragmatics. Reliance on such forms in writing would theoretically make writing development more efficient and should allow faster progress on the part of some children (those with the best developed oral language).

How related are writing and oral language? Much of the work on the relationships among the components of language comes from studies of atypical learners, usually those with serious deficiencies in one or another aspect of language. In a case study of a child who was a struggling language learner (Scott & Windsor, 2000), researchers sampled performance on various language tasks and concluded:

> A child with LLD [language learning disabilities] who behaves like the average LLD participant in the present study would find it difficult to meet basic language requirements of the classroom, and would certainly attract the attention of teachers and parents. The child would produce only 40%–60% of the volume of language of classmates in spoken or written discourse tasks. Compared to classmates, sentences would be less grammatically complex, particularly when writing, and especially when writing in an expository genre. The child still makes grammatical errors, perhaps noticeable in speaking, but certainly noticeable when writing, and blatant when writing expository material. (p. 336)

This kind of close description reveals the interconnections between oral and written language.

Another way to address the relationship of oral language and writing is to look at the relationship between IQ, or the verbal parts of IQ, and writing, because this would suggest how reliant on general verbal ability writing may be. The correlation of writing and oral language has been explored with various measures, usually resulting in moderate estimates of the degree of connection. For example, verbal IQ was correlated with composition *quality* for fourth- and fifth-grade students (.35 with narrative writing, and .42 with expository writing), but it was not found to be correlated with length of compositions in words or clauses (Berninger, Cartwright, Yates, Swanson, & Abbott, 1994). In other studies, volubility in oral language and writing were related (McCarthy, 1954; Harrell, 1957; O'Donnell, Griffin, & Norris, 1967), with steady increases in wordiness in both speaking and writing across the grade levels. Typically, the number of words is higher in oral language than in written language, but the amount of difference attenuates over time, with writing eventually catching up with oral composition. Similarly, there is a significant connection between the sophistication of grammar or syntax, in terms of density and embedding used in speech and writing, with oral development leading writing, but with the difference declining steadily across the elementary school years (Hunt, 1965; Loban, 1963; O'Donnell et al., 1967).

Writing is related to general language processing, but the nature of that relationship is less certain. One conception of this connection might be, for instance, that oral language and writing are dependent upon the same basic underlying cognitive abilities; therefore, those who are low in oral language would be low in writing, but there would be no functional value in knowing this, except that it would allow for writing and oral language to be treated equivalently for the purposes of identification and diagnosis of deficiencies. However, it appears that the reliance of written language on oral language is more direct and complex than this. For instance, it has been shown that even when early oral language problems are eventually overcome, written language continues to suffer (Naucler & Magnusson, 2002). This means that there is no threshold level of oral language performance that must be attained before writing proficiency can proceed.

Other studies have attempted to unpack or explain the connection between oral proficiency and writing by exploring the relations among the underlying abilities or component parts of language. Effective writing, for example, has been shown to be dependent upon verbal working memory (McCutchen, 1996; Swanson & Berninger, 1996); if this aspect of oral proficiency is underdeveloped, then students have difficulty producing well-formed compositions. Beginning writers, particularly young beginners, tend to be constrained in their ability to encode language fluently by hand (i.e., transcription, written encoding, text generation), which can overload their ability to hold much information in memory, giving their writing a choppy noncoherence and introducing certain kinds of syntactic errors (e.g., errors at the ends of sentences or T-units; Tetroe, 1984). Not surprisingly, young children are superior in oral composition or dictation as compared to writing, but as the limits of verbal memory expand (and some of the subprocesses such as handwriting become automatized), this difference diminishes (Bereiter & Scardamalia, 1987; Cox, Shanahan, & Tinzman, 1991; McCutchen, 1987). These studies show that verbal memory limitations impact not only the quantity of writing but also the quality. Additionally, there are similarities in beginning oral and written composing strategies (Berninger, Fuller, & Whittaker, 1996), such as selecting a topic and constructing a comment about it.

Even more cross-language mode work has been done in the area of cohesion—how speakers or writers affect coherence among the ideas they are communicating. Pappas (1985) has shown that first graders accom-

plish greater cohesive harmony in oral stories and less in writing, but with correlated performance, and Fink (1986) reports that children with oral language disabilities evidence weak cohesive harmony and density in both oral and written stories, though learning disabled children without oral language disabilities did not suffer this problem in oral language. Other studies have shown how the cohesion that develops earlier in oral language then bleeds into children's later writing (Cox, Shanahan, & Sulzby, 1990; Rentel, 1988).

Morphology is another area that has received attention with regard to the connections between oral language and writing. Children evidence earlier growth in oral morphology than in writing (Carlisle, 1994). Most investigations of morphological development—how children learn the combinations of phonemes that make up meaningful units of language—have focused on oral language learning (Berko, 1958; Brown, 1973). These investigations have shown that children shift from learning the inflections to learning morphemic derivations between school entry and grade four, an oral language change that Carlisle (1996) speculates might be explained by children's early experiences with written language, including writing. In a study that examined morpheme use in oral and written composition, Carlisle, (1996)found that oral language errors explained many, but not all, of the morphemic errors that occur in writing. Salience of morphological markers in the speech stream was an important determiner of how well students represented inflections in their writing. Other research has demonstrated this close match of oral and written language performance with regard to morphological development during the early school years (Green et al., 2003), and a similar pattern was evident in a study of five adult L2 (second language) learners as well—with the adults trying new morphemic (and syntactic) forms in their writing rather than in their oral language (Weissberg, 2000).

Oral language and writing are closely connected in a general way—with children who have well developed oral language doing better with writing. More particularly, writing appears to draw on oral language, such as in the development of cohesion. However, writing has been found to impact oral language as well—at least with later developing forms, such as morphemes, where the writing can make certain language characteristics more salient to the learner.

At this time, there is not much more to review on the connections between oral language and writing. This literature is more provocative than comprehensive. It is impossible to answer questions about whether programs aimed at oral language improvement would have an impact on writing achievement, or to track the connections of any aspect of development across the years. There simply has been too limited an amount of research into the connections of writing and oral language, with little attention devoted to instructional questions (e.g., whether students can use, in their writing, their oral language development to surmount problems that might be apparent in their reading skills).

Some of this inattention is likely due to the lack of focus on formal oral language development in schooling coupled with the historical neglect of writing instruction (Clifford, 1989). Modest amounts of school time have been devoted to speaking and listening instruction, so perhaps it has seemed that there is little reason to attend to these issues. Similarly, although there has been greater attention accorded to oral language during the preschool years, the correlations of early language growth and later writing may not be obvious. Research has shown that the correlations of preschool language development and primary grade reading are low, but that this relationship increases later (Strickland & Shanahan, 2004). Oral language skills seem to have little to do with the word recognition and production tasks that are paramount to early literacy development, but they are more implicated in later literacy growth. It is possible that some aspects of writing (e.g., certain syntactic forms) might develop more quickly through teaching that stresses oral composition, though it would be unwise to neglect the role writing may play in the growth of these oral forms. There is a need for more research into these issues.

How Writing Is Related to Reading

The relationships between writing and reading have a longer and more extensive re-search history, and this work has been reviewed numerous times (Berninger, Abbott, Abbott, Graham, & Richards, 2002; Berninger et al., 1994; Fitzgerald & Shanahan, 2000; Nelson & Calfee, 1998; Stotsky, 1983; Shanahan & Tierney, 1990; Tierney & Shanahan, 1996). The reason that researchers have been more concerned about the connections within written language than between oral and written language has much to do with theories that emphasize the unique qualities of literacy: Spoken language is ephemeral, or temporary, and takes place in real time, while literacy leaves a permanent record that can be pondered and reflected upon; oral language is fragmentary and social, while written language is not only more complete but also socially distant, because of the opportunities it allows a writer to revise; there are clear differences in vocabulary, grammatical structures, and discourse cohesion between oral and written language, and there is a much greater repertoire of intonation patterns and nonlinguistic features in oral language (Chafe, 1985; Garton & Pratt, 1998; Olson, 1994). Given this great chasm between literacy and oracy, researchers have tended to emphasize connections among the parts that seem most similar—both in terms of surface features and social uses.

Rather than attempting to recast all of the past research studies that have been synthesized, it would be more worthwhile to summarize and update some of the major points of these earlier reviews to provide a sound description of what has gone before, and to synthesize some of the newer empirical work that has accumulated concerning the relations of reading and writing.

One basic idea that has emerged repeatedly in this literature is that reading and writing are dependent upon common cognitive substrata of abilities (e.g., visual, phonological, and semantic systems or short- and long-term memory), and anything that improves these abilities may have implications for both reading and writing development (Berninger & Swanson, 1994; Ellis, 1985, 1987; Just & Daneman, 1992; McCutchen, 2000; Swanson & Berninger, 1996). The same can be said for the reliance of both reading and writing on a common base of knowledge (Fitzgerald, 1990, 1992). Given these commonalities, it should not be surprising that reading and writing are correlated with each other. In fact, in a study of beginning literacy learning, kindergartners' writing behaviors were found to be predictive of subsequent (grade 1) reading achievement, even after controlling for the effects of IQ (Shatil, Share, & Levin, 2000).

According to Fitzgerald and Shanahan (2000), readers and writers rely on four common knowledge bases. The most obvious of these—domain or content knowledge—has received the least attention from researchers interested in reading–writing relations. Although the need for knowledge is especially obvious in writing (Flower & Hayes, 1984; Hillocks, 1986)—because writing has to be about something, research has not often pursued the role of domain knowledge in composition, and when it has, the measured relationship has been rather attenuated (Langer, 1984). Our understanding of how domain knowledge is used by readers has received much greater attention, and it is clear that prior knowledge influences reading comprehension to a great extent (Spivey, 1997), with domain knowledge undergirding the ability to infer, organize, and remember information. Cognition appears to rely upon a single universe of substantive content knowledge that can be drawn upon for various functional purposes, including reading and writing. As with basic processes of memory, domain knowledge serves as a kind of generalizable substratum, available to both reading and writing.

The role of reading in learning content or domain knowledge is self-evident; in fact, learning new information is often given as one of the basic purposes for reading. The role of writing in the development of content knowledge is less secure. The idea that writing could increase content knowledge is widely discussed (Shanahan, 2004), and empirical study is somewhat supportive of this approach. In a meta-analysis of 48 writing-to-learn studies, researchers concluded that writing had a small, positive impact on various outcome measures of school learning (Bangert-Drowns, Hurley, & Wilkinson, 2004).

A second knowledge base that likely connects reading and writing is metaknowledge about written language, including pragmatics. "Metaknowledge refers to several subcategories of knowledge, including knowing about the functions and purposes of reading and writing; knowing that readers and writers interact; monitoring one's own meaning-making" (Fitzgerald & Shanahan, 2000). Tierney and Shanahan (1996) provided a thorough review of how being a writer can influence the process of reading (by giving readers insights into the intentions of the writer), and how being a reader helps a writer to anticipate confusion and miscommunication and, thus, to write better. To improve reading comprehension, it would make sense to encourage author awareness among readers; conversely, to improve writing, it is useful to inculcate audience awareness (Shanahan, 1992). However, it has been shown that certain cultural disassociations of reading and writing may limit these meta-knowledge connections. Brandt (1994) has shown that the settings in which reading and writing are learned and used, and the feelings surrounding early encounters with reading and writing, can differ dramatically: "People typically remembered their first reading experiences as pleasurable occasions, endorsed if not organized by adults. On the other hand, many early writing experiences . . . were remembered as occurring out of the eye of adult supervision and, often, feelings of loneliness, secrecy, and resistance" (p. 461).

A third area of investigation has been the study of the knowledge of specific features or components of written language that may underlie reading and writing. Studies have shown substantial correlations between linguistic features in reading and writing, including phonemic, orthographic, morphological, lexical, syntactic, and discourse features (Berninger, 2000; Shanahan, 1984; Shanahan & Lomax, 1986, 1988). Phonological and orthographic knowledge are closely linked in developing readers and writers (Abbott & Berninger, 1993; Shanahan, 1984), and handwriting is also implicated in spelling ability (Abbott & Berninger, 1993), but only for the younger children (Berninger et al., 1994). Word recognition skills provide a consistent, substantial prediction of the abilities to spell and write at all elementary grade levels (Abbott & Berninger, 1993; Berninger, Abbott, et al., 1998; Berninger, Vaughan, et al., 1998), and spelling is implicated in writing fluency at all elementary levels (Graham, Berninger, Abbott, Abbott, & Whittaker, 1997). Spelling also influences reading comprehension (Berninger et al., 2002; Shanahan, 1984), as do the vocabulary and discourse features of writing, including cohesion and organization (Cox et al., 1990, 1991; Shanahan, 1984). "In both children and adults the correlations between word recognition and word-level transcription factors were high, and the correlations between text-level reading comprehension and composition factors were high" (Berninger et al., 2002, p. 48).

Typically, the amounts of linguistic variance shared across reading and writing have rarely exceeded 50% (Fitzgerald & Shanahan, 2000), but in recent studies with multiple measures of *each* linguistic characteristic, estimates have risen to as high as 72–85% shared variance for word factors and about 65% for text factors (Berninger et al., 2002). Even in these best-case scenarios, it is evident that there are aspects of reading and writing that are unique rather than shared. This pattern of higher measurable relations among word-level as opposed to text-level variables is a consistent pattern across a wide range of populations and studies (Juel, 1988; Shanahan, 1984), and appears to be only weakly linked to age level (Berninger et al., 2002; Shanahan, 1984); however, some studies have reported variation in this pattern for adult literacy students versus comparable, in terms of reading level, normal developing children. Word recognition and spelling appear to be more closely linked for normal developing children, with the low-literacy adults showing much less use of phonological strategies—particularly for spelling (Greenberg, Ehri, & Perrin, 2002).

These linguistic feature relationships that connect reading and writing appear to be bidirectional (Berninger et al., 2002; Shanahan & Lomax, 1986, 1988). This means that not only can word recognition abilities of reading influence the spelling (and fluency) of composition, but also that learning to spell influences children's word recognition. Similar bidirectional patterns of growth were evident in the other linguistic features as well.

That so much linguistic knowledge underlies reading and writing, and that the use of such knowledge in one domain of language can facilitate performance in another is not to say that these relationships are symmetrical. Reading and writing draw on a common base of linguistic features, but it is likely not as simple as the sharing of domain knowledge. For example, students who are reading or writing about restaurants—and who know something about restaurants—might vary in their ability to draw on this knowledge in reading or writing (since in reading the author stimulates the reader to draw on prior knowledge and in writing the writer must self-stimulate these memories), but it is hard to imagine that the actual declarative knowledge about restaurants would vary much across reading and writing. The same does not appear to be true with regard to knowledge of language features, at least in terms of the phonemic and orthographic systems. It has been shown that there are different numbers and types of paths that run from analogous sounds to letters and from letters to sounds. For example, when a reader comes across a word such as *sure,* the potential underlying phonemic representations of the first letter would include /s/, /z/, and /sh/, as well as no specific sound ("a silent letter"). However, when a writer going from sound to letters wants to spell *sure,* he or she would choose only from the *s*, *sh*, or *ch* paths. The paths are not symmetrical, and reading and writing could not simply be inverse processes of each other (Cronnell, 1970; Ehri, 1997; Reed, 1981).

Finally, the shared knowledge underlying reading and writing includes procedural knowledge, which refers to knowing how to access, use, and generate information during reading and writing. This includes awareness of intentional strategies such as prediction, questioning, and summarizing. Langer (1986) conducted an analysis of the connections between these kinds of procedural actions during comparable reading and writing activities, and found similar levels of correlation to what was evident in the linguistic knowledge literature. This study had students carrying out think-alouds during and after various reading and writing activities. As with linguistic knowledge, a lack of symmetry was evident across reading and writing in procedural action. The reasons for these differences in knowledge use likely were bound up in the different purposes of reading and writing and the differences in starting places, since writers can begin with no more than a blank page and few constraints, while readers have to try to follow and stay within the leads and constraints placed on interpretation by the writer.

As should be obvious, empirical research has so far provided a much richer understanding of the connections between reading and writing than between oral language and reading. Unlike oral language research, with reading–writing connections, there are experimental studies showing that reading instruction can improve writing, and that writing instruction can have a positive impact on reading development (Tierney & Shanahan, 1996). For example, in an instructional study of reading–writing relationships, it was reported that instructional approach had an impact on reading (with traditional approaches to instruction having more impact than process or whole-language approaches), but that variations in writing performance were accounted for by reading achievement alone, not by the instruction (Stahl, Pagnucco, & Suttles, 1996). This kind of cross-domain language improvement is not found consistently, however, and there are published examples of such teaching impacting only the language domain that the instruction directly addressed (Shanahan, 1988).

A common finding has been that some reading-to-writing or writing-to-reading learning is possible, but that instruction targeting skills in one or the other tends to be most effective at improving that dimension. For example, handwriting instruction had a positive impact on word recognition skills, but not as much of an effect as is usually obtained from direct training in word recognition skills (Berninger et al., 1997). This, together with the earlier reviewed correlational data and a growing body of evidence that reveals both the overlapping but separable nature of reading and writing at a neurological level (Beaton, Guest, & Ved, 1997; Berninger et al., 2002; Boget & Marcos, 1997; Chan, 1992; Frith, 1980; Dejerine, 1891; Niemi, Poskiparta, Vaurus, & Maeki, 1998), suggests the complexity of combining reading and writing instructionally, and the need for design experiments that show how to do that most productively. Reading and writing instruction can be usefully combined, but instruction in one or the other is unlikely to be an adequate replacement for the other if the goal is to develop students who can read *and* write well.

There are two basic explanations for why it can be beneficial or more efficient to combine reading and writing instructionally. One has to do with the shared knowledge or skills required in reading and writing, and the cross-domain language practice that can occur through these literacy acts. For example, writers often read and reread what they are writing, and readers and writers certainly are practicing the use of a plethora of content information, linguistic features, and processes, though the differences in the nature of this practice may reduce its ultimate cross-language transfer potential, as earlier noted. A second benefit, however, may redound from the differences between reading and writing. One learning theory holds that learning is achieved through examining and reexamining information from a variety of cognitive perspectives (McGinley & Tierney, 1989). Within this theory, each reconsideration of information is deepened, not from repetition (that is a memory issue), but from thinking about the information in a new way. Since reading and writing have a somewhat different cognitive footprint, as shown in these various investigations, it is possible that reading and writing can provide these separate vantages for learning. In fact, research suggests that individuals combine reading and writing in different ways for various tasks, and that these interactions between reading and writing operate somewhat as this theory predicts, at least with regard to content information and metaknowledge (Tierney, Soter, O'Flahavan, & McGinley, 1989).

The separability or uniqueness of reading and writing is also an important issue within assessment design and interpretation when students are asked to show their reading comprehension through writing as opposed to oral reading or multiple-choice marking. Increasingly, large-scale assessments, such as the National Assessment of Educational Progress, use constructive response items that require students to write brief essays about stories or articles they have read. Even state accountability tests are using such formats on a large scale. This is potentially problematic, because the probability of doing well in both reading and writing is lower than the probability of doing well in either. This means that students will not appear to read as well as they can under other testing conditions, because writing may exacerbate the issue. If reading and writing possess unique qualities, the reading outcomes would be influenced deleteriously by the writing demands of the assessment. In fact, that is exactly what studies show (Jenkins, Johnson, & Hileman, 2004; McCormick, 1992):

> After controlling for word identification and listening, writing ability accounted for no variance in multiple-choice reading scores. By contrast, writing ability accounted for unique variance in reading ability, even after controlling for word identification and listening skill, and explained more variance in constructed-response reading scores than did either word identification or listening skill. (Jenkins et al., 2004, p. 125)

New Directions in Considering Relationships with Writing

Certainly one of the most important developments of the past 10–15 years has been the growing body of investigations into the nature of reading–writing relationships within children and adults who have problems learning to read. Historically, most of the reading and writing relationship studies were based on data drawn from regular classrooms and usually included a full performance range from the normal population. The burgeoning and high-quality work of Virginia W. Berninger and her colleagues over the last decade has helped to redress this imbalance to some extent. Their work has examined learning disabled populations but has avoided the problems of constrained variance usually evident with such groups (and constrained variance tends to lower correlations) through the careful identification of a large and varied population of research subjects and the estimation of parameters based on multiple measures. One of the most important and remarkable outcomes of this work is the insight that the patterns of reading–writing relationship tend not to differ much from those identified in a wider ranging population of subjects.

Of course, the neglect of special learners with regard to reading–writing relationships is due in part to the dearth of work on writing disabilities or similar topics. While there is a large literature devoted to the etiology,

identification, and remediation of various types of reading problems, no comparable literature of any scope has yet developed in the area of writing. If students struggle in reading lessons, they are likely to receive additional instruction, but no similar educational response is yet in place for writing.

Another relatively recent development in the study of reading–writing relationships has been the consideration of these relations with L2 learners. One of these studies (Ball, 2003) examined these relationships in children in grades 3–6. A series of statistical analyses revealed few differences between either the patterns of literacy development or how reading and writing related to each other for both native English or English-as-a-second-language students. However, this study found sizable differences in oral language performance for the two groups, an important finding, because the oral language measures were closely related to higher level reading comprehension and story construction. This suggests that greater oral language development might be needed to allow L2 students to progress successfully at the highest levels of literacy learning, but that the ways that reading and writing are taught and combined might not need to vary much from usual practice with native language learners. This finding contradicts theories reviewed earlier that posit a closer relationship among the written aspects of language, than between literacy and oral language. Furthermore, this study found that a composite measure of cognitive ability did not reveal differences across these groups, and this measure predicted comparable performance on both spelling and word recognition measures—the same pattern evident in first-language (L1) learners.

In another study of reading–writing relations, in this case, between composition quality and reading comprehension, measurable relationships were evident with English language learners (ELL) (from a variety of home languages) in the L2 (Carell & Connor, 1991). A somewhat different pattern was suggested in a third ELL study (Hedgcock & Atkinson, 1993), which attempted to connect various environmental reading variables in an L2, such as connecting how much pleasure reading and textbook reading was taking place to writing achievement in the L1 and L2. The reading measures were predictive of reading and writing performance in L1 but were not connected to L2 performance. The authors concluded that acquiring L2 literacy may be different than acquiring L1 literacy in terms of these particular relationships, and that lots of print exposure alone will not be sufficient to develop L2 writing skills.

Summary and Conclusions

Studies of the relationship of oral language and writing have demonstrated a clear and consistent connection between verbal intelligence and writing, and have provided sufficient evidence to suggest that both forms of language draw on a common set of cognitive abilities, including working memory, linguistic cohesion, and morphological knowledge. It is evident that early language problems are a harbinger to later writing problems, even when the early oral language deficiencies are overcome.

Unfortunately, there continues to be a paucity of research into the relations between oral language development and literacy, particularly with regard to studies that show how to use oral language toward better reading and writing skills or how to teach or support language development in ways that positively impact literacy. Although there are sufficient investigations into the oral language–writing relationship to suggest the potential value of these connections to understanding or improving literacy, there has not been a sufficiently ambitious program of research into these issues to provide a definitive portrait of the role of oral language within writing, and how reliance on oral language features can allow writers to surpass deficiencies from their reading skills that could block writing performance, or how oral language instruction can improve writing.

There are likely many reasons for this lack of attention to these issues, one of which may be the peculiar role of early vocabulary development—which is often used as the measure of oral language proficiency—in subsequent literacy skills. The pattern of relationship between this measure of oral language and early reading and writing skills is minimal, and this low correlation may suggest that early instructional emphasis on oral language development would be a waste of time in terms of literacy learning. However, the importance of this early vocabulary variable to reading and writing increases as attention turns toward text reading and writing, as opposed to word recognition and production. The message seems clear: Early and continued attention to oral language development may not be necessary for early literacy growth, but it is probably essential for sustaining that growth in the later school years. More research is clearly needed into issues of oral language and its role in literacy learning.

In contrast, there is a richer empirical research base available for examining the relationships between reading and writing. These studies show that reading and writing depend upon a common base of cognitive processes and knowledge, and we have a particularly fertile understanding of what kinds of linguistic knowledge are shared between reading and writing, how the patterns of this knowledge sharing change with development, and how reading and writing influence each other. These studies have revealed even closer relations between reading and writing than those previously found and have extended our understanding of the bidirectionality of these relations (e.g., the sharing of knowledge between reading and writing can go either way, from reading to writing, or from writing to reading), as well as of the nonsymmetrical nature of the relations. While recent research has expanded our notions of the potential sharing that can take place among reading, writing, spelling, and handwriting, anthropological and neurological investigations continue to expand our awareness of the ultimate separability of reading and writing; that is, it is possible to read without knowing how to write and vice versa.

Studies have shown that it is possible to teach reading so that it improves writing and to teach writing so that it improves reading, but we do not know how to do this consistently. We still lack a thorough understanding of how various reading or writing experiences may be beneficial to the other, though studies certainly show that such cross-language improvement is possible. However, it is also apparent that learning outcomes in reading and writing tend to be more powerfully influenced by direct instruction within those dimensions of language rather than across them. In other words, reading instruction does more for reading achievement, and writing instruction does more for writing achievement than would be expected from cross-language efforts. An exception to this may occur at the beginnings of literacy, when reading growth might actually be more important for writing achievement than writing instruction (Stahl et al., 1996). Particularly useful in sorting out this issue are the growing bodies of research on struggling learners and L2 learners. Although these studies often show similar patterns of performance across types of learners, there are some differences as well. For example, at the text levels of processing for L2 learners, comprehension and composition quality are more likely to depend upon oral language skills than upon the cross-domain aspects of reading and writing (this was not true for word-level processing, and it may not be true within an L1). In any event, there is a need for more theory development and systematic study of the nature of the relations within and across these special populations, because these efforts may reveal important insights for how reading and writing can be combined most productively within instruction.

References

Abbott, R. D., & Berninger, V. W. (1993). Structural equation modeling of relationships among developmental skills and writing skills in primary and intermediate grade writers. *Journal of Educational Psychology, 85,* 478–508.

Ball, S. E. (2003). *The relation between reading and writing development in English and ESL students.* Unpublished doctoral dissertation, University of Toronto, Toronto, Canada.

Bangert-Drowns, R. L., Hurley, M. M., & Wilkinson, B. (2004). The effects of school-based writing-to-learn interventions on academic achievement: A meta-analysis. *Review of Educational Research, 74,* 29–58.

Beaton, A., Guest, J., & Ved, R. (1997). Semantic errors of naming, reading, writing, and drawing following left-hemisphere infarction. *Cognitive Neuropsychology, 14,* 459–478.

Bereiter, C., & Scardamalia, M. (1987). *The psychology of written composition.* Hillsdale, NJ: Erlbaum.

Berko, J. (1958). The child's learning of English morphology. *Word, 14,* 150–177.

Berninger, V. W. (2000). Development of language by hand and its connections with language by ear, mouth, and eye. *Topics in Language Disorders, 20*(4), 65–84.

Berninger, V. W., Abbott, R. D., Abbott, S. P., Graham, S., & Richards, T. (2002). Writing and reading: Connections between language by hand and language by eye. *Journal of Learning Disabilities, 35,* 39–56.

Berninger, V. W., Abbott, R. D., Rogan, L., Reed, E., Abbott, R., Brooks, A., et al. (1998). Teaching spelling to children with specific learning disabilities: The mind's ear and eye beats the computer or pencil. *Learning Disability Quarterly, 21,* 106–122.

Berninger, V. W., Cartwright, A. C., Yates, C. M., Swanson, H. L., & Abbott, R. D. (1994). Developmental skills related to writing and reading acquisition in the intermediate grades. *Reading and Writing: An Interdisciplinary Journal, 6,* 161–196.

Berninger, V. W., Fuller, F., & Whittaker, D. (1996). A process approach to writing development across the life span. *Educational Psychology Review, 8,* 193–218.

Berninger, V. W., & Swanson, H.L. (1994). Modifying Hayes and Flowers' model of skilled writing to explain beginning and developing writing. In E. Butterfield (Ed.), *Children's writing: Toward a process theory of development of skilled writing* (pp. 57–81). Greenwich, CT: JAI Press.

Berninger, V. W., Vaughan, K., Abbott, R. D., Brooks, A., Abbott, S., Reed, E., et al. (1998). Early intervention for spelling problems: Teaching spelling units of varying size with a multiple connections framework. *Journal of Educational Psychology, 90,* 587–605.

Berninger, V. W., Vaughan, K., Abbott, R. D., Brooks, A., Abbott, S., Rogan, L., et al. (1997). Treatment of handwriting fluency problems in beginning writing: Transfer from handwriting to composition. *Journal of Educational Psychology, 89,* 652–666.

Bissex, G. L. (1980). *GNYS AT WRK: A child learns to read and write.* Cambridge, MA: Harvard University Press.

Boget, T., & Marcos, T. (1997). Reading and writing impairments and rehabilitation. In J. Leon-Carrion (Ed.), *Neuropsychological rehabilitation: Fundamentals, innovations and directions* (pp. 333–352). Delray Beach, FL: St. Lucie Press.

Brandt, D. (1994). Remembering writing, remembering reading. *College Composition and Communication, 45,* 459–479.

Brown, R. (1973). *A first language: The early stages.* Cambridge, MA: Harvard University Press.

Carlisle, J. F. (1996). An exploratory study of morphological errors in children's written stories. *Reading and Writing: An Interdisciplinary Journal, 8,* 61–72.

Carrell, P. L., & Connor, U. (1991). Reading and

writing descriptive and persuasive texts. *Modern Language Journal, 75,* 314–324.

Chafe, W. L. (1985). Linguistic differences produced by differences between speaking and writing. In D. R. Olson, N. Torrance, & A. Hildyard (Eds.), *Literacy, language, and learning: The nature and consequences of reading and writing* (pp. 105–123). Cambridge, UK: Cambridge University Press.

Chan, J. L. (1992). Alexia and agraphia in four Chinese stroke patients with review of the literature: A proposal for a universal mechanism model for reading and writing. *Journal of Neurolinguistics, 7,* 171–185.

Clifford, G. J. (1989). A Sisyphean task: Historical perspectives on writing and reading instruction. In A. H. Dyson (Ed.), *Collaboration through writing and reading* (pp. 25–83). Urbana, IL: National Council of Teachers of English.

Cox, B. E., Shanahan, T., & Sulzby, E. (1990). Good and poor elementary readers' use of cohesion in writing. *Reading Research Quarterly, 25,* 47–65.

Cox, B. E., Shanahan, T., & Tinzman, M. (1991). Children's knowledge of organization, cohesion, and voice. *Research in the Teaching of English, 25,* 179–218.

Cronnell, B. A. (1970). *Spelling-to-sound correspondences for reading vs. sound-to-spelling correspondences* (Technical Note No. 2–7–15). Los Alomitos, CA: Southwest Regional Laboratory.

Dejerine, J. (1891). Sur un cas de cecite verbale avec agraphie, suivi d'autopsie [On a case of word blindness with agraphia, follow-up autopsy]. *Memoires de la Societe Biologique, 3,* 197–201.

Ehri, L. (1997). Learning to read and having to spell are one and the same, almost. In C. A. Perfetti & L. Rieten (Eds.), *Learning to spell: Research, theory, and practice* (pp. 237–269). Mahwah, NJ: Erlbaum.

Ellis, A. (1985). The cognitive neuropsychology of developmental (and acquired) dyslexia: A critical survey. *Cognitive Neuropsychology, 2,* 169–205.

Ellis, A. (1987). Review on problems in developing cognitively transmitted cognitive modules. *Mind and Language, 2,* 242–251.

Fink, R. J. (1986). *A comparison of text characteristics in the narrative discourse of normal and learning disabled children.* Unpublished doctoral dissertation, University of Colorado, Boulder.

Fitzgerald, J. (1990). Reading and writing as "mind meeting." In T. Shanahan (Ed.), *Reading and writing together: New perspectives for the classroom* (pp. 81–97). Norwood, MA: Chrisopher-Gordon.

Fitzgerald, J. (1992). *Towards knowledge in writing: Illustrations from revision studies.* New York: Springer-Verlag.

Fitzgerald, J., & Shanahan, T. (2000). Reading and writing relations and their development. *Educational Psychologist, 35,* 39–50.

Flower, L., & Hayes, J. R. (1984). Images, plays, and prose: The representation of meaning in writing. *Written Communication, 1,* 120–160.

Frith, U. (1980). Unexpected spelling problems. In *Processes in spelling* (pp. 495–515). London: Academic Press.

Garton, A., & Pratt, C. (1998). *Learning to be literate: The development of spoken and written language* (2nd ed.). London: Blackwell.

Graham, S., Berninger, V. W., Abbott, R. D., Abbott, S., & Whittaker, D. (1997). The role of mechanics in composing of elementary school students: A new methodological approach. *Journal of Educational Psychology, 89,* 170–182.

Green, L., McCutchen, D., Schwiebert, C., Quinlan, T., Eva-Wood, A., & Juelis, J. (2003). Morphological development in children's writing. *Journal of Educational Psychology, 95,* 752–761.

Greenberg, D., Ehri, L. C., & Perrin, D. (2002). Do adult literacy students make the same spelling errors as children matched for word-reading age? *Scientific Studies of Reading, 6,* 221–244.

Harrell, L. E., Jr. (1957). A comparison of oral and written language in school-age children. *Monographs of the Society for Research in Child Development, 22*(3).

Harste, J. C., Woodward, V. A., & Burke, C. L. (1984). *Language stories and literacy lessons.* Portsmouth, NH: Heinemann.

Hauser, M. D. (1996). *The evolution of communication.* Cambridge, MA: MIT Press.

Hedgcock, J., & Atkinson, D. (1993). Differing reading–writing relationships in L1 and L2 literacy development? *TESOL Quarterly, 2,* 329–333.

Hildreth, G. (1936). Developmental sequences in name writing. *Child Development, 7,* 291–303.

Hillocks, G., Jr. (1986). The writer's knowledge: Theory, research, and implications for practice. In A. R. Petrosky & D. Bartholomae (Eds.), *The teaching of writing: 85th yearbook of the National Society for the Study of Education* (pp. 71–94). Chicago: National Society for the Study of Education.

Hunt, K. W. (1965). *Grammatical structures written at three grade levels* (Research Report No. 3). Urbana, IL: National Council of Teachers of English.

Jenkins, J. R., Johnson, E., & Hileman, J. (2004). When is reading also writing: Sources of individual differences on the new reading performance assessments. *Scientific Studies of Reading, 8,* 125–151.

Juel, C. (1988). Learning to read and write: A longitudinal study of 54 children from first through fourth grades. *Journal of Educational Psychology, 80,* 437–447.

Just, M., & Daneman, J. (1992). A capacity theory of comprehension: Individual differences in working memory. *Psychological Review, 99,* 122–149.

Langer, J. A. (1984). The effects of available information on responses to school writing tasks. *Research in the Teaching of English, 18,* 31–32.

Langer, J. A. (1986). *Children reading and writing: Structures and strategies.* Norwood, NJ: Ablex.

Lenneberg, E. H. (1967). *Biological foundations of language.* New York: Wiley.

Loban, W. D. (1963). *The language of elementary school children* (Research Report No. 1). Urbana, IL: National Council of Teachers of English.

McCarthy, D. A. (1954). Language development in children. In L. Carmichael (Ed.), *Manual of child psychology* (2nd ed., pp. 492–630). New York: Wiley.

McCormick, S. (1992). Disabled readers' erroneous responses to inferential comprehension questions: Description and analysis. *Reading Research Quarterly, 27,* 54–77.

McCutchen, D. (1987). Children's discourse skill: Form and modality requirements of school writing. *Discourse Processes, 10,* 267–286.

McCutchen, D. (1996). A capacity theory of writing: Working memory in composition. *Educational Psychology Review, 8,* 299–325.

McCutchen, D. (2000). Knowledge, processing, and working memory: Implications for a theory of writing. *Educational Psychologist, 35,* 13–24.

McGinley, W., & Tierney, R. J. (1989). Traversing the topical landscape: Reading and writing as ways of knowing. *Written Communication, 6,* 243–269.

Naucler, K., & Magnusson, E. (2002). How do preschool language problems affect language abilities in adolescence? In F. Windsor & M. L. Kelly (Eds.), *Investigations in clinical phonetics and linguistics* (pp. 99–114). Mahwah, NJ: Erlbaum.

Nelson, N., & Calfee, R. C. (Eds.). (1998). *The reading–writing connection. 97th yearbook of the National Society for the Study of Education* (pp. 1–52). Chicago: National Society for the Study of Education.

Niemi, P., Poskiparta, E., Vaurus, M., & Maeki, H. (1998). Reading and writing difficulties do not always occur as the researcher expects. *Scandinavian Journal of Psychology, 39,* 159–161.

O'Donnell, R. C., Griffin, W. J., & Norris, R. C. (1967). *Syntax of kindergarten and elementary school children: A transformational analysis.* Urbana, IL: National Council of Teachers of English.

Olson, D. R. (1994). *The world on paper.* Cambridge, UK: Cambridge University Press.

Pappas, C. C. (1985). The cohesive harmony and cohesive density of children's oral and written stories. In J. D. Benson & W. S. Greaves (Eds.), *Systemic perspectives on discourse* (Vol. 2, pp. 169–186). Norwood, NJ: Ablex.

Read, C. (1975). *Children's categorization of speech sounds* (Technical Report No. 197). Urbana, IL: National Council of Teachers of English.

Reed, C. (1981). Writing is not the inverse for reading for young children. In C. H. Frederickson & J. Dominick (Eds.), *Writing: The nature, development, and teaching of written communication* (Vol. 2, pp. 105–117). Hillsdale, NJ: Earlbaum.

Rentel, V. M. (1988). Cohesive harmony in children's written narratives: A secondary analysis. In J. L. Green & J. O. Harker (Eds.), *Multiple perspective analyses of classroom discourse* (pp. 281–307). Norwood, NJ: Ablex.

Schmant-Besserat, D. (1993). Before writing. *Science, 260,* 1670–1671.

Scott, C. M., & Windsor, J. (2000). General language performance measures in spoken and written narrative and expository discourse of school-age children with language learning disabilities. *Journal of Speech, Language, and Hearing Research, 43,* 324–339.

Shanahan, T. (1984). Nature of the reading–writing relation: An exploratory multivariate analysis. *Journal of Educational Psychology, 76,* 466–477.

Shanahan, T. (1988). The reading–writing relationship: Seven instructional principles. *Reading Teacher, 41,* 636–647.

Shanahan, T. (1992). Reading comprehension as a conversation with an author. In M. Pressley, K. R. Harris, & J. T. Guthrie (Eds.), *Promoting academic competence and literacy in school* (pp. 129–148). San Diego: Academic Press.

Shanahan, T. (2004). Overcoming the dominance of communication: Writing to think and to learn. In T. L. Jetton & J. A. Dole (Eds.), *Adolescent literacy research and practice* (pp. 59–74). New York: Guilford Press.

Shanahan, T., & Lomax, R. G. (1986). An analysis and comparison of theoretical models of the reading–writing relationship. *Journal of Educational Psychology, 78,* 116–123.

Shanahan, T., & Lomax, R. G. (1988). A developmental comparison of three theoretical models of reading–writing relationship. *Research in the Teaching of English, 22,* 196–212.

Shanahan, T., & Tierney, R. J. (1990). Reading–writing connections: The relations among three perspectives. In J. Zutell & S. McCormick (Eds.), *Literacy theory and research: Analyses from multiple paradigms: 39th Yearbook of the National Reading Conference* (pp. 13–34). Chicago: National Reading Conference.

Shatil, E., Share, D. C., & Levin, I. (2000). On the contribution of kindergarten writing to grade one literacy: A longitudinal study in Hebrew. *Applied Psycholinguistics, 21,,* 1–21.

Spivey, N. N. (1997). *The constructivist metaphor: Reading, writing, and the making of meaning.* San Diego: Academic Press.

Spufford, M. (1979). First steps in literacy: The reading and writing experiences of the humblest seventeenth-century spiritual autobiographers. *Social History, 4,* 407–435.

Stahl, S. A., Pagnucco, J. R., & Suttles, C. W. (1996). First graders' reading and writing instruction in traditional and process-oriented classes. *Journal of Educational Research, 89,* 131–144.

Stotsky, S. (1983). Research of reading/writing relationships: A synthesis and suggested directions. *Language Arts, 60,* 568–580.

Strickland, D., & Shanahan, T. (2004). Laying the groundwork. *Educational Leadership, 61,* 74–77.

Swanson, H. L., & Berninger, V. (1996). Individual differences in children's working memory and writing skills. *Journal of Experimental Child Psychology, 63,* 358–385.

Tetroe, J. (1984, April). *Information processing demand of plot construction in story writing.* Paper presented at the meeting of the American Educational Research Association, New Orleans, LA.

Tierney, R. J., Soter, A., O'Flahavan, J. F., &

McGinley, W. (1989). The effects of reading and writing upon thinking critically. *Reading Research Quarterly, 24,* 134–173.

Tierney, R. J., & Shanahan, T. (1996). Research on the reading–writing relationship: Interactions, transactions, and outcomes. In R. Barr, M. L. Kamil, P. Mosenthal, & P. D. Pearson (Eds.), *Handbook of reading research* (Vol. 2, pp. 246–280). Mahwah, NJ: Erlbaum.

Vygotsky, L. S. (1978). *Mind in society: The development of higher psychological processes.* Cambridge, MA: Harvard University Press.

Weissberg, B. (2000). Developmental relationships in the acquisition of English syntax: Writing vs. speech. *Learning and Instruction, 10,* 37–53.

Wood, B. S. (1981). *Children and communication: Verbal and nonverbal language development* (2nd ed.). Englewood Cliffs, NJ: Prentice-Hall.

Part III

INSTRUCTIONAL MODELS AND APPROACHES

Chapter 13

Strategy Instruction and the Teaching of Writing
A Meta-Analysis

Steve Graham

Although some historians claim that they can identify the exact year (1956) and date (September 11) that contemporary cognitive psychology began, such precision is not possible in trying to identify when the conceptual and methodological advances from the cognitive sciences were first applied to the area of writing. A seminal event, however, was an interdisciplinary conference in 1978 at Carnegie Mellon University aimed at synthesizing prior research on writing as well as showcasing new research. Publications of the papers from this meeting in the book *Cognitive Processes in Writing* (Gregg & Steinberg, 1980) generated considerable interest in the cognitive nature of writing.

An especially influential paper in the Gregg and Steinberg (1980) book presented a model of skilled writing, developed by asking adults to "think out loud" while composing (Hayes & Flower, 1980). Analysis of the participants' verbalizations provided the researchers with a window into the cognitive processes as well as other factors involved in writing. The resulting model included three basic ingredients. One component involved factors that were external to the writer but influenced the writing task. This included social elements, such as the writing assignment, and physical ones, such as the text produced so far. A second component provided a description of the mental operations involved

in writing, including planning what to say and how to say it, translating plans into written text, and reviewing to improve existing text. Planning, in turn, involved three processes-setting goals, generating ideas, and organizing ideas into a writing plan, whereas reviewing included reading and editing text. The third component encompassed the writer's knowledge about the topic, the intended audience, and general plans or formulas for accomplishing various writing tasks.

One of the reasons why this model had such a powerful impact on the field of writing is that it provided a viable mechanism for accounting for individual differences in how writers compose. In addition to cataloguing the mental operations involved in writing, Hayes and Flower (1980) proposed that the execution of these cognitive processes was under the writer's direct control, and that virtually any subprocess could interrupt or incorporate any other subprocess. Planning might interrupt translation, for example, if a writer identified the need to develop additional writing goals while producing a first draft. In contrast, another writer might combine translation and reviewing, generating a section and then revising it, then generating and revising a second section, and so on. Thus, a relatively small number of cognitive processes were able to account for a diverse set of mental operations during composing.

Not only did this model serve as the stimulus for additional research on the cognitive nature of writing, which eventually led Hayes (1996, 2004) to modify the original framework, but it also served as a spark for investigating the effectiveness of cognitive-oriented approaches to writing instruction. The purpose of such instruction is to change how writers' compose by helping them employ more sophisticated composing processes when writing. There are number of potential ways of achieving this objective. For example, it may be possible to induce more sustained and thoughtful writing behavior by carefully structuring the environment (as is done in the process writing approach), so that it is pleasant, supportive, and collaborative; so that writing assignments serve a real purpose; so that students share their work with each other; so that choice and ownership are emphasized; and so that a predictable classroom routine is established where students are encouraged to plan, revise, and edit their papers (Graham & Harris, 1996). More strategic behavior might also be facilitated through goal setting, because goals direct attention to what needs to be done and provide an incentive to mobilize and sustain effort (Locke, Shaw, Saari, & Latham, 1981). Teachers may further be able to help students carry out more sophisticated composing processes through procedural facilitation (Scardamalia & Bereiter, 1986), in which students receive some form of assistance designed to facilitate their execution of one or more cognitive processes when composing (e.g., providing students with a cue card during planning that prompts reflection). In addition, students can be directly and explicitly taught to use independently more sophisticated composing strategies (e.g., a student who does not plan in advance of writing might be taught how to brainstorm and to organize possible writing ideas before starting a first draft). This approach is typically referred to as strategy instruction.

In this chapter, I examine the effectiveness of one of these approaches, namely, strategy instruction. The effectiveness of environmental structuring, at least in terms of the process approach to writing instruction, is examined by Pritchard and Honeycutt in Chapter 19, this volume. We did not examine the effectiveness of procedural facilitation, because the practical implications of this research are currently limited. Many of the investigations in this area were conducted to examine theoretical issues (see, e.g., Graham, 1997; Scardamalia & Bereiter, 1983), involving treatments of very short duration, with little connection to the classroom or school curriculum. Finally, research examining the effectiveness of goal setting or other self-regulatory procedures, such as self-assessment of writing, was not included, because there are only a handful of studies in each of these areas.

I employed meta-analysis to examine the overall impact of strategy instruction on students' writing performance immediately following instruction and at maintenance. Generalization to different genres and across persons–settings was also examined. I attempted to (1) typify strategy instruction effects on posttest, maintenance, and generalization measures of writing performance, and (2) investigate the relationship between study features and study outcomes. This included examining whether study outcomes were related to student type (learning disability, poor writer, average writer, or good writer), grade (elementary or secondary), genre (narrative or expository), cognitive process (planning, revising/editing, or both), instructor (graduate assistant/researcher or teacher), and type of instruction (the Self-Regulated Strategy Development [SRSD] or other approaches).

Methods for the Review

Location and Selection of Studies

For the purpose of this review, strategy instruction studies in writing were defined as empirical investigations in which school-age students (grades 1–12) were taught one or more strategies for planning (including translating plans into text), revising, or editing text. This included the three cognitive processes—planning, translating, and reviewing—included in the model developed by Hayes and Flower (1980). Because the primary goal of strategy instruction is thoughtful and independent use of the target strategies, studies included in this review also had to meet the following criteria: (1) Students had to be shown how to use the strategy (i.e., modeling); (2) there were at least 3 or more days of instruction; and (3) instruction progressed toward students' independent use of the strategy.

Included in the review were experimental studies involving group comparisons (strategy instruction vs. control), as well as single-subject design investigations. The group studies included both true experiments (i.e., random assignment to treatments) and quasi-experiments (random assignment to treatments was not employed) that contained a control condition. Single-subject design studies were limited to multiple-baseline design investigations (see Kratochwill & Levin, 1992). With this type of design, treatment is systematically and sequentially introduced to each set of students at a time (a set can be one or more students). Prior to the introduction of the treatment, each student's writing is assessed over time to establish a baseline of typical performance. A functional relationship between the treatment (i.e., strategy instruction) and students' progress on the dependent measure is established if performance improves only after the introduction of treatment, and if the noninstructed students' performance stays at or near preintervention levels across baseline. I did not include single-subject studies involving reversal designs, because the effects of strategy instruction cannot be removed by terminating treatment (a basic assumption underlying such designs). Effect sizes were analyzed separately for group and single-subject design studies.

Multiple search procedures were used to select studies. The following databases were searched: ERIC and PsychInfo, using the descriptors "writing" and "strategy instruction." In addition, a hand search of the following journals was conducted from 1980 to Spring 2004: *British Journal of Educational Psychology, British Journal of Educational Research, Exceptional Children, Journal of Educational Psychology, Journal of Educational Research, Journal of Experimental Education, Journal of Learning Disabilities, Journal of Literacy Research, Journal of Research in Reading, Journal of Special Education, Learning Disabilities Quarterly, Learning Disabilities Research and Practice, National Reading Conference Yearbook, Reading Horizons, Reading Research and Instruction, Reading Research Quarterly, Remedial and Special Education, Research in the Teaching of English, Scientific Studies of Reading,* and *Written Communication.* As articles were retrieved, reference lists contained in them were searched for additional sources. I also included in the review unpublished papers presented at research conferences. Finally, books and other reviews about strategy instruction (e.g., Graham & Harris, 2003) were consulted to identify additional pieces.

Thirty-nine studies were located that were suitable for inclusion in this review (i.e., met the criteria noted earlier). Twenty of these investigations involved group comparisons, and the other 19 were single-subject design studies. Examples of studies not included in this review were component analysis of strategy instructional treatments in which there was no control condition (e.g., Graham & Harris, 1989a), strategy instructional studies in which no writing performance outcome measures were collected (e.g., Englert, Raphael, & Anderson, 1992), investigations in which strategy instruction was part of a larger treatment and its impact was not isolated (e.g., MacArthur, Graham, Schwartz, & Schafer, 1995), case studies of strategy instruction (e.g., MacArthur, Schwartz, Graham, Molloy, & Harris, 1996), investigations in which standard deviations were not reported (e.g., Sovik, Heggbergert, & Samuelstuen, 1996), studies in which less than 3 days of intervention were provided (e.g., Beal, Garrod, & Bonitatibus, 1993), group studies with no control condition (e.g., Wong, Butler, Ficzere, & Kuperis, 1997), and investigations in which strategy use was not modeled (e.g., Jampole, Mathews, & Konopak, 1994). Although Englert et al. (1991) did not report standard deviations in their paper, we were able to obtain these for most of their measures by contacting the authors.

The most common type of planning strategy taught in these studies involved planning a composition in advance of writing by brainstorming and organizing ideas for the basic parts of the composition (e.g., for persuasive writing, this usually involved generating possible ideas for reasons, counterreasons, examples, and elaborations) using the resulting plan to write the paper, and modifying and upgrading the plan while writing (see, e.g., De La Paz, 2001; Sawyer, Graham, & Harris, 1992). The most common revising strategy involved the use of specific criteria to evaluate the composition (see, e.g., Englert et al., 1991; Graham & MacArthur, 1988).

Coding of Study Features

Although the included studies all examined the effectiveness of strategy instruction on writing performance, they varied greatly. Students included in the studies ranged from second to 12th grade and involved poor, average, and good writers, as well as children with learning disabilities; the strategies taught were designed to improve children's planning (including analyzing source material and translating plans into text), revising, editing, or a combination of these processes; students were taught to use these strategies with a number of different types of writing, including stories, personal narratives, persuasion, compare-and-contrast, explanation, enumerative, sequential, and paragraphs; strategies were taught by research assistants, researchers, or teachers; and the approaches used to teach strategies varied (although the most common instructional approach was the SRSD instructional model developed by Harris and Graham [1996]). This variability in features is reflected in the description of studies provided in Tables 13.1 and 13.2.

Coding study features allows the meta-analyst to examine factors that account for variability in study outcomes. Following procedures used by Graham and Harris (2003), I coded studies on seven variables: design (group and single-subject design), student type (learning disability, poor writer, average writer, and good writer), grade (elementary and secondary), genre (narrative and expository), cognitive process (planning, revising, or both), instructor (research assistant/researcher and teacher), and instructional model (SRSD instruction and other). For grade, *elementary* was grades 1 through 5–6, whereas *secondary* was grades 6–12 (middle school and high school). If the study involved fifth- and sixth-graders, it was included under elementary, whereas studies with just sixth-graders or higher were coded as secondary. For genre, narrative included stories and personal narratives, whereas *ex-*

pository included persuasion, compare-and-contrast, explanation, enumerative, sequential, and paragraphs (none of the paragraph writing involved narration). For cognitive processes, planning involved several of the following processes: setting goals; generating, analyzing, and organizing ideas for writing; and translating and expanding the writing plan while writing. *Revising* included editing, as well as revising for substance, whereas *both* included teaching planning and revising strategies.

Calculation of Effect Sizes

For strategy instruction studies that involved group comparisons, effect sizes were computed by subtracting the posttest mean of the control group from the posttest mean of the strategy instruction group and dividing by the standard deviation for the control group. An effect size of 0.20 is typically considered small, 0.50 is medium, and 0.80 is large. For single-subject design studies, effect sizes were calculated using the percentage of overlapping data (PND) points recommended by Scruggs and Mastropieri (2001), which is "the proportion of data points in a given treatment condition that exceeds the extreme value in a baseline condition" (p. 230). PND scores above 90% represent very effective treatments; scores between 70% and 90% represent effective treatments; scores between 50% and 70% are of questionable effectiveness; and scores below 50% are ineffective. Because the PND metric was used, it was not possible to calculate effect size for all the variables collected in the single-subject design studies. PND can only be calculated when the data for each assessment point are provided. When multiple measures are collected in single-participant studies, such data was usually provided for only the most critical variables (usually in the form of one or more graphs). This was the case for most of the single-subject design studies reviewed here.

As can be seen in Tables 13.1 and 13.2, researchers used a variety of different measures to assess writing. The most common measures were length, elements, and quality. Length was the number of words in a composition. Elements assessed the inclusion of basic genre elements or parts in a composition. For the stories and narratives, elements

TABLE 13.1. Effect Sizes For Writing Strategy Instruction in Large Group Studies

Study	Genre (processes taught)	Grades	Students	Instructors	Posttests	ESs	Maintenance tests	ESs	Generalization tests	ESs
Harris, Graham, & Mason (in press)*	Story (planning)	2	Poor writers	GAs	Length Elements Quality	1.45 3.86 1.01	(8–10 weeks) Length Elements Quality	1.18 2.11 1.20	(Narratives) Length Elements Quality	0.52 2.65 0.20
	Persuasion (planning)	2	Poor writers	GAs	Length Elements Quality	1.53 4.64 3.18			(Informative) Length Quality (Classroom—Persuasion) Length Elements Quality	3.34 1.67 0.55 2.80 1.88
Harris, Graham, & Adkins (2005)*	Story (planning)	2	Poor writers	Teachers	Length Elements Quality	0.36 1.30 0.83	(8–10 weeks) Length Elements Quality	0.35 1.23 1.27	(Narratives) Length Elements Quality	0.94 1.23 1.17
Graham, Harris, & Mason (2005)*	Story (planning)	3	Poor writers	GAs	Length Elements Quality	2.21 1.76 1.90	(8–10 weeks) Length Elements Quality	0.49 1.16 0.82	(Narratives) Length Elements Quality	0.27 1.23 0.56
	Persuasion (planning)	3	Poor writers	GAs	Length Elements Quality	1.83 1.07 2.14			(Informative) Length Quality	1.58 1.15
Glaser (2004)*	Story (planning)	4	Normal writers	GAs	Elements Quality	2.30 1.24	(6 weeks) Elements Quality	2.58 1.64	(Retells) Ideas	0.44
Gambrell & Chasen (1991)	Story (planning)	4–5	Poor readers	Researchers	Story complexity Elements	1.55 0.9				

(continued)

191

TABLE 13.1. *(continued)*

Study	Genre (processes taught)	Grades	Students	Instructors	Posttests	ESs	Maintenance tests	ESs	Generalization tests	ESs
Englert et al. (1991)	Compare–contrast (planning and revising)	4–5	High acheivers	Teachers	# of comparisons Primary trait Quality Reader sensitivity	−0.34 0.56 0.29 5.41				
	Compare–contrast (planning and revising)	4–5	Low acheivers	Teachers	# of comparisons Primary trait Quality Reader sensitivity	0.21 0.18 0.11 0.45				
	Compare–contrast (planning and revising)	4–5	LD	Teachers	# of comparisons Primary trait Quality Reader sensitivity	0.32 0.81 0.37 —				
	Explanation (planning and revising)	4–5	High acheivers	Teachers	# of ideas Primary trait Quality Reader sensitivity	0.30 0.64 0.57 1.45				
	Explanation (planning and revising)	4–5	Low acheivers	Teachers	# of ideas Primary Trait Quality Reader sensitivity	0.09 0.79 0.49 1.58				
	Explanation (planning and revising)	4–5	LD	Teachers	# of ideas Primary trait Quality Reader sensitivity	0.29 0.49 0.41 0.35				
Troia & Graham (2002)	Stories (planning)	4–5	LD	GAs	Length Quality	0.07 0.24	(4 weeks) Length Quality	4.82 1.58	(Persuasion) Length Quality	1.08 −0.29

192

Study	Genre (process)	Grade	Group 1	Group 2	Measure	Effect size
MacArthur, Schwartz, & Graham (1991)*	Narrative (revising)	4–6	LD	Teachers	Total revisions S-Revisions NS-Revisions Spelling Punctuation Capitalization Quality	1.29 1.41 0.64 0.54 0.33 0.14 1.19
Sawyer, Graham, & Harris (1992)*	Story (planning)	5–6	LD	GAs	Story grammar Quality	3.52 1.47
Fitzgerald & Markham (1987)	Narrative (revising)	6	Normal writers	GAs	Total revisions S-Revisions MC-Revisions Additions Deletions Substitutions Quality	1.02 0.9 0.59 0.84 0.98 0.46 0.3
Welch (1992)	Paragraph	6	LD	Teachers	Elements	2.46
Welch & Jensen (1990)	Paragraph (planning)	6–8	Low acheivers	Teachers	Elements	0.59
Reynolds, Hill, Swassing, & Ward (1988)	Paragraph (editing and revising at sentence level)	6–8	LD	Teachers	Quality Mechanics	0.11 1.11
Yeh (1998)	Persuasion (planning)	7	Normal writers	Teachers	Conventions Voice Development	−0.14 0.46 −0.10
De La Paz & Graham (1997a)*	Persuasion (planning)	7–8	LD	GAs	(Task—Writing) Length Elements (2 weeks) (Task—Writing) Length Elements	0.32 0.55 0.58 1.53

(continued)

193

TABLE 13.1. *(continued)*

Study	Genre (processes taught)	Grades	Students	Instructors	Posttests	ESs	Maintenance tests	ESs	Generalization tests	ESs
De La Paz & Graham (1997a)* *(continued)*					Coherence	1.10	Coherence	1.19		
					Quality	0.48	Quality	0.48		
					(Task—Dictation)		(Task—Dictation)			
					Length	5.18	Length	1.38		
					Elements	3.74	Elements	2.11		
					Coherence	0.44	Coherence	0.40		
					Quality	1.43	Quality	0.90		
De La Paz & Graham (2002)*	Explanation (planning and revising)	7–8	Normal writers	Teachers	Length	0.82	(4 weeks) Length	1.07		
					Vocabulary	1.13	Vocabulary	0.94		
					Quality	1.71	Quality	0.74		
De La Paz (2005)*	Persuasion (analyzing source material and planning)	8	Normal writers	Teachers	Length	1.23				
					Elements	1.37				
					Quality	2.12				
					Historical	0.59				
Simons et al. (1994)	Story (planning and revising)	8	High acheivers	Teachers	Conventions	0.52				
					Ideas	0.46				
					Organization	0.30				
					Mode	0.67				
					Elements	0.60				
	Story (planning and revising)	8	Average acheivers	Teachers	Conventions	0.23				

194

	Story (planning and revising)	8	Low acheivers	Teachers	Ideas 0.26
					Organization 0.26
					Mode 0.38
					Elements 0.40
					Conventions 0.04
					Ideas 0.67
					Organization 0.38
					Mode 0.15
					Elements 0.51
Wong, Wong, Butler, Ficzere, & Kuperis (1996)	Persuasion (planning and revising)	8–9	LD/low achievers	Teachers	Clarity 9.05
					Cogency 7.38
Bryson & Scardamalia (1996)	Persuasion (planning and revising)	10	Normal writers	Researchers	Length 0.30
					Spelling errors 0.00
					Quality 0.74
					Argument level 1.54
					Reflectivity 1.15
			LD		Length 0.89
					Spelling errors −0.22
					Quality 2.41
					Argument level 1.77
					Reflectivity 1.50

Note. References with asterisk are Self-Regulated Strategy Development studies; ESs, effect sizes (calculated by subtracting the mean of the control from the mean of the strategy condition and dividing by the standard deviation for the control); LD, learning disability; GAs, graduate assistants; # of comparisons, number of comparisons; # of ideas, number of ideas; S-Revisions, surface-level revisions; NS-Revisions, non-surface-level revisions; MC-Revisions, meaning-changing revisions.

TABLE 13.2. Effect Sizes For Writing Strategy Instruction in Single-Subject Design Studies

Study	Genre (processes taught)	Grades	Students	Instructors	Posttests	ESs	Maintenance tests	ESs	Generalization tests	ESs
Saddler, Moran, Graham, & Harris (2004)*	Story (planning)	2	Poor writers	GAs	Elements	100%	(2–4 weeks) Elements	86%	(Narratives) Elements	83%
Cole (1992)	Paragraph (planning)	3–5	LD	GAs	Length Quality	100% 100%	(Up to 1 month) Length Quality	100% 100%	(Different Setting) Length Quality	100% 100%
Danoff, Harris, & Graham (1993)*	Story (planning)	4–5	LD	Teacher	Elements Story grammar	100% 100%	(2–4 weeks) Elements Story grammar	100% 100%	(Different Teacher) Elements Story grammar	100% 100%
		4–5	Normal writers	Teacher	Elements Story grammar	100% 100%	Elements Story grammar	100% 100%	Elements Story grammar	100% 100%
Troia, Graham, & Harris (1999)*	Story (planning)	5	LD	Researchers	Story grammar	100%	(3 weeks) Story grammar	67%	(Essays) Elements	75%
De La Paz & Graham (1997b)*	Persuasion (planning)	5	LD/gifted LD/MMR LD	Researcher	Elements	100%	(6–8 weeks) Elements	100%		
Graham, MacArthur, Schwartz, & Page-Voth (1992)*	Persuasion (planning)	5	LD	GAs	(Word Processing) Elements	100%	(4–15 weeks) (Word Processing) Elements	100%	(Stories) (Word Processing) Elements	88%
Sexton, Harris, & Graham (1998)*	Persuasion (planning)	5–6	LD	Researcher	Elements	70%	(3–8 weeks) Elements	33%	(Different Teacher) Elements	100%
Graham & MacArthur (1988)*	Persuasion (revising)	5–6	LD	GAs	(Word Processing) Total Revisions MC—Revisions MP—Revisions	60% 100% 30%	(4–9 weeks) (Word Processing) Total revisions MC—Revisions MP—Revisions	75% 100% 50%	(Persuasion) (Paper and Pencil) Total revisions MC—Revisions MP—Revisions	67% 100% 33%
Graham & Harris (1989b)*	Persuasion (planning)	6	LD	GAs	Elements	100%	(3–12 weeks) Elements	75%	(Classroom) Elements (Stories)	100% 100%

196

Study	Genre (planning)	Grade	Group	Researcher	(Home Setting)	%	(Maintenance)	%	(Generalization)	%
Albertson & Billingsley (2001)*	Story (planning)	6	Gifted	Researcher	Length Story Grammar Sentences Revising Time	71% 100% 100% 100%				
Harris & Graham (1985)*	Story (planning)	6	LD	GAs	Action verbs Adjectives Adverbs	100% 100% 88%	(2–14 weeks) Action verbs Adjectives Adverbs	50% 100% 75%	(Classroom) Action verbs Adjectives Adverbs	75% 100% 100%
Vallecorsa & deBettencourt (1997)	Story (planning)	7	LD	Teachers	Elements	88%			(Retelling Stories) Elements	87%
De La Paz (1999)*	Explanation (planning)	7–8	LD	Teachers	Length Elements Quality	89% 89% 89%	(4 weeks) Length Elements Quality	100% 100% 100%		
			Poor writers		Length Elements Quality	100% 100% 100%	Length Elements Quality	100% 100% 100%		
			Average writers		Length Elements Quality	100% 67% 100%	Length Elements Quality	100% 100% 100%		
			Good writers		Length Elements Quality	50% 83% 100%	Length Elements Quality	100% 100% 100%		
De La Paz (2001)*	Explanation (planning)	7–8	LD/gifted LD/MMR	Teachers	Elements	100%	(4 weeks) Elements	100%		
Moran, Schumaker, & Vetter (1981)	Enumerative Paragraph (planning)	7–8	LD	Teacher	Elements	100%			(Regular Class) Elements	100%
	Sequential Paragraph (planning)	7–8	LD	Teacher	Elements	100%			(Regular Class) Elements	100%
	Compare/Contrast Paragraph (planning)	7–8	LD	Teacher	Elements	100%			(Regular Class) Elements	100%

(continued)

197

TABLE 13.2. (continued)

Study	Genre (processes taught)	Grades	Students	Instructors	Posttests	ESs	Maintenance tests	ESs	Generalization tests	ESs
Stoddard & MacArthur (1993)*	Narrative (revising)	7–8	LD	Researcher	(Word Processing) NS-Revisions MNS-Revisions S-Revisions	 100% 100% 75%	(4–9 weeks) (Word Processing) NS-Revisions MNS-Revisions S-Revisions	 100% 100% 83%	(Paper and Pencil) NS-Revisions MNS-Revisions S-Revisions	 100% 83% 67%
Wallace & Bott (1989)	Paragraph (planning)	8	LD	Teacher	Elements	100%			(Different Setting) Elements	100%
Schumaker et al. (1982)	Paragraph (editing)	HS	LD	Teacher	(Edit Others' Work—Reading-Level Passages) Errors detected Errors corrected (Edit Others' Work—Grade-Level Passages) Errors detected Errors corrected (Edit Own Work) Errors corrected	 100% 100% 100% 100% 100%				
Tanhouser (1994)	Persuasion (planning)	12	LD	Researcher	(Word Processing) Length T-units Quality	 69% 46% 46%			(Different Classroom) (Word Processing) Length T-units Quality	 50% 60% 40%

Note. References with asterisk are Self-Regulated Strategy Development studies; ESs, effect sizes (the percentage of nonoverlapping data points); LD, learning disability; MMR, mild mental retardation; GAs, graduate assistants; MC-Revisions, meaning-changing revisions; MP-Revisions, meaning-preserving revisions; NS-Revisions, nonsurface revisions; MNS-Revisions, meaningnonsurface revisions; S-Revisions, surface revisions; HS, high school.

198

assessed the inclusion of main character(s), location, time frame, character goals, actions, expressed emotions, and ending. The measure story grammar (see Table 13.2) was a modification of this measure, assessing both the inclusion and quality of these elements. Elements tabulated in persuasive writing included the writer's premise, counterpremise, supporting reasons, refutation of counterreasons, elaborations, and ending. Quality measured the overall impact or value of a student's composition.

Five scores were created for the purpose of analysis. Quality involved the general merit of the composition and included the measures of quality, story complexity, primary trait, reader sensitivity, voice, development, coherence, historical accuracy, organization, mode, clarity, cogency, argument level, and reflectivity (see Tables 13.1 and 13.2). Elements concentrated on the inclusion of specific genre features and included the measures of elements and story grammar. Length focused on the amount of text written and included the measures of length, ideas, number of ideas, and number of comparisons. Revisions assessed changes in text and contained the measures of total revisions, surface-level revisions, non-surface-level revisions, meaning-changing revisions, meaning non-surface-level revisions, meaning-preserving revisions, revising time, additions, deletions, substitutions, errors detected, and errors corrected. Mechanics encompassed the skills involved in getting language onto paper and included measures of spelling, spelling errors, punctuation, capitalization, and conventions. Effect sizes for vocabulary (i.e., vocabulary, action verbs, adjectives, and adverbs) and syntax (T-units) were not included in these five scores.

Analysis

Analysis included presenting the average effect size for strategy instruction when the mean for all effect sizes was calculated at posttest, maintenance, and generalization (across genres and across persons–settings) for group and single-subject design studies separately. Means and standard deviations were also computed for each of the five composite variables (e.g., revisions) at posttest, maintenance, and generalization for four types of students (children with learning dis-

abilities, and students who were poor, average, and good writers). This allowed us to typify the general, as well as the more specific, impact of strategy instruction on students' writing.

To investigate the relationship between study features and writing outcomes for the group comparison studies, I conducted a series of analyses of variance (ANOVAs) in which the study feature was treated as the independent variable and the dependent variable was all of the calculated effect sizes at time of testing (either posttest or maintenance). The nonparametric Mann–Whitney U test was used to make these comparisons with the single-subject design studies, because the PND metric involves percentages. Even when combining all effect sizes at time of testing, the n's were too small to examine the relationship between study features and generalization, and in some instances, the relationship between a study feature and maintenance (no statistical analysis was run if any cell of an independent variable was less than 9).

Findings

Overall Impact of Strategy Instruction

GROUP STUDIES

Strategy instruction produced large effects on the writing of students in the 20 group comparison studies. When all effect sizes (ESs) were added together at posttest, the mean was 1.15 ($n = 110$) and the standard deviation was 1.44. Although maintenance was only assessed in 35% of the group comparison studies (all of these were investigations that employed the SRSD model), the average ES remained large: The mean for all effects was 1.32 ($n = 24$) and the standard deviation was .93. When generalization was assessed (20% of the studies, all involving SRSD), ESs were also large. The mean for all effects for generalization across genre was 1.74 ($n = 15$) and the standard deviation was 1.13, whereas the mean for all effects for generalization across persons–settings was 1.15 ($n = 3$) and the standard deviation was .93.

Table 13.3 presents means for four different types of students (children with learning disabilities (LDs), as well as students who

TABLE 13.3. Summary of Average Effect Sizes for Quality, Elements, Length, Revisions, and Mechanics for Strategy Instruction by Student Type Measures LD

Measueres	LD				Poor writers				Average writers			Good writers		All students
	Post.	Maint.	General. genre	General. P & S	Post.	Maint	General. genre	General. P & S	Post.	Maint.	General. P & S	Post.	Maint.	
Quality														
Group	1.03 (19)	0.90 (6)	—	0.47 (3)	1.88 (14)	1.24 (2)	1.01 (3)	1.88 (1)	0.82 (13)	1.19 (2)	—	1.15 (9)	—	1.16 (72)
SS	78% (4)	100% (2)	—	70% (2)	100% (1)	100% (1)	—	—	100% (1)	100% (1)	—	100% (1)	100% (1)	90% (13)
Elements														
Group	2.09 (7)	1.60 (3)	1.23 (1)	—	2.18 (5)	1.67 (2)	1.94 (2)	2.80 (1)	1.36 (3)	2.58 (1)	—	0.60 (1)	—	1.88 (26)
SS	96% (14)	86% (9)	84% (3)	100% (8)	100% (2)	93% (2)	83% (1)	—	89% (3)	100% (3)	100% (2)	92% (2)	100% (1)	92% (50)
Length														
Group	1.39 (8)	1.82 (4)	0.98 (3)	—	0.73 (5)	0.77 (2)	1.60 (3)	0.55 (1)	0.78 (3)	1.07 (1)	—	−0.02 (2)	—	1.10 (32)
SS	86% (3)	100% (2)	—	75% (2)	100% (1)	100% (1)	—	—	100% (1)	100% (1)	—	61% (2)	100% (1)	88% (14)
Revisions														
Group	1.11 (3)	—	—	—	—	—	—	—	0.80 (6)	—	—	—	—	0.90 (9)
SS	88% (11)	85% (6)	—	—	—	—	—	—	—	—	—	100% (1)	—	87% (18)
Mechanics														
Group	0.47 (5)	—	—	—	0.04 (1)	—	—	—	0.03 (3)	—	—	0.52 (1)	—	0.30 (10)
SS	—	—	—	—	—	—	—	—	—	—	—	—	—	—

Note. Post., posttest; Maint., maintenance; General. genre, generalization to different genre; General. P & S, generalization to different person or setting; LD, learning disability; Group, group design; SS, single-subject design studies; the number in parentheses following the ES is the number of ESs from which the average ES was computed.

200

were poor, average, and good writers) for each of the five composite variables described earlier. The number in the parentheses following each average ES specifies the n, or number of effect sizes used to compute that average. For all groups of students, the impact of strategy instruction on quality was large, because average ES exceeded 0.80 at posttest and at maintenance and generalization when scores were available. With one exception, similar effects were evident for elements; the effect size was moderate for good writers (0.60). The impact of strategy instruction on length was more variable, with large effect sizes for children with LD (all average ESs > 0.97), moderate to large effects for poor writers (all average ESs > 0.54), moderate to large effects for average writers (all average ESs > 0.78), and little impact on good writers (ES = −.002). Although the impact of strategy instruction on revisions was only assessed at posttest for children with LDs and average students, average effect sizes were large (exceeding 0.80). Last, for children with LDs, the impact of strategy instruction on mechanics was moderate at posttest (average ESs = 0.47), whereas this treatment had little effect on average writers' posttest mechanics (average ESs = 0.03). Only 1 ES was available for mechanics for poor and good writers. Thus, for the group comparison studies, strategy instruction consistently resulted in large improvements in writing quality, schematic structure (i.e., elements), and revisions across different types of students. The impact of such instruction on length and mechanics was more variable and generally not as strong.

SINGLE-SUBJECT DESIGN STUDIES

The overall impact of strategy instruction in the 19 single-subject design studies generally paralleled the findings from the group comparison studies. When all ESs were added together at posttest, the mean PND was 89% (n = 58) and the standard deviation was 19%. A mean PND of 90% or better indicates that the treatment is very effective. In contrast to the group comparison studies, maintenance was assessed in 74% of single-subject design studies, yielding a mean PND for all effects of 93% (n = 35) and a standard deviation of 16%. When generalization to different persons–settings was assessed (42%

of studies), the mean PND for all effects was again in the very effective range: Mean PND was 90% (n = 18) and the standard deviation was 20%. Generalization to a different genre, however, was only assessed in 16% of studies and was in the effective treatment range: Mean PND for all effects was 84% (n = 4) and the standard deviation was 6%.

In addition to presenting means for the group comparison studies by type of student, Table 13.3 also provides mean PND for the single-subject design investigations. The most common variable for which I was able to compute average PND was elements (this variable was graphed in 74% of the studies). With two exceptions, the mean PND was in the very effective range at posttest, maintenance, and generalization to persons–settings for all four groups of students. The two exceptions involved posttest performance for average writers and maintenance performance for students with LD; in both cases, mean PND was in the effective range. Generalization to a different genre was only assessed with poor writers and students with LDs, resulting in average PNDs for elements in the effective range. Quality, length, and revisions were only graphed in 16%,19%, and 19% of the single-subject design studies, respectively. With the exception of posttest length for good writers (which was in the questionable effectiveness range), all other average PNDs for different types of students at different times of testing (i.e., posttest, maintenance, and generalization to setting–persons) were in the effective to very effective range. Thus, for the single-subject design studies, strategy instruction was very effective to effective in improving the schematic structure of all students papers at posttest, maintenance, and on two different types of generalization. In contrast, it is difficult to draw any substantive conclusions about the impact of strategy instruction on quality, length, and revisions, because authors did not typically graph this type of data.

Relationship between Study Features and Writing Outcomes

Means, standard deviations, and number of ESs at posttest and maintenance for the six study features by type of research design (group comparisons and single-subject design) are presented in Table 13.4. Means

TABLE 13.4. Effect Sizes Averaged at Posttest and Maintenance by Student Type, Grade, Genre, Process, Instructor, and Type of Instruction

	Group studies								Single-subject design studies							
	Posttest			Maintenance					Posttest			Maintenance			
	M	SD	n	M	SD	n			M	SD	n	M	SD	n	
Student type															
LD	1.20	1.10	42	1.34	1.16	13			88%	20%	42	91%	19%	23	
Poor writers	1.63	2.32	25	1.22	0.56	6			100%	0%	4	97%	7%	4	
Average writers	0.78	0.62	30	1.39	0.74	5			93%	15%	5	100%	0%	5	
Good writers	0.88	1.42	13	—	—	—			86%	20%	7	100%	0%	3	
Grade															
Elementary	1.09	1.14	52	1.57	1.15	13			86%	24%	17	90%	20%	18	
Secondary	1.19	1.66	58	1.03	0.51	11			90%	16%	41	98%	7%	17	
Genre															
Narrative	0.91	0.82	47	1.57	1.15	13			93%	11%	20	93%	12%	9	
Expository	1.35	1.77	61	1.03	0.51	11			84%	22%	33	94%	17%	26	
Process															
Planning	1.53	1.27	41	1.38	.99	21			91%	16%	43	95%	15%	26	
Revising	0.74	0.42	16	—	—	—			83%	25%	15	90%	18%	9	
Both	0.58	1.68	53	0.92	0.17	3			—	—	—	—	—	—	
Instructor															
GA/Res.	1.45	1.21	46	1.45	1.04	18			83%	22%	30	87%	20%	18	
Teacher	0.93	1.55	64	0.93	0.35	6			95%	12%	28	100%	0%	17	
Instruction															
SRSD	1.57	1.19	42	1.15	0.58	22			88%	19%	42	93%	16%	33	
Other	0.89	1.52	68	3.20	2.29	2			91%	19%	16	100%	0%	2	

Note. M, mean; *SD*, standard deviation; *n*, number of ESs; LD, learning disability; GA/Res., graduate assistant or researcher; SRSD, Self-Regulated Strategy Development; Other, strategy instructional approaches other than SRSD.

202

were calculated using all of the calculated effect sizes. Statistical analyses were conducted for all six study features at posttest (with the exception of type of student for the single-subject design studies), but only for one half of the possible comparisons at maintenance (due to small n's in one or more cells of the independent variable).

STUDENT TYPE

Students who were struggling writers were most often the focal point of instruction in the 39 studies included in this meta-analysis (64% and 23% of studies involved students with learning LDs and poor writers, respectively). Average writers were included in 23% of the of the studies, whereas good writers were participants in just 10% of the investigations.

I was only able to examine the relationship between student type and writing outcome for the group comparison studies at posttest. There was no statistical difference between the average ES for the four different groups of students ($p = .15$).

GRADE

For both the group comparison and single-subject design studies, there was no statistically significant differences between studies involving elementary versus secondary students at posttest and maintenance (all p's > .16). Thus, the effects of strategy instruction were similar for younger and older students.

GENRE

For both the group comparison and single-subject design studies, there was no statistically significant differences between studies when narrative versus expository writing was the focus of instruction at posttest and maintenance (all p's > .25). Consequently, strategy instruction had similar effects on students' writing across these two genres.

PROCESS

For the group comparison studies at posttest and the single-subject design studies at posttest and maintenance, there were no statistically significant differences between studies that focused on teaching strategies for plan-

ning versus revising (or teaching both, in the case of the group comparison studies) (all p's > .08). It was not possible to examine the relationship between cognitive process and writing outcome at maintenance for group comparison studies due to the small number of calculated ESs for revising and the combination of planning–revising.

INSTRUCTOR

In 55% of the group comparison studies, teachers administered the treatment; this occurred in 37% of the single-subject design studies. Although there was no statistically significant difference at posttest in group comparison studies in which strategy instruction was delivered by teachers versus graduate assistant/researcher ($p = .06$), average PNDs in single-subject design studies were statistically larger at posttest and maintenance in studies in which teachers delivered treatment (both p's < .05). The relationship between instructor and writing outcome was not examined at maintenance for group comparison studies due to the small number of calculated ESs for teachers.

INSTRUCTION

The SRSD model was used to teach writing strategies in 45% of the group comparison studies and 68% of the single-subject design studies. Because this was the most frequent instructional model used to teach writing strategy, I examined whether there was a statistically significant difference between studies that used this model of strategy instruction and the other studies included in this meta-analysis.

With the SRSD model (Harris & Graham, 1996, 1999), there are five stages of instruction: Develop Background Knowledge (students are taught any background knowledge needed to use the strategy successfully), Describe It (the strategy and its purpose and benefits are described and discussed (a mnemonic for remembering the steps of the strategy may be introduced, too), Model It (the teacher models how to use the strategy), Memorize It (the student memorizes the steps of the strategy and any accompanying mnemonic), Support It (the teacher supports or scaffolds student mastery of the strategy), and Independent Use (students use the strategy with little or no supports). SRSD instruction is also characterized by explicit teaching, individualized instruction, and criterion-based versus time-based learning. Children are also treated as active collaborators in the learning process. Finally, students are taught a number of self-regulation skills (including goal setting, self-monitoring, self-instructions, and self-reinforcement) designed to help them manage the strategy, the writing process, and their behavior.

While the teaching regimens in the non-SRSD studies varied in their inclusion of the five instructional stages described earlier, the degree of individualization, and interactive learning, they were not criterion-based, nor did they emphasize the teaching of self-regulatory skills. As a result, I anticipated that SRSD studies would yield larger ESs than non-SRSD studies.

Although there was no statistically significant difference at posttest in single-subject design studies in which SRSD was employed versus all other studies ($p > .38$), the average ES for group comparison investigations using SRSD was statistically larger at posttest ($p < .02$). The average ES for SRSD studies was almost double that of the other studies. It was not possible to examine the relationship between instruction and writing outcomes at maintenance, because maintenance data were rarely collected in non-SRSD studies.

Conclusions

The primary finding from this meta-analysis was that strategy instruction is effective in improving students' writing performance. When all measures are added together, the mean ES immediately following strategy instruction in 20 group comparison studies was 1.15. When key measures, such as writing quality, elements, length, and revisions, were considered separately, the impact was still large, because ESs at posttest for these indices were 1.21, 1.89, 0.95, and 0.90, respectively. The impact of strategy instruction on writing mechanics was relatively weak (mean ES at posttest = 0.30), however, even though this was typically measured in studies where revising–editing strategies were taught. To place these ESs in context, the most successful intervention, the environ-

mental mode, in Hillocks's (1984) seminal meta-analysis of different methods for teaching writing had an average effect size of 0.44.

The findings from the 19 single-subject design studies support those from the group comparison studies. Immediately following instruction, the mean PND, when all variables are included in the tabulation, was 89% (90% or greater indicates that a treatment is very effective). For the most frequently graphed measure, elements, the posttest PND was 95%, and it was 89% for both writing quality and revisions.

A major issue in strategy instructional research is whether effects are maintained over time and are generalized to new tasks and situations (Graham, Harris, MacArthur, & Schwartz, 1991). Although the findings from this analysis must be viewed as tentative, since maintenance was only assessed in 54% of the studies reviewed and generalization (to genre or persons/settings) in just 38%, average ESs generally rivaled or exceeded those from baseline. For example, overall effects for the group comparison studies for maintenance, generalization to genre, and generalization to setting–person were 1.32, 1.13, and 0.93, respectively. For the single-subject design studies, mean PND at maintenance and for generalization to persons–settings was in the very effective range (above 90%). Thus, strategy instruction not only had a strong impact on students' writing immediately following instruction but these effects were also maintained over time and generalized.

The impact of strategy instruction appears to be extremely robust, because the effects on students' writing were not related to the type of student who received instruction, their grade-level placement, the type of cognitive process or strategy taught, or the genre that served as the focal point for instruction. There was a relationship, however, between magnitude of ES and how the writing strategies were taught in the group comparison studies. Investigations using the SRSD model (Harris & Graham, 1996, 1999) of instruction yielded a mean ES at posttest that was almost double the average ES obtained by researchers who did not use this approach. Such a relationship was not replicated in the analysis of single-subject design studies, however. Nevertheless, it is important to note that mean ES were large for both SRSD and non-SRSD groups and single-subject design studies.

There was also a relationship between ES and who delivered instruction (teachers vs. graduate assistants/researchers) in the single-subject design studies. When teachers delivered instruction, PND was larger at posttest and maintenance. This finding must be interpreted cautiously, however, because the variables included in calculating PND were limited only to those that were graphed by researchers, and PND does not measure magnitude of improvement (it only measures what percentage of posttreatment observations exceed the largest score during baseline). Furthermore, even though there was no statistically significant difference for type of instructor in the group comparison studies ($p = .06$), the mean ES for graduate assistants/researchers was one-half of a standard deviation larger at posttest than it was for teachers (a similar difference was evident at maintenance, but the number of ESs for teachers was too small to allow for a statistical comparison). Again, it is important to note that writing strategy instruction was effective no matter who delivered it.

Despite the positive impact of strategy instruction on students' writing, it is not as widely used in classrooms as other writing methods, such as the process approach to writing. However, as several studies have demonstrated (e.g., Danoff, Harris, & Graham, 1993; MacArthur, Schwartz, & Graham, 1991), it can be integrated with other forms of instruction to create a more effective writing program. Finally, additional research is needed to investigate more broadly the impact of strategy instruction. This includes developing and testing new strategies, extending strategy instructional research down into first grade, examining more fully its impact on average and good writers, and determining how to combine it with other writing approaches to maximize students' writing performance.

References

(References marked with an asterisk indicate studies included in the meta-analysis)

Albertson, L. R., & Billingsley, F. F. (2001). Using strategy instruction and self-regulation to improve gifted students' creative writing. *Journal of Secondary Gifted Education, 12,* 90–101.*

Beal, C., Garrod, A., & Bonitatibus, G. (1993). Fostering children's revision skills through training in comprehension monitoring. *Journal of Educational Psychology, 82,* 275–280.

Bryson, M., & Scardamalia, M. (1996). Fostering reflectivity in the argumentative thinking of students with different learning histories. *Reading and Writing Quarterly: Overcoming Learning Difficulties, 12,* 351–384.*

Cole, K. (1992). *Efficacy and generalization of instruction in sequential expository writing for students with learning disabilities.* Unpublished doctoral dissertation, Northern Illinois University, DeKalb, IL.*

Danoff, B., Harris, K. R., & Graham, S. (1993). Incorporating strategy instruction within the writing process in the regular classroom: Effects on the writing of students with and without learning disabilities. *Journal of Reading Behavior, 25,* 295–319.*

De La Paz, S. (1999). Self-regulated strategy instruction in regular education settings: Improving outcomes for students with and without learning disabilities. *Learning Disabilities Research & Practice, 14,* 92–106.*

De La Paz, S. (2001). Teaching writing to students with attention deficit disorders and specific language impairments. *Journal of Educational Research, 95,* 37–47.*

De La Paz, S. (2005). Teaching historical reasoning and argumentative writing in culturally and academically diverse middle school classrooms. *Journal of Educational Psychology, 97,* 139–158.*

De La Paz, S., & Graham, S. (1997a). Effects of dictation and advanced planning instruction on the composing of students with writing and learning problems. *Journal of Educational Psychology, 89,* 203–222.*

De La Paz, S., & Graham, S. (1997b). Strategy instruction in planning: Effects on the writing performance and behavior of students with learning disabilities. *Exceptional Children, 63,* 167–181.*

De La Paz, S., & Graham, S. (2002). Explicitly teaching strategies, skills, and knowledge: Writing instruction in middle school classrooms. *Journal of Educational Psychology, 94,* 291–304.*

Englert, C., Raphael, T., & Anderson, L. (1992). Socially mediated instruction: Improving students' knowledge and talk about writing. *Elementary School Journal, 92,* 411–445.

Englert, C., Raphael, T., Anderson, L., Anthony, H., Steven, D., & Fear, K. (1991). Making writing and self-talk visible: Cognitive strategy instruction writing in regular and special education classrooms. *American Educational Research Journal, 28,* 337–373.*

Fitzgerald, J., & Markham, L. (1987). Teaching children about revision in writing. *Cognition and Instruction, 4,* 3–24.*

Gambrell, L., & Chasen, S. (1991). Explicit story structure instruction and the narrative writing of fourth- and fifth-grade below-average readers. *Reading Research and Instruction, 31,* 54–62.*

Glaser, C. (2004). *Improving the fourth-grade students' composition skills: Effects of strategy instruction and self-regulatory procedures.* Unpublished doctoral dissertation, University of Pottsburg, Germany.*

Graham, S. (1997). Executive control in the revising of students with learning and writing difficulties. *Journal of Educational Psychology, 89,* 223–234.

Graham, S., & Harris, K.R. (1989a). A component analysis of cognitive strategy instruction: Effects on learning disabled students' compositions and self-efficacy. *Journal of Educational Psychology, 81,* 353–361.

Graham, S., & Harris, K. R. (1989b). Improving learning disabled students' skills at composing essays: Self-instructional strategy training. *Exceptional Children, 56,* 201–214.*

Graham, S., & Harris, K. (1996). Self-regulation and strategy instruction for students who find writing and learning challenging. In M. Levy & S. Ransdell (Eds.), *The science of writing: Theories, methods, individual differences, and applications* (pp. 347–360). Mahwah, NJ: Erbaum.

Graham, S., & Harris, K.R. (2003). Students with learning disabilities and the process of writing: A meta-analysis of SRSD studies. In H. L. Swanson, K. R. Harris, & S. Graham (Eds.), *Handbook of learning disabilities* (pp. 323–344). New York: Guilford Press.

Graham, S., Harris, K. R., MacArthur, C., & Schwartz, S. (1991). Writing and writing instruction with students with learning disabilities: A review of a program of research. *Learning Disability Quarterly, 14,* 89–114.

Graham, S., Harris, K. R., Mason, L. (2005). Improving the writing performance, knowledge, and motivation of struggling young writers: The effects of Self-Regulated Strategy Development. *Contemporary Educational Psychology, 30,* 207–241.*

Graham, S., & MacArthur, C. (1988). Improving learning disabled students' skills at revising essays produced on a word processor: Self-instructional training. *Journal of Special Education, 22,* 133–152.*

Graham, S., MacArthur, C., Schwartz, S., & Page-Voth, V. (1992). Improving the compositions of students with learning disabilities using a strategy involving product and process goal setting. *Exceptional Children, 58,* 322–334.*

Gregg, L., & Steinberg, E. (1980). *Cognitive processes in writing.* Hillsdale, NJ: Erlbaum.

Harris, K. R., & Graham, S. (1996). *Making the writing process work: Strategies for composition and self-regulation.* Cambridge, MA: Brookline.

Harris, K. R., & Graham, S. (1985). Improving learning disabled students' composition skills: Self-control strategy training. *Learning Disabilities Quarterly, 8,* 27–36.*

Harris, K. R., Graham, S. (1999). Programmatic intervention research: Illustrations from the evolution of self-regulated strategy development. *Learning Disability Quarterly, 22,* 251–262.

Harris, K. R., Graham, S., & Adkins, M. (in press). Classroom-based Self-Regulated Strategy Development instruction: Improving the writing performance and motivation of young struggling writers. *American Educational Research Journal.*

Harris, K. R., Graham, S., & Mason, L. (in press). Improving the writing performance, knowledge, and motivaiton of young struggling writers in second grade. *American Educational Research Journal.*

Hayes, J. (1996). A new framework for understanding cognition and affect in writing. In M. Levy & S. Ransdell (Eds.), *The science of writing: Theories, methods, individual differences, and applications* (pp. 1–27). Mahwah, NJ: Erbaum.

Hayes, J. (2004). What triggers revision? In L. Allal, L. Chanquoy, & P. Largy (Eds.), *Revision: Cognitive and instructional processes* (pp. 9–20). Boston: Kluwer.

Hayes, J., & Flower, L. (1980). Identifying the organization of writing processes. In L. Gregg & E. Steinberg (Eds.), *Cognitive processes in writing* (pp. 3–30). Hillsdale, NJ: Erlbaum.

Hillocks, G. (1984). *Research on written composition: New directions for teaching.* Urbana, IL: ERIC Clearinghouse on Reading and Communications Skills.

Jampole, E., Mathews, N., & Konopak, B. (1994). Academically gifted students' use of imagery for creative writing. *Journal of Creative Behavior, 28,* 1–15.

Kratochwill, T., & Levin, J. (1992). *Single-case research design and analysis: New directions for psychology and education.* Hillsdale, NJ: Erlbaum.

Locke, E. Shaw, K., Saari, L., & Latham, G. (1981). Goal setting and task performance: 1969–1980. *Psychological Bulletin, 90,* 125–152.

MacArthur, C., Graham, S., Schwartz, S., & Schafer, W. (1995). Evaluation of a writing instruction model that integrated a process approach, strategy instruction, and word processing. *Learning Disability Quarterly, 18,* 276–291.

MacArthur, C., Schwartz, S., & Graham, S. (1991). Effects of a reciprocal peer revision strategy in special education classrooms. *Learning Disability Research and Practice, 6,* 201–210.*

MacArthur, C., Schwartz, S., Graham, S., Molloy, D., & Harris, K.R. (1996). Integration of strategy instruction into a whole language classroom: A case study. *Learning Disabilities Research and Practice, 11,* 168–176.

Moran, M., Schumaker, J., & Vetter, A. (1981). *Teaching a paragraph organization strategy to learning disabled adolescents* (Research Report No. 54). Lawrence: University of Kansas Institute for Research in Learning Disabilities.*

Reynolds, C., Hill, D., Swassing, R., & Ward, M. (1988). The effects of revision strategy instruction on the writing performance of students with learning disabilities. *Journal of Learning Disabilities, 21,* 540–545.*

Saddler, B., Moran, S., Graham, S., & Harris, K. R. (2004). Preventing writing difficulties: The effects of planning strategy instruction on the writing performance of struggling writers. *Exceptionality, 12,* 3–18.*

Sawyer, R., Graham, S., & Harris, K. R. (1992). Direct teaching, strategy instruction, and strategy instruction with explicit self-regulation: Effects on the composition skills and self-efficacy of students with learning disabilities. *Journal of Educational Psychology, 84,* 340–352.*

Scardamalia, M., & Bereiter, C. (1983). The development of evaluative, diagnostic, and remedial capabilities in children's composing. In M. Martlew (Ed.), *The psychology of written language: Development and educational perspectives* (pp. 67–95). London: Wiley.

Scardamalia, M., & Bereiter, C. (1986). Written composition. In M. Wittrock (Ed.), *Handbook of research on teaching* (3rd ed., pp. 778–803). New York: Macmillan.

Schumaker, J., Deshler, D., Alley, G., Warner, M., Clark, F., & Nolan, S. (1982). Error monitoring: A learning strategy for improving adolescent performance. In W. Cruickshank & J. Lerner (Eds.), *Best of ACLD* (Vol. 3, pp. 170–183). Syracuse, NY: Syracuse University Press.*

Scruggs, T., & Mastriopieri, M. (2001). How to summarize single-participant research: Ideas and applications. *Exceptionality, 9,* 227–244.

Sexton, R. J., Harris, K. R., & Graham, S. (1998). The effects of self-regulated strategy development on essay writing and attributions of students with learning disabilities in a process writing setting. *Exceptional Children, 64,* 295–311.*

Simmons, D., Kame'enui, E., Dickson, S., Chard, D., Gunn, B., & Baker, S. (1994). Integrating narrative reading comprehension and writing instruction for all learners. In C. Kinzer & D. Leu (Eds.), *Multidimensional aspects of literacy research, theory, and practice* Chicago, IL: National Reading Conference.*

Sovik, N., Heggberget, M., & Samuelstuen, M. (1996). Strategy-training related to children's text production. *British Journal of Educational Psychology, 66,* 169–180.

Stoddard, B., & MacArthur, C. (1993). A peer editor strategy: Guiding learning disabled students in response and revision. *Research in the Teaching of English, 27,* 76–103.*

Tanhouser, S. (1994). *Function over form: The relative efficacy of self-instructional strategy training alone and with procedural facilitation for adolescents with learning disabilities.* Unpublished doctoral dissertation, Johns Hopkins University, Baltimore, MD.*

Troia, G., & Graham, S. (2002). The effectiveness of a highly explicit, teacher-directed strategy instruction routine: Changing the writing performance of students with learning disabilities. *Journal of Learning Disabilities, 35,* 290–305.*

Troia, G. A., Graham, S., & Harris, K. R. (1999). Teaching students with learning disabilities to mindfully plan when writing. *Exceptional Children, 65,* 215–252.*

Vallecorsa, A., & deBettencourt, L. (1997). Using a mapping procedure to teach reading and writing skills to middle grade students with learning disabilities. *Education and Treatment of Children, 20,* 173–188.*

Wallace, G., & Bott, D. (1989). Statement-pie: A strategy to improve the paragraph writing skills of adolescents with learning disabilities. *Journal of Learning Disabilities, 22,* 541–553.*

Welch, M. (1992). The PLEASE strategy: A metacognitive learning strategy for improving the paragraph writing of students with mild disabilities. *Learning Disability Quarterly, 15,* 119–128.*

Welch, M., & Jensen, J. (1990). Write, P.L.E.A.S.E.: A video-assisted strategic intervention to improve written expression of inefficient learners. *Remedial and Special Education, 12,* 37–47.*

Wong, B. Y. L., Butler, D. L., Ficzere, S. A., & Kuperis, S. (1996). Teaching low achievers and student with learning disabilities to plan, write, and revise opinion essays. *Journal of Learning Disabilities, 29,* 133–145.*

Wong, B. Y. L., Butler, D. L., Ficzere, S. A., & Kuperis, S. (1997). Teaching adolescents with learning disabilities and low achievers to plan, write, and revise compare-and-contrast essays. *Learning Disabilities Research and Practice, 12,* 2–15.

Yeh, S. (1998). Empowering education: Teaching argumentative writing to cultural minority middle-school students. *Research in the Teaching of English, 33,* 49–83.*

Chapter 14

Tenets of Sociocultural Theory in Writing Instruction Research

Carol Sue Englert, Troy V. Mariage, *and* Kailonnie Dunsmore

Sociocultural theory seeks to understand how culturally and historically situated meanings are constructed, reconstructed, and transformed through social mediation (Moll & Greenberg, 1990; Vygotsky, 1978; Wertsch, 1985, 1998). (See Prior, Chapter 4, this volume, for extended discussion of sociocultural theory.) Social mediation in activity settings through semiotic tools (e.g., speech, written language, diagrams, mnemonics, and drawings) forms the basic unit of analysis for understanding the genesis of psychological development. Rather than viewing knowledge as existing inside the heads of individual participants or in the external world, sociocultural theory views meaning as being negotiated at the intersection of individuals, culture, and activity. Higher psychological processes, such as writing and reading, have their origins in social processes that occur on an interpsychological plane, and that are mediated through language signs, symbols, actions, and objects (Vygotsky, 1978). Over time, these external semiotic mediators observed in their contextualized uses in activity settings become internalized and transformed to influence action (Bahktin, 1986). In this sense, while individuals are accorded agency for their actions, there remains a social quality to all higher psychological pro-

cesses. Through this mediated action, language begins to take on a unique role in psychological development as a mediator of cultural understanding and cognitive tools that can come under conscious realization to guide behavior (Bahktin, 1986; Gee, 1996).

This chapter does not present an exhaustive review of the many literatures that might contribute to a sociocultural approach to writing instruction; rather, it highlights specific studies that illustrate and anchor our discussions of particular themes relevant to the sociocultural perspective. In actuality, only a few writing instruction research programs have adhered to the rich traditions of a sociocultural approach, although many basic studies buttress the tenets of sociocultural theory through elucidation of central principles; that is, while many scholars have used sociocultural theory as a way to understand meaning construction in communities of practice and as an interpretive lens to analyze and discuss data, there has been less systematic effort to use it to inform the creation of learning environments and activity settings. Thus, this chapter draws from studies that use sociocultural theory as an interpretive lens and that offer evidence-based writing-instruction findings that support some of the basic tenets of sociocultural theory.

Three Significant Tenets

Three tenets of sociocultural theory are identified and guide the review of the literature, with emphases on (1) sociocognitive apprenticeships in writing; (2) procedural facilitators and tools; and (3) participation in communities of practice.

Sociocognitive Apprenticeships in Writing

The first pedagogical principle relates to the importance of offering cognitive apprenticeships that support novices in the participation and performance of a discipline, including the acquisition of the discourses, tools, and actions. Instructional discourse is a primary means by which cultural conventions and social practices are made accessible to individuals. Vygotsky's work suggests that effective teachers make tacit knowledge perceptible through think-alouds that make visible the discourse, thoughts, actions, decisions, struggles, and deliberations that are part of the writing process. Rogoff (1990) extended this view, with an emphasis on cognitive apprenticeship, and John-Steiner (2000) brought into focus the role of thought communities in the development of expertise and invention. Several aspects of instructional discourse are central to the design of teaching–learning contexts.

Sociocultural theory is replete with references to the role of adults, experts, and agents who provide access to strategies and tools through instructions, explanations, modeling, and think-alouds (Baker, Gersten, & Graham, 2003; Daniels, 2001; Scribner, 1997; Wells, 1999). Research supports a prominent view of teacher agency in the sharing of expertise in the teaching–learning process. Otherwise, students gain no insight into the way experts write and think (Daniels, 2001). Gersten and colleagues, for example, in a meta-analysis of experimental studies in writing, revealed that explicit teaching of the critical steps in the writing process had a substantial impact on writing performance (Baker et al., 2003; Gersten & Baker, 2001; Vaughn, Gersten, & Chard, 2000). Similarly, Hillocks's (1984) meta-analysis showed that explicit instruction, combined with activities that engaged students in understanding the purpose, content, and form of written discourse, was the most effective type of instruc-

tional mode. Although writing seems to be a solitary discipline, the roots of writing competence are developed in social interaction with teachers who can dramatize their thoughts, words, dilemmas, and actions in highly visible ways. Effective teachers create spaces to make available to students the full range of semiotic tools and discourses in constructing written texts. By forging concrete links among specific thoughts, words, and actions, teachers bring the relationship between "knowing and doing" into a plane of more active consciousness within an individual (Shotter, 1995).

The development of writing competence in a sociocultural model is closely aligned to another aspect of instructional discourse that is contextualized through effective pedagogical practice. Sociocultural theorists emphasize the importance of the provision of coparticipation and guided practice as a prominent feature in activity settings where expertise is distributed, practiced, and shaped in order to produce a common product or artifact. What begins as a teacher-centered discourse in authentic writing activity is succeeded by an interactive and collaborative discourse in which mental activity is distributed and shared between the teacher and student participants. In Vygotskian (1978) terms, cognitive processes are acquired on an intermental or social plane as the expert and novice jointly combine their mental resources to perform a process. The expert and novice take up relational positions with respect to each other: The novice takes increasing responsibility for performing facets of the writing activity for which he or she is capable, while the expert assists participation by stepping in to coach, perform, or support the actions and processes that lie beyond the independent attainment of the novice. Eventually, what was performed on the social plane of assisted performance is enacted on the intramental (individual) plane by the novice as the discourse and collaborative actions are turned inward to direct and assist the writer's own performance.

Arranging instructional settings to conform to the requirements of a participatory apprenticeship involves a highly orchestrated set of teaching moves. Englert and Dunsmore (2002), for example, reported on the discourse moves of a teacher skilled in apprenticing her students in the discourse and practices of skilled writers. In analyzing the teacher's moment-to-moment instructional moves in a collaborative writing task, they found that she used a combination of *step-in* and *step-back* moves that parallel the relational roles of teachers in an apprenticeship relationship. In the context of joint productive writing activity (Dalton & Tharp, 2002), the teacher stepped in to model, prompt, instruct, or think aloud when her students did not possess the requisite knowledge or strategies. Reciprocally, she stepped back to transfer control as she invited students to direct the specific language and problem-solving practices associated with writing activity (e.g., by asking students "How does the text sound?"; "What should we do?"; and "How can we do it?"). These step-back moves positioned her students in the role of experts and required them to explain, problem-solve, think aloud, and make decisions about the text, thereby creating a discursive space where students could exercise the discourse, strategies, practices, and skills of expert writers. Simultaneously, students had the benefit of the expertise of their peers and teacher. The orchestration of instructional moves was designed to accomplish several of the following teaching functions: assessing of students' knowledge; transferring control of self-regulation and discourse to students; providing metacognitive information about writing; providing access to explanations and strategies; and supporting students through coaching, explanations, prompts, and modeling.

Furthermore, although schools are not easily organized to foster the types of cognitive apprenticeships that allow master writers to work side-by-side with novice authors (Brophy, 2002; Wells, 1999), there are clear benefits for teachers and students in such arrangements. Student achievement is tied to the teacher's skill in assessing and matching his or her instructional moves to the child's level of development (Stone, 1998, 2002), and teachers can promote more sophisticated levels of metacognition and writing performance during interactive periods of text construction than during solitary periods. Mariage (2001; Mariage, Englert, & Garmon, 2000), for example, reported how a teacher used a combination of moves to promote involvement by explicitly transferring control of the meaning-making process

to students, while giving students deeper insight into particular aspects of the writing process based on the text and the changing literacy needs of the group. Students who showed the greatest level of participation and appropriation of the social discourse in collaborative activity with the teacher also showed the greatest gains on a writing measure that required independent problem solving to revise problematic texts. Joint involvement with adults in situated activity appeared to be responsible for improvements in performance levels (see Dalton & Tharp, 2002; Schaeffer, 1996).

In planning effective writing apprenticeships, interactive dialogues are not solely teacher-to-student; they can also feature student-to-student dialogues. Several studies have implemented interactive dialogues based on an instructional progression that moves from teacher modeling (thinking aloud) to collaborative planning and revising with a teacher or student partner, to independent writing (Englert, Berry, & Dunsmore, 2001; Englert & Dunsmore, 2002, 2004; Wong, Butler, Ficzere, & Kuperis, 1997). Working with peers helps students externalize covert processes, making them transparent to the implementor and to the other participants in the interaction. Wong and her colleagues (Wong et al., 1997) featured such forms of interactive discourse to support students' participation and performance in composing a compare–contrast text. Students engaged in interactive dialogues with the teacher and peers in four phases: text analysis, teacher modeling of the writing process, guided and collaborative student practice with peers, and independent writing. Wong et al. (1997) reported that working with partners in a collaborative phase supported the development of an elaborated dialogue. Likewise, they and other researchers reported that participation in a collaborative and interactive discourse fostered students' engagement in rehearsal and reflection, yielding alternative viewpoints of their texts and problem-centered conversations that resulted in texts that surpassed the quality of texts produced by any member of the student pairs when writing alone (Daiute & Dalton, 1993; Englert et al., 2001; Hillocks, 1995). Importantly, rates of student talk in small- and peer-group discussions have been found to exceed student rates in teacher-led arrangements, potentially offering greater opportunities for students to exercise and master the discourse, and to engage in legitimate reflection, reasoning, and creative responses to problems (Englert & Dunsmore, 2002; Hillocks, 1995; Hillocks et al., 1984).

Taken together, the studies of instructional discourse suggest that teachers can engage in a number of practices that make the writing apprenticeships within a sociocultural perspective a reality. These practices include (1) ensuring that there are numerous interactive, collaborative, and guided writing opportunities to make salient and visible the language of writing as one co-constructs written text with students; (2) monitoring in an apprenticeship arrangement one's role as a key knowledgeable other that incorporates both "step-in" moves when there is a need to model new writing conventions and provide explicit instruction, while also invoking "step-back" moves that alternate teacher and student roles to allow students to assume increasing ownership of the problem-solving activity; (3) monitoring the developmental levels of students and responding to their needs by providing access to the relevant conventions, tools, strategies, and dispositions; and (4) ensuring that there are multiple application spaces where students can be apprenticed and exercise their growing mastery of writing strategies and processes in constructing text with others in a variety of social settings (whole class, partners, individually). Throughout the instructional process, the heart of writing development is the dialogue in which teachers and students collaborate, inform, question, think aloud, self-correct, challenge, and construct meaning together (Gould, 1996). Rather than practicing writing skills in solitary situations, students acquire writing knowledge through discursive interactions with others, and through these dialogues talk their way into deeper understandings about writing practices. How students are positioned and supported in the interactive discourse influences their level of appropriation, application, internalization, and transformation of knowledge, discourse, and practices. Finally, influential in the acquisition process are the qualities of the social context, including the nature of assisted development, the mediational tools that are available, the nature of the relationship among participants, and the meaningfulness of the shared work. Further research needs to examine the features of the social and discursive context of writing that are consequential in what is internalized, transformed, and employed in future contexts.

Procedural Facilitators and Tools

A second pedagogical principle relates to the importance of supporting cognitive performance in advance of independent performance, through the provision of cultural tools (Stetsenko, 1999; Wertsch, 1998) and procedural facilitators to prompt students' use of cognitive tools and strategies. Procedural facilitation can scaffold performance by reminding students of the procedural steps, perspectives, tools, or higher order strategies that they can self-employ to plan, monitor, or revise their texts (Baker, Gersten, & Scanlon, 2002).

Tools include a variety of mental, linguistic, and physical devices used to enhance writers' performance, including notational systems, writing symbols, instruments, diagrams, graphic organizers, text structures, mnemonics, writing implements, procedures, rules of thumb, grammar and spell checkers, and any tool used in the transformation and construction process (Daniels, 2001; Kozulin, 2003; Pea, 1993; Wertsch, 1998; Wertsch & Toma, 1995). These tools support cognitive performance by helping writers to organize mental reasoning by offloading aspects of thought or functions onto the tool, and by making elements of the activity more visible, accessible, and attainable (Pea, 1993; Roth, 1998). Just as engineers use an array of tools to construct a well-formed building, writers use an array of tools to construct well-written text.

Problematically, many novice writers are unaware of the tools or procedures that they can apply to implement the tools in a situated writing activity. At that point, procedural facilitators can be employed to externalize the covert processes and to serve up strategic tools by cueing students to perform particular writing or self-regulatory processes. Bereiter and Scardamalia (1987) used procedural facilitation to support the writing performance of elementary school students. In their study, students were given cue cards that prompted planning and monitoring processes at various points as students wrote and revised. The results showed that experimental students showed an increased ability to monitor and analyze their texts, with a heightened sense of audience. Individuals operating with the mediational means afforded by the facilitators were able to perform at a level superior to what they could achieve otherwise. The procedural facilitator served as a type of social (intermental and symbolic) actor that allowed students to perform at advanced levels before they had attained independent competence.

Several programmatic studies illustrate the role of procedural facilitators and symbolic mediators in supporting writing performance. Cognitive Strategy Instruction in Writing (CSIW) (Englert, Raphael, Anderson, Stevens, & Fear, 1991) was a research program that emphasized the design of instructional activities using procedural facilitation and incorporating a number of principles emphasized in the sociocultural literature. First, in CSIW, teachers emphasized thinking aloud and modeling the strategies and inner talk related to the processes of writing (e.g., planning, organizing, writing, editing, and revision) to provide students with language or symbolic mediators to direct their own performance. Through these public demonstrations, teachers made it possible for students to witness the bottlenecks, false starts, dilemmas, actions, thoughts, and corrections of writers in the process of text monitoring and construction rather than experience the strategies in isolated contexts (Englert & Mariage, 2003). Second, teachers involved students in the joint construction of texts to transfer control of the strategies and talk to students, while assessing their performance and offering cognitive guidance and feedback on a moment-to-moment basis in the form of coaching, prompting, and modeling. Third, the teachers provided symbol systems and language tools to cue and support the internal (psychological) and external (physical) sides of writing activity. Teachers posted the mnemonic POWER as a type of procedural facilitator to remind students of the writing process (plan–organize–write–edit–revise) and associated strategies. Fourth, "think-sheets," a second type of procedural facilitator, were provided to externalize the self-talk, strategies, and key language that had been mod-

eled to support and prompt students at strategic points as they planned, organized, composed, and edited their own texts (Englert et al., 1991). Fifth, to assist students in organizing their texts, teachers provided a third type of procedural facilitator, graphic organizers, to represent the organization of the text structure (see Graham & Harris, 1989a, 1989b), then explicitly taught the conventions of each writing genre (e.g., compare–contrast, explanations) as part of the planning, organizing and editing process. All of these aforementioned instructional strategies offered social and organizational mediators that made visible and accessible the language and higher order strategies of writers (Vaughn et al., 2000).

The results showed that CSIW students significantly outperformed comparison students in their ability to produce well-organized texts that conformed to the requirements of the written genre. Interestingly, those who showed the greatest gains were students of teachers who were most effective in constructing activity settings that best represented the principles of the sociocultural model (Anderson, Raphael, Englert, & Stevens, 1991). Teachers who focused on the role of discourse and mediators as tools for communication and social action produced better outcomes than teachers who simply focused on the mechanical application of the structures and strategies, with little emphasis on their utilitarian role as part of a symbol or communication system. Although CSIW think-sheets and artifacts embodied the tools, discourses, functions, and meanings of the text, such cultural tools were ineffective when they were simply applied and practiced by students, without social interaction with others that featured the meaning, functions, self-regulatory, and communicative aspects of such tools. Writing development involved the acquisition of writing discourse and tools that were given meaning within the community of writers and readers.

De La Paz (1999; De La Paz & Graham, 2002) implemented an instructional model that featured several procedural facilitators for planning and writing strategies, semiotic tools, and text structures in writing instruction for middle school students. To support and scaffold performance, students were given cue cards that enhanced performance by reminding them how they might generate the macrostructure of the text, including the introductory paragraph (writing thesis statements and attention getters), the two to three body paragraphs (e.g., transition words to connect ideas); and the conclusion paragraph. Students were also taught specific strategies for engaging in the writing process, including the PLAN strategy (Pay attention to the prompt, List the main ideas, Add supporting Ideas, Number your ideas) and the WRITE strategy (e.g., students were cued to use their plans during writing, as well as prompted to transform their plans into well-organized texts). Throughout the study, teachers used several semiotic tools to increase students' competence in advance of independent performance, including the mnemonics that cued strategy use, the strategies that supported students in the planning and writing process, and the cue cards that offered self-instruction and language models to guide the talk and actions of expert writers. Writing plans generated by students scaffolded performance by offloading and storing ideas while writers engaged in other writing processes (writing, reviewing, and revising). At the conclusion of writing their first drafts, students met with peers to receive feedback on how to revise their essays to make them better. The intervention, which was implemented with 30 middle school students, was contrasted with a traditional control condition implemented with 28 students. Results showed that the intervention produced significant effects on writing performance, resulting in stories that were significantly longer, more complete, and qualitatively superior. Instruction that focused on producing well-organized texts using strategies and tools that supported students in planning and drafting their texts significantly impacted writing outcomes.

This study is an elegant example of how teachers used multiple semiotic systems to orchestrate the composition process to support writers. These semiotic systems were carefully designed to address the *cognitive* challenges that young writers face (e.g., developing metacognition, applying strategies and tools to help store and organize ideas, and using language to mediate thoughts and actions), the *social* conditions that provide access to knowledgeable others (e.g., peer

review, teaching modeling, and thinking aloud), and *motivational* aspects that impact focus and persistence (e.g., goal setting, positive self-talk).

Considerable educational research highlights the importance of procedural facilitators, such as think-sheets, graphic organizers, plans of action, and prompts and cues to support students' composition and learning from texts (Graham, 1997; Graham & Harris, 2003; Harris & Graham, 1996; MacArthur, Schwarz, & Graham, 1991; Wong, Harris, Graham, & Butler, 2003). Compatible with Vygotsky's thinking, procedural facilitators offer semiotic tools that enable teachers to make visible the character of the particular text forms, the strategies and procedures that underlie the text's construction and revision, and the discourse structures and language practices that permit writers to realize their writing goals. In collaboration with these representational systems, students gain access to writing actions and processes that deepen their participation and social position as competent language users in the broader sociocultural community (Coe, 2002). Procedural facilitators are particularly effective when linked to dialogic interactions with others about the content and quality of the written text, as well as writing techniques and processes (Baker et al., 2003).

Finally, this discussion of tools and procedural facilitators would be incomplete without attention to two aspects of cognitive influence in writing. From the learner's perspective, although the literature on cognitive strategies often remains separate from the sociocultural literature, Vygotsky's (1978) work renders a conceptual bridge, implicit in his emphasis on the role of semiotic or symbolic mediators in the regulation of psychological behavior. Without question, writing strategies serve as a primary form of procedural facilitation by offering language and psychological mediators that support students in advance of independent performance. Over time, the psychological tool or strategy, like many procedural facilitators, is internalized and comes to alter the flow of mental functions, mediating both the external actions and mental activities of writers through an internalized form of self-directed inner speech that writers use to guide covert and overt performance (Wells, 1999). Even after internalization, however, strategic tools and procedural facilitators always retain a social component, reflecting their social origins and the fact that they correspond to a form of distributed cognition that has progressed from existing as a joint enterprise shared between the individual and the expert or tool (intermental functioning) to a private phenomenon existing in the individual (intramental functioning). Strategies combined with procedural facilitators that scaffold implementation and self-regulation of the writing process offer vital means of social mediation that extend the visibility, power, and influence of the instruction.

From the teacher's perspective, the emphasis on tools and procedural facilitators provides another avenue for facilitating writing performance. Theoretically, the provision of tools is intended to bolster performance to levels that exceed what the individual can achieve alone—a performance gap that Vygotsky refers to as the zone of proximal development (ZPD). The ZPD reflects the difference in the level attained by students when they write with access to mediational tools and/or in collaboration with more knowledgeable others, and the level attained when they write independently, without access to mediational tools or agents. The ZPD is the most critical region of instructional sensitivity at which knowledge advancement can take place.

There are three implications for instructional design based on the collective work on ZPD. First, teachers are most effective when they lead cognitive development by teaching in advance of what students can accomplish alone and by presenting challenging material that invites problem solving and legitimate tool use. Second, within a student's ZPD, teachers should offer mental, physical, and procedural facilitators, as well as social tools or agents that scaffold and improve performance to levels that were previously unattainable by the student in independent and solitary writing arrangements. Third, as opposed to the assessment of students writing in solitary or unsupported conditions, sociocultural theory points to the importance of assessing students' performance in the context of tool-enabling conditions and situations (Wertsch, 1991, 1998; Gee, 1992). In this view, the assessment of individual writers must be expanded to assess the degree to which writing tools are provided, the types of tools implemented in the context of authentic writing activities in situated communities of practice, and the effects of tool use in augmenting writing performance.

Community of Practice

A third pedagogical principle is the establishment of communities of practice that emphasize knowledge construction and knowledge dissemination. Through participation in the literacy community's ongoing social practices, students come to share the community's conventions, standards, genres, and values (Roth, 1998). Central to participation in the community is the acquisition of language proficiency in speaking, reading, and writing (Dalton & Tharp, 2002), with opportunities to engage with others through written language and to receive feedback on one's written communications from teachers and peers. In these contexts, students experience legitimate reasons to communicate their knowledge, express their uncertainties, reveal their confusions, and request information or explanations from others who are more knowledgeable (Mercer, 2002). In such classrooms, students also learn to use texts and ideas as thinking devices that can be questioned and extended to create an elaborated knowledge reflective of the contributions of the group. In fact, Alvermann (2002) suggests that participatory approaches that actively engage students in their own learning, and that treat texts as tools for thought and reflection, are more likely to promote higher order thinking and critical literacy.

There are many examples of research projects in which writing is embedded in communities of practice such that students' facility in the use of literacy tools is developed simultaneously with growing expertise in disciplinary domains. One strand of instructional research from a sociocultural perspective is characterized by an emphasis on writing and written representational systems as part of a system of learning and communication in a discipline, such as science. Scardamalia and Bereiter (1994), for example, designed a computer-supported intentional learning environment (CSILE) that incorporated teaching emphases on intentional learning, distributed expertise, and discourse in constructing knowledge-building communities of learners. In the knowledge-building community, students studied and conducted inquiries into particular problems and questions, then advanced their theories about the problems based on their research for peer review. In CSILE, students constructed and shared their inquiry-based notes, questions, peer comments, and graphical representations in a computer-supported community knowledge space. The software supported knowledge building both in the creation of the notes and in the ways they were displayed and linked, and made textual objects the source of further work or study. Revisions, elaborations, and reorganizations in students' notes and texts over time not only offered an archival record of the group's scientific advances but also objectified the group's knowledge. All students had participatory roles as authors and respondents as they constructed and disseminated textual artifacts, shared their expertise, and questioned or pointed out the inadequacies in students' explanations or texts. A later adaptation of the software, the CSILE/Knowledge Forum, added scaffolds in the form of procedural facilitation to foster expertise in writing. This included scaffolds that defined roles and offered language support in processes such as theory refinement and constructive criticism. In both versions, the collaborative environment of CSILE exemplified a process of knowledge construction as a social and collective activity, not unlike that available to professionals in a scholarly discipline.

The results of evaluations of CSILE indicate that experimental students significantly surpassed control students on measures of depth of learning and understanding of learning processes. On standardized tests in reading, language, and vocabulary, CSILE students outperformed control students (Scardamalia and Bereiter, 1994). As a part of their research, Scardamalia and Bereiter identified at least five different contributions that written texts make in knowledge-building communities, including the provision of (1) writing and cognitive tools for reflection, communication, and disciplinary inquiry; (2) a publication/review process that encourages the type of evaluation, response, and revision that parallels the vetting of ideas in scholarly writing in a scientific discipline; (3) a cumulative, progressive set of artifacts or texts produced by the community that can be created, retrieved, modified, and archived; (4) multiple points of view and perspectives; (5) access to the distributed expertise and thoughts of others in the community of practice; and (6) expansion of the audience to include distant members beyond the classroom walls. Unlike a traditional classroom situation in which a single teacher took primary responsibility for providing feedback, the centralized storage and dissemination of student documents in the CSILE network created new possibilities for accessing and understanding the pragmatic functions and features of written communication.

Similar studies that have featured writing and representational systems in a community of inquiry have reported beneficial effects on students' written and academic performance. These include studies in the disciplinary subjects of science (Brown et al., 1993; Guthrie, Wigfield, & Perencevich, 2004; Palincsar, Magnusson, Marano, Ford, & Brown, 1998; Roth, 1998; Wells, 1999). In these studies, there exists a close connection between the collective activities of the sociocultural group (intermental plane) and the activities of individuals (intramental plane), with a dynamic and transformative relationship between the two (Mercer, 2002). Participation and communication in these communities is not just what students learn; it is how they learn and how they make sense of writing acts (Lemke, 2002). Roth (1998) elucidates the qualities of effective knowledge-building communities in disciplinary contexts, with their general emphases on (1) the assessment of students' states of knowledge as central to designing the curriculum; (2) the joint production, engineering, and reflection on the construction of artifacts, tools, and texts; (3) the presentation of ill-defined problems that invite design-based conversations and solutions; (4) the recognition of textual or student ambiguity as authentic and legitimate sites for problem solving and learning; (5) the public sharing and distribution of resources, tools, and strategies; and (6) the cultivation, recognition, and dissemination of the expertise of others, whether they are peers, teachers, or persons inside or outside the community.

A second body of related work featuring communities of practice focuses on the relationship between writers and readers in a sociocultural community of language users. This dialogic view of writers is based on the work of Bakhtin (1986), who proposed that each utterance, oral or written, is influenced and shaped by prior conversations and utterances in which speakers (writers) and listeners (readers) have taken part, as well as by the responses and utterances that are anticipated will follow. Written words are filled with dialogic overtones, because writers use ideas and texts as "thinking devices" to carry on conversations with the imagined readers and themselves. The construction of responsive words transforms the boundaries of the inner dialogues into print (Wells, 1999). In this manner, writing is an inherently social and multivoiced activity, with text construction being distributed and negotiated among writers and readers. Dialogic and symbolic interactions fill the writer's page with words.

There are several implications of this literature for instruction. First, according to Flower (2002; Flower & Hayes, 1981), students' participation and reflection on the acts of writing should provide access to constructive and metacognitive processes that are themselves the site of the multiple "voices" or kinds of knowledge that have shaped the representation of meaning. Writers need to learn to turn their attention to these multivoiced interactions during writing (either overtly or covertly) as they enter into a process of negotiating meanings among the participants, resulting in provisional resolutions and—at times—in restructured understandings and restructured texts (Flower, 2003). In this manner, as talk moves back and forth between the text and the respective stances of writers and readers, students are helped to think about the connection between intended and realized meanings, texts and contexts, tools and outcomes, convention and invention, as well as undertake divergent and inventive responses to repair communication problems and breakdowns.

Second, students who participate in design-based conversations about texts learn to treat printed words as thinking devices and are more likely to be successful in approaching their written texts as improvable objects (Roth, 1998; Wells, 1999). Such conversations draw attention to the medium of written language itself, with its own structure and organization (Wells, 1999). Third, students who interact frequently with other writers and readers have greater opportunities to understand and internalize the perspective of their audience, thereby laying the foundation for the development of dialogical skills that support text production, transformation, and revision. Fourth, authors and readers in collaboration with each another create ZPDs for one another, each providing the context for understanding and resolving contradictions and ambiguities through conversation, interpretation, and responsive action (Mahn & John-Steiner, 2002). Fifth, in the context of textual contradictions, writers can stretch and sometimes fundamentally transform their knowledge and practices, which can in turn, transform the knowledge and practices of the larger sociocultural community (Russell, 1997). Working on challenging texts and problems can make demands on writers to further their use of tools and practices, and even to invent new ones on their own (Wells, 1999). Finally, the notion of apprenticeship comes full circle when apprentices independently create new artifacts and tools that add to the cultural resources of the group (Wells, 1999). What remains to be crafted by teachers is a community that supports the development of creative responses in challenging activities, as well as the mutual sharing and distribution of resources that enrich the cultural capital of the community of practice.

Future Research Directions

This chapter has documented a qualitative and quantitative research base for understanding writing instruction from a sociocultural perspective. While the studies reviewed in this chapter reflect particular aspects of a sociocultural theory, relatively few studies have explicitly incorporated all aspects of the theory into either the design or evaluation of the studies. In this sense, sociocultural theory and its allied theories, such as activity theory (Engestrom, Miettinen, & Punamaki, 1999) and discourse theory (Gee, 1996; Halliday, 1998), have had significantly less impact than cognitive theories on our understanding of writing development. Sociocultural theory is currently underinvestigated in writing research, even though there is general acceptance of the inherently social nature of writing. Sociocultural theory can best inform future research as a theory that animates with other theoretical perspectives, methodological tools, and research practices. This section identifies a small sample of future research directions.

First, one of the most needed areas of research in the writing of school-age children continues to be the need for studies that draw upon both quantitative and qualitative methods to study writing development. Rich descriptions of how writing is socially constructed and reconstructed in classroom communities will allow teachers/educators to gain insight into the types of assisted development that advance writing. These studies should look at not only how writing is more than simply writing production or adherence to particular traits of specific genres, but also at the ways writing is used across the curriculum as a tool to accomplish meaningful goals and its impact on the dispositions students have toward writing and learning.

Second, research should also examine how teachers create writing contexts that support new participation structures, roles, rules, and collaborations. Manipulating and studying how activity settings in schools are consequential in improving writing, learning, and identity is a particularly ripe area of future research (Putney, Green, Dixon, Durain, & Yeager, 2000; Santa Barbara Discourse Group, 1992).

Third, the inherently social and historical roots of writing ensure that there will be a continuing need to study writing in relation to continuing cultural, societal, individual, and interindividual contexts. Writers, genres and social settings will continually influence the activity of writing (Kamberelis, 1999; Kamberelis & Bovino, 1999) as new activities, technologies, and discourses are juxtaposed (Bereiter, 2002; Scardamalia & Bereiter, 1994, 1999). As individuals have access to information on new technologies and through new media, the demand for new forms of literacy will be created. The very definition of what "counts" as literacy will constantly be interrogated as cultures, communities, activities, and individuals animate one another and reposition actors of all types to be responsive to a changing literacy landscape.

Fourth, while some writing research has focused on the microgenetic and ontogenetic development of writers, less attention has been paid to the role that larger social systems might play on communal and individual development. Schools themselves are made up of embedded communities of practice, but they are also subject to outside influences of parents, administrators, school boards, state curriculum standards, and federal mandates that impact the teaching context. A sociocultural and activity–theoretical perspective must account for how changes in these systems of influences impact more local meaning construction in the classroom. Manipulating the activity settings within and outside of school in an effort to develop more systemic coherence may prove to create a form of institutional memory and culture of writing that exceeds what is accomplished in one class with one teacher. Studying how the creation of both distal and proximal activity settings impacts the teaching of writing as a system of activity settings that come to privilege particular ways of knowing and valuing may impact the ways schools think about systemic reform (see Flower, 2002; Moje, 2002).

Fifth, any serious examination of writing from a sociocultural perspective must account for and attempt to understand the impact of culture and how different cultural groups are conventionalized by and transform culture. Writing is not value-neutral. Future studies of writing will need to be mindful of the role that writing plays in challenging or perpetuating social positions and injustices of members of various groups (Bell, 1997). The emergence of culturally responsive pedagogy, and the role that writing might play in these different ways of teaching and knowing, will help to elucidate how writing is used in communities to advance individual and communal goals in recursive cycles of activity.

Finally, a central aspect of the current educational landscape is the role that assessment and accountability have increasingly played in schooling. Vygotsky's interest in dynamic assessment as a critical element in assisting learning in advance of development provides the field with continued research challenges (Campione & Brown, 1987; Minick, 1987), especially as it relate to balancing our current obsession with measuring particular genres in decontextualized high-stakes environments. Equating effective writing with performance in specific genres may have the impact of artificially narrowing "what counts" as writing, literacy, and identity. Alternative forms of assessment that make light of learning in advance of development, including performance assessment and portfolio assessment (Valencia, 1998; Gearhart & Wolf, 1997), should continue to evolve and be traced back to how they mediate writing knowledge, performance, and disposition. Research can help to elucidate the role that assessment practices play in constructing what counts as writing for teacher and students. National and state writing assessments and standards are also particularly ripe sites for understanding how these policies impact local meaning construction at the district, building, teacher, and student levels.

Conclusion

Understanding writing development, teaching, and learning in social contexts requires a theoretical orientation that can reflect the intertextual, intercontextual, and intersemiotic aspects that influence writing (Lemke, 2003; Paxton-Buursma, 2004; Putney et al., 2000). Sociocultural theory attempts to account for how writing has become socially constructed in different cultural groups through attending to four genetic developments sociohistorically, including phylogenetically as human species evolve over time, sociogenetically as various cultural groups evolve, ontogenetically over the lifespan of an individual, and microgenetically as individuals interact with others on a moment-to-moment basis in activity settings. Continued research is needed to understand not only each developmental strata but also how these strata animate one another. Sociocultural theory may best be understood as a carrier of multiple complementary perspectives that are under constant construction in a dynamic tension. In this chapter, we have attempted to illuminate a portion of the substantial body of work that has informed a sociocultural theory of writing, while also acknowledging that it is in the imagined future that sociocultural theory may have its greatest impact on our understanding of writing development, teaching, and learning.

References

Alvermann, D. E. (2002). Effective literacy instruction for adolescents. *Journal of Literacy Research*, *34*, 189–208.

Anderson, L. M., Raphael, T. E., Englert, C. S., & Stevens, D. D. (1991, April). *Teaching writing with a new instructional model: Variations in teachers' practices and student performance.* Paper presented at the annual meeting of the American Educational Research Association, Chicago, IL.

Baker, S., Gersten, R., & Graham, S. (2003). Teaching expressive writing to students with learning disabilities: Research-based applications and examples. *Journal of Learning Disabilities*, *36*(2), 109–123.

Baker, S., Gersten, R., & Scanlon, D. (2002). Procedural facilitators and cognitive strategies: Tool for unraveling the mysteries of comprehension and the writing process, and for providing meaningful access to the general curriculum. *Learning Disabilities: Research and Practice*, *17*, 65–77.

Bakhtin, M. M. (1986). *Speech genres and other late essays* (V. W. McGee, Trans.). Austin: University of Texas Press.

Bell, L. A. (1997). Theoretical foundations for social justice in education. In M. Adams, L. A. Bell, & P. Griffin (Eds.), *Teaching for diversity and social justice: A sourcebook* (pp. 3–15). New York: Routledge.

Bereiter, C. (2002). *Education and mind in the knowledge age*. Mahwah, NJ: Erlbaum.

Bereiter, C., & Scardamalia, M. (1987). *The psychology of written composition*. Hillsdale, NJ: Erlbaum.

Brophy, J. (2002). Discussion. In *Social constructivist teaching: Affordances and constraints* (Vol. 9, pp. 333–358). Amsterdam: JAI Press.

Brown, A. L., Ash, D., Rutherford, M., Nakagawa, K., Gordon, A., & Campione, J. C. (1993). Distributed expertise in the classroom. In G. Salomon (Ed.), *Distributed cognition: Psychological and educational considerations* (pp. 188–288). New York: Cambridge University Press.

Campione, J. C., & Brown, A. L. (1987). Linking dynamic assessment with school achievement. In C. S. Lidz (Ed.), *Dynamic assessment: An interactional approach to evaluating learning potential* (pp. 82–115). New York: Guilford Press.

Coe, R. M. (2002). The new rhetoric of genre: Writing political briefs. In A. M. Johns (Ed.), *Genre in the classroom: Multiple perspectives* (pp. 197–210). Mahwah, NJ: Erlbaum.

Daiute, C., & Dalton, B. (1993). Collaboration between children learning to write: Can novices be masters? *Cognition and Instruction, 10*, 281–333.

Dalton, S. S., & Tharp, R. G. (2002). Standards for pedagogy: Research, theory and practice. In G. Wells & G. Claxton (Eds.), *Learning for life in the*

21st century: Sociocultural perspectives on the future of education (pp. 181–194). Malden, MA: Blackwell.

Daniels, H. (2001). *Vygotsky and pedagogy*. New York: Routledge.

De La Paz, S. (1999). Self-regulated strategy instruction in regular education settings: Improving outcomes for students with and without learning disabilities. *Learning Disabilities Research and Practice, 14*, 92–106.

De La Paz, S., & Graham, S. (2002). Explicitly teaching strategies, skills, and knowledge: Writing instruction in middle school classrooms. *Journal of Educational Psychology, 94*, 687–698.

Engestrom, Y., Miettinen, R., & Punamaki, R. (1999). *Perspectives on activity theory*. New York: Cambridge University Press.

Englert, C. S., Berry, R. A., & Dunsmore, K. L. (2001). A case study of the apprenticeship process: Another perspective on the apprentice and the scaffolding metaphor. *Journal of Learning Disabilities, 34*, 152–171.

Englert, C. S., & Dunsmore, K. (2002). A diversity of teaching and learning paths: Teaching writing in situated activity. In J. Brophy (Ed.), *Social constructivist teaching: Affordances and constraints* (Vol. 9, pp. 81–130). Amsterdam: JAI Press.

Englert, C. S., & Dunsmore, K. (2004). The role of dialogue in constructing effective literacy settings for students with language and learning disabilities. In E. R. Silliman & L. C. Wilkinson (Eds.), *Language and literacy learning in schools* (pp. 201–238). New York: Guilford Press.

Englert, C. S., & Mariage, T. V. (2003). The sociocultural model in special education interventions: Apprenticing students in higher-order thinking. In H. L. Swanson, K. R. Harris, & S. Graham (Eds.), *Handbook of learning disabilities* (pp. 450–470). New York: Guilford Press.

Englert, C. S., Raphael, T. E., Anderson, L., Stevens, D. D., & Fear, K. L. (1991). Making writing strategies and self-talk visible: Cognitive strategy instruction in writing in regular and special education classrooms. *American Educational Research Journal, 29*, 337–372.

Flower, L. (2002). Intercultural knowledge building: The literate action of a community think tank. In C. Bazerman, & D. Russell (Eds.), *Writing selves/writing societies: Research from activity perspectives*. Fort Collins, CO: WAC Clearinghouse. Available online at wac.colostate.edu/books/selves_societies/

Flower, L. S. (2003). Talking across difference: Intercultural rhetoric and the search for situated knowledge. *College Composition and Communication, 55*, 38–68.

Flower, L., & Hayes, J. R. (1981). A cognitive process theory of writing. *College Composition and Communication, 32*, 365–387.

Gearhart, M., & Wolf, S. A. (1997). Issues in portfolio assessment: Assessing writing processes from their products. *Educational Assessment, 4*, 65–296.

Gee, J. P. (Ed.). (1992). *The social mind: Language, ideology and social practice*. New York: Bergin & Garvey.

Gee, J. P. (1996). *Social linguistics and literacies: Ideology in discourses* (2nd ed.). London: Taylor & Francis.

Gersten, R., & Baker, S. (2001). Teaching expressive writing to students with learning disabilities: A meta-analysis. *Elementary School Journal, 101*, 251–272.

Gould, J. S. (1996). A constructivist perspective on teaching and learning in the language arts. In I. C. T. Fosnot (Ed.), *A constructivist perspective on teaching and learning in the language arts* (pp. 92–102) New York: Teachers College Press.

Graham, S. (1997). Executive control in the revising of students with learning and writing difficulties. *Journal of Educational Psychology, 89*, 781–791.

Graham, S., & Harris, K. R. (1989a). A components analysis of cognitive strategy instruction: Effects on learning disabled students' compositions and self-efficacy. *Journal of Educational Psychology, 81*, 353–361.

Graham, S., & Harris, K. R. (1989b). Improving learning disabled students' skills at composing essays: Self-instructional strategy training. *Exceptional Children, 56*, 201–216.

Graham, S., & Harris, K. R. (2003). Students with learning disabilities and the process of writing: A meta-analysis of SRSD studies. In H. L. Swanson, K. R. Harris, & Graham, S. (Eds.), *Handbook of learning disabilities* (pp. 323–344). New York: Guilford Press.

Guthrie, J. T., Wigfield, A., & Perencevich, K. C. (2004). *Motivating reading comprehension: Concept-oriented reading instruction*. Mahwah, NJ: Erlbaum.

Halliday, M. A. K. (1998) Linguistics as metaphor. In A.-M. Simon-Vandenbergen, K. Davidse, & D. Noel (Eds.), *Reconnecting language: Morphology and syntax in functional perspectives* (pp. 3–27). Amsterdam: Benjamins.

Harris, K. R., & Graham, S. (1996). *Making the writing process work: Strategies for composition and self-regulation* (2nd ed.). Cambridge, MA: Brookline Books.

Hillocks, G. (1984). What works in teaching composition : A meta-analysis of experimental treatment studies. *American Journal of Education, 93*, 133–170.

Hillocks, G. (1995). *Teaching writing as reflective practice*. New York: Teachers College Press.

John-Steiner, V. (2000). *Creative collaboration*. New York: Oxford University Press.

Kamberelis, G. (1999). Genre development and learning: Children writing stories, science reports, and poems. *Research in the Teaching of English, 33*, 403–460.

Kamberelis, G., & Bovino, T. D. (1999) Cultural artifacts as scaffolds for genre development. *Reading Research Quarterly, 34*(2), 138–170.

Kozulin, A. (2003). Psychological tools and mediated learning. In A. Kozulin, B. Gindis, V. S. Ageyev, & S. M. Miller, (Eds.), *Vygotsky's educational theory in cultural context* (pp. 15–38). New York: Cambridge University Press.

Lemke, J. L. (2002). Becoming the village: Education across lives. In G. Wells & G. Claxton (Eds.), *Learning for life in the 21st century: Sociocultural perspectives on the future of education* (pp. 34–45). Malden, MA: Blackwell.

Lemke, J. L. (2003, February). *Modeling change: The dynamics of place, time, and identity.* Paper presented at the 24th Annual Ethnography in Education Forum, University of Pennsylvania, Philadelphia.

MacArthur, C. A., Schwartz, S. S., & Graham, S. (1991). A model for writing instruction: Integrating word processing and strategy instruction into a process approach to writing. *Learning Disabilities Research and Practice, 6*, 230–236.

Mahn, H., & John-Steiner, V. (2002). The gift of confidence: A Vygotskian view of emotions. In G. Wells & G. Claxton (Eds.), *Learning for life in the 21st century: Sociocultural perspectives on the future of education* (pp. 45–58). Malden, MA: Blackwell.

Mariage, T. V. (2001). Features of an interactive writing discourse: Conversational involvement, conventional knowledge, and internalization in "Morning Message." *Journal of Learning Disabilities, 34*(2), 172–196.

Mariage, T. V.; Englert, C. S., & Garmon, M. A. (2000). The teacher as "more knowledgeable other" in assisting literacy learning with special needs students. *Reading and Writing Quarterly, 16*, 299–336.

Mercer, N. (2002). Developing dialogues. In G. Wells & G. Claxton (Eds.), *Learning for life in the 21st century: Sociocultural perspectives on the future of education* (pp. 141–153). Malden, MA: Blackwell.

Minick, N. (1987). Implications of Vygotsky's theories of dynamic assessment. In C. S. Lidz (Ed.), *Dynamic assessment: An interactional approach to evaluating learning potential* (pp. 116–140). New York: Guilford Press.

Moje, E. B. (2002). But where are the youth: Integrating youth culture into literacy theory. *Educational Theory, 52*, 97–120.

Moll, L. C., & Greenberg, J. B. (1990). Creating zones of possibilities: Combining social contexts for instruction. In L. C. Moll (Ed.), *Vygotsky and education: Instructional implications and applications of sociohistorical psychology* (pp. 319–348). Cambridge, MA: Cambridge University Press.

Palincsar, A. S., Magnusson, S, J., Marano, N., Ford, D., Brown, N. (1998). Designing a community of practice: Principles and practices of the GIsML Community. *Teaching and Teacher Education, 14*(1), 5–19.

Paxton-Buursma, D. J. (2004). *An apprenticeship in attuned discourse: Opening literacy affordances through multiple semiotics.* Unpublished doctoral dissertation, Michigan State University, East Lansing, MI.

Pea, R. D. (1993). Practices of distributed intelligence and designs for education. In G. Salomon (Ed.), *Distributed cognition: Psychological and educational considerations* (pp. 47–87). New York: Cambridge University Press.

Putney, L. G., Green, J., Dixon, C., Duran, R., & Yeager, B. (2000). Consequential progressions: Exploring collective–individual development in a bilingual classroom. In C. D. Lee & P. Smagorinsky (Eds.), *Vygotskian perspectives on literacy research: Constructing meaning through collaborative inquiry* (pp. 86–126). New York: Cambridge University Press.

Rogoff, B. (1990). *Apprenticeship in thinking: Cognitive development in social context.* New York: Oxford University Press.

Roth, W. M. (Ed.). (1998). *Designing communities.* Boston: Kluwer.

Russell, D. R. (1997). Rethinking genre in school and society: An activity theory analysis. *Written Communication, 14*, 504–554.

Santa Barbara Classroom Discourse Group. (1992). Constructing literacy in classrooms: Literate action as social accomplishment. In H. Marshall (Ed.), *Redefining student learning: Roots of educational change* (pp. 119–150). Norwood, NJ: Ablex.

Scardamalia, M., & Bereiter, C. (1994). Computer support for knowledge-building communities. *Journal of the Learning Sciences, 3*(3), 265–283.

Scardamalia, M., & Bereiter, C., (1999). Schools as knowledge building organizations. In D. Keating & C. Hertzman (Eds.), *Developmental health and the wealth of nations: Social, biological, and educational dynamics* (pp. 274–289). New York: Guilford Press.

Schaffer, H. R. (1996). Joint involvement episodes as context for development. In H. Daniels (Ed.), *An introduction to Vygotsky* (pp. 251–259). New York: Routledge.

Scribner, S. (1997). The cognitive consequences of literacy. In E. Tobach, R. J. Falmagne, M. B. Parlee, L. M. W. Martin, & A. S. Kapelman (Eds.), *Mind and social practice: Selected writings of Sylvia Scribner* (pp. 160–189). New York: Cambridge University Press.

Shotter, J. (1995). In dialogue: Social constructionism and radical constructivism. In L. P. Steffe & J. Gale (Eds.), *Constructivism in education* (pp. 41–56). Hillsdale, NJ: Erlbaum.

Stetsenko, A. (1999). Social Interaction, Cultural Tools and the Zone of Proximal Development: In search of a asynthesis. In S. C. M. Hedegaard, S. Boedker, & U. J. Jensen (Eds.), *Activity theory and social practice: Cultural–historical approaches* (pp. 235–253) Aarhus, Denmark: Aarhus University Press.

Stone, C. A. (1998). Should we salvage the scaffolding metaphor? *Journal of Learning Disabilities, 2,* 409–413.

Stone, C. A. (2002). Promises and pitfalls of scaffolded instruction for students with language learning disabilities. In K. G. Butler & E. R. Silliman (Eds.), *Speaking, reading, and writing in children with language learning disabilities: New paradigms in research and practice* (pp. 175–198). Mahwah, NJ: Erlbaum.

Toulmin, S. (1999). Knowledge as shared procedures. In Y. Engestrom, R. Miettinen, & R. Punamaki (Eds.), *Perspectives on activity theory* (pp. 53–64) New York: Cambridge University Press.

Valencia, S. W. (1998). *Literacy portfolios in action.* Orlando: Harcourt Brace.

Vaughn, S., Gersten, R., & Chard, D. (2000). The underlying message in LD intervention research: Findings from research syntheses. *Exceptional Children, 67*(1), 99–114.

Vygotsky, L. S. (1978). Mind in society: The development of higher psychological processes (M. Cole, V. John-Steiner, S. Scribner, & E. Souberman (Eds.). Cambridge, MA: Harvard University Press.

Wells, G. (Ed.). (1999). *Dialogic inquiry: Toward a sociocultural practice and theory of education* New York: Cambridge University Press.

Wertsch, J. (1985). *Vygotsky and the social formation of mind*. Cambridge, MA: Harvard University Press.

Wertsch, J. (1991). *Voices of the mind: A sociocultural approach to mediated action.* Cambridge, MA: Harvard University Press.

Wertsch, J. V. (Ed.). (1998). *Mind as action.* New York: Oxford University Press.

Wertsch, J. V., & Toma, C. (1995). Discourse and learning in the classroom: A sociocultural approach. In L. P. Steffe & J. Gale (Eds.), *Constructivism in education* (pp. 159–174). Hillsdale, NJ: Erlbaum.

Wong, B. Y. L., Butler, D. L., Ficzere, S. A., & Kuperis, S. (1997. Teaching adolescents with learning disabilities and low-achievers to plan, write and revise compare–contrast essays. *Learning Disabilities Research and Practice, 12,* 2–15.

Wong, B. Y. L., Harris, K. R., Graham, S., & Butler, D. L. (2003). Cognitive strategies instruction research in learning disaiblities. In H. L. Swanson, K. R. Harris, & S. Graham (Eds.), *Handbook of learning disabilities* (pp. 383–402). New York: Guilford Press.

Chapter 15

Response to Writing

Richard Beach *and* Tom Friedrich

In this chapter, we examine different strategies for written or oral responses to writing for the purpose of helping students improve their writing. We review the different functions and purposes for responding to writing, as well as research findings on the benefits of using certain methods of response to writing, leading to substantive revision and critical self-assessment, processes central to improving writing quality. Students not only engage in limited writing but they also do little extensive revision (National Writing Project, 2003). Analysis of a 12th-grade advanced composition class revealed that despite an emphasis on revising multiple drafts and peer feedback, 81.7% of revisions involved only surface and stylistic changes (Yagelski, 1995). Teachers may also find that revision remains a challenge for some students, requiring them to focus simply on formulating text (Schneider, 2003).

The research reviewed in this chapter includes studies of student writers and teachers at the primary, secondary, and college levels. Because student developmental level across these grade levels can itself be a factor shaping ability to revise and self-assess, we have identified students' grade levels in specific studies.

Methodologically, most of the research we reviewed consists of qualitative–interpretive analysis of teacher-written or oral response practices to student drafts, although some experimental studies compare the effects of different types of teacher response.

The Purpose and Function for Responding to Student Writing

A primary purpose for responding to students' writing is to help students improve the quality of their writing. More traditional approaches to teaching writing assumed that by "correcting" student errors on final drafts, students would improve their writing. However, focusing on final-draft errors only encouraged students to attend to matters of sentence structure and mechanics (Sommers, 1982). And the use of a formalist outline–draft–edit instructional model encouraged students to define initially their organization of content before writing as opposed to using writing to discover content/ideas (Hillocks, 1986). As a result, students engage in little substantive revision associated with rethinking their text.

How then can teachers foster substantive revisions? In her review of research on revision in composition, Fitzgerald (1992) found that epistemological notions of writing are central to understanding differences in the level and degree of revision. In a formalist model of writing instruction prevalent in the 1950s and 1960s, the primary focus was on teaching forms/templates based on the textbook model of outline, draft, and edit. Then, during the 1970s and 1980s, research on the revision process indicated that students' frequent focus on surface matters resulted in little substantive revision (Beach, 1976; Sommers, 1982). Moreover, cognitive processing research demonstrated that students revise according to the need to address problems in fulfilling specific rhetorical goals, problems that many beginning writers have difficulty articulating (Flower, Hayes, Carey, Schriver, & Stratman, 1986). Consistent with the "process" model then in favor, teachers shifted away from simply giving editing feedback to responding to students' development of ideas and drafts (Hillocks, 1986).

However, researchers in the 1980s found that when students focused solely on process without a sense of the social purpose or value, they simply "went through the motions" of the composing process (Faigley & Witte, 1981). The high school students Marshall (1987) studied employed the processes, but without a sense of the rhetorical purpose for making choices in revision or language, suggesting the need for socially purposeful assignments. There was also a growing concern about how minority students and English language learner (ELL) students fared in process settings given their lack of the linguistic and genre knowledge resources students acquire in middle-class-home contexts (Delpit, 1995).

It also became clear that the nature and quality of the teacher's feedback during the composing process is critical to whether students revise. Simply revising drafts does not necessarily result in an improvement in the quality of those drafts; a study of fifth- and sixth-grade students' revisions revealed that simply making revisions did not improve the quality of students' writing (Van Gelderen, 1997). If high school students receive feedback on only final drafts, they do not revise rough drafts (Yagelski, 1995). When a teacher shifted away from a focus on surface matters to provide open-ended comments on content, the college student in one study made more substantive revisions than when the teacher commented only on form (Mlynarczyk, 1996).

More recent research points to the additional need to help students learn to use feedback to self-assess their drafts. Analysis of 11 teachers' feedback to 64 middle school students' revisions of drafts revealed that most of the teacher feedback focused on editing matters (Matsumura, Patthey-Chavez, & Valdes, 2002). Students followed suit, with 58% of their revisions involving surface-level changes; only 34% were "content" revisions involving deleting, organizing, adding information, or responding to teacher questions. Content-based feedback only increased essay length, not improvement in quality across drafts, because most content feedback only requested further information. Adding that information did not necessarily improve the quality of students' writing. The few students who did make substantive revisions that improved writing quality received specific guidance on how to assess their use of evidence to support claims or formulation of a summary conclusion.

Helping students use that feedback to meet the rhetorical demands of specific social contexts points to the value of an "environmental" approach shown by Hillocks's (1986) meta-analysis of writing research to support greater writing achievement than formalist and traditional process approaches. Underlying this approach is a constructivist–sociocultural conception of knowledge as not being static or located "in the head," but rather as being continually redefined through social exchange of competing perspectives. Revision becomes more than simply making textual changes. It also involves entertaining alternative perspectives and testing out tentative "passing theories" or hypotheses about the world (Harris, 2003; Kent, 1993). Demonstrating to students how to use teacher and student feedback to reflect alternative perspectives on ideas and beliefs leads to a reenvisioning of one's beliefs, perspectives, and ways of knowing that are essential for revision (Lee, 2000). In this approach, teachers encourage students' engagement with alternative, competing voices to "help them transform these struggles into occasions for becoming" (Lensmire, 2002, p. 84).

All of this points to the importance of the social dynamics of the classroom in which teachers and students entertain competing perspectives associated with adopting different roles. Investigators in one study (Larson & Maier, 2000) found that a first-grade teacher assumed the roles of teacher, author, coauthor, and overhearer, modeling her own writing process as an author working together with students in constructing texts. Her students reciprocated by adopting similar roles through sharing texts with others as contributing members of an authoring community.

To support students' exploration of alternative perspectives, teachers can sidestep giving only "foreshadowing" comments that simply direct students on how to develop further an existing draft by providing "sideshadowing" comments that challenge and disrupt predictable directions or genre development (Welch, 1997). Welch argues that rather than simply fostering revision based on fulfilling predetermined intentions, teachers need to interrogate students' need for closure and certainty by highlighting alternative perspectives and dialogic tensions.

Teachers' social roles can also be implied by how they respond to student writing. In responding to students' drafts, teachers construct a students' identities based on interpretations of the personae projected in students' writing (Taylor, 2002). Given their perceptions of a student's identity, teachers project their own identities onto their constructions of the student persona. In responding to a college student's essay on obtaining a driver's license as an American cultural rite of passage, a female teacher from India had difficulty relating to what was portrayed as largely a male experience, leading her to adopt a more skeptical, critical stance about the student's writing, pitting her own identity *against* the identity portrayed in the text (Taylor, 2002). In constructing his or her own writing personae, a student either invites or deflects teachers' identification with that persona. This suggests that teachers need to reflect on how they construct students' personae, and on how students perceive teachers' identities— their beliefs, attitudes, and agendas—through teachers' feedback. Students may interpret a teacher's feedback as reflecting a negative perception of themselves as writers. Negative, stereotyped constructions of student identities may bias teachers' perceptions of their writing, leading to counterproductive feedback (Hyland, 1998).

Teachers are also responding to students' ability to employ genre tools to establish social connections with audiences (Chapman,

1999; Schneider, 2003). In an e-mail interaction between volunteer adults and third-grade students about a science unit, students' creative and unconventional uses of riddles to define the social and power relationships between themselves and the adults entailed use of the riddle genre to build positive relationships with their adult audiences (Britsch, 2004).

Genres function not only to foster alternative, competing perspectives but also shared, common norms leading to collaborative agreement. For example, to argue against closing their school, over an 8-week period, seventh-grade students collaboratively constructed a written speech to be delivered to the local school board (Sheehy, 2003). Drawing on Bakhtin (1981) for her analysis of the revision process, Margaret Sheehy (2003) examined two competing forces at work—a centripetal, unifying force of standardization versus alternative deviating, centrifugal challenges to standardization based on competing, diverse perspectives. The standardization forces involved the teacher's direct instruction of formalist models and genre conventions, and the students' uses of those models and conventions to pull together competing, alternative ideas into a cohesive text. At the same time, students were entertaining a range of alternative perspectives, including the idea that the school board would simply ignore their plea because, as students, they had little agency in the community. To bolster their rhetorical agency, the students recast their exploratory, informal, oral talk into more formal written prose, consistent with written speech genre conventions. As they worked, the teacher encouraged them to entertain both alternative, diverse perspectives leading to revision, leading students to organize and focus their ideas in a final speech that was consistent with their perceptions of board members' knowledge and needs. This points to the need for the teacher to encourage alternative perspectives and ways to synthesize these perspectives.

This study demonstrates the importance of students' perceptions of their audience's knowledge and beliefs operating in a social context—in this case, the school board. Knowing an audience's level of prior knowledge helps students to determine the amount, or sufficiency, of information necessary, leading to decisions about the need to add to, delete from, or clarify their writing (Beach, 1989). Knowing that an audience does not agree with their beliefs about a problem or issue leads them to engage in a form of "rival" hypotheses about alternative perspectives on a problem or issue (Flower, Long, & Higgins, 2001) or to include counterarguments (Leitão, 2003).

Teachers also need to formulate engaging assignments that entertain alternative perspectives that foster revision. In one study, more cognitively challenging assignments were predictive of elementary students' revisions and final draft content quality (Matsumura, Patthey-Chavez, & Valdes, 2002). Effective assignments also clearly articulate teachers' expectations (Wallace & Hayes, 1992) and help to avoid instances of students misunderstanding those expectations (Sperling & Freedman, 1987).

Also, teachers need to vary their assignments and feedback to accommodate individual differences in students' writing ability. One survey of 153 primary grade teachers found that while 42% made few or no adaptations to accommodate struggling writers' needs, most (85%) reported conferencing with struggling writers more often than with other students (Graham, Harris, Fink-Chorzempa, & MacArthur, 2003). Teachers need to recognize issues of language use faced by non-native speakers. While students generally prefer comments related to content (Storch & Tapper, 2000), ELL students may prefer feedback on content and language issues (Ferris, 1995, 1997).

Teachers also need to use their feedback to reference specific criteria or rubrics constituting the rhetorical demands of that assignment. Rather than importing generic criteria that may have little relevance to a unique classroom context, teachers should design criteria with that specific context in mind (Broad, 2003). And students need training on how to apply these criteria or rubrics. In one study, middle school students completed self-assessment rubrics in both experimental and control groups; students in the experimental group received two 40-minute instructional sessions in the application of the rubrics to their drafts (Andrade & Boulay, 2003). However, there were no significant treatment effects, suggesting the need for more extensive self-assessment instruction

beyond the minimal training provided in this study.

Techniques for Giving Feedback

Most of the research finds that teachers respond to student writing by making written comments. Unfortunately, these written comments are often too vague, pro forma, global, or inconsistent (Smith, 1997; Straub, 1996). High school students in one study preferred specific comments that provided explanations of feedback, including open-ended questions and use of backup conferences to elaborate on comments (Bardine, Bardine, & Deegan, 2000). In contrast to earlier findings that reported on teachers' attention to surface features in draft feedback, teachers are now using written comments to focus more on students' ideas and organization (Conrad & Goldstein, 1999; Ferris, 1997). Despite the limitations of written feedback, ELL students still prefer teacher-written feedback to that given by peers or in conference (Zhang, 1995). One analysis of the relationships between the level of revisions and the types of written comments given to ELL college students indicated that marginal notes, requests for clarification, and comments on grammar resulted in substantive revision (Ferris, 1997).

Researchers have also examined the efficacy of marginal versus final written comments. Final summative statements framed in generic, formulaic language or marginal comments such as "awk" are not perceived as useful by students (Smith, 1997).

Teachers can also provide feedback by taping comments on cassettes or digital tapes (Anson, 1997). In doing so, they can communicate considerably more information than that in written comments in the same time period, they have less difficulty communicating comments, and they can elaborate more on their comments (Anson, 1997). Huang (2000) found that a combination of taped and written comments by an ELL college teacher resulted in a greater quantity of feedback than the use of written feedback alone. In another study, investigators found that taped responses allowed college instructors to formulate critical responses from a safe distance (Mellen & Sommers, 2003).

Providing Reader-Based Feedback

In contrast to providing judgmental feedback, teachers can provide descriptive, "reader-based" feedback in which they describe how they as readers are responding to or processing students' writing (Elbow, 1981; Johnston, 1983). In doing so, they provide writers with a description of their processes in reading a draft:

- Engaged, entranced, moved, involved, disturbed, struck by, intrigued, puzzled, and so on ("In reading this, I was bothered, excited, confused, upset").
- Being overwhelmed; lost; besieged with; drowning in too much information, description, or different ideas/points, and so on.
- Being underwhelmed; missing something; wanting more, given a lack of information or description.
- Predicting or expecting subsequent text development associated with anticipating events, expecting support or evidence, and so on ("When I encounter opinions, I often expect some evidence supporting those opinions, which I didn't find in this draft").

Teachers also provide descriptive praise or commendation, although this praise is often too general and may lack any explanation of the positive comments (Straub, 1997).

This more indirect, facilitative, "reader-based" feedback leads students to learn to self-assess and formulate revisions on their own (Beach, 1976; Ferris, 1997; Johnston, 1983). Teachers are more likely to assume an indirect stance by adopting a conservational mode, particularly when responding to journal writing (Anson & Beach, 1997). In responding to her eighth-grade students' letters, Atwell (1998) reacts with her own return letters by posing questions to model question-asking heuristics for students to internalize for their own use in exploring or elaborating on topics. Students prefer dialogic feedback that focuses on specific points in their journal entries and builds positive teacher–student relationships (Todd, Mills, Palard, & Khamcharoen, 2001).

However, being indirect can be problematic when teachers mitigate direct criticism or pose questions, both of which can obscure teachers' intentions and confuse students (Hyland & Hyland, 2001). One study of Chinese- and Spanish-speaking students' perceptions of peers' responses indicated that they preferred negative comments that identified specific problems in their drafts (Nelson & Carson, 1998). In a comparison of two groups of developmental college students, students who were told directly where and how to make changes (a deductive approach) versus those who were asked questions (an inductive approach), the former were most likely to improve writing quality (Sweeney, 1999).

It is also important to examine the underlying intentions behind adopting a direct versus indirect stance. Analysis of five teachers' comments on the same drafts found that the teachers employed quite different strategies, in some cases using directive comments in ways that still respected students' autonomy (Straub, 1996). Straub (1996, 1997) argues that the distinction between direct and indirect approaches may be a false binary because teachers may adopt different stances for different reasons related to fostering students' revisions.

Regardless of the nature and quality of feedback, students often simply comply with what they perceive their teacher wants them to do in order to obtain a good grade, even though the teacher's suggestions may not help them improve their writing (Sperling & Freedman, 1987; Straub, 1996). Thus, distinctions between being directive or facilitative may not be useful if students adopt the stance of "Just tell me what to do" and perceive even indirect, facilitative feedback as directive. A teacher therefore needs to avoid foreseeing or foreshadowing what he or she believes a student's draft should become and allow the student's purposes to drive the direction of revisions instead (Welch, 1997). As Edward White (1999) notes, "We must convey to students that responsibility and control remain with them and that they need to do more than merely respond to our comments" (p. 130).

Modeling Self-Assessing

In giving feedback, teachers are also modeling a metacognitive vocabulary for describing rhetorical strategies students are employing, the fact that they are "identifying," "providing supporting evidence," "explaining," and so on (Beach, 1989). In modeling self-assessment, it may be more useful to model strategies for coping with problems rather than to simply demonstrate revisions (Zimmerman & Kitsantas, 2002). And in modeling self-assessment inviting revisions, teachers need to gear their language to fit the student's zone of proximal development (ZPD) (Vygotsky, 1978) by determining whether the student will be able to make the revisions implied by his or her responses and self-assessment (Ferris, 2003). If a student is totally incapable of making implied changes, then it makes little sense to provide feedback on problems he or she will not be able to address, as opposed to problems the student is capable of addressing within his or her ZPD.

In some cases, teachers provide students with extensive feedback related to a range of difficulties. However, too many comments can overwhelm students, suggesting the need for teachers to prioritize their comments by responding selectively to those aspects of a text that are perceived to be the most problematic or that deserve the most attention given their students' ZPD and language proficiency (Ferris, 2003). Earlier research on feedback consistent with process models of instruction posited that teachers should focus on issues of content and organization in responding to initial drafts, delaying a premature focus on editing until the editing phase (Sommers, 1982). It was assumed that prematurely focusing on issues of form, editing, or error correction dissuaded ELL college students from making more substantive revisions related to content and organization (Truscott, 1996). However, while content-focused feedback to ELL college writers resulted in greater improvement in draft quality than error-correction comments in one study (Kepner, 1991), another investigator found that delaying form feedback to ELL college writers resulted in no differences in draft quality (Ashwell, 2000). In fact, keeping these kinds of feedback separate is not necessary. In another study, feedback given to ELL college students that included both content and form–editing feedback simultaneously proved to be just as effective as giving content and form feedback in separate phases (Fathman & Whalley, 1990). Ultimately, just *when* certain kinds of feedback are provided matters less than the fact that

students understand *why* they are receiving certain types of feedback (Ferris, 1997, 2003).

Teachers and peers also need to vary their comments by determining each student's particular needs and difficulties (Ferris, 2003). In addition to noting consistent patterns of difficulties across different writings, teachers can also ask students to note what issues they face in their writing, then attempt to address those issues (Bauer & Garcia, 2002). A student may know how to develop a narrative, but note that he or she has difficulty portraying a setting or characters using descriptive details. By ascertaining students' difficulties, teachers can tailor their instruction to address those challenges.

Preferred Teacher Comments

Students seem to find two types of comments most helpful. First, they favor comments that suggest ways of making improvements (Ferris, 2003). Second, they prefer comments that *explain* why something is good or bad about their writing (Beach, 1989). A study of 172 first-year college students' preferences for certain types of teacher comments derived from actual comments on the sample first drafts supports these claims (Straub, 1997). Results showed that students preferred more specific or elaborate comments that provided clear direction for revisions rather than global, vague statements, or comments such as "just generalize" or "tighten up" the writing. Such specific comments pointed to careful teacher readings of student work, which the students also preferred. The students Straub studied also preferred comments focused on both global (ideas, development, etc.) and local (wording, sentence structure, etc.) matters, while disliking those that judged or challenged their ideas—an important distinction to draw, because comments perceived as punitive discouraged students from assuming responsibility for improving their writing, and those perceived as supportive had the reverse effect. This does not necessarily preclude providing critical feedback to students' ideas (Lee, 2000), but such feedback needs to be framed in a constructive as opposed to punitive mode.

Students' preferences are also related to their ability to use teachers' comments to make certain types of revisions based on the rhetorical strategy addressed in those comments. Students are more successful in making changes in response to requests for further information or for specific changes than in response to questions that challenge their ideas or argument (Conrad & Goldstein, 1999; Ferris, 2002). All of this suggests that written feedback may be particularly effective in fostering certain kinds of revisions, such as adding details/examples, improving coherence, or dealing with editing matters, because the written comments can focus on specific aspects of a draft (Conrad & Goldstein, 1999). With the larger issue of students' ideas or arguments, it may be more useful to use conference feedback to engage students in discussions about those ideas or arguments than to use written comments.

Teacher Conference Strategies

Use of teacher conferences with students has increased dramatically in the past three decades, to the point that many teachers perceive it as central to their instruction (Black, 1998). Conferences are particularly valuable for ELL students given their need to address language translation issues by verbalizing their thoughts to a teacher in the conference (Ferris, 2003).

In writing conferences, teachers can describe their intentions for providing feedback, offering explanations for comments or asking students for their perspectives (Frank, 2001). At the same time, students can voice their purposes, practice self-assessment, and formulate alternative revisions. If students are having difficulty with self-assessment, teachers can model the process, so that students use the conference to practice self-assessment (Beach, 1989).

Teachers may focus conference feedback on the specific issues facing a student. In "prewriting" conferences, they may employ heuristic strategies for exploring ideas or construction of the rhetorical context. In "drafting" conferences, they may focus on issues of organization and development of ideas. In "editing" conferences, they may focus on aspects of readability and clarity; specifically, they can have students read their drafts aloud, thus promoting self-editing,

although such oral approaches may only benefit more proficient readers (Moran, 1997).

Teachers also need to vary conference styles and strategies to accommodate for differences in students' ability to self-assess. For students who are readily able to self-assess, teachers may adopt a highly facilitative, open-ended style by simply asking students "what works" and "what needs work" (Glasswell, 2001). For students who have difficulty with self-assessment, a teacher may adopt a more directive style that addresses specific problems in their writing, model ways of reflecting on problems, and invite discussion of ideas and students' perceptions of the rhetorical context. In one study of college-level teacher–student conferencing, teachers adopted a more indirect style with stronger writers, allowing students to direct the conference and express opinions, while taking a more directive approach with weaker ones (Patthey-Chavez & Ferris, 1997). Finally, concluding conferences by negotiating a mutually agreed-upon plan for revisions can provide students with important direction for making subsequent revisions, particularly if students assume that there is no need for further revision (Black, 1998). For example, when elementary students considered their stories complete, a teacher's conference feedback aimed at supporting their revisions had little effect (Nickel, 2001).

More recently, teachers have employed online oral comments related to the use of online conferencing (Blair, 2003). Research comparing online to face-to-face conferencing suggests that online conferencing allows students to respond without concern for nonverbal reactions found in face-to-face conferencing, while requiring them to focus more on constructing the persona of the writer from the writing itself rather than from actual social or racial identities (Carabajal, LaPointe, & Gunawardena, 2003). Online feedback can be particularly supportive of self-assessment, because it can be saved for later reference when students are revising their drafts (Hewett, 2000). One study of ELL college students found that online feedback resulted in a larger number of comments and subsequent revisions than was the case with traditional feedback (Liu & Sadler, 2003).

Asynchronous online feedback through e-mail or message boards allows more time to reflect on and develop comments stored in a chat room database (Blair, 2003). On the other hand, synchronous interactions allow for real-time chat discussions about writing issues or potential revisions (Crank, 2002). ELL teachers also employ online feedback to correct grammatical errors (Melby-Mauer, 2003). Teachers using speech feedback and word prediction software to provide feedback to a seventh-grade, learning disabled student's journal writing resulted in production of longer, higher quality entries (Williams, 2002).

Teachers can reflect on their conferences by taping their responses and reflecting on their clarity of purpose, the quality of questions asked, the ratio of teacher-to-student talk, the uses of silence, and the use of scaffolding to help students self-assess (Power & Hubbard, 2001). Students can also write reflections on their revisions by making "revision memos" (Flash, 2002) or letters (Ferris, 1997, 2003) that they attach to their drafts to identify their revisions and what the teacher should be focusing on in responding to the draft.

Peer Conference Feedback

Teachers often do not have the time to devote to extensive conferencing with each student, so they need to rely on trained peers to supplement their conferencing in pair or small-group conferences, online conferences, or "read-arounds," in which students place papers on their desks and other students write comments on response sheets (Christian, 2000). In one study, high school students engaged in peer conferencing received higher writing quality scores on their portfolios than those who received only teacher comments (Simmons, 2003).

Peers can provide helpful feedback, but they need training on both strategies for providing specific, descriptive feedback and on group process skills for working cooperatively with peers (Dahl & Farnan, 1998; Fitzgerald & Stamm, 1990; Patthey-Chavez & Ferris, 1997). Without training, students may only give highly judgmental or negative feedback, or provide only praise out of concern for jeopardizing their social relationships. Trained students are better able to provide constructive feedback that leads to substantive revisions (Berg, 1999; Straub, 1997). One study of response groups composed of college-level, nonnative, and native English speakers illustrates the benefits of such training; while nonnative participants took fewer turns and produced fewer language functions during oral discussion of writing than the native speakers, due to the training, both groups' number of global comments was equivalent (Zhu, 2001). Such training requires a long-term commitment by teachers to continually model and scaffold feedback strategies across an entire school year (Simmons, 2003).

On the other hand, peer comments may not carry as much weight as teacher comments. Some second-language student writers come from cultures that perceive the teacher as the primary authority, so that they do not perceive peers as having authority to provide useful feedback (Nelson & Murphy, 1993). As a result, they may make less use of peer comments in making revisions (Zhang, 1995). However, students may still perceive peer comments as a useful option to just receiving teacher feedback (Jacobs, Curtis, Braine, & Huang, 1998). As Tsui and Ng show (2000), while secondary ELL writers who received both teacher and peer comments indicated that they favored teacher comments, they also valued peer comments for providing them with a clarified sense of audience, an understanding of their strengths and weaknesses, the value of collaborative learning, and a sense of ownership of their writing.

Students may also obtain feedback from school or university writing centers in which tutors receive extensive training on providing feedback (Boquet, 2002; Thanus, 2001). Central to the effectiveness of writing center feedback is the ability of tutors to accommodate to differences in students' abilities and needs, particularly for ELL writers who may not be obtaining assistance in their composition classes (Carino, 2003). Extensive training of tutors can enhance the quality of their feedback to students at high school (Tipper, 1999) and college levels (Friedrich, 2003).

Providing Editing Feedback

Teachers also respond to students' grammar, usage, and mechanics to assist them in editing final drafts for readability and clarity. It is important that such responses occur largely at the editing phase of writing, and not when students are attempting to formulate ideas or organize their drafts (Sommers, 1982). Effective editing feedback in conferences is particularly important in helping second-language students cope with the challenges of English syntax and vocabulary (Connor, 1996; Ferris, 2003; Harklau, Losey, & Siegal, 1999). On the other hand, focusing predominately on students' errors, particularly with less successful or second-language writers, can be counterproductive in that students become hyperconscious about writing for fear of making errors (Connors & Lunsford, 1988; Hull, 1985).

One of the difficulties that writing teachers face in responding to student errors is that they themselves are ambiguous about the validity of certain grammar and usage conventions that underpin "errors" (Anson, 2000; Ferris, 2003). Teachers vary widely relative to what they perceive to be serious errors—their perceptions largely reflect their individual judgments (Connors & Lunsford, 1988). Teachers may also frame errors as reflections of carelessness or incompetence, failing to determine reasons for consistent patterns of errors having to do with students' experimenting with unfamiliar, alternative genres or ways of thinking, both of which often result in increased frequency of errors (Briggs & Pailliotet, 1997; Weaver, 1996).

Teachers also need to respond to students' errors as reflecting particular uses of language, dialects, and registers within specific rhetorical contexts (Hull, 1985). Teachers may frame their responses on issues of language register by focusing on assumptions about writer–audience relationships, as well as on the fact that error is often based on arbitrarily defined social conventions (Horner, 1992; Newman, 1996).

A central question for teachers is whether they should correct students' errors or simply mark errors and have students make the corrections. One study that compared making corrections versus making descriptive comments only, in contrast to providing both corrections and descriptive comments to fifth-grade French-speaking students, found no differences in the effects of these treatments on the accuracy of corrections (Fazio, 2001). Some researchers have found that ELL students make fewer errors if they learn to identify and correct their own errors rather than have their errors corrected by a teacher (Ferris, 2002, 2003; Truscott, 1996). In a study comparing teacher correction of errors versus marking of errors for student self-correction versus describing error types on ELL college students' revisions, both teacher correction and simple underlining of errors were superior to describing the type of error, even with underlining, for reducing use of errors (Chandler, 2003). Teacher correction resulted in the most accurate revisions and was preferred by students for its efficiency, but students indicated that they learned more from self-correction based on teacher underlining of errors, which also requires less teacher time. In another study, ELL college students whose errors were underlined did just as well at self-editing as their peers whose underlined errors were linked to codes for five types of errors (Ferris & Roberts, 2001).

This research points to the value of having students learn to self-correct errors identified by teachers. However, this does not necessarily mean that students actually make appropriate corrections. Teacher correction of errors is most likely to result in accurate editing revisions and is preferred by students for its efficiency (Ferris, 2003). If students can see their errors corrected, they may better understand what constitutes correct revision and need not wait to learn whether their own corrections are accurate. On the other hand, students ultimately need to learn to self-correct on their own (Chandler, 2003; Truscott, 1996). Teachers can also mislabel errors, particularly at the sentence level, requiring a need for a larger "interlanguage perspective"—the ability to use language to organize and order sentences and text units, particularly in terms of reasons for constructing sentences in certain ways (Yates & Kenkel, 2002). This involves having ELL students draw on what they already know about social norms operating in conversations, for example, the need to be relevant in conversations (Grice, 1989), as it relates to determining the relevancy of information in written texts in order to delete irrelevant material.

Summary

The research on teacher response to student writing indicates that without effective feedback, students will not engage in the substantive self-assessment and revision that is essential to learning to improve their writing. Effective teacher feedback is specific, descriptive, nonjudgmental, and varied according to students' phases of development, developmental level, ZPD, language skills, perceived persona, and self-assessment ability. While written comments provide a record of reactions to specific aspects of a draft, teacher face-to-face or online conferences allow for discussion of ideas and practice of self-assessment. Editing feedback needs to encourage students to learn to self-correct, but teachers may also need to provide corrections. The effectiveness of any of this feedback is bolstered by assignments that include criteria, and training on the use of these criteria, as well as the use of trained peer conferences and writing center assistance. All of this points to the centrality of training teachers in effective methods for responding to student writing.

References

Andrade, H. G., & Boulay, B. A. (2003). Role of rubric-referenced self-assessment in learning to write. *Journal of Educational Research*, 97(1), 21–36.

Anson, C. M. (1997). In our own voices: Using recorded commentary to respond to writing. In P. Elbow & M. D. Sorcinelli (Eds.), *Learning to write: Strategies for assigning and responding to writing across the curriculum* (pp. 105–115). San Francisco: Jossey-Bass.

Anson, C. M. (2000). Response and the social construction of error. *Assessing Writing*, 7, 5–21.

Anson, C. M., & Beach, R. (1997). *Writing to learn: Using journals in the classroom.* Norwood, MA: Christopher Gordon.

Ashwell, T. (2000). Patterns of teacher response to student writing in a multiple-draft composition classroom: Is content feedback followed by form feedback the best method? *Journal of Second Language Writing*, 9(3), 227–257.

Atwell, N. (1998). *In the middle: New understandings about writing, reading, and learning* (2nd ed.). Portsmouth, NH: Heinemann.

Bakhtin, M. (1981). The dialogic imagination (C. Emerson & M. Holquist, Trans.). Austin: University of Texas Press.

Bardine, B., Bardine, M., & Deegan, E. (2000). Beyond the red pen: Clarifying our role in the response process. *English Journal*, 90(1), 94–101.

Bauer, E. B., & Garcia, G. E. (2002). Lessons from a classroom teacher's use of alternative literacy assessment. *Research in the Teaching of English*, 36(4), 462–494.

Beach, R. (1976). Self-evaluation strategies of extensive revisers and non-revisers. *College Composition and Communication*, 27, 160–164.

Beach, R. (1989). Showing students how to assess: Demonstrating techniques for response in writing conferences. In C. Anson (Ed.), *Writing and response: Theory, practice, and research* (pp. 127–148). Urbana, IL: National Council of Teachers of English.

Berg, E. C. (1999). The effects of trained peer response on ESL students' revision types and writing quality. *Journal of Second Language Writing*, 8(3), 215–241.

Black, L. J. (1998). *Between talk and teaching: Reconsidering the writing conference.* Logan: Utah State University Press.

Blair, L. (2003). Teaching composition online: No longer the second-best choice. *Kairos*, 8(2). Available online at english.ttu.edu/kairos/8.2/binder. html?praxis/blair/index.html

Boquet, E. (2002). *Noise from the writing center.* Logan: Utah State University Press.

Briggs, L., & Pailliotet, A. W. (1997). A story about grammar and power. *Journal of Basic Writing*, 16(2), 46–61.

Britsch, S. J. (2004). "Riddle me this, riddle me that": Genre as counterscript and the multiple spaces of dialogue. *Language Arts*, 81(3), 214–222.

Broad, B. (2003). *What we really value: Beyond rubrics in teaching and assessing writing.* Logan: Utah State University Press.

Carabajal, K., LaPointe, D., & Gunawardena, C. (2003). Group development in online learning communities. In M. G. Moore & W. G. Anderson (Eds.), *Handbook of distance education* (pp. 224–238). Mahwah, NJ: Erlbaum.

Carino, P. (2003). Power and authority in peer tutoring. In M. Pemberton & J. Kinkead (Eds.), *The center will hold: Critical perspectives on writing center scholarship* (pp. 96–113). Logan: Utah State University Press.

Chandler, J. (2003). The efficacy of various kinds of error feedback for improvement in the accuracy and fluency of L2 student writing. *Journal of Second Language Writing*, 12(3), 267–296.

Chapman, M. L. (1999). Situated, social, active: Rewriting genre in the elementary classroom. *Written Communication*, 16(4), 469–490.

Christian, B. (2000). The read-around alternative to peer groups. *Teaching English in the Two-Year College*, 27(3), 308–311.

Connor, U. (1996). *Contrastive rhetoric: Cross-cultural aspects of second-language writing.* New York: Cambridge University Press.

Connors, R. J., & Lunsford, A. (1988). Frequency of formal errors in current college writing, or Ma and Pa Kettle do research. *College Composition and Communication, 39*(4), 395–409.

Conrad, S. M., & Goldstein, L. M. (1999). ESL student revision after teacher-written comments: Text, contexts, and individuals. *Journal of Second Language Writing, 8*(3), 257–276.

Crank, V. (2002). Asynchronous electronic peer response in a hybrid basic writing classroom. *Teaching English in the Two-Year College, 30*(2), 145–155.

Dahl, K., & Farnan, N. (1998). *Children's writing: Perspectives from research.* Newark, DE: International Reading Association.

Delpit, L. (1995). *Other people's children: Cultural conflicts in the classroom.* New York: New Press.

Elbow, P. (1981). *Writing with power.* New York: Oxford University Press.

Faigley, L., & Witte, S. (1981). Analyzing revision. *College Composition and Communication, 32,* 400–414.

Fathman, A., & Whalley, E., 1990. Teacher response to student writing: Focus on form versus content. In B. Kroll (Ed.), *Second language writing: Research insights for the classroom* (pp. 178–190). New York: Cambridge University Press.

Fazio, L. L. (2001). The effect of corrections and commentaries on the journal writing accuracy of minority- and majority-language students. *Journal of Second Language Writing, 10*(4), 235–249.

Ferris, D. R. (1995). Student reaction to teacher response in multiple-draft composition classrooms. *TESOL Quarterly, 29,* 33–53.

Ferris, D. R. (1997). The influence of teacher commentary on student revision. *TESOL Quarterly, 31,* 315–339.

Ferris, D. R. (2002). *Treatment of error in second language student writing.* Ann Arbor: University of Michigan Press.

Ferris, D. R. (2003). *Response to student writing: Implications for second language students.* Mahwah, NJ: Erlbaum.

Ferris, D. R., & Roberts, B. (2001). Error feedback in L2 writing classes: How explicit does it need to be? *Journal of Second Language Writing, 10*(3), 161–184.

Fitzgerald, J. (1992). *Towards knowledge in writing: Illustrations from revision studies.* New York: Springer-Verlag.

Fitzgerald, J., & Stamm, C. (1990). Effects of group conferences on first graders' revision in writing. *Written Communication, 7*(1), 96–135.

Flash, P. (2002). Responding to students' writing. Minneapolis: University of Minnesota Center for the Study of Writing. Available online at cisw.cla.umn.edu/faculty/responding/index.htm

Flower, L. S., Hayes, J. R., Carey, L., Schriver, K., & Stratman, J. (1986). Detection, diagnosis, and the strategies of revision. *College, Composition, and Communication, 37*(1), 16–55.

Flower, L. S., Long, E., & Higgins, L. (2000). *Learning to rival: A literate practice for intercultural inquiry.* Mahwah, NJ: Erlbaum.

Frank, C. R. (2001). What new things these words can do for you: A focus on one writing-project teacher and writing instruction. *Journal of Literacy Research, 33*(3), 467–506.

Friedrich, T. (2003, March). *Tutors authoring transformation: Comparing peer tutors' responses to two self-evaluative projects as a means for charting shifts in subjectivity.* Paper presented at the Conference on College Composition and Communication, New York, NY.

Glasswell, K. (2001). Matthew effects in writing: The patterning of difference in classrooms K–8. *Reading Research Quarterly, 36,* 348–349.

Graham, S., Harris, K., Fink-Chorzempa, B., & MacArthur, C. (2003). Primary grade teachers' instructional adaptations for struggling writers: A national survey. *Journal of Educational Psychology, 95*(2), 279–292.

Grice, H. P. (1989). *Studies in the way of words.* Cambridge, MA: Harvard University Press.

Harris, J. (2003). Opinion: Revision as a critical practice. *College English, 65*(6), 577–592.

Harklau, L., Losey, K., & Siegal, M. (1999). *Generation 1.5 meets college composition: Issues in the teaching of writing to U.S.-educated learners of ESL.* Mahwah, NJ: Erlbaum.

Hewett, B. L. (2000). Characteristics of interactive oral and computer-mediated peer group talk and its influence on revision. *Computers and Composition, 17*(3), 265–288.

Hillocks, G. (1996). *Research on written composition.* Urbana, IL: National Council of Teachers of English.

Horner, B. (1992). Rethinking the "sociality" of error: Teaching editing as negotiation. *Rhetoric Review, 11*(1), 172–199.

Huang, J. (2000). A quantitative analysis of audiotaped and written feedback produced for students' writing and students' perceptions of the two feedback methods. *Tunghai Journal, 41,* 199–232.

Hull, G. (1985). Research on error and correction. In B. McClelland & T. R. Donovan (Eds.), *Perspectives on research and scholarship in composition* (pp. 162–184). New York: Modern Language Association.

Hyland, F. (1998). The impact of teacher written feedback on individual writers. *Journal of Second Language Writing, 7,* 255–287.

Jacobs, G. M., Curtis, A., Braine, G., & Huang, S. (1998). Feedback on student writing: Taking the middle path. *Journal of Second Language Writing 7*(3), 307–317.

Johnston, B. (1983). *Assessing writing*. Urbana, IL: National Council of Teachers of English.

Kepner, C.G. (1991). An experiment in the relationship of types of written feedback to the development of second-language writing skills. *Modern Language Journal, 75*(3), 305–313.

Kent, T. (1993). *Paralogic rhetoric*. London: Associated University Press.

Larson, J., & Maier, M. (2000). Co-authoring classroom texts: Shifting participant roles in writing activity. *Research in the Teaching of English, 34*(4), 468–497.

Lee, A. (2000). *Composing critical pedagogies: Teaching writing as revision*. Urbana, IL: National Council of Teachers of English.

Leitão, S. (2003). Evaluating and selecting counterarguments: Studies of children's rhetorical awareness. *Written Communication, 20*(3), 269–306.

Lensmire, T. (2002). *Powerful writing, responsible teaching*. New York: Teachers College Press.

Liu, J., & Sadler, R. W. (2003). The effect and affect of peer review in electronic versus traditional modes on L2 writing. *Journal of English for Academic Purposes, 2*(3), 193–227.

Marshall, J. (1987). The effects of writing on students' understanding of literary texts. *Research in the Teaching of English, 21*(1), 30–63.

Melby-Mauer, J. (2003). Using e-mail assignments and online correction in ESL instruction. *TESOL Journal, 12*(2), 37–38.

Mellen, C., & Sommers, J. (2003). Audiotaped response and the two-year-campus writing classroom: The two-sided desk, the "guy with the ax," and the chirping birds. *Teaching English in the Two-Year College, 31*(1), 25–39.

Mlynarczyk, R. W. (1996). Finding grandma's words: A case study in the art of revising. *Journal of Basic Writing, 15*(1), 3–22.

Matsumura, L. C., Patthey-Chavez, G. G., & Valdes, R. (2002). Teacher feedback, writing assignment quality, and third-grade students' revision in lower- and higher-achieving urban schools. *Elementary School Journal, 103*(1), 3–25.

Moran, M. (1997). Connections between reading and successful revision. *Journal of Basic Writing, 16*(2), 76–89.

National Writing Project. (2003). *Because writing matters: Improving student writing in our schools*. San Francisco: Jossey-Bass.

Nelson, G. L., & Carson, J. (1998). ESL students' perceptions of effective peer response groups. *Journal of Second Language Writing, 7*(2), 113–131.

Nelson, G. L., & Murphy, J. M. (1993). Peer response groups: Do L2 writers use peer comments in revising their drafts? *TESOL Quarterly, 27*(1), 135–142.

Newman, M. (1996). Correctness and its conceptions: The meaning of language form for basic writers. *Journal of Basic Writing, 15*(1), 23–38.

Nickel, J. (2001). When writing conferences don't work: Students' retreat from teacher agenda. *Language Arts, 79*(2), 136–147.

Patthey-Chavez, G. G., & Ferris, D. (1997). Writing conferences and the weaving of multi-voiced texts in college composition. *Research in the Teaching of English, 31*(1), 51–90.

Power, B., & Hubbard, R. (1999). Becoming teacher researchers one moment at a time. *Language Arts, 77*(1), 34–39.

Schneider, J. J. (2003). Contexts, genres, and imagination: An examination of the idiosyncratic writing performances of three elementary children within multiple contexts of writing instruction. *Research in the Teaching of English, 37*(3), 329–379.

Sheehy, M. (2003). The social life of an essay: Standardizing forces in writing. *Written Communication, 20*(3), 333–385.

Simmons, J. (2003). Responders are taught, not born. *Journal of Adolescent and Adult Literacy 46*(8), 684–693.

Smith, S. (1997). The genre of the end comment: Conventions in teacher responses to student writing. *College Composition and Communication, 48*(2), 249–268.

Sommers, N. (1982). Responding to student writing. *College Composition and Communication, 33*(2), 148–156.

Sperling, M., & Freedman, S. W. (1987). A good girl writes like a good girl: Written responses to student writing. *Written Communication, 9*(9), 342–369.

Storch, N., & Tapper, J. (2000). The focus of teacher and student concerns in discipline-specific writing by university students. *Higher Education Research and Development, 19*(3), 337–355.

Straub, R. (1996). The concept of control in teacher response: Defining the varieties of "directive" and "facilitative" commentary. *College Composition and Communication, 47*(2), 223–251.

Straub, R. (1997). Students' reactions to teacher comments: An exploratory study. *Research in the Teaching of English, 31*(1), 91–119.

Sweeney, M. (1999). Relating revision skills to teacher commentary. *Teaching English in the Two-Year College, 27*(2), 213–218.

Taylor, R. (2002). "Reading what students have written": A case study from the basic writing course. *READER, 46*, 32–49.

Thanus, T. (2001). Triangulation in the writing center: Tutor, tutee, and instructor perceptions of the tutor's role. *Writing Center Journal, 22*(1), 59–82.

Tipper, M. (1999). Real men don't do writing centers. *Writing Center Journal, 19*(2), 33–40.

Todd, R., Mills, N., Palard, C., & Khamcharoen, P. (2001). Giving feedback on journals. *ELT Journal, 55*(4), 354–359.

Truscott, J. (1996). The case against grammar correction in L2 writing classes. *Language Learning, 46*(2), 327–369.

Tsui, A. B. M., & Ng, M. (2000). Do secondary L2 writers benefit from peer comments? *Journal of Second Language Writing, 9*(2), 147–170.

Vygotsky, L. (1978). *Mind in society.* Cambridge, MA: Harvard University Press.

Van Gelderen, A. (1997). Elementary students' skills in revising: Integrating quantitative and qualitative analysis. *Written Communication, 14*(3), 360–397.

Wallace, D. L., & Hayes, J. R. (1992). Redefining revision for freshman. In J. R. Hayes (Ed.), *Reading empirical research studies: The rhetoric of research* (pp. 349–370). Hillsdale, NJ: Erlbaum.

Weaver, C. (1996). *Teaching grammar in context.* Portsmouth, NH: Boynton/Cook.

Welch, N. (1997). *Getting restless: Rethinking revision in writing instruction.* Portsmouth, NH: Boynton/Cook.

White, E. (1999). *Assigning, responding, evaluating: A writing teacher's guide* (3rd ed.). Boston: Bedford/St. Martin's.

Williams, S. C. (2002). How speech-feedback and word-prediction software can help students write. *Teaching Exceptional Children, 34*(3), 72–78.

Yagelski, R. (1995). The role of classroom context in the revision strategies of student writers. *Research in the Teaching of English, 29,* 216–338.

Yates, R., & Kenkel, J. (2002). Responding to sentence-level errors in writing. *Journal of Second Language Writing, 11*(1), 29–47.

Zhang, S. (1995). Re-examining the affective advantage of peer feedback in the ESL writing class. *Journal of Second Language Writing, 4*(3), 209–222.

Zhu, W. (2001). Interaction and feedback in mixed peer response groups. *Journal of Second Language Writing, 10*(4), 251–276.

Zimmerman, B., & Kitsantas, A. (2002). Acquiring writing revision and self-regulatory skill through observation and emulation. *Journal of Educational Psychology, 94*(4), 660–668.

Chapter 16

Writing to Learn
How Alternative Theories of School Writing Account for Student Performance

George E. Newell

What are the promises and challenges of empirical and theoretical studies of writing to learn, especially in light of recent efforts to consider how mental functioning is mediated by cultural, institutional, and disciplinary contexts (Wertsch, 1998)? This chapter addresses three general areas of research that are relevant to the question of the relationship between writing and learning in school contexts. First, rather than being a more efficient way to cover content and test for memory of that content, writing assignments can become ways of exploring and making sense of new ideas and experiences (Langer & Applebee, 1987; Marshall, 1987; Newell, 1984; Newell & Winograd, 1995). Second, with more efforts to teach writing in all content areas, students may become more aware of a full range of conventions and genres used in various contexts, especially in the discourse communities of various academic disciplines (Langer, 1992; Rose, 1989; Sheeran & Barnes, 1991). Third, writing-to-learn approaches to instruction alter the roles of both the teacher (from evaluator to collaborator) and students (from memorizers to meaning makers) and transform the content area information as facts to be absorbed into ways of understanding ourselves and our cultural communities through the study of various academic traditions (Applebee, 1996; Moje & O'Brien, 2001; Jones, Turner, & Street, 1999).

Theoretical Models

Some Common Ground: Constructivist Notions of Teaching and Learning

In spite of rather convincing arguments for the value of writing in academic learning, two interrelated issues have plagued writing to learn reforms. First, earlier conceptions of writing-to-learn based on process-oriented writing instruction neglected the fundamental issue of "what constitutes learning," focusing instead on the development of new activities and routines. Accordingly, "transmission" views of teaching and learning that emphasize memorization and recitation co-opted the more learner-centered underpinnings of writing for which theorists such as Janet Emig, James Britton, Donald Graves and Nancy Martin had argued. Second, although writing-to-learn approaches have provided insights into the role of writing as a tool for learning, they have largely ignored some of the unique ways of knowing and doing in various academic disciplines. This has led to two assumptions: (1) that writing should be the primary concern of the English teacher, who has the responsibility to teach generic strategies and forms for writing; and (2) that writing has no practical relevance to instruction in other content areas. Accordingly, any reform will have to consider not only how students make sense of disciplinary ways of knowing and doing but also the realities of schooling (e.g., testing) that often complicate shifts toward such fundamental change. The challenge is to develop a coherent view of teaching and learning that offers a conceptually powerful way of supporting process-oriented, learner-centered approaches to writing, as well as one that gives teachers an overarching framework for thinking about issues of teaching and learning in the content areas.

To offer new ways of conceptualizing models of teaching and learning, many educators and scholars are turning to constructivist theories of language and learning. With roots in fields as diverse as psychology, linguistics, sociology, history of science, and philosophy, constructivist approaches share a view of knowledge as an active construction, although some approaches focus on the constructions of individuals, whereas others focus on the construction of groups and even larger communities. A key principle of such a framework is that rather than viewing the content of the academic disciplines and students' learning as separate concerns, a constructivist sees learning in context—how knowledge develops within particular instructional contexts when students are actively engaged, such as, for example, when they take positions on topics and issues presented by others. This view of teaching and learning is compatible with some of the motives underlying process-oriented approaches to writing instruction, and it offers, in a principled way, a description of effective teaching and learning.

What then are some of tenets of constructivism that are relevant to a reconsideration of the role of writing to learn in the secondary school? Although constructivism has been discussed and examined from a range of perspectives, the view employed in much of the writing and learning theory and research has its roots in James Britton's (1970) discussions of the role of language in learning and in Douglas Barnes's (1992) notion of the "interpretation" view of learning, each of which integrates the act of communication with the process of knowing. Britton (1970) has argued that uses of expressive language (freewriting, journal keeping, etc.) in which the demands of formality are relaxed and audiences' judgments withheld are at once unstructured and open-ended, revelatory of the writer's own thinking, and com-

municative only to the extent that the writer and reader have a shared context. As an example of how interpretive teaching might foster students' active construction of meaning, Barnes (1992) has described the value of "exploratory talk." Barnes's analysis of successful small-group discussions indicates that the language students use in such contexts tends to be "marked by frequent hesitations, rephrasings, false starts and change of direction. . . . That is, such exploratory talk is one means by which the assimilation and accommodation of new knowledge to old is carried out" (p. 28).

Although the genesis of expressive uses of language and exploratory talk are part of a longer tradition of language and learning, they have come to represent elements of a larger orientation toward literacy instruction, often referred to as "process-oriented approaches." Such a view of teaching and learning has roots in constructivist approaches to learning in that it is based on the assumption that learning is not linear and sequential but instead involves false starts and tentative explorations. Understanding will grow and change as learning progresses. Premature evaluation will short-circuit the process and stall risk taking.

In the context of American schools and colleges, the works of Barnes and Britton have been instrumental in countering transmission approaches that Applebee (1996) has described as "knowledge-out-of-context" and as an "emphasis on memorization and rote learning." On the other hand, a more constructivist orientation toward teaching and learning can be described as "knowledge-in-action," that is, as ways of knowing that are a confluence of past and current ideas, concerns, and discussion. "Knowledge-in-action shapes our expectations about the future as well as our interpretation of the past" (Applebee, 1996, pp. 16–17).

This view of curriculum and instruction is developed more fully later in this chapter. My point for the moment is that when writing is construed as specialized genres that offer new ways of knowing and doing, the role of "literate thinking" is expanded and deepened to include both the learning of content and the process of critical analysis. However, given that transmission views of teaching and learning still are currently the common sense of schooling and the larger culture of which schools are a part, to implement writing-to-learn reforms requires a new perspective—which John Mayher (1990) has called "uncommon sense"—to guide teaching and learning toward constructivist orientations. As a field, composition has much work to do; to this point, the notion of writing to learn has been based more on favorite activities such as freewriting or dialogue journals rather than on broad principles of effective teaching across the content areas.

Thus far, this discussion of constructivist notions of writing to learn has assumed, as have many of my own studies, that writing is largely a psychological event that occurs within a social setting. A social-constructionist view, however, views writing as social events (not merely located in a social context) rather than simply psychological processes or a set of shared cognitive constructs mediated by social factors.

> When people interact with each other, which is what happens when people engage in reading and writing, they act on the world and they do so materially and historically, and this is so even when the substance of their interactions and actions is language. It is because social interaction is material and historical that reading and writing always involve a social and cultural ideology. (Bloome, 2001, p. 291)

The notion of writing and learning as social processes that establish how writing events are constituted and what their consequences may be has significance for all students, but especially for those students who find themselves at the bottom of the social, cultural, or political hierarchy. Given that American schools are founded in the basis of tolerance, diversity, nonsectarianism, and inclusiveness, and their academic mission is often defined in terms of thoughtfulness, reflection, and creativity, it seems clear that any agenda for writing and learning must likewise reflect such values.

A Functionalist Approach: "Writing Is Not Writing Is Not Writing"

As this aphorism taken from Langer and Applebee's (1987) study of school writing tasks warns, discussions of writing as learning go astray when they neglect to specify the kinds of learning various writing tasks might be expected to foster. Accordingly, in this section I continue the discussion of a theory of writing to learn, with a brief overview of Britton's and Applebee's theories of school writing tasks. I then review several key studies that have employed writing tasks developed from Britton's writing function system in order to understand the types of learning fostered by a range of writing tasks. If there is a point to be made in this part of the discussion, it is that not all writing tasks are equal, and that teachers' instructional decisions regarding when, how, and why to use writing-to-learn activities should depend on the kinds of learning in which they wish to engage their students.

In developing a discourse scheme for understanding the cognitive and linguistic demands of writing, Britton Burgess, Martin, McLeod, and Rosen (1975) based their theory on language function, that is, the universe of possible uses of language in general and written language in particular. Writing teachers are perhaps more familiar with the traditional modes of discourse—narration, description, exposition, argumentation, and sometimes poetry. Because these categories of writing assignments are based largely on fully formed, preordained structures rather than on the nature of the task itself or the demands it makes on the writer, Britton looked to extant theories of language function and intention to explore the intellectual value and complexities of school writing. For Britton, writing within a particular function (e.g., to tell a story, to report on an event) enables writers to organize meaning around intention and language use.

Beginning with the "great divide" between informational uses of writing on the one hand and poetic or literary uses on the other, the Britton et al. (1975) system proposed three main functions: transaction, expressive, and poetic. The transaction function includes expository and persuasive writing, with subcategories that constitute an abstractive scale from reporting to summarizing, analyzing, and theorizing. The expressive function is best understood as corresponding to informal talk among friends, where the rules of use are relaxed. The poetic function is essentially the literary uses of language as in poetry, fictional narratives, and drama used to represent the writer's experiences, and, in turn, a virtual experience for the reader. Applebee (1981, 1984a), in his adaptation of Britton's system, renamed the three overall categories as "informational," "personal," and "imaginative." He also refined and extended the system to include subcategories for both personal and imaginative writing, and streamlined and reconceptualized the subcategories for informational writing to characterize writing in American schools more accurately. Because his classroom observations and survey research revealed that a great deal of school writing required no composing, Applebee also added a category for "restricted" uses of writing, such as multiple-choice and short-answer exercises.

HOW WRITING SHAPES THINKING AND LEARNING

Thus far, my argument for the role of writing in academic learning has presumed a general or global effect of writing; that is, the process of writing will somehow lead inevitably to a better understanding of information gleaned from texts or from a teacher's presentation. As experienced writing teachers know, however, different writing assignments ask students to engage with ideas, information, and experiences in differing ways: Outlining the contents a book chapter is typically less demanding than selecting specific ideas from the same chapter for critical analysis. Consequently, writing research has examined under what conditions students learn from writing about texts, including the reasoning processes that accompany the generation and reformulation of ideas that enable students to understand and remember the information they read. The kind of understanding referred to in studies of the effects of writing function is conceptual, that is, knowledge of the concepts and the relationships among concepts gleaned from reading passages in a range of content areas. Note that this brief review is limited to writing about social studies texts in the secondary school and involves writing about a single reading passage (see reviews of other work in Ackerman, 1993; Bangert-Drowns, Hurley, & Wilkinson, 2004; Durst & Newell, 1989; McGinley & Tierney, 1989).

One caveat is that in the few studies of writing and learning from texts that have measured students' prior understanding of key concepts in reading passages, students' knowledge affects writing quality and influences how well they can organize their written responses (Langer, 1984a; Langer & Applebee, 1987; Newell & Winograd, 1995). For example, if students' knowledge of key concepts in a reading passage is well organized, they may be able to complete more complex tasks that require, for instance, a comparison and contrast of relevant ideas. If their knowledge is less well organized but extensive, then merely listing supporting evidence for a thesis is more manageable. Again, studies of the effects of prior knowledge on writing suggest that the teacher's instructional decision should consider what the students bring to the task: An effort to help students generate new information before writing may be significant or wasted depending on how well informed they are about the topic at hand.

This section examines the effects of three types of writing as described by Britton's (with Applebee's modifications) discourse theory: restricted writing (tasks requiring little or no composing; e.g., answering study questions), summary writing, and analytic writing. These three types of writing are not only assigned often in secondary schools but they also represent three distinct ways to engage students in thinking and reasoning about what they are assigned to read in various content areas. The underlying assumption that frames this discussion is that the extent to which information is manipulated enhances topic understanding. For example, writing tasks require more time to complete and more active engagement with the content of a reading passage than do nonwriting tasks such as mental review of a reading passage. In general, engagement is associated with the constraints of the writing task: Essay writing makes more demands on the writer than does answering study questions or fill-in-the-blank exercises. Accordingly, the greater the range of composing processes a writing task engenders, the more likely the writer will focus on the relationships among the ideas that give them coherence and structure, and thus develop more coherent topic understanding. A second assumption is that different tasks focus the writer's attention in specific ways, and the effects of writing on learning from text are limited to the ideas that are expressed during composing. For example, summarizing a reading passage is more likely to focus the writer's attention on a wide range of ideas but only superficially compared to analytic writing which is more likely to focus the writer's attention on a narrower range of ideas but in more substantial ways.

In answering study questions (assigned by the teacher or included in a textbook), students are usually asked to do so with a brief statement that suggests specific information in the passage. In the following excerpt from a transcript of a student thinking aloud while responding to a study question, we can see how the task shapes the student's responses to a reading passage.

What are the major manufacturing industries in the United Sates at the turn of the century? Uhm, looking down the page, factors of growth. No it's under. I'm reading over. I don't see any. . . . They're looking for specific factors uhhh, ok, I found it at the bottom of the page. In 1900, for example, the main manufacturing industries were meat packing. . . . (in Langer & Applebee, 1987, p. 97)

The student begins by reading the question, then searches for relevant information, reconsiders the question, and locates the answer in the text. Considering that this process is largely a transcription rather than an elaborated interpretation of the information, when might such a task be pedagogically useful? My own studies of teaching with writing (Newell, 1984; Newell & Winograd, 1995) suggest that study questions can provide useful means for students to prepare for a more complex task or to review several elements of a text prior to class discussion. As a learning tool per se, answering study questions is more appropriate for short-term retention of facts used to prepare for a more conceptually demanding task.

Summary writing can also provide the classroom teacher with a tool for reviewing previous learning or preparing for new tasks. However, when summarizing, students must consider text-based information somewhat differently than what is required by answering study questions. Two types of plans are necessary: plans for combining and integrating information from the text, and plans for representing the organization of the text in a succinct way. Studies of summarizing have

revealed that although students order information paragraph-by-paragraph, leading them to search for relationships among ideas, this task can result in a superficial understanding of content (Hidi & Anderson, 1986; Durst, 1987; Langer & Applebee, 1987). Analysis of the written products of summarizing suggest why this happens. Rather than evaluation or analysis of ideas, summaries begin with highly distilled descriptions of events and ideas discussed in a reading passage that then introduce more specific information. Although summarizing enables students to get a comprehensive or "bird's-eye view" of the information, such tasks tend to represent only the major ideas in a temporal order (as they occur in the reading passage), leading to only short-term retention of those ideas.

What then are the alternatives to tasks that require virtually no composing, or require restatements or paraphrasing of a reading passage? How might teachers, for example, foster students' reformulations and extensions of what they have read? How does this kind of learning differ from short-term recall of information? In secondary schools an entire range of both formal and informal writing assignments can be described as "analytic." In literature classrooms, this might entail explaining a character's motives; a history teacher might ask students to explain the significance of a historical event; and in science, students might be asked to examine the implications of weak environmental policies. In each case, students are required to move beyond transcribing selected information or summary statements to a more specific or focused explanations of why people behave as they do, or why specific ideas may be flawed or convincing.

With analytic writing, students have access to a different tool for understanding new ideas and information: a focused examination of relations among ideas and events. Across a set of studies anchored in Britton's discourse theory (Durst, 1987; Greene, 1993; Langer & Applebee, 1987; Marshall, 1987; Newell, 1984; Newell & Winograd, 1995), a consistent pattern has emerged of the kinds of thinking and reasoning fostered by analytic writing: a complex manipulation of ideas as a result of marshaling an argument to support a point of view and selecting language for representing it. Although analytic writing focuses on a narrower range of content in the reading passage when compared to tasks such as answering study questions or summarizing, a more lasting intellectual representation of that content seems to develop through an integration and reformulation of ideas.

These findings for the effects of various writing tasks raise an important issue that Peter Winograd and I (1995) articulated when we studied a U.S. history teacher's pedagogical uses of writing in a general track class and an academic track class. She worried that with analytic writing her general track students would have reviewed less information than if she assigned more review and summary tasks more regularly. This was exacerbated by the fact that her academic students were much better informed before they wrote analytically about U.S. history. "Knowing information and writing about it go hand-in-hand, but I still feel pressure— maybe it's just me—to make sure they know certain things and when they don't I try to get them caught up" (p. 160). The teacher's dilemma lies in deciding not only which writing task to assign but also how to balance content coverage with students' efforts to make sense of the content. This becomes a very real and important practical problem when teaching is conceived as content coverage and learning, as absorbing information, a view that is a legacy of building-block and transmission notions of curriculum and instruction (Langer, 1984b).

This discussion is intended not as a criticism of a particular teacher but to describe how a tradition of curriculum that Applebee (1996) has deemed "deadly" can shape a teacher's instructional decisions, in this case, a teacher who by all accounts was concerned by her students' independence as thinkers. Winograd and I concluded that for analytic writing tasks that ask students to reformulate and extend their understanding to have purchase in secondary schools, a large set of curricular problems needs to be resolved. Rather than just calling for more writing or for reading–writing connections, we suggested a broader analysis of what is essential to knowing and doing in each subject area, and of how such knowledge might be introduced in a coherent manner across the school year and across grade levels. To do so

implies a new set of promises and a new vision of what it means to teach and to learn in school settings.

After reading and analyzing the development in theory, research, and practice in writing to learn over a 25-year period, John Ackerman (1993) concluded that although it has been promised, we have yet to make an argument for writing to learn. Both Ackerman and Applebee (1984b) warned that "strong text" (Brandt, 1990; Street, 1984; Heath, 1983) versions of writing may simplistically assume that all writing is learning and that learning while writing may occur only under certain contextual conditions. A recent meta-analysis that studied the effects of writing on learning within a range of contexts provides more evidence that simply assigning more writing during classroom instruction does not automatically lead to learning—some studies even report negative effects for writing. Specifically, the project examined the results of 48 studies of students in elementary school, middle school, high school, and college in math, literature, social studies, sociology, earth science, chemistry, biology, history, and various professions (Bangert-Drowns et al., 2004). The analysis revealed that informational writing has a small, positive impact on "conventional measures of academic achievement"— 36 of the 48 studies yielded positive effects for writing. Perhaps most interesting in light of the long-standing beliefs derived from the British Model of writing to learn (Russell, 1991) is that learning from writing occurs

> at least in part, not so much from helping students find links between the content and their personal experiences as from scaffolding metacognitve processes, presumably in the service of developing self-regulation of learning strategies. Writing interventions in which students were asked to reflect on their current understandings, confusions, and learning processes typically yielded more positive results. (pp. 51– 52)

This finding suggests a more precise explanation of the effects of writing on learning in that instructional contexts that required students to reflect on what and how they understood the topic of their writing, what they found confusing, and what they were learning yielded positive results. Accordingly, the instructional contexts that teachers create for writing in various content areas and their concern for supporting their students with "metacogntive scaffolding" over long periods of time are significant implications of this meta-analysis of writing and learning. Additionally, the authors of the study suggest that the relationship between writing and learning might be better understood by sustained attention to contextual factors. "Qualitative research designs might be helpful for understanding the meanings that teachers and students bring to writing, how those meanings shift in the context of writing to learn, and how writing to learn changes students' relations with each other, with their teachers, and with the content they study" (p. 52).

Writing as a Way of Learning the Structure of Disciplinary Thought

The studies reviewed thus far focus mainly on the diverse purposes for writing, and it is clear that the functionalist view asserts that particular tasks both require and foster particular types of knowledge. Yet another way to envision the role of writing in school learning holds that even if one accepts the need for learning the various functions of writing, writers in different contexts and communities produce texts of similar structure in quite different ways because of the demands and customs of the particular communities in which they participate (Bizzell, 1992). Langer and Applebee (1987) have suggested that teachers need to know about the components of the disciplines they are teaching. After studying secondary teachers in a range of content areas over a 2-year period, they argued that teachers in disciplines other than English need to understand what is unique about writing that is specific to their discipline. (For a critique of the privileged status of writing as a psychological tool for the development of discipline-specific thinking and reasoning, see Smagorinsky, 1995.) Accordingly, in this section I examine theoretical and empirical work focused on the complexities of teaching and learning writing across the curriculum in the secondary school in particular. The assumption is that a variety of current problems in American education stem from an unrealistically narrow conceptualization of the nature of academic learning—one that

fails to take into consideration the uniquely discipline-specific ways of reasoning.

Two British scholars, Yanina Sheeran and Douglas Barnes (1991), have argued that one way to explain the differences in school success between working-class and middle-class children is that the latter have access to "ground rules" for what counts as academic success. Sheeran and Barnes discuss different types of ground rules: general rules for schooling as a whole (e.g., punctuality), for specific teachers (e.g., always type papers), and for particular subject areas or disciplines, such as conventions for a genre (e.g., a laboratory report in chemistry). Although such ground rules are for many students the commonplaces of schooling, they may not be for students who are not from privileged or middle-class backgrounds. Given that most people generally organize their behavior in familiar cultural situations (Grice, 1975), unstated ground rules may not seem unusual or problematic. However, in the context of schooling in which evaluations, both formal and informal, abound, the stakes are quite high, and students often pose the question, "What does the teacher really want?" And the teacher's response may not always be that helpful: The conceptualization of the nature of academic learning in American schools is typically underconceptualized in that it fails to take the uniquely discipline-specific ways of reasoning and writing into account (Langer & Applebee, 1987). Although teachers may be completely aware of how particular content knowledge differs across content areas, they do not always know the ways of reasoning that are appropriate and necessary for learning and understanding within the particular field (Langer, 1991).

Although Langer (1992) does not refer to "ground rules" for successful writing and knowing in academic disciplines, her study can be construed as a seminal effort to do so from three different perspectives: how writing and knowing are presented in the theoretical literature within the disciplines (biology, history, and literature), how they are emphasized in the pedagogical literature, and how teachers conceptualize the teaching of ground rules for academic knowing. As a result of critically reviewing the notions of disciplinarity from these three perspectives, Langer concluded that "in light of such results, previous findings about students' inability to engage in critical thinking in a variety of academic subjects come as no surprise. Students are unlikely to be learning how to gather evidence and develop effective arguments when their teachers (and the field in general) have not articulated such concerns to themselves" (1992, p. 84). In a follow-up study, Langer, Confer, and Sawyer (1993) examined ways of knowing and reasoning in academic course work (American literature, American history, biology, and physics), and the ways in which teachers' general goals are realized in their subject-specific pedagogical strategies. Using a case study approach, Langer, her research assistants, and eight high school teachers met as a collaborative team to consider similarities and differences in the teachers' goals and activities. The research assistants also observed and interviewed the teachers for in-depth considerations of the teachers' classroom practices. They also focused on issues surrounding students' reasoning and on ways to identify and talk about thinking in each subject area. Their findings were more positive than they had anticipated: Discipline-specific reasoning was being taught. However, the teachers did not recognize this reasoning in overt and explicit ways. Moreover, the teachers' disciplinary concerns (e.g., selecting evidence in biology) competed "with the more general pedagogical notions that are part of the field of education" (p. 38). In their conclusions, Langer and her associates raised the issue of how to foster wider change in teaching and learning that includes consideration of discipline-specific thinking and the sustainability of such a reform.

One Writing Across the Curriculum (WAC) movement at the secondary school level has achieved national recognition and even federal funding: the National Writing Project (NWP). Beginning in 1971 at the University of California at Berkeley, as the Bay Area Writing Project, instructors and administrators began a program to improve the writing of college freshmen by improving secondary school writing instruction. Rejecting the idea of supplying secondary teachers with "teacher-proof" materials or prescribing new methods using expert outsiders, the NWP's key to success is providing a forum for experienced and successful teachers to exchange ideas about writing instruction in a collegial

atmosphere. An effort is made to create the best blend of teachers' practical knowledge of schools and students and current composition theory and practice that seem relevant to writing in schools (Barr & Healy, 1988).

Gere's (1985) *Roots in the Sawdust* represents an example of a successful effort to do so. Classroom teachers from the Puget Sound Writing Program each contributed chapters to document the potential of writing-to-learn activities to transform classroom life. For the most part, these activities are informal in nature—response statements, freewriting, and journals—and short and ungraded. But there are also more formal assignments suggested that require attention to formal constraints such as writing for more critical and distant audiences. The essays in *Roots in the Sawdust* are each in their own right thoughtful excursions into the minds and classrooms of seemingly effective teachers, and each represents the best example of what has been described as "reflective practice." Yet one element that is overlooked in Gere's introduction and in the contributors' essays is that writing-to-learn assignments are likely to represent but a single element in a larger of configuration of social elements at work in the teachers' practices. For instance, each essay assumes the value of an intellectual community in classrooms, where students feel they can contribute to an ongoing exploration of ideas and experiences. Such a context seems just as necessary to successful teaching and learning as do imaginative writing and reading assignments.

A Sociocultural Turn: Writing as Academic Literacy Practice

At this point, I want to consider further a challenge to the idea that writing has exclusive and inherent potential as a mediational tool for developing thinking and understanding in all contexts for all people. Taking a sociocultural turn, Ackerman (1993) points out that writing in and of itself may or may not serve as a tool to promote learning. Although writing may at least potentially serve as a means for the development of thought, it can only do so within the complex and rich social contexts that have been restructured according to teachers' conceptions of learning and the school's values. To Ackerman, the writing-to-learn activities themselves are but one part of a complex set of values emerging out of social transactions that may lead to the success of process-oriented approaches to learning.

This point seems to be borne out in Bangert-Drowns et al.'s (2004) meta-analysis of the effects of writing-to-learn interventions on academic learning. Anchoring their claims in studies of metacognition, the researchers concluded,

> One might expect that, if the effectiveness of writing-to-learn is a result of metacognitive scaffolding, then longer-term treatments that give students more time to become adept at self-evaluation and perhaps even internalize a self-reflective posture would result in improved effectiveness. There is some evidence in this review that, in fact, longer interventions yield more positive effects. (p. 52)

Presumably, metacognitive scaffolding is most effective when a skilled teacher establishes an instructional context and sense of community that supports reflection and thoughtfulness that earlier claims about the advances of learning fostered by isolated writing-to-learn activities seemed to have ignored. Writing does enrich reasoning and learning but only to the extent that learning is situationally supported and valued. (See Clark, Chow-Hoy, Herter, & Moss, 2001, for an indepth case study analysis of how portfolio evaluation of writing can create "sites of learning" and reflective thinking.)

Elizabeth Moje (1996; Moje & O'Brien, 2001) has conducted a series of studies centered on the notion that "literacy . . . is more than reading, writing, speaking, and listening; literacy involves the practices in which these processes are embedded. Based on this sociocultural perspective, I defined reading, writing, speaking, and listening as tools for engaging in and making sense of social practices" (Moje, 1996, p. 175). Given some of the rather consistent findings that writing to learn is situated within certain kinds of social contexts, and given the range of linguistic and cultural backgrounds of American students, applying a literacy practices perspective to study writing and reading within secondary school content areas seems especially relevant to any discussion of writing to learn. Literacy practices shape the ways people engage in and make meanings from literacy

events, depending on how the events are situated in particular social, cultural, and historical arrangements (Street, 1984; Bloome, 2001). For example, in some classrooms, students might experience a writing workshop approach (Atwell, 1998) as an opportunity for developing close relationships with peers, while in another workshop context, students become silenced by the possibility of covert bullying and teasing (Lensmire, 2000). To study literacy practices within school contexts, ethnographic methods are appropriate because, as Erickson (1984) noted, ethnography is the study of "a social network forming a corporate entity in which social relations are regulated by custom" (p. 52). Accordingly, Moje's ethnographies of middle and secondary school writing offer valuable perspectives for understanding what Swanson-Owens (1986) has characterized as "sources of resistance" to curricular change.

One of Moje's (1996) studies is a particularly useful examination of the social situatedness of writing-to-learn in a secondary school subject area. Based on data collected over a 2-year period, Moje argued that the relationship between a chemistry teacher and her students motivated students to engage in literacy activities. Of particular relevance was her examination of how and why literacy strategies such as SQ3R for reading and summary writing were used within the high school chemistry classroom. Moje argued that rather than being valued as tools for learning in and of themselves, literacy practices were more or less valuable based upon (1) how well they fit the social needs and practices, such as studying for tests, getting assignments done quickly; and (2) how they enabled the teacher to develop a relationship of caring and respect with her students.

An Alternative Theoretical Framework: Writing as Participation in Curricular Conversations

Although there is a range of ways to conceptualize writing to learn (Applebee, 1984b; Durst & Newell, 1989; Langer, 1992; Moje, 1996; Sheeran & Barnes, 1991), in this chapter I assume that writing represents one way for students to enter and perhaps contribute to academic traditions of knowing and doing. Accordingly, the theory that I present grows out of a view of writing as a way to take action in a curricular domain—how to do science, for example, not simply to learn about it. This notion of writing as a means for learning content and procedures appropriate to a domain is based on the metaphor of "curriculum as conversation." "When we take this metaphor seriously, the development of curriculum becomes the development of significant domains of conversation, and [writing] instruction becomes a matter of helping students learn to participate in conversations within those domains" (Applebee, 1996, p. 3).

But what role might writing play in enabling students to enter into and participate in such conversations? If entering a curricular domain is contingent upon knowing the conventions of conversation of an academic domain—what is talked about, how, and why, learning to write within that domain must play a central role. Of course, participation will be partly oral, within the presentations and interactions that constitute the dialogue of instruction; but the opportunity for individuals to make extended contributions during classroom discussions will be necessarily limited. Writing then becomes both a primary and necessary medium for practicing the ways of organizing and presenting ideas that are most appropriate to a particular conversational domain within the content area. To enter the domain of literary studies, for example, students must be taught what kinds of interpretations are appropriate and how to marshal support for their arguments (Langer, 1995; Scholes, 1985).

Recent developments in "situated cognition" would seem to support Applebee's (1996) argument for knowledge-in-action as a way to engage students in significant cultural conversations. Lave and Wenger's (1991) situated learning and Brown, Collins, and Duguid's (1989) notion of cognitive apprenticeship are frameworks for understanding how students acquire, develop, and use cognitive tools (e.g., writing and reading) in authentic domain activity. Like Applebee (1996), they see the teacher as a mediator who guides students in their learning within academic traditions. Situated learning and knowledge-in-action also share another important feature: Each construct assumes that

conceptual knowledge be considered a tool that can only be fully understood through use. Specific content has meaning, not in itself, but as it is used and situated in the larger context of academic traditions in which it is embedded.

Studies of writing to learn in secondary school contexts have pointed out that if new writing activities stress one kind of knowledge but teachers look for other types of performances as evidence of learning, the new approaches make little difference (Langer & Applebee, 1987; Newell & Winograd, 1995). Some of the causes are institutional, tied to evaluation systems, public expectations, and conditions of instruction (Hillocks, 2002; Langer & Applebee, 1987). Others are more directly related to instruction—to what students are asked to learn and what teachers have learned to look for as evidence of the learning (Langer et al., 1993).

Implications for Teaching and Research: A New Agenda

Process-oriented approaches to writing instruction and related arguments about the value of writing to learn have taken us just so far: They enable the conceptualization of what might be useful in a lesson or what activities might be effective for a group of students. However, they do not address the issue of what knowledge is central or integral to learning in the content areas.

We can no longer expect to reconceptualize teaching and learning with theoretical arguments for and studies of writing and learning alone. This does not negate the value of studying what effective teachers know about writing and learning, but it does suggest the need to rethink our original assumptions about "strong text" versions that assume that studies of writing to learn in brief fragmented episodes are adequate.

Recent studies of school writing have examined the social (micro) contexts of specific classrooms within which writing occurs and develops; these studies suggest ways of studying writing to learn as socially situated. In these contexts, writers negotiate their places within the many communities of which they are a part, with a variety of resources and competing demands. Dyson (1995), for example, has argued explicitly that children's differentiation of ways of using language is linked directly to their differentiation of their own place within the social world. As a teacher–researcher in her own elementary classroom, Gallas (1994) has described how children use talking and writing as tools for integrating their personal knowledge of the physical world with the study of science: They learn how "to make things visible." Moje (1996) and her colleagues (Moje et al., 2004) have begun "to examine the ways these funds, or networks and relationships, shape ways of knowing, reading, writing, and talking—what Gee (1996) called Discourses—that youth use or try to learn in secondary schools" (p. 38). These studies and others discussed in this chapter suggest a new research agenda with its own list of guiding questions focused on how students use writing to make their own contributions to disciplinary conversations.

This chapter began with three questions, all concerned with the role of writing in the secondary schools and the possibilities of writing as a tool for school reform. If writing is to have a role in the intellectual development and academic life of all students, and in the practices of all teachers, how it functions within curricular conversations, as well as the social life of classrooms, both seem particularly important. This leads to a different set of research questions to shape both research and teaching agendas. For example, if we focus for a moment on the issue of assessment, it is apparent that writing can be a valuable means to examine how development and learning within a curricular domain are evaluated. However, our current notions of what constitutes writing development are limited to general notions of writing skills associated with fluency, appropriate uses of language, structural knowledge, and strategic processes (Applebee, 2000). As we enlarge our notions of learning across the curriculum, we will need to enlarge our notions of writing across the curriculum: Assessments must be based on what is valued in the disciplines and other systems of doing and knowing. This point leads to questions such as "What constitutes learning how to participate in and contribute to disciplinary conversations?" What is trivial and what is significant, and how can writing be a means for both learning and assessing how students know the difference?

However, if we are to include the ideas and voices of all students regardless of their linguistic and cultural backgrounds, we will need to study the intersections of disciplinary conversations with students' lives out of school. Our schools continue to be filled with adolescents who are disinterested and disengaged because "learning becomes a matter of memorization and recitation, where the teacher is seen as the provider of knowledge that the student is expected to replicate" (Applebee, 1996, p. 21). Thus, the central issue is motivation and engagement: We will also need to construct new notions of human agency within curricular domains if we want all students to participate. Clark et al.'s (2001) study of portfolios as "sites of learning" offers a compelling starting point for how we might reconceptualize both learning and assessment:

> In these classrooms, the portfolio process becomes one of the central shared practices as students negotiate the relationships between self, task, and fit. Learning, then, takes on a different end as students seek to become "writers" (among other "possible selves") and thus fully participating members in the communities of practice which are available in the portfolio context. (p. 232)

How might we study the "use value of increasing participation" (Lave & Wenger, 1991, p. 112) in curricular conversations? As students construct disciplinary knowledge, how do they also construct an identity that fosters efforts to catch on to the conversation?

The problem is that we have focused our research questions on narrow concerns, such as what constitutes effective teaching and learning, without asking the broader and more difficult question of how and why different kinds of curricular conversations in particular social contexts shape student learning. As we rethink curriculum and the role of writing in learning to take action within curricular domains, we will also have to understand writing to learn as participating in an increasingly wide array of culturally significant conversations. Additionally, we may also consider what goals and expectations students bring to these conversations—what experiences and factors shape how, if at all, they will engage in the issues and ideas teachers may proffer (Durst, 1999; Michie, 1999). In other words, as we consider what culturally significant ideas will be part of the curricular conversation, we must also know whom we are teaching: We will need to work top-down from a curricular perspective and bottom-up from our understanding of classroom life and the teachers and students who live there both materially and socially.

References

Ackerman, J. M. (1993). The promise of writing to learn. *Written Communication, 10*, 334–370.

Applebee, A. N. (1981). *Writing in the secondary school: English and the content areas* (Research Monograph No. 21). Urbana, IL: National Council of Teachers of English.

Applebee, A. N. (1984a). *Contexts for learning to write: Studies of secondary school instruction.* Norwood, NJ: Ablex.

Applebee, A. N. (1984b). Writing and reasoning. *Review of Educational Research. 54*, 577–596.

Applebee, A. N. (1996). *Curriculum as conversation: Transforming traditions of teaching and learning.* Chicago: University of Chicago Press.

Applebee, A. N. (2000). Alternative models of writing development. In R. Indrisano & J.R. Squire (Eds.), *Perspectives on writing: Research, theory, and practice* (pp. 90–110). Newark, DE: International Reading Association.

Atwell, N. (1998). *In the middle: Writing, reading, and learning with adolescents* (2nd ed.). Upper Montclair, NJ: Boynton/Cook.

Bangert-Drowns, R. L., Hurley, M. M., & Wilkinson, B. (2004). The effects of school-based writing-to-learn interventions on academic achievement: A meta-analysis. *Review of Educational Research, 74*(1), 29–58.

Barnes, D. (1992). *From communication to curriculum* (2nd ed.). Portsmouth, NH: Boynton/Cook.

Barr, M. A., & Healy, M. K. (1988). School and university articulation: Different contexts for writing across the curriculum. In S. H. McLeod (Ed.), *Strengthening programs for writing across the curriculum* (pp. 43–53). San Francisco: Jossey-Bass.

Bizzell, P. (1992). *What is a discourse community: Academic discourse and critical consciousness.* Pittsburgh: University of Pittsburgh Press.

Bloome, D. (2001). Boundaries on the construction of literacy in secondary classrooms: Envisioning reading and writing in a democratic and just society. In E. B. Moje, & D. G. O'Brien (Eds.), *Constructions of literacy: Studies of teaching and learning in and out of secondary school* (pp. 287–304). Mahwah, NJ: Erlbaum.

Brandt, D. (1990). *Literacy as involvement: The acts of writers, readers, and texts.* Carbondale: Southern Illinois University Press.

Britton, J. (1970). *Language and learning.* New York: Penguin Books.

Britton, J. N., Burgess, T., Martin, N., McLeod, A., & Rosen, H. (1975). *The development of writing abilities (11–18).* London: Macmillan.

Brown, J. S., Collins, A., & Duguid, P. (1989). Situated cognition and the culture of learning, *Educational Researcher, 18* 32–42.

Clark, C., Chow-Hoy, T. K., Herter, R., & Moss, P. A. (2001). Portfolios as sites of learning: Reconceptualizing the connections to motivation and engagement. *Journal of Literacy Research, 33* (2), 211–241.

Durst, R. (1987). Cognitive and linguistic demands of analytic writing. *Research in the Teaching of English, 21*, 347–376.

Durst, R. K., & Newell, G. E. (1989). The uses of function: James Britton's category system and research on writing. *Review of Educational Research, 59*(4), 375–394.

Dyson, A. H. (1995). Writing children: Reinventing the development of childhood literacy. *Written Communication, 12*(1), 4–46.

Erickson, F. (1984). What makes school ethnography "ethnographic"? *Anthroplogy & Education Quarterly, 15*, 51–66.

Gallas, K. (1994). *The language of learning: How children talk, write, dance, draw, and sing their understanding of the world.* New York: Teachers College Press.

Gee, J. P. (1996). *Social linguistics and literacies: Ideology in discourse* (2nd ed.). London: Falmer Press.

Gere, A. (1985). *Roots in the sawdust: Writing to learn across the disciplines.* Urbana, IL: National Council of Teachers of English.

Greene, S. (1993). The role of task in academic reading and writing in a college history course. *Research in the Teaching of English, 27*(1), 46–75.

Grice, H. P. (1975). Logic and conversation. In P. Cole & J. L. Morgan (Eds.), *Syntax and semantics* (Vol. 3, pp. 41–58). New York: Seminar Press.

Heath, S. B. (1983). *Ways with words: Language, life, and work in communities and classrooms.* Avon, UK: Cambridge University Press.

Hidi, S., & Anderson, V. (1986). Producing written summaries: Task demands, cognitive operations, and implications for instruction. *Review of Educational Research, 56,* 173–493.

Hillocks, G. (2002). *The testing trap: How state writing assessments control learning.* New York: Teachers College Press.

Jones, C., Turner, J., & Street, B. (1999). *Students writing in the university: Cultural and epistemological issues.* Philadelphia: Benjamin.

Langer, J. A. (1984a). The effects of available information on responses to school writing tasks. *Research in the Teaching of English, 18*, 27–44.

Langer, J. A. (1984b). Literacy instruction in American schools: Problems and perspective. *American Journal of Education, 93,* 107–132.

Langer, J. A. (1992). Speaking of knowing: Conceptions of understanding in academic disciplines. In A. Herrington & C. Moran (Eds.), *Writing, teaching, and learning in the disciplines* (pp. 69–85). New York: Modern Language Association of America.

Langer, J. (1995). *Envisioning literature: Literary understanding and literature instruction.* New York: Teachers College Press.

Langer, J. A., Confer, C., & Sawyer, M. (1993). *Teaching disciplinary thinking in academic coursework* (Report Series No. 2.19). Albany, NY: National Research Center on Literature Teaching and Learning.

Langer, J. A., & Applebee, A.N. (1987). *How writing shapes thinking.* Urbana, IL: National Council of Teachers of English.

Lave, J., & Wenger, E. (1991). *Situated learning: Legitimate peripheral participation.* Cambridge, UK: Cambridge University Press.

Lensmire, T. J. (2000). *Powerful writing, responsible teaching.* New York: Teachers College Press.

Marshall, J. D. (1987). The effects of writing on students' understanding of literary texts. *Research in the Teaching of English, 21,* 30–63.

Mayher, J. (1990). *Uncommon sense: Theoretical practice in language education.* Portsmouth, NH: Boynton/Cook.

McGinely, W., & Tierney, R. (1989). Traversing the topical landscape: Reading and writing as ways of knowing. *Written Communication, 6,* 243–269.

Michie, G. (1999). *Holler if you hear me: The education of a teacher and his students.* New York: Teachers College Press.

Moje, E. B. (1996). "I teach students, not subjects": Teacher–student relationships as contexts for secondary literacy. *Reading Research Quarterly, 31*(2), 172–195.

Moje, E. B., & O'Brien, D.G. (Eds.). (2001). *Constructions of literacy: Studies of teaching and learning in and out of secondary school.* Mahwah, NJ: Erlbaum.

Moje, E. B., Ciechanowski, K., Kramer, K., Ellis, L., Carrillo, R., & Collazo, T. (2004). Working toward third space in content area literacy: An examination of everyday funds of knowledge and discourse. *Reading Research Quarterly, 39,* 38–70.

Newell, G. E. (1984). Learning from writing in two content areas: A case study/protocol analysis. *Research in the Teaching of English, 18,* 365–387.

Newell, G. E., & Winograd, P. (1995). Writing about and learning from history texts: The effects of task and academic ability. *Research in the Teaching of English, 29,* 133–163.

Rose, M. (1989). *Lives on the boundary: The struggles and achievements of America's unprepared.* New York: Penguin Books.

Russell, D. (1991). *Writing in the academic disciplines, 1870–1990: A curricular history.* Carbondale: Southern Illinois University Press.

Scholes, R. (1985). *Textual power: Literary theory and the teaching of English.* New Haven, CT: Yale University Press.

Sheeran, Y., & Barnes, D. (1991). *School writing: Discovering the ground rules.* Philadelphia: Open University Press.

Smagorinsky, P. (1995). Constructing meaning in the disciplines: Reconceptualizing writing across the curriculum as composing across the curriculum. *American Journal of Education, 103,* 160–184.

Swanson-Owens, D. (1986). Identifying natural sources of resistance: A case study of implementing writing across the curriculum. *Research in the Teaching of English, 20,* 69–97.

Street, B. (1984). *Literacy in theory and practice.* Cambridge, UK: Cambridge University Press.

Wertsch, J. (1998). *Mind as action.* New York: Oxford University Press.

Chapter 17

The Effects of New Technologies on Writing and Writing Processes

Charles A. MacArthur

In a recent article in *The Washington Post* Sennett (2004) discussed the agonized reflections of a college student about whether her use of e-mail rather than the more casual instant messaging had scared away a potential date by conveying too much sense of commitment. In the high-stakes rituals of dating, where e-mails are edited by friends for the proper breezy tone before sending, her friends concluded that the e-mail had definitely been a mistake.

Electronic technologies are changing the forms by which people communicate with each other and understand the world. Changes in technology have and will continue to change the nature of literacy practices in society, and the cognitive and social skills needed to be considered fully literate. The process did not start with computers. Radio, television, and the movies dramatically altered the ways in which we receive news, entertain ourselves, consume goods, choose heroic figures, elect our leaders, and understand our culture. These popular media have had limited direct impact on schooling, though they may have had substantial indirect effects. Computer technologies may have a more direct influence on schooling and on literacy for two reasons. First, the integration of text and other media in hypermedia and the Internet means that schools, charged with responsibility for the important business of teaching reading and writing, cannot ignore them as they did television and the movies. The integration of text with graphics, video, and sound may encourage schools to expand the concept of literacy to include a variety of media. Second, electronic technologies engage students as writers or producers rather than just as readers or consumers. From publication of class newsletters to e-mail projects to hypermedia web pages, to blogs and zines, computers offer students opportunities to create new types of documents. At the same time, they are changing the ways in which traditional text is produced. New technologies promise to become increasingly important in our schools as tools for inquiry and learning, as well as means for communicating and composing.

In considering the impact of new technologies on writing, it is useful to begin with recent scholarship on the impact of writing on cognitive and social processes. Writing is itself a technology, a combination of a symbol system and various physical means of production, that makes possible the durable representation of language. Olson (1995) argued that written language, by capturing and communicating words with precision and separating them from the context of production, affords the opportunity to think in a more abstract and decontextualized way. The invention of the alphabet, which made literacy possible for more than the few, and of the printing press and paper, which supported wide literacy, had dramatic impacts on the nature of thinking in society—

supporting the development of a more rational approach in all fields of knowledge. Arguing against Olson's thesis, Scribner and Cole (1978) demonstrated, through study of users of an informal, nonschooled script used primarily for personal letters, that rational, decontextualized thought is not an inevitable consequence of the development of literacy but rather is a consequence of schooling. Thus, writing affords the opportunity for the development of more abstract thinking, but the actual impact on cognitive processes depends on the social context of use. This general principle applies to new technologies as well. New technological forms of writing afford opportunities for the development of cognitive skills and social interactions, but the actual effects of the technology depend on complex interactions among the technology, the social context, and individual users.

There is no shortage of theoretical work on the transformative effects of technology on literacy. Bolter (1998) argues that hypermedia, of which the Internet is the prime example, will have revolutionary effects on literacy for two reasons. First, the multilinear nature of hypertext challenges the rhetorical foundation of teaching writing (i.e., presenting a coherent point of view, with supporting arguments, by encouraging the presentation of multiple viewpoints). Second, hypermedia place greater emphasis on visual images than on verbal text, which will have dramatic effects on how knowledge is represented and manipulated mentally. Purves (1998) goes further, declaring that the impact of the digital media on literacy will have a historical weight equal to the invention of alphabetic writing and the printing press. He argues that the visual and organizational features of digital information convey meaning beyond the words. In particular, the emphasis on visual imagery will deemphasize the importance of language to meaning, and hypertext links will lead people to think in multidirectional rather than hierarchical ways.

In contrast, Bruce and Hogan (1998) argue that technology has quite variable effects depending on how it is embedded in a social context. Literacy technologies are ideological tools that are designed, accessed, used, and interpreted to further purposes that embody social values. In a classroom setting, the technology, the teacher's instructional methods, and student experiences will all interact in ways that determine the effects of technology as an innovation. Similarly, Perkins (1985) claimed that various media and technologies promote and require different types of thinking, because they use different symbol systems and afford various types of interaction. Regular use of any technology has effects on cognition that can be subtle and occur without awareness. However, how the affordances of technology are realized depends on conditions such as instruction, expertise, background knowledge, and design of the tools.

Despite the broad and interesting theoretical claims, empirical research on the cognitive and social effects of technology on writing is quite limited, and the results of that research are mixed. My purpose in this review is to examine empirical research on the impact of new technologies on writing and learning to write. Writing is defined broadly to include creation of hypertext or hypermedia, as well as traditional linear text, but not so broadly as to include video and film production. The review is limited to studies focused on writing, not on reading or the effects of technology on acquiring knowledge. It is also limited to work done in educational contexts, omitting the growing literature on out-of-school writing and popular media. Finally, it is limited to elementary and secondary education.

I begin the review by considering the effects of technology on producing traditional linear texts, including the cognitive processes involved, the development of skills, and how social interactions in instructional settings modify these effects. Sections address word processing, computer support for writing and learning to write, and assistive technology for struggling writers, then review the emerging research on composing hypermedia or hypertext. Finally, the review considers the effects of computer-mediated communication as it affects writing, including intercultural communication projects and the use of networked communication in writing classes.

Word Processing

One area of technology and writing that has seen extensive research is word processing. It was a common early application of computers in schools and is probably the most widely used application in the general population as well. It seems well adapted to contemporary theories about writing as a cognitive process involving recursive cycles of planning, drafting, and revising. Furthermore, it supports social processes by enhancing opportunities for publication and collaborative writing. A large number of studies of word processing were published in the late 1980s, followed by a slower but steady stream of publications to the present.

Two meta-analyses of the research have reported moderate positive effects of word processing in writing instruction on the length and quality of compositions. Bangert-Drowns (1993) found small to moderate effect sizes for quality (0.27) and length (0.36). [Note: Unless otherwise indicated, all effect sizes (ESs) reported in this chapter represent the common metric of mean difference divided by the standard deviation.] Though elementary, secondary, and college students were included, effects were not related to age. Interestingly, positive effects were found even when posttests were administered in handwriting, suggesting that whatever students had learned from instruction with word processing transferred to writing without computers. In a review of similar research since 1992, Goldberg, Russell, and Cook (2003) reported somewhat larger ESs for quality (0.41) and length (0.50).

Some evidence indicates that effects on quality are stronger for struggling writers than for average ones. The small effect on quality reported by Bangert-Drowns (1993) is better viewed as a combination of a moderate ES for nine studies of remedial instruction for struggling writers (0.49) and a nonsignificant ES for 11 studies with average writers (0.06). A few studies have shown positive effects of word processing in combination with instruction for students with learning disabilities (for a review, see MacArthur, 2000). It is important to note that few of the studies covered in these reviews effectively controlled for instruction to isolate the effect of the technology. Thus, it is probably more accurate to say that word processing in combination with instruction adapted to the technology had positive effects.

An important practical concern reflected in recent research is the impact of word processing or its absence on student performance on accountability tests. Wolfe, Bolton, Feltovich, and Niday (1996) compared test essays written via handwriting and word processing by high school students with high, medium, and low experience with word processing. No differences were found for quality or length for students with high or medium word-processing experience, but students with low experience wrote shorter, lower quality essays with word processing. Russell (1999; Russell & Plati, 2001) studied high school students taking tests involving multiple-choice questions, and paragraph and essay-length responses from state accountability tests on the computer, or with paper and pencil. No differences were found for multiple-choice questions, but students who were accustomed to writing with a word processor and had competent typing skills (20+ words per minute) performed substantially better on written responses when they used the word processor (ESs from 0.5 to 0.9). One of the studies (Russell, 1999) included students with a range of measured typing skills; students with below average typing scored significantly lower (ES = −0.4) with word processing, while those with above average typing scored significantly higher (ES = 0.5). Students who are used to writing with word processors may be at a substantial disadvantage if not permitted to use them on high-stakes tests.

Research on the impact of word processing on revising and other writing processes has been mixed. In early reviews, Cochran-Smith (1991) reported that word processing for elementary students resulted in more surface revision, but Hawisher (1987) and Bangert-Drowns (1993) found that results were too varied to draw any conclusions. One reason for conflicting results is variations in how revisions were measured. If revisions are only counted between drafts, then the extensive revisions often made during drafting with a word processor are missed. Another possible reason for variation in instructional studies is whether and how revising was taught. Experimental studies that compared handwriting and word processing without instruction with middle school students with learning disabilities (MacArthur & Graham, 1987), college students (Kellogg & Mueller, 1993), and expert adult writers (Van Waes & Schellens, 2003) have generally found more revisions during drafting with word processing, with most of those revisions focused on minor changes that did not affect meaning.

Early predictions that word processing would free writers from concern with the mechanics of text production and enable them to focus on higher level concerns (Daiute, 1986) have not been supported. In fact, the evidence on revision suggests that word processing increases attention to minor editing. Overall, the research is consistent with a view of the word processor as a flexible writing tool that has modest effects on writing processes, particularly revision, and that affords opportunities for learning if combined with effective instruction. Thus, the effects are largely dependent on the context in which word processing is used.

Computer Support for Planning and Revising Processes

Since the early days of research on word processing, educators have tried to design software that would supplement word processing by direct support of planning and revising processes. Most efforts have been based on cognitive models of composing processes (Hayes & Flower, 1980) and on Bereiter and Scardamalia's (1987) concept of procedural facilitation, or temporary supports to guide developing writers in using more sophisticated cognitive processes.

The most positive results to date were found in a study by Zellermayer, Salomon, Globerson, and Givon (1991). Their Writing Partner provided fairly extensive metacognitive support for planning, drafting, and revising. The planning tools asked students to answer questions about rhetorical purpose (e.g., Are you trying to persuade or describe?), topic, audience (e.g., Is your audience experts or beginners on this topic?), main ideas, and key words. While students worked on their draft, metacognitive questions appeared in random order, prompting students to consider purpose, organization, and elaboration; these prompts drew on information from the planning segment (e.g., descriptive or persuasive purpose). The revising questions included not only generic revising concerns but also drew on planning (e.g., asking about evidence, if the purpose was persuasive). High school students were ran-

domly assigned to one of three groups: writing partner with solicited guidance (SG) or with unsolicited guidance (USG), or regular word processing control (C). Both experimental groups received identical planning and revising support; the only difference was that the USG group saw the drafting prompts at random intervals without asking for them, whereas the SG group was directed to check the prompts by typing a special key. Pretest and posttest essays were written by hand without support in order to test the theory that the metacognitive support would be internalized. Both on essays written with support and on handwritten posttest essays, students in the USG group earned substantially higher quality ratings than the other two groups, which did not differ from each other (posttest ES about 1.5). The reason for the difference between the SG and USG groups is not clear. Planning and revising support were identical, and both groups saw about the same number of prompts during writing and recalled the same number of prompts on a posttest. Unfortunately, no further research was conducted with this tool to replicate or extend the findings.

Bonk and Reynolds (1992; Reynolds & Bonk, 1996) conducted two studies of a similar program that provided metacognitive prompts on planning and revising during composing. Students had a list of the eight types of prompts and could access them at any time; there was no unsolicited guidance condition. In the first study (Bonk & Reynolds, 1992), middle school students wrote three essays using the support tool and took a posttest with a regular word processor; a control group wrote three practice essays with a word processor. No effects were found on number of substantive revisions or on the quality of essays produced with support or on the posttest. In the second study (Reynolds & Bonk, 1996), first-year college students in a composition class received 9 weeks of instruction on planning and revising and were then assigned to experimental and control conditions, and wrote a paper using the support tool or a word processor. Students made significantly more substantive revisions and received higher quality ratings with the support tool; however, there was no correlation between the number of revisions and quality. No measure of transfer to writing without support was gathered. Differences in age, instruction, and outcome measures make it impossible to interpret the reasons for the different results across the two studies.

Rowley (Rowley, Carsons, & Miller, 1998; Rowley & Meyer, 2003) reported a series of studies of a computer program that provided prompts to support three aspects of writing: brainstorming ideas, setting goals and organizing ideas, and revising. All four studies were large quasi-experimental studies (500–1,200 students) in middle and high schools but with relatively small amounts of program use (6–15 hours over a semester or year) and poor treatment fidelity. The main outcome measure was writing quality on a posttest without support. The first three studies (Rowley et al., 1998) produced statistically significant effects when analyzed at the level of individual students rather than classes; except for one study in which the control group had no computer access, the effect sizes were extremely small (about 1% of variance accounted for). The fifth study found no significant effect.

Overall, the research on computer programs that provide metacognitive prompts to writers during the writing process has produced more negative than positive results, but there are too few studies to draw any firm conclusions. Zellermayer et al. (1991) was the only study to find improvements in the quality of writing on a transfer essay, but even their study included an unexpected and unexplained negative result for students receiving solicited guidance. Reynolds and Bonk (1996; Bonk & Reynolds, 1992) found increases in revision and writing quality on an essay written with support for college students but no effects on revision or quality for essays written with support or on a transfer essay for middle school students. Rowley et al.'s (1998) studies had design flaws and produced very small effect sizes.

More common in everyday life than prompts with an instructional purpose are tools designed to support planning, such as outliners and concept mapping programs. Despite the popularity among teachers of current concept mapping software, only one study of the effects of concept mapping software on writing was found. Sturm and Rankin-Erickson (2002) compared planning with concept mapping software, hand-drawn concept maps, and no maps in adoles-

cents with learning disabilities writing descriptive essays. Essays were longer and of higher quality in both concept map conditions than in the no-map condition.

A study by Crinon and Legros (2002) adopted a novel approach to supporting revision by novice writers. Arguing that lack of knowledge about good writing is a critical problem for novices, they provided access to a database of model texts to give students ideas about content and solutions to common problems such as how to begin a story. The database was an anthology of 250 excerpts from children's literature, ranging in length from a few lines to a page and half. The texts could be accessed through a search for theme (e.g., friendship, fighting), people and places, or technique (e.g., how to start a story, how to make readers laugh). In the study, 8- to 10-year-old children wrote a first draft in one session and used the database in a second session to help with revision. The database was compared to a paper condition in which children had access to eight story excerpts on the same theme as the assignment and to a no-support condition. The children using computers produced more propositions during rewriting and, in particular, more macrostructural propositions. Most of the additions were inventions rather than direct copies of text. No quality measures were used, and transfer to writing without support was not assessed. Research on using imitation of model essays in writing instruction has shown only modest effects (Hillocks, 1986). However, children writing collaboratively with peers have been shown to adopt techniques used by their peers for later independent writing (Daiute & Dalton, 1993) and modeling is well established as a basic method of learning. Perhaps this database of brief models is more effective than the typical use of models in writing instruction, because it gives writers ideas and helps them with particular problems during writing.

A new direction in computer support for writing development is the use of automated essay scoring (AES) systems to provide feedback to students on their writing in iterative cycles of revision and evaluation. Several AES systems have shown good interrater reliability with human raters (see Shermis & Burstein, Chapter 27, this volume). In addition, systems based on latent semantic analysis (LSA) are able to evaluate the semantic content of writing and how well it matches criterion texts (Landauer & Psotka, 2000). Such systems are able to evaluate the content coverage of an essay or the adequacy of a summary of a larger text. A common problem in writing instruction is that teachers do not have adequate time to provide detailed evaluations of large quantities of student writing. AES systems can provide repeated feedback on students' writing as they revise.

Kintsch, Steinhart, Stahl, Matthews, and Lamb (2000) described the development and initial evaluation of Summary Street, a program that provides feedback to students on how well their summary covers the various parts of a text, whether it meets length requirements, and which sentences might be redundant or irrelevant. In initial studies, sixth-grade students wrote better summaries with Summary Street than without support, but only on more difficult topics. Steinhardt (2001) conducted a controlled study in which 50 sixth-grade students wrote summaries using Summary Street or a simpler version that only gave feedback on length. Students spent significantly more time working on their summaries with Summary Street and received significantly higher ratings on content coverage and overall quality. Many issues remain to be investigated, including transfer to writing summaries without support and the effects on reading comprehension.

Overall, research on computer programs that provide metacognitive support, or procedural facilitation, has produced mixed results. Paper-based procedural facilitators have been shown to have effects on planning and revising processes, and the quality of writing in some studies (Bereiter & Scardamalia, 1987; Ferretti & MacArthur, 2001; Graham, MacArthur, & Schwartz, 1995). Thus, it is likely that computer-based versions could also be effective if appropriately designed and targeted on the needs of the students. Further research and development in this area should focus on the specifics of instructional design.

Another important area for research given the frequent use of graphic organizers and outlines in writing instruction is the design of instruction combined with computer versions of outlining and semantic mapping software. Crinon and Legros's (2002) concept of using a database of model texts to support writing instruction is a novel approach that deserves more research. Finally, applications of AES to writing instruction appear quite promising as ways to improve writing, especially writing in content areas.

Assistive Technology for Struggling Writers

Word processing, as noted earlier, appears to be especially helpful for writers with learning disabilities (LD) and other struggling writers, perhaps because they are in most need of the support it provides for motivation, mechanics, appearance, and revision. In addition to word processing, other computer tools, including spelling checkers, speech synthesis, word prediction, and speech recognition, can offer assistance to writers who struggle with transcription.

Spelling Checkers

Spelling checkers, as one might expect, do help students with LD to correct errors, but with significant limitations. In one study (MacArthur, Graham, Haynes, & De La Paz, 1996), middle school students with moderate to severe spelling problems corrected 37% of their spelling errors with a spelling checker compared to 9% unaided. The most severe limitations were that the spelling checker (1) failed to flag 37% of errors that were other words, including homonyms and other real words (e.g., *sad* for *said*), and (2) failed to include the correct word in the list of suggestions for 25% of errors. High school students with LD can correct more of their spelling errors if taught to use strategies for managing the limitations of spelling checkers (McNaughton, Hughes, & Ofiesh, 1997).

Speech Synthesis

Speech synthesis, or text-to-speech software, has potential as a tool to help students with revision. By listening to the text they have just written, students might be able to use their oral language skills to identify and correct errors they would miss on reading the text. Only one study with elementary and secondary students was found that addressed this potential. Borgh and Dickson (1992) had elementary school students write on a special word processor that prompted them to check for errors; half of the students used speech synthesis along with the prompts. No differences were found in overall amount of revision or the length and quality of papers.

Word Prediction

Word prediction software was originally developed to reduce keystrokes by individuals with physical disabilities, but it has also been applied with students with severe spelling problems. Word prediction software "predicts" what word the writer intends to type based on the initial letters and, for sophisticated software, syntax and individual patterns of word use. For example, if I have typed, "I went to the *s*," the program might offer a list of predictions including *store, show,* and *same.* If I continue by adding a *t* to the *s*, the program would update the list to include only words beginning with *st.* Most word prediction systems also provide speech synthesis to help students read the list of words.

MacArthur (1998, 1999) conducted a series of three studies of word prediction with 9- and 10-year-old students with severe spelling problems, using single-subject designs that support causal conclusions about the effects of treatment on individual students. Students wrote dialogue journals with their teachers, alternating among handwriting, word processing, and word prediction. Across the three studies, six of eight students demonstrated dramatic improvements in the legibility of their writing and spelling when using word prediction. During baseline, the writing of these six students ranged from 55 to 85% legible words (i.e., readable in isolation) and 42 to 75% correctly spelled words. All six increased their percentage of both legible and correctly spelled words into the 90 to 100% range. A more recent study (Handley-More, Deitz, Billingsley, & Coggins, 2003) with similar students (LD, age 10–11, severe spelling problems) and a similar research design found similar effects; two of three students made substantial improvements in legibility and spelling.

Thus, the available research supports the use of word prediction software with students with severe spelling problems. The studies also revealed that design issues, such as the size of the vocabulary, its match to the writing task, and complexity of the interface, make a difference in the impact. Further research is needed to replicate and extend the findings to other groups and to investigate the impact on vocabulary use.

Speech Recognition

Speech recognition software for dictation represents potentially the most complete solution to problems with spelling, handwriting, and overall fluency. However, despite steady improvements in the quality of speech recognition software, it still has significant limitations in comparison to dictation to a human (MacArthur & Cavalier, 2004). First, accuracy is still limited. Second, users must articulate carefully, dictate punctuation, and avoid extraneous vocalizations. Finally, users must learn to edit for new types of errors. On the other hand, one advantage of speech recognition over standard dictation to a secretary is that writers can see their text as they dictate.

Reece and Cummings (1996) studied the potential effects of speech recognition in a series of studies using a simulated speech recognition system with a hidden typist and visible computer screen. Two studies of fifth- and sixth-grade students, one with normally achieving students and another with students with writing problems, compared papers written via handwriting, normal dictation (to a tape recorder), and simulated speech recognition. For normally achieving students, handwritten and normally dictated papers were equivalent in quality, whereas poor writers did better with normal dictation than with handwriting. Both groups wrote better quality papers with the simulated speech recognition system than with either normal dictation or handwriting. However, in another study, in which normally achieving students were required to develop a plan before writing, the advantage of simulated speech recognition over normal dictation disappeared. The authors interpreted this finding to mean that planning made it less necessary to see the developing text. For students with writing problems, however, dictation in both forms was consistently better than handwriting.

Several studies of speech recognition with struggling writers have been reported. Though focused on college students with

LDs, Higgins and Raskind's study (1995) deserves mention as the earliest experimental comparison of speech recognition, dictation to a human transcriber, and unassisted composing (word processor or handwriting at students' choice). Quality ratings were significantly higher in the speech recognition than in the unassisted condition. Quinlan (2004) selected middle school students who had significantly lower written language than oral language scores (similar to a definition of LD) and compared them to students without such a discrepancy. All students learned to use speech recognition and then composed brief narratives using handwriting and speech recognition. Students with writing problems, but not the average writers, wrote longer papers using speech recognition. However, no statistically significant differences in quality were found by condition for either the poor or average writers.

MacArthur and Cavalier (2004) compared the effects of speech recognition, dictation to a person who typed on a visible screen, and handwriting on the writing of high school students with and without LD. All students received 6 hours of training and practice in the use of both speech recognition and a simple planning procedure for writing persuasive essays, then wrote essays in all three conditions. All students were able to use speech recognition to compose and edit essays. The students with LDs made fewer total errors with speech recognition than handwriting, and few words were unreadable. Their essays dictated using speech recognition were higher in quality than handwritten essays (ES = 0.42), and essays dictated to a person were even better (ES = 1.31). No statistically significant differences for condition were found for students without LDs.

Although the research on assistive technology is not extensive, it provides support for the use of some forms of technology to help students with LDs and other struggling writers compensate for problems with basic transcription. Word processing and spell checkers are clearly helpful and are readily available. Word prediction is promising for students with severe spelling problems. Speech recognition now has solid, if limited, support. One cautionary note is that all assistive technology tools, while removing one burden, impose some new burden. Word processing removes problems with handwriting, but students must learn to type. Speech recognition removes concerns with handwriting, typing, and spelling, but students must articulate carefully and edit for errors. Whether a new tool increases or decreases the overall burden of writing depends on the capabilities of the individual student, the training provided, and the demands of the setting. Thus, further research should investigate which students are most likely to benefit from particular tools.

Hypermedia

We turn our attention now from computer tools that support and instruct writers to technology that changes the nature of the written product. There is a rich literature on the design of hypermedia to enhance the content learning of users (for a review, see Dillon & Gabbard, 1998). In this chapter, discussion is limited to research on the cognitive processes involved in composing hypermedia, or hypertext, and the learning consequences of such composing. The term "hypermedia" is used for studies that involve multiple media, including text, connected by a network of links; "hypertext" is used for research focused on linked text with no other media.

Composing hypermedia and linear text differ in some ways and are similar in others. Both are composing processes with communicative purposes and, as such, require considering the audience, setting goals, organizing with attention to content and rhetorical purpose, presenting content clearly, and evaluating and revising. Hypermedia differ from written text in two major ways: the linked structure and the inclusion of multiple media. These two differences potentially affect all aspects of composing. For example, the multiple purposes of audiences need to be considered in planning the organizational structure of hypermedia (Bromme & Stahl, 2002). Multiple links among segments of content, as well as navigation through the document as a whole, must be considered. The content of individual segments is affected, because the writer cannot count on the reader's having read previous segments. Careful consideration needs to be given to the use of multiple media. In addition, visual design issues play an important role in usability.

Investigations of the effects of composing hypermedia have been primarily case studies of instruction in classrooms. Experimental studies of the effects of composing hypermedia are difficult to design because of two considerations. First, media comparison studies, like those comparing handwriting and word processing, make no sense because of the lack of comparability of hypermedia and text documents. Second, experimental comparisons of content learning as an outcome of composing hypermedia are confounded by the amount of effort and time devoted to creating hypermedia, not to mention motivational factors. However, a number of case studies have investigated the cognitive and social processes involved in composing hypermedia and changes in students' understanding of the composing, or design, process. In addition, a few recent experimental studies have investigated cognitive processes.

Lehrer, Erickson, and their colleagues (Carver, Lehrer, Connell, & Erickson, 1992; Erickson & Lehrer, 1998, 2000) have conducted a number of classroom studies of collaborative inquiry projects based on authoring hypermedia. In their studies, students worked collaboratively to investigate topics within a classroom unit of instruction and made hypermedia presentations to teach their peers what they learned. Students received instruction in the hypermedia authoring tools, and explicit instruction and guidance in the design process. The researchers developed a theoretical model of the design skills, or cognitive processes, required for hypermedia composition and argued that those design skills were important educational outcomes. The model described a wide range of cognitive skills covering research skills, planning and management, organization, presentation, evaluation, and revision. They then used the model to design the curriculum, to document exposure to instruction in design skills, and to assess students' conceptual understanding of the design skills, their use of design skills in class projects, and their transfer of skills to novel tasks. Carver and colleagues (1992) reported case studies of a ninth-grade class that worked directly with the researchers, and a group of three eighth-grade classes taught by

their teachers. Both groups participated in 10-week units and 4-week follow-up projects to assess transfer. Analysis of student discourse, self-report measures, and design performance on the transfer tasks demonstrated gains in design skills in both sites. However, students taught by their regular teachers received less explicit instruction in the design process and developed less independence in design, especially regarding the overall research process.

Erickson and Lehrer (1998) conducted a 2-year longitudinal study with a group of sixth- and seventh-grade students who participated in a series of hypermedia inquiry projects in social studies. They documented changes in students' understanding of what constituted good research questions and what characterized good hypermedia design. Understanding of research questions evolved from simple factual questions to thought-provoking questions that required interpretation. Standards for hypermedia design evolved from a focus on display features and content information to a greater focus on clarity of communication and consideration of audience. For example, students devoted more attention to multiple representations of content, and the purpose and organization of links. The analysis also revealed the extent to which student development of design knowledge depended on explicit instruction, based on assessment of student understanding.

Erickson and Lehrer (2000) conducted a more detailed analysis of students' developing understanding of links and the hypermedia space. They based their analysis on Bereiter and Scardamalia's (1987) theory that knowledge-transforming writing results from an interaction between the content-problem space and the rhetorical-problem space, as writers revise and extend their understanding of content by wrestling with the necessity of communicating ideas clearly to readers. Detailed analysis of the development of 10 students over the course of a year showed a change from an exclusive emphasis on content links to a greater rhetorical emphasis on facilitating navigation and organizing content for readers by using links that indicated specific relationships among content.

Liu (1998) and colleagues (Liu & Hsiao, 2002; Liu & Pedersen, 1998) conducted a series of studies with high school, middle school, and elementary school students working on multimedia design projects. Though they used a rationale similar to that of Erickson and Lehrer (1998, 2000), and used a variation of their design questionnaire to measure gains in design knowledge, their projects differed in that they focused on the design of hypermedia as done by professional designers, with an emphasis on presentation rather than on the inquiry process of research and communication. This narrower emphasis on designing presentations limits the application of Erickson and Lehrers' argument for the relevance and importance of design skills. In addition, the studies were primarily pretest–posttest designs with single classes, with limited analysis of qualitative data. Results on the quantitative measures were mixed. They found increases in motivation and design knowledge in the high school class but mixed results in the middle school and elementary school studies. Qualitative analysis of interviews and observations showed that students were engaged and developed knowledge of design, but their claims should be interpreted cautiously.

Other case studies of educational projects with hypermedia have taken different approaches. Myers, Hammett, and McKillop (1998) discussed the use of hypermedia to support critical pedagogy. In their case studies, high school students used hypermedia to construct critical commentaries on literature. By linking images and commentary to texts, they created juxtapositions that involved reinterpreting the texts, questioning the underlying assumptions, and reflecting on culture and ideology. Although Myers and her colleagues believed that hypermedia afforded the opportunity to critique texts, they acknowledged that the effects of the technology were dependent on the ways in which teachers and students used them.

Daiute and Morse (1994) reported a case study of a class of reluctant writers who produced simple multimedia documents based on pictures or sounds that they brought to school because they had personal meaning. They compared such multimedia writing to the drawing in which primary students are commonly engaged. The case studies of individual students revealed high levels of engagement and increased production of text.

Baker (2001; Baker & Kinzer, 1998; Baker, Rozendal, & Whitenack, 2000) reported a series of analyses of an ethnographic case study of a fourth-grade class in an intensive technology environment with a 1:1 ratio of computers to students plus five multimedia stations. Students worked on collaborative inquiry projects in science and social studies that often involved hypermedia presentations and engaged in a variety of writing activities during language arts time. In this setting, the composing process was highly recursive, with students brainstorming, searching for information, composing, and revising repeatedly in various orders (Baker & Kinzer, 1998). Often students revised hypermedia products they had completed and presented much earlier. One apparent reason for this recursive activity was the public nature of composing on the computer screen (Baker et al., 2000). Students were often observed to comment on each other's work or to stop and talk as they walked by a peer's computer. The classroom offered pervasive opportunities for interacting with a peer audience through presentations, solicited and unsolicited feedback, and frequent viewing of others' screens, often without comment. The teacher saw not only positive value in this public nature of writing, in that students got ideas from each other and received lots of support in revising, but also potentially negative implications in the lack of opportunity to write privately in journals. Another issue about the impact of technology was the effects of publication and presentation. Students in this class were highly motivated by the presentational tools at their disposal. However, the teacher expressed some concern about an overemphasis on presentation to the detriment of substance. A common theme of her conferences with students was encouraging them to find more content for their reports.

One experimental study with high school students investigated the cognitive processes involved in composing hypermedia. Braaksma, Rijlaarsdam, Couzijn, and van den Bergh (2002) compared the cognitive processes involved in composing hypertext to the processes involved in composing standard linear text. They used artificial tasks designed to represent the key processes of hierarchicalization for hypertext and linearization for standard text. The hypertext task required students to take a paragraph-length argument and draw a diagram of the thesis, arguments, and subordinate arguments. The linearization task required students to take such a hierarchical diagram and write a short argumentative paragraph. Think-aloud data were gathered, and the quality of products was assessed. Each student did two tasks of each type, one easier and the other harder. The overall quantity of think-aloud statements was greater in the hypertext task. In terms of proportions, the hypertext task elicited more analysis, planning, goal setting, and meta-analysis, while the linear task led to more writing and rereading statements. For both tasks, the amounts of planning and analysis were positively correlated with the quality of products. The authors interpreted the results as evidence of considerable similarity in the general types of cognitive processes involved in composing text and hypertext, and suggested that composing hypertext may have a positive effect on linear writing skills by promoting more planning and analysis.

In summary, research on the effects of composing hypermedia is at an early stage. The case studies have demonstrated the potential of instructional models that combine technology and collaborative inquiry, and have analyzed some of the cognitive processes and instructional factors involved. They have avoided unproductive media comparisons. After all, research on models of collaborative inquiry without the use of technology, such as Group Investigation (Shachar & Sharan, 1994), has shown positive effects on student content learning and learning of inquiry processes. Instead of asking about the effects of technology, these case studies have investigated how to use hypermedia effectively. The studies have illuminated some of the cognitive processes involved in using hypermedia, such as an understanding of how to divide content into segments and link them in ways that are responsive to readers' needs, or how to use multiple media to communicate effectively rather than simply to make a flashy presentation. They have also pointed to important social considerations, such as the impact of the public nature of technology on interaction with peers. Finally, they have drawn important conclusions about the importance of instruction guided by a model of the cognitive processes and learning outcomes desired.

Experimental study of particular aspects of hypertext composing has just begun. The case studies and experimental studies together show that composing hypermedia requires high-level cognitive processes and can help to develop those processes. Though perhaps somewhat different in emphasis, the cognitive processes seem similar to those required for writing, involving setting goals, considering audience needs, generating and organizing content, evaluating, and revising. Continued research is needed to understand these cognitive processes in more detail and to develop effective classroom environments that include hypermedia composing.

Computer-Mediated Communication

The term "computer-mediated communication" (CMC) covers a diverse range of technologies and contexts for use, unified only by the idea of interactive communication over the Internet or local networks, primarily via writing, though sometimes supplemented with other media. It includes everyday professional and personal use of e-mail, listservs, instant messaging, and chat rooms, as well as specific instructional and professional uses, such as online and distance courses, online discussions in traditional courses, and collaborative work groups and meetings. The large body of writing on CMC is primarily practical and descriptive but also includes theoretical and empirical work. Social-psychological research has examined interaction patterns in CMC (see a review from the point of view of composition by Eldred & Hawisher, 1995). The use of synchronous and asynchronous CMC in online courses or distance education has generated a body of examples and principles for practice (see the multiple-volume edited set by Berge & Collins, 1998). Linguists have conducted descriptive research on the syntax, semantics, and pragmatics of communication via email and instant messaging (e.g., Baron, 1998). CMC has been widely used in college writing courses (for a historical review, see Palmquist, 2003; for research on one extensive project, see Bruce, Peyton, & Batson, 1993).

Because CMC is communication conducted via writing, all of this work is relevant to some degree to this chapter. However, this chapter is confined to a review of studies that looked specifically at the effects of CMC on writing processes and writing products in the context of writing instruction. At the elementary and secondary school level, this research has focused on telecommunication projects, often involving classrooms from different cultures or geographical areas.

Intercultural communication projects using the Internet have been proposed as ways to improve students' writing skills, develop greater cultural awareness, and prepare students for an increasingly globally connected world (Garner & Gillingham, 1996; Fabos & Young, 1999). The scope of projects varies from simple pen pal communications to collaborative curriculum projects that involve sharing of data and written products. Such projects offer substantial opportunities to communicate in writing for authentic purposes with age peers from culturally different backgrounds. Communication with distant peers may cause students to think more carefully about audience, and to be more explicit and elaborative in their writing. The authenticity of the writing and the technology may also motivate students to write more. However, little empirical research has tested these possibilities.

Cohen and Riel (1989) had two classes of seventh-grade students in a repeated measures design write papers on the same topic for the teacher for a grade and for a distant audience of peers. These students had no prior experience with email or writing for distant peers. The papers written for the distant audience were rated higher on all five aspects of an analytic scale and given higher grades by the teacher. Gallini and Helman (1995) collected writing samples from fifth-grade students who had experience in an intercultural communication project. Students were randomly assigned to write papers for their teacher, for a self-selected classmate, or for distant peers. The papers written for distant peers were rated significantly higher than others on several elements of an analytic scale—organization, elaboration, and interest. These studies provide preliminary support for the value of writing to distant audiences, but both studies were small and involved a single writing sample.

Case studies of intercultural communication projects have also been reported. Based on a series of six case studies of innovative teachers using the Internet, Garner and Gillingham (1996) argued that intercultural communication projects encourage more social-constructivist methods by supporting collaboration and student inquiry. The teachers in these cases changed their teaching by devoting more effort to inquiry methods that drew on student interests and real-world concerns. The researchers found high levels of motivation for writing, substantial amounts of writing, and evidence of children attempting to understand cultural differences and to consider audience needs. Case studies have also revealed some of the institutional and social complexities of establishing Internet communication projects. For example, Neilson (1998) discussed a large telecommunications project in a rural high school. A variety of institutional barriers and difficulties in managing projects resulted in an implementation that reached only a few students who were especially interested in technology.

Fabos and Young (1999) wrote a highly critical review of telecommunications projects, pointing out the lack of empirical research on outcomes, and urging educators to look critically at the political and social forces that support such global communication projects. Case studies have demonstrated the potential of intercultural communication projects, but given the popularity of such projects, much more research is needed to document their effects on writing and other types of learning, and to gain understanding of the factors required for successful projects.

Concluding Comments

In considering research on technology and writing, it is helpful to divide it into two parts: research on the use of technology to support traditional writing outcomes, and research on new forms and contexts for writing. Research on traditional outcomes has asked whether writing processes or the quality and quantity of written products are affected by the use of word processing or programs that support writing by providing metacognitive prompts, organizational support, automated evaluative feedback, or support with transcription. The answer, it turns out, is, "It depends." Word processing by itself has minimal impact on written products, but in combination with instruction, it can help students develop better writing skills. Research on software that provides metacognitive prompts or procedural facilitators has produced mixed results, which suggests that the key issue is instructional design. Research on promising areas, such as the use of automated evaluation systems to provide feedback, is just beginning, but it seems likely that the design of the feedback and the surrounding instruction will be critical. Assistive technology has been shown to be effective under certain conditions, but it has important limitations that make the effects dependent on the match of student and tool, as well as instructional support. Computers are powerful, flexible tools for writing and writing instruction, but their effects depend on the design of the software and ways that instruction takes advantage of computer capabilities.

Questions about the educational impact of new forms of writing, such as hypermedia, and new social contexts for writing, such as CMC, have been more difficult to define and to answer, and the research is quite limited. A few studies of intercultural communication have asked questions about the effect on traditional written products. A more common approach has been to use qualitative methods to describe the social and cognitive processes that occur in classrooms using hypermedia or CMC. Research on CMC at the elementary and secondary level is limited primarily to case studies of intercultural communication. Case studies of classrooms using hypermedia have provided evidence about some of the cognitive processes required for creating hypermedia, as well as the impact on social interactions. They have also pointed out the importance of instruction guided by a model of the cognitive processes and learning outcomes desired.

It is possible that most of technology's impact on writing will come, not through direct use of technology in school, but rather through the changed experiences of students outside of school and new requirements for skills needed after school. In addition to more research on the educational interventions discussed in this review, research is needed on the impact of these larger societal factors.

References

Baker, E., & Kinzer, C. K. (1998). Effects of technology on process writing: Are they all good? In T. Shanahan & F. V. Rodriquez-Brown (Eds.), *47th yearbook of the National Reading Conference* (pp. 428–440). Chicago: National Reading Conference.

Baker, E. A. (2001). The nature of literacy in a technology-rich, fourth-grade classroom. *Reading Research and Instruction, 40,* 159–184.

Baker, E. A., Rozendal, M. S., & Whitenack, J. W. (2000). Audience awareness in a technology-rich elementary classroom. *Journal of Literacy Research, 32,* 395–419.

Bangert-Drowns, R. L. (1993). The word processor as an instructional tool: A meta-analysis of word processing in writing instruction. *Review of Educational Research, 63*(1), 69–93.

Baron, N. S. (1998). Letters by phone or speech by other means: The linguistics of email. *Language and Communication, 18,* 133–170.

Bereiter, C., & Scardamalia, M. (1987). *The psychology of written expression.* Hillsdale, NJ: Erlbaum.

Berge, Z. L., & Collins, M. P. E. (1998). *Wired together: The online classroom in K–12* (Vols. 1–4). Cresskill, NJ: Hampton Press.

Bolter, J. D. (1998). Hypertext and the question of visual literacy. In D. Reinking, M. C. McKenna, L. D. Labbo, & R. D. Kieffer (Eds.), *Handbook of literacy and technology* (pp. 3–13). Mahwah, NJ: Erlbaum.

Bonk, C. J., & Reynolds, T. H. (1992). Early adolescent composing within a generative–evaluative computerized prompting framework. *Computers in Human Behavior, 8,* 39–62.

Borgh, K., & Dickson, W. P. (1992). The effects on children's writing of adding speech synthesis to a word processor. *Journal of Research on Computing in Education, 24*(4), 533–544.

Braaksma, M. A. H., Rijlaarsdam, G., Couzijn, M., & van den Bergh, H. (2002). Learning to compose hypertext and linear text: Transfer or interference? In R. Bromme & E. Stahl (Eds.), *Writing hypertext and learning: Conceptual and empirical approaches* (pp. 15–37). Oxford, UK: Elsevier Science.

Bromme, R., & Stahl, E. (2002). Learning by producing hypertext from reader perspectives: Cognitive flexibility theory reconsidered. In R. Bromme & E. Stahl (Eds.), *Writing hypertext and learning: Conceptual and empirical approaches* (pp. 63–72). Oxford, UK: Elsevier Science.

Bruce, B. C., & Hogan, M. P. (1998). The disappearance of technology: Toward an ecological model of literacy. In D. Reinking, M. C. McKenna, L. D. Labbo, & R. D. Kieffer (Eds.), *Handbook of literacy and technology* (pp. 269–282). Mahwah, NJ: Erlbaum.

Bruce, B. C., Peyton, J. K., & Batson, T. (Eds.).

(1993). *Network-based classrooms: Promises and realities*. New York: Cambridge University Press.

Carver, S., Lehrer, R., Connell, T., & Erickson, J. (1992). Learning by hypermedia design: Issues of assessment and implementation. *Educational Psychologist, 27*, 385–404.

Cochran-Smith, M. (1991). Word processing and writing in elementary classrooms: A critical review of related literature. *Review of Educational Research, 61*, 107–155.

Cohen, M., & Riel, M. (1989). The effect of distant audiences on students' writing. *American Educational Research Journal, 26*, 143–159.

Crinon, J., & Legros, D. (2002). The semantic effects of consulting a textual database on rewriting. *Learning and Instruction, 12*, 605–626.

Daiute, C. A. (1986). Physical and cognitive factors in revising: Insights from studies in computers. *Research in the Teaching of English, 20*, 141–159.

Daiute, C., & Dalton, B. (1993). Collaboration between children learning to write: Can novices be masters? *Cognition and Instruction, 10*, 281–330.

Daiute, C., & Morse, F. (1994). Access to knowledge and expression: Multimedia writing tools for students with diverse needs and strengths. *Journal of Special Education Technology, 12*(3), 221–256.

Dillon, A., & Gabbard, R. (1998). Hypermedia as an educational technology. *Review of Educational Research, 68*, 322–349.

Eldred, J. C., & Hawisher, G. E. (1995). Researching electronic networks. *Written Communication, 12*, 330–359.

Erickson, J., & Lehrer, R. (1998). The evolution of critical standards as students design hypermedia documents. *Journal of the Learning Sciences, 7*, 351–386.

Erickson, J., & Lehrer, R. (2000). What's in a link?: Student conceptions of the rhetoric of association in hypermedia composition. In S. P. Lajoie (Ed.), *Computers as cognitive tools: No more walls* (Vol. 2, pp. 197–226). Mahwah, NJ: Erlbaum.

Fabos, B., & Young, M. D. (1999). Telecommunications in the classroom: Rhetoric versus reality. *Review of Educational Research, 69*, 217–287.

Ferretti, R. P., & MacArthur, C. A. (2001). The effects of elaborated goals on the argumentative writing of students with learning disabilities and their normally achieving peers. *Journal of Educational Psychology, 92*, 694–702.

Garner, R., & Gillingham, M. G. (1996). *Internet communication in six classrooms: Conversations across time, space, and culture*. Mahwah, NJ: Erlbaum.

Gallini, J. K., & Helman, N. (1995). Audience awareness in technology-mediated environments. *Journal of Educational Computing Research, 13*, 245–261.

Goldberg, A., Russell, M., & Cook, A. (2003). The effect of computers on student writing: A meta-analysis of studies from 1992 to 2002. *Journal of Technology, Learning, and Assessment, 2*(1), 1–51.

Graham, S., MacArthur, C. A., & Schwartz, S. S. (1995). The effects of goal setting and procedural facilitation on the revising behavior and writing performance of students with writing and learning problems. *Journal of Educational Psychology, 87*, 230–240.

Handley-More, D., Deitz, J., Billingsley, F. F., & Coggins, T. E. (2003). Facilitating written work using computer word processing and word prediction. *American Journal of Occupational Therapy, 57*, 139–151.

Hawisher, G. E. (1987). The effects of word processing on the revision strategies of college freshmen. *Research in the Teaching of English, 21*, 145–159.

Hayes, J. R., & Flower, L. S. (1980). Identifying the organization of writing processes. In L.W. Gregg & E. R. Steinberg (Eds.), *Cognitive processes in writing* (pp. 3–30). Hillsdale, NJ: Erlbaum.

Higgins, E. L., & Raskind, M. H. (1995). Compensatory effectiveness of speech recognition on the written composition performance of postsecondary students with learning disabilities. *Learning Disability Quarterly, 18*, 159–174.

Hillocks, G. (1986). *Research on written composition: New directions for teaching*. Urbana, IL: ERIC Clearinghouse on Reading and Communication Skills.

Kellogg, R. T., & Mueller, S. (1993). Performance amplification and process restructuring in computer-based writing. *International Journal of Man–Machine Studies, 39*, 33–49.

Kintsch, E., Steinhart, D., Stahl, G., Matthews, C., & Lamb, R. (2000). Developing summarization skills through the use of LSA-based feedback. *Interactive Learning Environments, 8*(2), 87–109.

Landauer, T. K., & Psotka, J. (2000). Simulating text understanding for educational applications with latent semantic analysis: Introduction to LSA. *Interactive Learning Environments, 8*(2), 73–86.

Liu, M. (1998). A study of engaging high-school students as multimedia designers in a cognitive apprenticeship-style learning environment. *Computers in Human Behavior, 14*, 1–29.

Liu, M., & Hsiao, Y.-P. (2002). Middle school students as multimedia designers: A project-based learning approach. *Journal of Interactive Learning Research, 13*, 311–337.

Liu, M., & Pedersen, S. (1998). The effect of being hypermedia designers on elementary school students' motivation and learning of design knowledge. *Journal of Interactive Learning Research, 9*, 155–182.

MacArthur, C. A. (2000). New tools for writing: Assistive technology for students with writing difficulties. *Topics in Language Disorders, 20*, 85–100.

MacArthur, C. A. (1998). Word processing with speech synthesis and word prediction: Effects on the dialogue journal writing of students with learning disabilities. *Learning Disability Quarterly, 21*, 1–16.

MacArthur, C. A. (1999). Word prediction for students with severe spelling problems. *Learning Disability Quarterly, 22*, 158–172.

MacArthur, C. A., & Cavalier, A. (2004). Dictation and speech recognition technology as accommodations in large-scale assessments for students with learning disabilities. *Exceptional Children, 71*, 43–58.

MacArthur, C., & Graham, S. (1987). Learning disabled students' composing under three methods of text production: Handwriting, word processing, and dictation. *Journal of Special Education, 21*, 22–42.

MacArthur, C. A., Graham, S., Haynes, J. A., & De La Paz, S. (1996). Spelling checkers and students with learning disabilities: Performance comparisons and impact on spelling. *Journal of Special Education, 30*, 35–57.

McNaughton, D., Hughes, C., & Ofiesh, N. (1997). Proofreading for students with learning disabilities: Integrating computer use and strategy use. *Learning Disabilities Research and Practice, 12*(1), 16–28.

Myers, J., Hammett, R., & McKillop, A. M. (1998). Opportunities for critical literacy and pedagogy in student-authored hypermedia. In D. Reinking, M. C. McKenna, L. D. Labbo, & R. D. Kieffer (Eds.), *Handbook of literacy and technology* (pp. 63–78). Mahwah, NJ: Erlbaum.

Neilson, L. (1998). Coding the light: Rethinking generational authority in a rural high school telecommunications project. In D. Reinking, M. C. McKenna, L. D. Labbo, & R. D. Kieffer (Eds.), *Handbook of literacy and technology* (pp. 129–144). Mahwah, NJ: Erlbaum.

Olson, D. R. (1995). Conceptualizing the written word: An intellectual autobiography. *Written Communication, 12*(3), 277–297.

Palmquist, M. (2003). A brief history of computer support for writing centers and writing-across-the-curriculum programs. *Computers and Composition, 20*(4), 395–413.

Perkins, D. N. (1985). The fingertip effect: How information-processing technology shapes thinking. *Educational Researcher, 14*(7), 11–17.

Purves, A. (1998). Flies in the web of hypertext. In D. Reinking, M. C. McKenna, L. D. Labbo, & R. D. Kieffer (Eds.), *Handbook of literacy and technology* (pp. 235–252). Mahwah, NJ: Erlbaum.

Quinlan, T. (2004). Speech recognition technology and students with writing difficulties: Improving fluency. *Journal of Educational Psychology, 96*, 337–346.

Reece, J. E., & Cummings, G. (1996). Evaluating speech-based composition methods: Planning, dictation, and the listening word processor. In C.

M. Levy & S. Ransdell (Eds.), *The science of writing: Theories, methods, individual differences, and applications* (pp. 361–380). Mahwah, NJ: Erlbaum.

Reynolds, T. H., & Bonk, C. J. (1996). Facilitating college writers' revisions within a generative–evaluative computerized prompting framework. *Computers and Composition, 13*(1), 93–108.

Rowley, K., Carsons, P., & Miller, T. (1998). A cognitive technology to teach composition skills: Four studies with the R-WISE writing tutor. *Journal of Educational Computing Research, 18*, 259–296.

Rowley, K., & Meyer, N. (2003). The effect of a computer tutor for writers on student writing achievement. *Journal of Educational Computing Research, 29*, 169–187.

Russell, M. (1999). Testing writing on computers: A follow-up study comparing performance on computer and on paper. *Educational Policy Analysis Archives, 7*(20). Available online at epaa.asu.edu/epaa/v7n20/

Russell, M., & Plati, T. (2001). *Effects of computer versus paper administration of a state-mandated writing assessment.* Teachers College Record online at www.tcrecord.org, ID No. 10709.

Scribner, S., & Cole, M. (1978). Literacy without schooling: Testing for intellectual effects. *Harvard Educational Review, 48*, 448–461.

Sennett, A. J. (2004, July 5). Romance at first click?: Ha. *The Washington Post*, p. B1.

Shachar, H., & Sharan, S. (1994). Talking, relating, and achieving: Effects of cooperative learning and whole-class instruction. *Cognition and Instruction, 12*(4), 313–353.

Steinhart, D. (2001). *Summary Street: An intelligent tutoring system for improving student writing through the use of latent semantic analysis.* Unpublished dissertation, Institute of Cognitive Science, University of Colorado, Boulder.

Sturm, J. M., & Rankin-Erickson, J. L. (2002). Effects of hand-drawn and computer-generated concept mapping on the expository writing of students with learning disabilities. *Learning Disabilities Research and Practice, 17*, 124–139.

Van Waes, L., & Schellens, P. J. (2003). Writing profiles: The effect of the writing mode on pausing and revision patterns of experienced writers [Special issue: Pragmatics of Writing], *Journal of Pragmatics, 35*(6), 829–853.

Wolfe, E. W., Bolton, S., Feltovich, R., & Niday, D. M. (1996). The influence of student experience with word processors on the quality of essays written for a direct writing assessment. *Assessing Writing, 3*, 123–147.

Zellermayer, M., Salomon, G., Globerson, T., & Givon, H. (1991). Enhancing writing-related metacognitions through a computerized writing partner. *American Educational Research Journal, 28*, 373–391.

Chapter 18

"I Guess I'd Better Watch My English"
Grammars and the Teaching of the English Language Arts

Michael W. Smith, Julie Cheville, *and* George Hillocks, Jr.

Sitting on a plane and chatting with the person next to us, we all have been asked, "What do you do for a living?" If we respond, "I teach English" or "I teach those who want to be teachers of English," the inevitable response is something like, "Oh, I guess I'd better watch my English, then." This exchange shows the close association in the public imagination between teaching grammar and teaching English, an association that persists despite the fact that for a century, research has consistently shown that the teaching of grammar as a separate subject has little or no effect on students' language development. In this chapter, we discuss some of the pressures that might account for the continuation of a practice that has been so roundly criticized. Then we briefly review the research that informs that criticism. Finally, we discuss research and theory that might identify some directions for future research and teaching. But before we do so, some definitions are in order.

The Meanings of Grammar

Part of the problem with discussions of "grammar" is that the term itself has so many meanings. Building on an important article by Francis (1954), Hartwell (1985) argues that the term is used to mean many different things. Two meanings seem especially important to understanding the gap between research and theory. One meaning of grammar is the systematic description, analysis, and articulation of the formal patterns of a language. Modern linguists of different theoretical perspectives seek to provide that description, analysis, and articulation in different ways. Grammar is also the term used to refer to a set of rules governing how one ought to speak or write. While modern grammars eschew this kind of prescription, traditional school grammar (TSG) combines the explanatory function of grammar with prescription. "Parts of speech" and other terms, for example, purport to identify the function of words, phrases, and clauses in English. Mechanics and usage rules (e.g., "Adverbial conjunctions that join independent clauses take semicolons") prescribe a standard for correctness.

The Pressure Teachers Face

It is easy to see why a grammar that has a prescriptive function would be attractive to teachers in an era of high-stakes assessments. Such assessments typically include some kind of editing task in addition to a writing sample. Although test designers seem to recognize the importance of writing as an indication of students' problem solving, reasoning, and critical thinking by including these writing samples on their tests, the diagnostic method employed in these assessments focuses on surface-level features (Powers, Burstein, Chodorow, Fowles, & Kukich, 2002). In short, current tests place a high emphasis on the standard of correctness that TSG is designed to provide.

As Hillocks (2002) explains, the desire for the expedient processing of student essays by human scorers accounts for the focus on surface-level errors and prompt-specific cues rather than richer indications of students' composing ability. In recent years the desire for reliable and efficient scoring has led to design of automated scoring systems to replace those human scorers. This development will likely increase the focus on surface features of texts.

In one such system, teachers can access an online library of 108 writing prompts spanning all grade levels in narrative, expository, and persuasive modes. This topic function allows teachers to use prompts that have been already tested and scored. Because these prompts are calibrated to test-trialed 4- and 6-point rubrics and their representative benchmark essays, a scoring engine offers writers an immediate, or real-time, response just seconds after students submit an essay online. Responses focus on the following areas:

- Grammar, that is, fragments, garbled sentences, subject–verb agreement, verb-form errors, pronoun errors, possessive errors, wrong or missing words.
- Usage, that is, article errors, confused words, wrong form of word, faulty comparison, and nonstandard verb or word.
- Mechanics, that is, spelling, missing capitalization of proper nouns, missing initial capital letter in a sentence, missing question mark, missing final punctuation, missing apostrophe, missing comma, missing hyphen, fused words, compound words, and duplicate words.
- Style, that is, repetition of words, inappropriate words or phrases, sentences with passive voice, long sentences, short sentences, and sentences beginning with coordinating conjunctions.
- Organization and development, that is, introductory material, thesis statement, main ideas, supporting ideas, conclusion,

and transitional words and phrases (ETS Technologies, Inc. 2002).

A writer receives both a holistic score and descriptive feedback for each submitted essay. Essays return with highlighted portions of text flagging particular errors. By clicking on highlights, students receive additional "diagnostic analysis." For instance, a short sentence within a paragraph consisting of several other short sentences might be flagged for potential stylistic flaws with the suggestion that the student might be able to improve his or her sentence structure through sentence combining (ETS Technologies, Inc., 2002). Regarding content organization and development, the diagnostic analysis is geared to transitional cues according to the computational assumption that words like "first, second, third" and phrases like "in summary" and "in conclusion" are topic-related vocabulary signaling content development and coherence. In the absence of an introductory cue, for instance, the flagged portion in an expository lead might read: "Is this your thesis?"

In summary, if high-stakes tests focus increasingly on errors of various sorts enumerated in the first three categories mentioned earlier, it is easy to understand why teachers would persist in a focus of instruction that seems designed to eliminate those errors, especially if the method also held the promise of helping students with their problems in the last two areas. Unfortunately, however, there is a wealth of evidence that TSG does neither.

The Problems with TSG

TSG is an Inadequate Description of the Way Language Works

In the first place, the categories that TSG proposes simply are not useful. Fries (1952) argues that the analytic method associated with TSG is so restrictive that it fails to orient students to many crucial features of English (e.g., phonology, morphology, pitch, stress, and juncture), features which inevitably affect meaning. He also demonstrates that a focus on parts of speech and other restrictive categories of language proves hopelessly ambiguous. TSG presents definitions that cannot function with desired results unless the person using them has more information about language than the definition provides. For example, TSG tells us that a noun is the name of a person, place, or thing (some add idea to the list). Blue, red, and yellow are the names of colors but would not be considered nouns in the phrase, the blue shirt. Fries points out that a large part of this difficulty arises because the definitions are not parallel; that is, a word like blue is the name of a color but, at the same time, can be used to modify a noun. It fits two definitions.

The problematic nature of parts of speech is made manifest by the discussion of nouns offered by Riley and Parker (1998). Although they recognize that many words do not clearly fit into the traditional definition of noun, they posit that "words like *shirt, horse,* and *Frank* easily fit the semantic definition of a noun since they name specific entities in the real world" (p. 72). What then to make of "shirt factory," "horsing around," or the "Frank Lloyd Wright Foundation" (to say nothing of a "frank discussion" or the "franking privilege")? Even the words chosen by experts for the express purpose of providing an unproblematic illustration of a term are in fact problematic.

Moreover, TSG holds that language conventions, including standard dialectal features, are inviolable. Lexical and syntactic elements associated with vernacular dialects are identified as errors, which risks the inference among teachers and students that they are inherently flawed—an inference that does not stand up to scholarly investigations of those dialects. In the case of black English vernacular (BEV), for example, Labov (1972) argues forcefully that the dialect is not the mass of error it was sometimes thought to be. On the contrary, he shows that BEV is "a distinct subsystem within the larger grammar of English" (pp. 63–64) with its own regular conventions and a few clearly different rules for the production of utterances. In addition to demonstrating the internal regularities of BEV and how failures to comprehend it lead to serious misunderstandings by educators, linguists have also demonstrated that speakers of BEV develop a finely honed sense of logic and argument within their own language conventions (pp. 201–240). Since this work, researchers have also indicated how teachers' assumptions of deficit undermine language learners' esteem and developmental progress (Fasold, 1984; Shuy & Fasold, 1973; Trudgill, 1975).

In contrast to the view that conventions are both fixed and nonnegotiable, sociolinguists insist that the explicit study and negotiation of language variety facilitates children's language development. In her descriptive portrait of distinct *speech communities* (Hymes, 1974), Heath (1983) illuminates the interdependence of language, culture, and thought, a focus that has welcomed broader interest in discourse (Cazden, 1988; Purcell-Gates, 1995). In 1996, the school board of the Oakland Unified School District (CA) approved a resolution implementing the use of contrastive pedagogies for African American students whose primary language is Ebonics. The unfortunate misreading of both the initiative and its intent doomed curricular reform but has not forestalled research that continues to indicate how the negotiation of dialectal variety in the context of meaningful reading activities and writing processes supports literacy development (Delpit, 1988; Harris-Wright, 1999; Ladson-Billings, 1994; Wolfram, 1999; Wolfram & Creech, 1996).

Students Have Difficulty Learning TSG

But even if TSG were an excellent description of the language, studying it would be problematic because of the difficulty students have learning it. The most persuasive study that makes this point was done by Macauley (1947). His participants, Scottish students of varying academic levels, had studied grammar for 30 minutes a day for 4 years. He presented these students sets of sentences and asked that they identify the nouns, verbs, adjectives, and adverbs. With passing set at 50% correct, only one student passed. He administered the same test to students completing the elite senior secondary school, which, in Scotland, admitted only the top 20% of junior secondary school graduates. These students had studied grammar for 9 years. Of these top students, only 42% were able to identify 50% of the items correctly.

TSG Has No Impact on Student Writing

It might be worth teaching and reteaching TSG if doing so had instructional benefits. The evidence is quite clear that it does not. In their 1963 review of research in written composition, Braddock, Lloyd-Jones, and Schoer make this unequivocal declaration: "The teaching of formal grammar has a negligible or, because it usually displaces some instruction and practice in actual composition, even a harmful effect on the improvement of writing" (pp. 37–38). Hillocks (1986) makes an equally strong statement some two decades later:

> School boards, administrators, and teachers who impose the systematic study of traditional school grammar on their students over lengthy periods of time in the name of teaching writing do them a gross disservice which should not be tolerated by anyone concerned with the effective teaching of good writing. (p. 248)

Other reviews of the teaching of grammar (see, e.g., Hillocks & Smith, 2003) discuss a whole range of studies upon which these judgments are based. The most compelling of these was done by Elley, Barham, Lamb, and Wyllie in 1976. They considered the achievement of New Zealand high school students as they moved through the third, fourth, and fifth forms (grades 9–11) and in a follow-up 1 year after the completion of instruction. The sample was large (248 students at the outset and 166 after 3 years) and carefully controlled. Students were divided into eight classes matched on the basis of four test scores, sex, ethnicity, contributing school, and subject option. Three of these classes studied the Oregon curriculum, which included generative (transformational) grammar. Three other classes studied the same curriculum, replacing the study of transformational grammar with extra literature and creative writing. (We discuss alternative grammars later in the chapter.) The final two classes studied TSG. The instruction in literature for these classes was centered on the study of six to eight sets of popular fiction. During each year of the study, teachers taught a different treatment so that no one method was taught by the same teacher for more than 1 year. The researchers used a variety of measures after each year of the study: tests of reading, listening, English usage, spelling, English literature, and sentence combining; criterion-referenced scales on essays the students had written; and attitude surveys.

The findings are notable for how few differences were found. At the end of the first year, no significant differences among groups existed on any of the measures. At the end of the second year, the TSG group's essay content was significantly better than the no grammar group, and the generative grammar group's attitude toward writing and literature was significantly worse than that of the other two groups. At the end of the third year, the generative grammar group and the no-grammar group performed significantly better on the sentence combining test. Both grammar groups performed significantly better on the English usage test. However, there were no significant differences in the quality or correctness of students' actual writing. The fact that the differences among groups were small is clear. Indeed, even the superiority of the grammar groups on the test of English usage is questionable, because it "was dispersed over a wide range of mechanical conventions, and was not clearly associated with sentence structure" (Elley et al., 1976, p. 15). This advantage must be weighed against the negative effect of studying grammar on students' attitudes toward English.

Students' strong negative reaction to the teaching of grammar has been documented by other scholars as well. For example, Hillocks (1971) surveyed attitudes toward English of over 3,000 high school students in three predominantly blue-collar suburban communities. He reports that students rated the study of TSG and mechanics as the least interesting part of their English programs.

So What to Do?

Given the strong evidence that instruction in TSG does little to facilitate language development, but recognizing the increasing emphasis on error in an increasingly high-stakes environment, it is important to examine what alternatives teachers have available. Theory and research have identified two possible responses: teach alternative grammars, or teach TSG in a way that maximizes its benefits while minimizing its harms.

Alternative Grammars

In this section, we consider three grammars that have had some influence in the teaching of English: structural grammars, transformational–

generative grammar (TGG), and systemic functional linguistics (SFL).

STRUCTURAL GRAMMARS

Structural linguists collect samples of the spoken language of native speakers and analyze them at three levels: the phonemic (significant sounds or alphabet), the morphological (words and parts of words that carry distinctive meaning), and the syntactic (sentence structures and substructures; e.g., clauses and phrases). They work to identify the elements of these levels through structural features. At the phonemic level, for example, they show that different consonants are voiced in different ways.

In a similar way, structural linguists analyze parts of speech through structural features. For example, they point out that nouns take plural and possessive inflections; use certain derivational affixes, such as *-er, -ism*, and *-tion*; and fit in frames of the following kind: One _____ is here. A complete analysis of any form class in English is quite complex (see, e.g., Francis, 1958, pp. 237–288).

Structural linguists examine syntax most commonly through immediate constituent analysis, a technique based on the assumption that linguistic structures may be analyzed by dichotomous cuts to the level of individual words and sometimes meaningful segments of words. Although this analysis helps to show certain relationships among the words and phrases that constitute sentences, the rules for making the cuts were never clearly laid out. Structural grammars do not provide much insight into syntax.

Certain basic assumptions of structural linguistics were to come under sharp criticism. One was its rejection of meaning as a criterion for the analysis of language. Some critics argued that the structuralists' own techniques contradicted this belief; that is, although a linguist may not know the meaning of a language, the native informant's identification of contrastive features depends upon the informant's knowledge of meaning. A second important assumption inherent in its descriptive procedures also came under attack: the philosophical view that language is what comes out of the mouth of a speaker. Assuming that to be true, then no matter how large a sample of language is collected, it will remain a tiny proportion of what may

be spoken. However, structural grammars do not explain how speakers are able to produce utterances that they have not heard but that will be recognized by other native speakers as grammatical.

Although structural grammars do not currently have much effect on school curricula, some schools did incorporate them in years past as an alternative to TSG. Research on teaching structural grammar, however, does not provide a ringing endorsement of their effect. Working with classes from 21 schools, Smith and Sustakowski (1968) compared the effects of a structural grammar to the effects of traditional grammar. They report large gains on the Modern Language Aptitude Test (MLAT) by the group that studied structural grammar. This is understandable because the MLAT measures sensitivity to phonological, morphological, and syntactic structures, something the structural group studied but the traditional group did not. Much like TSG, however, there was not transfer to situations that are of greater concern for teachers of English: The researchers did not find significant differences on a variety of measures of correctness.

TGG

A grammar that has had more influence on schools is transformational–generative grammar (TGG). The fundamental question that TGG seeks to answer is the one that structural grammars do not take up: how a speaker whose experience with language is finite "can produce or understand an indefinite number of new sentences" (Chomsky, 1957, p. 15).

TGG rejects the view that the whole of language is contained in actually observed utterances. The task of transformational grammarians is to make explicit phrase and transformational rules that explain native speakers' intuitive knowledge and use of grammar. (It is important to note that the use of the term *rule* here has nothing to do with rules for correctness found in TSG.) In TGG, phrase rules explain the surface structure of sentences, while transformational rules examine the relation of deep structure to meaning. The purpose of studying grammar, then, is to develop the rules that will explain how surface structures are generated from deep structures and to state these rules so that they have the widest possible generality in their application (Hillocks, McCabe, & McCampbell, 1971, p. 427).

While the object of structural linguistics is to identify, through constituent analysis, the minimal grammatical categories that combine to form utterances, TGG moved beyond phrase structure rules that delineate minimal structures (e.g., labeling trees) to rules that identify how transformations of deep structure result in particular minimal units and meanings. Unlike the empirical focus on language production that characterized structural grammar, TGG linguists were interested in the infinite productivity of all languages and in documenting the transformations that languages make possible.

Because TGG focuses on the generation of new structures, it might seem that knowledge of TGG would transfer to writing. Indeed, Mellon (1969) finds that applying a knowledge of transformational grammar to concrete sentence combining (SC) problems results in a significant increase in students' syntactic complexity. O'Hare (1973), however, argues that the gains in Mellon's experimental group were the result of SC practice rather than knowledge of transformational grammar, a hypothesis confirmed by his research. O'Hare's finding jibes with that of Elley and his colleagues (1976), which, as we explained earlier, calls into question whether the explicit teaching of the principles of TGG benefits students' writing. As a consequence of these results, researchers turned their investigations away from teaching transformational grammar and toward investigation of SC instruction that did not employ transformational terminology.

In SC activities, students are asked to transform kernel sentences into sentences that are more syntactically complex. Strong (1973), who has developed a corpus of instructional materials using SC, defines the kernel sentence as "the basic stuff of sentences." He explains that English has between 4 and 10 patterns of kernels, depending the system for identifying kernels to which one subscribes. Strong illustrates the idea by providing this set of three kernels:

The writer is young.
The writer is developing.
The writer works with options. (p. 4)

These kernels can be transformed into more complex structures in a number of ways, for example, "The young, developing writer works with options," or "The writer who is young and developing works with options."

The research on the use of SC strongly suggests that SC is effective in increasing students' syntactic maturity, typically measured by analyzing the numbers of words per clause and the number of clauses per sentence. In their review, Hillocks and Mavrogenes (1986) report that "the overwhelming majority of these studies have been positive, with about 60 percent of them reporting that work in sentence combining, from as low as grade 2 through the adult level, results in significant advances (at least $p < .05$) on measures of syntactic maturity" (pp. 142–143).

These findings, however, do not provide unqualified support for using SC. Most significantly, they do not establish whether longer clauses mean better writing. In fact, Hake and Williams (1979) argue that when students who were initially judged to be incompetent writers become competent writers, their T-unit length decreases. Other studies (see, e.g., Nold & Freedman, 1977) have also shown a very low correlation between mean clause length and quality ratings. In addition, research (see, e.g., Crowhurst & Piche, 1979) suggests that syntactic complexity is a function of the writer's purpose in a specific piece of writing. If so, syntactic complexity cannot be an effective measure of writing ability unless there is some control for writer's purpose.

Even if gains in syntactic complexity are important, there are questions about whether those gains are maintained. Strong (1986) labels the Morenberg, Daiker, and Kerek (1978) study "probably the best designed, best funded, and most carefully executed SC study to date" (p. 7). Morenberg et al. report that the experimental group that studied SC scored significantly higher on holistic and analytic measures than the control group, whose instruction focused on modes of discourse. They also report that these gains were maintained for several months. However, 28 months after the instruction, Kerek, Daiker, and Morenberg (1980) gave their subjects a delayed posttest and found that, while the experimental group's scores did not decline, the control group gained significantly, without specific instruction. These results suggest that syntactic fluency may be, in part, the result of maturity. They raise a question of the ultimate benefits of accelerating what may be natural development.

A related question is whether SC actually increases students' skill in manipulating syntax or rather simply cues them to make use of resources they already have. Smith and Combs (1980) studied this question. They presented three assignment conditions to college freshmen: the assignment, with no cue about structure; the assignment plus an overt cue indicating that the audience would be impressed with long, complex sentences; and 2 days of SC, which they argue, would covertly suggest the desire for longer sentences. Their results indicate that a combination of the overt and covert cues over 1 week produced mean gains in words per clause comparable to those gains produced by a semester of SC practice in other studies.

Other studies took a more direct approach to examine the effect of SC on writing quality. Hillocks (1986) included four SC studies that had measures of writing quality in his meta-analysis of composition research and found that they had a highly homogeneous effect size (ES) of 0.35 standard deviations. This effect is significantly greater than the average effect of grammar (–0.29), freewriting (0.16), and the study of models (0.22). The mean ES of SC is approximately the same as the ES of treatments using rating scales (0.36). Only the inquiry focus (0.56) has a significantly greater ES than SC.

If SC is designed to promote syntactic complexity and if syntactic complexity, is at best a problematic indicator of writing quality, what might account for these positive findings? Research by Bereiter and Scardamalia (1982) provides one possible explanation. They found that when children revise, they avoid changing basic sentence plans. Shaughnessy's (1977) analysis of sentence consolidation errors suggests that basic writers are plagued by the same tendency. Perhaps SC provides students with a more systematic repertoire of syntactic choices and helps them avoid this difficulty. Crowhurst (1983) offers three possible explanations. She notes that the increase in writing quality may be the result of increased practice in writing sentences, greater facility in constructing sentences, and increased attention to other aspects of composing as a conse-

quence of students' facility in constructing sentences. Strong (1986) supports Crowhurst's third alternative. He believes that "SC may help with automaticity in syntax, freeing up mental energy so that learners can concentrate on planning and composing" (p. 3). He also argues that revising and editing are the main skills affected by SC practice. Freedman (1985) believes that SC promotes skill in perceiving relationships on the T-unit level and that this skill transfers to the whole-text level. She contends that because SC causes students to search for these relationships, they develop a habit of mind that, in turn, extends conceptual knowledge.

Another area of concern for researchers is the effect of SC on error. And here the findings are a mixed bag. For example, Schuster's (1976, 1977) experimental groups exhibited fewer errors on their posttest essays, both in usage and mechanics. On the other hand, Maimon and Nodine (1978, 1979) find that SC practice results in more errors on a rewriting passage, though this is not true for freewriting, and Hake and Williams (1979) report a higher "flaw count" with increased T-unit length. Perhaps these contradictory findings are to be expected. If instruction results in students' experimenting with more complex structures, errors are bound to result. On the other hand, if SC practice focuses on producing specific structures and learning how to punctuate those structures, it is likely to prove effective.

SYSTEMIC FUNCTIONAL LINGUISTICS

Systemic functional linguistics (SFL) is a system of language analysis developed by M. A. K. Halliday and his colleagues. Though it resembles structural grammar in some ways, it moves into territory never explored by the older structural grammars. While structural grammar rejected meaning as a means of analysis, SFL makes meaning one of its chief means of analysis. The concern for meaning is what the term *functional* conveys. Furthermore, while the other grammars we have discussed treat words, clauses, or sentences as the units of analysis, SFL moves beyond clauses to a consideration of how texts and genre work to make meaning.

SFL's focus on meaning can be seen in Halliday's (1985) analysis of the following three sentences:

1. The duke gave my aunt this teapot. (p. 32)
2. This teapot my aunt was given by the duke. (p. 35)
3. My aunt was given this teapot by the duke. (p. 35)

Halliday argues that the position of "the duke" at the beginning of sentence 1 has the effect of announcing, "I am going to tell you something about the duke. He gave my aunt this teapot." This position results in what he calls the *psychological subject* or *theme*, a notion of subject that has been included in TSG, such as when a teacher explains, "The subject tells you what the sentence is about."

The "duke" is also the subject in that he is the doer of the act in question. Halliday (1985) calls this the *logical subject* or *actor*. In addition, sentence 1 is a proposition about the duke; the question that it generates is "Did the duke give my aunt this teapot?" Halliday calls this function the *grammatical subject*. In sentence 1, all three senses of the traditional concept of subject are fulfilled by a single term. In idealized sentences, the kind we find in TSG books, one term frequently fulfills all three functions. The question that arises is whether that is a necessary condition. Sentence 2 demonstrates that it is not:

2. This teapot my aunt was given by the duke. (p. 35)

In this sentence, the three functions are split among three separate terms. The shift of "this teapot" to the beginning of the sentence announces, "I am going to tell you something about this teapot." The sentence also adds a new semantic dimension by indicating the idea of exclusivity with two possibilities of meaning, depending on the tonal pattern of the noun phrase. With primary stress on the word *this*, it indicates that *this particular and no other teapot* was given my aunt by the duke. A primary stress on *teapot* indicates that the duke gave my aunt the teapot and no other item. Sentence 1, on the other hand, allows for the possibility that the duke may have given my aunt something in addition to the teapot.

In short, *teapot* fulfills the role of theme in the sentence, while the *duke* remains the actor and *aunt* becomes the grammatical subject, that about which something is predicated. This discussion, which Halliday extends, illustrates how SFL demonstrates the multiple coding of language.

Halliday (1985) also shows how clauses are organized as messages. He uses the term *theme* to designate the topic of a clause and *rheme* to indicate the comment on the topic. For example, in sentence 2, "this teapot" is the theme, and the rheme is the remainder of the sentence. This analysis of clause Halliday refers to as *clause as message*. The analysis of patterns of themes and rhemes provide a major means of examining the ways in which texts are conceptualized and organized, and has been widely used by those interested in teaching clearer sentence structure and stronger passage flow (e.g., Williams, 1999).

Halliday (1985) also discusses the clause in terms of its

> role as a means of representing patterns of experience. A fundamental property of language is that it enables human beings to build a mental picture of reality, to make sense of their experience of what goes on around them and inside them. Here again the clause is the most significant grammatical unit, in this case because it is the clause that functions as the representation of processes. (p. 101)

Halliday argues that a process consists essentially of three components: the actor, the process, and the goal. Halliday designates clauses that may be analyzed as material processes as those that express the "notion that some entity 'does' something—which may be done 'to' some other entity" (p. 103). To use one of his examples, the clause "Geoffrey flew the kite" may be probed by questions such as the following: "What did Geoffrey do?" "What did the kite do?"

However, other clauses may not be analyzed in this way. For example, the clause "Geoffrey liked the kite" cannot be probed with either *do* or *happen*. We cannot say that *Geoffrey* is is doing something to the kite. To explain such clauses, Halliday (1985) posits the category of *mental processes*. In mental process clauses, there is always one participant who is human or, alternatively, one who is endowed with consciousness. Because mental processes are not processes of doing or happening, as are the material processes, the terms *actor, process,* and *goal* do not apply. Halliday offers *senser, process,* and *phenomenon* (thing or fact) as the primary components of mental processes.

Halliday (1985) identifies four other types of processes:

1. Relational, which involve identification and attribution, as in "He is the flyer" or "The kite is red."
2. Behavioral, which have to do with physiological and psychological behavior, such as breathing, coughing, and so forth.
3. Verbal, which have to do with symbolic exchanges of meaning (e.g., saying).
4. Existential, which assert that something exists (e.g., "There is a skunk in the drive").

Each of these, like material and mental processes, may be distinguished from the others and shown to be systematically different in their requirements and functioning.

These categories and their extensions and elaborations permit SFL theorists to analyze how genres differ from one another. For example, Halliday (1993) demonstrates how scientists made use of linguistic resources that were latent in English to transform material and mental process clauses into nominalizations that could be used as themes in other material, mental, and relational clauses. These nominalizations allow scientific discourse to portray facts as things that can act on other things. In addition, the nominalization of previously stated clauses allows for the logical progression of theme–rheme arrangements so that the discourse moves forward in a logical and clear, step-by-step fashion. Halliday (1993) puts it this way:

Newton and his successors were creating a new variety of English for a new kind of knowledge; a kind of knowledge in which experiments were carried out; general principles [were] derived by reasoning from these experiments, with the aid of mathematics; and these principles in turn tested by further experiments. The discourse had to proceed step by step, with a constant movement from "this is what we have established so far" to "this is what follows from it next"; and each of these two parts, both the "taken for granted" part and the new information, had to be presented in a way that would make its status in the argument clear. The most effective way to do this, in English grammar, is to constrict the whole step as a single clause, with the two parts turned into nouns, one at the beginning and one at the end,

and a verb in between saying how the second follows from the first. (p. 81)

Followers of Halliday have begun to use his insights to understand the challenges distinct genre pose for student writers. For example, Schleppegrell (1998) investigated the extent to which students writing in science class met the genre expectations of scientific description. She argues that functional approaches "can reveal the particular grammatical structures that are useful" (p. 207) for a particular task and students' ability to manipulate those structures. Wollman-Bonilla (2000) made use of a similar sort of analysis to evaluate how family message journals affect young children's understanding of the conventions of science writing and their ability to use them flexibly. These studies suggest that SFL can be a valuable resource for teachers to identifying target structures. Though advocates of such analyses argue that students must be taught the specialized structures they need to write in a particular genre (see, e.g., Kamberelis, 1999), their research does not provide a clear picture of how that teaching ought to be done.

More Progressive Approaches to TSG

More progressive approaches to TSG also use grammatical insights to help students produce target structures. Rather than emphasize grammar as a means of analysis, as TSG has traditionally done, these approaches help students to employ grammatical knowledge in a more synthetic way.

Noguchi (1991) argues that situating grammar instruction in the context of writing requires limitations on the scope and sequence of TSG. By eliminating the memorization of nomenclature and the identification of constituent parts unrelated to writing development, grammar instruction can occur during the writing process. According to Noguchi, it should focus on problems associated with organizing and punctuating the following minimal categories: (1) the sentence and (2) the nonsentence, which includes the fragments of modifier, subject, and verb (p. 34). Because students are intuitively familiar with these categories, such an orientation makes sensible the operational knowledge required of writers. Offering sentence formation strategies adapted from

TGG, Noguchi identifies specific strategies that can help students recognize, punctuate, and manipulate the structures most closely associated with syntactic correctness and maturity. In his conclusion, Noguchi admits limitations: "The very focus on the syntactic structure of sentences ensures that grammar instruction will have much to say about the form and style of sentences but very little to say about the content and organization of writing, areas which extend beyond the borders of the sentence unit and—more significantly—count more in actually enhancing writing quality" (p. 106).

As we have noted, one potential problem with SC activities is that in the process of synthesizing clauses, students may actually create new problems in semantic and syntactic fluency. And, as Noguchi (1991) warns, manipulation at the level of the sentence unit does not assist writers to understand the patterning of whole texts. Attentive to this problem, Noden (1999) recommends an alternate approach to TSG that emphasizes the relation of syntax and rhetorical structures. Consonant with the expressivist model of composing that views the writer as artist (Berlin, 1988), Noden's approach begins with writers' imitating and generating modifiers, or "brushstrokes," in the context of writing and revising sentences and passages in narrative and poetic genres. The emphasis at this stage is on understanding modifiers as elaborating not just syntax but meaning. In their narrative writing, for instance, students learn how single or multiple-word brushstrokes do not simply vary the sounds of sentences but, most importantly, elaborate the image denoted by the simple subject and verb. Once students are able to create modifiers that elaborate images and ideas in an abbreviated context, they are prepared to consider how this local patterning contributes to an essay's rhetorical structure. In other words, image grammar serves a broader structural grammar that coordinates and subordinates paragraph units. In a final chapter addressing the revision of drafts, Noden offers limited, if not insufficient, attention to the correction of surface-level grammatical errors.

In her own response to TSG, Weaver (1996, 1998) broadens the study of minimal categories to include parts of speech and attends in much greater detail to surface-level syntactic, morphemic, and mechanical problems. Framing her approach in constructivist theory, Weaver reconceptualizes the nature and function of grammatical error. Suggesting the dangers of a predominant emphasis on correctness, Weaver concurs with those who claim that error is an opportunity to understand the assumptions and textual patterns of writers (Kroll & Schafer, 1978). For Weaver, the study and negotiation of error are central to writing development, and she offers both strategies and lesson plans for developing an instructional sequence that orients students to the patterns of error they commit in and across writing assignments.

No empirical evidence yet suggests that alternative approaches to TSG actually contribute to students' writing development. This may be due, in part, to the relatively recent implementation of these approaches in language classrooms. Nevertheless, anecdotal evidence offered by teachers at regional and national conferences indicates, at the very least, the considerable professional interest in synthetic approaches that situate grammar instruction in the context of process instruction. Future research employing both quantitative and qualitative tools needs to document the efficacy of these approaches. In addition, researchers must consider the effects of automated scoring technologies currently available in web-based writing programs, noting how a surface-level orientation to error influences the writing quality and perceptions of elementary and secondary school computer users.

References

Bereiter, C., & Scardamalia, M. (1982). From conversation to composition: The role of instruction in a developmental process. In R. Glaser (Ed.), *Advances in instructional psychology* (Vol. 2, pp. 1–64). Hillsdale, NJ: Erlbaum.

Berlin, J. (1988). Rhetoric and ideology in the writing class. *College English, 50,* 477–494.

Braddock, R., Lloyd-Jones, R., & Schoer, L. (1963). *Research in written composition.* Champaign, IL: National Council of Teachers of English.

Cazden, C. (1988). *Classroom discourse: The language of teaching and learning.* Portsmouth, NH: Heinemann.

Chomsky, N. (1957). *Syntactic structures.* The Hague: Mouton.

Chomsky, N. (1965). *Aspects of the theory of syntax.* Cambridge, MA: MIT Press.

Crowhurst, M. (1983). Sentence combining: Maintaining realistic expectations. *College Composition and Communication, 34,* 62–72.

Crowhurst, M., & Piche, G. L. (1979). Audience and mode of discourse effects on syntactic complexity in writing at two grade levels. *Research in the Teaching of English, 13,* 101–109.

Delpit, L. D. (1988). The silenced dialogue: Power and pedagogy in educating other people's children. *Harvard Educational Review, 58,* 280–298.

Elley, W. B., Barham, I. H., Lamb, H., & Wyllie, M. (1976). The role of grammar in a secondary school English curriculum. *Research in the Teaching of English, 10,* 5–21.

ETS Technologies, Inc. (2002). *Criterion: Online writing evaluation.* Princeton: Author.

Fasold, R. (1984). *The sociolinguistics of society.* Oxford, UK: Blackwell.

Francis, W. N. (1954). Revolution in grammar. *Quarterly Journal of Speech, 4q,* 299–312.

Francis, W. N. (1958). *The structure of American English.* New York: Ronald Press.

Freedman, A. (1985). Sentence combining: Some questions. In A. Freedman (Ed.), *Carleton papers in applied language studies* (Vol. 2, pp. 17–32). (ERIC Document Reproduction Service No. ED 267 602)

Fries, C. C. (1952). The *structure of English.* New York: Harcourt, Brace & World.

Hake, R. L., & Williams, J. M. (1979). Sentence expanding: Not can, or how, but when. In D. A. Daiker, A. Kerek, & M. Morenberg (Eds.), *Sentence combining and the teaching of writing* (pp. 134–146). Conway: University of Akron and University of Central Arkansas.

Halliday, M. A. K. (1985). *An introduction to functional grammar.* London: Edward Arnold.

Halliday, M. A. K. (1993). Some grammatical problems in scientific English. In M. A. K. Halliday & J. R. Martin (Eds.), *Writing science: Literacy and discursive power* (pp. 69–85). Pittsburgh: University of Pittsburgh Press.

Harris-Wright, K. (1998). Enhancing bidialectalism in urban African American students. In C. Adger, D. Christian, & O. Taylor (Eds.), *Making the connection: Language and academic achievement among African American students* (pp. 55–60). Arlington, VA: Center for Applied Linguistics.

Hartwell, P. (1985). Grammar, grammars, and the teaching of grammar. *College English, 47,* 105–127.

Heath, S. B. (1983). *Ways with words: Language, life, and work in communities and classrooms.* New York: Cambridge University Press.

Hillocks, G., Jr. (1971). *An evaluation of Project Apex, a nongraded phase-elective English program.* Trenton, MI: Trenton Public Schools.

Hillocks, G., Jr. (1986). *Research on written composition: New directions for teaching.* Urbana, IL: National Conference on Research in English and ERIC.

Hillocks, G., Jr. (2002). *The testing trap: How state writing assessments control learning.* New York: Teachers College Press.

Hillocks, G., Jr., & Mavrogenes, N. (1986). Sentence combining. In *Research on written composition: New directions for teaching* (pp. 142–146). Urbana, IL: National Conference on Research in English and ERIC.

Hillocks, G., Jr., McCabe, B. J., & McCampbell, J. F. (1971). *The dynamics of English instruction: Grades 7–12.* New York: Random House.

Hillocks, G., Jr., & Smith, M. W. (2003). Grammars and literacy learning. In J. Flood, J. Jensen, D. Lapp, & J. Squire (Eds.), *Handbook of research on teaching the English language arts* (2nd ed., pp. 721–737). Mahwah, NJ: Erlbaum.

Hymes, D. (1974). *Foundations in sociolinguistics: An ethnographic approach.* Philadelphia: University of Pennsylvania Press.

Kamberelis, G. (1999). Genre development and learning: Children writing stories, science reports, and poems. *Research in the Teaching of English, 33,* 403–460.

Kerek, A., Daiker, D., & Morenberg, M. (1980). Sentence combining and college composition. *Perceptual and Motor Skills, 51,* 1059–1157.

Kroll, B. M., & Schafer, J. C. (1978). Error-analysis and the teaching of composition. *College Composition and Communication, 29,* 242–248.

Labov, W. (1972). *Language in the inner city: Studies in the black English vernacular.* Philadelphia: University of Pennsylvania Press.

Ladson-Billings, G. (1995). *The dreamkeepers: Successful teachers of African American children.* San Francisco: Jossey-Bass.

Macauley, W. J. (1947). The difficulty of grammar. *British Journal of Educational Psychology, 17,* 153–162.

Maimon, E. P., & Nodine, B. F. (1978). Measuring syntactic growth: Errors and expectations in sentence-combining practice with college freshmen. *Research in the Teaching of English, 12,* 233–244.

Maimon, E. P., & Nodine, B. F. (1979). Words enough and time: Syntax and error one year after. In D.A. Daiker, A. Kerek, & M. Morenberg (Eds.), *Sentence combining and the teaching of writing* (pp. 101–108). Conway: University of Akron and University of Central Arkansas.

Mellon, J. C. (1969). *Transformational sentence-combining: A method for enhancing the development of syntactic fluency in English composition.* Urbana, IL: National Council of Teachers of English.

Morenberg, M., Daiker, D., & Kerek, A. (1978). Sentence combining at the college level: An experimental study. *Research in the Teaching of English, 12,* 245–256.

Noden, H. (1999). *Image grammar: Using grammat-*

ical structures to teach writing. Portsmouth, NH: Boyton/Cook.

Nold, E. W., & Freedman, S. W. (1977). An analysis of readers' responses to essays. *Research in the Teaching of English, 11*, 164–174.

Noguchi, R. R. (1991). *Grammar and the teaching of writing: Limits and possibilities*. Urbana, IL: National Council of Teachers of English.

O'Hare, F. (1973). *Sentence combining: Improving student writing without formal grammar instruction*. Urbana, IL: National Council of Teachers of English.

Powers, D. E., Burstein, J. C., Chodorow, M. S., Fowles, M. E., & Kukich, K. (2002). Comparing the validity of automated and human scoring of essays. *Journal of Educational Computing Research, 26*, 407–425.

Purcell-Gates, V. (1995). *Other people's words: The cycle of low literacy*. Cambridge, MA: Harvard University Press.

Riley, K., & Parker, F. (1998). English grammar: Prescriptive, descriptive, generative, performance. Boston: Allyn & Bacon.

Schleppegrell, M. J. (1998). Grammar as a resource: Writing a description. *Research in the Teaching of English, 32*(2), 184–211.

Schuster, E. H. (1976, October). *Forward to basics through sentence combining*. Paper presented at the Annual Meeting of the Pennsylvania Council of Teachers of English, Harrisburg. (ERIC Document Reproduction Service No. ED 133 774)

Schuster, E. H. (1977, November). *Using sentence combining to teach writing to inner-city students*. Paper presented at the Annual Meeting of National Council of Teachers of English, New York. (ERIC Document Reproduction Service No. ED 150 614)

Shaughnessy, M. P. (1977). *Errors and expectations: A guide for the teacher of basic writing*. New York: Oxford University Press.

Shuy, R. W., & Fasold, R. W. (Eds.). (1973). *Language attitudes: Current trends and prospects*. Washington, DC: Georgetown University Press.

Smith, H. L., Jr., & Sustakowski, H. J. (1968). *The application of descriptive linguistics to the teaching of English and a statistically-measured comparison of the relative effectiveness of the linguistically-oriented and traditional methods of instruction*. Buffalo: State University of New York. (ERIC Document Reproduction Service No. ED 021 216)

Smith, W. L., & Combs, W. E. (1980). The effects of overt and covert cues on written syntax. *Research in the Teaching of English, 14*, 19–38.

Strong, W. (1973). *Sentence combining: A composing book*. New York: Random House.

Strong, W. (1986). *Creative approaches to sentence combining*. Urbana, IL: National Council of Teachers of English.

Trudgill, P. (1975). *Accent, dialect and the school*. London: Edward Arnold.

Weaver, C. (1996). *Teaching grammar in context*. Portsmouth, NH: Boynton/Cook.

Weaver, C. (1998). *Lessons to share on teaching grammar in context*. Portsmouth, NH: Boynton/Cook.

Williams, J. M. (1981). The phenomenology of error. *College Composition and Communication, 32*, 152–168.

Williams, J. M. (1999). *Style: Ten lessons in clarity and grace* (6th ed.). New York: Addison-Wesley.

Wolfram, W. (1999). Repercussions from the Oakland Ebonics controversy—the critical role of dialect awareness programs. In C. Adger, D. Christian, & O. Taylor (Eds.), *Making the connection: Language and academic achievement among African American students* (pp. 61–80). Arlington, VA: Center for Applied Linguistics.

Wolfram, W., & Creech, K. (1996). *Dialects and Harkers Island speech*. Raleigh: North Carolina Language and Life Project.

Wollman-Bonilla, J. E. (2000). Teaching science writing to first graders: Genre learning and recontextualization. *Research in the Teaching of English, 35*, 35–65.

Chapter 19

The Process Approach to Writing Instruction
Examining Its Effectiveness

Ruie J. Pritchard *and* Ronald L. Honeycutt

Our goal in this chapter is to review theory and research on the writing process, as well as research concerning the influence of the National Writing Project (NWP) in training teachers and in advancing the pedagogical principles associated with the writing process. First, we provide a historical overview of the writing process. Then, we critique studies that evaluate the writing process in terms of its impact on K–12 students and on how writing is taught. This is followed by a review of the research on the NWP model for professional development. Finally, we make suggestions for needed research.

Our literature review reveals that most of the articles and reports on the writing process are not research reports. Many raise questions that are not empirically answerable. Moreover, numerous published works that address the writing process and deal with empirically answerable questions do not employ empirical methodology to answer the question(s). In this chapter, we include only research reports from the professional literature that describe an attempt to attain empirical information about a specific question related to the writing process. Furthermore, we report in this chapter only studies in which the research process is clearly described. The research designs include experimental, quasi-experimental, comparison, pre- and postassessments, survey,

correlational, and case study. For the most part, our sources are research articles published in professional journals; however, our review of the literature also extends to dissertations and research published in edited books. We have sought to include an information base drawn from diverse fields such as psychology, English, rhetoric, regular and special education, and education of English language learners (ELLs). We limit the research to studies that address kindergarten-through high school-age subjects, even though the bulk of research on composing is with college students and adults.

The understanding of what constitutes the writing process instructional model has evolved since the 1970's, when it emerged as a pedagogical approach. In the early years, it was regarded as a nondirectional model of instruction with very little teacher intervention. In his review of research on composition from 1963 to 1982, Hillocks (1984) concluded that the teacher's role in the process model is to facilitate the writing process rather than to provide direct instruction; teachers were found "*not* to make specific assignments, *not* to help students learn criteria for judging writing, *not* to structure activities based on specific objectives, . . . *not* to provide exercises in manipulating syntax, *not* to design activities that engage students in identifiable processes of examining data"

(p. 162; emphasis in original). It is not surprising that the research Hillocks summarizes showed minimal impact on the quality of writing products as a result of this "natural process mode."

In the formative years, the process approach model was regarded as applying mainly to stories, was linear and prescriptive, merged proofreading and editing as the same thing, and usually did not involve direct instruction—a sort of anything-goes model whereby the process was valued over the product. In this early model, a simplistic pedagogy resulted: After their teacher describes the four stages, students recall and rehearse the steps, use the process to produce a story, and get into groups to share their stories and gain feedback. In the literature in special education, such instruction to help students plan, organize, and carry out a writing task is called teaching "plans of action" (Gersten & Baker, 2001). Such plans comprise only some of the procedural tasks of the current process model.

Today, most researchers of the process model recognize that it involves both procedural knowledge and many other kinds of strategies that can be nurtured and directly taught, including activating schemata to access prior knowledge; teaching self-regulation strategies; helping students understand genre constraints; guiding students in re-visioning and in editing surface errors; providing structured feedback from teachers and peers; teaching the differences between reader- and writer-based prose; developing audience awareness and effects of audience on style, content, and tone; and dealing with emotional barriers, to name a few. In general, those studies that view the process model as encompassing more teacher direction in the process show positive effects on the quality of students' writing, on their view of themselves as writers, and on their understanding of the writing process. For example, a meta-analysis of 13 studies with learning disabled students (Gersten & Baker, 2001) concluded that an effective comprehensive writing program in special education should entail explicit teaching of "(a) the steps of the writing process and (b) the critical dimensions of different writing genres . . . as well as (c) structures for giving extensive feedback to students on the quality of their writing from either teachers or peers"

(p. 251). Our review of the literature reveals that these elements also characterize effective writing instruction within regular education classroom settings.

Furthermore, current researchers recognize that as a writer matures and internalizes the overall procedures and strategies for producing texts in various genres, these become automatized. They occur more efficiently throughout the writing process, and not in sequential steps, as noted in the change in the professional literature in referring to the writing process as "recursive." Furthermore, the emphasis today on state academic standards is influencing how the process model is implemented and tested. In his argument that assessment creates artificial conditions for applying the writing process, Schuster (2004) sarcastically says that state writing tests should really be labeled "state drafting tests" (p. 378). As a result of new theories, new research, and the changing status of writing in the curriculum, the process model has evolved. Teaching the process model now demands careful scaffolding and creating lessons that traverse the entire process; researching the process model in all its inclusiveness is a multilayered process demanding a variety of research methodologies. As we learn more about what is entailed in teaching and learning the writing process, the definition and the pedagogy of the process model are likely to change.

Historical Overview of the Writing Process

The key ideas and foundational practices of the writing process can be traced back to early Greek and Roman models of teaching rhetoric (Bloodgood, 2002; Winterowd & Blum, 1994). The professional literature does not mention the writing process until Day's (1947) discussion of the seven steps of the writing process. Mills (1953) argued that "the basic failure in our teaching centers, in my judgment, is our unwillingness or incapacity to think of writing in terms of process" (p. 19). Later, a description of a four-stage writing process garnered from interviews with 16 published writers appeared in the introduction to a book edited by Cowley (1958).

Many of these published writers spoke of meeting regularly with other writers to share their works in progress, though this was a rare practice in the schools until the 1970s. The idea of planning instruction along the lines of how real writers write is frequently attributed to the seminal contributions of Peter Elbow, Janet Emig, Donald Graves, Donald Murray, and Mina Shaughnessy (Jensen, 2002; Smith, 2000a, 2000b). In the 1970s, a group of teachers in the San Francisco Bay Area began to share their own writing. They compared the model for how professional writers compose with how writing was commonly taught in the schools, labeling their nontraditional instructional model "the process approach" (Gray, 2000; Wilson, 1994). These early proponents of the process model emphasized a balance in instruction between writing processes and products. Since the 1980s, the process approach to teaching writing has emerged as the primary paradigm, so much so that many state and local school systems have mandated it as the gold standard for instruction in K–12 classrooms (Patthey-Chavez, Matsumura, & Valdés, 2004). Textbooks often translate the process into a prescriptive, linear formula for producing a paper, which is not truly representative of the stop-and-start, recursive process used by professional writers, who are also writing for authentic audiences and not for classroom teachers.

Over the past 30 years, the definition and elements of the writing process have been reinterpreted. Initially, most researchers proposed a three-stage writing process. Rohman's (1965) model of prewrite, write, and rewrite is the most widely referenced explication of the writing process. However, in his dissertation about the composing process of four high school honor students, Brozick (1976) concluded that the writing process is much more dynamic and is contingent upon numerous variables and influences such as purpose, audience, type of writing, and the writer's personality type. Larsen (1983) argued in her dissertation documenting the history of the writing process that by the mid-20th century, writers were encouraged to compose recursively. However, it was not until the work of cognitive researchers, such as Flower and Hayes (1980, 1981), and Bereiter and Scardamalia (1987), that most researchers and practitioners questioned the linear–prescriptive view of the composing process and embraced one that is recursive

and more complex. Numerous other writing experts have noted that the writing process is individualized and does not occur in any fixed order (de Beaugrande, 1984; Bridwell, 1980; Witte, 1987). Chapter 2 of this volume is devoted to cognitive theories of writing development.

Researchers who subscribe to this paradigm regard the writing process as mainly a series of problem-solving tasks (Braaksma, Rijlaarsdam, van den Bergh, & van Hout-Wolters, 2004; Bereiter & Scardamalia, 1987). Goldstein and Carr (1996), authors of the summary report of National Assessment of Educational Progress (NAEP), describe a process in which writers make multiple decisions:

"Process writing" refers to a broad range of strategies that include pre-writing activities, such as defining audience, using a variety of resources, planning the writing, as well as drafting and revising. These activities, collectively referred to as "process-oriented instruction," approach writing as problem-solving. (p. 1)

Most educators today hold this view that producing a written text is a mental recursive process coupled with procedural strategies for completing writing tasks. Consequently, the instructional strategies associated with the process model have changed. Now they commonly include explicit instruction in self-regulation, searching prior knowledge, goal setting, and other strategies not included when the process instructional approach was introduced.

In terms of research, examining a student's declarative knowledge of steps makes for a clean study; however, it does not account for all the facets of the recursive process model and its accompanying pedagogy that we recognize today. Furthermore, as Lipson, Mosenthal, Daniels, and Woodside-Jiron (2000) discovered in their research, even those who subscribe to a definition of the writing process as recursive vary in how they implement the writing process in their classrooms. This variation further complicates interpreting the effects of using the process approach in research studies or generalizing across studies.

Jensen (1993) quotes Colette Daiute as saying "The major contribution to understanding writing in the past 30 years has been the realization that writing, like reading, is a complex process, influenced by many factors" (p. 292). The writing process approach was validated in 1992 by the National Council of Teachers of English and the International Reading Association, when they defined Content Standard 5 for the English Language Arts, K–12: Students are expected to use writing process elements strategically (De La Paz, 1999).

Early Studies of the Writing Process

The most well-known and cited study on the writing process is Janet Emig's (1971) dissertation on the composing processes of 12th-grade writers. Emig employed case study methodology to interview eight students to delineate the processes they went through when completing writing assignments. Additionally, on three separate occasions, Emig asked the subjects to complete a writing assignment, composing aloud while she recorded each subject. Emig concluded that writers engage in two distinctive modes of composing—extensive, to convey a message; and reflexive, to explore one's feelings. Each entailed its characteristic process.

Over a 5-month period, Donald Graves (1973) gathered data during five distinct phases of his research. First, he examined the writing folders of 94 students, looking at their thematic choices, the frequency of their writing, and the types of writing. In the second phase of his study, he observed 14 different children while they were composing. During the third phase of the research, Graves interviewed 9 boys and 8 girls about their views of their own writing and the concept of a good writer. Finally, he conducted a case study on 6 boys and 2 girls who were purported to be representative of 7-year-old children. In his study, and similar to the later findings of numerous researchers (e.g., Brozick, 1976; Gundlach, 1977), Graves concluded that multiple variables, frequently unknown to the writer, influence the writing process.

Based on his personal experiences of writing in college, Peter Elbow (1973) challenged the emerging concept of the writing process that basically viewed writing as a linear, two-step process of writing and editing. He argued for a flexible prewriting stage, noting that it was counterproductive to have a clear picture in one's mind of a finalized version before one began writing. Elbow viewed the writing process as a series of problem-solving steps one goes through in order to discover what he or she knows and feels about a subject. The writer is thereby freed from having to know all of his or her meaning before writing any of it. Elbow has had a powerful influence on practices, even though his study was a reflection on his own experiences as a struggling writer and, like Graves's study (1973), did not employ experimental design.

One criticism during this era of research on the writing process was that the model is based on the processes that professional writers use. Smagorinsky (1987) noted that the definition of "professional writers" was narrow, including mainly literary figures. Because the theory behind the process model relied on the genre of narratives about personal experiences, Australian researchers challenged the implicit assumption in the American model that children have an innate understanding of genre structures (Cope & Kalantzis, 1993; Hicks, 1997). Other criticisms issued from educators who argued that it is a major pedagogical leap to assume that immature writers, who are at a different developmental stage, as well as writing primarily for classroom audiences, are able to apply principles of process writing at the same level as adult writers. Over time, the understanding of the process model, and thus the research, grew to encompass more genres and broader based pedagogy.

Research Studies on the Effectiveness of the Writing Process

Commenting on the 1992 NAEP assessment, officials asserted that "teaching the cluster of writing techniques known collectively as 'writing process' is associated with higher average writing proficiency among students" (Goldstein & Carr, 1996, p. 1). Their analysis is based on the self-reports of 29,500 students in 1,500 schools, which indicate that students whose teachers implement writing process techniques "almost every day" consistently obtain the highest average writing scores on the NAEP writing assessment. The 1998 NAEP writing assessment of 17,286 fourth-grade teachers and 14,435 eighth-grade teachers revealed that, across the United States, considerable time is devoted each week to working with students on the writing process (Greenwald, Persky, Campbell, & Mazzeo, 1999). The data from the NAEP assessments in 1998 and 2002 that correlate the amount of time spent on the writing process with student achievement are still unavailable. Except for the NAEP assessments, few large-scale studies are specifically designed to study the relation of the process instructional approach to the quality of written products. Fewer yet use an experimental and control group design.

Even the NAEP data are so broad that they do not give us clear evidence about what kind of instruction is regarded as "process writing." Patthey-Chavez et al. (2004) concluded that "students appear to respond to the type of feedback they receive, and when they are asked to standardize their writing rather than to develop it, that is precisely what they do" (pp. 469–470). So if teachers embrace a standardized linear model of the writing process, or an open-ended recursive model, or a direct instruction model, or an integrated model, or a writing as problem-solving model, their students will respond accordingly. The authors of one of the studies we reviewed (MacArthur, Schwartz, Graham, Molloy, & Harris, 1996), cite a similar comment by Michael Fullan (1982) that "teachers may reject innovations not consonant with their current beliefs and practices" (p. 169). This principle pertains to how teachers—and, ultimately, researchers—define the writing process and interpret findings.

In our review of the research, we found that researchers hold surprisingly different views of what the process approach entails. For example, some see it as a loosely monitored series of steps, a "natural process" in the context of authentic tasks, without explicit instruction in planning, revising, and other strategies (MacArthur et al., 1996). In this view, "process writing [is] primarily based on indirect rather than direct methods of instruction" (Graham & Harris, 1997, p. 252). On the other hand, others regard direct strategy instruction and guided practice integrated into the writing process as crucial to the definition of the process approach (Applebee, 1986; Atwell, 1987; Calkins, 1986;

Cramer, 2001; DeFoe, 2000; Honeycutt & Pritchard, 2005; Poindexter & Oliver, 1998/1999). Cramer (2001) sees the writing process as "a set of theories, procedures, and activities which emphasize the operations, changes and procedures by which writing is accomplished" (p. 53). Applebee (1986) construed the writing process as "strategies that writers employ for particular purposes. For difficult tasks, writers will use different strategies, and for some tasks these strategies may involve no more than the routine production of a first and final draft" (p. 106). Hence, the process writing that researchers have studied may be a routine first and final draft devoid of specific strategy instructions, or it may be a framework in which strategies and skill development are embedded.

To complicate matters even more, the basic definition of the process model has evolved in the theoretical literature, so that now it is regarded quite differently than in its early years, when, for example, explicit instruction, reflection, guided revision, and self-assessment were not commonly associated with the process model. These varying views of the process approach alert us to the potential bias exerted by a researcher's paradigm and definition of the writing process.

An ERIC (Educational Resources Information Center) search of dissertation abstracts on the writing process, as well as a search for studies in electronic educational databases, reveals that during the 1970s and 1980s, research focused on how components of the writing process are related to specific variables, such as syntactic complexity (Moriarity, 1978); catalysts for the writing process (Schwartz, 1980); writing apprehension (Butler, 1980); language ability skills (Hayes, 1984); journal writing (Robinson-Metz, 1985); thought and emotions (Miller, 1985); prior knowledge (DeGroff, 1985); ELLs (So, 1986; Watkins-Goffman, 1986); and verbal skills (Robbins, 1986). All of these studies show some positive association of the writing process with the variables being studied. However, the variables did not always include improved products.

From the late 1980s through 2003, research increased that was specifically designed to measure the quality of students' written products as a result of using the writing process. Robinson (1986) conducted an experimental study with 120 fifth-grade students to investigate the effects of process writing instruction on the number and levels of revision as a result of 1- and 2-day lessons on revision. She found that students taught using the process approach scored higher on final writing samples and engaged in 2.5 times more revisions than students taught using a traditional method of composing. Croes (1990) used a nonequivalent control group design to study the efficacy of the writing process in helping 157 learning disabled students in grades 1–5 improve their overall writing performance. Harris (1992) investigated the relationship between writing quality and attitudes toward writing in a study of 34 third-graders randomly assigned to one of four treatment groups. These last two studies indicate some positive effects of the writing process on the variables examined.

More recent studies have involved the use of personal correspondence and the writing process by 236 second-grade children in traditional and process approach classrooms (Hamilton, 1992); the writing process as the context for developing 16 "nonnative" students' writing ability (Chiang, 1992); a case study of the development of writing skills over 1 year for three first graders using a process approach (Eitelgeorge, 1994); a comparison between the effects of using traditional and process approaches on second graders' written retellings of stories (Boydston, 1994); a description by gender of writing processes and attitudes about writing of 41 first graders (Billman, 1995); the effects of explicitly teaching the writing process to improve the writing skills of 15 seventh-grade Title I students (Dean-Rumsey, 1998); and the impact of direct teaching of writing strategies and skills to middle school students to facilitate their execution of the writing process (De La Paz & Graham, 2002). Again, all of these studies show to varying degrees positive results on writing products by using the writing process.

The following examinations of two experimental and two qualitative studies with K–12 students are illustrative of research designed specifically to measure how instruction in the writing process affects the overall quality of the products.

Scannella (1982) conducted a yearlong experimental study of the effects of the writing-as-process model on the writing of 121 average and above ninth- and tenth-grade students. Students assigned to the experimental group received instruction in the process approach to writing based on Emig's research; the control groups received instruction using the standard methods of teaching composition at the time (textbooks, worksheets, teaching grammar in isolation, providing the topic to students, giving assignments and due dates). Scannella found that, overall, students taught in the process method evidenced greater improvement in their expository writing, but not in their creative writing, than did students in the control group. Furthermore, the experimental group evidenced a statistically significant increase in positive attitudes toward writing, whereas the control group showed a slight decrease in overall positive attitudes toward writing.

In an experimental study with 654 third-, fourth-, and fifth-grade students, Bruno (1983) compared the writing achievement of students taught using the writing process method with that of students taught using the textbook and workbook method. Using pre- and posttests, Bruno found that the writing of students taught using the writing process approach was rated superior to that of students using the traditional method, especially in terms of the overall organization and format.

A research team funded by the National Institute of Education (Graves, 1984) published 26 articles about the writing behaviors of 16 children in five elementary classrooms in a New Hampshire school. A contribution of this qualitative study was the research method of observing children while they write, rather than using retrospective analyses of written products and postcomposing interviews. One member of this team, Lucy Calkins, used direct observations of children composing, field notes, transcripts of interviews with children and teachers, collections of all drafts, and videotapes of children during composing and conferencing. In her 2-year longitudinal case study of one child's writing development in a writing workshop, Calkins (1982; 1983) charted writing samples for changes in punctuation, handwriting, spelling, topic, structure, flow, and readability. She observed the child's daily writing behaviors through third and fourth grades, documenting the child's gradual grasp of the revision process, her development of the writer's executive functions, and her internalization of writing and revising strategies. Calkins's findings indicate that as the child internalized a repertoire of process writing strategies, especially revising strategies, her writing products steadily improved. Considering how limited Calkins's research was—just one child's processes—her research has had enormous impact on how the writing process is implemented in the elementary grades.

The work of Graves and Calkins is regarded as contributing to theory from a practitioner's perspective, but since the samples are small and the designs are not experimental, this research has been criticized. Smagorinsky (1987), for example, states that the case study methodology that Graves and his colleagues advocated is merely "reportage" (p. 333). Validity concerns are legitimate. Graves and Calkins employed an early application of qualitative research that did not specifically address the numerous types of validity that are now expected. Recent qualitative research is more rigorous in addressing types of validity, such as construct validity, internal validity, external validity, democratic validity, process and outcome validity, catalytic validity, and dialogic validity (Anderson, Herr, & Nihlen, 1994; Bogdan & Bilken, 1998; Erlandson, Harris, Skipper, & Allen, 1993).

Honeycutt's research design (2002; Honeycutt & Pritchard, 2005) explains how he triangulated the data, kept field notes to record any researcher biases that might emerge, and transcribed video and audio records that were reviewed with the subjects for accuracy. His purpose was to create a grounded theory about good readers who are poor writers but have no identifiable learning or behavioral disability. His definition of the process model includes explicit strategy instruction, such as schema strategies for story grammar and searching prior knowledge, as well as guided practice, peer group feedback, teacher–student conferencing, and the usual stages for producing a draft. In examining the impact of a process-based model on improving student written products over 16 weeks of instruction, Honeycutt used quantitative data such as standardized and teacher-developed pre- and posttests, and scores on a writing test and on the Writer's Self-Perception Scale (WSPS)

(Bottomley, Henk, & Melnick, 1997/1998), as well as qualitative data consisting of teacher lesson plans, student writing portfolios, written reflections by students, instructor's notes on conferences, and individual and focus-group interviews with 11 fifth-grade students and seven teachers. Three types of procedures (Denzin, 1989) were used to verify the data: (1) across collection methods (document analysis, scores on the writing samples and the Writer Self-Perception Scale, individual interviews, and focus groups), (2) across data sources (students and teachers), and (3) across investigators (two researchers, formal member checking in focus groups, and informal member checking with individuals). In the context of a writing workshop, Honeycutt (2002) examined the effects of explicit instruction and practice in how to apply writing process strategies and strategies for dealing with negative emotions that arise during various stages of the writing process. Pre- and posttests indicated that the overall quality of students' texts improved when students (1) internalized specific strategies for prewriting, writing, and revising; (2) employed self-regulation strategies to monitor the development of a text; and (3) activated strategies for dealing with negative emotions that arise during the composing process.

Like Calkins's (1982) case study subject, the students in the Honeycutt study (2002) practiced specific processes until the processes became automatized during composing. Honeycutt's research introduced a grounded theory about what subprocesses and specific instructional aspects of the writing process exert the most influence on students' writing dispositions and writing products. More studies are needed to study and refine this theory, especially in light of the recognition that some practitioners using the process approach do not see it as encompassing explicit instruction or dealing with emotional issues.

Although most researchers agree that the strategies and mental processes involved in the writing process are recursive and interlocked, many have discovered that studying one component at a time makes an enormously complex research task more manageable. Thus, to date, the vast majority of the research has investigated specific components of the writing process, especially prewriting and revising.

Affording time and presence to prewriting in the classroom is a major consequence of the process approach. Until the advent of the process model, prewriting was usually not addressed apart from a teacher making the assignment and giving due dates. Now, prewriting is explicitly addressed, with the purpose of teaching students to develop personalized strategies that they can apply not only to develop content—as was the focus originally—but also to create structure and organization. In the early years of the process model, prewriting was considered one step in the process—the writer did it and dispensed with it. Now, as with the other stages of the process approach, prewriting is regarded as recursive; prewriting strategies may emerge during the revising stage, for example. Moreover, prewriting can take the form of inquiry, a method that Hillocks (1986) found to be over 2.5 times more effective than the study of writing models, a traditional prewriting activity. Although inquiry can occur anytime during the writing process, it constitutes an effective prewriting strategy in that students' focus is on transforming raw data.

Like prewriting, revision instruction was largely neglected in composition classes until the process approach. Before this, revision was usually provoked as a mandate to students to "improve your paper," made after the paper was complete and had been turned in to the teacher. The results were usually editing, not a true re-visioning of the paper, as noted in the title of Lee O'Dell and Joanne Cohick's (1975) article, "You Mean, Write It Over in Ink?" Today, the counterpart would be, "You mean, run spell check and laser print it?" Numerous researchers and writers view revision as the most important part of the composing process; it has also been the most researched subprocess of the writing process. Generally, revision has been understood not as a step in which the author corrects errors, but as a process of discovering what one has to say and adapting the text to maximize the clarity of the message (Calkins, 1986; Elbow, 1973; Graves, 1983; Murray, 1985; Sommers, 1982).

Taken together, these studies of the impact of using the process approach on student achievement indicate mainly positive effects, but they are based on uneven implementations of the writing process. In their review of the research on process writing, Dyson and Freedman (2003) noted that even though the 1998 NAEP found a strong correlation between higher scores and application of the writing process, it is "difficult to evaluate the degree to which the approach in [the United States] as a whole has improved student writing" (p. 976). Furthermore, Dyson and Freedman argued that the research on the writing process does not offer any "simple prescriptions for practice, but it can offer a vocabulary for talking about the nature of writing" (p. 974). Cramer (2001) asked whether there is sufficient weight in the criticisms to abandon the process model. As a result of our review of the literature, we agree with his answer:

> It is best to face this truth: the writing process has its weaknesses; it is poorly implemented in many instances; it is not a panacea. But it is a better candidate for improving writing performance than the traditional approach. . . . We must listen to the critics; we must be willing to rethink and adjust our theories, procedures, and practices. But there is not sufficient evidence to cause us to abandon the writing process. (p. 39)

Research on the Impact of the National Writing Project Professional Development Model

As an exemplary professional development model with roots in the 1973 Bay Area Writing Project, the NWP "eschews a singular formula for teaching writing" (Friedrich & LeMahieu, 2004, p. 19). However, "the fundamental belief of the NWP that the process of writing needs to be taught deliberately, systematically, and extensively in the classroom has deeply affected writing instruction at all grade levels during the decade of the 1980's" (Inverness Research Associates, 1997, p. 19). Our review of the current literature indicates that the process pedagogy has continued to affect writing instruction in the new millennium

The NWP summer institute is the enterprise most closely identified with the process approach. Blau (1988) characterizes the salient features of NWP institutes: "Teacher consultants emphasized teaching writing as a process, spoke of an instructional sequence that proceeded from fluency to form to correctness, practiced the use of writing response groups, and explored the various ways that writing can be used as an instrument for learning" (p. 30). As already noted, these have been studied as teaching techniques in separate investigations, as well as collectively in an instructional approach called the process model.

The NWP has compiled statistical data measuring its far-reaching influence on teachers and schools. Reporting to the 2003 NWP meeting, Inverness Research Associates (St. John, 2003) shared these figures:

1. The steadily growing NWP network consists of more than 175 college-based sites in 50 states, Washington, DC, Puerto Rico, and the U.S. Virgin Islands, annually serving approximately 125,000 K–16 teachers (roughly 1 out of 40 teachers in the United States) in all disciplines.
2. Over 30 years, the NWP has served approximately 3.5 million teachers, nearly the same as the total number of teachers in the United States today.

The literature on the NWP is replete with positive testimonies of the impact of NWP training on teacher attitudes and on their confidence as writers and as teachers of writing. There is no doubt that the NWP has been a major force in accentuating the role of writing in learning, in reinvigorating teacher enthusiasm, in garnering respect for what teachers of writing accomplish in their classrooms, and in professionalizing the teacher as leader, teacher consultant (TC), and researcher. These numerous studies are not addressed in this chapter. Instead, the focus is on those studies about NWP impact on teacher practices and on student achievement.

Empirical evidence of the impact of NWP training on teacher practices and student achievement is relatively thin, as compared to reading. This is largely due to the "messy process" of studying staff development in general (Pritchard & Marshall, 2002a; Wilson & Berne, 1999), and writing in particular (Daiute, 1993; De La Paz & Graham, 2002; van den Bergh & Rijlaarsdam, 2001). A recent publication (National Writing Project & Nagin, 2003) devotes an entire chapter to the multiple challenges faced by educators in teaching writing. To that, we can add researching writing.

Do NWP teachers implement the strategies for teaching writing that they learn and prac-

tice in the institutes and in outreach projects? The particular classroom practice that is most influenced by training evolves as the sophistication of NWP participants grows. In the early years of the NWP, prewriting was a new concept; later, it was sentence combining, the use of rubrics, revision strategies, portfolios, the reading–writing connection, and writing across the curriculum. Now, the role of reflection, the subprocesses of writing, standardized assessments, writing with special populations, and technology and blogs in the writing class have emerged as topics in the summer institutes. That NWP institutes change as schools and communities develop is a strength of the NWP network; it is also a reason why documenting NWP impact in highly controlled empirical studies is difficult. Most studies have focused on impact on teachers rather than on students. In this section, we define "teacher impact" as influences of the NWP on teaching practices rather than on teachers' attitudes, creativity, leadership skills, their own writing, and other dimensions abundantly addressed in numerous descriptive publications and dissertations.

In a study of a writing project in the Midwest, Pritchard (1987) used a questionnaire administered 3 years after teachers participated in NWP training to compare the teaching strategies of NWP-trained and nontrained teachers, and found statistical differences between groups for only 22% of the strategies. Studies using surveys indicate that trained teachers use a greater variety of activities (Pritchard & Marshall, 1994), and that trained teachers show notable changes in how they teach writing, especially in the amount of time devoted to writing (Bates, 1986; Carter, 1992; Fanscali, Nelsestuen, & Weinbaum, 2001; Fischer, 1997; Hampton, 1990; Laub, 1996; Roberts, 2001; St. John, Dickey, Hirabayashi, & Stokes, 2001; Swenson, 1992; Tindall, 1990; Vaughan, 1992; Wilson, 1988, 1994). Large-scale studies by Inverness Research Associates (St. John et al., 2001) show that 95% of the teachers report gaining new teaching strategies from NWP training. Similarly, a 2-year in-depth study of six teachers (Lieberman & Wood, 2003; Wood & Lieberman, 2000) identifies significant impact of NWP training on teaching strategies.

In one study (Pritchard, 1987), a survey of 19 trained and 39 nontrained teachers about their classroom practices revealed that trained teachers averaged significantly *more* time in writing lessons, and significantly *less* time in more traditional activities, such as using references and teaching spelling and vocabulary, than did nontrained teachers. One interpretation derived from this study was that perhaps the absence of certain practices is what enhances writing growth rather than the presence of certain practices. Furthermore, Pritchard concluded that a process orientation does not preclude attention to the product, and that the "environmental mode" that Hillocks (1984) ascribes to the NWP does not replace the "presentational" mode of more traditional classrooms.

Across two decades of studies, the positive effects of NWP training on teaching practices have been well established. But do students write better as a result of their teachers' implementing new practices after NWP training? NWP principles are so instantiated in schools, and in textbooks, that it is a challenge even to define a control group unaffected by the NWP in order to conduct experimental studies about its impact on student achievement. Of the published statistical studies, all main results favor the NWP approach over traditional approaches (DiStephano & Olson, 1980; Haugen, 1982; Hawkins & Marshall, 1981; Marshall, 1983; Penfield, 1979; Pritchard, 1987; Pritchard & Marshall, 2002b; Roberts, 2001; Shook, 1981; Shortt, 1986; Zemelman & Wagner, 1982). Two studies were designed to examine impact of the same students 1 year and 2 years after their teachers were trained. Researchers collected more than 18,582 papers for study of impact on 1,622 students after 1 year (Hawkins & Marshall, 1981; Marshall, 1983), and more than 4,000 essays from a sample of 509 of the same students for a study of impact after 2 years (Pritchard, 1987). The strength of these studies from the 1980s is that researchers examined complete data sets for each student (six essays each the first year; nine essays each the second year) rather than one pre- and postsample, as well as determined impact on students in buildings where trained teachers taught (the spinoff group). Students of trained teachers achieved the highest mean scores, followed by students in the schools where trained teachers taught, and then by students of nontrained teachers. This is a testimony to

the teachers-teaching-teachers principle of the NWP outreach philosophy.

In another large-scale study, Pritchard and Marshall (1994) evaluated 7,838 pre- and posttest essays of students of trained and nontrained teachers using 11 analyses for comparison among grade level, district, treatment, and control groups. In 9 of 11 analyses, significant differences were found in favor of the students of trained teachers at all levels, with middle school students achieving the highest mean scores, followed by elementary students, and then high school students. Another large-scale study showing the positive impact of the NWP involved 1,900 students in five states (Fanscali & Silverstein, 2002), with essays collected over 3 years.

In a comprehensive study (Pritchard & Marshall, 2002a, 2002b, 2005) of professional development practices in healthy and unhealthy school districts in which NWP outreach programs had been offered, nearly 3,000 writing samples were elicited from students in randomly selected classrooms in randomly selected schools, in 18 randomly selected districts across the United States. Student achievement in writing was used as one measure of impact of the professional development. The students in districts rated as having high health obtained significantly higher mean writing achievement results than students in districts rated as having low health. This study advances the idea that impact of NWP training, or any professional development activity, is highly tied to the culture of support at the district level.

In 2004, the NWP launched a multiyear research agenda using the following criteria: (1) All studies must include a focus on student learning, and in particular, student writing performance; (2) the assessment of student writing must involve direct (as opposed to indirect) assessment of student writing; and (3) each study must include some form of "comparative reference" to allow the logic of the research design to dispel at least some of the most common alternative (and irrelevant to the attribution of impact) hypotheses regarding explanations for observed findings. The design is either comparison groups, or mixed method, or quasi-experimental method. These studies under way should provide data responsive to the local context of particular sites, as well as data that can be aggregated to evaluate impact across sites to provide a national picture of NWP impact.

Where Do We Go from Here?

Critics of the process approach argue that attention to the processes of creating texts has made writing products into by-products. "The process has become so ubiquitous as to mean anything, or perhaps more precisely, it has come to mean almost nothing. Tragically, the art and soul of writing have been lost in the 'process'" (Baines, Baines, Stanley, & Kunkel, 1999, p. 72). Proponents of the process approach say it is only through valuing the process that we help our students find the art and soul of writing.

Our reading of the current literature reveals that most researchers assert that writing and the writing process are best understood as complex phenomena that include not only procedural strategies for going through the writing process to generate text but also a multitude of other strategies to develop specific schemata. These include strategies to help writers understand the context for writing, to tap general background knowledge and reading ability, to sharpen cognitive processes for problem solving, to create emotional dispositions and attitudes about writing, to develop micro-level skills such as spelling, transcription, and sentence construction, as well a macro-level understanding about organization, conventions, cohesion, audience, genre, and topic, to name a few. To complicate matters, findings from reports on the various subprocesses of the writing process contradict one another (van den Bergh & Rijlaarsdam, 2001). These strategies and subprocesses need to be explored in conjunction with the process model; since writing proficiency is recognized as a developmental process, longitudinal studies are especially needed.

A concomitant finding of much of the early research was that multiple factors influence the writing process, such as the finding that there are social benefits in using peer groups. In other words, best practices in the teaching of writing include not only improving writing products but also developing positive dispositions, social behaviors, problem solving, and other skills that have value

in and of themselves. Although teasing out the effects of these aspects of the process approach requires complicated research designs, these issues need to be explored in qualitative and quantitative studies.

As a result of the complexity of studying writing processes that are so inclusive, multi-layered, and overlapping, few purely experimental studies have been conducted, and fewer yet on a large scale or with the same population over time. Even when variables are highly controlled, researchers in writing concede that their studies cannot account for all the factors that influence the final product. For example, some studies suggest, but have not proven, that the process approach is most applicable to creating narratives. Theorists have surmised that as the writing process approach evolved, it became fused with personal writing, and this flawed understanding of the process model has persisted with practitioners and researchers (Stotsky, 1995). Needed, and in some cases under way, are studies about the comparative impact of the process approach to teaching various genres of writing. Another persisting misconception is that the process model does not entail direct instruction. In the beginning, the holistic emphasis on developing a writer's ownership of his or her writing, of creating authentic audiences, and of providing multiple sources of feedback somehow dominated educators' interest. Studies of the subprocesses of writing were not prominent in the research and still need to be studied as variables influencing writing products.

Since the process approach provided an instructional alternative at a time when traditional methods grounded in rhetorical theory were being challenged, the process model evolved in practice more quickly than did supporting research and theories. Many theories have been used to study writing, such as the cognitive process theory of Flower and Hayes (1981), the natural process model of Peter Elbow (1973) and Donald Murray (1985), and the mental growth model of James Moffett (1981, 1992). Not all derived from or were tested by research. Practitioners still need theories of teaching writing that are firmly grounded in research. This, in turn, should provide a foundation for what professionals consider best practices for enhancing student writing performance.

References

Anderson, G. I., Herr, K., & Nihlen, A. S. (1994). *Studying your own school: An educator's guide to qualitative practitioner research.* Thousand Oaks, CA: Corwin Press.

Applebee, A. (1986). Problems in process approaches: Toward a reconceptualization of process instruction. In A. R. Petrosky & D. Bartholomae (Eds.), *The 85th yearbook of the National Society for the Study of Education.* Chicago: University of Chicago Press.

Atwell, N. (1987). *In the middle: Writers reading and learning with adolescents.* Portsmouth, NH: Boynton/Cook.

Baines, L., Baines, C., Stanley, G. K., & Kunkel, A. (1999). Losing the product in the process. *English Journal, 88*(5), 67–72.

Bates, A. M. (1986). The short term effects of the Western Pennsylvania Writing Project on twelve teachers' attitudes and practices in teaching composition. *Dissertation Abstracts International, 47*(06A), 2126. (UMI No. AAI8620271)

Bereiter, C., & Scardamalia, M. (1987). *The psychology of written composition.* Hillsdale, NJ: Erlbaum.

Billman, L. K. (1995). An exploration of the gender differences associated with 6 and 7 year old children's process writing activities in three classrooms at the first-grade level. *Dissertation Abstracts International, 56*(12A), 4654. (UMI No. AAI9611399)

Blau, S. (1988). Teacher development and the revolution in teaching. *English Journal, 77*(4), 30–35.

Bloodgood, J. W. (2002). Quintillion: A classical educator speaks to the writing process. *Reading Research and Instruction, 42*(1), 30–43.

Bogdan, R. C., & Bilken, S. K. (1998). *Qualitative research in education: An introduction to theory and method* (3rd ed.). Boston: Allyn & Bacon.

Bottomley, D. M., Henk, W. A., & Melnick, S. A. (1997/1998). Assessing children's view about themselves as writers using the Writer Self-Perception Scale. *Reading Teacher, 51*(4), 286–295.

Boydston, R. C. (1994). Written retellings of narratives as an instructional strategy in traditional and writing process second-grade classrooms. *Dissertation Abstracts International, 55* (12A), 3736. (UMI No. AAI9512249)

Braaksma, M. A., Rijlaarsdam, G., van den Bergh, H., & van Hout-Wolters, B. (2004). Observational learning and its effects on the orchestration of writing processes. *Cognition and Instruction, 22*(1), 1–36.

Bridwell, L. (1980). Revising strategies in twelfth grade students' transactional writing. *Research in the Teaching of English, 14*(3), 197–222.

Brozick, J. R. (1976). An investigation into the composing processes of twelfth grade students: A case studies based on Jung's personality types, Freudian psychoanalytic ego psychology and cognitive functioning. *Dissertation Abstracts International, 38*(01A), 31. (UMI No. AAI7715206)

Bruno, D. D. (1983). The writing process method verses the traditional textbook–worksheet method in the teaching of composition skills to third, fourth, and fifth grade students. *Dissertation Abstracts International, 44*(09A), 2663. (UMI No. AA18400878)

Butler, D. A. (1980). A descriptive analysis of the relationship between writing apprehension and the composing process of selected secondary students. *Dissertation Abstracts International, 49*(09A), 3854. (UMI No. AAI8102603)

Calkins, L. M. (1982). Lessons from a child: A case study of one child's growth in writing. *Dissertation Abstracts International, 43*(06A), 1828. (UMI No. AAI8226743)

Calkins, L. M. (1983). *Lessons from a child: On the teaching and learning of writing.* Portsmouth, NH: Heinemann.

Calkins, L. M. (1986). *The art of teaching writing.* Portsmouth, NH: Heinemann.

Carter, L. C. (1992). A descriptive study of a writing workshop modeled from the National Writing Project on writing pedagogy. *Dissertation Abstracts International, 53*(04A), 1127. (UMI No. AA9225100)

Chiang, Y. S. (1992). The process-oriented writing workshop and "non-native" speakers of English: A teacher–researcher study. *Dissertation Abstracts International, 53*(09A), 3090. (UMI No. AAI9237657)

Cope, B., & Kalantzis, M. (Eds.). (1993). *The powers of literacy: A genre approach to teaching writing.* London: Falmer Press.

Cowley, M. (Ed.). (1958). *Writers at work: The Paris Review interviews.* New York: Viking.

Cramer, R. (2001). *Creative power: The nature and nurture of children's writing.* New York: Longman.

Croes, M. J. (1990). The efficacy of employing a writing process approach for the instruction of language arts with learning disabled elementary students. *Dissertation Abstracts International, 51*(12A), 4083. (UMI No. AAI9115193)

Day, A. G. (1947). Writer's magic. *American Association of University Professors Bulletin, 33,* 269–278.

Dean-Rumsey, T. A. (1998). Improving the writing skills of at-risk students through the use of writing across the curriculum and writing process instruction. *Dissertation Abstracts International, 37*(06A), 1598. (UMI No. AAI1395724)

de Beaugrande, R. (1984). *Advances in discourse processes: Vol. 11. Text production: Toward a science of composition.* Norwood, NJ: Ablex.

DeFoe, M. C. (2000). *Using directed writing strategies to teach students writing skills in middle grades language arts.* (ERIC Document Reproduction Services No. ED444186)

DeGroff, L. J. (1985). The relationship of prior knowledge to the content of text and peer conference comments in process approach lessons. *Dissertation Abstracts International, 46*(12A), 3595. (UMI No. AAI8603755)

De La Paz, S. (1999). Teaching writing strategies and self-regulation procedures to middle school students with learning disabilities. *Focus on Exceptional Children, 31*(5), 1–16.

De La Paz, S., & Graham, S. (2002). Explicitly teaching strategies, skills, and knowledge: Writing instruction in middle school classrooms. *Journal of Educational Psychology, 94*(4), 687–698.

Denzin, N. K. (1989). *The research act* (3rd ed.). Englewood Cliffs, NJ: Prentice-Hall.

DiStefano, P., & Olson, M. C. (1980). Describing and testing the effectiveness of a contemporary model for in-service education in teaching composition. *English Education, 12*(2), 69–76.

Dyson, A. H., & Freeman, S. W. (2003). Writing. In J. Flood, D. Lapp, J. R. Squire, & J. M. Jensen (Eds.), *Handbook of research on teaching the English language arts* (2nd ed., pp. 967–992). Mahwah, NJ: Erlbaum.

Elbow, P. (1973). *Writing without teachers.* New York: Oxford University Press.

Emig, J. (1971). *The composing processes of twelfth graders.* Urbana, IL: National Council of Teachers of English.

Eitelgeorge, J. W. (1994). Writing development: A longitudinal study of multiple continua of conceptual understandings within the writing process as displayed by first-graders. *Dissertation Abstracts International, 55*(03A), 494. (UMI No. AAI9420946)

Erlandson, D. A., Harris, E. L., Skipper, B. L., & Allen, F. D. (1993). *Doing naturalistic inquiry: A guide to methods.* Newbury Park, CA: Sage.

Fanscali, C., Nelsestuen, K., & Weinbaum, A. (2001). *National Writing Project: Year-two evaluation report.* New York: Academy for Educational Development.

Fanscali, C., & Silverstein, S. (2002). *National Writing Project: Final evaluation report.* New York: Academy for Educational Development.

Fischer, R. O. (1997). An investigation of the long-term effects on teachers of participation in the 1991 summer institute of the Metropolitan Area Writing Project (NWP) on effective teaching. *Dissertation Abstracts International, 58*(06A), 2166. (UMI No. AAI9735262)

Flower, L., & Hayes, J. R. (1980). The cognition of discovery: Defining a rhetorical problem. *College Composition and Communication, 31*(1), 21–32.

Flower, L., & Hayes, J. R. (1981). A cognitive process theory of writing. *College Communication and Composition, 32*(4), 365–387.

Friedrich, L., & LeMahieu, P. (2004). New NWP study explores teachers' learning, leadership, and legacy. *The Voice, 9*(1), 1, 19.

Fullan, M. (1982). *The meaning of educational change.* New York: Teachers College Press.

Gersten, R., & Baker, S. (2001). Teaching expressive writing to students with learning disabilities: A meta-analysis. *Elementary School Journal, 101*(3), 251–272.

Goldstein, A., & Carr, P. G. (1996, April). Can students benefit from process writing? *NAEPfacts, 1*(3), Washington, DC: National Center for Education Statistics. Retrieved March 12, 2004, from nces.ed.gov/pubs96/web/96845.asp

Graham, S., & Harris, K. R. (1997). Whole language and process writing: Does one approach fit all? In J. W. Lloyd, E. J. Kameenui, & D. Chard (Eds.), *Issues in educating students with disabilities* (pp. 239–258). Manwah, NJ: Lawrence Erlbaum Associates.

Graves, D. H. (1973). Children's writing: Research hypotheses based on an examination of the writing processes of seven-year-old children. *Dissertation Abstracts International, 34* (6497A). 6255 (UMI No. AAI17408375)

Graves, D. H. (1983). *Writing teachers and children at work.* Portsmouth, NH: Heinemann.

Graves, D. H. (1984). *A researcher learns to write: Selected articles and monographs.* Exeter, NH: Heinemann.

Gray, J. (2000). *Teachers at the center: A memoir of the early years of the National Writing Project.* Berkeley, CA: National Writing Project.

Greenwald, E. A., Persky, H. R., Campbell, J. R., & Mazzeo, J. (1999). *The NAEP 1998 writing report card for the nation and the states* (NCES Report No. 19990462). Washington, DC: US Department of Education, Office of Educational Research and Improvement.

Gundlach, R. A. (1977). The composing process and the teaching of writing: A study of an idea and its uses. *Dissertation Abstracts International, 38*(11A), 6497A. (UMI No. AAI 805271)

Hamilton, A. C. (1992). Performance assessment of personal correspondence on the development of written language use and functions in traditional and process writing second-grade classrooms. *Dissertation Abstracts International, 53*(07A), 2235. (UMI No. AAI9234729)

Hampton, S. B. (1990). Changing instructional practice: Principles of andragogy and the ongoing education of writing teachers. *Dissertation Abstracts International, 52*(02A), 393. (UMI No. AAI9118128)

Harris, E. A. (1992). The relationship of attitudes and writing abilities to computer writing and peers critique of writing. *Dissertation Ab-*

stracts International, 53(06A), 1828. (UMI No. AAI9224268)

Haugen, N. (1982, March) An investigation of the impact of the Wisconsin Writing Project on student composition. Paper presented at the annual meeting of the American Educational Research Association, New York. (ERIC Document Reproduction Services No. ED214203)

Hawkins, M. L., & Marshall, J. C. (1981). Evaluating writing grades 3–12. Ferguson, MO: Ferguson–Florissant School District.

Hayes, B.L. (1984). The effects of implementing process writing into a seventh grade English curriculum. Dissertation Abstracts International, 45(09A), 2743. (UMI No. AAI8425249)

Hicks, D. (1997). Working through discourse genres in school. Research in the Teaching of English, 31(4), 459–485.

Hillocks, G. (1984). What works in teaching composition: A meta-analysis of experimental treatment studies. American Journal of Education, 93(1), 133–170.

Hillocks, G. (1986). Research on written composition: New directions for teaching. Urbana, IL: ERIC clearinghouse on reading and communication skills and the national conference on research in English.

Honeycutt, R. L. (2002). Good readers/poor writers: An investigation of the strategies, understanding, and meaning that good readers who are poor writers ascribe to writing narrative text on-demand. Unpublished doctoral dissertation, North Carolina State University, Raleigh.

Honeycutt, R. L., & Pritchard, R. J. (2005) Using a structured writing workshop to help good readers who are poor writers. In G. Rijlaarrsdan, H. van den Bergh, & M. Couzijin (Eds.), Studies in writing, Vol. 14. Effective teaching and learning of writing (2nd ed., pp. 141–150). Amsterdam: Kluwer.

Inverness Research Associates. (1997). National Writing Project annual report, 1996–97. Berkeley: University of California Press.

Jensen, J. M. (1993) What do we know about the teaching of writing of elementary school children? Language Arts, 70(4), 290–294.

Jensen, J. M. (2002). Teaching writing on the shoulders of giants. Language Arts, 79(4), 357–362.

Larsen, E. K. (1983). A history of the composing process. Dissertation Abstracts International, 45(05A), 1381. (UMI No. AA10410240)

Laub, H. D. (1996). The effect of participation in a writing institute on selected teachers. Dissertation Abstracts International, 57(10A), 4332. (UMI No. AAI9708252)

Lieberman, A., & Wood, D. (2003). Inside the National Writing Project. New York: Teachers College Press.

Lipson, M. Y., Mosenthal, J., Daniels, P., & Wood-

side-Jiron, H. (2000). Process writing in the classrooms of eleven fifth-grade teachers with different orientations to teaching and learning. Elementary School Journal, 101(2), 209–231.

MacArthur, C., Schwartz, S., Graham, S., Molloy, D., & Harris, K. (1996). Integration of strategy instruction into a whole language classroom: A case study. Learning Disabilities Research and Practice, 11(3), 168–176.

Marshall, J. C. (1983, April). Student achievement in the holistic teaching of writing: Project impact and diffusion. Paper presented at the annual meeting of the American Educational Research Association, Montreal, Canada.

Miller, C. L. (1985). The experience of eleventh grade writers: The interaction of thought and emotion during the writing process. Dissertation Abstracts International, 46(12A), 3638. (UMI No. AAI8602622)

Mills, B. (1953). Writing as process. College English, 15(1), 19–56.

Moffett, J. (1981). Active voice. Montclair, NJ: Boynton/Cook.

Moffett, J. (1992). Detecting growth in language. Portsmouth, NH: Heinemann.

Moriarity, D. J. (1978). An investigation of the effect of instruction of five components of the writing process on the quality and syntactic complexity of student writing. Dissertation Abstracts International, 38(05A), 2727. (UMI No. AAI7819765)

Murray, D. (1985). A writer teaches writing (2nd ed.). Boston: Houghton Mifflin.

National Writing Project, & Nagin, C. (2003). Because writing matters. San Francisco: Jossey-Bass.

Odell, L., & Cohick, J. (1975). You mean, write it over in ink? English Journal, 64(9), 48–53.

Patthey-Chavez, G. G., Matsumura, L. C., & Valdés, R. (2004). Investigating the process approach to writing instruction in urban middle schools. Journal of Adolescent and Adult Literacy, 47(6), 642–476.

Penfield, E. (1979). Faculty development and the teaching of writing: A local adaptation of the National Writing Project. Baton Rouge: Louisiana Writing Project. (ERIC Document Reproduction Service No. ED200960)

Poindexter, C. C., & Oliver, I. R. (1998/1999). Navigating the writing process: Strategies for young children. Reading Teacher, 52(4), 420–423.

Pritchard, R. J. (1987). Effects on student writing of teacher training in the National Writing Project model. Written Communication, 4(1), 51–67.

Pritchard, R. J., & Marshall, J. C. (1994). Evaluation of a tiered model for staff development in writing. Research in the Teaching of English, 28(3), 259–285.

Pritchard, R. J., & Marshall, J. C. (2002a). Professional development in "healthy" vs. "unhealthy" districts: Top 10 characteristics based on research.

School Leadership and Management, 22(2), 113–141.

Pritchard, R. J., & Marshall, J. C. (2002b, Summer). Do NWP teachers make a difference?: Findings of research on district-led staff development. *NWP Quarterly, 24*(3), 32–38. Berkeley, CA: National Writing Project. Available online at www.writingproject.org.

Pritchard, R. J., & Marshall, J. C. (2005). School and district culture as reflected in student voices and student achievement. *School Effectiveness and School Improvement: An International Journal of Research, Policy and Practice, 16*(2), 153–177.

Robbins, J. T. (1986). A study of the effect of the writing process on the development of verbal skills among elementary school children. *Dissertation Abstracts International, 47*(08A), 2930. (UMI No. AAI8627505)

Roberts, C. A. (2001). The influence of teachers' professional development at the Tampa Bay Area Writing Project on student writing performance. *Dissertation Abstracts International, 63*(05A), 1792. (UMI No. AAI3052666)

Robinson, M. E. (1986). The writing performance and revision behavior of fifth grade process and non-process writing students during one-day and two-day writing sessions. *Dissertation Abstracts International, 49*(09A), 2536. (UMI No. AA18813469)

Robinson-Metz, J. M. (1985). A case study of the journal writing process: Three 11th grade journal writers. *Dissertation Abstracts International, 46*(09A), 2604. (UMI No. AA18521895)

Rohman, D. G. (1965). Pre-writing: The stage of discovery in the writing process. *College Composition and Communication, 16*(2), 106–122.

Scannella, A. M. (1982). A writing-as-process model as a means of improving composition and attitudes towards composition in high school. *Dissertation Abstracts International, 43*(08A), 2582. (UMI No. AA18301605)

Schuster, E. H. (2004). National and state writing tests: The writing process betrayed. *Phi Delta Kappan, 85*(5), 375–378.

Schwartz, M. (1980). Six journeys through the writing process. *Dissertation Abstracts International, 41*(04A), 1450. (UMI No. AAI8023624)

Shook, J. (1981). The Gateway Writing Project: An evaluation of teachers teaching teachers to write. *Research in the Teaching of English, 15*(1), 282–284.

Shortt, T. L. (1986). Teacher classroom behaviors and their effects on student achievement in secondary classrooms. *Dissertation Abstracts International, 48*(12A), 3087. (UMI No. AII8802908)

Smagorinsky, P. (1987). Graves revisited: A look at the methods and conclusions of the New Hampshire study. *Written Communication, 4*(4), 331–342.

Smith, C. B. (2000a). *Writing instruction: Changing views over the years* (ERIC Digest 155). Bloomington: Indiana University (ERIC Document Reproduction Service No. ED449337)

Smith, C. B. (2000b). *Writing instruction: Current practices in the classroom* (ERIC Digest 156). Bloomington: Indiana University (ERIC Document Reproduction Service No. ED446338)

So, W. Y. (1986). Integrating first language and second language approaches to writing. *Dissertation Abstracts International, 47*(04A), 1308. (UMI No. AAI8613337)

Sommers, N. (1982). *Revision strategies of student writers and experienced adults.* Washington, DC: National Institute of Education. (ERIC Document Reproduction Services No. ED220 839)

St. John, M. (2003, November). *NWP update report.* Delivered to the annual meeting of the National Writing Project, San Francisco, CA.

St. John, M., Dickey, K., Hirabayashi, J., & Stokes, L. (2001, Dec.). *The National Writing Project: Client satisfaction and program impact: Results from a follow-up survey of participants at summer 2000 invitational institutes.* Inverness, CA: Inverness Research Associates.

Swenson, J. M. (1992). Changes in teaching practices related to the Colorado Writing Project, 1987–1991. *Dissertation Abstracts International, 53*(10A), 3438. (UMI No. AAI9304607)

Stotsky, S. (1995). The uses and limitations of personal or personalized writing in writing theory, research, and instruction. *Reading Research Quarterly, 30*(4), 758–776.

Tindall, M. E. (1990). Process-oriented writing instruction: The effect of training on instructional practice. *Dissertation Abstracts International, 52*(02A), 511. (UMI No. AAI9118946)

van den Bergh, H., & Rijlaarsdam, G. (2001). Changes in cognitive activities during the writing process and relationships with text quality. *Educational Psychology, 21*(4), 373–385.

Vaughan, S. C. (1992). Writing in the classroom: A study of Northwest Inland Writing Project teacher's beliefs and practices. *Dissertation Abstracts International, 53*(11A), 3876. (UMI No. AAI9309076)

Watkins-Goffman, L. F. (1986). A case study of the second language writing process of a sixth grade writing group. *Dissertation Abstracts International, 47*(08A), 2932. (UMI No. AAI8625662)

Wilson, D. E. (1988). Teacher change and the Iowa Writing Project. *Dissertation Abstracts International, 50*(04A), 926. (UMI No. AAI8913252)

Wilson, D. E. (1994). *Attempting change: Teachers moving from Writing Project to classroom practice.* Portsmouth, NH: Boynton/Cook.

Wilson, S., & Berne, J. (1999). Teacher learning and the acquisition of professional knowledge: An examination of research on contemporary professional development. In A. Iran-Nejaf & P. D. Pearson (Eds.), *Review of research in education* (Vol. 24, pp. 173–209). Washington, DC: American Educational Research Association.

Winterowd, W. R., & Blum, J. (1994). *A teacher's introduction to composition in the rhetorical tradition.* Urbana, IL: National Council of Teachers of English.

Witte, S. P. (1987). Pre-text and composing. *College Composition and Communication, 38*(4), 397–425.

Wood, D. R., & Lieberman, A. (2000). Teachers as authors: The National Writing Project's approach to professional development. *International Journal of Leadership in Education, 3*(3), 255–273.

Zemelman, S., & Wagner, B. J. (1982). *Application for validation.* Elmhurst, IL: Chicago Area Writing Project.

Part IV

WRITING AND SPECIAL POPULATIONS

Chapter 20

Teaching Writing in Culturally Diverse Classrooms

Arnetha F. Ball

In 1987, Freedman and Dyson published a report, *Research in Writing: Past, Present, and Future*, in which they noted that "the past twenty years have brought about dramatic changes in writing research—in the questions asked, the approaches used to answer those questions, and the kinds of implications drawn for teaching and learning" (p. 1). They elaborated on how much of the research in the 1970s was concerned with written product, replaced with writing process during the late 1970s, then shifted to a focus on context in the 1980s. Researchers were beginning to show how uses of writing differed on academic and nonacademic tasks. They were also beginning to focus more on how language and writing differs among subcultures. As schools and communities in the United States were becoming more culturally diverse, researchers were focusing more attention on the ways in which culture manifests itself within classrooms and in the cultural lives of students from diverse backgrounds. In their 1987 report, Freedman and Dyson challenged their readers to envision future research that would go beyond the current insights of any given research paradigm or instructional system and to attend to the connections between the powerful forces of cognition, context, and language. They proposed that such work would call for a broad research agenda informed by a cross-disciplinary approach to the study of writing.

That same year, Delpit (1987) published an article entitled "Skills and Other Dilemmas of a Progressive Black Educator." In this article, Delpit discussed writing programs that focused on fluency and proposed that they did not meet the needs of poor and minority students. She challenged her readers to consider the notion that if we are to effect needed changes that will allow minorities to progress, writing programs for them must insist on skills development within the context of critical and creative thinking. Today, almost 20 years after the publication of these two documents, teaching writing to culturally diverse, poor, and marginalized students is still a point of great concern, because many of these students continue to fare poorly on every measure of writing proficiency and academic achievement. A review of the research on teaching writing in culturally diverse classrooms since 1987 reveals that we are still seeking cross-disciplinary approaches to the study of writing that will inform a broad research agenda to assist us in effectively teaching students from culturally diverse backgrounds in critical and creative ways.

The report of the National Assessment of Educational Progress National Center for Educational Statistics (NAEP, 1998, 2003) on writing in urban schools indicates that far too many students who attend schools in poor and underresourced communities still have not yet mastered the writing skills needed to excel in today's technologically advanced society. In 2002, the writing scores for eighth graders in very diverse communities such as Los Angeles and the District of Columbia were considerably lower than the national average (NAEP Trial Urban District Assessment [TUDA], 2003). The National Center for Education Statistics published the *Long-Term Trends in Student Writing Performance* in 1998. This report traditionally discusses changes in the differences in performance among subgroups as determined by race/ethnicity and gender from a long-term perspective. After looking at these trends over the past decade, NAEP concluded that there had been no improvement in the writing performance of these subgroups. With the considerable attention that had been given to product versus process writing, basic writing, and cultural influences on writing in the literature, this finding was cause for great concern. Realizing that good writing skills are needed to assist students in meeting the communicative requirements of today's increasingly global society and the increasingly complex demands of the workplace and postsecondary learning environments, there is no doubt that many questions remain about how best to facilitate the improvement of writing skills among culturally diverse students. In an effort to address these concerns, researchers are asking many questions, including the following:

1. What is the influence of classroom and/or community *context* on the teaching of writing to culturally diverse students?
2. What is the influence of students' *culture* and home discourses on students' writing performance inside and outside of school?
3. What are the effects of various *teaching strategies* or pedagogical approaches on the writing and *assessment* of culturally diverse students?
4. How can educators, curriculum developers, and policymakers develop practices and policies that build upon the existing resources that students from diverse backgrounds bring from their culturally rich home environments—to scaffold their learning and help them to meet the communicative demands of today's workplace and academic environments?

These are but a few of the questions that command the attention of researchers whose work focuses on teaching writing in culturally diverse classrooms, but they represent four critically important areas that these researchers investigate.

Since the Delpit and the Freedman and Dyson publications in 1987, scholarship on the writing of culturally diverse students has become even more prominent in our field. A recent search of the Educational Resources Information Center (ERIC) database from 1987 to 2004 generated 938 entries using the descriptors *teaching writing* and *culture*. When the descriptors were expanded to include other keywords relevant to the topic *teaching writing in culturally diverse classrooms*, I found that a wide assortment of labels is used to categorize scholarship in this area. Limiting the search from 1987 forward and cross-listing the keywords *teaching writing* and *culture* with four additional terms, I found that 137 entries were generated using the terms *teaching writing, culture*, and *multicultural*; 123 entries were generated using the terms *teaching writing, culture, and diversity*; 105 entries were generated using the terms *teaching writing, culture*, and *minority*; and 71 entries were generated using the terms *teaching writing, culture*, and *ethnic groups*. Looking closely at the entries generated, I found that many of the results were duplicate entries, some focused on second language learners (a topic covered in another chapter of this handbook), and some others that were literature reviews, how-to pieces, or theoretical in nature. Looking only at publications based on empirical studies that focused on K–12 students who are considered racial or ethnic minorities in this country, or on multicultural students who come together to make up diverse classroom populations, I selected over 50 studies that became the focus of the discussions in the sections that follow.

Predominant Theoretical Models That Frame the Research

Since the late 1980s, several theoretical models have been used to frame the research conducted on teaching writing to culturally diverse students. Over the last two decades, the most common theoretical models used to ground the research on teaching writing to culturally diverse learners emphasize the impact of the social context on writing. Sociocultural, sociocognitive, sociolinguistic, and social-constructivist frameworks have been dominant in the literature. Critical theory, cognitive models, and other perspectives have also been used to guide this research, but they appeared less frequently in the literature I reviewed. The predominance of theoretical models that stress social influences on writing practices and writing development is of little surprise given the social and political events that have taken place during these times. In the 1960s, following the War on Poverty, social and cultural models emerged to dominate the literature. By the 1980s, 1990s, and into the new millennium, these theories have again dominated the literature in the form of theoretical frames such as sociocultural and sociocognitive theory. These theoretical frameworks acknowledge the influence of an individual's prior experiences, values, beliefs, and context on what and how students learn.

Guided by such theoretical perspectives, the research on teaching writing to culturally diverse students has generally fallen into several categories: (1) the influences of teachers, classrooms, and/or community *contexts* on teaching writing to diverse students; (2) the influences of the students' *culture* or home discourse styles on their writing; and (3) the effects of particular *teaching strategies* or pedagogical approaches on the writing and assessment of culturally diverse students. Using these three categories to organize the information—context, culture, and strategies for teaching and assessment—this review focuses on frequently occurring questions that have guided the research, the methods used to explore these questions, and the major findings that have emerged in these studies. In the concluding section of this chapter, I discuss some of the implications of this work for writing instruction in culturally diverse classrooms and proposed directions for future research.

Context

One primary area of study in the research on teaching writing in culturally diverse classrooms focuses on the importance of con-

text in teaching and learning writing. This research helps us to understand that the individuals within the classroom are but one factor that influences a student's learning and/or achievement. Studies confirm that additional factors include—but are not limited to—school characteristics, learning environments, class activities, parental input, instructional characteristics, and even students' imaginative worlds. All of these factors play important roles in the ultimate achievement of students in culturally diverse classrooms. Dyson (1989, 1991) conducted a 2-year descriptive and interpretive study of the social and imagined worlds of Anglo, African American, Hispanic, African–Anglo, and Hispanic–Anglo K–3 children to understand better the multiple functions of the imaginary world of children when learning to write. Her research confirmed that the imaginative worlds that children construct are embedded in their social worlds, and both play central roles in students' writing development. Schneider (2003) also conducted a descriptive and interpretive study of students' writing in an elementary classroom, focusing on context, genre, and imagination. Schneider observed second- and third-grade students in a yearlong study that recasts one African American and two European American children's writing as performance within differing instructional contexts designed to support it. This study examined the complex interplay between teachers' instructional strategies and the students' writing strategies, revealing the idiosyncratic nature of students' writing performances. In an attempt to help teachers understand some of the complex influences of context on students' writing, Moore and O'Neill (2002) published *Practices in Context: Situating the Work of Writing Teachers,* which includes a collection of essays composed by writing teachers themselves. The authors envisioned this book as a collection designed to meet the needs of new teachers as they encounter new students, new courses, new institutions, and engage with new experiences.

Sperling and Woodlief (1997) conducted a study of two 10th-grade classrooms serving African American, European American, and Asian American students in an urban multicultural setting and a suburban white setting. They used discourse analysis to compare the characteristics of the classroom writing communities in the urban, multiracial setting and the suburban setting. These researchers found that in the multiracial urban school, writing was treated primarily as a means for students to explore and better understand their lived experiences, while in the suburban classroom, although students' experiences were the basis for the work, these experiences were created for the purpose of the assignment rather than using experiences students already possessed. In the urban multiracial classroom, where efforts were made to diminish hierarchical boundaries between the teacher and students, space was provided for students' lived experiences to be regarded as a valued source of information through autobiographical essays, thereby making the students the experts. In the suburban classroom, where students were seen as equals to each other but the teacher maintained the role of "expert," the assignment required students to conduct interviews and complete projects that drew on other sources as expert resources. While the findings of the study confirmed the notion that multiple factors influenced the writing produced be these students, the design of the study did not allow the researchers to make causal claims.

Mavrogenes and Bezruczko (1993) used data from the Longitudinal Study of Children at Risk (Reynolds, Bezruczko, Hagemann, & Mavrogenes, 1991) that involved 1,225 African American students to identify correlations between student writing samples, teacher reports, parent reports, and self-reports from the students themselves. Mavrogenes and Bezruczko concluded that students' motivation, maturity, attitude, and the marital status of their parents (with children of married parents performing better than children of unmarried parents) all seemed to have a significant influence on students' writing development. They also concluded that, while the teacher and student reports were important, the parent reports had a significant influence on students' writing development.

Needels and Knapp (1994) conducted a large-scale study involving 1,123 underserved students to examine how various school characteristics influence student writing. They hypothesized a relationship between student outcomes and preselected variables, including degree of emphasis on teaching component skills in context and on

the meaningful use of writing, degree of connection between writing and students' backgrounds, degree of student interaction while writing, problem-solving processes involved in the writing task, and frequency of opportunities to write extended texts. The findings revealed that these six pedagogical principles explained 44% of the variance in the writing competency scores and 21% of the variance in the writing mechanics scores. Needels and Knapp concluded that these six variables should be considered when designing writing programs to benefit low-income students.

Langer (2001) conducted a study involving 25 middle and high schools, 44 teachers, and students from diverse cultural backgrounds enrolled in 88 classrooms. This study was designed to investigate environments and activities that foster success among students from diverse cultural backgrounds. This study of the English/Language Arts programs in these 25 middle and high schools showed distinct differences between schools that were "beating the odds" (those whose student bodies were performing better on standardized writing assessments than other schools with a comparable student body). Langer found that high-performing schools had the following characteristics: They integrated skills instruction within purposeful assignments, revised their school literacy curriculums to incorporate the skills and content required by standardized tests, made connections with instructional content across subject matter and within student's lives outside of school, had teachers who were explicit with their expectations and evaluation procedures, treated learning as an activity that went beyond mere skills acquisition to a deeper and continuing understanding of concepts and ideas, and frequently allowed students to work together in groups to challenge and critique each other's ideas. Langer found that these six characteristics worked in concert to create a positive learning context. She also found that having one or two of the six characteristics in place did not lead to a school having comparable scores on high-stakes standardized writing assessments.

While the majority of the studies that emerged from my search on the importance of context in teaching writing to culturally diverse students focused on in-school factors, the work of Ball (1995), Mahiri (1998), and Schultz (2002) helps us to understand the influences of community and/or out-of-school contexts on the writing of diverse students. They make links to teaching writing in culturally diverse classrooms as well. Gaining an understanding of the literacy practices that take place outside of schools can help us to build bridges that strengthen students' academic writing (Hagemann, 2001). In a 3-year ethnographic study of three community-based organizations, Ball (1995) found a variety of oral and written communication practices used by African American vernacular English (AAVE) speakers in community-based organizations. The three organizations included in this study all emphasized collaborative work on oral and written assignments, high standards, and dedicated commitment to important oral and written skills on the part of both participants and their instructors. In translating the findings of this research into classroom practices to support the writing development of culturally diverse students, Ball suggests that teachers should provide students with opportunities both to speak and to write in mainstream ways, as well as in ways that use local literacies that reflect their cultural background. This is a departure from more traditional teaching practices used in many writing classrooms. The oral language used in these community-based organizations turned out to be an important factor in students' writing successes. Teachers in community-based organizations used oral language to engage students' interest *and* as a precursor to successful writing activities. This approach required that teachers be willing to take risks. Ball recommended that in-school writing teachers should emphasize collaborative work among students, standards of high expectations, and commitment to generative and critical thinking on the part of both teachers and students.

Mahiri (1998) brings classroom and community issues to the forefront as he looks at students struggling for voice through the development of writing skills. In *Shooting for Excellence,* Mahiri describes two teachers, both African Americans, who teach English in the same inner-city high school. One teacher had astounding success with her students, while another teacher's students were frequently disruptive and even fell asleep in class. Through a series of vignettes, Mahiri probed deeply the causes of the differences and demonstrated how the students' African American and youth culture cannot be ignored if we are to effect change in their patterns of educational success. Mahiri brought together classroom and community-based research to explore language learning that influences students' writing development as well. He showed how building on African American youth culture and experiences fostered student ownership and achievement, and proposed that it is the task of teachers to apply creative social and cultural awareness to students' cultures, in order to address their historically oppositional nature. As Mahiri looked at the students' teacher-aided struggle for voice through the development of writing skills, he recommended that teachers must make viable connections between "the streets" (students' community lives) and schools to create more meaningful cultural worlds for learning—which can lead to changes in classroom discourse, culture, and ways of reflecting diversity in the curriculum. Mahiri concluded by imagining new century schools as building on students' cultural diversity yet aiming for cultural transformation by teaching students the knowledge, skills, and values that promote nonoppressive human interactions that increase their prospects of finding their personal gold, as well as achieving their personal goals.

Schultz (2002) reports on a longitudinal study of three seniors in an urban high school. Situated within a Black and Latino community, Schultz looks at multiracial students' writing practices outside of low-income schools, where almost 79% of the students received Aid to Families with Dependent Children. She argued for a focus on students' writing practices both in and out of school to develop a more comprehensive understanding of students' capabilities. Like Ball (1995) and Mahiri (1998), Schultz (2002) found that despite students' reluctance to write in school, many of them wrote outside of school in ways more similar to academic writing than is generally assumed. These and other studies help us to understand how the contexts in which writing occurs play an important role in students' learning to write and their transformative uses of writing in a wide range of contexts.

Most importantly, they help us to understand that the learning community that is created within culturally diverse classrooms can vary depending on the characteristics of the school context and the student body, parental involvement, structuring of the classroom environment, the nature of teachers' assignments, out-of-school experiences, and students' imaginative worlds. These, however, are but a few of the factors that shape how a student experiences school and the development of writing skills in classrooms.

Some of the studies in this section on context raise questions concerning the belief of some educators that it is essential to emphasize explicit instruction and basic writing skills to poor students who attend under-resourced schools. They suggest that researchers and practitioners alike should maintain a broad and flexible view of what communities of learners can and should look like in writing classrooms. In addition, this research suggests that school curricula should provide more opportunities for students to write, that teachers should be required to receive training in teaching writing and composition to diverse students, and that teachers should be sensitive to the many other context-related factors that affect students' learning, such as their levels of self-confidence and their perceptions of the usefulness of the writing they are asked to do within schools.

Culture

In 1979 a federal court judge in Detroit ruled that, to meet federal guidelines for nondiscrimination, a school must consider the language practices of a student's home culture, even when that language varies from the linguistic system used by most middle-class Americans. More than 20 years after that seminal ruling, the challenge remains for teachers to use extensive amounts of writing in their classrooms and to find ways to support the learning of all students in a culturally and linguistically diverse society. A long-standing concern has been to develop classroom cultures that promote equity in opportunity and accessibility to learning for individuals across boundaries of class and ethnicity. Acting upon this concern can be difficult, however, for many teachers, who feel overwhelmed when faced with the task

of teaching writing to students from cultural backgrounds different from their own. The Ann Arbor case, however, made it clear that school districts and teachers are responsible for rethinking pedagogy and curriculum in ways that make learning accessible to all students, regardless of their racial or ethnic backgrounds.

While most school curricula and research on teaching writing continue to reflect the values and interests of middle-class European Americans and omit the cultural experiences of racially, ethnically, and linguistically diverse students, some researchers have worked to help us understand the influences of the students' culture and home discourse styles on their writing. The seminal work of researchers such as Farr Whiteman (1981), Heath (1983), Michaels (1987), and Gilmore and Glatthorn (1982) confirms the notion that culture is an important factor that can and should be considered when teaching writing in culturally diverse classrooms. In 1986, Farr and Daniels provided examples of culturally-related conflicts in the writing of many African American students at the phonological, syntactic, semantic, pragmatic, and discourse levels. Over the past 20 years, Staton, Shuy, Kreeh & Payton, and Reed and colleagues (1988), Ball (1992, 1996, 1999), Smitherman (1994), Stein, Dixson, and Isaacson (1994), Fecho (2000), and Rosaen (2003) are but a few of the researchers who have continued this tradition of helping us to understand the critical importance of culture in the writing of culturally diverse students. In addition, other researchers, including Moll (1987, 1990), Gutierrez (1992), Lee (1992), Nieto (1992), Redd (1992), Srole (1994), and Au (1993, 1997, 1998), have contributed to our understanding of the language and literacy resources that diverse student populations bring to their classroom life experiences and the importance of considering these resources when planning and implementing writing instruction.

Staton and colleagues (1988) studied the use of dialogue journals in a sixth-grade classroom in a multicultural section of Los Angeles. The students in the classroom came from diverse cultures and spoke 13 different languages. Their teacher, who had been using dialogue journals for 17 years, asked her students to write, in English, daily entries in their journals, to which she wrote short responses. Even those students who had minimal literacy skills in mainstream academic English were asked to write, as best they could, at least three sentences per day. The teacher did not evaluate this writing; instead, she responded to it as a natural form of communication between two people who were writing and reading rather than talking. Analysis of the journals over the course of a year showed substantial growth in the students' writing ability, including an increase in quantity, elaboration of student-initiated topics, fluency, and control of academic English and syntax. Moreover, these students experienced, some for the first time, writing and reading for a purpose of their own within the context of the classroom. They eagerly read the teacher's responses to their entries and wrote copiously, some even ending the year with several filled notebooks comprising their yearlong dialogue journal.

The research on language variation and writing has identified particular linguistic features characteristic of the "home language" of various groups that speak nonmainstream varieties of English that occur in the writing of students from various groups. Through a close analysis of the writing of one African American high school student, Ball (1999) described the culturally influenced features revealed in the writing of this student and discussed the implications this work has for understanding the writing of students from other backgrounds (e.g., Latino and Native American bilinguals), and deaf users of American sign language.

Smitherman (1994) published a chapter entitled " 'The Blacker the Berry, the Sweeter the Juice': African American Student Writers." In this study, she analyzed the degree to which African American verbal traditions survived in the classroom writing lives of African American students across a generational time span. A total of 867 essays from the 1984 and the 1988/1989 NAEP were subjected to primary trait and holistic scoring analysis and were ranked in terms of the degree of African American discourse found in the texts. These scores were compared to the scores given by NAEP raters, and to scores from the 1969 and 1979 NAEP. Results indicated that (1) no correlation existed between a discernibly African American discourse style and the production of Black

English Vernacular (BEV) syntax, supporting results of earlier studies of 1969 and 1979 NAEP essays; (2) the more discernibly African American the discourse, the higher the primary trait and holistic scores, and the less discernibly African American the discourse, the lower the primary trait and holistic scores, contrary to earlier studies; and (3) "imaginative/narrative" essays continued to be black students' strong suit. Findings suggested that students who employed a black expressive discourse style in their classroom writing received higher NAEP scores than those who did not. Smitherman encouraged writing instructors to capitalize on the strengths of African American cultural discourse; encourage students toward the field dependency style, which enables them to produce more powerful, meaningful, and more highly rated essays; and deemphasize concerns about BEV grammar.

In "Analyzing the Role of the Vernacular in Student Writing: A Social Literacies Approach," Blackburn and Stern (2000) drew on the cultural practices that students bring from home and used a social literacies perspective to analyze a rap written by a high school student. The researchers examined students' use of AAVE and "standard" English, and concluded that teachers and researchers must engage students' literacy practices in order to enrich classroom life and to conduct meaningful and socially just research. The study reinforced the need to continue the scholarly debate about the wisdom and efficacy of trying to impose "standard" English on all speakers and writers, and argued that new ways to validate alternative literacies should be found that can be used as a means of helping students to become proficient users of dominant literacies.

Much of the research reported here on writing in culturally diverse classrooms deals with researchers' desire to explore ways to improve educational practice, classroom life, and writing instruction, and points toward changing teachers' perceptions about bringing students' culture into the classroom and generating new ways to reduce educational failure of students in culturally diverse classrooms. Researchers confirm the notion that language is one of the primary representations and expressions of culture, and that it reflects one's worldview, beliefs, values, and conscious and unconscious expectations.

Michaels's (1987) study examined the oral interaction of a first-grade student and her teacher during sharing time and the written interaction between a fifth-grade student and his teacher during the development of an essay. Michaels found a dis-connect based on cultural expectations. Other researchers have built on this research to show how culturally based variations in speech patterns and styles of communication influence students' writing. In 1992 Ball found that while the fifth and sixth graders in her study did not insist on using a particular preference for expressing discourse patterns, the high school students did. The high school students in this study showed a clear preference for using circumlocution or narrative interspersion, two of the vernacular, culturally based organization patterns African American students used to organize their expository texts. Among the remaining high school students in the study almost three-fourths used a topic net when organizing expository texts in academic settings, while all of the African American high-school students preferred the culturally based writing patterns in academic and nonacademic settings. Ball noted the educational implications of all of the students' preferences and demonstrated a bias in teachers' evaluation practices that favored the use of academic-based patterns in school settings (Ball, 1992, 1996).

Since the 1979 Ann Arbor Black English case, scholars have cautioned teachers that they must be aware of the presence of AAVE in their students' written texts. Ball (1999) provided an example of a student's written text that had several characteristic AAVE features. She rendered a close linguistic analysis of this student's writing that can help teachers realize what it means to understand students' culturally based influences on their writing and the presence of AAVE in a student's writing. In this analysis, Ball found syntactic, semantic, phonological, and stylistic patterns in the student's text that reflected patterns typical in the speech of AAVE speakers. Ball recommended several principles to guide teachers in teaching writing to culturally diverse students.

Sperling (1995) conducted a study of five African American, white, and Chinese American 10th-grade students to investigate students' discourse and writing based on an examination of a classroom discussion. Sperling found that the various roles that

students took on during this discussion (observer, historian, prognosticator, critic, and philosopher) were based on relationships within the classroom community, in the broader society, or in the texts themselves. Sperling's (1996) publication builds on a discussion that centers on speech and discourse patterns, and provides a review of research that assists us in better understanding the precise connection between writing and speaking. Because all individuals learn to talk according to the norms of their culture, speaking can be viewed as a rich cultural resource to build upon in writing instruction for students from diverse cultures. Many culturally diverse students receive skills-based instruction in schools. However, their understanding of academic writing is quite different from the literacy practices present in their home communities. Sperling highlights the fact that culture influences students' and teachers' conscious and unconscious interactions and expectations in the classroom, and recommends clear and open dialogue between students and teachers to support the development of students' writing.

In 1992 Heller conducted a study to show how African American students wrote, published, and shared their culture through writing. Looking closely at different styles of writing from diverse students, Heller concluded that language is one of the primary representations and expressions of culture. Several years later, Ball (1995) provided a detailed text analysis of the expository writing patterns of four academically successful African American high school students. Using text analysis, Ball revealed that students had the ability to manipulate AAVE, mainstream, and academic English skillfully during their oral discussions and written assignments. They also demonstrated the ability to intersperse culturally influenced literacy patterns into their expository writing in ways that enriched their classwork. Green (1997) reports on a study of two kindergarten Appalachian students' reading and writing development. Green found that both students developed unique styles and approaches to literacy that stemmed from home and cultural influences and a supportive, constructivist, whole-language classroom. Researchers have confirmed that there is a close link between students' uses of oral language and their writing. Fecho's (2000) critical inquiry into language in an urban classroom situates teachers as cultural workers (Freire, 1970). This teacher–research study used interpretive methods to help culturally diverse African American and Caribbean America high school students investigate the impact of language on their lives through writing. Fecho found that as students deepened their awareness of themselves as inquirers into language, they simultaneously problematized their perspectives on language and became theorizers about language and power in their society. Fecho recommends that teachers find ways to celebrate students' home lives and home languages in their classrooms while teaching students about the culture of power in our society.

The researchers who focus on writing and writing instruction in culturally diverse classrooms have confirmed the fact that the interrelationships between language, culture, and writing are strong. Their findings indicate that culture influences students' and teachers' classroom practices, as well as their conscious and unconscious interactions and expectations. In addition, these researchers help us to understand how students' community-based discourse patterns can help to inform teachers and allow them to create curricular bridges that link students' home, community, and school communication practices and demands. Writing teachers can also build upon the range of roles students already take on in their home communities. Students' experiences can be brought into the classroom to connect their community lives with their school lives to enhance the curriculum and enrich students' learning experiences. More importantly, teachers have a great impact on students' writing achievement by creating a sense of "classroom community" through their pedagogical practices, and through the relationships they establish with their students around writing.

Instruction and Assessment

Research confirms that the pedagogical approaches and instructional strategies teachers choose to employ in their classrooms can have long-lasting effects on the writing development and assessment results of culturally diverse students. The greatest number of studies I found in my literature review on teaching writing in culturally diverse classrooms focused on these areas. Yeh and Stuart

(1998) investigated the teaching of argument to 116 Hispanic American, African American, Asian American, and European American middle school students and found that students who were explicitly taught argumentative strategies made statistically significant gains in that area and in the development of voice. They concluded that explicit instruction in argument form and argument structure sharpens students' judgment about the organization of argumentative texts and improves their writing of arguments—particularly among minority students. These researchers recommended that a replication study be conducted that compares a larger, more balanced sample of students of color with white students to increase the possibility of attaining statistically significant findings regarding the impact of explicit instruction on students from culturally diverse backgrounds. Davis, Clarke, and Rhodes (1994) examined the impact of giving extended writing opportunities to students in 39 culturally diverse fourth- and fifth-grade classrooms in the western United States. In this study, classes that emphasized extended writing were contrasted with skills-oriented classrooms, which tended to have more instruction focused around worksheets requiring only short answers. Their findings revealed that students in the classrooms where extended writing opportunities were emphasized received significantly higher scores on their writing samples, both in content and conventions, and they even scored somewhat higher on the standardized test they took. It was presumed that students in the "skills-centered" classrooms would outperform students in the classrooms emphasizing extended writing, since activities in the skills-centered classrooms mirrored the multiple-choice writing tasks that appear on most standardized tests. However, the researchers did not find a statistically significant difference between the two groups on standardized tests. The researchers concluded that not only students of color but also all students benefit from classrooms that provide them with opportunities to write extended texts.

Agee (1995) discussed the strategies she used to help her culturally diverse students to make connections between their personal lives and poetry. The purpose of these strategies—including multicultural ballads and narrative poems—was to help students move beyond their prior conceptions of poetry and to explore their own ways of representing the creative side of poetry. Students shared their personal responses to poetry in class. They were also asked to create an original ballad or narrative poem based on a dramatic experience or story that had occurred in their lives and to write a short paper based on a log of their creative process (see also Jocson, 2005). Agee found this to be an effective strategy when teaching writing to culturally diverse students.

Blake (1998) used a critical reader–response approach in an urban classroom to create cultural texts designed to engage diverse readers. The critical response model that she used was designed to encourage diverse readers to respond to texts that focused on cultural issues. The model was based on the idea that through a certain ideology or stance, it is possible to examine critically a text's or an author's assumptions and perspective around areas such as gender, race, and class. As students wrote their texts, they linked the stories of their own lives and experiences, and shaped their texts as they shaped their identities. The researchers proposed that responding to these texts would encourage the students' desire to understand different people, times, and dilemmas. They also felt that this would help them to learn to use their own cultural resources to make connections with themselves and others as well as with texts. Responding to other students' writing helped these students to challenge stereotypes, and responding critically to their own texts helped to prepare them to become critical of other texts and to learn to challenge dominant societal discourses (see also Appleman, 2000).

Carbonaro and Gamoran (2002) conducted a study of 8,157 Asian American, African American, and Latino 8th- to 12th-grade students. They investigated four aspects of high-quality literacy instruction in these students' classrooms, including quality of assignments, coherence of instruction, student voice in curricular and pedagogical issues, and content of instruction. Their analysis indicated that greater emphasis on analytical writing was associated with greater growth in reading scores.

Kong and Fitch (2003) used book clubs to engage fourth- and fifth-grade culturally and linguistically diverse learners in reading, writing, and talking about books. The researchers used a program that comprised four major elements of book clubs, including community share, reading, individual writing, and minilessons. The teacher also taught minilessons to provide explicit instruction on topics of literary elements and reading responses, to introduce writing prompts to help students set up purposes for the reading, and to provide support on composing strategies. The researchers concluded that the program was a success, because the teacher held high expectations, created a classroom learning community, provided time and space for students to write, provided direct instruction, and modeled and scaffolded students' participation within their zones of proximal development.

A particular challenge to teachers in culturally diverse classrooms is the assessment of writing produced by students from diverse racial, ethnic, and linguistic backgrounds. These students often receive unclear messages from teachers, because teachers are often unaware of, or unwilling to acknowledge, the influences of culture on the teaching and learning of writing. Because of their lack of knowledge about the cultural practices that diverse students bring into the classroom, some teachers are unable to explain explicitly how the classroom rules of participation differ from the students' rules of participation or the culture of power in which students are expected to participate in society and in many classrooms. This situation often contributes to students' failure in classrooms that require them to demonstrate their knowledge through writing. Improving this situation depends a great deal on improving cross-cultural communication and understanding and on changing the attitudes of many teachers who hold negative attitudes toward the use of nonmainstream forms of cultural expression. It also depends on our ability to provide teachers with information that can help them to develop instructional strategies and assessment approaches that support the writing development of all their students.

One thread that runs through the literature on teaching writing to culturally diverse students focuses on assessment and considers how best to evaluate writing in culturally diverse classrooms. Research indicates that cultural expectations and preferences play a key role in teachers' assessment practices. Ball (1997) reported a study that illustrated the assessment practices of teachers from different cultural groups and highlighted the value of including the voices of teachers from diverse backgrounds in discussions on writing assessment. The inclusion of such voices can help not only to inform but also to re-shape current assessment practices, research priorities, and policy debates that focus on finding solutions to problems of assessment, particularly as they relate to diverse populations. In a two-part study, Ball (1997) compared the assessment practices of four European American teachers and four African American teachers and found that European American and African American teachers hold some consistently different views about the assessment of diverse students' written texts. Ball found that European American teachers consistently rated the writing of European American students as superior to that of African American students, while African American teachers rated African American students' writing as superior to that of European American students. Both groups of teachers rated the writing of Latino students the lowest. Ball followed the holistic writing evaluations with teacher interviews that revealed the concerns of the African American teachers who participated in this study. Through candid and reflective comments, these teachers shared deeply felt concerns and made specific suggestions concerning writing assessment. The African American teachers all reported concerns about the low levels of the students' writing, anxieties about the teaching and assessments that students of color receive, and uncertainties about how the research is helping us to assess better the writing of students of color. These teachers discussed with certainty, however, their feelings that content and the students' ideas should be emphasized in assessments, along with a balanced focus on the conventions and forms of writing, and they called for more research that addresses the teaching of writing to students from culturally diverse backgrounds. Ball noted that including the voices of teachers from culturally diverse backgrounds can be useful for broadening debates about the reform of writing assessment for all students, but for culturally and linguistically diverse students in particular. Ball (1999) also discussed is-

sues of assessment with AAVE-speaking students and provided examples to assist us in distinguishing between characteristic features of spoken AAVE that appear in a student's written text at the phonological, syntactic, semantic, and discourse levels, and errors.

In statewide standardized writing assessments, race consistently emerges as a variable that has a distinctive effect on students' achievement. Gabrielson, Gordon, and Englehard (1995) took a broad look at writing assessment from the students' perspective. They used data from the Georgia state writing assessment of 11th graders in 1993 to analyze the effects of "task choice" in standardized assessments. That data included 34,200 students: 52% female, 48% male, 67% European American, and 33% African American. To the researchers' surprise, there was a nonsignificant trend in their findings suggesting that, by itself, *choice in writing task as a variable on standardized assessment* did not have a significant impact on students' writing scores. What the researchers found, however, was that gender and race, when combined with choice, had an impact on student scores, particularly in the areas of writing conventions and sentence formation as opposed to content, organization, and style. When females were compared to males and when African American students were compared to European American students, females and Black students tended to write better when given a choice of writing topics. The differences in these conditions, however, were slight and not statistically significant.

In Ball's (1992, 1997) study of African American students, teachers demonstrated differences in their patterns of assessments for African American and European American students. When this research is considered along with the trend in findings of Gabrielson et al. (1995), it appears that students' choice of topics and their preferred patterns of organizing their ideas may have an important influence on assessments. This research could have some important implications, particularly for high school students of color and warrants further investigation. Future research of this nature—analyzing the relationship between culture, instructional strategies, and writing assessment—should be conducted to include a larger sample of teachers, larger samples of students, and should look at the roles and perspectives of teachers from a wide range of cultural backgrounds. This information can be useful for broadening debates about the reform of writing assessment for all students.

Implications for Instruction and Future Research

Several important implications for writing instruction in culturally diverse classrooms drawn from the research discussed in this chapter can serve as a motivation for further study. The implications of Yeh and Stuart's (1998) study speak to the value of explicit instruction on argumentative writing. In this study, the explicit instruction that students received went along with an "immersion" experience though class debates. Yeh and Stuart recommended that a replication study be conducted that compares a larger and more balanced sample of students of color and White students to increase the possibility of attaining statistically significant findings regarding the impact of explicit instruction on the learning of students from culturally diverse backgrounds. According to the Davis et al. (1994) study, students who have more opportunities to write extended texts in their classes scored higher in the areas of content and conventions. This suggests that teachers should allow students numerous opportunities to write extended texts, and Davis et al. noted that such opportunities are commonly overlooked in skills-based classrooms. Similarly, Mavrogenes and Bezruczko (1993) recommend that school curricula provide more opportunities for students to write and that teachers be required to receive training in teaching composition and be sensitive to factors such as students' levels of self-confidence.

On the other hand, Needels and Knapp (1994) have raised questions concerning the belief of some educators that it is essential to emphasize explicit instruction on basic writing skills to poor, underserved students of color. They recommend that more studies be conducted to investigate different kinds of writing that call on students' higher order thinking skills, in addition to the analytic writing that they focused on in their study. They also suggested that the voices of students be heard through student interviews to supplement other data and to inform the design and interpretation of future research.

Langer's (2001) study of schools that are "beating the odds" on standardized writing assessments identified six factors that should be considered by those who teach writing in culturally diverse classrooms. Langer proposed that all six influences worked together to create an environment in which students are able to perform above average on high-stakes standardized assessments. School districts can play a key role in helping increase students' achievement by adopting district-wide approaches that integrate these six factors to support teachers and students alike. Langer suggests that researchers conduct an experimentally designed study that introduces additional instructional interventions to lower performing schools that have been found effective in higher performing schools.

The work of Sperling and Woodlief (1997) implies that researchers and practitioners should maintain a broad and flexible view of what communities of learners should look like in writing classrooms. Another implication is that we should recognize that when viewed from a sociocultural perspective, students have understandings that may be inconsistent with larger societal understandings and with those understandings that teachers might regard as valuable. A follow-up study of the students in Sperling and Woodlief's study might provide a more complex view of these understandings and a more complete picture of how classroom contexts impact what students are prepared to do beyond the school settings. An implication of Sperling's (1995) is that writing teachers can build upon the range of roles that students already take on in their home communities. Rather than attempting to create artificial roles and audiences for students to write for, teachers can build upon these roles to motivate authentic and meaningful writing. In this way, students' experiences can be brought into the classroom to connect their community lives with their school lives.

When looking at issues of writing assessment, Ball (1997) analyzed the relationship between culture and writing assessment and highlighted the importance of including the voices of teachers from culturally diverse backgrounds in policy discussions about writing evaluations and assessments at the school, state, and national levels. Gabrielson et al.'s (1995) study of the Georgia High

School Writing Test suggested that student choice on writing task did not have a significant affect on students' writing scores. However, when focusing specifically on female students and on African American students, choice tended to positively impact their assessment scores. Ball's (1992, 1999) examinations of the oral and written discourse preferences of African American adolescents provides teachers with a line-by-line analysis of a student's text, and suggests that culture and age are important factors in students' preferred writing patterns, and that a clearer understanding of students' community-based discourse practices can help to inform teachers' instructional and assessment practices. An understanding of these factors will allow teachers to create curricular bridges that link student's home, community, and school communication practices and demands. Ball recommends that writing conferences be recognized as a valuable source of communication between students and teachers, so that each can better understand and better meet the other's expectations related to writing.

The principles that emerged from all of the research reported in this chapter support the call for *ethnosensitivity* on the part of teachers, defined as "viewing social topics and practices from the cultural perspectives of students who come from cohesive social groups" (Baugh, 1988). Ball noted that it is critical that teachers gain insight and understanding concerning the characteristic features of students' oral language, so they can be sensitive to the appearance of these patterns in their students' writing. Ball (1999) recommends that for basic writers, teachers should not only emphasize conventions in their assessments but also that attention to content and student's ideas should be the central goal of assessments early on.

Conclusions

This review of research on teaching writing to culturally diverse students over the past two decades reveals that much research has focused on issues related to context, culture, and instructional and assessment strategies. While over 50 studies were reviewed in these areas, the scarcity of the emergence of studies in several other areas warrants mentioning. Although I am confident that some work

is being conducted in these other areas, my mention of these topics is an appeal for further research in these areas that are crucial to the development of successful writing skills for students in culturally diverse classrooms.

One area of great need is further research on distinguishing between the differences in the needs of culturally diverse struggling writers who have learning disabilities and the needs of underachieving students in culturally diverse classrooms in underresourced schools who have been denied access to excellent instruction by fully qualified teachers. Fisher and Frey (2003) looked at writing instruction for struggling adolescent readers and concluded that teachers should focus on both the reading and writing skills of these students to support the literacy development of these struggling adolescents. Initiatives such as the No Child Left Behind Act of 2001 pressure teachers to focus on the reading abilities of students in culturally diverse classrooms. However, the writing needs of these students are often neglected.

A second area of concern is the development of voice in the writing of culturally diverse students. Brockman and Garfield (2000) concluded that voice is an important attribute that is facilitated through students' extended writing, and that literacy educators should find ways to ensure that students can develop their voices through writing— allowing them to respond to cultural conflicts through writing and to form positive images of themselves as writers. Blair (1991) asserts that reading and writing autobiographies can help both native and language-minority students to develop a fluent narrative voice and to become better writers. She describes a unit called Voices in American Literature, in which the students read and write autobiographies, keep reading logs, and share their ideas in group discussions. She recommends that more of this type of work be done by teachers of culturally diverse students.

A third area that needs more attention is the balancing of instructional focus on process writing versus skills development. Since Delpit's (1987) publication, researchers have continued to question the writing process and its use with culturally diverse students (see also Delpit, 1995). Carney (2000) discussed process writing in secondary schools as a compromise that should be further investigated. Gutierrez (1992) noted the necessity to broaden current writing process curricula when working with diverse student populations. Patthey-Chavez et al. (2004) have investigated the process approach to writing instruction in urban middle schools. They concluded that effective implementation of writing process pedagogies requires more staff development than is currently being provided—staff development that stresses the importance of giving appropriate teacher preparation, effective teacher intervention, and useful feedback to students from diverse backgrounds.

In today's technologically advanced global society, it is critically important that a great deal more attention be devoted to the use of computer technology in writing classes for culturally diverse students. In 1998, the National Center for Education Statistics noted that "one issue to consider when looking at student writing performance is the use of computers in education" (p. 3), and in 2003, the National Commission on Writing recommend that the private sector should "work with curriculum specialists, assessment experts, and state and local educational agencies to apply emerging technologies to the teaching, development, grading, and assessment of writing" (p. 30). However, among researchers who focus on the teaching of writing to culturally diverse students, it is evident that technology's potential has not been fully explored, realized, maximized, or even been made fully accessible to students from culturally diverse backgrounds. Pinkard (1998) is one of few researchers who focuses specifically on the development of computer-based visualizations to support teacher analysis of practice and student learning, and on increasing our understanding of how culture influences the design and use of learning environments. "Say, Say Oh Playmate" is but one of the computer-based tools developed by Pinkard that is specifically designed to teach and enhance the literacy skills of African American girls who have not been motivated to read. Pinkard found that few instructional materials are designed with the African American child in mind, and few computer-based learning programs are specifically designed for girls in general, and African American girls in particular. She noted that "Since technology is playing and will play an even greater role in the way our kids are educated, I'm interested in making

sure that technology becomes a key factor in how all students, particularly ethnic students, are educated" (Pinkard, 2003). Pinkard provides an excellent model for other developers by basing her software development on the lived experiences of African American students, so that they can identify with the characters on the screen. She notes that if the technology can hold these students' attention, then they are more willing to sit down to engage with the materials and develop their literacy skills.

In 1997, Fairbanks examined the use of writing as a tool for social and cultural inquiry. In 1990, Sinatra's research combined visual literacy, text understanding, and writing for culturally diverse students. Blue and Collins (1998) conducted a 2-year urban school–university writing collaboration that engaged fifth graders in the reexamination of social studies textbook topics from alternative materials that emphasized the perspectives of African Americans and native people from the same historical time periods. A much needed direction for future research would combine the work of Pinkard (1998), Fairbanks (1997), Sinatra (1990), and Blue and Collins (1998) to use writing as a tool for social and cultural inquiry employing computer-based technology and visual literacies that simulate historical and present-day lived experiences of students of color as a key factor for improving the writing of culturally diverse students.

A final area in need of further research focuses on the realization that teachers are faced with an urgent responsibility to transform their curricula, teaching practices, and approaches to assessment. This area of research should focus on the development of teachers who have the skills, attitudes, dispositions, and desire to become excellent writing teachers for culturally diverse students. Rosaen (2003) conducted a study of her own efforts as a teacher–educator to transform her curriculum, teaching, and assessment practices to support the learning of an increasingly diverse cultural and linguistic student population and to better prepare beginning teachers for diverse classrooms. She used poetry to help teacher candidates explore aspects of their own culture, to share their knowledge with one another, and to find connections between their personal lives and texts that support meaningful learning (see also Jocson, 2005). In addition, Ball (in press) reported the results of a cross-national action research study of a teacher education course designed to instill in teachers critical thinking and positive attitudes about using writing in their own professional development and in teaching culturally diverse students. The study involved more than 100 multicultural South African and U.S. teachers. Using discourse analysis, Ball documented the effect of the course on teachers' discourses and classroom practices, based on their journal writing, reflective essays, responses to classroom readings, transcripts of classroom discussions, and observations of the teachers' classroom teaching. The book reports on these South African and U.S. teachers' changes in classroom practices—during and following the course—in teaching both students of color and students from poverty backgrounds, and it shares the teachers' reports of what happened in their teacher education course that significantly developed their teaching. This book brings together a 10-year program of research in the United States and South Africa, and reports on Ball's efforts as a teacher–educator to develop a powerful course that facilitates the development of teachers who use writing as a pedagogical tool to motivate, facilitate, and document teacher change, and who envision themselves in the process of becoming effective teachers of students from diverse racial, ethnic, and language backgrounds.

While we know that writing is one of the best indicators of students' successful transition from secondary to postsecondary schooling and into the workplace, we know very little about the actual day-to-day writing practices of culturally diverse, underachieving, low-income adolescents outside of schools that can serve as a scaffold for teaching academic writing skills within school settings (some exceptions do exist, e.g., Ball [1995], Hagemann [2001], Mahiri [1998], and Schultz [2002] mentioned earlier in this chapter). While writing had been a focus of close scrutiny at the national level in past decades, it has recently been referred to as "the neglected R" (National Commission on Writing, 2003). This report published by the College Board, states:

> Writing, education's second "R," has become the neglected element of American school reform. . . . American education will never realize its potential until a writing revolution puts language and communication in their proper place in the classroom. Although many models of effective ways to teach writing exist, both the teaching and learning of writing are increasingly shortchanged throughout the school and college years. . . . Of the three "Rs," writing is clearly the most neglected. . . . The nation's leaders must place writing squarely in the center of the school agenda, and policymakers at the state and local [and might I add the national] levels must provide the resources required to improve writing. (pp. 3, 9)

Although this report mentions immigrants and second-language learners, and recommends a focus on developing a national writing agenda, time, measurement of results, technology, and professional development, it does not spend much time addressing issues of teaching writing to culturally diverse students. In addition, when we look for detailed reports about teaching writing to culturally diverse students, we find that although information has been published about writing in elementary schools, there is much less information about teaching writing to poor, underachieving students from culturally diverse backgrounds in the middle and high school grades. If we are committed as a nation to improving the teaching of writing in culturally diverse classrooms, closing the achievement gap between white students and students of color, and reaping the full benefits of the great democratization of learning in the United States (see National Commission on Writing, 2003, p. 9), then more research is urgently needed that focuses on teaching writing to culturally diverse students in secondary classrooms, making links between writing and technology, writing in the content areas, writing practices of second language and second dialect learners, preparing teachers to teach writing to culturally diverse students, and studying the cognitive and perceptual mechanisms that influence writing development among poor and underachieving students of color. Researchers have produced a wide variety of studies that include many small-scale studies of our practice. As has been pointed out by Sleeter (2001a, 2001b), often researchers do not systematically connect their work with other studies that have asked very similar questions. Unconnected small studies do not necessarily produce convergent findings. We need to conduct more research that can help us to understand strategies that actually make a significant difference, and the methods of effective teachers of writing in culturally diverse classrooms. In other words, we need to know what features matter most, according to the research. To bring new insights to the field, such research will require interest from a diverse and committed research community and increased funding to support large-scale and longitudinal studies conducted by researchers from culturally and linguistically diverse backgrounds as well as by mainstream researchers.

Acknowledgments

I am grateful to Julie Wilson, Christine Montanez, Laurie Stapleton, and Pamela Ellis for their assistance with the research needed to complete this chapter.

References

Agee, J. (1995). Making connections with poetry: Multicultural voices in process. *Teaching English in the Two-Year College, 22,* 54–60.

Appleman, D. (2000). *Critical encounters in high school English: Teaching literacy theory to adolescents.* New York: Teachers College Press.

Au, K. (1993). *Literacy instruction in multicultural settings.* Forth Worth, TX: Harcourt Brace.

Au, K. (1997). Changing views of literacy instruction and teacher development. *Teacher Education and Special Education, 20,* 74–82.

Au, K. (1998). Social constructivism and the school literacy learning of students of diverse backgrounds. *Journal of Literacy Research, 30,* 297–319.

Ball, A. F. (1992). Cultural preferences and the expository writing of African American adolescents. *Written Communication, 9,* 510–532.

Ball, A. F. (1995). Text design patterns in the writing of urban African American students: Teaching to the cultural strengths of students in multicultural settings. *Urban Education, 30*(3), 253–289.

Ball, A. F. (1996). Expository writing patterns of African American students. *English Journal, 85*(1), 27–36.

Ball, A. F. (1997). Expanding the dialogue on culture as a critical component when assessing writing. *Assessing Writing, 4,* 169–202.

Ball, A. F. (1999). Evaluating the writing of culturally and linguistically diverse students: The case of the African American vernacular English speaker. In C. R. Cooper & L. Odell (Eds.), *Evalu-*

ating writing (pp. 225–248). Urbana, IL: National Council of Teachers of English.

Ball, A. F. (2005). *Carriers of the torch: Addressing the global challenge of preparing teachers for diversity.* New York: Teachers College Press.

Baugh, J. (1988). Review of twice as less: Black English and the performance of Black students in mathematics and science by Eleanor Wilson Orr. *Harvard Educational Review, 58,* 395–403.

Blackburn, M. & Stern, D. (2000). Analyzing the role of the vernacular in student writing: A social literacies approach. *Working Papers in Educational Linguistics, 61*(1), 53–69.

Blair, L. (1991). Developing student voices with multicultural literature. *English Journal, 80*(8), 24–28.

Blake, B. (1998). "Critical" reader response in an urban classroom: creating cultural texts to engage diverse readers. *Theory into Practice, 37*(3), p. 238–243.

Blue, E., & Collins, J. (1998). Learning to co-construct critical learning processes in an urban school–university partnership. *Urban Education, 32*(5), 577–590.

Brockman, S., & Garfield, S. (2000) Students find their voices in writing. *Journal of Adolescent & Adult Literacy, 43*(5), 484–488.

Carbonaro, W., & Gamoran, A. (2002). The production of achievement inequality in high school English. *American Educational Research Journal, 34*(4), 801–827.

Carney, B. (2000). Process writing and the secondary school reality: A compromise. In R. Robinson, M. McKenna, C. Michael, & J. Wedman (Eds.), *Issues and trends in literacy education* (2nd ed.). Boston: Allyn & Bacon.

Davis, A., Clarke, M. A., & Rhodes, L. K. (1994). Extended text and the writing proficiency of students in urban elementary schools. *Journal of Educational Psychology, 86,* 556–566.

Delpit, L. (1987). Skills and other dilemmas of a progressive black educator. *Equity and Choice, 3*(2), 9–14.

Delpit, L. (1995). *Other people's children.* New York: Norton.

Dyson, A. (1989). *Multiple worlds of child writers: Friends learning to write.* New York: Teachers College Press.

Dyson, A. (1991). *The social worlds of children learning to write.* New York: Teachers College Press.

Fairbanks, C. (1997). Writing for our lives: Literacy through social and cultural inquiry. *Teacher Education and Practice, 13*(1), 52–63.

Farr, M., & Daniels, H. (1986). *Language diversity and writing instruction.* Urbana, IL: National Council of Teachers of English.

Farr Whiteman, M. (1981). Dialect influence in writing. In M. Farr Whiteman (Ed.). *Variations in writing: Functional and linguistic–cultural differences.* Hillsdale, NJ: Erlbaum.

Fecho, B. (2000). Critical inquiries into language in an urban classroom. *Research in the Teaching of English, 34*(3), 368–395.

Fisher, D., & Frey, N. (2003). Writing instruction for struggling adolescent readers: A gradual release model. *Journal of Adolescent and Adult Literacy, 46*(5), 396–406.

Freedman, S. W., & Dyson, A. H. (1987). *Research in writing: Past, present, and future* (technical report). Berkeley, CA: Center for the Study of Reading and Writing.

Freire, P. (1970). *Pedagogy of the oppressed.* New York: Continuum.

Gabrielson, S., Gordon, B., & Engelhard, G. (1995). The effects of task choice on the quality of writing obtained in a statewide assessment. *Applied Measurement in Education, 8*, 273–290.

Gilmore, P., & Glatthorn, A. (Eds.). (1982). *Children in and out of school: Ethnography and education.* Washington, DC: Center for Applied Linguistics.

Green, C. (1997). Literacy development in an Appalachian kindergarten. *Reading Horizons, 37*(3), 215–232.

Gutierrez, K. (1992). A comparison of instructional contexts in Writing Process Classrooms with Latino children. *Education and Urban Society, 24*(2), 244–262.

Hagemann, J. (2001). A bridge from home to school: Helping working class students acquire school literacy. *English Journal, 90*(4), 74–81.

Heath, S. B. (1983). *Ways with words: Language, life and work in communities and classrooms.* Cambridge, UK: Cambridge University Press.

Heller, C. (1992). Written worlds: Students Share Culture through writing. *Teaching Tolerance, 1*(2), 36–43.

Jocson, K. (2005). "Taking it to the mike": Pedagogy of June Jordan's poetry for the people in partnership with an urban high school. *English Education, 37*(2), 44–60.

Kong, A., & Fitch, E. (2002). Using Book Club to engage culturally and linguistically diverse learners in reading, writing, and talking about books. *The Reading Teacher, 56*(4), 352–362.

Langer, J. A. (2001). Beating the odds: Teaching middle and high school students to read and write well. *American Educational Research Journal, 38*, 837–880.

Lee, C. D. (1992). Literacy, cultural diversity, and instruction. *Education and Urban Society, 24,* 279–291.

Mahiri, J. (1998). *Shooting for excellence: African American and youth culture in new century schools.* New York: Teachers College Press.

Mavrogenes, N. A., & Bezruczko, N. (1993). Influences on writing development. *Journal of Educational Research, 86,* 237–245.

Michaels, S. (1987). "Sharing time": Children's narrative styles and differential access to literacy. *Language in Society, 10,* 423–442.

Moll, L. C. (1987). Change as the goal of educational research. *Anthropology and Education Quarterly 18*(4), 300–311.

Moll, L. (Ed.). (1990). *Vygotsky and education: Instructional applications of sociohistorical psychology.* Cambridge, UK: Cambridge University Press.

Moore, C., & O'Neill, P. (Eds.). (2002). *Practice in context: Situating the work of writing teachers.* Urbana, IL: National Council of Teachers of English.

National Center for Educational Statistics, National Assessment of Educational Progress. (1998). *The nation's report card, NAEP Facts: Long-term trends in student writing performance.* Washington, DC: U.S. Department of Education, Office of Educational Research and Improvement.

National Center for Education Statistics (2003). *The nation's report card, writing highlights 2002.* Washington, DC: U.S. Department of Education, Institute of Educational Sciences.

National Assessment of Educational Progress Trial Urban District Assessment. (2003). *The nation's report card.* Washington, DC: U.S. Department of Education, Office of Educational Research and Improvement.

National Commission on Writing in America's Schools and Colleges. (2003). *The neglected "R": The need for a writing revolution.* Washington, DC: College Board.

Needels, M. C., & Knapp, M. S. (1994). Teaching writing to children who are underserved. *Journal of Educational Psychology, 86,* 339–349,

Nieto, S. (1992). *Affirming diversity: The sociopolitical context of multicultural education.* New York: Longman.

Patthey-Chavez, G., Matsumura, L., & Valdés, R. (2004). Investigating the process approach to writing instruction in urban middle schools. *Journal of Adolescent Literacy, 47*(6), 462–477.

Pinkard, N. (1998). *Leveraging background knowledge: Using popular music lyrics to build beginning literacy skills.* Unpublished doctoral dissertation, Northwestern University, Evanston, IL.

Redd, T. (1992, April). *Untapped resources: "Styling" in black students' writing for black audiences.* Paper presented at the annual Meeting of the American Educational Research Association, San Francisco.

Rosaen, C. (2003). Preparing teachers for diverse classrooms: Creating public and private Spaces to Explore Culture Through Poetry Writing. *Teachers College Record, 105*(8), 1437–1485.

Reynolds, A. J., Bezruczko, N., Hagemann, M., & Mavrogenes, N. (1991). *Multiple influences on early school adjustment: Results from the Longitudinal Study of Children at Risk.* Symposium presented at the annual meeting of the American Educational Research Association, Chicago.

Schneider, J. (2003). Context, genres, and imagination: An examination of the idiosyncratic writing performances of three elementary children within multiple context of writing instruction. *Research in the Teaching of English, 37,* 329–379.

Schultz, K. (2002). Looking across space and time: Reconceptualizing literacy learning in and out of school. *Research in the Teaching of English, 36,* 356–380.

Sinatra, R. (1990). Combining visual literacy, text understanding, and writing for culturally diverse students. *Journal of Reading, 33*(8), 612–617.

Sleeter, C. E. (2001a). Epistemological diversity in research on preservice teacher preparation for historically underserved children. *Review of Research in Education, 25,* 209–250.

Sleeter, C. E. (2001b). Preparing teachers for culturally diverse schools: Research and the overwhelming presence of whiteness. *Journal of Teacher Education, 52*(2), 94–106.

Smitherman, G. (1994). "The blacker the berry, the sweeter the juice": African American student writers. In A. H. Dyson & C. Genishi (Eds.), *The need for story: Cultural diversity in classroom and community* (pp. 80–101). Urbana, IL: National Council of Teachers of English.

Sperling, M. (1995). Uncovering the role of role in writing and learning to write. *Written Communication, 12,* 93–133.

Sperling, M. (1996). Revisiting the writing–speaking connection: Challenges for research on writing and writing instruction. *Review of Educational Research, 66,* 53–86.

Sperling, M., & Woodlief, L. (1997). Two classrooms, two writing communities: Urban and suburban tenth-graders learning to write. *Research in the Teaching of English, 31,* 205–239.

Srole, C. (1994). Pedagogical responses to student diversity: History and language. *History Teacher, 28,* 49–55.

Staton, J., Shuy, R., Kreeft Payton, J., & Reed, L. (1988). *Dialogue journal communication: Classroom, linguistic, social, and cognitive views.* Norwood, NJ: Ablex.

Stein, M., Dixon, R., & Isaacson, S. (1994). Effective writing instruction for diverse learners. *School Psychology Review, 23*(3), 392–405.

Yeh, S. S., & Stuart, S. (1998). Empowering Education: Teaching argumentative writing to cultural minority middle-school students. *Research in the Teaching of English, 33,* 49–83.

Chapter 21

Influence of Gender on Writing Development

Shelley Peterson

Studies of the influence of gender on student writing have been motivated by competing concerns. Some researchers have highlighted the silencing of female voices and the privileging of masculine writing styles in peer audience and teacher feedback on students' classroom writing. In contrast, other researchers, concerned about gender disparities privileging girls in the scores of large-scale writing tests, have highlighted the ways in which students and teachers constructed masculine identities of resistance to authority and lack of writing competence.

In all cases, researchers have perceived writing as one of the ways in which children learn the meanings of their culture, exploring and constructing their respective gender roles through and in their writing. As such, these researchers have viewed writing as a social practice that shapes and is shaped by gender. To study the influence of gender on writing development, many researchers have considered the local and the wider social and political contexts within which students were writing. They have examined the social meanings taken up by girls and boys in their construction of gender in their classroom writing, and have attempted to understand the ways in which classroom writing contributed to and challenged stereotypical gender dualities.

Research in the field of gender and writing development has clustered around several themes, which are used to organize this review: Much of the research has highlighted developmental gender patterns in characterization and in the themes and linguistic features of students' writing. Other studies have examined students' self-perceptions and teachers' views of girls' and boys' relative writing competencies. Research also examined the ideologies that shape girls' and boys' writing and writing behavior in terms of their use of writing for social purposes, and the dominance of singular gender models in classrooms. A final group of research studies has explored ways in which teachers can create spaces for students to write against traditional gender positions. In this chapter, the research studies are described in these five categories. In the final pages of the chapter, I summarize the major findings and discuss the implications for practice and further research.

Research Findings

Developmental Gender Patterns in Students' Writing and Writing Processes

Much of the research in the field of gender and writing has investigated differences between boys' and girls' writing from early childhood through adolescence. The research has been primarily quantitative, because researchers have created gender taxonomies to identify the presence of dualistic gender traits in the characters and relationships among characters in selected writing samples. Based on Chodorow's (1978) theory of identity development, these taxonomies differentiated between feminine characteristics of relationship and connectedness, and masculine characteristics of autonomy and independence in the writing.

A number of researchers assessed writing that had been submitted to young authors' contests in their states. Tuck, Bayliss, and Bell (1985) examined 84 fifth- and sixth-graders' submissions, Romatowski and Trepanier-Street (1987) analyzed 180 first-through sixth-graders' submissions, and Many (1990) analyzed 102 samples of writing from kindergartners through 12th-graders. In all of these studies, children tended to create characters of their own sex and frequently stereotyped these characters. These stereotypes were variations of the traits that Tuck et al. (1985) used to analyze the writing in their study: Male characters were heroic, brave, assertive, competent, and independent; female characters were nurturing, dependent, sensitive, emotionally expressive, and interested in their appearance. Male characters were assigned more occupational roles than were female characters in girls' and boys' writing across the grades (Many, 1990; Romatowski & Trepanier-Street, 1987). In both studies, researchers used Erickson's (1963) notion of the early adolescent's discovery of a sense of self-identity to explain the children's propensity to write about characters of their own sex. Many (1990) also drew on Condry's (1984) work to explain that the students were learning and trying out various roles associated with their gender through writing about characters of their own sex.

The only developmental effect on gender found in Many's (1990) and Romatowski and Trepanier-Street's (1987) studies occurred in girls' writing. The older girls in each study assigned more attributes to female characters than to male characters and created active, problem-solving female characters more frequently than did their younger peers. In addition, Many (1990) found that high school boys assigned a greater number of attributes to male characters, but fewer attributes to female characters than did younger boys. Burdick's (1997) study of high school students' biography writing also showed that girls were more likely than boys

to demonstrate flexibility and wide ranges of choice in the sex of their narrative and non-fiction characters.

Researchers in two studies structured a writing task to determine the ways in which students cast male and female characters into stereotypical and nonstereotypical gender roles (Gray-Schlegel & Gray-Schlegel, 1995–1996; Trepanier-Street, Romatowski, & McNair, 1990). Sixth-grade girls' and boys' writing included characters demonstrating more high-intensity and aggressive actions than did third-grade children's writing, with male characters being more active and violent than female characters. Sixth-grade boys' writing contained the highest level of aggressive behavior. At both grade levels, protagonists of boys' narratives usually acted independently and were problem-solvers, whereas protagonists of girls' narratives generally acted in conjunction with others. The fate of protagonists in girls' writing was more positive than that of protagonists in boys' writing, with the margin being greater in sixth-grade children's writing.

Four studies (Graves, 1973; Kamler, 1994; Kanaris, 1999; Rogers, 1996) looked at gender features beyond characterization. Rogers's (1996) Canadian study assessing the reliability of a taxonomy of gender differences in identifying girls' and boys' writing drew on the gender development theories of Chodorow (1978), Gilligan (1982), and Belenky, Clinchy, Goldberger, and Tarule (1986). The taxonomy's two content characteristics, theme and characterization, were the strongest indicators of gender in student writing. These two elements were dichotomized as being either relationship-oriented or independent-action oriented. When analyzing the structural elements of the writing, Rogers found consistent gender differences in terms of focus and details. Boys' writing tended to focus on outer scenes, whereas girls' writing focused on inner experience. Boys' writing used graphic and visual details, whereas girls' writing used other sensory images. Similarly, Graves (1973, 1975) found that primary-age girls tended to write about themes related to home and school experiences (primary territory). He observed that although teachers in his study tended to assign writing on topics within primary territory, boys' assigned and unassigned writing tended to be on themes that extended beyond their homes and schools (secondary and extended territories). The more developmentally advanced girls did write about topics within secondary and extended territories, however.

Two studies identified gender differences in the linguistic features of students' writing (Kamler, 1994; Kanaris, 1999). The studies were based on a social semiotic perspective (Halliday, 1978), proposing that children learn gender roles as they learn and use language. The linguistic choices that children make when reconstructing their experiences in their writing reflect their attempts to position themselves as female or male. Kamler (1994) used Halliday's (1985) systemic functional grammar and Martin's (1986) models of genre and register to analyze the freechoice writing of two Australian children: Peter, in his kindergarten and grade 1 classes, and Zoe, in her kindergarten through grade 2 classes. Kanaris (1999) examined writing about a recent school excursion from 29 girls and 25 boys in an Australian grade 3–4 class.

In both studies, boys generally constructed identities as actors, using first-person singular pronouns more often than the girls. Girls generally used third-person references to position themselves as observers in their narratives. Girls used almost twice as many adjectives as boys, with the most frequently used adjectives being possessives. Boys framed their texts in terms of "material processes," and girls focused on detail and description. In Kanaris's (1999) study, additional gender differences were found; girls' texts were longer and more complex in terms of words per T-unit. Gender similarities were found in Kamler's (1994) study, however; Peter and Zoe wrote on topics within primary territory, and both used the observation genre (reconstructing personal experience and offering an evaluation of the experience) most frequently.

Four research studies considered the interaction of gender discourses with discourses of popular culture, race, and social status in their analyses of student writing (Gilbert, 1993; MacGillivray & Martinez, 1998; Moss, 1993; Sumida, 2000). Sumida's analysis of unassigned writing by a third-grade girl of Hawaiian ancestry, for example, revealed that Ka'iulani had appropriated traditional gender discourses through the use of popular culture in her writing (e.g., the mermaid character, taken from a Disney movie, was subordinate to the male character), and use of classical literature genres (e.g., her story was an epic tale similar to Homer's *Odyssey*, with a male character experiencing the adventure). She did present alternative views of families, however, because the protagonist married his girlfriend, who was a single mother.

MacGillivray and Martinez (1998) highlighted the complexities of gender construction in a story written by a female primarygrade student whose parents encouraged her to be critical of gender portrayals in mass media. In their analysis of the story about a lonely princess who committed suicide because she did not have appropriate clothes or a ticket for the ball, the researchers identified the violence as a masculine characteristic. However, even though the story contained no male characters, the female character was positioned as a victim.

The writing of third- and fourth-grade children in an affluent suburban school was influenced not only by gender expectations, but also by the constraints of classroom social status (Anderson, 2002). In the writing of a class play, for example, a girl who was a competent writer and held high social status enjoyed agency in crossing gender boundaries and in working out social relationships in her play writing. Girls and boys with less status did not enjoy this wide sense of agency in their writing, nor in taking up roles in peers' plays.

Further complexities in students' gender construction in their writing were discussed in Moss's (1993) U.K. study. Angelique, a 15-year-old Jamaican girl in Moss's classroom, wrote a romance narrative for homework. The story provided alternative gender relationships to those in traditional romance storylines, because it reflected what Angelique would do, not what protagonists in the romance novels she read would do (e.g., the girl rejected the boy because she was unwilling to tolerate his untrustworthiness). Angelique created a white protagonist, because she felt that her teachers would not accept Jamaican patois in student writing, and because her only models for this genre were romance stories with white protagonists.

Focusing on boys' writing, Gilbert (1993) deconstructed a violent narrative written by five 10-year-old boys during a writers' workshop in an Australian school. She used various lenses, including a sex-difference lens (Tuck et al., 1985) and a poststructuralist lens (Weedon, 1987). A sex-difference perspective highlighted the high-intensity action, violence, and problem solving associated with male characters and the contrasting passivity of the silent, dull-witted female characters. Gender alternatives were presented, however, as one female character attacked the villains, and some of the male characters were victims in the story. Gilbert's poststructuralist analysis of the story showed the ways in which boys positioned characters bearing names of girls and socially unpopular boys in the classroom in less powerful positions, in contrast to the characters bearing the names of the five socially popular writers and their friends. Femininity was constructed as "flirtatious, stupid, and romantic" (Gilbert, 1993, p. 29) by the male writers. Boys who were not part of the writers' social group were positioned as outsiders to masculine culture by being involved in activities such as enjoying the company of girls (these boys were killed holding hands, murmuring sweet nothings or getting married).

In summary, marked gender differences were found in much of the research examining boys' and girls' writing in primary through middle grades. Although a few studies showed gender differences in linguistic features, characterization and theme in narrative writing were the strongest indicators of gender. Girls tended to write about nurturing, relationship-oriented female characters on themes relating to primary territory, and boys tended to write about heroic, independent male characters on themes within secondary territory. Individual students who did cross gender lines in their writing were often girls. Social status, race, and popular culture influenced the degree to which the girls created alternative gender meanings and relationships in their writing.

Students' and Teachers' Perceptions of Boys' and Girls' Writing Competencies

Studies of students' and teachers' perceptions of girls' and boys' writing competence were often motivated by a desire to understand the gender disparity favoring girls in scores on large-scale writing tests. These studies were primarily quantitative, because

researchers gathered data using surveys of large groups of students across a number of grade levels. Theories showing a positive correlation between students' self-perceptions and their performance (Pajares, 1997) underpinned studies of students' perceptions (Gambell & Hunter, 2000; Hansen, 2001; Pajares & Valiante, 2001; Peterson, 2000; Pottoroff, Phelps-Zientarski, & Skovera, 1996). Theories showing a positive correlation between teachers' expectations and students' performance (Rosenthal & Jacobson, 1968) framed studies of teachers' perceptions (Peterson, 1998; Peterson & Bainbridge, 1999; Roen, 1992).

Pajares and Valiante (2001), in a survey of students in grades 6–8, found that students with a feminine orientation, regardless of their sex, earned higher grades in writing classes. They were more likely to view themselves as successful writers and to attribute their success to personal competencies appropriate to their academic levels. Similarly, Gambell and Hunter (2000), using data from a Canadian test of 13- and 16-year-old students' literacy and their literacy proclivities, habits, and tastes, found that girls showed greater self-confidence as writers than did boys. Girls adopted a more formal approach to writing (preplanning, revising and editing, and using dictionaries) than did boys, particularly at age 16.

Students in grades 2, 4, 6, and 8 in Pottoroff, Phelps-Zientarski, and Skovera's (1996) study, and teachers and students in grades 4 and 8 in Peterson's (2000) study, perceived girls to be better writers than boys. The gender disparity was the greatest at the eighth-grade level in both studies. In Peterson's study, students felt that girls' writing strengths lay in their use of writing conventions and description. Boys felt that their writing strengths were creativity and audience appeal, whereas girls that felt this was an area in which they needed to improve as writers. Developmental differences appeared in the conventions category; fourth-grade students felt that their spelling needed improvement, and eighth-grade students felt that their grammar needed improvement.

In Hansen's (2001) New Zealand high school study, boys viewed writing as less satisfying and were less positive about the perceived value of writing in comparison to girls. In Cleary's (1996) American study, in contrast, male high school students derived greater satisfaction from their writing and felt a greater sense of self-determination and autonomy than did their female counterparts. They were more inclined to balance their own communicative intentions with teachers' expectations for high grades, whereas girls tended to subordinate their purposes to their teachers' expectations in order to earn higher grades.

In research on students' writing processes conducted in four primary classrooms, Graves (1973, 1975) found that boys tended to be more "reactive," showing erratic problem-solving strategies, using overt language to accompany composing, and rarely reviewing their writing and revising at the word level. Their self-evaluations seldom went beyond the affective domain. They completed more unassigned writing than did their female peers, however. The girls tended to be reflective writers who used little overt language to accompany their writing, frequently reread their writing to revise at the word or phrase level, and supported their self-evaluations with examples, as well as affective reasons. Burdick's (1997) observations of 47 female and 56 male high school students' writing processes during a 2-month research project differed from those of Graves (1973, 1975). Boys were more comfortable and more detailed than girls in identifying what they had done independently to complete the research papers and in describing how their writing was original. In spite of the contrasting levels of self-confidence and specificity in describing their writing processes, girls and boys were equally able to formulate a focus for their research papers.

Teachers' gender perceptions were the focus of research in Canada and the United States. In Peterson and Bainbridge's (1999) study, Canadian third-, sixth-, and ninth-grade teachers participated in interviews and described gender markers that helped them to identify the writer's gender within five narratives written by students at their grade levels. Teachers in the study explained that their own potential gender biases did not influence their evaluation of student writing, because they consciously distanced themselves from the content of the writing by attending to the objective criteria in the scoring rubric. In their identification of gender markers in the writing, however, teachers

privileged girls' writing, explaining that girls used more descriptive words and phrases, emotional language, detail, wide vocabulary, clarity, and correct mechanics than did boys. In their actual evaluation of the five student narratives, teachers' guesses about the gender of writers did not influence their scoring of the writing except in one sixth-grade narrative in which a girl crossed gender lines. Teachers who identified the writer as a boy scored the paper significantly lower than did teachers who believed that the writer was a girl (Peterson, 1998).

There was an interaction of teacher's sex and student writer's sex in Roen's (1992) American study, in which teachers showed same-sex appreciation; that is, they assigned significantly higher scores to persuasive letters identified by the researcher as having been written by students of their own sex. Participating teachers also showed greater respect for the writers' opinions, their intelligence, the confidence they inspired, their experience with the topic, their qualifications to write about the subject, and their truthfulness when the writer's names on the papers matched their own sex.

Much of the research examining students' and teachers' gender perceptions revealed an expectation that girls are better writers than boys in terms of their written products (e.g., more descriptive, better use of conventions), their writing processes (e.g., girls adopt a more formal, reflective approach to planning, revising, and editing their writing), their views on the value and satisfaction derived from writing, and their self-confidence as writers. Only two studies of high school students' perceptions showed that boys felt a greater sense of self-determination and creativity as writers than did girls.

Students Using Writing for Social Purposes

Feminist theory (Belenky et al., 1986; Gilligan, 1982), poststructuralist theory (Weedon, 1987), and dialogic theory (Bakhtin, 1981) provided the underpinnings of case study research focusing on small groups of girls (Blair, 1998; Finders, 1997; Laidlaw, 1998; Phinney, 1994; Schultz, 1996). Concepts of voice and identity were central to the researchers' analyses of students' writing and classroom behavior connected to writing. The researchers were concerned with not only gender but also the ways in which race, sexuality, religion, social status, and socio-economic class influenced students' identity construction and their expression of voice in their writing. These studies highlighted boys' and girls' social motivations for their writing choices in school-sanctioned and non-school-sanctioned writing, as well as in writing completed outside of school.

Two studies in kindergarten classes showed young girls to be very conscious of the ways in which they could use their writing to create and maintain relationships with high-status peers. Five girls in Phinney's (1994) observational study fulfilled school goals by writing animal stories, realistic fiction, and fairytales. The girls also fulfilled their own social goals by including characters in their stories with peers' names. Being included in each other's stories was symbolic of their membership within the peer group. Similarly, in Laidlaw's (1998) Canadian study, one girl, Jennifer, used writing as an important tool to gain social acceptance. She was of mixed racial heritage and from a lower socioeconomic class than the European Canadian girls she attempted to befriend. Laidlaw was concerned, however, that Jennifer did not use writing to express her own voice and value her own identity. Unlike the five girls in Phinney's study, Jennifer did not attempt to assert her own status through her writing. Those five girls named the "littlest" characters in stories after themselves or were able to negotiate the naming of the "littlest" characters in peers' stories after themselves in order to gain status. They explained that the source of power in being the "littlest" characters came from being freed from responsibility and being able to get attention.

The use of writing to maintain social relationships and status played out in similar ways in an American seventh-grade classroom (Finders, 1997) and in a Canadian eighth-grade classroom (Blair, 1998). Four girls in a seventh-grade class found that their "underlife" and out-of-school writing provided more currency and gave them greater power within their social worlds than did school-sanctioned writing (Finders, 1997). One group of girls, whom Finders dubbed the "queens," used note and graffiti writing to create a boundary around their group of friends, compete for social status, and defy authority. Similarly, in Blair's (1998) study,

many of the 16 girls in the class wrote notes to same-sex friends in an effort to create boundaries around their social groups. They also covered their desks with colored paper and wrote comments on the paper, and on their clothing and binders, such as "You're a cool chick," to create these allegiances.

Private writing was important to all the girls in Blair's (1998) study; they had either written in diaries or were writing in diaries at the time of the study. Their classroom writing was about personal topics, such as friendship and romance; philosophical topics; and social issues, such as family violence. The girls wrote more fiction than any other genre, but they also wrote poetry and nonfiction. They wrote for their female peers, because they were uncomfortable about having boys read or hear their writing. The Native Canadian girls handed in far fewer completed pieces than did their non-Native peers. They neither saw their culture represented in written texts in the classroom nor did they value their own knowledge.

Social class played a role in restricting two girls' writing in Finders's (1997) study. These two "tough cookies" used out-of-school poetry and narrative writing for playing and escaping from domestic chores. To the two girls, writing was a private, solitary endeavor. They resisted working in groups and found sharing their writing with others to be unproductive. The girls attempted to fulfill their teacher's expectations in their school-sanctioned writing and deliberately veiled their thoughts and emotions in an effort to protect themselves from peer ridicule. In contrast, their socially adept peers, the "queens," did not see the social value in school-sanctioned writing, and they completed written assignments with little regard for quality.

Schultz (1996) conducted a 2-year ethnographic study of the role of writing in the lives of urban high school girls from minority working and nonworking poor families during their final year of high school and their first year in postsecondary institutions or working in a job. One girl, who had just had a baby, attributed her ability to stay focused on a career, and to take the steps to achieve her goals, to writing in a journal outside of school, a practice initiated by a substitute teacher in a summer school class. She found some assigned writing practices useful to her goals for her future: opinion logs written in American government class, essays connecting personal experiences to literature in English class, and a research project on a topic of students' choice. Schultz used additional examples of the ways in which young women used a range of genres to "help them imagine the future and construct plans to reach their goals" (p. 538) to support her assertion that reconceptualizing school literacies that will support young people in their lives beyond high school must go beyond the discrete skills needed to accomplish particular jobs.

Case studies of girls writing to achieve social purposes showed that some girls of minority ethnicities and low socioeconomic status shrouded their thoughts and emotions in school-sanctioned writing. They valued private writing in journals and writing that could be shared with other girls. In contrast, naming characters after peers in school-sanctioned writing in primary grades and engaging in writing graffiti and notes to peers in middle-grade classrooms were ways in which socially popular girls used writing to establish and maintain social relationships.

Dominance of Singular Gender Models in Classrooms

Ethnographic studies conducted in grade 1 (Henkin, 1995), 2 (Fleming, 1995; Orellana, 1995), 4 (Peterson, 2001), and 8 (Peterson, 2002) classrooms, and of two adolescent boys' writing (Newkirk, 2000) showed how particular gender styles of writing predominated within certain contexts, constraining students' writing choices. Researchers in these studies drew on poststructural theories (Davies & Banks, 1992; Gilbert, 1993) to understand how some ways of demonstrating gender through writing were recognized, accepted, rewarded, and maintained, while others were questioned, reproached, ridiculed, and extinguished/diluted within classrooms. The primarily ethnographic studies used analyses of students' writing, field notes of observations, transcripts of student interactions, focus groups, and interviews with teachers and students as data sources.

An undervaluing of girls' writing topics and styles was observed in Henkin's (1995) study. First-grade boys worked in same-sex groups while writing, because they viewed girls as inadequate in understanding boys' topics and in being able to provide useful

feedback on their writing. The girls in the class sensed this deprecation of their contributions to boys' writing and chose same-sex groups for feedback on their writing as well. First-grade girls' and boys' writing in Fleming's (1995) study reproduced gender dichotomies; girls wrote relationship-oriented stories on topics within primary territory, and boys wrote heroic stories within secondary and extended territories in both teacher-assigned and unassigned writing. Peer and teacher response reflected a privileging of the conflict resolution models of boys' writing over the descriptive, celebratory model of girls' writing. The story of one boy, who eschewed the heroic tale for a descriptive story with a collaborative resolution, and the stories of girls who used descriptive story models were not published, whereas stories by peers who followed the conflict resolution model were published.

In Orellana's (1995) study of two Spanish–English bilingual primary classrooms, the majority of students in a student-directed classroom chose to work in same-sex partner groups and wrote on topics that reproduced gender stereotypes typical of their sex. In the more teacher-directed classroom, however, the teacher created mixed-sex writing groups and the students wrote on assigned topics. Boys and girls produced similar writing, because the teacher's expectations established norms that privileged masculine writing styles and topics as the "supposedly gender-neutral norm" (Orellana, 1995, p. 697).

Assuming that gender dualities were a natural part of classroom social life, students in Peterson's (2001, 2002) research felt it was ludicrous and even dangerous for students, particularly boys, to take up topics, themes, and styles of the opposite sex or of homosexuality. Such writing brought into question, in the eyes of peers, the writer's identity as a girl or boy. Students defined the constraints on their writing with a unified voice. It was acceptable for girls to take up masculine topics and themes, such as sports, violence, and competition, but it was beyond the realm of possibility for boys to take up feminine topics and themes, such as romance. Boys were seen to be abandoning a position of power if they chose to write on feminine topics, whereas girls were viewed as trying out possible identities within the more powerful gender position if they chose to write on masculine topics. Similarly, Newkirk's (2000) study of two boys' writing indicated that the topics and themes of the writing were constrained by boys' desire to present themselves as masculine to their peers. He explained that violent writing and parody were considered masculine traits, in part because they resisted authority within parameters acceptable to their teachers and other adults in their lives.

Ethnographic research examining the ways in which students and their teachers negotiated what was acceptable for boys' and girls' writing within the classroom showed that rigid gender expectations constrained both girls' and boys' writing choices. Because boys' writing topics and conflict resolution models were valued in three primary classrooms, girls' writing was not carried through to publication for classroom reading, and boys' writing styles and topics became the classroom norm for all students. Studies examining writing expectations in middle-grade settings showed that boys' writing was constrained to a greater extent than girls' writing, because it was socially acceptable for girls to take up masculine styles of writing, but socially dangerous for boys to take up feminine themes and topics, particularly romance.

Creating Spaces to Write against Traditional Gender Positions

Poststructuralist theories (Davies & Harré, 1996; Walkerdine, 1990) and sociocultural theories (Bakhtin, 1981; Barton & Hamilton, 2000) framed research studies that moved beyond identifying gender differences in an attempt to understand the social practices that played roles in constructing gender differences (Blake, 1997; Egan-Robertson, 1998; Harper, 1998; Luce-Kapler, 1999; Peterson & Ladky, 2001). The studies were ethnographic; analyses of students' writing were triangulated with field notes of on-site observations, transcripts of student interactions, and interviews with teachers and students. In four of the five studies, researchers facilitated writing groups with a small group of girls. For the most part, these groups provided safe places for the girls to construct gender identities that opened up "multiple possibilities for understanding and acting"

(Luce-Kapler, 1999, p. 267). The competing importance of private and public writing in girls' construction of their gender identities is a theme permeating these studies.

Fifth-grade girls used writing within a once- or twice-weekly meeting with a female researcher, as well as response journals and letters to peers, to develop a sense of community, and to express and develop voices of their own (Blake, 1997). Through this more private writing, the girls explored issues of domesticity, family life, and sexuality that they felt they could not discuss in their classroom. In their writing and talking about issues and events in their daily lives, the girls used powerful voices, sometimes taking on activist voices to offer solutions to the violence and injustices in their lives. Egan-Robertson (1998) also observed a small-group writing club of eighth-grade girls who took up issues of gender and race through their writing. They read and heard about the work of teenage ethnographers and designed their own ethnographic studies. Their findings were published in a number of genres and compiled in an edited volume. Similarly, Luce-Kapler (1999) and Sidonie, a high school English teacher, facilitated a writing group of nine high school girls from a suburban Canadian school. The girls participated in activities such as writing about memories evoked by a button selected from a collection that the facilitators provided, and reading and writing about genres and topics that stretched beyond what the girls usually wrote. The girls accepted an invitation to take part in a public reading of their work at a local café.

In one study, a small writing group was not as successful in encouraging young women to use public writing to explore more powerful gender identities than those available in traditional gender discourses. Harper (1998) met with a group of six 17-year-old girls once or twice a week during her English class in a Canadian high school. Group members read, discussed, and wrote in response to feminist works that offered a range of unconventional uses of language, literary form, and theme by contemporary French, Anglo, black, and Native Canadian women. Rather than using the feminist literature as a model for public writing, the girls expressed a preference for private writing that allowed them to work through individual feelings that were unconnected to larger social or political conditions.

Peterson and Ladky (2001) found numerous examples of gender-crossing in 26 girls' and 28 boys' eighth-grade narrative writing following instruction that encouraged, but did not require, students to draw on personal experiences in their writing. Some stories written by boys were based on collaborative relationships among friends, cousins, or immediate family members. A number of girls wrote sports stories in which female characters were positioned in powerful roles. One girl wrote an overtly violent story, positioning a female character and her younger brother as victims of male perpetrators. Gender stereotypes were also present; however, because collaboration was more frequently an element of girls' writing, and competition was most frequently found in boys' writing.

A number of studies showed how mixed-sex groups created opportunities for students to write in less stereotypical ways (Anderson, 2002; Dyson, 1997; McAuliffe, 1994; Marsh, 1998; Simmons, 1997; Strough & Diriwächter, 2000; White, 1990). In one primary classroom, for example, students carried out open-ended composing activities, frequently performed their narratives in Author's Theater, and discussed their writing with peers and their teacher (Dyson, 1997). A few of the girls created gender-hybrid stories in which superhero female characters were involved in romantic heterosexual relationships. The characters demonstrated nurturing behaviors but also engaged in independent, heroic actions. When talking about peers' writing in formal discussion groups, the girls sometimes questioned the boys' positioning of female characters as victims and the superfluous violence in their stories. An African American boy in the class, who usually wrote violent, action-filled stories about male, popular-culture superheroes in order to fit in with his male peers, crossed gender lines when he wrote a story about a female hero, Rosa Parks. He also found a way to maintain relationships with girls in his classroom, while maintaining status with the boys by including X-Men women whose strength equaled that of the male X-Men.

McAuliffe (1994) and Simmons (1997) examined the ways in which gender characteristics of student writing changed through reading aloud and inviting feedback on students' writing within mixed-sex groupings. Following several months of such interaction around their writing, some of the boys' and girls' narrative writing moved from being stereotypically gendered to containing both male and female characteristics. These cross-gendered stories were the class favorites.

Strough and Diriwächter (2000) assessed narrative writing in response to book illustrations of 104 sixth-graders while working within a same-sex or a mixed-sex dyad. White (1990) and Marsh (1998) examined the writing of older children who wrote for younger children of either the same sex or the opposite sex in a British classroom. In all three studies, mixed-sex collaboration and writing for the opposite sex mitigated the reproduction of gender stereotypes in students' writing. In Strough and Diriwächter's (2000) study, prosocial ideas were more prevalent in mixed-sex dyads and girl-only dyads than in boy-only dyads. Overt and verbal aggression were characteristics of mixed-sex and boy-only dyads. In White's (1990) study, girls who wrote for younger boys wove themes of domesticity and morality into their science fiction and adventure stories. Boys who wrote for younger girls cast female characters in humorous and dangerous positions as tomboys. Similarly, 6-year-old girls and boys in Marsh's (1998) study chose adventurous topics for male readers and relationship-oriented topics for female readers. Girls' stories written for boys introduced emotional responses that were not observed in the boys' stories for other boys. Unlike the girls' stories written for other girls, boys' stories written for girls cast heroines as self-sufficient and independent.

Several research studies have shown that opportunities to write with and for students of the opposite sex create space in classrooms for students to explore alternatives to gender stereotypes in their writing. Within the contexts of Author's Theater, mixed-sex collaborative writing groups, and writing for younger students of the opposite sex, elementary-age students crossed gender lines and tempered the gender stereotypes that did appear in their writing. Other research studies created small-group forums for girls to move beyond the typically feminine private writing toward writing with powerful voices about issues of racial and gender identity in more public arenas, such as published books and café readings.

Summary and Implications

Underlying research examining the influence of gender on writing development is a view that writing is a social practice that shapes and is shaped by gender meanings. Writers of all ages construct gender identities through their writing. Much of the early research in this area has identified gender dualities in student writing, writing processes, and in perceptions of boys' and girls' relative competencies as writers. These studies have contrasted feminine nurturing and affiliation themes and a tendency to write in ways that teachers value, with masculine competition and independence themes, and a tendency to resist teachers' expectations for good writing.

More recent research has examined social interactions and social purposes that provide a context for students' writing. In these studies, socially popular girls used sanctioned and nonsanctioned writing to maintain social relationships in the classroom. These social purposes for writing were not available to marginalized girls, whose voices were often silenced in assigned classroom writing for a peer audience. Other studies have shown that students' writing was constrained by the presence of a dominant model of good writing in the classroom. In some cases, the dominant model privileged boys' writing, and girls' writing was disregarded. In other cases, the dominant model constrained boys' writing, because the boys felt the need to demonstrate their masculinity by avoiding styles, themes, characters, and genres that their peers might construe as feminine.

A final body of research observed how students responded to instruction that created space for students to take up alternatives to typical gender styles in their writing. Elementary-age students who had opportunities to write with and for students of the opposite sex took up the styles of the opposite sex to make their writing more appealing to their audience. In other studies, small groups of girls who examined nontraditional

gender identities challenged the typical feminine writing style by writing for a public audience about topics of social justice.

These trends in the research questions and approaches that studies of gender and writing development have taken up, as well as the patterns in research findings, provide starting points for suggested further research and considerations for instruction.

Implications for Further Research

Research on gender and writing development should continue to go beyond the examination of dualistic gender characteristics in students' writing and move toward contextualizing gender construction through examining classroom interactions that influence students' writing. This research supports contemporary views of writing as a social practice that is inevitably and profoundly influenced by gender. In addition, new research should take up questions of the interactions of gender with social class, race, social status, and sexuality in students' writing, furthering the work of researchers such as Blake, (1997), MacGillivray and Martinez (1998), and Egan-Robertson (1998). Students' *and* teachers' gender ideologies should be examined in these studies, moving beyond the volume of research that has primarily examined the students' gender ideologies.

Guzzetti, Young, Gritsavage, Fyfe, and Hardenbrook (2002), in their study of research on gender, literacies, and oral language, suggested a need for further examination of the ways in which particular classroom contexts maintain traditional gender ideologies, and others create and support wider ranges of possible gender ideologies. Supported by researchers cited in this chapter, such research could explore teachers' formal and informal interactions, together with students' interactions that foster writing against gender stereotypes.

Finally, much of the research on creating environments for students to express and develop their voice has involved case studies and action research with groups of girls. Further research should focus on writing instruction for girls *and* boys. Such instruction would foster boys' and girls' confidence and competence in using writing to explore and challenge restrictive gender ideologies.

Implications for Practice

In an effort to create classroom environments that open up opportunities for girls and boys to flourish as writers, teachers need to gain an awareness of their own gender ideologies and the ways these ideologies are communicated and shaped through their verbal and written responses to student writing. This awareness is likely to lead to instruction and assessment that honor girls' and boys' writing styles, and that communicate the valuable roles that writing might play in boys' and girls' lives. Instruction that provides opportunities for girls to express and develop their voices might involve groups of girls, such as those in Blake's (1997) study, engaged in private writing that encourages the exploration of issues relevant in girls' lives. Such instruction might also support girls in expressing powerful voices in public writing, as in Egan-Robertson's (1998) group of girls engaged in ethnographies that resulted in published writing and Luce-Kapler's (1999) group of girls reading their writing at a local café. Instruction that provides opportunities for boys to construct identities as successful writers might involve the rethinking of evaluation criteria to include qualities that boys say are their strengths: creativity and evoking strong audience response. It may also involve honoring the genres (e.g., parody, action and adventure stories, and nonfiction) and topics (e.g., sports, cartoons, and video games) that boys enjoy writing (Newkirk, 2000).

Classroom instruction fostering boys' and girls' valuing of writing would create space for students to use their writing to create and maintain social relationships within parameters that ensure some students do not feel isolated and excluded. Teachers might set expectations for students' writing, so that not just individuals like the socially powerful girl in Anderson's (2002) study could enjoy a wide sense of agency in constructing gender in their writing.

Teachers' efforts to expand the gender identities available to students in their writing might take up the challenge posed by Fairclough's (1989) assertion that ideology is most pernicious when its workings are least visible. Teachers might engage students in deconstructing a variety of texts, including students' and the teacher's writing, to make gender ideologies visible and open to students' questioning, challenging, and resisting.

Teachers might use collaborative writing in mixed-sex groups to encourage students to explore alternative gender constructions in their writing, as did students in a number of research studies (Marsh, 1998; Strough & Diriwächter, 2000; White, 1990). Students' use of a variety of writing forms (see Luce-Kapler's 1999 study), as well as multimodalities such as visual art, drama, film, and technological media, might create spaces for a wider range of gender meanings in students' writing as well.

References

Anderson, D. D. (2002). Casting and recasting gender: Children constituting social identities through literacy practices. *Research in the Teaching of English, 36*(3), 391–428.

Bakhtin, M. M. (1981). Discourse in the novel. In C. Emerson & M. Holquist (Eds.), *The dialogic imagination: Four essays by M. Bakhtin* (pp. 259–422). Austin: University of Texas Press.

Barton, D., & Hamilton, M. (2000). Literacy practices. In D. Barton, M. Hamilton, & R. Ivanic (Eds.), *Situated literacies: Reading and writing in context* (pp. 7–15). New York: Routledge.

Belenky, M. F., Clinchy, B. M., Goldberger, N. R., & Tarule, J. M. (1986). *Women's ways of knowing: The development of self, voice, and mind.* New York: Basic Books.

Blair, H. (1998). They left their genderprints: The voice of girls in text. *Language Arts, 75*(1), 11–18.

Blake, B. E. (1997). *She say, he say: Urban girls write their lives.* Albany: State University of New York Press.

Burdick, T. (1997, Fall). Snakes and snails and puppy dog tails: Girls and boys expressing voice in information research project. *Youth Services in Libraries,* pp. 28–35.

Chodorow, N. (1978). *The reproduction of mothering: Psychoanalysis and the sociology of gender.* Berkeley: University of California Press.

Cleary, L. M. (1996). I think I know what my teachers want now: Gender and writing motivation. *English Journal, 85*(1), 50–57.

Condry, J. (1984). Gender identity and social competence. *Sex Roles, 11,* 485–511.

Davies, B., & Banks, C. (1992). The gender trap: A feminist poststructuralist analysis of primary school children's talk about gender. *Journal of Curriculum Studies, 24*(1), 1–25.

Davies, B., & Harré, R. (1996). Positioning: The discursive production of selves. *Journal for the Theory of Social Behavior, 20,* 43–63.

Dyson, A. H. (1997). *Writing superheroes: Contemporary childhood, popular culture, and classroom literacy.* New York: Teachers College Press.

Egan-Robertson, A. (1998). Learning about culture, language and power: Understanding relationships among personhood, literacy practices, and intertextuality. *Journal of Literacy Research, 30*(4), 449–487.

Erikson, E. (1963). *Childhood and society.* New York: Norton.

Fairclough, N. (1989). *Language and power.* London: Longman.

Finders, M. J. (1997). *Just girls.* New York: Teachers College Press.

Fleming, S. (1995). Whose stories are validated? *Language Arts, 72*(8), 590–596.

Gambell, T., & Hunter, D. (2000). Surveying gender differences in Canadian school literacy. *Journal of Curriculum Studies, 32*(5), 689–719.

Gilbert, P. (1993). *Gender stories and the language classroom.* Victoria, Australia: Deakin University Press.

Gilligan, C. (1982). *In a different voice: Psychological theory and women's development.* Cambridge, MA: Harvard University Press.

Graves, D. H. (1973). Sex differences in children's writing. *Elementary English, 50*(7), 1101–1106.

Graves, D. H. (1975). An examination of the writing processes of seven year old children. *Research in the Teaching of English, 9*(3), 227–241.

Gray-Schlegel, M., & Gray-Schlegel, T. (1995–1996). An investigation of gender stereotypes as revealed through children's creative writing. *Reading Research and Instruction, 2*(35), 160–170.

Guzzetti, B. J., Young, J. P., Gritsavage, M. M., Fyfe, L. M., & Hardenbrook, M. (2002). *Reading, writing, and talking gender in literacy learning.* Newark, DE: International Reading Association and National Reading Council.

Halliday, M. A. K. (1978). *Language as social semiotic: The social interpretation of language and meaning.* London: Edward Arnold.

Halliday, M. A. K. (1985). *An introduction to functional grammar.* London: Edward Arnold.

Hansen, S. (2001, July). *Boys and writing: Reluctance? Reticence? Or rebellion?* Paper presented at the annual meeting of the Education Research Network, Spetses, Greece.

Harper, H. (1998). Dangerous desires: Feminist literary criticism in a high school writing class. *Theory into Practice, 37*(3), 220–228.

Henkin, R. (1995). Insiders and outsiders in first-grade writing workshops: Gender and equity issues. *Language Arts, 72*(6), 429–434.

Kamler, B. (1994). Gender and genre in early writing. *Linguistics and Education, 6*(2), 153–182.

Kanaris, A. (1999). Gendered journeys: Children's

writing and the construction of gender. *Language and Education, 13*(4), 254–268.

Laidlaw, L. (1998). Finding "real" lives: Writing and identity. *Language Arts, 75*(2), 126–131.

Luce-Kapler, R. L. (1999). As if women writing. *Journal of Literacy Research, 31*(3), 267–291.

MacGillivray, L., & Martinez, A. M. (1998). Princesses who commit suicide: Primary children writing within and against gender stereotypes. *Journal of Literacy Research, 30*(1), 53–84.

Many, J. C. (1990). Sex roles from a child's point of view: An analysis of children's writing. *Journal of Research in Childhood Education, 5,* 60–72.

Marsh, J. (1998). Gender and writing in the infant school: Writing for a gender-specific audience. *English in Education, 32*(1), 10–18.

Martin, J. R. (1986). *English text: System and structure.* Unpublished manuscript, Department of Linguistics, University of Sydney, Australia.

McAuliffe, S. (1994). Toward understanding one another: Second graders' use of gendered language and story styles. *Reading Teacher, 47*(4), 302–310.

Moss, G. (1993). The place for romance in young people's writing. In L. K. Chistian-Smith (Ed.), *Texts of desire: Essays in fiction, femininity, and schooling* (pp. 106–125). Washington, DC: Falmer Press.

Newkirk, T. (2000). Misreading masculinity: Speculations on the great gender gap in writing. *Language Arts, 77*(4), 294–300.

Orellana, M. F. (1995). Literacy as a gendered social practice: Tasks, texts, talk and take-up. *Reading Research Quarterly, 30*(4), 674–708.

Pajares, F. (1997). Current directions in self-efficacy research. In M. Maehr & P. R. Pintrich (Eds.), *Advances in motivation and achievement* (Vol. 10, pp. 1–49). Greenwich, CT: JAI Press.

Pajares, F., & Valiante, V. (2001). Gender differences in writing motivation and achievement of middle school students: A function of gender orientation? *Contemporary Educational Psychology, 26,* 366–381.

Peterson, S. (1998). Evaluation and teachers' perceptions of gender in sixth-grade student writing. *Research in the Teaching of English, 33*(2), 181–208.

Peterson, S. (2000). Grades four and eight students' and teachers' perceptions of girls' and boys' writing competencies. *Reading Horizons, 40*(4), 253–271.

Peterson, S. (2001). Gender identities and self expression in classroom narrative writing. *Language Arts, 78*(5), 451–457.

Peterson, S. (2002). Gender meanings in grade eight students' talk about classroom writing. *Gender and Education, 14*(4), 351–366.

Peterson, S., & Bainbridge, J. (1999). Teachers' gendered expectations and their evaluation of student writing. *Reading Research and Instruction, 38*(3), 255–271.

Peterson, S., & Ladky, M. (2001). Collaboration, competition and violence in eighth-grade students' classroom writing. *Reading Research and Instruction, 41*(1), 1–18.

Phinney, M. Y. (1994). Gender, status, writing, and the resolution of kindergarten girls' social tensions. *Linguistics and Education, 6,* 311–330.

Pottoroff, D. D., Phelps-Zientarski, D., & Skovera, M. E. (1996). Gender perceptions of elementary and middle school students about literacy at school and home. *Journal of Research and Development in Education, 29*(4), 203–211.

Roen, D. H. (1992). Gender and teacher response to student writing. In N. H. McCracken & B. Appleby (Eds.), *Gender issues in the teaching of English* (pp. 126–141). Portsmouth, NH: Boynton/ Cook.

Rogers, J. M. (1996). *Two sides to a story: Gender difference in student narrative.* Winnipeg: Inkshed.

Romatowski, J. A., & Trepanier-Street, M. L. (1987). Gender perceptions: An analysis of children's creative writing. *Contemporary Education, 59*(1), 17–19.

Rosenthal, R., & Jacobson, L. (1968). *Pygmalion in the classroom: Teacher expectation and pupils' intellectual development.* New York: Holt, Rinehart & Winston.

Schultz, K. (1996). Between school and work: The literacies of urban adolescent females. *Anthropology and Education Quarterly, 27*(4), 517–544.

Simmons, J. (1997). Attack of the killer baby faces: Gender similarities in third-grade writing. *Language Arts, 74*(2), 116–123.

Strough, J., & Diriwächter, R. (2000). Dyad gender differences in preadolescents' creative stories. *Sex Roles, 43*(1/2), 43–60.

Sumida, A. Y. (2000). Reading a child's writing as a social text. *Language Arts, 77*(4), 309–315.

Trepanier-Street, M. L., Romatowski, J. A., & McNair, S. (1990). Children's written responses to stereotypical and non-stereotypical story starters. *Journal of Research in Childhood Education, 5*(1), 60–72.

Tuck, D., Bayliss, V., & Bell, M. (1985). Analysis of sex stereotyping in characters created by young authors. *Journal of Educational Research, 78*(4), 248–252.

Walkerdine, V. (1990). *Schoolgirl fictions.* London: Verso.

Weedon, C. (1987). *Feminist practice and post-structuralist theory.* Oxford, UK: Blackwell.

White, J. (1990). On literacy and gender. In R. Carter (Ed.), *Knowledge about languages and the curriculum* (pp. 181–196). London: Hodden & Stroughton.

Chapter 22

Writing Instruction for Students with Learning Disabilities

Gary A. Troia

According to data from the 2002 National Assessment of Educational Progress, only 28% of fourth-graders, 31% of eighth-graders, and 24% of 12th-graders performed at or above a proficient (i.e., competent) level of writing achievement for their respective grade levels (Persky, Daane, & Jin, 2003). There are at least three reasons why so many children and youth appear to find writing challenging. First, composing text is most certainly a complex and difficult undertaking that requires the deployment and coordination of multiple affective, cognitive, linguistic, and physical operations to accomplish goals associated with genre-specific conventions, audience needs, and communicative purposes. Gene Fowler, celebrated author, editor, and journalist, epitomized the inherent difficulty of composing with his comment, "Writing is easy; all you do is sit staring at a blank sheet of paper until the drops of blood form on your forehead" (The Quotations Page, n.d.).

Second, the profile of the typical classroom in the United States has undergone dramatic changes in the recent past. Many more students today come from impoverished homes, speak English as a second language, and have identified or suspected disabilities (Persky et al., 2003). This increasing diversity of the school-age population has occurred within the context of the standards-based education movement and its accompanying high-stakes accountability testing. As a consequence, more demands for higher levels of writing performance and for demonstration of content mastery through writing are being made of students and their teachers; simultaneously, teachers are facing a higher proportion of students who struggle not only with composing but also with basic writing skills. Unfortunately, many teachers feel ill-equipped for handling these competing pressures, in part because they lack the requisite pedagogical knowledge, instructional capabilities, and valued resources for teaching writing, and in part because writing curricula, which exert a strong influence on teachers' writing instruction, tend to be underdeveloped and misaligned with other curricula (Troia & Maddox, 2004).

Third, the quality of instruction that students receive is a major determinant of their writing achievement (Graham & Harris, 2002a). In some classrooms, writing instruction focuses almost exclusively on text transcription skills, such as handwriting and spelling, with few opportunities for meaningful, authentic text composing (e.g., Palinscar & Klenk, 1992). In others, there are frequent and varied opportunities for completing personally relevant and engaging writing tasks using the writing process, but little time is devoted to teaching important writing skills and strategies, because it is assumed these can be mastered through incidental teaching and learning (e.g., Westby & Costlow, 1991). In still other classrooms, virtually no time is devoted to writing instruction or writing activities (e.g., Christenson, Thurlow, Ysseldyke, & McVicar, 1989). In perhaps a minority of classrooms, students are taught by exemplary educators who blend process-embedded skills and strategy instruction with writing workshop elements such as minilessons, sustained writing, conferencing, and sharing (e.g., Bridge, Compton-Hall, & Cantrell, 1997; Troia, Lin, Cohen, & Monroe, in preparation; Wray, Medwell, Fox, & Poulson, 2000). Yet for students with disabilities, who tend to develop or exhibit chronic and pernicious writing difficulties, even this type of instruction may be inadequate. What these students need is considerably more intensive, individualized, and explicit teaching of transcription skills and composing strategies that incorporates effective adaptations to task demands, response formats, student supports, and teacher practices (Troia & Graham, 2003; Troia, Lin, Monroe, et al., in preparation). The writing difficulties of students with learning problems, in terms both of their use of the processes associated with accomplished writing and their written output, and the metacognitive and motivational underpinnings of their writing problems, are summarized in the next section. This information offers insights into the kind of writing instruction that is most likely to lead to stronger writing outcomes for students with learning disabilities (LDs), which is the focus of this chapter, though the research findings and instructional recommendations are likely to be relevant for other poor writers.

Writing Difficulties and Instructional Research

Characteristics of LD Students' Writing Products and Processes

Compared to the texts of their more accomplished peers, papers written by writers with LDs are shorter, incomplete, poorly organized, and weaker in overall quality (e.g., Englert & Raphael, 1988; MacArthur & Graham, 1987; Nodine, Barenbaum, & Newcomer, 1985; Thomas, Englert, & Gregg, 1987). In addition, these students' composi-

tions typically contain more mechanical and grammatical errors (Graham, 1990; MacArthur & Graham, 1987; Thomas et al., 1987). These problems may be attributed, in part, to difficulties in executing and regulating the processes underlying proficient writing, including planning, content generation, revising, and text transcription (e.g., Graham, Harris, & Troia, 1998). Each of these processes is considered in greater detail below.

PLANNING

Planning behavior, especially the amount of time spent planning, is a critical part of the composing process and is linked to the quality of written papers (Bereiter & Scardamalia, 1987; Hayes & Flower, 1980). Planning involves three subprocesses: (1) formulating, prioritizing, and modifying both abstract and highly delineated goals and subgoals to address task and genre demands, and perceived audience needs; (2) generating ideas; and (3) selecting and organizing valuable ideas for accomplishing established goals (Hayes & Flower, 1980). Many expert writers engage in planning while they are producing text rather than beforehand, pausing up to 70% of the total time they spend writing, especially during the initial phases of composing (Hayes & Flower, 1980; Gould, 1980). However, planning in advance of writing may help circumvent potential attention and memory disruptions when composing tasks require the satisfaction of both content and structural demands (Hayes & Flower, 1980; Kellogg, 1986). Conversely, advance planning may restrict exploration of new ideas and organizational schemes that arise while drafting and may be counterproductive, unless the writer already knows what ideas should be included in the text (Elbow, 1981; Torrance, Thomas, & Robinson, 1991). Regardless of when it might be best to plan, students with LDs do very little planning spontaneously or even when prompted (MacArthur & Graham, 1987).

Why do struggling writers frequently bypass planning? Research evidence suggests that students with LDs tend to rely on a knowledge-telling tactic for many writing tasks, generating content in an associative, linear fashion (Bereiter & Scardamalia,

1987; Gould, 1980; Hayes & Flower, 1980; McCutchen, 1988, 1995). They start to write immediately after being given a writing assignment and pause perhaps only briefly (typically less than a minute) to formulate their first sentence so that it is related to the topic and conforms to the requirements of the genre, but they do not appear to consider broader rhetorical or personal goals for their compositions and the constraints imposed by the topic and text structure (Bereiter & Scardamalia, 1987; Graham, 1990; McCutchen, 1988). They use this retrieve-and-write process primarily for two reasons: They are overwhelmed by the demands of text transcription (Graham, 1990; Graham & Harris, 1997; Graham et al., 1998; McCutchen, 1988, 1996), and they are frequently asked to complete writing assignments that do not necessitate overt planning of content, because the tasks entail a familiar genre and common format. When poor writers do allocate time for planning, they typically list potential content in a first draft format, one that hinders the elaboration and exploration of ideas. More adept writers, however, plan extensively and recursively to organize, develop, and reflect on their thoughts at a more abstracted level of representation within a framework that meets specific task and audience demands, and personal goals (Bereiter & Scardamalia, 1987). When explicitly taught, a number of planning strategies are effective in improving the schematic structure, length, and quality of papers written by students with LDs, including (1) brainstorming words and ideas (e.g., Troia, Graham, & Harris, 1999); (2) generating and organizing content with text structure prompts prior to writing (e.g., De La Paz & Graham, 1997; Sawyer, Graham, & Harris, 1992; Wong, Butler, Ficzere, & Kuperis, 1996, 1997); and (3) setting planning goals (e.g., De La Paz, 1999; Page-Voth & Graham, 1999).

CONTENT GENERATION

Students with LDs frequently generate less content for their papers than other students of the same age; simultaneously, they including more superfluous or nonfunctional material in their texts (Graham, 1990; MacArthur & Graham, 1987; Thomas et al., 1987). They may do so because (1) they are less capable of sustaining their memory search for topic-relevant material (Englert & Raphael, 1988); (2) their topic knowledge is incomplete or fragmented (Graham & Harris, 1997); or (3) they are less knowledgeable about text structures for particular genre patterns, such as narration and persuasion (Englert & Raphael, 1988; Graham, 1990; Thomas et al., 1987). For example, Graham and Harris (1989) found that fifth- and sixth-grade students with LDs excluded several important text structure elements from their written stories and persuasive essays. Often, the omitted elements included the setting of a story and the premise of an essay, suggesting that these students were insensitive to the reader's perspective, presupposing shared referential information that was not established. Nodine et al. (1985) reported that upper elementary school-age students with LDs were less proficient than their normally achieving peers in writing narratives that included a basic plot; nearly half of the students with LDs provided simple descriptions of picture prompts.

Simply asking students with LDs to write more or providing them with text frames to help them organize the retrieval of content does increase the length, organization, and quality of their papers. Graham (1990), for instance, found that students with LDs typically spent 6–7 minutes writing argumentative essays, but when asked to write more, they generated up to four times more content, half of which was new and useful. Teaching students with learning difficulties to establish goals concerning the length of their papers and to self-monitor their productivity also can increase the amount and quality of their writing (e.g., Harris, Graham, Reid, McElroy, & Hamby, 1994). These findings suggest that poor writers have access to more information that could be included in their papers (Englert & Raphael, 1988; Graham, 1990; Graham & Harris, 1989).

REVISING

Text appraisal and revision also pose a considerable challenge for students with LDs. In general, poor writers spend very little time revising and focus on more localized concerns, such as changing word and phrase selections and editing mechanical errors (Graham, 1997; MacArthur & Graham, 1987;

McCutchen, 1995). These minor revisions have little impact on the quality of students' texts (e.g., Graham, MacArthur, & Schwartz, 1995; MacArthur & Graham, 1987). In fact, less than 20% of the revisions made by students with LDs are substantive (Graham, 1997; Graham et al., 1995; MacArthur & Graham, 1987).

One potential reason that poor writers are not adept at making revisions is that they often fail to detect mismatches between what they intended and what they wrote (e.g., Graham, 1997). However, having poor writers read a text aloud can help them locate and correct more grammatical errors than if they read the same text silently (Espin & Sindelar, 1988). Likewise, peer feedback regarding text clarity can facilitate changes in the revising behavior of students with LDs (MacArthur, Schwartz, & Graham, 1991; Stoddard & MacArthur, 1993), as can procedural facilitators in the form of questionnaires or rating scales (e.g., Stoddard & MacArthur, 1993). Another potential explanation rests in poor writers' limited ability to assume their readers' perspective (Bereiter & Scardamalia, 1987). A strong emphasis on mechanics by teachers who work with students with disabilities also may serve to bias students' views of writing, leading them to believe that text appearance is paramount (Englert & Raphael, 1988; Graham, 1990; MacArthur & Graham, 1987; Palincsar & Klenk, 1992). Thus, when asked what constitutes good writing, students with LDs stress form over content more often than their peers who write well (Graham, Schwartz, & MacArthur, 1993; Lin, Monroe, & Troia, in press).

TEXT TRANSCRIPTION

Students with disabilities have extraordinary difficulty with the mechanics of translating content into written text. For example, the compositions written by students with LDs are fraught with more spelling, capitalization, and punctuation errors than those written by their typically developing peers (e.g., Fulk & Stormont-Spurgin, 1995). In addition, the handwriting of students with LDs is slow and uneven (Graham & Weintraub, 1996), and their papers are less legible than those written by normally achieving students (MacArthur & Graham, 1987). These dis-

ruptions in lower-level text production skills hobble students' ability to engage in higher order composing behaviors such as planning and revising (Graham, 1990; Graham & Harris, 1997). When students with writing difficulties have to devote substantial cognitive resources to spelling and handwriting, often with limited success, attention to content, organization, and style becomes minimized (McCutchen, 1996). It is little wonder then that handwriting and spelling performance account for a sizable portion of variance in writing quality and fluency (Graham, Berninger, Abbott, Abbott, & Whitaker, 1997).

Characteristics of LD Students' Metacognition and Motivation

Many students with LDs possess limited metacognitive awareness—awareness of domain-specific knowledge, skills, and strategies, how to apply them, and when to deploy them for effective and efficient task performance (Ellis, Lenz, & Sabornie, 1987; Garner, 1990; Troia, 2002). Thus, students with LDs tend to overestimate their capabilities and discount the necessity for strategic effort (Ellis, 1986; Paris & Winograd, 1990). For example, they may not appreciate the value of a strategy (Ellis, 1986), or may believe that a strategy is too time-consuming or arduous to use (Wong, 1985, 1988). Even if they select and deploy an appropriate strategy, students with LDs may corrupt its effectiveness, because they do not adequately regulate their thoughts, feelings, and behaviors (Wong, 1985). Writing instruction that incorporates self-management procedures, such as goal setting, self-monitoring, self-evaluation, and self-reinforcement, enables students to reflect on their writing capabilities and empowers them to make modifications to their tactics as the need arises (Garner, 1990; Harris & Graham, 1992; Paris & Winograd, 1990). A number of studies have shown that teaching self-regulation in conjunction with task-specific strategies is more effective than teaching such strategies in isolation (e.g., Sawyer et al., 1992).

In one particularly illustrative case, Sawyer et al. (1992) compared the use of Harris and Graham's (1992) Self-Regulated Strategy Development (SRSD) instructional model, with and without explicit self-regulation training, to teach fifth- and sixth-grade students with LDs a multistep planning strategy that prompted them to generate and organize writing content by responding to a series of questions about the basic parts of a story. The SRSD model employs a metascript in which six individual instructional stages can be reordered, combined, modified, or omitted to meet particular students' needs (Graham, Harris, & Troia, 2000). The SRSD model has been used to teach a variety of planning and revising strategies to students with and without disabilities. These include brainstorming, semantic webbing, generating and organizing writing content using text-structure organization (e.g., story grammar), revising with the use of peer feedback, and revising for both mechanics and substance. Instruction in these strategies has led to improvement in four aspects of students' performance: quality of writing, knowledge of writing, approach to writing, and attitudes about writing (e.g., Graham & Harris, 2002b; Graham et al., 2000, 1993; Troia et al., 1999).

In the study conducted by Sawyer and his colleagues (1992), students were assigned to either one of the two strategy instructional conditions (i.e., full SRSD and SRSD without explicit instruction in goal setting and self-monitoring) or a third condition in which students were taught the planning strategy using a direct teaching approach in which no self-instructional statements or explicit self-regulation procedures were included. Results regarding generalization offered support for the full SRSD model, because students in this condition received significantly higher story structure scores on the generalization probe administered in their resource room than did students in the other instructional conditions. Although no significant differences between the three strategy instruction groups were obtained for story grammar elements on probes administered 2–4 weeks following the conclusion of instruction, more of the students who received full SRSD used the planning strategy than those who received SRSD without explicit self-regulation instruction, who in turn used the strategy more than participants in the direct teaching condition.

It is well documented that positive motivation is associated with strategic behavior (Kuhl, 1985), task persistence (Zimmerman & Ringle, 1981), and academic achievement (Kuhl, 1985; Paris & Winograd, 1990). Students with LDs, unfortunately, often exhibit pervasive motivational problems—a lack of will and effort to tackle the demands of challenging tasks such as writing. In particular, they tend to attribute their successes and failures to factors that are not under their volitional control (e.g., luck and teacher assistance for success, poor ability for failure) rather than to effort or the lack thereof, and consequently possess negative self-efficacy beliefs (e.g., Ellis et al., 1987). Because of their repeated academic failures, students with learning problems come to devalue academic tasks, doubt their own capabilities, and expend little effort (Schunk, 1984). Thus, they avoid challenging assignments, which further limits their potential for skillfully choosing, modifying, or creating strategies, ultimately forming a cycle of avoidance and missed learning opportunities (Garner, 1990; Paris & Winograd, 1990; Wong, 1988, 1994). They also tend more often to pursue performance goals rather than learning goals, attempting to display their ability publicly rather than master the demands of challenging tasks. While in the pursuit of performance goals, students with LDs tend to avoid tasks that may lead to failure and negatively reflect on their ability (Bandura, 1989).

Fortunately, teachers can help counteract these students' motivational problems in a number of ways. First, they can persuade them to (1) redirect their attributions for success to effort and strategy use; (2) use self-statements that reflect these positive attributions (e.g., "Good writing takes hard work"); and (3) monitor their writing behaviors, writing performance, and strategy use to improve productivity and on-task behavior (e.g., Harris et al., 1994). Second, they can provide struggling writers with opportunities to complete writing tasks that are interesting and that connect with their background experiences, yet encourage further exploration of a topic. Students are more likely to be motivated to attempt writing assignments in which they themselves have a personal stake because the topics are self-selected rather than teacher imposed (e.g., Garner, 1990). Third, they can ensure that writing tasks are perceived as challenging enough to warrant effort and strategic behavior, but not perceived as so demanding as to be overwhelming and impossible to manage successfully (Graham & Harris, 1994a). Fourth, teachers can help students explicitly connect strategy use and improved task performance through gradually ceding responsibility for monitoring and evaluating their strategy use and corresponding achievement gains through graphing (Bandura, 1989). When an effortful strategy is judged worthwhile through direct evidence of its impact on task performance, students are more likely to continue to marshal effort and to apply the strategy (e.g., Wong, 1985). Conversely, if it is evident that the strategy is not having the desired effect on achievement, then the data serve as a signal that the strategy should be modified or abandoned and replaced. Fifth, they can capitalize on constructivist learning principles and students' innate curiosity by inviting students with LDs to resolve communicative tension that is created when critical information is undisclosed (e.g., Wong, 1994). A study completed by Troia et al. (1999) exemplifies this last way of improving students' motivation to apply writing strategies.

Troia et al. (1999) taught three fifth-grade students with LDs to use three advance planning strategies (goal setting, brainstorming, and content sequencing) for writing stories within the SRSD framework. However, in contrast to previous research based on the SRSD model, students were forced to construct their own knowledge about the essential features, rationale, and value of the strategies through a process of task deconstruction and comparison. In this modified version of SRSD, the instructor modeled the use of the strategies in diverse tasks without informing the students about the nature of the strategies, creating communicative tension that students needed to resolve by discovering the critical similarities and differences of the tasks and of the planning strategies used for each (for discussion, see Troia, 2002; Wong, 1994). The SRSD model was modified in a second manner as well; self-identified homework assignments for applying the planning strategies to additional tasks were completed.

After intervention, all three students used the advance planning strategies for all of their posttreatment stories and, with one exception, postinstructional generalization essays. The schematic structure and length of stories increased dramatically following treatment, but there were only minimal improvements in story quality. These changes in writing performance were generally maintained 3 weeks later. Interestingly, stories written by all three students received their highest quality ratings at maintenance. Analogous changes in essay writing performance were noted with respect to the number of functional essay elements. Increases in composition length were evident for the essays written by all three students immediately after instruction and for essays written by two of the students 3 weeks later. Although the quality of essays written by students after instruction dropped for one child, remained stable for another, and increased slightly for the third, two of the students received their highest quality ratings on the essay maintenance probe.

As we have seen, students with LDs face a number of obstacles to achieving competence in writing. They produce far fewer ideas for content than their typically developing peers, in some cases because they lack knowledge about text organizational structures that cue writing ideas, and in other cases because they have impoverished or poorly organized knowledge about the topics they are assigned or choose. They are not particularly adept at developing conceptually anchored and flexible plans for writing that will produce informative, provocative, or entertaining work that is satisfying to the audience as well as the writer. They make superficial revisions to text, if at all, because they fail to recognize their errors, the perspective of their audience, and the need for balance between content and form. The mechanics of writing, most notably spelling and handwriting, are particularly challenging for these students. Finally, struggling writers are not motivated to write; they perceive themselves as incapable of becoming better writers given their sense of powerlessness and lack of awareness of the utility of strategic effort.

Researchers have demonstrated our capacity to address these obstacles and help students attain higher levels of writing achievement. Powerful strategy intervention models such as SRSD (Harris & Graham, 1992), Strategic Content Learning (SCL; Butler,

1998), and Cognitive Strategies Instruction in Writing (CSIW; Englert & Mariage, 1991) can help students develop the knowledge, skills, and will to plan and revise in purposeful and effective ways. When coupled with writing tasks that are interesting, relevant, and sufficiently demanding, as well as other procedures for increasing motivation, most students with LDs make substantial gains in their writing. Of course, strategy instruction is only one part of a comprehensive writing program. To address the chronic planning, revising, and transcription problems of struggling writers, a writing program must be comprehensive, well organized, challenging, sustained across the grades, and responsive to the needs of each child. Moreover, a creative and engaging balance of meaning, process, and form must be maintained through formal and informal teaching methods (Graham & Harris, 2002a; Graham, Harris, & Larsen, 2001). Although such a program is not easy to develop and implement, and will not eliminate all writing difficulties, it is advantageous for three reasons (Graham et al., 2001). First, it helps to optimize the writing development of each child. Second, it decreases the number of students who experience writing problems as a consequence of poor instruction. Third, it serves to ameliorate the severity of writing difficulties experienced by students with disabilities. The next section describes the essential components of a comprehensive writing program that meets the needs of students with LDs.

A Comprehensive Writing Program for Poor Writers

What are the most salient characteristics of a strong writing program for students with diverse abilities? First, text production skills, planning, and revising, the three most troublesome aspects of writing for most struggling writers, are explicitly taught within a process writing framework. However, their relative emphasis is adjusted according to the needs of each student, because not all struggling writers exhibit the same writing problems. For example, Juel (1988) found that some students who were poor writers had difficulties with both form (e.g., spelling) and process (e.g., content generation), whereas others had difficulty with just one or the other. This implies that teachers should

communicate the equal importance of form, process, and meaning, but their instruction should emphasize those aspects that are most problematic for any given student (Graham & Harris, 1997). Such individualized instruction may be delivered in the form of teacher–student conferences, teacher-directed minilessons on specific skills and strategies, peer tutoring lessons, and differentiated feedback on students' work.

Second, the writing tasks are meaningful, varied, and challenging (Graham & Harris, 1994b; Troia, 2002). Students need to have the opportunity to write for real audiences and for broad purposes, such as writing a letter to a school board president to request reconsideration of a controversial policy, authoring a poem to commemorate an important event or person, creating an advertisement for a school fund-raiser, and writing a report about the emergence of democratic governments in the former Soviet Union. Authentic writing activities help students appreciate the power and influence of writing and foster a positive motivational regard for writing (Atwell, 1987; Calkins, 1986). One particular way to ensure that writing tasks are meaningful and challenging is to use content area topics and children's literature read in the classroom as source material for writing assignments. Poorly conceived writing tasks undermine teachers' efforts to develop students' knowledge about the craft of writing, their writing skills, their motivation to write, and their ability to self-regulate the writing process. All too often, students with and without LDs are given writing assignments that demand little strategic negotiation (e.g., writing a straightforward personal narrative), because the tasks entail a familiar genre and common format, inviting them to generate content without much forethought (Bereiter & Scardamalia, 1987). Students' limited facility with various forms of exposition, such as compare–contrast, as well as argumentation, underscores the ubiquitous nature of narrative prose in typical classroom writing instruction (e.g., Applebee, Langer, Mullis, Latham, & Gentile, 1994). Of course, simple writing tasks have their place in any writing program, but students need to attempt more sophisticated tasks that require deftness at weaving topic knowledge, knowledge of writing formats and conventions, and both general heuristics and task-specific strategies (Hillocks, 1986).

Third, a predictable writing routine is evident in which planning, revising, and editing are expected and reinforced. More importantly, specific strategies for carrying out these processes are explicitly taught (Harris & Graham, 1999; Wong, 1997). Strategy instruction is well suited for addressing the particular needs of struggling writers, because (1) it provides students with cognitive routines for managing the complexities of writing tasks, (2) it can help them gain greater awareness of their writing strengths and limitations and consequently be more strategic in their attempts to accomplish writing tasks, and (3) when it incorporates self-regulation procedures, such as goal setting, self-monitoring, self-evaluation, and self-reinforcement, strategy instruction enables students to reflect on their writing capabilities, adequately manage paralyzing thoughts, feelings, and behaviors, and empowers them to make adaptations to strategies when necessary (see Harris & Graham, 1992).

Fourth, sufficient time is devoted to explicitly teaching text transcription skills to increase students' spelling and handwriting accuracy and fluency. According to Graham (1999), effective spelling instruction includes four components. One, students need to be taught how to spell words they frequently use when writing. Two, students need to learn how to generate plausible spellings for unknown words. Teachers can facilitate the development of this skill by explicitly teaching phonemic awareness, grapheme–phoneme correspondences, common spelling patterns, highly generalized spelling rules, dictionary skills, and strategies for becoming "spelling detectives," such as spelling by analogy (e.g., Cunningham & Hall, 1998; Englert, Hiebert, & Stewart, 1985). Three, students need to know how to check and correct any spelling miscues that occur. This includes learning to use spell checkers and other aides, such as a dictionary, soliciting editing assistance from others, and applying strategies such as reading text aloud in reverse order to locate misspellings. Four, students need to develop a sensible desire to spell correctly. Teachers can promote such a desire by modeling correct spelling and by providing numerous opportunities for students to display their work in a public forum (e.g., a school newspaper) in which correctness is expected.

Similarly, effective handwriting instruction includes four components (Troia & Graham,

2003). One, letter and word formation, pencil grip, and paper positioning need to be explicitly modeled, practiced, and reviewed. Two, students need to be provided with facilitative supports for attaining legible handwriting. Such supports include numbered arrows that depict correct letter stroke sequences, verbal descriptions of strokes, hand-over-hand physical assistance, reminders to use good handwriting, paper positioning marks on students' desks, tripod grip molds, and raised- or colored-lined paper. Three, students must develop the capacity to independently evaluate and improve their handwriting. Teachers can assist in this development by immediately reinforcing qualitatively superior handwriting attempts, and by asking students to apply similar criteria while making their own judgments. They also can encourage students to keep track of their handwriting performance, set goals for improving it, and correct poor handwriting attempts. Four, students need to be taught to produce handwriting fluently. Teachers can help students increase their handwriting speed (without concomitant decrements in legibility) by providing ample opportunities to write by hand, and by administering speed trials during which students try to copy texts 5–10% faster on each subsequent trial. After students have mastered basic handwriting skills, they should be permitted to create more efficient, personalized ways of forming letters and words by eliminating or modifying redundant and expendable strokes, and by electing to use manuscript, cursive, or a combination of the two, to complete written assignments.

Even with all of the components of effective writing instruction in place in a classroom, some students with LDs are likely to continue to struggle with written expression. Consequently, teachers must thoughtfully and skillfully make adaptations to the instructional environment, their teaching methods, the materials they select, and their expectations for these students (Graham & Harris, 2002a). In the next section, recommendations for such adaptations are presented based on the available research.

Instructional Adaptations for LD Students

Graham, Harris, Fink, and MacArthur (2003) surveyed a nationwide sample of primary grade teachers to identify the types of adaptations they made for struggling writers. Teachers reported devoting more time to teaching handwriting, phonics for spelling, and capitalization and punctuation skills to weaker writers than to average writers. Teachers also were more likely to reteach writing skills to struggling writers, provide minilessons responsive to their needs, and conference with them about their writing. In addition to providing extra instruction, teachers helped students overcome text transcription difficulties by developing personalized spelling lists for weaker writers, directly helping them to spell unknown words, providing resources (e.g., word banks) designed to facilitate correct spelling, or bypassing text transcription difficulties by allowing poor writers to dictate their compositions or write with a keyboard. Likewise, teachers provided additional support for planning and revising by having struggling writers discuss their ideas before writing, use graphic organizers to generate and sequence ideas, draw pictures to prompt recall of events, and revise with the assistance of the teacher, a peer, or a checklist. Other adaptations included help with selecting writing topics, shorter or easier writing assignments, small-group instruction, additional homework, and extra instruction on grammar and sentence-writing skills. Many of these adaptations have also been observed in teacher practice (Dahl & Freepon, 1991; Troia, Lin, Cohen, et al., in preparation).

Unfortunately, almost 20% of the teachers in the sample reported making no adaptations, whereas another 24% reported making only one or two adaptations. Moreover, not all of the reported adaptations were positive ones. For example, in comparison to their average writing peers, poor writers were less likely to share their writing with classmates, to help others, to select their own writing topics, or to complete assignments at their own pace.

Research findings suggest that some technological adaptations can be expected to have substantial impact on the writing of students with disabilities, if used in conjunction with strong writing instruction. Most of these assistive technologies are designed to compensate for struggling writers' poor text transcription skills. Word processing, for instance, can support students with LDs by making it easier for them to revise a document, because it eliminates tedious recopying (MacArthur, 1996; MacArthur & Graham, 1987). However, unless students know how to revise and how to type accurately and quickly, word processing has no appreciable effect on writing quality (see MacArthur, Ferretti, Okolo, & Cavalier, 2001). Spelling checkers permit students to identify and correct more spelling errors than if they simply copyedited without assistance, but they have serious limitations, including an inability to distinguish homonyms and other real words substituted for intended words, and a limited capacity for suggesting correct spellings, especially for severely misspelled words (MacArthur, Graham, Haynes, & De La Paz, 1996). Word prediction software is especially beneficial for students with LDs when the software dictionary is individualized and well suited for the writing task. Several studies have found significant improvements in students' spelling performance when using word prediction software (see MacArthur et al., 2001, for a summary). Research suggests that speech recognition technology often yields higher quality papers by students with disabilities when compared with their handwritten or typed papers (cf. Graham, 1990; MacArthur & Cavalier, 2004; MacArthur & Graham, 1987; Quinlan, 2004). Nevertheless, speech recognition does have notable limitations: Inaccuracies are present even after extensive system training, the software demands clear and deliberate speech input, and text formatting (e.g., capitalization and punctuation) must be dictated outright (MacArthur & Cavalier, 2004). Other possibilities for using technological adaptations in writing include outlining and semantic mapping software and collaboration through the use of online computer networks, although these remain largely unexplored by researchers.

In the final section of this chapter, potential ideas for future research in writing instruction for students with LDs are discussed. These suggestions are based, in part, on the limitations of the extant literature.

Future Directions for Writing Instruction Research

In many writing strategy investigations, not all students (in some cases, fewer than half) who are taught a strategy actually use it after treatment is discontinued, and among those who do, there is frequently some corruption of the strategy, especially when a number of steps have to be followed. Moreover, although changes in writing behaviors and performance can be maintained up to a month following treatment, they frequently dissipate beyond that point. Additionally, although generalization of treatment effects to different instructional contexts is rather easily accomplished, transfer to different tasks, such as writing in a different genre, is not. Last, students' attitudes about writing and perceived competency beliefs with respect to writing are difficult to alter meaningfully. These results suggest that strategy maintenance and generalization remain elusive goals (see Gersten & Baker, 2001, for a meta-analysis of writing intervention studies with students with LDs and similar conclusions). Apparently, many students with LDs are not particularly adept at bringing to bear the cognitive and motivational resources and introspective processes required to generalize spontaneously and effectively the knowledge, skills, and strategies they acquire (Ellis, 1986; Garner, 1990; Wong, 1988, 1994).

There may be a number of reasons why writing strategy interventions are not more successful in helping struggling writers maintain and generalize the strategies they acquire. First, strategy instruction research often is conducted over a period of several weeks or months, but students with learning difficulties may need a prolonged period of intervention to accrue demonstrable benefits in affect, behavior, and performance (Wong, 2000). Second, in many cases, writing strategy interventions are conducted outside of the regular classroom writing block or in classrooms in which students are not exposed to a strong and comprehensive writing program. As such, students may have limited opportunity to apply what they have learned, either because they have not acquired pathways for strategy transfer to educationally relevant contexts, or because those contexts offer few supports for engaging in strategic writing behavior. Consequently, future research should examine the effectiveness of a combination of writing strategy instruction and the components of a strong writing program, with particular emphasis on how writing strategies and performance can be maintained over time and generalized across writing assignments. Third,

there has been a tendency to examine the effectiveness of writing strategies in isolation: Planning strategies rarely have been investigated in conjunction with revision or editing strategies to determine their impact on writing behavior and performance, both separately and in combination. Fourth, the impact of writing strategies often has been assessed with discrete writing tasks that are not well articulated with the general education curriculum in terms of the variety of writing activities or content area mastery. It is likely that embedding strategy training in more meaningful writing activities will produce more impressive outcomes in the fidelity, maintenance, and transfer of writing strategies.

This chapter has identified a number of causes of poor writing achievement among students with LDs, including lack of planning, constrained content generation, limited revision, poor text transcription, underdeveloped metacognitive awareness, and weak motivation. Fortunately, educators can do much to help students attain competence in writing, primarily by using a comprehensive writing program that contains just the right balance of basic writing skills instruction, composing strategies training, and suitable instructional adaptations embedded in a process writing framework that incorporates the best elements of writing workshop (e.g., Fletcher & Portalupi, 2001). Although the writing instruction research literature has far to go to attain a depth and breadth equal to that in reading, based on the studies discussed in this chapter, we know quite a bit about what works for students who perform the least well in writing.

References

Applebee, A. N., Langer, J. A., Mullis, I. V., Latham, A., & Gentile, C. (1994). *NAEP 1992: Writing report card.* Washington, DC: U.S. Government Printing Office.

Atwell, N. (1987). *In the middle: Reading, writing, and learning from adolescents.* Portsmouth, NH: Heinemann.

Bandura, A. (1989). Regulation of cognitive processes through perceived self-efficacy. *Developmental Psychology, 25,* 729–735.

Bereiter, C., & Scardamalia, M. (1987). *The psychology of written expression.* Hillsdale, NJ: Erlbaum.

Bridge, C. A., Compton-Hall, M., & Cantrell, S. C. (1997). Classroom writing practices revisited: The effects of statewide reform on writing instruction. *Elementary School Journal, 98,* 151–170.

Butler, D. L. (1998). The strategic content learning approach to promoting self-regulated learning. In D. H. Schunk & B. J. Zimmerman (Eds.), *Self-regulated learning: From teaching to self-reflective practice* (pp. 160–183). New York: Guilford Press.

Calkins, L. (1986). *The art of teaching writing.* Portsmouth, NH: Heinemann.

Christenson, S., Thurlow, M., Ysseldyke, J., & McVicar, R. (1989). Written language instruction for students with mild handicaps: Is there enough quantity to ensure quality? *Learning Disability Quarterly, 12,* 219–229.

Cunningham, P. M., & Hall, D. P. (1998). The four blocks: A balanced framework for literacy in primary classrooms. In K. R. Harris, S. Graham, & D. Deshler (Eds.), *Teaching every child every day: Learning in diverse schools and classrooms* (pp. 32–76). Cambridge, MA: Brookline.

Dahl, K., & Freepon, P. (1991). Literacy learning in whole language classrooms: An analysis of low socioeconomic urban children learning to read and write in kindergarten. In J. Zutell & S. McCormick (Eds.), *Learner factors/teacher factors: Issues in literacy research and instruction* (pp. 149–158). Chicago: National Reading Conference.

De La Paz, S. (1999). Self-regulated strategy instruction in regular education settings: Improving outcomes for students with and without learning disabilities. *Learning Disabilities Research and Practice, 14,* 92–106.

De La Paz, S., & Graham, S. (1997). Strategy instruction in planning: Effects on the writing performance and behavior of students with learning difficulties. *Exceptional Children, 63,* 167–181.

Elbow, P. (1981). *Writing with power: Techniques for mastering the writing process.* Oxford, UK: Oxford University Press.

Ellis, E. S. (1986). The role of motivation and pedagogy on the generalization of cognitive training by the mildly handicapped. *Journal of Learning Disabilities, 19,* 66–70.

Ellis, E. S., Lenz, B. K., & Sabornie, E. J. (1987). Generalization and adaptation of learning strategies to natural environments: Part 1. Critical agents. *Remedial and Special Education, 8*(1), 6–20.

Englert, C. S., Hiebert, E., & Stewart, S. (1985). Spelling unfamiliar words by an analogy strategy. *Journal of Special Education, 19,* 291–306.

Englert, C. S., & Mariage, T. V. (1991). Shared understandings: Structuring the writing experience through dialogue. *Journal of Learning Disabilities, 24,* 330–342.

Englert, C. S., & Raphael, T. (1988). Constructing well-formed prose: Process, structure and metacognitive knowledge. *Exceptional Children, 54,* 513–520.

Espin, C., & Sindelar, P. (1988). Auditory feedback and writing: Learning disabled and nondisabled students. *Exceptional Children, 55,* 45–51.

Fletcher, R., & Portalupi, J. (2001). *Writing workshop: The essential guide.* Portsmouth, NH: Heinemann.

Fulk, B. M., & Stormont-Spurgin, M. (1995). Spelling interventions for students with disabilities: A review. *Journal of Special Education, 28,* 488–513.

Garner, R. (1990). When children and adults do not use learning strategies: Toward a theory of settings. *Review of Educational Research, 60,* 517–529.

Gersten, R. & Baker, S. (2001). Teaching expressive writing to students with learning disabilities: A meta-analysis. *Elementary School Journal, 101,* 251–272.

Gould, J. D. (1980). Experiments on composing letters: Some facts, some myths, and some observations. In L. W. Gregg & E. R. Steinberg (Eds.), *Cognitive processes in writing: An interdisciplinary approach* (pp. 97–127). Hillsdale, NJ: Erlbaum.

Graham, S. (1990). The role of production factors in learning disabled students' compositions. *Journal of Educational Psychology, 82,* 781–791.

Graham, S. (1997). Executive control in the revising of students with learning and writing difficulties. *Journal of Educational Psychology, 89,* 223–234.

Graham, S. (1999). Handwriting and spelling instruction for students with learning disabilities: A review. *Learning Disability Quarterly, 22,* 78–98.

Graham, S., Berninger, V. W., Abbott, R. D., Abbott, S. P., & Whitaker, D. (1997). The role of mechanics in composing of elementary school students: A new methodological approach. *Journal of Educational Psychology, 89,* 170–182.

Graham, S., & Harris, K. R. (1989). A components analysis of cognitive strategy training: Effects on learning disabled students' compositions and self-efficacy. *Journal of Educational Psychology, 81,* 353–361.

Graham, S., & Harris, K. R. (1994a). The role and development of self-regulation in the writing process. In D. Schunk & B. Zimmerman (Eds.), *Self-regulation of learning and performance: Issues and educational applications* (pp. 203–228). Hillsdale, NJ: Erlbaum.

Graham, S., & Harris, K. R. (1994b). Implications of constructivism for teaching writing to students with special needs. *Journal of Special Education, 28,* 275–289.

Graham, S., & Harris, K. R. (1997). It can be taught, but it does not develop naturally: Myths and realities in writing instruction. *School Psychology Review, 26,* 414–424.

Graham, S., & Harris, K. R. (2002a). Prevention and intervention for struggling writers. In M. Shinn, H. Walker, & G. Stoner (Eds.), *Interventions for academic and behavior problems: II. Preventive and remedial techniques* (pp. 589–610). Washington, DC: National Association of School Psychologists.

Graham, S., & Harris, K. R. (2002b). The road less traveled: Prevention and intervention in written language. In K. G. Butler & E. R. Silliman (Eds.), *Speaking, reading, and writing in children with language learning disabilities: New paradigms in research and practice* (pp. 119–217). Mahwah, NJ: Erlbaum.

Graham, S., Harris, K. R., Fink, B., & MacArthur, C. A. (2003). Primary grade teachers' instructional adaptations for struggling writers: A national survey. *Journal of Educational Psychology, 95,* 279–292.

Graham, S., Harris, K. R., & Larsen, L. (2001). Prevention and intervention of writing difficulties for students with learning disabilities. *Learning Disabilities Research and Practice, 16,* 74–84.

Graham, S., Harris, K. R., & Troia, G. A. (1998). Writing and self-regulation: Cases from the self-regulated strategy development model. In D. H. Schunk & B. J. Zimmerman (Eds.), *Self-regulated learning: From teaching to self-reflective practice* (pp. 20–41). New York: Guilford Press.

Graham, S., Harris, K. R., & Troia, G. A. (2000). Self-regulated strategy development revisited: Teaching writing strategies to struggling writers. *Topics in Language Disorders, 20*(4), 1–14.

Graham, S., MacArthur, C. A., & Schwartz, S. S. (1995). The effects of goal setting and procedural facilitation on the revising behavior and writing performance of students with writing and learning problems. *Journal of Educational Psychology, 87,* 230–240.

Graham, S., Schwartz, S. S., & MacArthur, C. A. (1993). Knowledge of writing and the composing process, attitude toward writing, and self-efficacy for students with and without learning disabilities. *Journal of Learning Disabilities, 26,* 237–249.

Graham, S., & Weintraub, N. (1996). A review of handwriting research: Progress and prospects from 1980 to 1994. *Educational Psychology Review, 8,* 7–87.

Harris, K. R., & Graham, S. (1992). Self-regulated strategy development: A part of the writing process. In M. Pressley, K. R. Harris, & J. Guthrie (Eds.), *Promoting academic competence and literacy in school* (pp. 277–309). New York: Academic Press.

Harris, K. R., & Graham, S. (1999). Programmatic intervention research: Illustrations from the evolution of Self-Regulated Strategy Development. *Learning Disability Quarterly, 22,* 251–262.

Harris, K. R., & Graham, S., Reid, R., McElroy, K., & Hamby, R. (1994). Self-monitoring of attention versus self-monitoring of performance: Replication and cross-task comparison studies. *Learning Disability Quarterly, 17,* 121–139.

Hayes, J., & Flower, L. (1980). Identifying the organization of writing processes. In L. Gregg & E. Steinberg (Eds.), *Cognitive processes in writing: An interdisciplinary approach* (pp. 3–30). Hillsdale, NJ: Erlbaum.

Hillocks, G. (1986). *Research on written composition: New directions for teaching.* Urbana, IL: National Conference on Research in English.

Juel, C. (1988). Learning to read and write: A longitudinal study of 54 children from first through fourth grade. *Journal of Educational Psychology, 80,* 437–447.

Kellogg, R. T. (1986). Writing method and productivity of science and engineering faculty. *Research in Higher Education, 25,* 147–163.

Kuhl, J. (1985). Volitional mediators of cognition–behavior consistency: Self-regulatory processes and action versus state orientation. In J. Kuhl & J. Beckmann (Eds.), *Action control: From cognition to behavior* (pp. 101–128). New York: Springer-Verlag.

Lin, S. C., Monroe, B. W., & Troia, G. A. (in press). Development of writing knowledge in grades 2–8: A comparison of typically developing writers and their struggling peers. *Reading and Writing Quarterly.*

MacArthur, C. A. (1996). Using technology to enhance the writing performance of students with learning disabilities. *Journal of Learning Disabilities, 29,* 344–354.

MacArthur, C. A., & Cavalier, A. R. (2004). Dictation and speech recognition technology as accommodations in assessments for students with learning disabilities. *Exceptional Children, 71,* 43–58.

MacArthur, C. A., Ferretti, R. P., Okolo, C. M., & Cavalier, A. R. (2001). Technology applications for students with literacy problems: A critical review. *Elementary School Journal, 101,* 273–301.

MacArthur, C. A., & Graham, S. (1987). Learning disabled students' composing with three methods: Handwriting, dictation, and word processing. *Journal of Special Education, 21,* 22–42.

MacArthur, C. A., Graham, S., Haynes, J. A., & De La Paz, S. (1996). Spelling checkers and students with learning disabilities: Performance comparisons and impact on spelling. *Journal of Special Education, 30,* 35–57.

MacArthur, C. A., Schwartz, S. S., & Graham, S. (1991). Effects of a reciprocal peer revision strategy in special education classrooms. *Learning Disabilities Research and Practice, 6,* 201–210.

McCutchen, D. (1988). "Functional automaticity" in children's writing. *Written Communication, 5,* 306–324.

McCutchen, D. (1995). Cognitive processes in children's writing: Developmental and individual differences. *Issues in Education: Contributions from Educational Psychology, 1,* 123–160.

McCutchen, D. (1996). A capacity theory of writing:

Working memory in composition. *Educational Psychology Review, 8,* 299–325.

Nodine, B., Barenbaum, E., & Newcomer, P. (1985). Story composition by learning disabled, reading disabled, and normal children. *Learning Disability Quarterly, 8,* 167–181.

Page-Voth, V., & Graham, S. (1999). Effects of goal setting and strategy use on the writing performance and self-efficacy of students with writing and learning problems. *Journal of Educational Psychology, 91,* 230–240.

Palincsar, A. S., & Klenk, L. (1992). Fostering literacy learning in supportive contexts. *Journal of Learning Disabilities, 25,* 211–225.

Paris, S. G., & Winograd, P. (1990). Promoting metacognition and motivation of exceptional children. *Remedial and Special Education, 11*(6), 7–15.

Persky, H. R., Daane, M. C., & Jin, Y. (2003). *The Nation's Report Card: Writing 2002.* Washington, DC: National Center for Education Statistics.

Quinlan, T. (2004). Speech recognition technology and students with writing difficulties: Improving fluency. *Journal of Educational Psychology, 96,* 337–346.

Quotations Page. (n.d.). Retrieved March 14, 2005, from www.quotationspage.com/search.phps?author=gene+fowler&file=other

Sawyer, R., Graham, S., & Harris, K. R. (1992). Direct teaching, strategy instruction, and strategy instruction with explicit self-regulation: Effects on learning disabled students' composition skills and self-efficacy. *Journal of Educational Psychology, 84,* 340–352.

Schunk, D. H. (1984). The self-efficacy perspective on achievement behavior. *Educational Psychologist, 19,* 199–218.

Stoddard, B., & MacArthur, C. A. (1993). A peer editor strategy: Guiding learning disabled students in response and revision. *Research in the Teaching of English, 27,* 76–103.

Thomas, C. C., Englert, C. S., & Gregg, S. (1987). An analysis of errors and strategies in the expository writing of learning disabled students. *Remedial and Special Education, 8,* 21–30.

Torrance, M., Thomas, G. V., & Robinson, E. J. (1991). Strategies for answering examination essay questions: Is it helpful to write a plan? *British Journal of Educational Psychology, 61,* 46–54.

Troia, G. A. (2002). Teaching writing strategies to children with disabilities: Setting generalization as the goal. *Exceptionality, 10,* 249–269.

Troia, G. A., & Graham, S. (2003). Effective writing instruction across the grades: What every educational consultant should know. *Journal of Educational and Psychological Consultation, 14,* 75–89.

Troia, G. A., Graham, S., & Harris, K. R. (1999). Teaching students with learning disabilities to

mindfully plan when writing. *Exceptional Children, 65,* 235–252.

Troia, G. A., Lin, S. C., Cohen, S., & Monroe, B. W. (in preparation). *Implementing a strong model of writing workshop at one elementary school: The confluence of district, school, and classroom variables.*

Troia, G. A., Lin S. C., Monroe, B. W., & Cohen, S. (in preparation). *The effects of a strong model of writing workshop on the writing knowledge, motivation, and performance of good and poor elementary-aged writers.*

Troia, G. A., & Maddox, M. E. (2004). Writing instruction in middle schools: Special and general education teachers share their views and voice their concerns. *Exceptionality, 12,* 19–37.

Westby, C., & Costlow, L. (1991). Implementing a whole language program in a special education class. *Topics in Language Disorders, 11,* 69–84.

Wong, B. Y. L. (1985). Metacognition and learning disabilities. In T. G. Waller, D. Forrest-Pressley, & G. E. MacKinnon (Eds.), *Metacognition, cognition, and human performance* (pp. 137–175). New York: Academic Press.

Wong, B. Y. L. (1988). An instructional model for intervention research in learning disabilities. *Learning Disabilities Research and Practice, 4,* 5–16.

Wong, B. Y. L. (1994). Instructional parameters promoting transfer of learned strategies in students with learning disabilities. *Learning Disability Quarterly, 17,* 110–120.

Wong, B. Y. L. (1997). Research on genre-specific strategies for enhancing writing in adolescents with learning disabilities. *Learning Disability Quarterly, 20,* 140–159.

Wong, B. Y. L. (2000). Writing strategies instruction for expository essays for adolescents with and without learning disabilities. *Topics in Language Disorders, 20*(4), 29–44.

Wong, B. Y. L., Butler, D. L., Ficzere, S. A., & Kuperis, S. (1996). Teaching low achievers and students with learning disabilities to plan, write, and revise opinionessays. *Journal of Learning Disabilities, 29,* 197–212.

Wong, B. Y. L., Butler, D. L., Ficzere, S. A., & Kuperis, S. (1997). Teaching adolescents with learning disabilities and low achievers to plan, write, and revise compare-and-contrast essays. *Learning Disabilities Research and Practice, 12,* 2–15.

Wray, D., Medwell, J., Fox, R., & Poulson, L. (2000). The teaching practices of effective teachers of literacy. *Educational Review, 52,* 75–84.

Zimmerman, B. J., & Ringle, J. (1981). Effects of model persistence and statements of confidence on children's efficacy and problem solving. *Journal of Educational Psychology, 73,* 485–493.

Chapter 23

Multilingual Writing in Preschool through 12th Grade
The Last 15 Years

Jill Fitzgerald

Multilingual writing is a "hot" topic these days in bilingual, foreign language, English-language learner (ELL), and applied linguistics fields. Textbooks and concept pieces abound, and theories of multilingual writing processes have emerged and are debated. Historically, interest in multilingual writing has been rooted in the study of college and adult students. But what research has been done on multilingual writing for preschool- and school-age students? What issues have been addressed, and how thick is the evidence to support various contentions and theoretical positions about multilingual writing?

These are the major questions I address in this chapter by comprehensively examining published preschool through 12th-grade research conducted from 1988 through 2003. I use the terms "multilingual writing" and "second-language writing" to mean ability or competency in process or product, to whatever extent, in writing in two or more languages (cf. Buckwalter & Lo, 2002; Dworin, 1998).

Several features of the collected research made synthesis of the research findings difficult. There was a tendency toward low levels of research rigor, and coverage of a wide range of research issues, many of which were narrow in scope, resulted in topic clusters that were not deeply researched. Although I have tried to push toward synthesis where possible, on the whole, this chapter stands more as a compendium of studies and my critique of that body of work.

Methods for the Review

The following databases were searched: ERIC (for published research only), PsychInfo, and all bibliographies provided in *Journal of Second Language Research* (a regular feature of the journal). As articles and books were retrieved and read, reference lists contained in them were scanned for additional pieces. Keywords used in database searches were: English-as-a-second-language writing, L2 composition, bilingual writing, L2 writing, foreign-language writing, English-as-a-second-language composition, bilingual composition, foreign-language composition, L2 composition, Latino writing/composition, Hispanic writing/composition, and Spanish writing/composition.

Very few criteria were applied for inclusion in this review. Research purpose or question had to be stated or easily inferred; data on writing had to have been collected; participants had to be of preschool through 12th-grade age; the study had to have undergone editorial or peer review and been "published" (which excluded technical reports,

337

ERIC documents, etc.); and I had to be able to identify the work as fitting my aforementioned definition of multilingual writing. Also, I located two potential articles written in a language other than English that I could not read, and these were excluded. Fifty-six studies were selected. I analyzed studies using a systematic interpretive procedure, similar to a constant-comparative method used in qualitative research (Glaser, 1978). Readers may assess the reliability of my characterization using criteria set forth by Moss (1994).

Results

Summary of Studies

Table 23.1 provides selected summary information about the 56 studies. It is possible that outcomes in studies are affected by selected aspects of the studies, such as the extent of native-to-new-language linguistic differences, participant situations, including whether they are immigrants immersed in a new language culture or university-bound students learning a foreign language, and/or the degree of knowledge about and experience with both native and new language. At the same time, it is possible that much can be learned about multilingual writing by considering research that is broadly situated. Consequently, as I conducted the work of the present review, I was mindful of the potential impact of varied situations within which the research was conducted upon drawing conclusions across studies. Readers of this review might also find it useful to keep the research conditions in mind, and referring to Table 23.1 might assist in this regard.

In brief, there were similar numbers of reports at all three age/grade levels (18 to 20). In all, there were 27 studies done in the United States or Hong Kong (or Hong Kong and Britain), 8 in the United Kingdom (or the United Kingdom and Australia), 4 in Fiji/Singapore, 5 in Canada, 2 each in Germany and Finland, and 1 each in Denmark, Iceland, Kenya, Mexico, Morocco, New Zealand, Norway, and Spain. In the majority of studies (27), participants could be labeled English-as-a-second (or third-) language learners, 13 as English-as-a-foreign-language learners, 13 as bilingual, and 3 as French- or Spanish-as-a-foreign-language learners. In all but 12 studies, researchers only examined

new-language writing. Most studies were qualitative in nature, and many involved very small numbers of participants.

Some features distinguished studies at the secondary level from those at the two lower age/grade levels. The secondary-level research was done predominantly in Hong Kong (or Hong Kong and Britain) (7), tended to be classified primarily as studies of English as a foreign language (11), originated in many different countries, and demonstrated some breadth in type of methodology. The research at the two lower age/grade levels was mostly done in the United States (18), tended to be discussed as studies of English-as-a-second- (or third-) language learners (19), and involved less variability in country of study origin and type of methodology than was evident in the secondary-level research.

Critique of Methodologies Used

In general, few of the 56 studies demonstrated methodological rigor that might be judged by many to be "sufficient." Of course, "rigor" is defined somewhat differently according to the particular research paradigm used. Evidence of rigor in quantitative work includes issues such as the need for counterbalancing across measures or prompts/topics, assertion of treatment fidelity, controlling time on task across treatment groups, use of multiple texts to guard against confounding of results due to topic, determination of unit of analysis (e.g., class vs. individual), ensuring reliability and validity of measures, and otherwise formulating designs to protect against alternative explanations of results. Criteria for rigor in qualitative work should be reflected in reports in at least the following ways: detail how the study was done (e.g., an audit trail); reveal multiple perspectives and/or other forms of complexity; show researcher reflectivity; address alternative explanations (how this is done varies greatly by genre); present primary data, quotes, stories, scenes, and so on; state conclusions about what has been learned, that is, show evidence of learning from the study rather than the study validating the author's original beliefs; and point to how the "learnings" relate to a wider discourse (G. Noblit, personal communication, January 18, 2004).

TABLE 23.1 Selected Information for Reports

Author(s)	Grade/age (n)	Label/country(native language)	New language proficiency level	Methodology
		Preschool through Primary Grades		
Arab-Moghaddam & Sénéchal (2001)	2nd/3rd(55)	Bilingual/Canada(Persian)	Not specifically given; lived in English-speaking Canada 4 yr.	Correlational
Blanton (1998)	5 and 6 yr (focus on 4 and 2 teachers)	ELL/Morocco (French, Arabic/ French, Arabic/English/French)	Had been in English immersion 1 or 2 yr.	Ethnography
Buckwalter & Lo. (2002)	5 yr (1)	ELL/US (Taiwanese)	Moved from Taiwan 5 mo. prior; spoke no English before moving.	Case study
Davis, Carlisle, & Beeman (1999)	1st–3rd (51)	Bilingual/US (Spanish)	"Varied widely but was below average in relation to developmental expectations in English and Spanish . . ." (p. 242). Scores on selected tests provided in a table.	Quasi-experimental
Elley (1994)	6–8 yr (512–5,000 for varied analyses)	ELL/Singapore (Native language[s] not specifically given)	Not specifically given; students began learning English in primary grades in school.	Experimental
Everatt, Smythe, Adams, & Ocampo (2000)	7–8 yr (30)	Bilingual/England (Sylheti)	Not specifically given.	Quasi-experimental
Ferroli & Shanahan (1993)	2nd/3rd (47)	Bilingual/US (Spanish)	Not specifically given; had only Spanish reading/writing instruction for at least 1 yr; just beginning to receive English;	Descriptive
Fitzgerald & Noblit (1999)	1st (2)	ELL/US (Spanish, Spanish/ Tarascan Indian)	1 scored "limited English speaking," 1, no prior English.	Descriptive; case analysis
Franklin & Thompson (1994)	1st (1)	Bilingual/US (American Indian Dakotan, English)	English levels not specifically given; 1st grade read simple stories in English and writing in English; Dakotan oral.	Child study
Garrett, Griffiths, James, & Sholfield (1994)	10–11 yr (56)	Bilingual classrooms, learning English/UK (Punjabi, Welsh)	Not specifically given.	Experiment
Huss (1995)	5 and 6 yr (3)	ELL/England (Pakistani, Punjabi)	Not specifically given, but reference to range of language and literacy developmental levels.	Ethnography

(continued)

339

TABLE 23.1. (continued)

Author(s)	Grade/age (n)	Label/country(native language)	New language proficiency level	Methodology
Jackson, Holm, & Dodd (1998)	3–10 yr (71)	Bilingual/Britain and Australia (Cantonese)	Not specifically given, but only students who could "communicate fluently in English" were chosen (p. 84).	Quasi-experimental
Maguire & Graves (2001)	8 yr (3)	English as 3rd language/ Canada (Arabic/Persian, Indonesian/ Javanese)	New arrivals.	Examined language; descriptive
Nathenson-Mejia (1989)	1st (12)	Bilingual/Mexico(Spanish)	Not specifically given; 1st year of formal English, 3; preschool years "informal."	Descriptive
Neufeld & Fitzgerald (2001)	1st (3)	ELL/US (Spanish)	English oral proficiency test, 2 classified "limited. English speakers," 1 "non-English."	Case analyses
Rudden & Nedeff (1998)	K–5 (8)	ELL/US (not given)	In the U.S. for 1–3 yr.	Ex'd writing; descriptive
Samway (1993)	2nd–6th (9)	ELL/US (implied Turkish and Spanish)	"Low" on English proficiency test; none recent arrival; "communicated quite comfortably" in English (p. 234).	Observations, interviews; descriptive
Seow (1997)	Primary 3, secondary 5 (US 3rd–10th) (400)	ELL/Singapore (Chinese, Indian, Malay)	Not specifically given. "At the primary level, the number of contact hours in learning of English Language . . . varied between 6½ and 7½ hours per week, and at the secondary level, it was 5-5½" (p. 151).	Ex'd writing; descriptive
Wade-Woolley & Siegel (1997)	2nd (73)	ELL/Canada (Cantonese, Mandarin, Gujarati, Urdu, Punjabi)	Not specifically given; 2 half-day and 2 full-day yr in English-speaking schools.	Quasi-experimental
Zutell & Allen (1988)	2nd–4th (108)	Bilingual/U.S. (Spanish)	None specifically given.	Descriptive
		Intermediate grades		
Bermúdez & Prater (1994)	4th (37)	ELL/US (Spanish for 36; 1 English at home)	Not specifically given; 18 in ESL classes; 19 "already mainstreamed" (p. 50).	Ex'd writing; descriptive
Carlisle (1989)	4th, 6th (62)	Bilingual, ELL/US (Spanish 42; rest English)	Not specifically given.	Experimental

340

Study	Grade (N)	Population/Country (Language)	English Proficiency	Description	Type
Elley (1994)	9–11 yr (> 500)	ELL/Fiji (Fijian or Hindi)	Not specifically given.		Experimental
Fazio (2001)	5th (110)	French as 2nd language/Canada (Arabic, Chinese, Creole, English, Farsi, Italian, Khmer, Hindi, Lingala, Polish, Punjabi, Portuguese, Romanian, Somali, Spanish, Thai)	Not specifically given.		Experimental
Gomez, Parker, Lara-Alecio, & Gomez (1996)	5th (48)	ELL/U.S. (Spanish)	Not specifically given.		Experimental
James & Klein (1994)	12–13 yr (185)	EFL/Germany (German)	Not specifically given; "near beginner[s]" (p. 39).		Descriptive
Lanauze & Snow (1989)	4th/5th (38)	Bilingual/US (Spanish)	Not specifically given; teachers labeled students good or poor in each language.		Quasi-experimental/correlational
Lumme & Lehto (2002)	12–13 yr (66)	EFL/Finland (Finnish)	Not specifically given, but some measures in the study provide information.		Correlational
Maguire (1994)	Middle grades (2)	Bilingual/Canada (French/English; English)	Not specifically given.		Ex'd writing; descriptive
Patthey-Chavez & Claire (1996)	4th (5)	Bilingual/US (Spanish)	Not specifically given; represented heterogeneity of English in the class.		Descriptive
Peyton (1993)	6th (6)	ELL/US (Burmese, Cantonese, Korean, Italian)	Not specifically given; arrived within the past yr and classified as ELL.		Ex'd writing; descriptive
Peyton, Staton, Richardson, & Wolfram (1993)	6th (12)	ELL/US (Chinese, Spanish)	4 judged (teacher/test) "middle-level," 4 "highly proficient," 4 "low" (p. 201); in US school 1 mo.–5 yr.		Ex'd writing; descriptive
Prater & Bermúdez (1993)	4th (40)	ELL/US (Ethnicities Asian American, Hispanic)	Not specifically given; ESL/bilingual education classrooms once, regular classrooms now, limited English (teacher said).		Experiment
Reynolds (2002)	5th–8th (735)	ELL/US (Spanish, Vietnamese, "other East Asian")	Not specifically given.		Ex'd writing; descriptive
Samway & Taylor (1993)	6th, 8th (3)	ELL/US (Farsi, Hindi)	Not specifically given.		Interviewed, ex'd writing; descrip1tive

(continued)

341

TABLE 23.1. (continued)

Author(s)	Grade/age (n)	Label/country(native language)	New language proficiency level	Methodology
			Intermediate grades (continued)	
Schleppegrell (1998)	7th–8th (128)	ELL/US (Ethnicities African American, Chinese, East Indian, European American, Hmong, Lao, Latino, Native American)	Not specifically given; approximately two thirds spoke language other than English at home.	Ex'd writing; descriptive
Trenchs (1996)	6th (3)	Spanish as foreign language/US (English)	Not specifically given; "beginning" language learners.	Case study
		High school		
Albrechtsen (1997)	9th (1)	EFL/Denmark (Danish)	Not specifically given; "fairly high"English.	Think-aloud
Berman (1994)	17–18 yr (126)	EFL/Iceland (Icelandic)	Not specifically given.	Experimental
Franken & Haslett (1999)	High school (20)	ESL/New Zealand (Cantonese, Chinantec, Chinese, Croatian, Hakka, Hindi, Korean, Macedonian, Malay, Serbian, Spanish)	Not specifically given; in NZ 4 mo–4 yr.	Quasi-experimental
Hyland & Milton (1997)	Secondary (1,670)	EFL/Britain and Hong Kong (British-English, Cantonese)	Grades on high school English exam from A to failing, with E ~ = to EFL score of ~450 and A = 600.	Ex'd writing; descriptive
Lai (1993)	9th (52)	EFL/Hong Kong	Not specifically given; "two or more years of English learning."	Experimental
Lam & Pennington (1995)	9th (17)	EFL/Hong Kong (Cantonese)	Not specifically given.	Experimental
Mäkinen (1992)	9 yr (24)	EFL/Finland (Finnish)	Not specifically given; learning English since age 9 (2–3 times per wk).	Ex'd writing; descriptive
Nyamasyo (1994)	Secondary (not given)	EFL/Kenya (perhaps variety of Kenyan languages)	Not specifically given.	Ex'd writing; descriptive
Olsen (1999)	Secondary (39)	EFL/Norway (Norwegian)	Not specifically given.	Ex'd writing; descriptive

342

Pennington, Brock, & Yue (1996)	7th–12th (291)	EFL/Hong Kong (Cantonese)	Not specifically given.	Descriptive
Reichelt (1997)	13th (10)	EFL/Germany (German)	Not specifically given.	Case study
Roca de Larios, Marín, & Murphy (2001)	High school (7) (compared to 7 college and 7 college grads)	EFL/Spain (Spanish)	Scored 100–108 on test for which 110 is "usually" about "elementary" level.	Think-aloud
Sengupta (1998)	Secondary (6)	Authors says ELL/Hong Kong	Not specifically given.	Descriptive
Sengupta (2000)	Secondary (118)	Author: Hong Kong English is neither ELL nor EFL; inferred ELL/Hong Kong (Cantonese)	Not specifically given.	Experimental
Silver & Repa (1993)	Secondary (66)	ELL/U.S. (Chinese/ Korean; Chinese/Korean/English; English; English/other; French/ English; French/other; Spanish; Spanish/ English)	Not specifically given.	Experimental
Sparks, Ganschow, Artzer, & Patton (1997)	High school (15)	Spanish as foreign language/US (implied English)	Not specifically given.	Experimental
Tarone et al. (1993)	8th, 10th, and 12th (83) (compared to 45 college)	ELL/US (Cambodian, Lao, Hmong, Vietnamese)	Not specifically given; ELL "levels 3 and 4" (not further defined); mean age on arrival 15–16 yr old, mean length time in the US for levels 3 and 4, 1.6 yr and 2.8 yr.	Descriptive; correlational
Tsui & Ng (2000)	12th and 13th (27)	"English as the medium of instruction," ELL inferred/Hong Kong (Chinese)	Not specifically given.	Ex'd writing; questionnaire/ interview; descriptive
Wong (1993)	Secondary (43)	ELL inferred/Singapore (Native language[s] not given)	Not specifically given.	Think-aloud

Note. Ex'd, examined; ELL, English-language learner; EFL, English as a foreign language.

Some specific methodological issues about the 56 studies can be noted (others have commented upon similar issues, primarily referring to adult second language writing research; cf. Ferris, 2003; Goldstein, 2001; Krapels, 1990; Polio, 2001; Reichelt, 2001). First, as I have already noted, certain factors embedded in the research situation may be critical to interpretation of findings. At minimum, investigators must obtain reliable data and report the following: participant ages and/or grade levels, and native and new language background, including information from measures of oral and literate proficiencies; and length of time learning the new language. Participants' proficiency particularly is undeniably linked to the meanings of findings, a necessary feature if we are to place results into broader theoretical networks about multilingual writing. Very few investigators provided such information. Among the exceptions, Buckwalter and Lo's (2002) descriptions were exemplary in this regard.

Second, complete information must be reported for all measures used in a study, including: names of tests and complete references for them; procedures used with participants; illustrative items; how items were scored; how variables were created; and reliability estimates. Without such information, it is difficult to understand what findings actually mean. Again, very few researchers provided such information. Reports by Carlisle (1989) and Prater and Bermúdez (1993) were among the notable exceptions here. Also, as investigators consider measures, an analysis of measures used to assess second-language writing development provided by Wolfe-Quintero, Inagaki, and Kim (1998) might prove helpful, though many measures they discuss are ones used in studies of adults.

Third, related to the preceding point, when investigators examine writing to code selected features, at minimum, intercoder reliability estimates for determining units of analysis and codes for the units must be obtained and reported. Believability of results is dependent upon ways of coding that are not idiosyncratic to particular investigators. Again, very few researchers who used coding actually reported reliability estimates. Among exemplary exceptions were reports by Berman (1994), DeLarios, Marin, and Murphy (2001), and Hyland and Milton (1997).

Fourth, methods of analysis must be fully detailed, and they must meet commonly accepted standards of rigor according to the paradigm used. It is impossible to interpret results if the methods of analysis and their level of rigor are not known. Many of the investigators did not report how analyses were done. DeLarios et al.'s (2001) report was one of a few notable exceptions.

Finally, it is imperative that investigators assess second-language writing through at least two writing samples in a way that enables at least one to be considered a replicate of another. It is well known that topic seriously affects results in literacy research. Consequently, studies of second-language writing must demonstrate that the same results are obtained across "like" writing samples. Decisions about ways of structuring the writing tasks to make them as "alike" as possible are often difficult, but some attempt should be made. Carlisle (1989) was one of the rare investigators who accomplished such replication of writing samples.

Preschool and Primary Grades

• How do selected features of second-language writing develop, and/or how do patterns of second-language writing development compare to those of first-language writing development? Each of five studies of 5- or 6-year-olds who were native speakers of Arabic, French, Pakistani, Punjabi, Spanish, Tarascan Indian, and Taiwanese provided detailed descriptions of several aspects of students' English writing development (Blanton, 1998; Buckwalter & Lo, 2002; Neufeld & Fitzgerald, 2001; Fitzgerald & Noblit, 1999; Huss, 1995). One study (Buckwalter & Lo, 2002) additionally described aspects of writing development in the native language. Because the researchers tended to focus on different writing features, it was not possible to synthesize across the studies to portray a common set of features. Though not all of the sets of researchers specifically inferred comparison of their accounts of the students' English writing development to that of native English speakers', their descriptions tended to appear highly similar to ones described for similar-age native English-speaking students in prior literature (cf. Fitzgerald & Shanahan, 2000). Buckwalter and Lo (2002), Fitzgerald and Noblit (1999), and Neufeld and Fitzgerald (2001) specifically make such an inference. Additionally, Buckwalter and Lo (2002) suggested that their student's Chinese writing development could be described using phases of development previously delineated by Chan and Louie (1992).

Two sets of researchers reported contradictory findings about spelling development in the early grades. In a cross-sectional study of native Spanish-speaking students learning English, Davis, Carlisle, and Beeman (1999) found a large advancement in English writing abilities from first to second grade, and a large advancement in Spanish writing abilities from second to third grade. On the other hand, Zutell and Allen (1988), reporting a cross-sectional analysis, found no early grade differences for English spelling outcomes for native Spanish-speaking students.

Sociocultural contexts in one study strongly influenced three 8-year-old native speakers of Arabic, Javanese, Indonesian, and Persian English-as-a-third-language writing, with each participant developing personal sense of agency, voice, and identity in relation to different social situations (Maguire & Graves, 2001). In a final study in this category (Seow, 1997), there were few suggestions of a developmental acquisition order for the different verb patterns in English-as-a-second-language writing for native Chinese, Indian, and Malay speakers. Results for the second-language writers, even for the youngest of them, were similar to those of adults and professional native English writers.

• Is there transfer of knowledge/skills between first- and second-language writing? For a 5-year-old ELL native Taiwanese student, concepts of print developed in one language transferred to the other (Buckwalter & Lo, 2002). Likewise, spelling abilities transferred from Spanish native language to English, or vice versa, in four studies of primary grade/age children (Davis et al., 1999; Ferroli & Shanahan, 1993; Nathenson-Mejia, 1989; Zutell & Allen, 1988).

• What is the relationship between phonological awareness and spelling or how do bilinguals' phonological awareness and spelling compare to monolinguals'? In two studies second-language English phonological processing was related to English spelling for native speakers of Persian and Sylheti (Arab-Moghaddam & Sénéchal, 2001; Everatt, Smythe, Adams, & Ocampo, 2000). However, another set of researchers found a contradictory result, with native Cantonese, Mandarin, Gujarati, Urdu, and Punjabi speakers' English phonological processing abilities (sound mimicry and phoneme deletion) less developed than their counterpart native English-speaking peers, but the two groups performed similarly in spelling (Wade-Woolley & Siegel, 1997). Reasons for discrepant results were not clear. Jackson, Holm, and Dodd (1998) reported that their bilingual Cantonese–English and monolingual English preschoolers performed equivalently on several phonological awareness and spelling measures, except for onset–rime awareness, where the bilinguals performed more poorly. For grades 1 through 5, monolinguals outperformed the bilinguals on spelling unfamiliar words and on complex manipulation of phonemic information.

• *Are particular instructional interventions effective?* Provision of lots of books in English was, on the whole, more effective for new-language English writing (native languages were not identified, but the country of study was Singapore) than a matched-group treatment using an audiolingual approach that emphasized oral language (Elley, 1994). A second set of researchers (Garrett, Griffiths, James, & Scholfield, 1994) found few effects of prewriting activities done in mother-tongue Punjabi and Welsh (compared to those done in English) in students' writing about how to play a word game.

• *Other issues.* (1) A Dakota Indian bilingual girl's main themes in writing over her first-grade year were about relationships, cultural commitment to the Dakota Oyate, and romance (Franklin & Thompson, 1994). She also used a variety of genres, including personal narratives and realistic and romantic fiction. (2) Second- through sixth-grade ELLs (implied to speak Turkish and Spanish) were highly reflective when evaluating their own stories, emphasizing means of putting ideas into print (Samway, 1993). (3) Eight books written by K–5 ELL students (with unidentified native languages) tended to include features suggested by experts as important in both informational and narrative texts (Rudden & Nedeff, 1998).

Intermediate Grades

• Is second-language writing process similar to, or different from, that of first-language writing process? Maguire (1994) examined two middle-grades native French–English speakers' written stories in English Language Arts and again in French Immersion. There was little difference in writing processes used by the students across the two languages. Maguire suggested the data supported "a unity of process across the two languages" (p. 140), such that processes used in one language were also used in the other. Similarly, German students learning English used visual and phonemic access routes for both German and English spelling (James & Klein, 1994).

• *How do selected features of second-language writing develop, and/or how do patterns of second-language writing development compare to those of first-language writing development?* Reynolds (2002) compared development of causality marker use in descriptive writing cross-sectionally for native speakers of Spanish, Vietnamese, and "other East Asian" languages in grades 5 through 8, as well as ELL students' usage compared to that of students in "regular language arts" classes. On average, there were not developmental effects for use of the causality markers investigated, but in general, the ELL students used more causality markers than did students in "regular language arts classes." Also, the ELL students tended to use the causality markers in similar ways across two different topics, whereas the other students did not.

• *Is there transfer of knowledge/skills between first- and second-language writing?* For 12- and 13-year-old German students learning English as a foreign language, spelling knowledge used in native language transferred to English (James & Klein, 1994). Lanauze and Snow (1989) reported transfer of Spanish native-language abilities to English descriptive writing, and results also led to an inference that, for at least some students, transfer was not dependent upon well-developed oral capabilities in the new language.

• *Are particular instructional interventions effective?* One study provided support for the contention that bilingual education may tend to help native Spanish-speaking in-termediate grades students' English *and Spanish* writing more than do submersion situations. Carlisle (1989) compared the English expressive, narrative, and persuasive writing of native English- and native Spanish-speaking fourth and sixth graders who were in regular classrooms (native English speakers), in bilingual education classrooms for at least 2 years (native Spanish speakers), or in submersion classrooms (native Spanish speakers in all-English settings through parental choice). Students in the regular education classrooms outperformed the others on rhetorical effect, overall quality, and error frequency, but the students from bilingual education, where writing was first learned in the native language, outperformed those in submersion situations on syntactic maturity and productivity. Also, bilingual education students wrote significantly better papers in Spanish than in English.

Neither of the two studies examining feedback for writing revealed substantial treatment effect. Fazio (2001) employed three feedback conditions examining journals in French immersion classes for fifth-grade native speakers of 16 different languages: form-focused, content-based focused, or a combination of both. Feedback was given in the journals by a francophone elementary teacher who was not a teacher at the students' school. There was not a significant effect of type of feedback on students' "accuracy in grammatical spelling." Prater and Bermúdez (1993) used a pre–posttest experimental-comparison group design to assess the effect of teaching students to provide responses to authors in small groups. The students' ethnicities were Asian American and Hispanic. There were no differences between the treatment groups for quality of personal writing or for number of sentences written. There were, however, differences favoring the experimental group for number of words and number of idea units written.

Over the course of 1 year, Patthey-Chavez and Clare (1996) traced the development of ideas in five native Spanish-language fourth graders' writing during reading lessons that were conducted as "Instructional Conversations" (Goldenberg, 1992/1993). "Instructional Conversations" lessons are guided by a set of principles and steps, and are designed "to facilitate discussions to enhance student reading comprehension," and they served as anchoring activities for "negotiation of joint meaning" (Patthey-Chavez & Clare, 1996, p. 515). "Ideas and interpretations from these discussions reappeared in the students' writings" (p. 515).

In a substudy reported in Elley (1994), eight schools carried out an experimental treatment involving a book flood with either silent reading or shared book reading, and four comparison schools used an audio-lingual method with readers for learning English. The treatments were compared annually for 3 years, each year for "more than 500" 9- to 11-year-old native speakers of Fijian or Hindi. Experimental and comparison schools were matched on reading scores, racial composition, and resources. Significant differences between experimental and comparison treatments, favoring the book flood treatment, were found for written communication for only 1 of the 3 years.

Finally, Structured Writing instruction, as compared to Freewrite instruction, was associated with significant growth over a summer for fifth-grade native Spanish speakers for analytic and holistic overall quality scores (Gomez, Parker, Lara-Alecio, & Gomez, 1996).

• *Other issues.* (1) Comparing English persuasive writing of fourth-grade Latino students in ELL classes to those who were "already mainstreamed into the regular English classroom," Bermúdez and Prater (1994, p. 50) found no differences between the two groups for number or type of appeal or for writing quality. The only significant effects were for gender differences, favoring females. (2) Peyton (1993) analyzed ELL teachers' and native Burmese, Cantonese, Korean, and Italian students' questions in dialogue journals and pointed to the authenticity of teachers' questions that prompted sixth-grade students' exploration of their own opinions and thoughts. Additionally, teachers' questions appeared related to increasing student-initiated questions and ongoing interaction through the year. (3) Analyzing all of the extended writing done by 12 sixth-grade students during one week, Peyton, Staton, Richardson, and Wolfram (1993) asserted that native Chinese- and Spanish-speaking students' dialogue journal writing was complex in ways that approximated the formality of assigned texts, such as the degree to which it contained extended

texts focused on one topic and the extent to which it was cohesive. At the same time, the dialogue journal writing was different from other writing in that there were more clause connectors—perhaps because there were more opportunities to do dialogue journaling—and more advanced cohesive relations. Finally, when the writing task was less closely tied to personal knowledge, it was more difficult. (4) Three sixth- and eighth-grade ELLs, who were native Farsi and Hindi speakers, often utilized knowledge from reading in their own writing (Samway & Taylor, 1993). (5) After conducting a functional grammar analysis on descriptive writing for seventh- and eighth-grade students, some of whom were native English speakers and some of whom were ELLs (with eight different ethnicities represented), Schleppegrell (1998) delineated some possible weaknesses in the ELLs' writing, with the "weakest" having difficulty with the verb "be," and some students incorrectly using the third-person singular and/or using a phrasal construction with "of." (b) Examination of e-mail activity (in Spanish) of three sixth-grade native English speakers learning Spanish as a foreign language revealed that students kept audience in mind, had a purpose for their writing, and varied their discourse accordingly (Trenchs, 1996). (7) Finnish pseudoword spelling correlated with English story-writing ability for 12- and 13-year-old Finnish students learning English (Lumme & Lehto, 2002).

Secondary Grades

• Is second-language writing process or product similar to, or different from, that of first-language writing process? Four sets of researchers noted highly similar selected composing processes across native and second-language writing or across participants who wrote in both languages while doing think-alouds. In several cases, some differences were also found. When writing in both languages, one native Danish speaker, learning English as a foreign language (described as "very able") used prewriting and extensive initial planning when writing, and exhibited similar commenting, reading aloud, writing, and verbatim verbalizations (Albrechtsen, 1997). The researcher suggested that differences across languages were likely due to differences in essay topics and the extent of distractions in the participant's working environment. Likewise, Roca de Larios, Marín, and Murphy (2001) emphasized the similarity of selected composing processes for their seven high school native Spanish-speaking participants' argument writing in Spanish and in English as a foreign language. The researchers focused on "formulation" processes, or "pretexts," that covered "both the verbalization of written material and those other utterances . . . (lexical units, syntactic structures, etc.) . . . [that] could be considered clear candidates for becoming part of the text" (pp. 510–511). Participants spent equal amounts of time formulating when writing in the native and the new language. However, there was also a quantitative difference in at least one aspect of writing process across the two languages: Fluent formulation was twice as common as problem-solving formulation when writing in a second language, whereas it was five times as common when writing in the native language. Similarly, more and less effective Singaporan writers used meaning-construction strategies in their persuasive writing in both native their language and in English (Wong, 1993). Finally, in an examination of ability to express doubt and uncertainty in English, highly similar patterns were noted in the written products of native English speakers in Britain and native Cantonese speakers who were learning English in Hong Kong (Hyland & Milton, 1997). Both groups of students were heavily dependent upon a narrow range of devices, principally for modal verbs and adverbs. However, manipulation of doubt and certainty was particularly difficult for the ELLs. They used syntactically "simpler constructions, relied on a more limited range of devices, offered stronger commitments to statements and exhibited greater problems in conveying a precise degree of certainty" (p. 201).

• *How can the development of selected features of second-language writing be described, and/or how do patterns of second-language writing development compare to those of first-language writing development?* For a participant subgroup of Southeast Asian speakers of Cambodian, Lao, Hmong, and Vietnamese, who were learning English in mainstream classes, there were no significant differences in measures of accuracy, flu-

ency, coherence, and organization for one English descriptive essay across 8th-, 10th-, and 12th-grade levels, suggesting unusually flat development (Tarone, Downing, Cohen, Gillette, Murie, & Dailey, 1993). Compared to mainstream ELLs at each grade level, participants in the lower-level ELL class scored significantly lower on all four measures. The pupils in the highest level scored significantly lower than the mainstream 8th- and 10th-grade ELLs on accuracy and fluency, and significantly lower than the 10th-grade ELLs on coherence. On the whole, mainstreamed ELLs outperformed those in ELL classes.

• *Is there transfer of knowledge/skills between first- and second-language writing?* Two studies suggested transfer of selected abilities between first- and second-language writing, and a third highlighted transfer interference from native language to second-language spelling. Olsen (1999) analyzed Norwegian students' English texts for orthographic, morphological, syntactic, and lexical errors and concluded that the students' native language knowledge influenced their English writing. Wong's (1993) Singaporan pupils doing persuasive writing in Chinese and English transferred meaning-construction strategies from one language to the other. However, in a spelling study of Kenyan students learning English, Nyamasyo (1994) found transfer interference, with a large number of misspelled words in English evidently due to the difference in phonetic inventories of Kenyan and English.

• *What are the differences between better and poorer second-language writers' compositions?* Mäkinen (1992) divided "reflective" essays written by native Finnish 19-year-olds who had studied English as a foreign language for 10 years into good-, middle-, and poor-quality categories, and then did a topical structure analysis. Good writers were better able to develop the topics more evenly across several topic levels than middle or poor writers. Good writers were also more homogeneous as a group in handling topics at higher levels than either of the other two groups, and they returned to higher topic levels at the end of their pieces more often than did others. There was, however, no significant relationship between topic depth and quality group.

• *Are particular instructional interventions effective?* Ten sets of investigators examined seven different intervention topics. Icelandic students taught with English as the language medium improved their English essay organization more than those not taught essay writing (some persuasive), but students taught in Icelandic did not write better essays in English than those not taught essay writing (Berman, 1994). Also, those taught in their native language made the greatest gains (compared to the other two groups) on most organizational features in the Icelandic essays.

Cantonese student response to English-as-a-foreign-language classroom instruction in process writing instruction was mixed, with academically achieving all-girl classes judging the intervention most positive, two lower achieving mixed-gender classes judging it negative, with the remaining classes judging it as a mix of positive and negative (Pennington, Brock, & Yue, 1996). They also found that teacher disposition toward the process writing approach was positively related to student disposition.

English-as-a-second-language students (representing 11 different native languages) in an intervention group with no peer interaction outperformed those who had partners to talk with on grammatical accuracy and complexity of writing. Also, greater text resource support for writing (as opposed to lesser text support) was associated with enhanced grammatical accuracy and complexity of writing, communicative quality, and ideas and organization (Franken & Haslett, 1999).

Three sets of investigators explored revision issues within some type of instructional context. Tsui and Ng (2000) examined the extent to which native Chinese speakers incorporated teacher and/or peer comments in English essays (one persuasive, the other either descriptive or persuasive) during the last two of four cycles of process writing instruction done in English. While some learners incorporated high percentages of both teacher and student comments into their compositions, all learners favored teacher comments. Similarly, Sengupta (1998) had students in Hong Kong do self-evaluations and peer evaluations for their English compositions and then looked at the students' revisions in six pairs of student compositions. Students were unable to value peer comments as much as teacher comments. In another study, Sengupta (2000) concluded that students

(native Cantonese speakers) who received revision instruction made more gains in writing quality on English compositions than did a comparison group.

Two reports delineated the effects of computers. A group of native Cantonese speakers who learned word processing and wrote using the computer outscored a group who used pen and paper on vocabulary, language use, mechanics, and total score, but not on content or organization for English compositions (Lam & Pennington, 1995). Similarly, in another study (Silver & Repa, 1993), students (representing five different native languages) who learned and used word processing wrote English essays (both on the computer and using pen) judged significantly better in quality than did a comparison group that only used pen and paper. There were no differences between the two groups for self-esteem.

Hong Kong students who took a 4-week summer reading program showed significant growth in English writing speed, wrote more error-free T-units, and improved their style (Lai, 1993). Effects were largely attributable to a high-ability group of students.

Finally, U.S. students at risk for learning Spanish as a foreign language and those not at risk received special instruction designed to target phonology and orthography in the new language (Sparks, Ganschow, Artzer, & Patton, 1997). Both groups made significant gains on phonological and orthographic measures during the first year, but not the second. There were minimal differences between the two groups on semantic and verbal memory measures, which the investigators interpreted to mean that native language differences were less likely to distinguish between those at risk for learning a foreign language and those not at risk than were phonological, orthographic, and/or syntactic abilities.

• *Other issues.* German students learning English, who chose to write an exit exam in English, commented upon positive experiences of taking an English class and writing in English (Reichelt, 1997). They also suggested that "despite the fact that they had had English instruction since at least the fifth grade, vocabulary, text comprehension and 'getting into' the language were all major concerns for them" (p. 282).

Dependable Contentions and Agenda Setting

On the whole, too few studies were alike with regard to contextual situations (e.g., studies within a particular country, with participants of the same native language background learning the same new language under similar circumstances) to draw many generalizations. In the following sections, I present and discuss contentions that appear relatively dependable and end with possibilities for multilingual writing research agendas.

Dependable Contentions?

What contentions about preschool through 12th-grade students' multilingual writing might reasonably and dependably arise from the research done to date? The short answer is, "Very few." There may be only three possible assertions, and even these are based upon very small numbers of studies and participants:

1. For very young children, features of early English-as-a-second-language writing may develop in ways that are quite similar to certain features of early writing development of native English young children (seven studies).
2. For primary- and intermediate-grade students, knowledge/skill can transfer between first- and second-language writing (seven studies).
3. For secondary- and/or intermediate-level bilingual students or students learning English as a foreign language, selected composing processes may be highly similar across native and second-language writing, though differences may also exist (five studies).

Discussion of Contentions

The first of the three preceding assertions is reminiscent of that made by some researchers studying young children's multilingual reading development. For instance, several investigators have pointed to very young children's capabilities for making strong progress in developing early reading strategies in English as a second language, noting how similar such progress can be as compared to that of typically developing native English children (e.g., Araujo, 1997; Fitzgerald & Noblit, 1999, 2000; Geva & Yaghoub-Zadeh, 2000; Weber & Longhi, 1996). At a presentation in fall 2003, representatives of the National Literacy Panel on Language Minority Children and Youth (August, 2003) also tentatively concluded there was sufficient evidence to assert such capabilities and similarities.

The meaning of transfer in the second assertion is that individuals develop knowledge or skill in one language and then use it in another. At a rudimentary level, revelation of specific kinds of knowledge transfer, such as phonological knowledge, affirm facets of Cummins' (1979) contentions about linguistic interdependence. The finding in one study of transfer, even when new-language oracy was only minimally developed, also deserves more study.

The third assertion brings to mind a similar conclusion from prior reviews of second-language writing research done with adults. For instance, Silva (2001) and Krapels (1990) concluded that there are similar processes, but in another piece, Silva (1997) tended to point to differences more than similarities. Krapels (1990) suggested that unskilled second-language writers' processes are similar to those of native language unskilled writers and that skilled second-language writers' processes are similar to those of native-language skilled writers. She concluded that when second-language writers have difficulties, the difficulties are more related to individual composing competencies rather than being inherently linked to language factors. Manchón-Ruiz (1997) indicated that adult second-language composing, like first-language composing, is a "recursive and problem-solving process" (p. 197), but that adult second-language writing processes can also be different in some ways from first-language processes, such as in strategic use of native language to reread text being produced in the second language.

Given the history and somewhat advanced state of research and theory on native-language composing of school-age students, it is surprising to find the paucity of research on multilingual composing at school-age levels. Perhaps one explanation lies in the history of multilingual interests, which has tended to originate with linguists and faculty in English departments, where an adult focus and a view of literacy as successor to oracy have previously been embraced.

Research Agenda Possibilities

How might the field move forward? Because the work is in its infancy, there seem to be countless means of advancement. I suggest here ways that appear to be particularly important. First, multilingual writing research will make a substantial impact when it furthers the construction of multilingual writing theory (see Fitzgerald, 2003, for a similar argument). This means that researchers should start their work with theory, either their own or previously published ones. Explicit positioning, and even implicit positioning, of research in relation to theory was rare among the 56 studies I reviewed.

To date, a few theorists have suggested detailed possibilities for second-language writing theory. Grabe (2001), Grabe and Kaplan (1996), Matsuda (2001), and Silva (2001) are among those frequently cited as positing theory and proposing key variables, their functions, and their relationships. When researchers ground their thinking in such theories, the questions and issues take on more focus, research becomes more programmatic and planful, findings feed back to theory, and theory becomes more or less supported and instantiated. When theories are supported, teachers can be more confident about the ways in which they engage their students. A resultant effect can be improved instruction for school-age students.

Second, all of the concerns I noted in an early section of this chapter, "Critique of Methodologies Used," should be addressed by investigators in every study and every report. Journal editors and reviewers also bear responsibility for holding the highest of standards for rigorous research and detailed reporting.

Third, the most pressing of practical preschool through school-age multilingual writing issues deserve priority attention. My own view is that these tend to be questions that are grounded in, or related to, current theory of multilingual writing. In at least some countries, such as the United States, the United Kingdom, and Canada, these are also tied to sociopolitical issues. For preschool and school-age children:

1. What *are* second-language writing processes? How can they be described?
2. Are cognitive processes involved in writing in a new language similar or different to those involved in writing in a native language? If so, in what ways? Does one theory of composing process sufficiently describe multilingual writing, or are separate theories necessary?
3. Which composing processes transfer across native and second-language writing?
4. In what ways do sociopolitical situations impact second-language writing processes and products?
5. How can second-language writing development be described? Is it different according to age/grade, sociopolitical circumstances, such as immigrant status versus university-bound students learning a foreign language, native to new language particulars, and/or native-language composing abilities?
6. What features of second-language composing can be taught explicitly?
7. Does learning to write in a native language first facilitate learning to write in another language? Can students learn to write well in a new language without learning to write in native language?
8. How is oral language development in a native and a new language related to composing in the new language?
9. Are there "special" aspects of second-language writing processes, features that are not present in native-language writing, that students should be taught to use to their advantage?
10. What facets of cultural background (e.g., genre familiarity) in relation to the new language culture impact writing processes and products?

As immigration and emigration increase around the world, as is certainly the North American case at least, the stakes for global citizenry grow higher and higher. The importance of multilingualism, including multilingual composing, will blossom. In some circumstances, such as when children are suddenly immersed in new language cultures and classrooms in which their native languages are not supported, second-language writing ability looms large in students' academic development. In such situations, second-language composing is critical to educational advancement and future opportunities. Forging solid multilingual writing research agendas that engage investigators and theorists from historically divided disciplines such as linguistics, psychology, sociology, and education is one immediate response to the serious needs of our children.

References

Albrechtsen, D. (1997). One writer two languages: A case study of a 15-year-old student's writing process in Danish and English. *International Journal of Applied Linguistics, 7,* 223–250.

Arab-Moghaddam, N., & Sénéchal, M. (2001). Orthographic and phonological processing skills in reading and spelling in Persian/English bilinguals. *International Journal of Behavioral Development, 25,* 140–147.

Araujo, L. (1997, December). *Making the transition to English literacy.* Paper presented at the annual meeting of the National Reading Conference, Scottsdale, AZ.

August, D. (Chair). (2003, December). *National Literacy Panel on Language Minority Children and Youth: Findings from the panel's research synthesis.* Symposium presented at the annual meeting of the National Reading Conference, Scottsdale, AZ.

Berman, R. (1994). Learners' transfer of writing skills between languages. *TESL Canada Journal, 12,* 29–46.

Bermúdez, A., & Prater, D. (1994). Examining the effects of gender and second language proficiency on Hispanic writers' persuasive discourse. *Bilingual Research Journal, 18,* 47–62.

Blanton, L. L. (1998). *Varied voices: On language and literacy learning.* Boston, MA: Heinle & Heinle.

Buckwalter, J. K., & Lo, Y. G. (2002). Emergent biliteracy in Chinese and English. *Journal of Second Language Writing, 11,* 269–293.

Carlisle, R. (1989). The writing of Anglo and Hispanic elementary school students in bilingual submersion and regular programs. *Studies in Second Language Acquisition, 11,* 257–280.

Chan, L., & Louie, L. (1992). Developmental trend of Chinese preschool children in drawing and writing. *Journal of Research in Childhood Education, 6,* 93–99.

Cummins, J. (1979). Linguistic interdependence and the educational development of bilingual children. *Review of Educational Research, 49,* 222–251.

Davis, L. H., Carlisle, J. F., & Beeman, M. (1999).

Hispanic children's writing in English and Spanish when English is the language of instruction. *Yearbook of the National Reading Conference, 48,* 238–248.

Dworin, J. E. (1998, April). *Biliteracy development: Perspectives from research in children's reading and writing.* Paper presented at the annual meeting of the American Educational Research Association, San Diego, CA.

Elley, W. B. (1994). Acquiring literacy in a second language: The effect of book-based programs. In A. H. Cumming (Ed.), *Bilingual performance in reading and writing* (pp. 331–366). Ann Arbor, MI: Research Club in Language Learning.

Everatt, J., Smythe, I., Adams, E., & Ocampo, D. (2000). Dyslexia screening measures and bilingualism. *Dyslexia, 6,* 42–56.

Fazio, L. L. (2001). The effect of corrections and commentaries on the journal writing accuracy of minority- and majority-language students. *Journal of Second Language Writing, 10,* 235–249.

Ferris, D. R. (2003). *Response to student writing: Implications for second language students.* Mahwah, NJ: Erlbaum.

Ferroli, L., & Shanahan, T. (1993). Voicing in Spanish to English knowledge transfer. *Yearbook of the National Reading Conference, 42,* 413–418.

Fitzgerald, J. (2003). Multilingual reading theory. *Reading Research Quarterly, 38,* 118–122.

Fitzgerald, J., & Noblit, G. W. (1999). About hopes, aspirations, and uncertainty: First-grade English-language learners' emergent reading. *Journal of Literacy Research, 31,* 133–182.

Fitzgerald, J. & Noblit, G. W. (2000). Balance in the making: Learning to read in an ethnically diverse first-grade classroom. *Journal of Educational Psychology, 92,* 1–20.

Fitzgerald, J., & Shanahan, T. (2000). Reading and writing relations and their development. *Educational Psychologist, 35,* 39–50.

Franken, M., & Haslett, S. J. (1999). Quantifying the effect of peer interaction on second language students' written argument texts. *New Zealand Journal of Educational Studies, 34,* 281–293.

Franklin, E., & Thompson, J. (1994). Describing students' collected works: Understanding American Indian children. *TESOL Quarterly, 28,* 489–506.

Garrett, P., Griffiths, Y., James, C., & Scholfield, P. (1994). Use of the mother-tongue in second language classrooms: An experimental investigation of the effects on the attitudes and writing performance of bilingual UK school children. *Journal of Multilingual and Multicultural Development, 15,* 371–383.

Geva, E., & Yaghoub-Zadeh, Y. (2000). *Understanding individual differences in word recognition skills of ESL children.* Manuscript submitted for publication.

Glaser, B. (1978). *Theoretical sensitivity: Advances*

in the methodology of grounded theory. Mill Valley, CA: Sociology Press.

Gomez, R., Jr. Parker, R., Lara-Alecio, R., & Gomez, L. (1996). Process versus product writing with limited English proficient students. *Bilingual Research Journal, 20*, 209–233.

Goldenberg, C. (1992/1993). Instructional conversations: Promoting comprehension through discussion. *Reading Teacher, 46*, 316–326.

Goldstein, L. (2001). For Kyla: What does the research say about responding to ESL writers? In T. Silva & P. K. Matsuda (Eds.), *On second language writing* (pp. 73–89). Mahwah, NJ: Erlbaum.

Grabe, W. (2001). Notes toward a theory of second language writing. In T. Silva & P. K. Matsuda (Eds.), *On second language writing* (pp. 39–57). Mahwah, NJ: Erlbaum.

Grabe, W., & Kaplan, R. (1996). *Theory and practice of writing: An applied linguistics perspective.* New York: Longman.

Huss, R. (1995). Young children becoming literate in English as a second language. *TESOL Quarterly, 29*, 767–774.

Hyland, K., & Milton, J. (1997). Qualification and certainty in L1 and L2 students' writing. *Journal of Second Language Writing, 6*, 183–205.

Jackson, N. E., Holm, A., & Dodd, B. (1998). Phonological awareness and spelling abilities of Cantonese–English bilingual children. *Asia Pacific Journal of Speech, Language, and Hearing, 3*, 79–96.

James, C., & Klein, K. (1994). Foreign language learners' spelling and proof-reading strategies. *Papers and Studies in Contrastive Linguistics, 29*, 31–46.

Krapels, A. R. (1990). An overview of second language writing process research. In B. Kroll (Ed.), *Second language writing research: Insights for the classroom* (pp. 37–56). New York: Cambridge University Press.

Lai, F. (1993). The effect of a summer reading course on reading and writing skills. *System, 21*, 87–100.

Lam, F., & Pennington, M. (1995). The computer vs. the pen: A comparative study of word processing in a Hong Kong secondary classroom. *Computer Assisted Language Learning, 8*, 75–92.

Lanauze, M., & Snow, C. E. (1989). The relation between first- and second-language writing skills: Evidence from Puerto Rican elementary school children in bilingual programs. *Linguistics and Education, 1*, 323–339.

Lumme, K., & Lehto, J. E. (2002). Sixth grade pupils' phonological processing and school achievement in a second and the native language. *Scandinavian Journal of Educational Research, 46*, 207–217.

Maguire, M. (1994). Cultural stances informing storytelling among bilingual children in Quebec. *Comparative Education Review, 38*, 115–143.

Maguire, M. H., & Graves, B. (2001). Speaking personalities in primary school children's L2 writing. *TESOL Quarterly, 35*, 561–593.

Mäkinen, K. (1992). Topical depth and writing quality in student EFL compositions. *Scandanavian Journal of Educational Research, 36*, 237–247.

Manchón-Ruiz, R. M. (1997). Learners' strategies in L2 composing. *Communication and Cognition, 30*, 91–113.

Matsuda, P. K. (2001). Contrastive rhetoric in context: A dynamic model of L2 writing. In T. Silva & P. K. Matsuda (Eds.), *Landmark essays on ESL writing* (pp. 241–255). Mahwah, NJ: Erlbaum. Reprinted from Contrastive rhetoric in context: A dynamic model of L2 writing, *Journal of Second Language Writing, 6*, 45–60, by P. K. Matsuda, 1997.

Moss, P. A. (1994). Can there be validity without reliability. *Educational Researcher, 23*(2), 5–12.

Nathenson-Mejia, S. (1989). Writing in a second-language: Negotiating meaning through invented spelling. *Language Arts, 66*, 516–526.

Neufeld, P., & Fitzgerald, J. (2001). Early English reading development: Latino English learners in the "low" reading group. *Research in the Teaching of English, 36*, 64–109.

Nyamasyo, E. (1994). An analysis of the spelling errors in the written English of Kenyan pre-university students. *Language, Culture, and Curriculum, 7*, 79–92.

Olsen, S. (1999). Errors and compensatory strategies: A study of grammar and vocabulary in texts written by Norwegian learners of English. *System, 27*, 191–205.

Patthey-Chavez, G., & Clare, L. (1996). Task, talk, and text: The influence of instructional conversation on transitional bilingual writers. *Written Communication, 13*, 515–563.

Pennington, M., Brock, M., & Yue, F. (1996). Explaining Hong Kong students' response to process writing: An exploration of causes and outcomes. *Journal of Second Language Writing, 5*, 227–252.

Peyton, J. K. (1993). Teacher questions in written interaction: Promoting student participation in dialogue. In J. K. Peyton & J. Staton (Eds.), *Dialogue journals in the multilingual classroom: Building language fluency and writing skills through written interaction* (pp. 155–172). Norwood, NJ: Ablex.

Peyton, J. K., Staton, J., Richardson, G., & Wolfram, W. (1993). The influence of writing task on ESL students' written production. In J. K. Peyton & J. Staton (Eds.), *Dialogue journals in the multilingual classroom: Building language fluency and writing skills through written interaction* (pp. 196–221). Norwood, NJ: Ablex.

Polio, C. (2001). Research methodology in second language writing research: The case of text-based studies. In T. Silva & P. K. Matsuda (Eds.), *On second language writing* (pp. 91–115). Mahwah, NJ: Erlbaum.

Prater, D., & Bermúdez, A. (1993). Using peer response groups with limited English proficient writers. *Bilingual Research Journal, 17*, 99–116.

Reichelt, M. (1997). Writing instruction at the German Gymnasium: A 13th grade English class writes the Abitur. *Journal of Second Language Writing, 6*, 265–291.

Reichelt, M. (2001). A critical review of foreign language writing research on pedagogical practices. *Modern Language Journal, 85*, 578–598.

Reynolds, D. W. (2002). Learning to make things happen in different ways: Causality in the writing of middle-grade English language learners. *Journal of Second Language Writing, 11*, 311–328.

Roca de Larios, J., Marin, J., & Murphy, L. (2001). A temporal analysis of formulation processes in L1 and L2 writing. *Language Learning, 51*, 497–538.

Rudden, J. F., & Nedeff, A. R. (1998). ESL learners: Process writing and publishing good literature. *Reading Horizons, 38*, 181–202.

Samway, K. (1993). "This is hard, isn't it?": Children evaluating writing. *TESOL Quarterly, 27*, 233–258.

Samway, K., & Taylor, D. (1993). Inviting children to make connections between reading and writing. *TESOL Journal, 2*, 7–11.

Schleppegrell, M. J. (1998). Grammar as resource: Writing a description. *Resarch in the Teaching of English, 32*, 182–211.

Sengupta, S. (1998). Peer evaluation: "I am not the teacher." *ELT Journal, 52*, 19–27.

Sengupta, S. (2000). An investigation into the effects of revision strategy instruction on L2 secondary school learners. *System, 28*, 97–113.

Seow, A. (1997). Relative frequencies of use of English verb patterns in narrative writing. In V. Berry, B. Adamson, & W. Littlewood (Eds.), *Applying linguistics: Insights into language in education* (pp. 151–175). Hong Kong: English Centre at the University of Hong Kong.

Silva, T. (1997). Differences in ESL and native English speaker writing: The research and its implications. In C. Severino, J. C. Guerra, & J. E. Butler (Eds.), *Writing in multicultural settings* (pp. 209–219). New York: Modern Language Association of America.

Silva, T. (2001). Toward an understanding of the distinct nature of L2 writing: The ESL research and its implications. In T. Silva & P. K. Matsuda (Eds.), *Landmark essays* (pp. 191–208). Mahwah, NJ: Erlbaum. (Reprinted from *TESOL Quarterly, 27*, 657–675, by T. Silva, 1993)

Silver, N., & Repa, J. (1993). The effect of word processing on the quality of writing and self-esteem of secondary school English as a second language students: Writing without censure. *Journal of Educational Computing Research, 9*, 265–283.

Sparks, R. L., Ganschow, L, Artzer, M., & Patton, J. (1997). Foreign language proficiency of at-risk and not-at-risk learners over 2 years of foreign language instruction: A follow-up study. *Journal of Learning Disabilities, 30*, 92–98.

Tarone, E., Downing, B., Cohen, A., Gillete, S., Murie, R., & Dailey, B. (1993). The writing of Southeast Asian-American students in secondary school and university. *Journal of Second Language Writing, 2, 149–172.*

Trenchs, M. (1996). Writing strategies in a second language: Three case studies of learners using electronic mail. *Canadian Modern Language Review, 52*, 464–497.

Tsui, A. B. M., & Ng, M. (2000). Do secondary L2 writers benefit from peer comments? *Journal of Second Language Writing, 9*, 147–170.

Wade-Woolley, L., & Siegel, L. S. (1997). The spelling performance of ESL and native speakers of English as a function of reading skill. *Reading and Writing: An Interdisciplinary Journal, 9*, 387–406.

Weber, R. M., & Longhi, T. (1996, December). *Moving into ESL literacy: Three learning biographies.* Paper presented at the annual meeting of the National Reading Conference, Charleston, SC.

Wolfe-Quintero, K., Inagaki, S., & Kim, H. Y. (1998). *Second language development in writing: Measures of fluency, accuracy and complexity.* Honolulu: University of Hawaii Press.

Wong, R. Y. L. (1993). Strategies for construction of meaning: Chinese students in Singapore writing in English and Chinese. *Language, Culture, and Curriculum, 6*, 291–301.

Zutell, J., & Allen, V. (1988). The English spelling strategies of Spanish-speaking bilingual children. *TESOL Quarterly, 22*, 333–340.

Part V

METHODOLOGY AND ANALYTIC TOOLS

Chapter 24

Qualitative Research on Writing

Katherine Schultz

Seated at his desk in his fifth-grade classroom on a warm September day in Philadelphia, Michael conjured up memories of Cambodia. His assignment was to write a poem entitled "Where I'm From,"[1] and he was given examples from his teachers and classmates about the kinds of images he might want to include in this poem. It was not difficult for him to begin. He was reminded every day of where he is from; that aspect of his identity is central to how he introduces himself to his teacher and peers in his urban public school. He began with his own title "I Am From" and continued mixing and blending his old and new worlds:

I am from killing fields, animals all around, riding bikes, and shared love.
I am from rice, egg rolls, and noodles. I am from DVDs and songs and CDs, movies and model cars.
I am from poor and rich. I am from sickness and hardness.
I am from a loving heart and grandparents love of us part.
I am from the flag that I love. The flag is of the love in our country. I am from red and blue. I am from Cambodia.

His classmate, Samay, who also recently immigrated to the United States from Cambodia, looked silently at Michael's composition and returned to his own writing. Another peer gasped at the opening words, failing to comprehend the meaning of the phrase "kill-

ing fields," immediately associating it instead with the steady stream of gunfire and threats in her neighborhood.

Later in the year, Michael was given a different, yet related assignment. For a final and cumulative project, he was instructed to compose a multimedia story of his past, present, and future. He and his classmates were asked to represent where they were from, what they experienced during their fifth-grade year in school, and their aspirations for the future, through images, words, and music. Once again, Michael turned to his family and his home country as a source of ideas. He brought to school a single drawing from home of a relative who had died recently in Cambodia, images and maps from a computer, and several photographs. The drawing exemplified his respect for this relative and represented the essence of where (and who) he is from. The photographs contextualized his life. He selected music from his country and narrated a story into a tape recorder. His final project, a 2-minute iMovie, captured his past, present, and future in a dream-like sequence that embodied the sadness he had carried with him throughout the year.

This brief vignette, drawn from a yearlong study of multimedia storytelling (Schultz & Vasudevan, 2005), suggests several of the possibilities for using qualitative research methodologies for the study of writing. The vignette points to current and future directions for writing research, at the same time that it captures many of the research questions and directions of the past 30 years. It illustrates the way that research questions of the past continue to animate current research projects even as they are transformed by new technologies and media.

For instance, drawing on research beginning in the 1970s, current researchers might focus on Michael's composing processes, asking him to narrate each of his decisions as he selected words and crafted his poem. Alternatively, reflecting another strand of research at that time, researchers might investigate the connections between Michael's writing and his home and community contexts, focusing on questions such as: What is the range and variation of his written products, his purposes, and audiences? Drawing on more recent research that focuses on the social nature of writing, research questions might center on Michael's relationships and conversation with his peers during his composing processes. For instance, researchers might ask: Where do his images come from, and how are they shaped by the communicative context of the classroom? Turning to the work of Soviet literary theorist Mikhael Bakhtin (e.g., 1981), researchers might examine how Michael takes up and transforms the available discourses in his classroom. Researchers might ask how his various identities—as a young Cambodian boy, as a fifth-grade student, as a member of a close-knit family—shape both what and how he composes. Finally, following the recent visual turn in writing research, researchers might focus on the multiple modalities Michael draws on to represent his ideas in each of his compositions. How is his story told through images and sound? How does his access and command of these resources and tools alter his composing processes and products, and his ability to craft a message? Each of these questions and research directions reflects a different emphasis of writing research over the past three decades, and each suggests new directions for writing research and the teaching of writing at the present time.

Since the early 1970s, researchers have used a wide range of qualitative studies and methodologies to address an evolving set of research questions. These qualitative studies have added immeasurably to knowledge about writing, schooling, and a range of ed-

ucational topics. While not the exclusive methodology for writing research, many of the most significant advances in the writing field in recent years have come from qualitative studies (Hull & Schultz, 2001). As Sperling and Freedman (2001) assert, there is a trend in current research on writing to replace experimental research studies with ethnographic case studies and teacher research. For instance, development in writing, once thought to be reflected solely in the written products of a child, has recently been understood as located in the composing processes of individual writers (e.g., Emig, 1971; Perl, 1979) and in the social interactions between and among peers (e.g., Dyson, 1988, 1989; Lensmire, 1994; Schultz, 1997). While text analysis was useful to understand the increasing complexity of written products, qualitative methods allow researchers to document and analyze the writing processes of individuals and groups. Visual methodologies and the use of multimedia in composing, along with attention to writers' identities, have further shifted the current understanding of writing development. Growth or development in writing is thought by some to be reflected in the choices of media and modalities writers make as they compose (e.g., Jewitt & Kress, 2003; Kress, 2001, 2003) in addition to the sophistication or complexity of the writing process and product.

Despite significant advances in writing research from qualitative studies, there is a growing movement to identify outcomes-based scientific research as the only valid methodology for research in education. For instance, the No Child Left Behind Act of 2001 (U.S. Department of Education, 2001), which has had an unprecedented impact on classroom practice, relies on outcomes-based research based on quantitative methodologies. Given this recent trend, this is a particularly opportune time to highlight the past and current contributions of qualitative research to our knowledge of writing and to suggest promising research directions. The current emphasis on reading and math in many schools precludes teachers from including writing in their curricula, especially in schools and districts where the curriculum is tied to high-stakes testing. What is perhaps most alarming to writing educators and researchers about this reliance on high-stakes testing is that many writing tests—and the curriculum that prepares students to take them—encourage narrow and formulaic writing, and the teaching of writing merely as a skill. At the same time that the teaching of writing has disappeared from many classrooms, the new writing section of the SAT exam is likely to lead to an increased demand for the teaching of writing in the near future (National Commission on Writing in America's Schools and Colleges, 2003). In addition, although it may be difficult to find writing instruction in schools, youth are finding new ways to use and transform texts in their out-of-school lives (Hull & Zacher, 2004; Moje, 2000; Schultz, 2002; Schultz & Fecho, 2005). Qualitative methodologies offer researchers tools to investigate writing across the boundaries of the school and the community, and beyond prescribed understandings and uses of texts to inform classroom practices and research.

This chapter traces the major conceptual advances in writing research, drawing on key studies to illustrate what we have learned from this research and to elaborate on the questions raised in the opening vignette. To introduce the chapter, I provide a brief discussion of the contribution of qualitative research methodologies to understanding the teaching of writing. I describe the particular strengths of this approach in elucidating and pushing forward the field. In the following three sections, I illustrate several shifts in qualitative research in writing. First, I offer a historical overview of the methodological turn to qualitative research through two narratives that each begin in the early 1970s and derive from different, yet overlapping, academic disciplines. Next, I offer four recent examples of writing research that highlight the social turn in writing research. Finally, I draw on my own research to suggest one future direction of writing research that reflects the current visual turn in writing and research. With its focus on qualitative methodology and, specifically, the discussion of what research questions, and thus insights, have been possible through the use of qualitative methods in writing research, this review adds a new dimension to the published histories of writing research (e.g., Dyson & Freedman, 1990; Freedman, 1994b; Freedman, Dyson, Flower, & Chafe, 1987; Freedman & Sperling, 1985) and qualitative stud-

ies of education (e.g., Athanases & Heath, 1995; Bloome, 2003; Green & Bloome, 1997; Green, Dixon, & Zaharlick, 2003).

Contributions of Qualitative Research Methodologies to Writing Research

Qualitative research methods in education—including ethnography—are most often used to understand the cultural or everyday practices of individuals and social groups, the ways that these practices affect the access to and distribution of resources across time and space, and the consequences of this distribution of resources (Green et al., 2003; Ortner, 1984; see also Barton & Hamilton, 1998). Researchers use qualitative methods—often called interpretive methodology—to investigate how particular people in particular social contexts interpret or make sense of everyday interactions (Dyson, 1987; Erickson, 1986; Geertz, 1973). This review includes examples of several different types of qualitative research, including long-term theoretically driven ethnographies, case studies, narrative analyses, observational studies, and descriptive surveys. Erickson (1986) explains that there are many terms for qualitative research, including "ethnographic," "participant observational," "case study," "symbolic interactionist," "phenomenological," "constructivist," or "interpretive research," adding that

> these approaches are all slightly different, but each bears strong family resemblance to the others. . . . What makes such work interpretive or qualitative is a matter of substantive focus and intent, rather than of procedure in data collection, that is, a research *technique* does not constitute a research *method*. (pp. 119–120; emphasis in original)

Rather than an explication of each type of research method, this section describes some of the characteristics of qualitative research that have led to advances in our understanding of writing, including a focus on insiders' perspectives; an emphasis on social context; the means to look across settings, including home, school, and community contexts; the study of situated communication and language; and the use of nuanced, descriptive language. Many qualitative studies of writing are long-term ethnographies. As a result, several of these characteristics are particularly reflective of that methodology.

Qualitative research, and particularly ethnographic methodology, often emphasizes and builds on the perspectives of participants in the research setting. Ethnographic research in education often focuses on what group members need to know, do, predict, and interpret in order to participate in everyday life within their social groups or communities, which might include classrooms, schools, or educational settings outside of school (Heath, 1982). In addition, ethnography can be characterized by its comparative frame, its emphasis on long-term participation and observation in a research site, its use of multiple methods, and its focus on the generation of theory (Athanases & Heath, 1995). Other types of qualitative studies tend to be shorter term and do not necessarily emphasize the comparative analysis of more than one setting. Through a focus on the emic, or participants' perspectives, qualitative researchers, including ethnographers, gain critical knowledge about writing practices. For instance, qualitative research methods have helped researchers inform teaching practices and curricula by exploring students' understandings of the meanings and nature of writing in their lives, in and out of school (e.g., Schultz, 2002). Drawing on their lived knowledge of classroom life, teacher researchers have made significant contributions to our understandings of the teaching of writing (e.g., Fecho & Allen, 2003).

A second contribution of qualitative research has been its emphasis on the cultural, historical, social, and ideological contexts of teaching and learning. For instance, in their book, *Writing Ourselves*, which describes the Mass-Observation Project in Great Britain (discussed later in this chapter), Sheridan, Street, and Bloome (2000) write:

> Our interest in writing is inseparable from our interest in the social conditions within which people write, the social purposes they use writing for, and how writing fits in with their life histories, all of which define writing itself. We are also interested in how writing is implicated in power relations, both those involved in the daily lives of people and those among people and the dominant institutions of our society. We are interested in how writing is used to establish identities and to transform social situations and relationships. (p. 1)

Qualitative methods allow for the inclusion of the multiple contexts in which writing occurs and inform our understanding of writing as situated or deeply embedded in these various contexts. Anthropologists of education have used ethnographic methods to describe in detail the functions and uses of writing and other literacy practices in and out of school, and across community and cultural contexts (e.g., Gilmore, 1983; Heath, 1983; Schultz, 2002; Skilton-Sylvester, 2002). These studies have extended our understandings of writing beyond school walls (Hull & Schultz, 2001) and outside of the canonized texts. This methodology reminds researchers that their questions reflect the social and political climate in which the research is designed and carried out (Sperling & Freedman, 2001). For instance, Shaughnessy's (1976, 1977) findings about the importance of studying errors as a window into students' thinking grew out of her work with ethnically and linguistically diverse students who were in her college classes as a result of the new open admissions policies of the times (Schultz & Fecho, 2000).

Qualitative methods have allowed researchers to investigate writing across contexts, including the boundaries between home, school, and the community. Researchers have been able to investigate the many resources individuals bring to writing, replacing the more typical focus on deficits with an understanding of an individual or group's repertoire and strengths. Using qualitative methods, researchers have also looked across individuals, documenting interactions between and among teachers and students. For instance, researchers such as Dyson (e.g., 1997b, 1999, 2003) have used these methods to explore the interactions between peers, texts, and contexts to provide a complex description of the development of writing abilities.

Drawing from theoretical perspectives from anthropologists and linguists in a methodology called the ethnography of communication (e.g., Gumperz & Hymes, 1972), qualitative research has added a focus on language and communication in social contexts to the study of writing. Researchers have used this set of methods to examine the interrelationships between oral and written language and the ways language is tied to social and cultural contexts (e.g., Heath, 1983; Philips, 1983; Scribner & Cole, 1981). More recently, qualitative researchers have examined the range and variation of communicative modalities, media, and contexts that are available to youth for composing texts (e.g., Hull & Zacher, 2004; Moje et al., 2004; Schultz & Vasudevan, 2005).

The reporting of qualitative research relies on rich, descriptive language. In writing research, qualitative research methodologies have led researchers to complicate definitions of terms such as "language," "literacy," "literature," "learning," and "culture" (Bloome, 2003). Understanding, in qualitative research, comes from the insiders' perspective, which is derived through inductive research and reported through nuanced, textured description and writing that is often more accessible to educators, including teachers and administrators. This has led to the suggestion that this methodology is more likely to result in changes in practice.

Perhaps most significantly, qualitative research in writing has led researchers to use the term "literacy" to refer to more than the acts of reading, writing, and speaking, and to consider the ways in which these acts are intimately tied to social, cultural, economic, historical, and political contexts. In addition, researchers often make distinctions between writing events and practices. A focus on the term "literacy practices," for instance, draws from the anthropological tradition to describe ways of acting and behaving that reflect power positions and structures (Hull & Schultz, 2001). Street (2001) makes a distinction between practices and events, explaining that one could photograph an event but not a practice. Literacy practices, according to Street, embody folk models and beliefs, while events might be repeated occurrences or instances in which interaction surrounds the use of text (cf. Barton & Hamilton, 2000).

Qualitative research has contributed new knowledge to writing research in several areas. This research methodology has led to several research questions that are elaborated later in the chapter. Dyson (1987) illustrates the directions qualitative research can take in her example of the kinds of definitional questions researchers might ask, such as: What is writing or literacy? Where should we look for it? What are the boundaries? Is writing synonymous with the words on the page? Is it the meaning communicated to an audience? The genre? How are the purposes of writing in a particular cultural event connected to ideology or to societal discourses? This review focuses on writing researchers' questions and the knowledge obtained over the past few decades through qualitative research, beginning with a short history of the use of qualitative methods for the study of writing.

The Methodological Turn to Qualitative Research: Historical Overview

There are two dominant narratives of the turn to qualitative research on writing in the United States: One comes from literacy and composition researchers, and the other, from anthropologists and sociolinguists interested in language and literacy. Literacy and composition researchers tell the following story to describe the shift to qualitative research methodologies: In 1971 Janet Emig published her study, *The Composing Processes of Twelfth Graders*, demonstrating what could be learned by using qualitative research methods for the study of writing, and dramatically shifting the focus of research on writing. Emig's use of case study methods and her pioneering use of think-aloud protocols, coupled with qualitative interviews with students about their experiences with writing, introduced new approaches to understanding writing as a process. Until that time, most writing research either focused on textual analyses of writing done by "experts" or used experimental treatments to test the efficacy of particular teaching techniques. Typical studies included descriptions of written products from students at various age levels and tests of classroom treatments to determine which would produce better products (e.g., Braddock, Lloyd Jones, & Shoer, 1963). Emig's research not only gave writing researchers new insights but also suggested questions that might be asked about writing as a process to add to knowledge gained by the examination of written products. As a result of Emig's work and other related studies, researchers began to ask questions such as: What are the cognitive processes of an individual writer, and how do these processes vary across individuals and contexts? What factors influence the decisions writers make as they compose? This new focus on the writing process shaped instructional practices and led researchers and teachers to focus on the process of learning to write rather than a single focus on final products. Researchers' gazes turned away from the texts and teachers, toward the student.

Emig's study was notable not only for its use of qualitative methods and, in particular, case study methodologies based on protocol analysis, but also for its focus on typical students—eight "average" or "above average" 12th graders—rather than relying on the study of expert writers to guide the direction of instruction. In addition to gathering data about the composing processes of these students, she asked them about their interests and their out-of-school writing, further extending the domain of writing research. She learned that composing is recursive rather than linear, and that it is more learned than taught. This description of writing helped to shift the discussion about how to teach writing away from a focus on model texts, toward an analysis and description of ordinary writing (Nystrand & Duffy, 2003).

Cognitive perspectives on writing dominated most mainstream composition research in the 1970s and 1980s (Sperling & Freedman, 2001). Following Emig's landmark study, several researchers examined writers' thinking processes as they wrote. Central to the writing research of this time was the work by Flower and Hayes (1981; Hayes & Flower, 1980; see also Scardamalia & Bereiter, 1986), who contended that "the process of writing is best understood as a set of distinctive thinking processes which writers orchestrate or organize during the act of composing" (Flower & Hayes, 1981, p. 366). This work made visible the individual cognitive processes involved in writing. While the authors acknowledged the role of context in their models, context remained in the background in these early studies. Over time, models of writing have become more elaborate. For instance, drawing on the work of Bakhtin, Nystrand (1986, 1989) offers a social-interactive model of writing in which

the meaning is neither in writer's intentions nor in the text. Instead, texts are dynamic; their meaning evolves when they are read by a reader or writer.

During this same time period, the ethnic diversity and educational backgrounds of college students in urban public universities increased dramatically as a result of open admissions policies. Responding to the need to understand these students, and building on Labov's (e.g., 1972) early work on "nonstandard" English, Mina Shaughnessy (1976, 1977) sought to understand the logic, patterns, and history of students' writing in her basic writing classes. Her focus on students' errors as a window into their thinking redefined the commonplace analysis of these students as cognitively deficient, refocusing the discussion of how to teach students the rules they need to enter into the social and cultural norms of the academy. This shift from prescription to description followed the research trajectory begun by Emig. Both sought to explain the cognitive processes of writers as they composed texts (Nystrand & Duffy, 2003).

When the Center for the Study of Writing, affiliated with the University of California–Berkeley and Carnegie Mellon, was formed in 1985, one of its central goals was to develop a sociocognitive theory of writing (Freedman et al., 1987). The researchers associated with this center sought to merge the research on cognitive processes and studies of social contexts. They argued that writing is more than a skill; it is a purposeful social act connected to membership in the social life of one's community, school, or workplace. For instance, they wanted to understand how the social relationships writers form with their peers and teachers shape their learning or cognition (Freedman et al., 1987). Glynda Hull and Mike Rose's (e.g., 1989, 1990) work illustrates this sociocognitive research on writing. Through qualitative research methods, these researchers documented the knowledge that underprepared learners bring to the complex tasks of interpreting literacy texts (Hull & Rose, 1989) and writing summaries (Hull & Rose, 1990). Their research exemplifies this new direction in writing research that they termed sociocognitive studies of writing, in which students' decisions have a history and a logic, arguing for a close analysis of students' thinking in context. This work was based on think-aloud protocols that revealed cognitive moves and also an understanding of thinking in social context. Rather than locating failure in individuals, this research argues for new conceptual frameworks that highlight cognitive competence and difference (cf. Flower, 1994; Hull, Rose, Losey, & Castellano, 1991).

Deborah Brandt (1992) used think-aloud protocols with graduate students in English to show how students continuously justify what they have done and what they are going to do as they compose. Her findings include a description of how students merge their own beliefs with those they think will make sense to the group. She concludes that writers continuously and simultaneously construct and justify their social worlds. Sarah Freedman and her colleagues' (1994a; Freedman & McLeod, 1988) cross-national study of secondary teachers in the United States and United Kingdom examined how students learn to write in urban schools in these two countries. They found significant differences in the expectations of U.S. and U.K. teachers, especially in the ways that they adapted (or failed to adapt) the curriculum to each classroom community. Their research adds a sociocultural dimension to the sociocognitive study of writing, paying particular attention to family, community, and language variety.

A second narrative about the turn to qualitative research in writing from this same time period is told primarily by anthropologists and sociolinguists interested in the study of language and writing. These scholars wanted to document the contrasting patterns of language use of members of various racial and ethnic groups, with a focus on the differences between home and school as a means to explain failure (e.g., Cazden, John, & Hymes, 1972). This narrative begins in 1962, when Dell Hymes proposed the concept of an "ethnography of communication" to focus on the communicative patterns of a community and a comparison of these patterns across communities (Gumperz & Hymes, 1964). While Hymes intended the ethnography of communication to include writing and literacy, the early focus on speaking led many to believe that his emphasis was on spoken language (Hornberger, 1995). Drawing on the theoretical perspectives from ethnography of communication (e.g., Gumperz & Hymes,

1964), researchers began to look at the interrelationships between oral and written language, with a focus on the social contexts of these discourse practices (e.g., Gilmore & Glatthorn, 1982; Heath, 1983; Philips, 1983; Shuman, 1986, 1993).

Following this initial work in language and speaking, Keith Basso (1974) suggested that an ethnography of writing should be the centerpiece of ethnographies of communication. He called for a study of writing as it is distributed across a community rather than a single focus on the classroom, introducing the term "writing event" to emphasize that writing, like speaking, is a social activity. A few years later, folklorist John Szwed (1981) called for ethnographies of literacy and proposed that rather than a single continuum or level of literacy, we should imagine a variety of configurations or a plurality of literacies. Szwed's focus on an ethnography of writing was a response to the "literacy crisis" of the 1980s. He suggested that despite the claims of a crisis of "illiteracy," we had not yet conceptualized what literacy means, nor did we know how literacy or reading and writing were used in social life. He claimed that ethnographic methods are "the only methods for finding out what literacy is and what can be validly measured" (p. 20). Rather than a focus on the composing processes of individual writers, Szwed suggested that researchers pursue the following questions: How is the ability to write distributed in a community? How do these abilities vary according to age, gender, socioeconomic class, race, and the like? What do people write? To whom? When and for what purposes? How is writing related to certain roles and relationships in a community? How is writing taught in and out of schools? How do individuals learn to write? When? Under what circumstances? He concluded that researchers should examine the positions that reading and writing hold in the entire communicative economy and the range of their social and cultural meanings (p. 20).

During this same time period, Shirley Brice Heath (1982) suggested the importance of documenting the social history of writing, for which she coined the phrase, "ethnohistory of writing." Like Szwed (1981), Heath made explicit linkages between writing in social or family settings and methods of writing instruction in school. Using preliminary data from what would become a groundbreaking ethnography, Heath (1983) described ethnographic research begun in response to complaints made by junior and senior high school teachers that it was impossible to teach students to write. According to the teachers, their classrooms were filled with students who planned to work in the textile mills, where reading and writing were not needed for work. Heath concluded that although there was a debate about how to teach writing in schools, there was little systematic description of the functions of writing for specific groups of people. Her study suggests the possibility of using ethnographic studies of writing to reorganize schooling with potentially dramatic results. This early work supported the notion of teacher and student research, and prompted both teachers and students to research the functions and uses of literacy in their communities to inform classroom practice.

At the same time that ethnographic researchers were documenting writing and literacy practices in communities (e.g., Heath, 1983; Taylor, 1983; Taylor & Dorsey-Gaines, 1988) and at the intersection of schools and communities (e.g., Gilmore, 1983; Gilmore & Glatthorn, 1982), Susan Florio and Chris Clark (1982; Clark & Florio, 1981) were investigating many of these same issues inside schools. In their study of the literacy events in second- and sixth-grade classrooms, these researchers developed an analytic framework to document the functions and uses of writing throughout the school day. Their research addressed the following questions: What is the nature of writing activities in a classroom? What variety of functions does writing serve in a second-grade classroom? They concluded that researchers knew little about the role of writing in the lives of children inside and outside of school (Florio & Clark, 1982). Furthermore, they suggested:

> By means of study of classrooms as working social units with needs for communication, we can begin to illuminate their unanalyzed writing curricula. In so doing we can provide the tools and insights needed to take advantage of activities already occurring in their classrooms and to shape those activities to help children expand and extend their written expressive repertoires and their beliefs about writing and its power. (p. 129)

These researchers sought to understand the functions and uses of writing in classrooms and the potential implications for classroom practice.

My own research (e.g., Schultz, 2002) extends these ideas, investigating students' writing across space and time, illustrating how students' use of writing and their identities as writers shift as they move between school and their home and work communities, and suggesting that teachers consider students' writing beyond the school walls in order to encourage them to continue to write after they leave school. Rather than looking for writing in either school or the community, I suggest that researchers conceptualize writing as circulating practices in order to investigate its transformation as it crosses geographic and temporal locations (cf. Hull & Schultz, 2001; Schultz, 2004).

Beginning in the late 1960s, qualitative studies of writing shifted researchers' and teachers' attention away from texts, toward students and the processes of composing texts. Furthermore, this research emphasized the cognitive processes of composing, as well as the social context surrounding these practices. Researchers focused on the identification of resources and promise rather than on deficits or mistakes. This methodology allowed researchers and teachers to understand not only how people write but also the genres, themes, and forms of their writing. With its emphasis on description and investigation, and its focus on explanations rather than cause and effects, qualitative research led to the following questions: What are the processes of writing? What are the range and variation of students' writing in and out of school? What are the functions and uses of writing across contexts? What are the roles of writing in people's lives? What is the nature and function of writing in diverse cultural settings? What is the nature of writing development? Current researchers draw on both strands of research to understand why and where people write, and the knowledge that people bring to their writing. These current qualitative studies of writing join the two traditions of writing research by bringing together the foci on cognition and culture to emphasize the social nature of writing, as described in the next section.

One way to conceptualize the change in writing research over time is as a historical progression from a focus on text analysis and an analysis of instructional strategies to achieve ideal texts, to a focus on individual composing processes and cognitive development, with a later exploration of sociocognitive perspectives, to an understanding of writing as embedded in complex social and cultural systems, and, finally, to the study of writing across multiple media and modalities. Of course, this is not a linear sequence; the research directions are overlapping and recursive. Researchers today are still asking many of the questions that were initiated several decades ago. One focus of this review is to explore the questions that qualitative research methodology has enabled researchers to pursue in each of these areas of research (see Table 24.1 for a summary of this historical overview).

The Social Turn: Recent Qualitative Research in Writing

James Gee (2000a) wrote that in the past several decades, literacy research, like the research in several disciplines, has taken a "social turn" away from a focus on the study of individuals to an emphasis on social and cultural interaction. Gee's own work (e.g., 1996, 2000b) goes beyond the inclusion of sociocultural contexts in the study of writing

to emphasize the ways in which contexts are mutually constitutive (Gee, 2000a; Hull & Schultz, 2002). Focusing on Discourses rather than writing, he claims that Discourses are inherently ideological, embedded in social hierarchies, and reflect the distribution of power. Writing in the mid-1980s, Linda Brodkey (1987) made a similar point in response to the dominance of cognitive studies at that time, arguing that context is always present and must be taken into account in the study of writing. As she explained,

In the field of composition, where it seems patently obvious that both writing abilities and opportunities to write are unevenly distributed, researchers could do a great deal worse than to begin by presuming the unit of "analysis" to be social. When protocol analyses ignore the social, historical, and economic circumstances that are likely to bear on the ways in which, say, children, minorities, and women think about writing, it is not only writers and writing, but *research* on writers and writing that is being decontextualized, and then recontextualized, as a social scene conveniently known as a laboratory. ... There is always a context. And, in order to understand social variation in writing better, one would need to explore how writers and readers conceptualize one another and negotiate their relationships in a given social context. (p. 35; emphasis in original)

TABLE 24.1 Historical Progression of Writing Research

Research focus	Sample research questions
• Text analysis • Exemplary instructional practices	• What are the features of texts written by expert or proficient writers? • How does treatment A (one form of writing instruction) compare to treatment B?
• Individual composing processes • Cognitive perspectives • Sociocognitive perspectives	• What are the decisions an individual makes as she he or composes texts? • How do individuals move through the multiple stages of the composing process? • What are the understandings and knowledge individuals bring to their composing processes?
• Writing as embedded in sociocultural practices and identities	• How are an individual's writing practices and identities shaped by the social, cultural, and ideological contexts he or she inhabits? How does his or her writing, in turn, shape these contexts?
• Writing across multiple media and modalities	• How do people author texts and communicate their messages through a range of multiple modalities? How does the composer adopt and transform the available tools and resources to convey meaning?

In order to emphasize the embedded nature of writing as social practices, as well as the interconnections between writing, reading, and talk (and, more recently, visual and aural modalities such as pictures and music), researchers often use the term "literacy" in place of "writing." Barton and Hamilton (2000), among others, use the term "literacy practices" to emphasize the socially embedded nature of reading and writing and to focus on what people *do* with literacy (cf. Street, 1995, 1996, 2001). Furthermore, they articulate the interplay of structure and agency, focusing on the insiders' perspectives of what constitutes local practices and the ways in which these practices reflect and shape social structures (Barton, Hamilton, & Ivanic, 2000). This use of the term "literacy practices" draws from the anthropological tradition to describe ways of acting and behaving that reflect power positions and structures.

To illustrate recent trends in writing research that use qualitative methods, in this section I describe four research projects that reflect different, yet overlapping aspects of the social turn in this field. First, Anne Dyson (e.g., 1987, 1997b, 2003) has explored the social nature of literacy practices for more than two decades in classroom-based studies of young children located in multiracial, urban public schools. While her research questions have changed over time and with each research project, a consistent focus has been to explore writing as a mediational tool between individuals and their peers, and also as a tool for children to reflect on and remake peer culture. Second, using the term "funds of knowledge," Luis Moll and his colleagues (e.g., Moll & Diaz, 1987) have explored the ways that literacy practices act as mediational tools between individuals and their communities in working-class Mexican American neighborhoods and bilingual schools. Like Dyson, these researchers are interested in understanding how literacy meditates between individuals and their social worlds. Third, begun in 1937, the Mass Observation Project and Archive (Sheridan, Street, & Bloome, 2000) is often characterized as "a people's anthropology" of life in Britain. In this longitudinal project spanning several decades, literacy practices are viewed as a mediating tool between individuals and the historical, cultural, and political moment in which they

compose. Fourth, several researchers have recently explored the ways that literacy is used to position oneself in relation to others (e.g., Blackburn, 2002/2003; Fecho & Green, 2004; Ivanic, 1994; Moje, 2000; Schultz, 1999). Using the phrase "literacy performances" to describe the relationship between literacy and identity, Mollie Blackburn (2002/2003) investigates literacy practices at a youth-run center for lesbian, gay, bisexual, transgender, and queer (LGBTQ) youth. Each of these four studies raises a series of questions that, taken together, characterize some of the recent trends in qualitative research in writing.

Dyson's early work (1987) focused on the role of talk in composing. Rather than conceptualizing writing as an individual, cognitive process, Dyson illustrated the role of peers in children's literacy development. As she explored the social contexts of literacy in classrooms, she focused on the interactions between children through their talk, writing, and drawing. Literacy was a mediational tool that allowed children to negotiate their academic and social worlds, and their relationships between their work and their acceptance and participation in the worlds of their peers. As she studied literacy through this lens, Dyson's initial questions were specifically focused on writing: What is writing and where is writing located (1997a, p. 171)? Drawing on the theoretical perspectives articulated by Vygotsky (1962, 1978), which described how children use language as a tool for learning societal ways of thinking, Dyson posed the question: How does writing function as a useful tool within the social lives and symbolic repertoire of students and their peers (p. 174)? She found that children composed by drawing on symbolic resources and social intentions shaped by the available social structures and interactional possibilities of a classroom.

Dyson's (e.g., 1997b, 1999, 2003) more recent focus has been on understanding children's appropriation of textual practices from outside of school (e.g., songs, films, and television) to use in their school writing. This research draws on theoretical frames based on the work of Bakhtin (1981), who explained that writers not only use words and write in particular situations to interact with others; they also adopt, transform, or resist these words. Her questions emerging from this work include "What is the nature of the interplay between the changing interactional and ideological dynamics of children's classroom lives and the changing nature of the writing processes and products?" (Dyson, 1997a, p. 177). Over the past decade, one of Dyson's many contributions to writing research has been her focus on children as key to understanding new directions in literacy learning and teaching. She urges us to pay attention to the various resources children bring to school, including popular culture and commercial media, in order to understand writing development.

Beginning with research located in communities, Moll and his colleagues have explored ways in which teachers can learn about the knowledge from the community that students bring to the classroom. These researchers use the generative term "funds of knowledge" to describe the networked expertise woven into community practices (Moll & Diaz, 1987; Moll & Greenberg, 1990; Moll, 1992; see also Vásquez, 1993). This work, built on theoretical frames from sociohistorical psychology and cultural psychology, provides illustrations of how learning can be redefined in ways that lead to changes in instructional practices (e.g., Moll & Diaz, 1987). Students are given new "tools" that include materials and practices, as well as ways to mediate between individual and social worlds. Several general questions frame this research: What resources do students bring to school, and how can teachers build their pedagogy and curriculum on this knowledge? What happens to literacy and learning when children are given opportunities to bring their language into the classroom? How can this knowledge shift classroom practices and provide more opportunities for these youth to succeed in school? Moll and his colleagues illustrated how students changed the ways they participated in instructional events and wrote stronger essays that reflected their community funds of knowledge once teachers shifted their practice in response to their understanding of students' home and community lives.

The Mass-Observation Project, begun in the 1930s and revived in 1981, provided a window into the nature of writing in Britain in the late 20th century (Sheridan et al., 2000). Over the past several decades, organizers of the project have recruited ordinary citizens from all over Britain to write about their lives in diaries or in response to specific questions related to a variety of topics, including experiences in school and historical events. The archive now contains over 1 million pieces of writing representing over 2,500 writers since 1981, and a wealth of information about literacy and writing experiences. This project, along with other, more recent studies (e.g., Barton & Hamilton, 1998; Knobel, 1999; Prinsloo & Breier, 1996), makes visible the ordinary, everyday literacy practices of individuals located in particular contexts and specific moments in history. In addition to an archive of written products, through interviews and the responses individuals have written to prompts, the Mass-Observation Project documents the writing processes, purposes, and functions of writing in the lives of citizens in and outside of school contexts, as well as the shifting patterns of writing over a long period of time. As Heath (2000) explains in her foreword to a book detailing the project, "Autobiography, case study, memoir, and ethnography all come together to make up the corpus of [Mass-Observation Project] writing" (p. xii).

In their analysis of the accumulated writing from this project, Sheridan et al. (2000) raise questions:

> What is being reported? Who is doing the reporting? What kind of report is it? What is the nature of the knowledge in the report? What kinds of knowledge are being transmitted? What contexts of knowledge are being implied? What kind of reader is being imagined? In what way is the knowledge from different reports cumulative? What limitations are there about the knowledge being transmitted? (p. 197)

This long-term study gives insight into individuals' own understanding of the role of literacy in their lives and the ways these practices have changed over time for them and for British society as a whole. It raises questions about what can be learned from the study of "ordinary" people reporting on their own practices and about the significance of making usually invisible practices a site of research and a source of knowledge about writing, teaching, and learning.

In her work exploring literacy and identity in a youth-run center for LGBTQ youth, Mollie Blackburn (2002/2003) introduces the term "literacy performances" to "refer to a series of performances in which words and worlds are read and written" (p. 312). As she explains, "Any one performance is among innumerable others, each of which is both similar to and different from all of the others, both confirming and disrupting one another" (p. 312). Blackburn describes how youth use and transform literacy practices to claim and perform social identities while working, at times, for social change. Specifically, she elaborates a particular time and place where she joined the youth at this center to explore "the relationships among literacy performances and identity work in ways that disrupted the hegemonic heteronormative" (p. 312). Blackburn's work reminds us of the power of literacy to provide opportunities for youth to work toward social change and personal transformation, and the importance of paying close attention to and creating spaces for youth's passions in classrooms and community locations.

Blackburn raises several questions: How do youth use literacy to shape, express, and transform their identities? What are the spaces that enable youth to perform identities through reading, writing, and talk, in ways that are respectful and important to them? How do educators foster such opportunities? How do they pay attention to the knowledge and resources that youth bring to their literacy practices and performances in and outside of classrooms? Finally, how can educators acknowledge the privilege we assign to certain literacy practices and remain open to seeing and hearing the alternative practices youth might introduce into our schools, homes, and communities? These questions urge us to look beyond classrooms and textual practices to the interests and passions youth express that are often outside of our purview and beyond our understanding.

The social turn in research on writing has shifted our focus away from texts to the individual interactions and larger cultural, social, and historical contexts of writing practices leading to the more common use of the term "literacy." This research suggests that a single composition cannot be understood apart from the particularities of its creation or its surround. Written texts from classrooms, for instance, always reflect not only the audiences and purposes of the author and his or her readers, but also the history, values, and intentions the composer brings to the piece, as well as the assignment and context in which it was written. In addition, writing positions the writer in a particular way, enabling him or her to take on new identities. Qualitative research has captured the layers of context that are a part of composing processes and texts themselves and has contributed to knowledge about writers and writing, extending our understanding of what we mean by writing, how it is taught and learned, and where and how it occurs across the boundaries of school, home, and community. A focus on literacy, rather than writing, helps us to understand the ways in which the social, cultural, and historical contexts of writing are mutually constitutive (Gee, 2000a) and as such helps us to reimagine research, teaching, and learning about writing.

The Visual Turn: Future Directions in Qualitative Studies of Writing

With the advent of new technologies, writing researchers are thinking broadly about composition and exploring new venues, including visual images transmitted on screens, digital stories written on computers, and poetry slams performed for packed audiences (e.g., Alvermann, 2002; Gee, 2003; Hull, 2003; Hull & Zacher, 2004). Researchers suggest that, in the past, although writers most often relied on available materials rather than adapting or changing those materials or resources, today we might ask how a composer uses and adapts the resources to communicate a message (Kress, 2003). As Kress explains, in the age of multiple modalities, "there are now choices about how what is to be represented should be represented: in what mode, in what genre, in what ensembles of modes and genres on what occasions" (p. 117). A focus on the choices writers make suggests new research directions and methodologies.

My own work has included an exploration of how digital technologies shape research methods (Schultz, 2004). The methods I have explored with my colleagues in a recent project that documents the use of multimedia storytelling with urban fifth graders (Schultz & Vasudevan, 2005; Schultz, Vasudevan, Bateman, & Coleman, 2004) are variously called visual methodologies and image-based research, and are drawn from disciplines such as anthropology, sociology, and cultural studies (cf. Grimshaw, 2001). In addition to the collection of data through standard qualitative methods in our current research, we work collaboratively with teachers and students to combine media in forms such as iMovies in order to collect and analyze data such as video, student- and researcher-produced photographs, and audio recordings. Through our research, we have explored what it means to represent students' literacies and learning through multiple modalities. Among other questions, we ask: How does storytelling across multiple modalities help us to capture—with youth—the practices, identities, relationships, experiences, and knowledge that cross the boundaries of school, home, and community? Furthermore, we ask how can we use multimodal and multimedia research methods to document these literacy practices?

While the questions asked by writing researchers in the past will continue to shape the directions of qualitative research in writing in the future, new research is likely to push past a focus on words on the page. As Hull (2003) writes, "Ours is an age in which the pictoral turn has supplanted the linguistic one, as images push words off the page and our lives become increasingly mediated by a visual popular culture" (p. 230). This suggests that in our current time period, in which visual images are featured prominently in our daily lives, the vocabulary we use for researching and teaching writing practices will begin to change dramatically. We need a vocabulary to help students, teachers, and researchers recognize the different representational demands of a variety of texts (Bearne, 2003; Bearne & Kress, 2001).

This vocabulary is likely to include terms such as "modality," "media," and "affordances." In addition, we need terms to describe learning and development, and the nuances of texts composed across multiple domains. Representational modes include the various formats for composing meaning such as writing, speech, images, gestures, and music. The current forms of media include books, magazines, computer screens, video, film, radio, and the like. Used in this sense, the term "affordances" indicates what is possible through various modes and media, and what is inhibited or con-

strained. As writing researchers look to the future, research agendas might focus on investigating the affordances connected to different forms of representation, modalities, and media, and the ways in which learning and development are closely tied to available resources and local contexts.

Questions that will shape future research agenda include the following: What forms of media and which modalities are particularly suited to convey messages and meaning to various audiences? Furthermore, how is the selection and choice of materials, genres, technologies, and modalities agentive and transformative? Qualitative research methods are particularly suited to capturing the new directions that literacy, technology, and learning are moving in our new digital age. Not only have researchers used qualitative methodologies to deepen our knowledge of the role of literacy in people's lives, a focus on the engagement of multiple modalities in literacy research has added new dimensions to an understanding of the situatedness of these practices. As researchers invent and use multiple modes of inquiry to document and analyze these practices with students and teachers, we create possibilities for understanding new literacy practices through a bricolage of multilayered stories (Vasudevan, 2004).

We live in a time when there are new semiotic possibilities for representing ideas and conveying meaning. Schools lag behind community spaces outside of school, where much of this experimentation is occurring (Hull & Schultz, 2001; Hull & Zacher, 2004; Moje et al., 2004; Vasudevan, 2004). It is incumbent upon writing researchers and educators to look to youth in order to understand what they know, value, and seek to understand. As we sketch out an agenda for writing research in the future, we can ask along with Allan Luke (2003),

> How will literacy practices be redefined in relation not only to the emergence of digital technologies but also to the emergent, blended forms of social identity, work, civic and institutional life, and the redistributions of wealth and power that accompany economic and cultural globalization? (p. 133)

The chapter opened with a poem written by a student on one of the first days of his fifth-grade school year. The poem captured the notion of cultural globalization in its merging of images of the killing fields of Cambodia with current songs on U.S. radios. In his final composition of the year—a layered text that juxtaposed music, text, and images to convey meaning, Michael asserted his identities as a Cambodian son and as a youth living in the United States. In composing his iMovie, Michael carefully selected how he would tell his story and the media that would convey his message. Beginning with images, and moving back and forth between those images and his poetry, he wove together a multilayered story. As researchers, we documented his work across the year in several different forms drawing on new visual methodologies. These media afforded us ways to engage youth in the documentation of their literacy practices, decentering the role of the researcher in the collection, production, and representation of data, thus opening up the research to a myriad of perspectives of what literacy is and why literacy matters in the lives of youth and adults (Schultz & Vasudevan, 2005; Vasudevan, 2004).

This work reminds us of the potential of youth, of teachers and classrooms that build on their knowledge and deep interests, and of research methodologies that seek to inform and transform our existing knowledge and practice. It points to possible future directions in research in writing and to the potential of qualitative research methodologies to contribute understanding and create opportunities for the education of youth in and out of schools.

Acknowledgments

I gratefully acknowledge the helpful feedback and commentary from Charles MacArthur, Anita Chikkatur, Anne Burns Thomas, Lalitha Vasudevan, Mollie Blackburn, and Judith Green. Thanks also to Mrs. Betty Deane for editorial assistance.

Note

1. This assignment was adapted from Linda Christensen's (2000) description in *Reading, Writing and Rising Up* and is used in K–12 and university classrooms across the country.

References

Alvermann, D. E. (Ed.). (2002). *Adolescents and literacies in a digital world*. New York: Peter Lang.

Athanases, S. Z., & Heath, S. B. (1995). Ethnography in the study of the teaching and learning of English. *Research in the Teaching of English*, 29(3), 263–287.

Bakhtin, M. (1981). *The dialogic imagination* (C. Emerson & M. Holquist, Trans.). Austin: University of Texas Press.

Barton, D., & Hamilton, M. (1998). *Local literacies: Reading and writing in one community*. London: Routledge.

Barton, D., & Hamilton, M. (2000). Literacy practices. In D. Barton, M. Hamilton, & R. Ivanic (Eds.), *Situated literacies: Reading and writing in context* (pp. 180–196). London: Routledge.

Barton, D., Hamilton, M., & Ivanic, R. (Eds.). (2000). *Situated literacies: Reading and writing in context*. London: Routledge.

Basso, K. (1974). The ethnography of writing. In R. Bauman & J. Sherzer (Eds.), *Explorations in the ethnography of speaking* (pp. 425–432). Cambridge, UK: Cambridge University Press.

Bearne, E. (2003). Rethinking literacy: Communication, representation and text. *Reading, Literacy and Language*, 37, 98–103.

Bearne, E., & Kress, G. (2001). Editorial. *Reading, literacy and language*, 35(3), 89–93.

Blackburn, M. V. (2002/2003). Disrupting the (hetero)normative: Exploring literacy performances and identity work with queer youth. *Journal of Adolescent and Adult Literacy*, 46(4), 312–324.

Bloome, D. (2003). Anthropology and research on teaching the English language arts. In J. Flood, D. Lapp, J. R. Squire, & J. M. Jensen (Eds.), *Handbook of research on teaching the English language arts* (2nd ed., pp. 53–66). Mahwah, NJ: Erlbaum.

Brodkey, L. (1987). Writing ethnographic narratives. *Written Communication*, 4(1), 25–50.

Braddock, R., Lloyd Jones, R., & Shoer, L. (1963). *Research in written composition*. Urbana, IL: National Council of Teachers of English.

Brandt, D. (1992). The cognitive as the social: An ethnomethodological approach to writing process research. *Written Communication*, 9(3), 315–355.

Cazden, C., John, V., & Hymes, D. (Eds.). (1972). *Functions of language in the classroom*. New York: Teachers College Press.

Christensen, L. (2000). *Reading, writing, and rising up: Teaching about social justice and the power of the written word*. Milwaukee, WI: Rethinking Schools.

Clark, C. M., & Florio, S. (1981). *Diary time: The life history of an occasion for writing*. East Lansing, MI: Institute for Research on Teaching.

Dyson, A. H. (1987). The value of "time-off task": Young children's spontaneous talk and deliberate text. *Harvard Educational Review, 57,* 396–420.

Dyson, A. H. (1988). Negotiating among multiple words: The space/time dimensions of young children's composing. *Research in the Teaching of English, 22*(4), 355–391.

Dyson, A. H. (1989). *Multiple worlds of child writers: Friends learning to write.* New York: Teachers College Press.

Dyson, A. H. (1997a). Children out of bounds: The power of case studies in expanding visions of literacy development. In J. Flood, S. B. Heath, & D. Lapp (Eds.), *Handbook of research on teaching literacy through the communicative and visual arts* (pp. 167–180). New York: Macmillan.

Dyson, A. H. (1997b). *Writing superheroes: Contemporary childhood, popular culture, and classroom literacy.* New York: Teachers College Press.

Dyson, A. H. (1999). Coach Bombay's kids learn to write: Children's appropriation of media material for school literacy. *Research in the Teaching of English, 33*(4), 367–402.

Dyson, A. H. (2003). The stolen lipstick of overheard song: Composing voices in child song, verse, and written text. In M. Nystrand & J. Duffy (Eds.), *Towards a rhetoric of everyday life: New directions in research on writing, text and discourse* (pp. 145–186). Madison: University of Wisconsin Press.

Dyson, A. H., & Freedman, S. W. (1990). *On teaching writing: A review of the literature.* (Occasional Paper No. 20). Berkeley: University of California, Center for the Study of Writing.

Emig, J. (1971). *The composing processes of twelfth graders* (Research Report No. 13). Urbana, IL: National Council of Teachers of English.

Erickson, F. (1986). Qualitative methods in research on teaching. In M. C. Whittrock (Ed.), *Handbook of research on teaching* (3rd ed., pp. 119–161). New York: Macmillan.

Fecho, B. (with Green, A.), (2004). Learning as Aaron. In B. Fecho (Ed.), *"Is this English?": Race, language, and culture in the classroom* (pp. 91–112). New York: Teachers College Press.

Fecho, B., & Allen, J. (2003). Teacher inquiry into literacy, social justice and power. In D. Lapp & J. Flood (Eds.), *Handbook of research on the English language arts* (pp. 232–246). Mahwah, NJ: Erlbaum.

Florio, S., & Clark, C. (1982). The functions of writing in an elementary classroom. *Research in the Teaching of English, 16,* 115–129.

Flower, L. (1994). *The construction of negotiated meaning: A social cognitive theory of writing.* Carbondale: Southern Illinois University Press.

Flower, L., & Hayes, J. (1981). A cognitive process theory of writing. *College Composition and Communication, 32,* 365–387.

Freedman, S. W. (1994a). *Exchanging writing exchanging cultures: Lessons in school reform from the United States and Great Britain.* Urbana, IL: National Council of Teachers of English, and Cambridge, MA: Harvard University Press.

Freedman, S. W. (1994b). *Moving writing into the 21st century* (Occasional Paper No. 36). Berkeley: University of California, Center for the Study of Writing.

Freedman, S. W., Dyson, A. H., Flower, L., & Chafe, W. (1987). *Research in writing: Past, present, and future* (Technical Report No. 1), Berkeley: Center for the Study of Writing.

Freedman, S. W., & McLeod, A. (1988). *National surveys of successful teachers of writing and their students: The United Kingdom and the United States* (Technical Report No. 14). Berkeley: University of California, Center for the Study of Writing.

Freedman, S. W., & Sperling, M. (1985). Teacher student interaction in the writing conference: Response and teaching. In S. W. Freedman (Ed.), *The acquisition of written language: Response and revision* (pp. 106–130). Norwood, NJ: Ablex.

Gee, J. P. (1996). *Social linguistics and literacies: Ideology in discourses* (2nd ed.). London: Falmer Press.

Gee, J. P. (2000a). The new literacy studies: From "socially situated" to the work of the social. In D. Barton, M. Hamilton, & R. Ivanic (Eds.), *Situated literacies: Reading and writing in context* (pp. 180–196). London: Routledge.

Gee, J. P. (2000b). New people in new worlds: Networks, the new capitalism and schools. In B. Cope & M. Kalantzis (Eds.), *Multiliteracies: Literacy learning and the design of social futures* (pp. 43–68). London: Routledge.

Gee, J. P. (2003). *What video games have to teach us about learning and literacy.* New York: Palgrave Macmillan.

Geertz, C. (1973). *The interpretation of cultures.* New York: Basic Books.

Gilmore, P. (1983). Spelling "Mississippi": Recontextualizing a literacy event. *Anthropology and Education Quarterly, 14*(4), 235–256.

Gilmore, P., & Glatthorn, A. A. (Eds.). (1982). *Children in and out of school: Ethnography and education.* Washington, DC: Center for Applied Linguistics.

Green, J. L., & Bloome, D. (1997). Ethnography and ethnographers of and in education: A situated perspective. In J. Flood, S. B. Heath, & D. Lapp (Eds.), *Handbook on teaching literacy through the visual and communicative arts* (pp. 181–202). New York: Macmillan.

Green, J. L., Dixon, C. N., & Zaharlick, A. (2003). Ethnography as a logic of inquiry. In J. Flood, D. Lapp, J. R. Squire, & J. M. Jensen (Eds.), *Handbook of teaching the English language arts* (pp. 201–224). Mahwah, NJ: Erlbaum.

Grimshaw, A. (2001). *The ethnographer's eye: Ways*

of seeing in modern anthropology. New York: Cambridge University Press.

Gumperz, J. J., & Hymes, D. (1964). *The ethnography of communication.* Washington, DC: American Anthropological Association.

Gumperz, J. J., & Hymes, D. (Eds.). (1972). *Directions in sociolinguistics: The ethnography of communication.* New York: Holt, Rinehart, & Winston.

Hayes, J., & Flower, L. (1980). Identifying the organization of writing processes. In L. W. Gregg & E. R. Steinberg (Eds.), *Cognitive processes in writing* (pp. 31–50). Hillsdale, NJ: Erlbaum.

Heath, S. B. (1982). Ethnography in education: Defining the essentials. In P. Gilmore & A. A. Glatthorn (Eds.), *Children in and out of school: Ethnography and education* (pp. 33–55). Washington, DC: Center for Applied Linguistics.

Heath, S. B. (1983). *Ways with words.* New York: Cambridge University Press.

Heath, S. B. (2000). Foreword. In D. Sheridan, D. Bloome, & B. Street (Eds.), *Writing ourselves: Mass-observation and literacy practices.* Cresskill, NJ: Hampton Press.

Hornberger, N. H. (1995). Ethnography in linguistic perspective: Understanding school processes. *Language and Education, 9*(4), 233–248.

Hull, G. (2003). Youth culture and digital media: New literacies for new times. *Research in the Teaching of English, 38*(2), 229–233.

Hull, G., & Rose, M. (1989). Rethinking remediation: Toward a socio-cognitive understanding of problematic reading and writing. *Written Communication, 6,* 139–154.

Hull, G., & Rose, M. (1990). "This wooden shack place": The logic of an unconventional reading. *College Composition and Communication, 41,* 287–298.

Hull, G., Rose, M., Losey, K., & Castellano, M. (1991). Remediation as social construct: Perspectives from an analysis of classroom discourse. *College Composition and Communication, 42,* 299–329.

Hull, G., & Schultz, K. (2001). Literacy and learning out of school: A review of theory and research. *Review of Educational Research, 71*(4), 575–611.

Hull, G., & Schultz, K. (Eds.). (2002). *School's Out!: Bridging out-of-school literacy with classroom practices.* New York: Teachers College Press.

Hull, G., & Zacher, J. (2004). What is after-school worth? Developing literacies and identities out-of-school. *Voices in Urban Education.* Annenberg Institute for School Reform. Providence, RI: Brown University. Retrieved March 7, 2005, from www.annenberginstitute.org/VUE/Spring04/Hull.html

Ivanic, R. (1994). I is for interpersonal: Discoursal construction of writer identities and the teaching of writing. *Linguistics and Education, 6,* 3–15.

Jewitt, C., & Kress, G. R. (Eds.). (2003). *Multimodal literacy.* New York: Peter Lang.

Knobel, M. (1999). *Everyday literacies: Students, discourse, and social practice.* New York: Peter Lang.

Kress, G. R. (2001). *Multimodal discourse: The modes and media of contemporary communication.* New York: Oxford University Press.

Kress, G. R. (2003). *Literacy in the new media age.* London: Routledge.

Labov, W. (1972). *Language in the inner city: Studies in the black English vernacular.* Philadelphia: University of Pennsylvania Press.

Lensmire, T. (1994). *When children write: Critical re-visions of the writing workshop.* New York: Teachers College Press.

Luke, A. (2003). Literacy and the other: A sociological approach to literacy research and policy in multilingual societies. *Reading Research Quarterly, 38*(1), 132–141.

Moje, E. B. (2000). "To be part of the story": The literacy practices of "gangsta" adolescents. *Teachers College Record, 102,* 652–690 .

Moje, E. B., Mcintosh Ciechanowski, K., Kramer, K., Ellis, L., Carrillo, R., & Collaz, T. (2004). Working toward third space in content area literacy: An examination of everyday funds of knowledge and discourse. *Reading Research Quarterly, 39*(1), 38–71.

Moll, L. C. (1992). Bilingual classroom studies and community analysis: Some recent trends. *Educational Researcher, 21*(3), 20–24.

Moll, L. C., & Diaz, S. (1987). Change as the goal of educational research. *Anthropology and Education Quarterly, 18,* 300–311.

Moll, L. C., & Greenberg, J. B. (1990). Creating zones of possibilities: Combining social context for instruction. In L. C. Moll (Ed.), *Vygotsky and education: Instructional implications and applications of sociohistorical psychology* (pp. 319–348). Cambridge, UK: Cambridge University Press.

National Commission on Writing in America's Schools and Colleges (2003). *The neglected "R": The need for a writing revolution.* New York: College Board.

Nystrand, M. (Ed.). (1986). *The structure of written communication.* Orlando, FL: Academic Press.

Nystrand, M. (1989). A social-interactive model of writing. *Written Communication, 6,* 66–85.

Nystrand, M., & Duffy, J. (Eds.). (2003). *Towards a rhetoric of everyday life: New directions in research on writing, text and discourse.* Madison: University of Wisconsin Press.

Ortner, S. (1984). Theory in anthropology since the sixties. *Comparative Studies in Society and History, 26*(1), 126–166.

Perl, S. (1979). The compositing processes of unskilled college writers. *Research in the Teaching of English, 13,* 317–336.

Philips, S. U. (1983). *The invisible culture: Communication in classroom and community on the*

Warm Springs Indian Reservation. New York: Longman.

Prinsloo, M., & Breier, M. (1996). *The social uses of literacy: Theory and practice in contemporary South Africa*. South Africa: Bertsham, SACHED Books.

Scardamalia, M., & Bereiter, C. (1986). Research on written composition. In M. C. Whittrock (Ed.), *Handbook of research on teaching* (3rd ed., pp. 778–803). New York: Macmillan.

Schultz, K. (1997). "Do you want to be in my story?": Collaborative writing in an urban elementary school classroom. *Journal of Literacy Research, 29*(2); 253–287.

Schultz, K. (1999). Identity narratives: Stories from the lives of urban adolescent females. *Urban Review, 31*(1), 79–106.

Schultz, K. (2002). Looking across space and time: Reconceptualizing literacy learning in and out of school. *Research in the Teaching of English, 36*(3), 356–390.

Schultz, K. (2004, March). *The visual turn in educational research: Re-envisioning qualitative methods through multimodalities*. Paper delivered to the National Academy of Education, Meeting of Postdoctoral Fellows, Philadelphia, PA.

Schultz, K., & Fecho, B. (2000). Society's child: Social context and writing development. *Educational Psychologist, 35*(1), 51–62.

Schultz, K., & Fecho, B. (2005). Literacies and adolescence: An analysis of policies from the United States and Queensland, Australia. In N. Bascia, A. Cumming, A. Datnow, K. Liethwood, & D. Livingstone (Eds.), *International Handbook of Educational Policy* (pp. 677–694). Dordrecht, The Netherlands: Kluwer.

Schultz, K., & Vasudevan, L. (2005, February). *Representing literacies and lives: Multimedia storytelling with urban adolescent youth*. Paper presented at the National Council of Teachers of English Assembly on Research, Columbus, OH.

Schultz, K., Vasudevan, L., Bateman, J., & Coleman, A. (2004). *Storytelling across multiple modalities as method*. Philadelphia: Ethnography in Education Forum.

Scribner, S., & Cole, M. (1981). *The psychology of literacy*. Cambridge, MA: Harvard University Press.

Shaughnessy, M. (1976). Diving in: An introduction to basic writing. *College Composition and Communication, 27*(3), 234–39.

Shaughnessy, M. (1977). *Errors and expectations*. New York: Oxford University Press.

Sheridan, D., Street, B. V., & Bloome, D. (2000). *Writing ourselves: Mass-Observation and literacy practices*. Cresskill, NJ: Hampton Press.

Shuman, A. (1986). *Storytelling rights: The uses of oral and written texts among urban adolescents*. Cambridge, UK: Cambridge University Press.

Shuman, A. (1993). Collaborative writing: Appropriating power or reproducing authority? In B. V. Street (Ed.), *Cross-cultural approaches to literacy* (pp. 247–271). Cambridge, UK: Cambridge University Press.

Skilton-Sylvester, E. (2002). Literate at home but not at school: A Cambodian girl's journey from playwright to struggling writer. In G. Hull & K. Schultz (Eds.), *School's out!: Bridging out-of-school literacies with classroom practice* (pp. 61–90). New York: Teachers College Press.

Sperling, M., & Freeman, S. W. (2001). Teaching and writing. In V. Richardson (Ed.), *Handbook of research on teaching* (4th ed., pp. 370–387). Washington, DC: American Educational Research Association.

Street, B. V. (1995). *Social literacies: Critical approaches to literacy in development, ethnography and education*. London: Longman.

Street, B. V. (1996). Preface. In M. Prinsloo & M. Breier (Eds.), *The social uses of literacy: Theory and practice in contemporary South Africa* (pp. 1–9). Bertsham, South Africa: SACHED Books.

Street, B. V. (2001). Literacy "events" and literacy "practices": Theory and practice in the "new literacy studies." In M. Martin-Jones & K. Jones (Eds.), *Multilingual literacies: Comparative perspectives on research and practice* (pp. 17–29). Amsterdam: John Benjamins.

Szwed, J. F. (1981). The ethnography of literacy. In M. F. Whiteman (Ed.), *Writing: The nature, development, and teaching of written communication, part 1* (pp. 13–23). Hillsdale, NJ: Erlbaum.

Taylor, D. (1983). *Family literacy: Young children learning to read and write*. Exeter, NH: Heinemann.

Taylor, D., & Dorsey-Gaines, C. (1988). *Growing up literate: Learning from inner-city families*. Portsmouth, NH: Heinemann.

U.S. Department of Education. (2001). *No Child Left Behind Act of 2001*. Washington, DC: U.S. Government Printing Office.

Vásquez, O.A. (1993). A look at language as resource: Lessons from La Clase M·gica. In B. Arias & U. Casanova (Eds.), *Bilingual education: Politics, research, and practice* (pp. 119–224). Chicago: National Society for the Study of Education.

Vasudevan, L. (2004). *Telling different stories differently: The possibilities of (counter)storytelling with African American adolescent boys*. Unpublished doctoral dissertation, Philadelphia: University of Pennsylvania.

Vygotsky, L. S. (1962). *Thought and language* (Ed. and Trans., E. Hanfmann & G. Vakar). Cambridge, MA: MIT Press.

Vygotsky, L. S. (1978). *Mind in society: The development of higher psychological processes*. Cambridge, MA: Harvard University Press.

Chapter 25

Statistical Analysis for Field Experiments and Longitudinal Data in Writing Research

Robert D. Abbott, Dagmar Amtmann, *and* Jeff Munson

In this chapter we begin with a focus on the strengths of randomization and experiments in writing research, and discuss statistical implications for power and type I error rates when scaling laboratory or small-scale research up to field experiments. Because statistical methods for exploratory and confirmatory analysis of cross-sectional data are well known, we then focus on statistical analysis and the design of newer *longitudinal* approaches that are useful in research on growth in writing processes. These longitudinal methods include latent variable growth mixture modeling for change when measures are continuous and latent transition analysis (LTA) for change when measures of change are stages or categories. We have minimized the number of equations in the text, instead pointing readers to the relevant sources in the statistical literature. In many ways, this chapter is a complement to Abbott, Amtmann, and Munson (2003), where the reader can find discussion of graphical and quantitative (e.g., factor analysis) exploratory methods of analysis for cross-sectional data, confirmatory methods for measured and latent variable structural equation modeling of cross-sectional data, and new directions in confirmatory methods, including permutation-based statistics and graph–theoretic approaches to causal modeling.

Consequently, we make only brief reference to these methods in this chapter.

Researchers investigating writing processes have used a variety of qualitative and quantitative methods (Allal, Chanquoy, & Largy, 2004; Beach & Bridwell, 1984; Kamil, Langer, & Shanahan, 1985; Rijlaarsdam, van den Bergh, & Couzijn, 1996). The complementary nature of qualitative and quantitative methods is well illustrated by the work of MacArthur, Graham, and Harris (2004), whose program of research on revising draws on theory about writing processes, descriptive interview studies, and randomized experimental studies to tease apart the multiple processes involved in revising.

While complementary and compatible within a broader epistemological framework (MacArthur, 2003), applications of qualitative and quantitative methods in writing research need to be evaluated based upon the standards of construct validity, internal validity, statistical conclusion validity, and external validity (Levin & O'Donnell, 1999; Mosteller & Boruch, 2002; Shadish, Cook, & Campbell, 2002) or their translation into scientifically based research standards (Eisenhart & Towne, 2003). As research on effective strategies in teaching writing is extended into experiments in schools and classrooms, researchers need to continue to focus on issues of internal validity (Feuer, Towne, & Shavelson, 2002). Random assignment to condition minimizes selection bias and makes it unlikely that individuals in the various conditions vary *systematically* for reasons other than that created by the manipulation of the experiment. This is a strength of the randomized experiment. Some researchers reject qualitative methods for this reason and calls for randomized experiments grow stronger (Levin & O'Donnell, 1999; Mosteller & Boruch, 2002) and now influence federal funding (Eisenhart & Towne, 2003). Qualitative and quantitative methods are not mutually exclusive, though, and we see research on writing that incorporates both (e.g., Gere & Abbott, 1985; MacArthur et al., 2004) as making important contributions to our understanding of writing processes.

Design of Randomized Field Experiments in Research on Writing

Randomized experiments are well discussed in statistical texts (Maxwell & Delaney, 1990) and have a long tradition in studies of writing processes. However, scaling up these randomized experiments (often short-term studies in controlled environments) by extending them into classrooms in field experiments is challenging (Mosteller & Boruch, 2002) when considerations of internal validity and statistical conclusion validity are important. Shadish et al. (2002) do an outstanding job of discussing threats to internal and external validity in such randomized field experiments. Cook and Payne (2002) respond to objections to using random assignment in field experiments and address epistemological, ethical, and political concerns. Because we think that the step of scaling up research-supported strategies and procedures is important, we next discuss issues pertinent to statistical analyses and the design of randomized field experiments in research on writing.

Design Issues and Statistical Conclusion Validity

Beyond the many practical realities of bringing research to scale (Cook & Payne, 2002) considerations of internal validity, type I error rate, and power are paramount. For ex-

ample, assume that we have a set of writing instructional strategies that we want to test using a randomized field experiment. Our focus is on the outcomes of the program *compared to* what would have happened in the absence of the program (the counterfactual).

One aspect of planning the design is that we need to make decisions about how many classrooms and how many children in each classroom should be included in the experiment. In randomized field experiments, classrooms often are going to be randomly assigned to condition, so that spillover effects are minimized and we have efficient service delivery. In such designs, classrooms are randomly assigned to condition, and individuals are not randomly assigned to condition. Statistical analysis that ignores the clustering effects of children within the classroom has disastrous effects on type I error rate even in the context of contemporary views of null hypothesis testing (Wainer & Robinson, 2003). For example, assume that you have three classrooms of 30 children each, with a classroom randomly assigned to each of the three conditions, a commonly used but inappropriate design (Murray, 1998). If you do a *one-way analysis of variance* (ANOVA) assuming independence of children with 87 degrees of freedom and if you have an intraclass correlation of .10, your actual type I error rate is .34 not .05 (Scariano & Davenport, 1987). If you do not model the multilevel nature of the data (students nested within randomly assigned classrooms), and you have 10 classrooms with 30 children in each classroom, the type I error rate is .69, not .05. Clearly, your statistical decision to reject the null hypothesis will be wrong more often that you thought. Researchers must perform such analyses using hierarchical modeling (Murray, 1998; Raudenbush & Bryk, 2002) that correctly models the intraclass correlation and holds alpha close to .05.

In such randomized field experiments, thinking about the power of your statistical test for reasonable effect sizes leads to the recognition that it is important to randomize an adequate number of groups (Raudenbush, 1997; Siemer & Joormann, 2003; Wampold & Serlin, 2002) and that it is less important how many individuals per group you have (Murray, 1998; Raudenbush &

Liu, 2000; Varnell, Murray, Janega, & Blitstein, 2004). Deciding how many classrooms to assign to control and treatment conditions is complex (Snijders & Bosker, 1993; Liu, 2003; Murray, Varnell, & Blitstein, 2004). Raudenbush and Liu's (2000) Optimal Design software program helps the researcher plan such multilevel studies assuming estimates of the intraclass correlation and effect size. In their approaches to power analyses, Liu (2003) and Snijders and Bosker (1993) incorporate considerations of the relative cost of adding another classroom or adding more students, as well as the value of having different numbers of classrooms in control and experimental conditions. These are important design considerations for randomized field experiments examining the effectiveness of writing curricula and writing instruction, especially considering that maintaining treatment fidelity and obtaining reliable measurement for a large number of students are costly and important considerations (Allison, Allison, Faith, Paultre, & Pi-Sunyer, 1997).

Small-*n* Studies and Writing Research

Many quantitative studies in writing research examine a few students intensively. While the methods of applied behavior analysis and intensive experiments for small-*n* studies (Kazdin, 1982; Richards, Taylor, Ramasamy, & Richards, 1999) are often used by writing researchers, group-based statistical methods for small samples are also useful. Hoyle (1999) edited a collection of chapters discussing many of the available methods. We have found permutation-based methods (Agresti, 1992) to be more appropriate than asymptotic χ^2 tests in our small-*n* writing research that has involved brain scanning.

Small-sample tests are available today for a great variety of types of data and research questions including ordered categorical data (Agresti, Mehta, & Patel, 1990) and recent statistical and computing developments in Monte Carlo estimation (Senchaudhuri, Mehta, & Patel, 1995) have made accurate approximation of exact tests and estimation of distributional characteristics and confidence intervals computationally feasible for

a variety of data types. Given that much research about writing processes only includes a small number of children or measurements with non-normal error distributions, statistical tests that do not rely on asymptotic assumptions may be more appropriate in such cases and are often more powerful when such assumptions are not consistent with the data. StatXact (2004) and LogXact (2002) are two statistical software packages that provide researchers with modern approaches to calculating these exact p-values and confidence intervals.

Longitudinal Data in Writing Research

While cross-sectional experimental studies on writing are important, longitudinal studies of the development of writing processes and the effects of experimental manipulations on such processes allow the modeling of hypotheses not testable with cross-sectional data. Furthermore, evaluating the outcomes of experimental studies based on repeated observations in longitudinal data gives the researcher more power (Fan, 2003; Raudenbush, 2001a, 2001b) for the detection of effects. Methods focusing on longitudinal growth also allow the modeling of individual differences in growth, as well as the opportunity to relate these individual differences in growth to other characteristics of the learner or treatment conditions.

Modeling Change in Writing Processes

Analysis of change is a complex task (Collins, 2001; Singer & Willett, 2003). To model changes in behavior, repeated measurements of individuals over time allow the researcher to study intraindividual change across time without confounding it with the interindividual differences in change (Raudenbush, 2001a). Longitudinal designs often present specific measurement and statistical issues that traditional statistical methods, such as repeated-measures ANOVA are not equipped to address. Such ANOVA methods are suitable for balanced experimental designs with discrete independent variables and restrictive assumptions, which are typical for small-scale experiments. The assumptions of these univariate ANOVA methods become problematic when the data are unbalanced and some or all predictors are continuous. Furthermore, multiple observations for individuals violate the assumption of independence of residuals (Raudenbush & Bryk, 2002). If such data are analyzed inappropriately, the assumption violations result in inaccurate significance tests due to biased estimates of standard errors (Hanushek & Jackson, 1977; Scariano & Davenport, 1987; Murray, 1998). Research on the development of writing processes includes considerations of growth as measured by quantity (e.g., length of composition) as well as stage-based categorical growth (e.g., Stein and Glenn's (1989) stages of narrative story grammar). In this chapter, we discuss methods for both kinds of growth.

Designing research to model change involves many design decisions (Singer & Willett, 2003). When doing an experiment, the researcher makes decisions about the definition of treatments and their random assignment to individuals. Outcomes must be measured that vary systematically over time either quantitatively or in a stage-like fashion. Measurements must be comparable across time and equally valid at all measurement occasions. The researcher must decide whether everyone will be measured at the same points in time (time-structured data) or whether each person will have a flexible schedule of repeated measurements. Collection of three or more waves of data allows the separation of measurement error from estimates of true change and provides information about the shape of trajectory. The timing of the repeated measurements can be at equal intervals or at theoretically relevant occasions depending upon the hypothesized shape of the trajectory. Time can be measured in multiple ways, such as grade, age, weeks, or number of sessions. In many analysis methods, all of the available data from a person are included in the analysis, and persons are not deleted from the analysis if they are missing some data.

Quantitatively Measured Growth

For quantitatively measured growth, latent variable growth curve methodology, including structural equation modeling (SEM) and hierarchical linear modeling (HLM), explicitly models correlations among the residuals. By doing so, these methods not only provide valid significance tests but also summarize the degree to which individuals systematically differ in their mean levels and their rates of change (Raudenbush & Bryk, 2002). In addition to modeling dependence correctly, multilevel modeling allows us to examine how explanatory variables at each level contribute to outcomes. Both predictors that vary at each time point (time varying) and predictors that are constant at each time point (time invariant) can be included in these models (Raudenbush & Bryk, 2002; Muthen & Muthen, 2004).

While allowing for some across-individual heterogeneity, many analyses assume that all individuals come from the same population. Other research questions, however, involve grouping individuals based on their developmental trajectories into categories that include individuals who are similar to each other but have a trajectory that differs from that of individuals in other categories (Muthen, 2001). For example, researchers modeling individuals' responses to a writing intervention may also be interested in identifying subgroups of learners, because membership in these classes or subgroups might provide opportunities for differential interventions (Muthen & Curran, 1997).

Multiple sample or multiple group growth analyses involve fitting a different trajectory in each group. Group-based mixture modeling strategies can then be used to analyze questions about developmental trajectories that are inherently categorical, to describe how patterns of growth vary throughout a population, and to test whether latent classes of trajectories predicted by group-based theories are present. In writing research, situations are common where group membership is not known a priori, and finding individuals with common trajectories is highly desirable, because early identification provides opportunities for differential intervention. Group-based mixture modeling analyses can be used to identify individuals who will immediately benefit from a particular approach to writing instruction and those whose growth is likely to be slower.

Psychology as a discipline has a long tradition in the development of group-based theories of development. Examples of group-based theories include Holyoak and Spellman's (1993) theories of learning, Markman's (1989) theories of language and conceptual development, and Moffitt's (1993) theories of antisocial behaviors, such as delinquency. These theories propose that certain groups of people tend to have distinctive developmental trajectories and, based on these trajectories, we can make predictions about individuals' membership in a certain group. Similar predictions would be made by writing theorists who classify writers in different categories. Although growth modeling methods have not been widely used to model growth in writing, they have been used to model developmental trajectories in reading and math achievement (e.g., Rescorla & Rosenthal, 2004; Williamson, Appelbaum, & Epanchin, 1991).

Researchers analyzing mixtures of developmental trajectories in writing processes can choose among methods that cluster similar individual trajectories into groups: (1) multilevel analysis of models of individual growth (Raudenbush & Bryk, 2002) in conjunction with a grouping procedure (e.g., cluster analysis), (2) latent growth curve mixture modeling (Muthen, 2001), and (3) semiparametric, group-based modeling (Nagin, 1999). All methods provide the posterior probability of group membership for evaluating the precision of group assignment. The semiparametric group-based approach and latent growth curve mixture modeling also provide an integrated approach for determining the number of latent trajectory groups that best fit the data.

In this chapter we focus on latent growth curve mixture modeling (Muthen, 2001) for two main reasons. First, the current version of the software based on the semiparametric group modeling approach (Nagin, 1999) includes the assumption that within-class variances equal zero, and does not allow the researcher to test this assumption. When the assumption that individuals within each distinct trajectory group vary little around the group trajectory is supported by the data, the model based on semiparametric mixture fits the data equally as well as a model based on latent growth curve mixture model approaches that allow for within-class variation. However, when the assumption of no variance within classes does not hold, the latent variable growth mixture model that estimates within-trajectory class variation is more accurate.

Second, multilevel analyses of models of individual growth (e.g., HLM and other modeling methods that utilize the random coefficient approach) draw on statistical estimation procedures that have been thoroughly studied and tested over time. This approach can easily handle any number of unequally spaced waves of longitudinal data; allows the shape of individual growth trajectories to be linear or curvilinear; can model multiple predictors of change; provides a variety of goodness-of-fit statistics, parameter estimates, and standard errors; and allows testing of complex hypotheses about change over time through the analysis of contrasts and the program's ability to restrict individual growth parameter variances to zero (Muthen & Muthen, 2000). One of the main advantages of multilevel modeling approaches is that analysis of models of individual growth does not require time-structured data (Raudenbush & Bryk, 2002), although Version 3 of the SEM program Mplus (Muthen & Muthen, 2004) can model data that are not time structured. Additionally, latent growth curve mixture modeling offers greater flexibility in investigating systematic interindividual differences in change and modeling error covariance structures. When models can be fit by both methods, parameter estimates and standard errors obtained by both methods are identical, or almost identical (Singer & Willett, 2003).

For researchers whose aim is to find different categories of trajectory subgroups, HLM analysis of models of individual growth provides a trajectory intercept and slope for each individual, but a different approach (e.g., cluster analysis) has to be used to explore whether reliable subgroups can be found, a procedure that can be problematic (Beauchaine & Beauchaine, 2002). In contrast, latent growth curve mixture modeling and the software used to estimate latent variable models (Muthen & Muthen, 2004) can handle both research questions if used appropriately (Bauer & Curran, 2003).

Latent Growth Curve Mixture Modeling

Latent variable growth mixture modeling builds on conventional growth modeling. In growth modeling using a SEM framework, random coefficients that capture individual variation are continuous latent variables or growth factors. The goal of growth modeling is to estimate the variation of the growth factors and to study the influence of other variables on this variation. Latent growth models represent one subset of models that can be fitted within the flexible framework of SEM. Categorical latent variable mixture modeling has been developed by Muthen (2001) as a methodology for capturing heterogeneity that corresponds to qualitatively different development. Using this methodology—referred to as growth mixture modeling, each individual obtains a posterior probability estimate for being a member of each underlying latent class. The probability estimate is a function of the model estimates and the values of each individual on the observed measurements. By obtaining posterior probability estimates for each person, the class to which the individual is most likely to belong can be determined. Such approaches can be very useful in early diagnosis or evaluation of preventive interventions, in which early identification of problematic development and intervention is essential.

Growth Mixture Modeling: An Example

In this section we illustrate the use of latent variable growth mixture modeling by examining growth in the accuracy of the spelling in compositions written by students at risk for writing disabilities (Berninger et al., 1998). Many different approaches have been developed to remediate spelling difficulties, but spelling problems are generally resistant to remediation, and different intervention strategies may improve the spelling performance of some students, but not others. It is also often unclear what characterizes students who benefit from instructional interventions. In this study, intervention programs with 24 lessons were taught over 12 weeks to 128 children at risk for writing disabilities. The number of words spelled correctly in a composition written during each of the 24 sessions was obtained for 127 of the children. This research design was developed to test the efficacy of seven different randomly assigned treatments for remediating spelling problems compared to a contact control. See Berninger et al. (1998) for

descriptions of the experimental design and seven treatments and a contact control.

In this chapter we are using these data to investigate three research questions: Can students at risk for writing disabilities be assigned into reliably different trajectory groups based on their response to the spelling interventions over the 24 sessions? How many different trajectory groups can be reliably identified? Is membership in a trajectory group related to treatment or preintervention differences among the students?

Figure 25.1 illustrates the corresponding analysis model. In the diagram, time 1 to time 24 represents the 24 measurements during the 24 sessions in the experiment. Measurement error at each of the 24 time points was modeled but not represented in the diagram. The mean and variance of the latent factors of intercept and slope represent the group and individual variations in slope and intercept. The Latent Class represents the modeling of latent trajectory classes that potentially differ in intercepts and slopes. Orthographic and Phonological Coding represent predictors of latent class membership. Again, residuals are modeled but not represented in the diagram. This model does assume full mediation of the effects of these predictors, although other models are testable (Stoel, van den Wittenboer, & Hox, 2004).

Model testing proceeded systematically, first by examining the basic fit of competing models that included increasing numbers of trajectory classes, second by examining both linear and quadratic models over the time points, and then by testing for evidence of systematic heterogeneity in growth trajectories. The number of latent trajectory classes was determined iteratively, specifying an increasing number of trajectory classes and evaluating the results in terms of model fit, interpretability, and meaningfulness of trajectory classes. Models were tested using several start values to ensure a proper solution (Muthen & Muthen, 2004).

The processes described by Muthen and Muthen (2000) were followed to determine the number of latent trajectory classes. As a first step, the Bayesian information criterion (BIC) statistic was used to assess the model fit. BIC reflects both the likelihood value of a model and the number of parameters estimated. A low BIC value indicates a well-

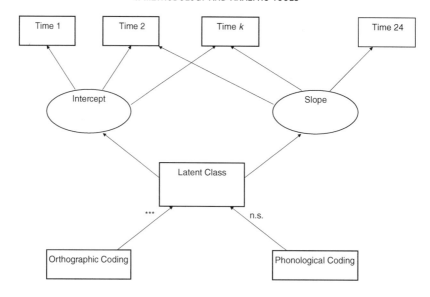

FIGURE 25.1. Growth mixture model with orthographic and phonological coding predictors.

fitting model and can be achieved by models that fit the data well without using many parameters. We used the guidelines provided by Kass and Raftery (1995) to judge the degree of evidence for differing numbers of trajectory groups provided by the BIC difference between two models(Kass & Raftery, 1995). According to the guidelines, a difference of 0–2 BIC points provides weak evidence, a difference between 2 and 6 points provides positive evidence, a 6- to 10-point difference suggest strong evidence, and a difference larger than 10 is considered very strong evidence for H_1. We also considered the results from the Lo, Mendell, and Rubin (2001) likelihood ratio test.

As a second step, the average posterior probabilities were examined. Each student should have a considerably higher average posterior probability for the trajectory group to which he or she is most likely to belong than for any other trajectory group. As a third step, the practical and theoretical usefulness of the latent trajectory classes is considered. This step involves examining the trajectory shapes for similar trends, the number of individuals in each trajectory group, the number of parameters estimated, and the differences in prediction of consequences (e.g., the importance of distinguishing between different trajectory classes in terms of prevention or treatment). Measurements should also be assessed for non-normality, since

extreme non-normality can lead to analyses that estimate spurious classes (Bauer & Curran, 2003; Muthen, 2003).

The goal of the analysis was to find different trajectory classes corresponding to groups of individuals who responded differently to the spelling interventions. Table 25.1 lists the BIC values for the linear model with the within-class variability allowed to vary.

We decided upon the four-class model even though the three-class model had the absolute lowest BIC, because the four-class model classified students similarly to the three-class model and differed only by identifying eight students who started out with high scores as a fourth latent trajectory class.

TABLE 25.1 BIC Values for the Linear Model with Free Growth Factor Variances for Students at Risk for Writing Disabilities

Number of classes	BIC values
1	19,762
2	19,764
3	19,752
4	19,760
5	19,773
6	19,771
7	19,862

The three- and four-class models had similar posterior probabilities. Although the number of children in the fourth class is small, separating out the growth trajectories of these children with high initial scores (and who might not be as impacted by the treatment) was theoretically interesting. Figure 25.2 shows the trajectories for the four latent classes.

As a next step we examined whether the within-class variability needed to be modeled or could be set to zero. To test the difference between the four-class H_0 (within-class variability restricted to zero) and four-class H_1 (within-class variability allowed to vary for some classes and restricted to be the same within other classes), the log likelihood value (χ^2) of the difference was multiplied by -2 (Duncan, Strycker, Li, & Aepert, 1999). The difference between the number of estimated parameters (degrees of freedom) between the models gives the correct degrees of freedom for testing H_0 and H_1. Chi-square was statistically significant, suggesting that the model with the released within-class variability fit the data significantly better than the model that assumes no variance within groups: $\chi^2(3, n = 101) = 290, p < .001$. Using Nagin's (1999) semiparametric group modeling would

not have allowed us to model this variability within trajectory groups.

The classification quality of the four-class solution was also evaluated by examining the posterior probabilities. For the four-class solution, the mean posterior probability for each class was high.

Next, we examined the number of individuals in each class, the parameter estimates, and evaluated the usefulness of the latent classes in practice, as well as the practical consequences of belonging to a specific class. Table 25.2 shows the values of the slope, intercept, and the number of children for each trajectory class in the four-class model. These values are the basis for the trajectories in Figure 25.2.

In the four-class solution, students in the first trajectory class start high and make progress spelling correctly, on average, seven more words than they spelled correctly at the beginning of the intervention study. Students in second trajectory class started lower than class 1 students and improved faster, spelling, on average, 10 more words correctly at the end of the study. Students in class 3 started lower than students in classes 1 and 2, but did not improve much. Class 4 included students whose performance at the

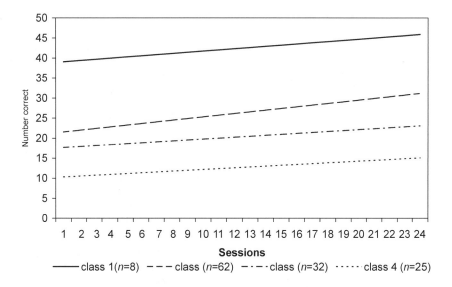

Best fitting linear four-class model

FIGURE 25.2. Growth mixture trajectories for the best fitting linear four-class model.

TABLE 25.2 Intercept and Slope for the Four-Class Model with Free Growth Factor Variances for Students at Risk for Writing Disabilities

	Class			
	1	2	3	4
Intercept	39.08	21.55	17.64	10.33
Slope	.30	.42	.24	.21
n	8	62	32	25

beginning of the study was lowest and improved the least.

These results also inform us about the effects of the randomly assigned treatments in the study. The treatment focusing on whole-word recognition and onset-rime had 69% of its students in classes 1 or 2, and 0% of its students in class 4, with the lowest growth trajectories. In contrast, 50% of the students in the contact control were in trajectory group 4, the lowest performing group.

Another way of viewing these trajectory groups would be to use them to identify pre-experimental predictors of trajectory group membership. For example, many researchers point to the role of phonological coding in literacy and would predict that children low in phonological coding would make the least progress, and children higher in phonological coding would make the most progress. While this is an interesting hypothesis, the data do not support the hypothesis, because there were no significant differences across the four trajectory groups in the preexperimental Rosner phoneme deletion scores, $F(3,123) = 1.79$, $p = .15$. Furthermore, the four trajectory groups did not significantly differ in their Wechsler Intelligence Scale for Children (WISC) Verbal IQ, $F(3,123) = 1.67$, $p = .17$. What did predict faster growth (membership in groups 1 or 2) was orthographic coding, $F(1,123) = 5.84$, $p < 001$, and score on the alphabet transcription task, $F(1,123) = 2.89$, $p < .04$. See Berninger et al. (1998) for an explanation of these measures and their relationship to the theory underlying the interventions.

In summary, in this example with a quantitatively measured outcome, latent variable growth mixture modeling allows us to model individual growth over the 24 sessions in the experiment, identify four latent trajectory classes of growth, and relate these classes to treatment and preexisting differences among the children at risk for writing disabilities.

Growth in Latent Stages

Our discussion of latent variable growth mixture modeling assumes that growth in the targeted writing process can be measured by a quantitative indicator of the process. In this section we discuss longitudinal methods that are appropriate for modeling growth in writing processes that occurs when the writer moves from one qualitative stage to another, for example, if we were modeling children's growth in the development of narrative story grammar (Stein & Glenn, 1979). In the Stein and Glenn model, children's response to narrative prompts is theorized to move from a stage characterized by descriptive story sequence (knowledge listing) to a stage characterized by a linear action sequence, to one described by an internally reactive story sequence, and finally to a stage with the narrative characterized as being a goal-directed single episode. Narratives are classifiable according to dimensions within each of these stages, but the transition between stages has not been statistically modeled.

Modeling transitions between such stages is possible using latent transition analysis (LTA), an approach for fitting stage-sequential models in longitudinal panel data (Graham, Collins, Wugalter, Chung, & Hansen, 1991; Collins & Wugalter, 1992; Collins, Fidler, Wugalter, & Long, 1993; Collins, 2001; Muthen & Muthen, 2004). LTA is a statistical procedure for modeling complex multiway contingency tables where underlying latent classes are hypothesized. As a type of latent class model, LTA combines features of contingency table analysis and some features of latent variable methods. The ratings of the narrative serve as indicators of an unobserved latent class. In LTA analyses of longitudinal data, individuals may dynamically change their latent class membership over time. It is possible to identify different classes of children that move through the developmental stages in different orders or at different rates. It is also possible to test hypotheses: Children randomly assigned to one instructional treatment may progress more quickly through Stein and Glenn's (1979) stages of story grammar than children randomly assigned to a different treatment. LTA also allows the examination of the hypothesis that children in one treatment might skip stages and move directly to goal-directed, single-episode narrative writing. In LTA, growth is being modeled as growth between qualitatively different stages.

Summary

In this chapter we have described statistical methods that writing researchers might consider in addition to classical linear model approaches. We have argued for the role of randomized field experiments when scaling up laboratory interventions and have suggested resources to help the researcher design such studies. We have also described longitudinal methods for the analysis of change for both quantitative and categorical measures. We hope that we have touched on methods new to readers and that they will consider how these methods might help them clarify research questions and examine the consistency of data with models derived from competing theoretical perspectives.

Acknowledgments

Robert D. Abbott's work on this chapter was supported by the Statistics Core for the Learning Disciplinary Center: Links to Schools and Biology, Grant No. P50 HD33812-07; Interventions for Component Writing Disabilities, Grant No. HD25858-11; the Statistics Core of the UW STAART Center of Excellence in Autism, Grant No. U54 MH0066399; and the Statistics Core of the Autism Program Project: Neurobiology and Genetics of Autism, Grant No. HD 35465. Dagmar Amtmann was supported by Grant No. H224A930006 from the U.S. Department of Education, National Institute on Disability and Rehabilitation. Jeff Munson was supported by Grant Nos. HD 35465 and U54 MH0066399.

References

Abbott, R. D., Amtmann, D., & Munson, J. (2003). Exploratory and confirmatory methods in learning disabilities research. In H. L. Swanson, K. R. Harris, & S. Graham (Eds.), *Handbook of learning disabilities* (pp. 471–482). New York: Guilford Press.

Agresti, A. (1992). A survey of exact inference for contingency tables. *Statistical Science, 7,* 131–177.

Agresti, A., Mehta, C. R., & Patel, N. R. (1990). Exact inference for contingency tables with ordered categories. *Journal of the American Statistical Association, 85,* 453–458.

Allal, L., Chanquoy, L., & Largy, P. (Eds.). (2004). *Revision: Cognitive and instructional processes.* New York: Kluwer.

Allison, D., Allison, R., Faith, M., Paultre, F., & Pi-Sunyer, F. (1997). Power and money: Designing statistically powerful studies while minimizing financial costs. *Psychological Methods, 2,* 20–33.

Bauer, D. J., & Curran, P. J. (2003). Distributional assumptions of growth mixture models: Implications for over-extraction of latent trajectory classes. *Psychological Methods, 8,* 338–363.

Beach, R., & Bridwell, L. S. (1984). *New directions in composition research.* New York: Guilford Press.

Beauchaine, T. P., & Beauchaine, J. B. (2002). A comparison of maximum covariance and K-means cluster analysis in classifying cases into known taxon groups. *Psychological Methods, 7,* 245–261.

Berninger, V. W., Abbott, R. D., Rogan, L., Reed, E., Abbott, S. P., Brooks, A., et al. (1998). Teaching spelling to children with specific learning disabilities: The mind's ear and eye beat the computer or pencil. *Learning Disabilities Quarterly, 21,* 106–122.

Collins, L. M. (2001). Reliability for static and dynamic categorical latent variables: Developing measurement instruments based on a model of the growth process. In L. Collins & A. Sayer (Eds.), *New methods for the analysis of change* (pp. 271–288). Washington, DC: American Psychological Association.

Collins, L. M., Fidler, P. L., Wugalter, S. E., & Long, J. D. (1993). Goodness-of-fit testing for latent class models. *Multivariate Behavioral Research, 28,* 375–389.

Collins, L. M., & Wugalter, S. E. (1992). Latent class models for stage-sequential dynamic latent variables. *Multivariate Behavioral Research, 27,* 131–157.

Cook, T. D., & Payne, M. R. (2002). Objecting to the objections to using random assignment in educational research. In F. Mosteller & R. Boruch (Eds.), *Evidence matters: Randomized trials in education research* (pp. 150–178). Washington, DC: Brookings Institute.

Duncan, T. E., Duncan, S. C., Strycker, L. A., Li. F., & Alpert, A. (1999). *An introduction to latent variable growth curve modeling.* Mahwah, NJ: Erlbaum.

Eisenhart, M., & Towne, L. (2003). Contestation and change in national policy on "scientifically based" education research. *Educational Researcher, 32,* 31–38.

Fan, X. (2003). Power of latent growth modeling for detecting group differences in linear growth trajectory parameters. *Structural Equation Modeling, 10,* 380–400.

Feuer, M. J., Towne, L., & Shavelson, R. J. (2002). Scientific culture and educational research. *Educational Researcher, 31,* 4–14.

Gere, A. R., & Abbott, R. D. (1985). Talking about writing: The language of writing groups. *Research in the Teaching of English, 19,* 362–385.

Graham, J. W., Collins, L. M., Wugalter, S. E., Chung, N. K., & Hansen, W. B. (1991). Modeling transitions in latent stage-sequential processes: A substance use prevention example. *Journal of Consulting and Clinical Psychology, 59,* 48–57.

Hanushek, E. A., & Jackson, J. E. (1977). *Statistical methods for social scientists.* New York: Academic Press.

Holyoak, K., & Spellman, B. (1993). Thinking. *Annual Review of Psychology, 44,* 265–315.

Hoyle, R. (Ed.). (1999). *Statistical strategies for small sample research.* Thousand Oaks, CA: Sage.

Kamil, M. L., Langer, J. A., & Shanahan, T. (1985). *Understanding reading and writing research.* Boston: Allyn & Bacon.

Kass, R. E., & Raftery, A. E. (1995). Bayes factor. *Journal of the American Statistical Association, 90,* 773–795.

Kazdin, A. E. (1982). *Single case research designs: Methods for clinical and applied settings.* New York: Oxford University Press.

Levin, J. R., & O'Donnell, A. M. (1999). What to do about educational research's credibility gaps? *Issues in Education, 5,* 177–229.

Liu, X. (2003). Statistical power and optimum sample size allocation ration for treatment and control having unequal costs per unit of randomization. *Journal of Educational and Behavioral Statistics, 28,* 231–248.

Lo, Y., Mendell, N. R., & Rubin, D. B. (2001). Testing the number of components in a normal mixture. *Biometrika, 88,* 767–778.

LogXact 5. (2002). *Software for exact logistic regression.* Cambridge, MA: Cytel Software.

MacArthur, C. (2003). What have we learned about learning disabilities from qualitative research?: A review of studies. In H. L. Swanson, K. R. Harris, & S. Graham (Eds.), *Handbook of learning disabilities* (pp. 532–549). New York: Guilford Press.

MacArthur, C. A., Graham, S., & Harris, K. R. (2004). Insights from instructional research on revision with struggling writers. In L. Allal, L. Chanquoy, & P. Largy (Eds.), *Revision: Cognitive and instructional processes* (pp. 125–137). New York: Kluwer.

Markman, E. M. (1989). *Categorization and naming in children: Problems of induction.* Cambridge, MA: MIT Press.

Maxwell, S. E., & Delaney, H. D. (1990). *Designing experiments and analyzing data: A model comparison perspective.* Belmont, CA: Wadsworth.

Moffitt, T. E. (1993). Adolescence-limited and life-course persistent antisocial behavior: A developmental taxonomy. *Psychological Review, 100,* 674–701.

Mosteller, F., & Boruch, R. (Eds.). (2002). *Evidence matters: Randomized trials in education research.* Washington, DC: Brookings Institute.

Murray, D. M. (1998). *Design and analysis of group-randomized trials.* New York: Oxford University Press.

Murray, D. M., Varnell, S. P., & Blitstein, J. L. (2004). Design and analysis of group-randomized trials: A review of recent methodological developments. *American Journal of Public Health, 94,* 423–432.

Muthen, B. O. (2001). Second-generation structural equation modeling with a combination of categorical and continuous latent variables: New opportunities for latent class/latent growth modeling. In L. M. Collins & A. G. Sayer (Eds.), *New methods for the analysis of change* (pp. 289–322). Washington, DC: American Psychological Association.

Muthen, B. O. (2003). Statistical and substantive checking in growth mixture modeling: Comment on Bauer and Curran (2003). *Psychological Methods, 8,* 369–377.

Muthen, B. O., & Curran, P. J. (1997). General longitudinal modeling of individual differences in experimental design: A latent variable framework for analysis and power estimation. *Psychological Methods, 2,* 371–402.

Muthen, B. O., & Muthen, L. K. (2000). Integrating person-centered and variable-centered analyses: Growth mixture modeling with latent trajectory classes. *Alcoholism Clinical and Experimental Research, 24,* 882–891.

Muthen, L. K., & Muthen, B. O. (2004). *Mplus 3.0 user's guide.* Los Angeles: Author.

Nagin, D. S. (1999). Analyzing developmental trajectories: A semi-parametric, group-based approach. *Psychological Methods, 4,* 139–157.

Raudenbush, S. (1997). Statistical analysis and optimal design for cluster randomized trials. *Psychological Methods, 2,* 173–185.

Raudenbush, S. W. (2001a). Comparing personal trajectories and drawing causal inferences from longitudinal data. *Annual Review of Psychology, 52,* 501–525.

Raudenbush, S. W. (2001b). Toward a coherent framework for comparing trajectories of individual change. In L. M. Collins & A. G. Sayer (Eds.), *New methods for the analysis of change* (pp. 33–64). Washington, DC: American Psychological Association.

Raudenbush, S., W., & Bryk. A. S. (2002). *Hierarchical linear models: Applications and data analysis methods* (2nd ed.). Thousand Oaks, CA: Sage.

Raudenbush, S., & Liu, C. (2000). Statistical power

and optimal design for multi-site randomized trials. *Psychological Methods, 5*, 199–213.

Rescorla, L., & Rosenthal, A. S. (2004). Growth in standardized ability and achievement test scores from 3rd to 10th grade. *Journal of Educational Psychology, 96*, 85–96.

Richards, S. B., Taylor, R. L., Ramasamy, R., & Richards, R. Y. (1999). *Single subject research: Applications an in educational and clinical settings.* San Diego: Singular.

Rijlaarsdam, G., van den Bergh, H., & Couzijn, M. (Eds.). (1996). *Theories, models, and methodology in writing research.* Amsterdam: Amsterdam University Press.

Scariano, S., & Davenport, J. (1987). The effects of violation of the independence assumption in the one way ANOVA. *American Statistician, 41*, 123–129.

Senchaudhuri, P., Mehta, C. R., & Patel, N. R. (1995). Estimating exact *p*-values by the method of control variables, or Monte Carlo rescue. *Journal of the American Statistical Association, 90*, 640–648.

Shadish, W., Cook, T.D., & Campbell, D. T. (2002). *Experimental and quasi-experimental designs for generalized causal inference.* New York: Houghton Mifflin.

Siemer, M., & Joormann, J. (2003). Power and measures of effect size in analysis of variance with fixed versus random nested factors. *Psychological Methods, 8*, 497–517.

Singer, J. D., & Willett, J. B. (2003). *Applied longitudinal data analysis: Modeling change and event occurrence.* New York: Oxford University Press.

Snijders, T., & Bosker, R. (1993). Standard errors and sample sizes for two-level research. *Journal of Educational and Behavioral Statistics, 18*, 237–259.

StatXact. (2004). *StatXact-6.0 statistical software.* Cambridge, MA: Cytel Software.

Stein, N. L., & Glenn, C. G. (1979). An analysis of story comprehension in elementary school children. In R. Freedle (Ed.), *Advances in discourse processing 2: New directions in discourse processing* (pp. 53–120). Norwood, NJ: Ablex.

Stoel, R. D., van den Wittenboer, G., & Hox, J. (2004). Including time-invariant covariates in the latent growth curve model. *Structural Equation Modeling, 11*, 155–167.

Varnell, S. P., Murray, D. M., Janega, J., & Blitstein, J. L. (2004). Design and analysis of group-randomized trials: A review of recent practices. *American Journal of Public Health, 94*, 393–432.

Wainer, H., & Robinson, D. H. (2003). Shaping up the practice of null hypothesis significance testing. *Educational Researcher, 32*, 22–30.

Wampold, B. E., & Serlin, R. C. (2000). The consequences of ignoring a nested factor on measures of effect size in analysis of variance. *Psychological Methods, 5*, 425–433.

Williamson, G. L., Appelbaum, M., & Epanchin, A. (1991). Longitudinal analysis of academic achievement. *Journal of Educational Measurement, 28*, 61–76.

Chapter 26

Text Structure as a Window on the Cognition of Writing
How Text Analysis Provides Insights in Writing Products and Writing Processes

Ted J. M. Sanders *and* Joost Schilperoord

Text analysis in writing research

Many teachers believe that the best and the worst essays written in class differ in organization. The best one is clearly structured, whereas the worst one is hard to follow. What can writing research tell us about this observation? Not much, until recently, because text structure was hardly studied seriously in the context of writing research. Traditionally, writing researchers have paid relatively little attention to the role of text analysis. In Flower and Hayes's (1981) cognitive approach, for instance, the characteristics of the text (e.g., style or structure) are almost completely neglected. However, Bereiter and Scardamalia (1983, 1987) have shown the way to an interesting interaction between psychological models and text linguistic research, which, in our view, is of crucial importance to writing research. They argued that "research is needed to discover what rules less skilled writers actually use and how these rules differ from those of experts." They even pointed to the remedy for this deficiency in studies of writing: text analysis (Bereiter & Scardamalia, 1983, pp. 11, 23). By analyzing the texts writers have produced, the rules they use in composing can be discovered.

In this chapter we show how text analysis can be used to identify such composition rules. We argue that an adequate analysis of the product of writing—the text—reveals significant traces of the writer's cognitive representation, even of online text planning. In order to gain insight into the writer's representations, we analyze the *structure* of texts and try to give a cognitive interpretation of this analysis. Furthermore, we show how data of online writing processes corroborate this cognitive interpretation of text structure.

Why Text Structure?

In his overview of the psycholinguistic processes involved in language production, Levelt (1989) distinguishes between conceptual processes (e.g., macroplanning) and linguistic processes (e.g., syntactic formulation). The few linguistically oriented writing research studies that were carried out, often focused on "lower" levels of text, such as syntax (Hunt, 1970) or the presence of connectors (Lintermann-Rygh, 1985; see Van Wijk, 1992, for further discussion). However, if we want to gain insights into the cognition of writing, that is, both in the processes involved and in the writer's representation, we need to focus on conceptual processes. More specifically, if we use text analysis as a research method, it is imperative that it deal with the essential characteristics of a text and its un-

386

derlying representation. Text structure and discourse coherence are such characteristics. They are constituting principles of text; without them, texts would be nothing but a random set of utterances (see, among many others, Brown & Yule, 1983; Hobbs, 1990; Mann & Thompson, 1988; Sanders, Spooren, & Noordman, 1992; Van Dijk, 1977). For this reason, a cognitively interpretable text analysis should focus on text structure rather than, for instance, on stylistic or syntactic characteristics.

Types of Text-Analytic Methods and Their Application

"Text analysis" can be defined as the unfolding of a unity, the text, in its constituent parts. In text linguistics, a number of text-analytic methods have been developed over the past 30 years. We discuss a representative selection below.

MACROSTRUCTURE AND SUPERSTRUCTURE

In the context of a psychological model of text processing, Kintsch and Van Dijk (1978) and Van Dijk and Kintsch (1983) distinguished between three aspects of text representation: microstructure, macrostructure, and superstructure. Micro- and macrostructure concern the text *content*. The basic building block of these representations are *propositions* (i.e., a unit of meaning that consists of a predicate and connected arguments). For instance, the proposition underlying sentence (1) would be (1'), where HAVE is the predicate and HE and BEARD are the arguments.

(1) He has a beard
(1') [HAVE, (HE, BEARD)]

The microstructure is a network of propositions like these, which represents the textual information in a bottom-up fashion: sentence-by-sentence. On the basis of such a microstructure or *text base,* a macrostructure can be built: an abstract representation of the global meaning structure, which would reflect the gist of the text. This is achieved by applying macrorules to the detailed meaning representation of the microstructure. *Deletion, generalization,* and *construction* are such macrorules, which produce macropropositions: the main ideas

in the text (see especially Van Dijk, 1980). This idea of producing the macrostructure on the basis of the details of the microstructure is certainly appealing. However, the theoretical and empirical status of this part of the Van Dijk and Kintsch (1983) theory has remained unclear over the years.

Where micro- and macrostructure represent the text content, the superstructure is the global structure that is characteristic of a text type: the form in which the macrostructure is presented. The superstructure "provides a kind of overall functional syntax for the semantic macro-structures" (Van Dijk & Kintsch, 1983, p. 242). An example of such a superstructure is that of the type *news discourse,* in which superstructural categories of this type are distinguished: *headlines, lead, context, and event.*

Let us briefly evaluate the macro- and superstructure from the point of view of *usability in writing research*. If a content analysis is needed, the macrostructure analysis is a possibility, even though the exact way in which it is produced is unclear. Another disadvantage of the use of content analyses in the context of writing research is that they do not enable a comparison of different texts, because they will always result in content-specific, incomparable analyses. By contrast, analyses focusing on structure *do* provide this possibility. Superstructures certainly seem useful in this respect, even though they are specific to certain genres.

RHETORICAL STRUCTURE THEORY

In the 1980s and 1990s, Mann and Thompson (1988) presented rhetorical structure theory (RST), which is a functional theory of text organization developed in the context of linguistics and cognitive science. At the heart of RST are the so-called rhetorical relations, including meaning relations such as *cause, elaboration,* and *evidence.* These relations are identified between adjacent text segments (say, clauses) up to the top level of the text. The top level of an RST tree organizes the text as a whole: a relationship that dominates the total text structure. Figure 26.1 illustrates the three highest levels of the RST structure of the expressive text in (2), a letter to the editor, taken from a magazine and broken down into segments on a clause-by-clause basis (Sanders, 1997).

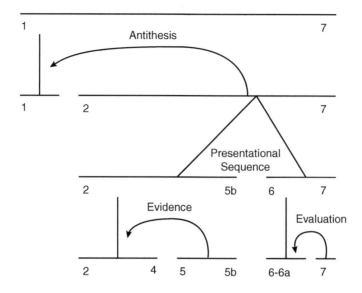

FIGURE 26.1. The three highest levels in the RST analysis of the expressive text (2).

(2)

(1) As are the other ladies of the board of the Dutch Society of Housewives, I am very pleased with the products of *Albert Heijn* and with the great variety. (2) One thing, however, keeps bothering us, (3) namely the self-service when taking and weighing certain products. (4) This is an unhygienic situation, especially with the sweets. (5) We have observed, for instance, (5a) that customers use their hands to grope about in the storage bins, (5b) and children eat sweets from the supplies. (6) We also want to bring it to your attention (6a) that it happens (6aa) that mothers let their small children take place in the shopping cart with their shoes on. (7) This is not very nice, either.

(Source: *Allerhande* [Magazine])

RST has proven to be a useful analytic tool. One of the benefits is that it allows for a complete text analysis of whatever text type: expository, argumentative, or narrative. The system has been applied to many real-life texts. An RST-analysis always starts with an inspection of the *entire* text. The analysis does not proceed in a fixed way; it proceeds bottom-up (from relations between clauses to the level of the text), or top-down (the other way around), or follows both routes (Mann, Matthiessen, & Thompson, 1992).

The analysis results in a hierarchical structure that encompasses the entire text and has a label attached to each of its branches. The exact number and meaning of the different labels have been a much-debated issue, but proposals seem to converge on a basic set of about 30 relations (Hovy, 1990) that can be categorized in a taxonomy (Sanders, 1992; Sanders et al., 1992).

Although RST defines rhetorical relations in a fairly exact way, the assignment of a label is ultimately based on observed "plausibility." Four general constraints are the guidelines: completedness, connectedness, uniqueness, and adjacency (Mann & Thompson, 1988, pp. 248–249). How the analysis actually proceeds is left to the intuitions of the analyst.

PROCEDURES FOR INCREMENTAL STRUCTURE ANALYSIS

Inspired by RST, Sanders and Van Wijk (1996a, 1996b) developed procedures for incremental structure analysis (PISA). PISA incorporates both intuitions about structural regularities in the corpus texts and insights from the text analytical literature, especially with respect to hierarchical aspects of text structure. The two texts in (3) are taken from the PISA-corpus. They were both written by 12-year-old boys, in response to a request to explain to someone who knows nothing about the subject, who Saint Nicholas is. The texts are translated from Dutch in a rather literal way. They were also divided into segments, roughly corresponding to clauses (see Sanders & Van Wijk, 1996a). The hierarchical structures of the texts in (3a and 3b) are shown in Figures 26.2a and 26.2b.

(3a)

(1) Every year Saint Nicholas comes (2) that is on the 4th of December (3) That day he comes by steamboat (4a) When he arrives in the Netherlands (4) then everyone waves to him (5) At night (5a) when it is pitch-dark (5) Saint Nicholas rides over the roofs with Black Peter (6) and throws lots of presents through the chimney (7) while the children sing a song (7a) such as: "Sinterklaas Kapoentje" . . . (8) Saint Nicholas gives lots of presents (9) but he always gets something in return (10) That is either a carrot for the horse or a bit of water, also for the horse (11) On the 5th of December Saint Nicholas really has his birthday (12) on that day he brings the presents (13) and then he leaves again. (14) He also looks into the red book with the cross on it. (15) There it says whether you have been naughty or not (16a) When Saint Nicholas leaves again (16) the children sing Bye bye Saint Nicholas.

(3b)

(1) Saint Nicholas is an old man (2) He has a white-grey beard (3) He has a steamboat with a lot of little black men (4) They are called Black Peter (5a) When it is

the 5th of December (5) the time has come.(6) The day of Saint Nicholas is a Big Festival. (7) The Peters have a birch. (8) A birch is a bundle of swishing branches. (9) They also have a sack (10) that is a kind of wool and a shape. (11) The children in all villages and towns got ginger-nuts. (12) And ginger nuts are four-sided blocks, with sugar. (13) That is candy (13a) that children like. (14) Well, Saint Nicholas is an old man, with white hair. (15) He wears a red robe. (16) And wears a sort of shirt. (17) He also has a whitish grey. (18) A grey is a horse. (18a) (noble animal) (19) Just now I was talking about a steamboat. (20) A steamboat is a big ship, (21) a steamboat often has got a big funnel (21a) from which the steam comes (22) The children sing songs on the 5th of December, (23) that is because there is a big feast.

The texts in (3) illustrate two different ways of arranging information in an explanatory text. The first one follows the *temporal order* of events: first this, then that, and so on. The writer of the second text has chosen a different way to solve the problem of explanation: He focuses on the topic of the text and mentions all kinds of *properties* of Saint Nicholas in a rather associative way.

Clearly, these two texts differ in their global structure. The first one is dominated by an *action-line*: a temporal sequence of actions. The second one is dominated by a *property-line*: a list of characteristics of the topic. The general idea is that text structures reflect the way in which the writer has orga-

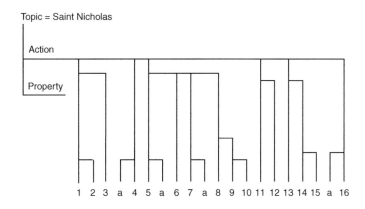

FIGURE 26.2a. Hierarchical structure of text (3a), an explanatory text dominated by a sequence of actions.

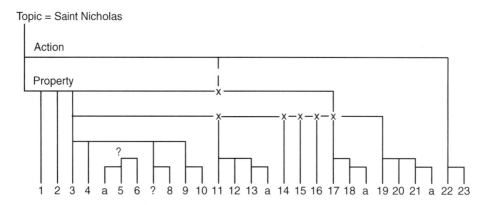

FIGURE 26.2b. Hierarchical structure of text (3a), an explanatory text dominated by a list of properties.

nized the information during the production of the text. For example, the first text can be produced by running through episodic memory; the actions or events are mentioned in temporal succession, and the text ends with the closing of an episode. The second text, on the other hand, is probably produced by searching semantic memory in an associative way. It resembles brainstorming; it lists information related to the topic, which is potentially relevant to explain it.

These two structures dominate the explanatory texts in the PISA-corpus. The research question then was as follows: Is it possible to analyze text structure in terms of notions like *action-* and *property-lines*, and can this be done in an objective, reliable way? PISA was developed in answer to this question. In a series of publications (Sanders, Janssen, Van der Pool, Schilperoord, & Van Wijk, 1996; Sanders & Van Wijk, 1996a, 1996b; Schilperoord, 1996; Van der Pool, 1995; Van Wijk & Sanders, 1999), it was argued that the product of this text-analytical method is cognitively interpretable. For that reason, we elaborate on it in the next section.

How Text Structure Provides Insight into the Writer's Cognitive Representation: An Example

Basics of Hierarchical Structure

The most important features of PISA are the following: First, it aims at psychological plausibility. Two features of mental processes have been incorporated. To begin with, people do not process language with-

out any guidance: In production, they have plans; in perception, expectations. These have been implemented as discourse schemes. Two of these determine the global organization of the topic's explanation [see (4)]:

(4) *Action-line*: What happens, what does the topic do, how is it used, how does it work, and so on?

Property-line: What are its features, parts, properties etc.?

Topic = ...
    |Action _____
    |Property _____

In addition, language users tend to process language in an incremental way (i.e., with little preplanning) (Levelt, 1989). This idea has been incorporated by processing text segments in their linear surface order, without a preceding global inspection of the text. It is this feature of incrementality that sets PISA apart from RST.

Second, PISA has a well-defined knowledge base. It depends upon linguistic and lexical knowledge only. PISA is procedural, because it specifies exactly which actions an analyst should undertake in certain circumstances. This procedural character is defined in terms of CONDITION–ACTION PAIRS. A very simple example is a rule such as: *If CONNECTOR (<{or}>) = True, then coordinate current segment with preceding segment.*

How does a PISA-analysis proceed? It takes the segments one after the other and decides on two issues. First, the position in the hierarchical structure: To which segment does this one connect, and how does it connect (subordination, coordination)? And second, the labeling in the relational structure: What is the meaning of the connection in terms of coherence relations (*cause*, *problem–solution*, *contrast*, etc.)?

For the moment, we only consider the hierarchical structure. Basically, there are four ways in which segments can be connected:

1. As an *action-line* to the discourse topic.
2. As a *property-line* to the discourse topic.
3. As a *response line*.
4. As a local *elaboration*.

The first two lines were introduced earlier, the last two were not. *Response-lines* are made up of a piece of text that begins with the statement of a goal or a problem, and continues with a specification of how the goal is to be achieved or the problem is to be solved. *Response-lines* may show up anyplace in a text. An *elaboration* on a neighboring segment may fulfill many functions, such as the specification of an object introduced in a preceding segment, a *concession* or *condition* with respect to the content of an earlier segment, *evidence* for it, and so on.

Some Linguistic Markers of Hierarchical Structure

How do linguistic features point out the structures that can be identified by PISA (see Figure 26.2 and 26.2b)? Let us start with the *action-line*. Its content is directly related to the text-topic. This line is built up of segments denoting actions or events. The main criterion used to decide this is the semantics of the main verb. This is the distinction between action and nonaction verbs, derived from the notions "stative" verb and "event" verb, introduced by Vendler (1967). The second criterion is the presence of temporal markers indicating temporal succession (*then, the next day, later, in the evening*).

The text-structurally very important function of the preposed subordinative clause is accounted for here. Especially the function of *if–when* clauses and purpose clauses depends on their placement in relation to the main clause. In a medial or final position, their role is indeed a local one, but in an initial position, their role becomes one of foregrounding information. They signal how to interpret the segments that follow directly,

and how to attach them to the preceding text. So preposed subordinated clauses are checked as possible temporal markers for the action expressed in the main clause.

In the example text (3a), the crucial events telling the temporally ordered story are the following segments (henceforth indicated with s); the linguistic markers are in italics.

s1,s1a	He comes, *on the 4th of december*
s4a,s4	*When he arrives*, everyone waves
s5	*At night*, he rides over the roofs
s11	*On the 5th of december* Saint Nicholas has his birthday
s13	*and then* he leaves again
s16a16	*When he leaves again*, the children sing

We have now discussed the top level of the text structure. How is the rest of the structure built up? There are some straightforward *local elaborations*, which are connected to the first antecedent and marked by referring expressions, such as in s2 (*that is*), s3 (*That day*) and s10 (*That is*). Also, we see some segments connected to the preceding text because of the hypotactic connectors, like s9 (*but he always gets something in return*).

Some other segments express actions, but they denote *temporal overlap* and are therefore coordinated to the preceding segment. An example is s6. This is not a new event but rather a subsequence about "riding the roofs," identified because of the grammatical construction: contraction of the subject in the second clause. The subject is shared with the first clause (s5), so s6 is coordinated to s5, and it is not placed on the *action-line*.

One thing in the global organization of text (1) is particularly remarkable: the lack of a *property-line*, which is strikingly present in text (2). The *property-line* and many elaborations are made up of segments with a similar syntactic form: a simple subject–predicate connection established by a nonaction verb. They only differ in the antecedent of the subject. The *property-line* consists of all characteristics attributed to the text-topic. Elaborations further specify a concept or idea mentioned earlier in the text.

What features are decisive for the structural analysis of text (36)? s1–s3 clearly constitute the *property-line*: stative verbs that express information about the text-topic. In s4, *They* refers back to an antecedent in last position (*little black men*). This leads to a subordination, whereas, for example, s7 refers back to the *Black Peters* in s4; they are in first position in the sentence frame; therefore, s7 is coordinated to s4. This same rule is very important in the case of s11 and s13a, two segments connected to the *action-line*. s22 and s11 are very solitary connections to the *action-line*. The linguistic indicators are the temporal marker *on the 5th of december* and the verbs *sing* and *got* the nuts. Also, there are a few problematic connections. s5 cannot be connected; *the* time has come for what? s19 has to be connected to the steamboat mentioned in s3, so it leads to a *discontinuity*.

This concludes a very concise overview of the relevant linguistic features (see Sanders & Van Wijk, 1996a, for more details).

Interpretation of the Structures: Strategies and Evaluation

Let us return for a moment to the rather peculiar areas of the structure of text (3b). There are two organizational problems in this text: One segment cannot possibly be connected to other segments in the text, and another one can only be connected in a discontinuous way. A good thing for this writer is that he signals this discontinuity in s19, but he also has trouble in the case of s14, which reopens the *property-line* after it was just closed off. Note that this sentence is almost literally the same as the opening sentence of the text, and that it is introduced by the pop marker *Well* (*Nou* in the original Dutch text) (cf. Polanyi, 1988), indicating a hierarchical "jump" in the text structure. Such discontinuities can be structurally defined in the following way [see (5)].

(5)

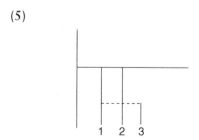

S3 is attached to s1. However, the two segments are separated from each other by the "intervening" s2. Structural discontinuities have been shown to be typical "errors" occurring in the writing products of immature writers (Sanders, 1992; Sanders & Van Wijk, 1996a, 1996b). Their writings often contain cases that go back to information mentioned earlier.

More in general, the corpus analyses show that writing strategies can be described in terms of text structures. Some writers stick to *property-lines*, others to *action-lines*, while still others combine the two. A purely indicative observation is that texts dominated by *property-lines* often tend to be rich in specific information but show organizational problems as well, probably due to the writer's lack of a clear plan. Texts dominated by *action-lines* are often clearly organized but do not contain much specific information.

Text Structure and Writing Development: Text-Analytical Study 1

In this section and the next, we discuss two text-analytical studies in the field of cognitive research on writing processes. While the first study, by Van der Pool (1995), attempts to uncover aspects of the *development* of writing proficiency, the second study, by Schilperoord and Sanders (1999), explores retrieval processes in *expert* writing. Both studies exemplify how (structural) text analysis contributes to the construction and testing of theories of writing.

From Conversation to Composition

Bereiter and Scardamalia (1987) typify learning how to write as a process of going "from conversation to composition." Writing is difficult for children due to the absence of a communicative partner. If they *tell* a certain story, their retrieval processes are guided by responses of their interlocutors ("Tell me more about that!"; "Why do think that?"). When such responses are absent, they have to solve the problem of adjusting the text to the reader's needs entirely by themselves. However, children will gradually become aware of the demands of the specific communicative circumstances in which the text is to operate. Because this development leaves its traces at the level of textual content and structural make up, the question is: What do these traces tell us about developmental aspects of writing?

To study this question, Van der Pool (1995) used a corpus of writing products of children ages 10, 12, and 15. They were asked to describe a person they would like to resemble, and were urged to tell things about that person, such as their age, character, looks, and profession. Both the content and the structure of the texts were analyzed according to the PISA algorithm, which allowed Van der Pool to rephrase the developmental issue into text-analytical terms: How does (choice of) content and structure of texts differ among children ages 10, 12, and 15? In the next sections, we examine these differences and see what they imply for the development of writing skills.

Content and Structure of Children's Texts

Text (6)[1] is an example of an actual person description, written by a 10-year-old boy.

(6)

1	He is a teacher in Heervarebeek
2	He teaches children to learn
2a	like arithmetic Language History Geography
3	He is round 40 years old
4	He wears a suit and a white skirt, and black shoes
5	and looks healthy
6	On Sundays, Wednesdays and Saturdays cycling
6a	Correcting notebooks
6b	Walking in the woods
7	His name is Uncle Harrie
8	Sometimes he goes to Tilburg to the families
8a	and window-shopping on Sundays as well.

Informal observation tells us that this text shows considerable flaws, both in content and structure. First, only after seven clauses does the writer reveal whom this text is about (s7: His name is Uncle Harrie). Sec-

ond, the information seems to be selected rather arbitrarily; the text structure suggests an almost accidental order of idea retrieval. Finally, the text ends quite abruptly, as if the writer could not think of anything else to write about Uncle Harrie.

With this in mind, we now turn our attention to a person description produced by an older writer.[2] This text differs from the one in (6) in a number of ways. The first difference is shown in (7).

(7)

1	I would,
1a	if forced to make a choice
2	like to be like Ed Nijpels

Unlike the 10-year-old, this writer starts by properly *introducing* the topic of his text: Ed Nijpels, the man he would like to resemble. After the introduction comes the main part of the text: the actual person description. However, rather than summing up a couple of features, the writer presents an ordered list of characteristics that he would like to have. For example, following his description of various of Nijpels's activities, he adds a comment to it [see (8)].

(8)

1	It is this variation that appeals to me very much

In addition, he brings his text properly to a close by including a *recapitulation* [see (9)].

(9)

1	Summarizing, I must say that in any case it looks as if Ed Nijpels feels comfortable with himself
2	Or
2a	to put it informally
2	"he likes who he is"
3	and that is something worth striving for!

Properties like these provide a first impression of how texts of mature writers differ from those of immature writers. To further refine this impression, let us now see what a PISA-analysis reveals about the hierarchical and relational structure of the various texts. The overall hierarchical structure, or the *superstructure* of a person description written by a *mature* writer consists of three parts: introduction (I), description (D), and conclusion (C). This structure is shown in Figure 26.3.

Figure 26.3 represents the *discourse schematic knowledge* a mature writer puts to use in producing a person description (see section Basics of hierarchical structure), or his writing *plan*.[3] So, by examining how text (6) relates to this discourse scheme, we get an impression of the kind of writing plan an *immature* writer uses to produce a person description. This plan is shown in Figure 26.4.

Figure 26.4 shows us that the descriptive part of this text is little more than a set of arbitrarily selected elements with respect to the topic. The topic is not introduced before s7; furthermore, no introduction is provided, nor does the text contain a conclusion.

The immature nature of this text becomes even more apparent if we look at the *contents* of the segments and their *relational* structure, and compare these features to those of the mature text. The successive segments of the immature text inform us about the person's career (s1–2a), a personal particular (s3), his appearance (s4), his career again (s5), his hobby (s6–6b), another personal particular (s7), and another hobby (s8–8a). Hence, the list is poorly ordered, because it displays two discontinuities (see Interpretation of the Structures: Strategies and Evaluation): 1,2a–5, and 6,6a–8,8a.

Finally, labeling the relations between the segments (see section Basics of hierarchical structure), results in the list shown in (10).

Topic = person

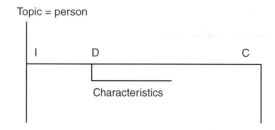

FIGURE 26.3. Discourse scheme for person descriptions.

Topic = Uncle Harrie

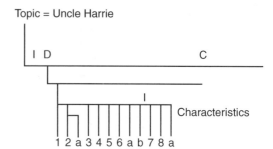

FIGURE 26.4. Hierarchical structure of a person description by a 10-year-old.

(10)

Segment	Relation
1	SPECIFICATION (unknown topic)
2	CONSEQUENCE (1/teaches)
2a	LIST (specification)
3	LIST specification (unknown topic)
4	LIST specification (unknown topic)
5	LIST specification (unknown topic)
6	LIST specification (unknown topic)
a	LIST specification (unknown topic)
b	LIST specification (unknown topic)
7	LIST specification (topic)
8	LIST specification (topic)
a	LIST specification (topic)

Hence, the main goal of the immature writer's plan has been to *list* specifications regarding his topic. The text's overall coherence fully depends on *topical connectivity*: All segment are subordinated to an overall topical entity and no between-segment relations are realized.

Now let us compare these characteristics to those of the mature text. Its relational structure is presented in (11), together with the full text.

(11)

	Segments	Relation
1	I would	SPECIFICATION (topic)
1a	if forced to make a choice,	CONDITION (1)
1	like to be Ed Nijpels	SPECIFICATION (1)
2	He looks quite nice,	LIST specification (1)
3	is well dressed,	LIST specification (1)
4	and expresses himself quite well	LIST specification (1)

5	Besides, he has undertaken all kinds of activities alongside his varied career.	EVALUATION (5)
6	It is this variation that appeals to me much.	LIST specification (1)
7	His main job at the moment is being mayor of Breda,	CONTRAST (7)
8	but as a compere on TV he holds his own as well.	LIST specification (1)
9a	When he relaxes after his busy work,	LIST specification (9a)
9	he can be found on the tennis court	LIST specification (9a)
10	and the evenings he likes to be with friends or on his own reading a nice book	LIST specification (1)
11	Because of his open character he makes friends easily	LIST specification (1)
12	and makes contacts easily.	LIST specification (1)
13	As a mayor he tries to stand close to people.	LIST specification (1)
14	The age of Ed Nijpels	LIST specification (14)
14a	(round about 40)	EVALUATION (14)
14	is an age which has many advantages:	EVALUATION (14)
15	one has had the chance to make something of one's life.	CONCLUSION (1)
16	One doesn't need to be a "he-man" anymore.	ALTERNATIVE (17)
	Summarizing, I must say that it looks as if Ed Nijpels feels comfortable,	CONCLUSION (1)
17	or to put it informally	EVALUATION (18)
	"he likes who he is"	
18a	and that is something worth striving for.	
18		
19		

Like the other text, this text also lists personal characteristics, but the relational structure of the descriptive part (s2–16) shows that there is a lot more going on than just listing. Coherence relations are also realized *between* segments (e.g., s5 and s6, s14, s15, and s16, etc.), so the relational structure does not rely on listed segments attached to a superordinate topic. In addition, the content of the segments shows that the writer actu-

ally *addresses* personal characteristics rather then just listing a couple. He first describes the person's appearance (s2, 3), provides personal particulars (s4), and then he informs the reader about the person's career (s5–8), his hobbies (s9a–10), his character and his age (s14–16). In addition, as we already saw, the descriptive part is properly introduced (s1–1a) and brought to a close (s17–19). Hence, all parts of the superstructure (see Figure 26.3) are realized. Finally, unlike the immature text, the core part of this text shows several layers of descriptions (i.e., a main line of listed features, together with several local elaborations and evaluations).

From Text Structure to Text Planning

The previous section has shown us which differences between the texts of immature and mature writers are revealed by text structure analysis. Let us now examine what these differences tell us about the development of writing skills.

Writing a proper personal description includes *introducing* the topic of the text, *characterizing* it by listing/elaborating various themes (career, personal characteristics, character, etc.), and *bringing it to a close* by some concluding statements. Mature writers also develop themes further, for example, by *elaborating* on them, *evaluating* them, or *adding context* to them. Introducing, characterizing, evaluating, and so on, can thus be seen as *a repertoire of retrieval strategies* that mature writers have apparently mastered.

Now, apart from *listing* characteristics, these strategies are almost completely absent in the writing processes of young children. Van der Pool's data (1995) show that their retrieval processes rely almost entirely on "list" strategies, often at the expense of "evaluate" strategies. This contrasts sharply with the retrieval processes of 15-year-old writers, which are properly balanced between the various strategies. For example, 15-year-olds add context and elaborations three times more often than do 10-year-olds.

Van der Pool (1995) also found age-related effects on text structuring. For example, although structural discontinuities remain present in the writings of 10-, 12- and 15-year-old writers, they vanish almost completely in the writing products of older writers. Hence, mature writers seem to be able to structure information in accordance with their *communicative intentions*, whereas young writers structure information according to the (random) *order of their retrieval*. Structural planning abilities thus seem to come with age and therefore make up an important feature of the development of writing abilities. Text analysis has brought this feature to light, as it did with respect to developmental aspects of *conceptual* processes. Because both relational and hierarchical aspects of text structure are constitutive text principles, text analysis indeed provides a window on the cognition of writing.

Text Structure and Retrieval in Expert Writing: Text-Analytical Study 2

This section examines what text analysis reveals about *retrieval processes* of expert writers producing routine texts: in this case, lawyers producing simple judicial letters. Though limited to this text genre, their writing processes represent a state of writing proficiency that has resulted from sustained effort and repeated performance on certain writing tasks. This writing is fully driven by discourse schemes, which specify content categories and ways to arrange them. One particularly important characteristic of expert writing is its predominantly *linear* mode of processing, with almost no online revisions (Schilperoord, 1996, p. 56ff).

Retrieval and Pausing during Writing

One particularly transparent feature of retrieval, even in expert writing, is that it is *discontinuous*. New elements tend to be retrieved *incrementally*. This is especially manifest by the patterning of writing *pauses*. If we actually observe an expert writer, this is what we see (12).

(12)

Translating pausing translating pausing . . .
$\rightarrow$ time

Periods of scribal inactivity, or pauses, alternate with periods of translating: actually putting words on paper or typing them on screen. At the very least, it seems plausible to

assume that a writer pauses *in order to* retrieve conceptual information that is *subsequently* translated and added to the text produced so far. Retrieving information from longterm memory (LTM) probably requires a certain amount of time-consuming effort, so it seems that a *causal relation* between a "pause–translate"/"retrieve–execute" pair can be inferred: What is executed at stage X is retrieved during the stage immediately preceding X.[4]

How can we further characterize these retrieval processes? As our first case study has already demonstrated, the method of structural text analysis can be employed to that end. However, in our second case study, we go one step further: We also examine how retrieval processes can be characterized in terms of the *amount of cognitive effort required by different kinds of retrieval processes*. Our approach is to combine pause time data with text analysis, that is, to combine *process data with product data*. In the next sections, we first look at the distribution of pause time. Next, we examine the hierarchical structure of judicial letters. Finally, we use these structures as input in order to reconstruct retrieval processes in judicial writing, and relate these processes to the distribution of pause time.

Pause Time Distribution

Whatever cognitive process is reflected by pauses, one thing is immediately clear: Pauses differ in length. In psycholinguistics, it is widely agreed that such differences correlate with the intensity of cognitive processes. The longer a pause, the more effort is required by the process that this pause reflects. With this in mind, let us now look at an actual piece of text production. Figure 26.5 shows us about 35 seconds of (dictated) text production, represented in terms of the "pause (off time)–translate (on time)" alternation.

In Figure 26.5, both pausing and translating have been plotted cumulatively over the total production time. The horizontal axis represents *translating time* (adding up to about 11 seconds) and the vertical axis, *pausing time* (about 23 seconds).

Note that pausing time is far from being equally distributed across the total production time. There are three periods dominated

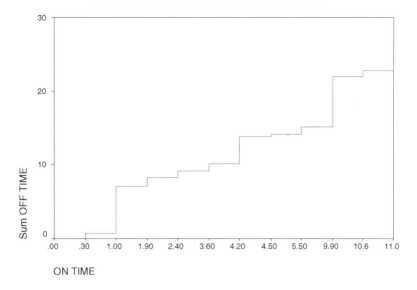

FIGURE 26.5. Pausing (off time) and translating (on time).

by pausing, one after 1 second, another after 16 seconds, and a third after about 25 seconds. Now, if we combine these observations with features of the surface text, it turns out that the two longest pauses (the first and the third one) occur between *paragraphs*, whereas the second, somewhat shorter pause occurs between two *sentences* within a paragraph. So it would seem that certain *structural* features of the text *determine* the distribution of pause time. In fact, the pattern observed in Figure 26.5 turns out to be a remarkably stable one: Our analysis of pause time distribution in a large corpus of writing processes shows that, on average, writers pause about 8 seconds before a new paragraph, while they pause only 3 seconds before a new sentence (Schilperoord 1996, p. 89). In addition, paragraph and sentence boundaries particularly attract pause activity. Here, writers pause almost all the time, whereas pauses occur only at about 60% at other locations. Granting the correlation between pause-time variation and cognitive effort, it would thus seem that *structural* features of the text predict at what moments during writing extensive retrieving will take place. A promising prospect indeed!

However, there is a catch. Although the division of texts into paragraphs and sentences suggests some kind of hierarchical organization, it is not all that informative to state: "Longer pauses occur before paragraphs, so

conceptualizing paragraphs is more costly." One would like to probe deeper into the nature of these processes and their cognitive costs. At this point the PISA-algorithm comes into play, in that it allows us to examine the hierarchical structure of judicial letters in far more detail.

The Hierarchical Structure of Routine Judicial Letters

To examine their hierarchical structure, a corpus of judicial letters was analyzed using the PISA method (Schilperoord & Sanders, 1999). In (13), part of one of these letters is shown.[5]

(13)

1	Dear confrere (my learned friend),
2	On behalf of Mr. NAME,
2a	living at ADRESS,
2	I hereby strongly object to the summary dismissal given to him by FIRM.
3	First of all, this dismissal cannot be motivated
3a	Considering your client's letter to my client,
3	as you are well aware.
4	And second, there is no motive at all.
5	The fact that my client was in jail for a couple of days in connection with a case dating from long before he started working for your firm, is of no significance in this case.
6	You have also informed me that my client has used abusive language,

6a   that is, that he started to taunt and rave
6b   after he was given his dismissal.
7   He allegedly cursed your client.
8   Again this is no reason for a dismissal,
8a   quite apart from the fact that he was given his dismissal beforehand
9   I hereby summon your client to withdraw the summary dismissal by return post. (. . .)

An analysis of various of these letters reveals that their hierarchical structure (the discourse scheme) can be characterized as illustrated in Figure 26.6. This discourse scheme contains three levels (indicated by Roman numerals). The first level (I) is the superstructure of judicial letters. It specifies parts such as "greeting," "introduction," "append signature," and so on. The second level (II) constitutes the letters *core part*, which displays a highly regular structure. Lawyers perform two kinds of *speech acts*: They make certain *judgments*, and they *appeal* to their opponents to take certain actions. This structural pattern therefore consists of a *judgment* line, and an *appeal* line. A judgment line is made up of segments expressing the judgment itself, and of segments justifying that judgment. The same is true for the appeal line.

Finally, the third hierarchical level (III) constitutes various kinds of *local elaborations*. Often, segments expand or elaborate on segments expressing judgments or appeals. These segments make up the part of the text that cannot be predicted by the hierarchical structure in Figure 26.6. Their inclusion depends on how the lawyer, more or less "on the fly," estimates the need his readers will have for further information or clarification.

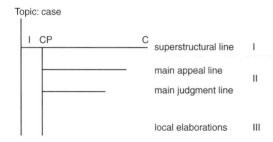

Topic: case

I CP — C superstructural line   I

main appeal line   II

main judgment line

local elaborations   III

FIGURE 26.6. Discourse scheme for judicial letters (I, introduction; CP, core part; C, conclusion).

All these levels can be easily found in the example text (13). For instance, s1 expresses a "greeting," hence constituting the introduction part of the superstructure. The letter's core part starts with s2 expressing a judgement, which so *opens* the judgement line. s3, s4, s6, and s8 serve to justify the lawyer's judgement and so *constitute* the judgement line. s9 expresses an appeal (the lawyer *demands* that his opponent revoke the dismissal), so here the main *appeal line* is opened. Finally, s2a, s3a, s5, s6a, s6b, and s7 express various kinds of local elaborations, all located at the third hierarchical level. In the next section, we apply the three hierarchical levels in order to reconstruct different kinds of retrieval processes.

Hierarchical Structures and Retrieval Processes

Cognitive text analysis claims that tree structures, such as the one in Figure 26.6, assess the writer's mental representation of a text. In other words, the tree structure represents the writer's plan for retrieving information from LTM. This enables us to reconstruct retrieval processes in terms of this structure. A suitable way to do this is to model these processes in terms of *production rules*. A production rule is an IF–THEN pair: the IF-part defines some processing goal, or state of affairs, whereas the THEN-part defines some processing action to be taken. Some of these rules are shown in (14).[6]

(14)

IF the goal is:	→	THEN retrieve information specifying:
1. PRODUCE {core part}	→	JUDGE {topic} & APPEAL {topic}
2. JUDGE {topic}	→	judgement & JUSTIFY {judgement}
3. JUDGE {topic} is finished	→	SWITCH {APPEAL {topic}}
4. APPEAL {topic}	→	appeal & JUSTIFY {appeal}
5. JUSTIFY {judgement}	→	reasons & fixme/- denials & ELABORATE {reason/ ± denials}
6. ELABORATE {reason}	→	[context] & [specification] & [tinge] & [. . .]

[ ] = optional; capital letters denote processes; lower-case letters denotes content elements.

Production rule 1 "says": If you want to produce a core part, start by judging the topic and proceed by stating an appeal with respect to it. This rule is responsible for retrieval processes that resulted in the entire core part of the letter: s2–9 in the example text. This rule is decomposed into two recursive production rules (2 and 3). Rule 2 guides retrieval operations that have resulted in s2–8a of the letter. A special production rule 3 is responsible for switching from judgements to appeals. It activates rule 4.

Note that this way of modeling retrieval processes results in rules that are *structured hierarchically*. Lower order rules are embedded into higher order rules. Suppose the writer decides to add elaborating information to the text (e.g., s2a, s3a, and s5). The process responsible for retrieving elaborating information (adding context, specifications, etc.) can then be modeled as (15).

(15) (PRODUCE {core part} *embeds*
    (JUDGE {topic} *embeds*
      (JUSTIFY {reason} *embeds*
        (ELABORATE {reason})))).

Because our primary interest in this case study concerns the *cognitive effort* required by various types of retrieval processes, this way of modeling retrieval processes allows for various hypotheses. The guiding principle is: The more a certain rule is controlled by higher order rules (or: the deeper it is embedded), the less cognitive effort is required for its application. Technically speaking: we hypothesize the hierarchical order of retrieval processes to show *top-down facilitation.*[7]

If this hypothesis is basically correct, then several interesting predictions follow. First, it would lead us to predict that ELABORATE-processes are relatively cheap, whereas rules

guiding a switch between main lines (e.g., from judging to appealing) reflect major attention shifts in retrieving and therefore are costly. Second, production rules are closely intertwined with the text in which they result. Applying the production rule JUDGE {topic}, for example, takes place right before the second segment, but also before all segments constituting the judgement main line in the text. Hence, we predict retrieval to be relatively costly at these locations.

As we already noted, hypotheses like the ones just put forth can be tested by looking at the *pause times* relative to the various segments in the text. By combining the kind of process data shown in Figure 26.5 with various production rules for retrieval, our hypotheses can be stated in terms of pause times: The cheaper the operation, the shorter the pause. Table 26.1 shows the *order* of rules in terms of the *predicted declining* pause times (first column). Each rule is furthermore located relative to the text in terms of corresponding segments (second column). Finally, Table 26.1 shows the actual (average) pause times for each kind of retrieval process and text location (third column).

There is one obvious mismatch between the predicted pause times and those actually observed: The retrieval operation PRODUCE {core part} takes less pause time to execute than was hypothesized. Arguably, the opening of a core text part also marks a transition at the level of the text's superstructure. Maybe for expert writers the switch from the *Introduction* to the *Core* part is so well entrenched that retrieval processes at this stage proceed with greater ease than our model predicts. However, all remaining predictions are actually borne out by the data. Finally, one may wonder whether the cognitive costs required by executing retrieval processes such as those in (14) exceeds those occurring else-

TABLE 26.1. Retrieving Processes, Locations, and Pause Times

Retrieving processes	Locations (segment number)	Pause time (msec)
PRODUCE {core part}	2	4,085
SWITCH from JUDGE {topic} to APPEAL {topic}	9	9,283
JUDGE {topic}/APPEAL {topic}	3, 4, 6, 8	5,979
ELABORATE {judgment/appeal/reason}	2a, 3a, 5, 6a, 6b, 7	1,856

where. To check whether this was indeed the case, we measured the duration of pauses occurring *within* segments. The average length of within-segment pauses turned out to be about 0.7 seconds.

Conclusion

The most important contribution of this chapter concerns the correspondence between the hierarchical text structure on the one hand, and developmental aspects and online retrieving processes on the other. This relationship suggests that cognitive writing activities are—at least to a certain extent—reflected in the hierarchical structure of the text produced. This underlines the merits of combining text analysis and empirical research on writing processes. It is the combination of various kinds of data that promises to provide the tools we need in order to develop testable psycholinguistic models and theories of language production at the text level. By way of concluding this chapter, we summarize two of the main virtues of the method of text analysis for cognitive research on writing.

1. *It allows us to characterize retrieval processes in great detail.* As we noted in Pause time distribution, structural units such as "paragraphs" and "sentences" have little to tell us about the nature of retrieval processes. In fact, the level of detail of reconstructing these processes is severely restricted (see 16).

(16) RETRIEVE {paragraph}
     RETRIEVE {sentence}

As our two case studies have demonstrated, the quite scarce level of detail of the rules in (16) contrasts sharply with the level of detail obtained when PISA-derived text structures are used as input for reconstructing retrieval operations.

2. *It allows us to locate these processes relative to the growing text and model cognitive effort required.* If hierarchical text structure is used as input for reconstructing retrieval processes, we are able to locate precisely these processes relative to the growing text. Let us once again look at the hierarchical structure of the example text discussed in

(13) and "zoom in" on the production of s4 and s5 (see Figure 26.7).

The relation between s4 and s5, and their position within the hierarchical framework can be assessed as follows: At level III, s4 and s5 are related in terms of reason–elaboration; at level II, s4 is a segment attached to the main judgment line, and at level I, the main judgement line is part of the core part of the text. Each hierarchical level can be used to reconstruct retrieval processes. Hence s5 and s4 result from applying the rules in (17).

(17)

ELABORATE →	[context] & [specification] &
{reason}	[tinge] & [. . .]
JUSTIFY →	reasons & ± denials &
{judgement}	ELABORATE {reason/± denials}

Together, this part of the texts results from applying (18).

(18)

1. PRODUCE →	JUDGE {topic} & APPEAL
{core part}	{topic}
2. JUDGE →	judgement & JUSTIFY
{topic}	{judgement}

[ ], optional; capital letters denote processes; lower case letters denote content elements.

By bringing together the kinds of data discussed so far, that is, text structural data and processing data, we are able to *reconstruct* retrieval processes, *locate* them relative to the growing text, and test hypotheses regarding their *cognitive efforts*. This is how text structure analysis provides a window on the cognition of writing.

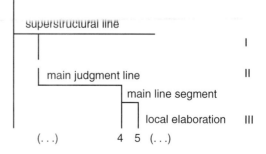

Topic: dismissal client

superstructural line — I

main judgment line — II

main line segment

local elaboration — III

(. . .)   4 5 (. . .)

FIGURE 26.7. Production of s4–5.

Acknowledgments

We would like to thank Steve Graham, Marion Tillema, and Daphne van Weijen for comments on earlier versions of this chapter, and Margriet van der Meulen for editorial assistance.

Notes

1. We have omitted all spelling and grammatical errors, since they are not relevant for the present discussion. See Van der Pool (1995, p. 3) for a translation of the original text, including English counterparts of these errors.
2. The full text will be given later on. Here we stick to those parts of it that are absent in the former text.
3. Discourse schemes have been identified for a number of text genres, including scientific papers (Van Dijk & Kintsch, 1983), expository texts (Sanders & Van Wijk, 1996a, 1996b), judicial letters (Schilperoord, 1996), and argumentative texts (Van Wijk, 1999).
4. Apart from retrieving words, or concepts from LTM, pauses may reflect processes such as considering two alternative wordings, aligning already retrieved concepts into a well-formed sentence, structuring information into a section, or monitoring parts of the text produced so far. So, just on "the face of it," we cannot tell what cognitive process a particular pause reflects. However, because of the predominantly linear nature of expert writing, it seems safe to assume that the vast majority of pauses indeed reflect retrieval operations. One compelling piece of evidence is the fact that in expert writing, up to 90% of all pauses are in fact followed by a period of translating (Schilperoord 1996, p. 58; see also Schilperoord, 2002).
5. The letter is the one that actually resulted from the production process depicted in Figure 26.5. We observe the production of the final part of s3a , s4 and s5, and the first part of s6. The two long pauses shown in Figure 26.6 precede s4 and s6, whereas the somewhat shorter pause precedes s5.
6. For further details about this way of modeling retrieval processes, see Van der Pool (1995), Schilperoord (1996), and, especially, Van Wijk (1999).
7. A theoretical account of this hypothesis can be found in Schilperoord (1996, p. 208ff.) and Anderson (1983, p. 146).

References

Bereiter, C., & Scardamalia, M. (1983). Levels of inquiry in writing research. In P. Mosenthal, L. Tamor, & S. Walmsley (Eds.), *Research on writing: Principles and methods* (pp. 3–25). New York: Longman.

Bereiter, C., & Scardamalia, M. (1987). *The psychology of written composition.* Hillsdale, NJ: Erlbaum.

Brown, G., & Yule, G. (1983). *Discourse analysis.* Cambridge, UK: Cambridge University Press.

Flower, L. S., & Hayes, J. R. (1981). A cognitive process theory of writing. *College Composition and Communication, 32,* 229–243.

Hobbs, J. R. (1990). *Literature and cognition.* Menlo Park, CA: Centre for the Study of Language and Information, Stanford University.

Hovy, E. H. (1990). Parsimonious and profligate approaches to the question of discourse structure relations. In *Proceedings of the 5th International Workshop on Natural Language Generation* (pp. 128–136). East Stroudsburg, PA: Association for Computational Linguistics.

Hunt, K. (1970). Syntactic maturity in school children and adults. *Monographs of the Society for Research in Child Development, 35,* 1–67.

Kintsch, W., & van Dijk, T. A. (1978). Toward a model of text comprehension and production. *Psychological Review, 85,* 363–394.

Levelt, W. J. M. (1989). *Speaking: From intention to articulation.* Cambridge, MA: MIT Press.

Lintermann-Rygh, I. (1985). Connector density—an indicator of essay quality? *Text, 5,* 347–357.

Mann, W. C., Matthiessen, C. M. I. M., & Thompson, S. A. (1992). Rhetorical structure theory and text analysis. In W. C. Mann, & S. A. Thompson (Eds.), *Discourse description: Diverse linguistic analyses of a fund-raising text* (pp. 39–78). Amsterdam: Benjamins.

Mann, W. C., & Thompson, S. A. (1988). Rhetorical structure theory: Toward a functional theory of text organization. *Text, 8,* 243–281.

Polanyi, L. (1988). A formal model of the structure of discourse. *Journal of Pragmatics, 12,* 601–638.

Sanders, T., Janssen, D., Van der Pool, E., Schilperoord, J., & Van Wijk, C. (1996). Hierarchical text structure in writing products and writing processes. In G. Rijlaarsdam, H. van den Bergh & M. Couzijn (Eds.), *Theories, models and methodology in writing research* (pp. 472–493). Amsterdam: Amsterdam University Press.

Sanders, T., & Van Wijk, C. (1996a). PISA—a procedure for analyzing the structure of explanatory texts. *Text, 16*(1), 91–132.

Sanders, T., & Van Wijk, C. (1996b). Text analysis as a research tool: How hierarchical structure gives insight in the writer's representation. In C. Levy & S. Ransdell (Eds.), *The science of writing* (pp. 251–270). Mahwah, NJ: Erlbaum.

Sanders, T. J. M. (1992). *Discourse structure and coherence: Aspects of a cognitive theory of discourse representation.* Unpublished doctoral dissertation, Tilburg University, The Netherlands.

Sanders, T. J. M. (1997). Semantic and pragmatic sources of coherence: On the categorization of coherence relations in context. *Discourse Processes, 24,* 119–147.

Sanders, T. J. M., Spooren, W. P. M., & Noordman, L. G. M. (1992). Toward a taxonomy of coherence relations. *Discourse Processes, 15,* 1–35.

Schilperoord, J. (1996). *It's about time: Temporal aspects of cognitive processes in text production.* Amsterdam: Rodopi.

Schilperoord, J. (2002). On the cognitive status of pauses in discourse production. In T. Olive & C. M. Levy (Eds.). *Contemporary tools and techniques for studying writing* (pp. 61–90). Dordrecht, The Netherlands: Kluwer.

Schilperoord, J., & Sanders, T. (1999). How hierarchical structure affects retrieval processes: Implications of pause and text analysis. In G. Rijlaarsdam & E. Esperet (Series Eds.) and M. Torrance & D. Galbraith (Eds.), *Knowing what to write: Conceptual processes in writing* (Studies in Writing, Vol. 4, pp. 13–30). Amsterdam: Amsterdam University Press.

Van der Pool, E. (1995). *Writing as a conceptual process: A text analytical study of developmental aspects.* Unpublished doctoral dissertation, Tilburg University, The Netherlands.

Van Dijk, T. A. (1977). *Text and context: Explorations in the semantics and pragmatics of discourse.* New York: Longman.

Van Dijk, T. A. (1980). *Macrostructures.* Hillsdale, NJ: Erlbaum.

Van Dijk, T. A., & Kintsch, W. (1983). *Strategies of discourse comprehension.* Orlanda, FL: Academic Press.

Van Wijk, C. (1992). Information analysis in written discourse. In J. De Jong & L. Verhoeven (Eds.), *The construct of language proficiency* (pp. 85–99). Amsterdam: Benjamins.

Van Wijk, C. (1999). Conceptual processes in argumentation: A developmental perspective. In G. Rijlaarsdam & E. Esperet (Series Eds.) and M. Torrance & D. Galbraith (Vol. Eds.), *Knowing what to write: Conceptual processes in writing* (Studies in Writing, Vol. 4, pp. 31–51). Amsterdam: Amsterdam University Press.

Van Wijk, C., & Sanders, T. (1999). Identifying writing strategies through text analysis. *Written Communication, 1,* 52–76.

Vendler, Z. (1967). Verbs and times. In Z. Vendler (Ed.), *Linguistics in philosophy* (pp. 97–121). Ithaca, NY: Cornell University Press.

Chapter 27

Applications of Computers in Assessment and Analysis of Writing

Mark D. Shermis, Jill Burstein, *and* Claudia Leacock

It has been almost 40 years since Ellis "Bo" Page prophesized the imminence of grading essays by computer. As a former high school English teacher, he envisioned a world where computers could assist in reducing the burden of grading written English. Later, as a seminal educational researcher, his desire was to implement a system that would operationalize what 50 years of research has shown us: Students become better writers by writing more. His landmark article in *Phi Delta Kappan* (Page, 1966) forecast this, but it took another 7 years to produce a working model (Ajay, Tillett, & Page, 1973) using FORTRAN code and a large mainframe computer. The result was Project Essay Grade (PEG). In order to submit text to the essay grader, written documents had to be transferred to awkward IBM 80-column punched cards, an overwhelming task for the technology of the day. Beyond this handicap, the technology performed as well or better than the ratings assigned by humans (Ajay et al., 1973).

In the early 1990s, Page refashioned PEG with a more sophisticated parser, real-time calculations, and a Web-based interface (Shermis, Mzumara, Olson, & Harrington, 2001). The details of this new format are explored further in this chapter, demonstrating the way automated essay scoring (AES) works, the kinds of software programs it uses, and some emerging applications.

AES is the evaluation of written work via computers. Initial research restricted AES to English but has recently extended to Japanese (Kawate-Mierzejewska, 2003), Hebrew (Vantage Learning, n.d.), Bahasa (Vantage Learning, 2002), and other languages. The interfaces are predominantly Internet-based, though there are some implementations that use CD-ROMs.

Most packages place documents within an electronic portfolio. They provide a holistic assessment of the writing, which can be supplemented by trait scores based on an established rubric, and may provide qualitative critiques through discourse analysis. Most use ratings from humans as the criterion for determining accuracy of performance, though some of the packages will permit validation against other sources of information (e.g., large informational databases).

Obviously, computers do not "understand" written messages in the same way that humans do, a point that may be unnerving until one reflects on ways alternative technologies achieve similar results. Thus, cooking was once associated primarily with convection heating, a form of heating external to the food. But by thinking "outside the box," we can see that the same outcome can be achieved by a technology not based on convection, but on molecular activity within the uncooked items (i.e., the microwave oven).

The computer scores essays according to models of what human raters consider desirable and undesirable writing elements. Collections of these elements are referred to as "traits," the intrinsic characteristics of writing called "trins"; the specific elements are called proxies or "proxes" (Page and Petersen, 1995).

The differentiation of "trins" and "proxes" is parallel to that of "latent" and "observed" variables in the social sciences: thus, the score on an IQ test might be thought of as a "prox" (specific element) for the underlying characteristics of the "trin" (conceptualization) intelligence.

AES software packages include computer programs that parse the essay text for the purpose of identifying hundreds of prox variables ranging from simple to complex. A deceptively simple variable is essay length. Although raters value this attribute, the relationship to good writing is not linear but rather is logarithmic (i.e., raters value the amount of writing output up to a point, but then they look for other salient aspects of writing once the quantity threshold is met). Similarly, the number of occurrences of "because" is a relevant feature. Although seemingly a superficial feature, it importantly serves as a proxy for the beginning of a dependent clause. And this, in turn, is reflective of sentence complexity.

When human raters comprise the criterion against which rating performance is judged, AES engines work off of a statistical model developed using the following procedures:

1. Obtain a sample of 500 essays with human ratings (4–8) on each essay.
2. Randomly select 300 essays and regress the human ratings against the variable set available from various computational analyses of a text.
3. Use a subset of consolidated feature variables, or the factor structure underlying a set of feature variables, in order to formulate a regression equation. The equation does not have to have a linear basis, but linear models are easier to explain.
4. Cross-validate the regression equation on the 200 remaining essays to determine whether the original regression line has suffered from shrinkage.

Reliability and Validity of Automated Essay Scoring Systems

As is true with most performance assessments, the indices for reliability and validity are generally lower than those associated with multiple-choice tests, but they fall well within the realm of psychometric acceptability. And as Bennett and Bejar (1998) point out, attempts to maximize reliability of performance assessments may undermine validity. For example, if raters are asked to concentrate their attention on, say, six traits of writing, the consequence may be that they ignore other aspects essential to differentiating good from poor writing performance. Issues of reliability and validity with human raters are covered elsewhere (Cizek & Page, 2003; Keith, 2003).

Reliability

Most of the literature on reliability for objective tests is either focused on measures of internal consistency or examines changes in test performance over time (test–retest). These types of assessments do not make sense in the context of automated essay scoring since, for example, test–retest reliability is perfect under machine-scored conditions (i.e., one will get the same score for the essay no matter when one asks the automated essay scorer to evaluate it). In a performance assessment such as AES, where the criterion is drawn from human ratings, the concern is not so much that the ratings are "reliable" but rather that the raters are in agreement with one another regarding their observations. So it is possible to have perfect covariation among a set of ratings (i.e., perfect reliability) but little in the way of actual agreement.

Accordingly, two indices are commonly provided for agreement: exact and adjacent. Exact agreement is an estimate of the level of agreement among either a set of raters or among both an AES engine and set of raters' evaluation of writing. If, for example, a 6-point scale were used, a 3 from Rater A and a 3 from Rater B would count as a "match" for the purposes of calculating exact agreement.

Adjacent agreement stipulates that scores from adjacent categories are equivalent. So a

3 from Rater A and a 4 from Rater B, on the hypothetical 6-point scale, are viewed as equivalent. This tradition arises from the way in which human-scored essays are often handled. With discrepancies of more than one point between two raters, a third rater resolves the disagreement. Otherwise, the ratings are found to be close enough to make an overall decision about the quality of writing.

Most of the evidence suggests that AES evaluations are equivalent to or better than evaluations of reliability with human raters (Elliot, 2003; Landauer, Laham, & Foltz, 2003; Shermis, Koch, Page, Keith, & Harrington, 2002; Shermis et al., 2001). All AES engines have obtained exact agreements with humans in the mid 80's and adjacent agreements in the mid-high 90's—slightly higher than the agreement coefficients for trained human raters. The slight edge for AES may be a function of the fact that the statistical models are based on more raters than one would typically find in a rating enterprise.

Validity

It is perhaps true that everyone has their own criteria for good composition because they have written something. Whether true or not, a variety of trait rubrics have emerged as the standard by which to assess writing performance. Most mainstream efforts coalesce into the "Big Five": content, creativity, style, mechanics, and organization (Page, 2003). One popular trait rubric for the assessment of writing is the 6+1 Traits™ from the Northwest Regional Education Laboratory (1999), which is broken down as follows: ideas, organization, voice, word choice, sentence fluency, and conventions.

Despite these efforts, the discipline is unable to articulate a "gold standard" of the constituents of good writing, or even good writing at various developmental levels. Even if a "gold standard" were to be formulated, it is unclear that human raters could adhere to it without some modification. For example, in one high-stakes statewide accountability assessment, the rubric allows for expressions of nonstandard English dialects without penalty. However, after many years of trying, the state department concluded that it was impossible to train human raters

to read such essays without undervaluing them. The point here is that human evaluators may at times apply subjective criteria regardless of any written standards.

One way in which the construct validity of automated essay scoring has been assessed is through confirmatory factor analysis. Shermis, Koch, Page, Keith, and Harrington (2002) used confirmatory factor analysis (CFA) with data from a PEG study on 386 essays, each evaluated by six judges. The normal standard for such comparisons is "pairs of judges." Accordingly, five CFAs were performed to compare the PEG ratings with all possible pairs of human judges. The Amos 4.0 (Arbuckle, 1999) computer program and maximum-likelihood estimation using the raw data were employed in this analysis. Five separate covariance analyses were conducted to avoid overlapping judge pairs. For each analysis, there was one latent variable, the presumed true essay score, and four measured variables (three judge pairs and the PEG ratings). Model identification was achieved by constraining the unstandardized factor loading for the first judge pair to 1. Thus, the first analysis compared judge pairs 1 and 2, 3 and 4, and 5 and 6 to PEG ratings; the second CFA compared judge pairs 1 and 3, 2 and 5, and 4 and 6 to PEG ratings, and so on. All five models showed a good fit to the data using conventional criteria (e.g., goodness-of-fit and comparative-fit indices above .95).

For the five CFAs, the standardized loadings for the human judge pairs ranged from .81 to .89, with a median loading of .86. In comparison, the loading of PEG ratings on the latent essay true score were .88 to .89 (median = .89). Thus, the computer ratings of essays appeared to be at least as valid a rating from *pairs* of human judges.

Keith (2003) examined the convergent and discriminant validity of seven PEG data sets in the following way. He took the statistical models from each data set and used each one to predict the score outcomes on the other data sets, then correlated the score results. The results across data sets, which differed on a number of variables (essay content, writing populations, number of essays, and number of judges), are summarized in Table 27.1. Convergent validity coefficients ranged from .69 to .90, demonstrating that

TABLE 27.1 The Generalized Validity of PEG: Scoring Formulae Developed from One Set of Essays Were Applied to Another Set of Essays

Essay scored	Source of training formula							
	Other	GRE	Praxis	IUPUI	Hi-School	NAEP-90	Write-America	n of judges
Other	**.88**	.82	.81	.78	.77	.81	.79	5
GRE	.79	**.86**	.81	.76	.76	.80	.75	2
Praxis	.77	.81	**.86**	.79	.72	.79	.81	6
IUPUI	.70	.71	.72	**.78**	.68	.70	.72	2
Hi-School	.78	.79	.78	.80	**.90**	.81	.77	Varied
NAEP-90	.80	.83	.81	.79	.77	**.88**	.76	8
Write-America							**.69**	2
n of judges	5	2	6	2	Varied	8	2	

Note. Data from Keith (2003). Columns show the source of the scoring formula, and rows show the set of essays to which they were applied. The diagonal shows the calibration correlation between PEG and human judges. See text for additional detail.

the model was accounting for common variance.

Finally, a few studies have shown that automated essay writing interventions have had a positive impact on writing production. Attali (2004), in a national study using e-rater®, observed improvements in essay length, essay development, and rating scores based on subsequent revisions of e-rater-evaluated submissions. Shermis, Burstein, and Bliss (2004) using the same technology, but in an urban setting only, also found improvements in essay length and reductions of number and types of errors over subsequent essay submissions. The aforementioned studies help to establish the linkage between automated essay scoring and scoring in typical writing instruction, a form of empirical validity beyond face validity.

Overall, AES has done as well or better than humans in the rating of essays for high- and low-stakes tests on the psychometric issues. Since humans typically form the ultimate criterion in AES, replications of human errors can contribute to decrements in overall reliability and validity. As was alluded to in the example with ratings of nonstandard English, AES may be able to overcome some of the biases that humans bring to the assessment enterprise.

Many of the variables defined in the statistical model for AES are "coachable," but their combination is what contributes to high essay scores in most models. If one had mastery of them all (or a good portion of

them), one would most likely be deemed a "good writer." Interestingly, when attempts have been made to generate "bad faith" essays intended to "trick" the AES engine into giving a poor essay a good score, it has been found that a poor essay can get a good score, but only good writers can generate the "bad faith" essay that does so (Shermis et al., 2002).

In the following sections, the four most popular AES software packages are described. These packages may be "bundled" with other software components, such as an electronic portfolio in which essays are kept and maintained, or combined with ancillary services, such as a plagiarism check. The focus of the following descriptions, however, is on the essay grading software.

Automated Essay Evaluation Systems

Project Essay Grade

PEG software is the original automated essay scoring system (Page, 1966). Initially developed to run on mainframe computers in the 1960s, PEG software was completely re-engineered in the mid-1990s to take advantage of more capable PC systems, object-oriented programming methodologies, web-based technologies, and advanced statistical techniques.

True to Page's original tenets, PEG software relates the intrinsic characteristics ("trins") of good writing (e.g., diction, grammar, fluency, logic, and cohesion) with mathematical approximations ("proxes"). Over the course of 30 years of research, Page identified more than 300 measurable characteristics (variables and their derivatives) that contribute to the mathematical representation of a particular essay.

Basically, PEG calculates scores for selected variables represented in a training set of essays already scored by professional readers. A mathematical formula is derived by PEG to describe, in statistical terms, the role that a given variable plays in the scoring decision. The formulae are combined into a model that simulates the scoring decisions of professional readers and issues a predicted score (known as a PEGScore™).

The quality and effectiveness of the predictive model depends on the quality of the human judgments being modeled. Critical in this process is the focus on training and monitoring the output of experienced professional readers, who score essays used in calibrating PEG's scores; "drift," for example, is eliminated through use of well-defined rubrics and validation testing to ensure that the score itself reflects the collective judgment of readers as the best approximate of a "true score."

Although most automated scoring systems assume a normal distribution of scores across a population, experience suggests that the distribution does not always fit a neat, bell-shaped curve. PEG model formulation has been modified to better fit expected distributions.

In addition, it has been recognized that a single holistic score provides few clues for students seeking to improve their writing skills. Accordingly, PEG has the ability to generate trait scores to provide greater insight into the component characteristics (e.g., organization or mechanics) that shape the essay's overall impression. Efforts to chart new directions for the future of PEG include enhanced content analysis and model development that reflect discrete differences among modes of discourse such as persuasive versus narrative essays.

e-rater v.2.0

e-rater® v.2.0, developed at Educational Testing Service (ETS), is a state-of-the art AES system that uses *natural language processing*

techniques to identify various features of writing in student essays (Attali & Burstein, 2004; Burstein, Chodorow, & Leacock, in press). Natural language processing is a subfield of computer science that deals with automated evaluation of text and speech.

This new system builds on earlier versions of e-rater (Burstein, 2003; Burstein et al., 1998). It learns to score student essays holistically, based on human-reader-scored writing samples. e-rater uses the following two model-building (calibration) approaches: *prompt-specific* and *grade-specific*. Prompt-specific models are customized for a particular test question. In addition, an innovative modeling method has been introduced, in which the system can assign a score to an essay based on a test-taker's grade level. This is called a *grade-specific* (generic) modeling. The advantage of this method is that once a model has been built for a test-taker population, the system can score data on any new topic for the given population. Practically speaking, what this means is that additional samples of human-scored data do not have to be collected when a new topic is introduced onto a test, or within an instructional system (Burstein, Chodorow, & Leacock, 2003).

E-RATER V.2.0 FEATURES

A central difference between e-rater v.2.0 and previous versions of the system is that many of the features in the updated system are directly related to *Critique* writing analysis tools. *Critique* is an automated feedback system and also a companion application to e-rater within *Criterion*SM, ETS's online essay evaluation service (Burstein, Chodorow, et al., 2003). *Critique*'s feedback is closely aligned with features addressed in human-reader-scoring guides. This close alignment of e-rater features with the scoring guide contributes to increased validity of the scoring system.

The 12 features used by the system include various features related to these six areas of analysis: errors in grammar, usage, and mechanics (Leacock & Chodorow, 2003); comments about style (Burstein & Wolska, 2003); identification of organizational segments, such as *thesis statement* (Burstein, Marcu, & Knight, 2003); and vocabulary content (Attali & Burstein, 2004). With the exception of the vocabulary content category, the remaining five categories correspond to feedback provided by *Criterion*. Eleven of the individual features derived from these five feedback categories reflect essential characteristics in essay writing and are aligned with human scoring criteria. The importance of this alignment is that it increases the validity of the scoring system, in that the system actually does what is intended, in this case, measuring the quality of writing. For our users, writing teachers and the larger assessment community, validity is a crucial consideration. Specifically, the features[1] are (1) proportion of grammar errors, (2) proportion of word usage errors, (3) proportion of mechanics errors, (4) proportion of style comments, (5) number of required discourse elements, (6) average length of discourse elements, (7) score assigned to essays with similar vocabulary, (8) similarity of vocabulary to essays with score 6, (9) number word types divided by number of word tokens, (10) log frequency of least common words, (11) average length of words, and (12) total number of words.

The first six features are derived from the *Critique* writing analysis tools. Features 1–3 are based on the number of errors in grammar, usage, and mechanics that *Critique* has identified in the essay. Similarly, feature 4 derives from *Critique*'s style diagnostics. Features 5 and 6 are based on *Critique*'s analysis of the essay's organization and development. Feature 5 counts how many discourse elements are present in the essay relative to a typical 8 units: a thesis, 3 main ideas, 3 supporting ideas, and a conclusion. If an essay has 1 thesis, 4 main points, and 3 supporting ideas, it gets credit for 7 units, since it is missing a conclusion. An extra main idea does not contribute to the count, because the program is looking for a particular development structure, not just identifiable discourse units in any category. Feature 6 is the average length of the discourse elements as a proportion of the total number of words in the essay. This provides an indication of the relative amount of discourse development.

To capture an essay's topical content, e-rater uses content vector analyses that are based on the vector-space model (Salton, Wong, & Yang, 1975) that is often used in information retrieval. A set of essays used to train the model are converted into vectors of word frequencies. These vectors are transformed into word weights, where the weight of a word is directly proportional to its frequency in the essay but inversely related to the number of essays in which it appears. To calculate the topical analysis of a novel essay, e-rater represents each of the six score points with a vector of word weights based on the training essays. To calculate feature 7, e-rater converts the novel essay into a vector of word weights and conducts a search to find the training vectors that are most similar to it. Similarity is measured by the cosine of the angle between two vectors. The second topical, content-based feature (feature 8) is the cosine between the vocabulary of the essay and the vocabulary of the very best training essays—those to which readers have assigned a score of 6.

The remaining features are word based. For feature 9, e-rater computes the ratio of number of word types to tokens. The number of word *types* is the size of the vocabulary used in the essay (the number of different words it contains). The number of word *tokens* is the total number of word occurrences. For example, if a word appears three times in an essay, it increases the type count by one and the token count by three. The type–token ratio can reveal a number of important characteristics of writing, including the level of repetitive word use.

Word frequency is closely associated with word difficulty (Breland, Jones, & Jenkins 1994; Breland 1996), and word frequency information is commonly used to help develop assessments that evaluate verbal ability. To capture whether the writer is comfortable using relatively difficult words, e-rater incorporates an index based on word frequency as feature 10. These frequencies were collected from a general corpus of about 14 million words, and e-rater calculates the logarithm of the frequency of the least common words in the essay.

Feature 11 calculates the average word length in characters across all words in the essay as an additional indicator of the sophistication of vocabulary. Finally, feature 12 is a count of the total number of word tokens in the essay. Since word count is a strong predictor of essay score, the weight of the word count feature is controlled. The standardized weight of the word count feature is set to some proportion of the sum of all 12 weights. This sum is determined only after the sum of the other 11 features weights is determined by the regression equation. Let us say, for example, that we want the weight of the word count feature to be 30% of the total sum of the 12 feature weights. If the sum of the 11 optimal weights (based on the regression equation) is 1.4, then this would be 70% of the value that will be our total sum. This sum, 1.4, is 70% of 2.0, and 2.0–1.4 = 0.6, or 30% of 2.0. Therefore, the final weight for the word count feature would be 0.6.

In theory, this weight can be any proportion of this sum, so the highest performing weight for word count must be empirically determined on a particular data set during training.

MODEL BUILDING, SCORE ASSIGNMENT, AND PERFORMANCE

e-rater models human reader judgments for the prompt-specific method by considering papers on a particular topic, whereas for the grade-specific method, it examines papers across many topics but at a specific grade level. e-rater then reads a sample of scored essays across the range of score points. The model-building sample size might vary from 200 essays to larger samples, but this is somewhat dependent on data availability and whether the task is prompt-specific or grade-specific. The system uses a number of computer programs to identify linguistically based features in the essay text that are aligned with those in holistic scoring guides. Next, each essay in the sample is converted to a list (vector) of features, where each list represents one essay. The vectors of features for the model-building sample are submitted to a *multiple regression*. The regression assigns a weight to each e-rater feature. Once the e-rater model is built for a particular test question, or grade level, e-rater uses this model to score new essays. For more system details, see Attali and Burstein (2004).

System performance is evaluated by degree of agreement between e-rater-assigned scores and human reader scores, and interrater human scores. Independent data sets (approximately $n = 200$) of essays are used to cross-validate an e-rater model. Across these data sets, e-rater agreement with human readers is comparable to interrater human agreement.

IntelliMetric

IntelliMetric™, similar to other AES systems, emulates processes demonstrated by human scorers. It draws on the traditions of cognitive processing, artificial intelligence, natural language understanding, and computational linguistics in the process of evaluating written text. Like e-rater, its evaluative focus is on grading content, with human raters' processes as the ultimate criterion.

IntelliMetric incorporates a natural language processing (NLP) parser and a feature extractor that identifies approximately 400 semantic, syntactic, and discourse-level features to understand the syntactic and grammatical structure of the language in which the essay is written. Each sentence is identified with regard to parts of speech, vocabulary, sentence structure, and concept expression. Several techniques are employed to make sense of the text, including morphological analysis, spelling recognition, collocation grammar, and word boundary detection. A 500,000-word unique vocabulary and 16 million-word "concept net" are referenced to form an understanding of the text.

The information gleaned is then used by a series of independent mathematical judges, or mathematical models to "predict" the human expert scores, and then optimized to produce a final predicted score.

Rather than relying on a single "judge," IntelliMetric employs multiple mathematical judges ("virtual judges") that vary according to conditions under which it is used. Nevertheless, they all share certain things in common: At the highest level, features extracted from the text are associated with the scores assigned in the training set in order to make accurate scoring judgments about essays with unknown scores. Judges differ with regard to specific information used to score an essay and, more importantly, with regard to the underlying mathematical model used to make judgments. Several statistical, artificial intelligence (AI) and machine-learning methodologies are used to create judges. In the development stage for a new prompt or topic, this step actually creates the mathematical models or "judges" to be used. After the models have been created, this step would simply apply the mathematical understanding to a novel essay response.

The primary source of information used to obtain the approximately 400 features is the sample essays on which the engine has been trained. In addition, reliance on the word "concept net" permits linking words thematically or by function, for example, recognizing that car and automobile are similar even though only the word *car* was used in the training essays.

The Intellimetric scoring model is optimized when the essays represent various cut points across a rubric. Multiple raters evaluate each essay to increase reliability. It is important that essays represent each scale point on the rubric; 25 or more essays at each scale point produce the best results; however, strong models have been calculated with as few as three essays representing each of the end points of the scale. The spread of essay scores essentially maximizes the variability of the essays and allows for a more efficient weighting process. Unlike some of the other AES model-building strategies, IntelliMetric relies on several mathematical models for its series of judges, including linear and nonlinear statistical models, machine-learning algorithms, and genetically optimized algorithms. If the algorithms for the essay scoring do not cross-validate well, they are adjusted, and a new, independent sample of papers is drawn until the model replicates within acceptable parameters.

As mentioned previously, the empirical models can be adjusted in a variety of ways. For instance, the Intellimetric parser can be set to flag "bad faith" essays (e.g., inappropriate use of vulgar language), to check for plagiarism, or to identify the writer's intent to do harm to him- or herself or to others.

Information from previous models can be employed to adjust or supplement information from current models. This can be particularly helpful when trying to create scoring models in which samples are small and the writing model is likely to conform to some existing set of parameters.

Intelligent Essay Assessor

The Intelligent Essay Assessor (IEA) is an AES system for scoring the quality of open-ended expository and discursive writing and for returning diagnostic tutorial feedback on the adequacy of knowledge and its expression. IEA uses a statistical combination of several measures to produce an overall score. It differs from Intellimetric and e-rater in that it does not rely solely on empirical data from human raters but can incorporate corpus-statistical measures rather than ones motivated by traditional AI or linguistic theory. Its greatest difference lies in its use of a machine-learning model of human understanding of text called Latent Semantic Analysis (LSA; Landauer & Dumais, 1997), by which it constructs mathematical representation of the meanings of words and passages in the language and knowledge domains of the desired essay. The model accurately mimics the degree of similarity in the meaning of two texts even when the two use entirely different words (Landauer, Laham, & Foltz, 1998).

The content variable is based on a *direct prediction* of the score that expert humans would give to an essay—a score whose independent variables are natural human judgments of student essays and parts or aspects thereof. Direct prediction scores are not theoretical or empirical index variables, or proxies such as the ones that predict human scores from hundreds of index variables computed from sample texts and then used in place of human judgments. By contrast, through LSA-based measures of overall similarity of meaning, direct prediction uses human scores to predict other human scores. Such scores are easily applied to many properties of an essay other than its overall quality simply by having human readers make judgments of a particular property according to a common notation or scale, for example, in judging the persuasive quality of the essay as a whole or within a section.

In stepwise fashion, the standard procedure follows:

1. Apply the language model to extensive background text covering the language of the test, the domain of knowledge, and the concepts expected in answer to prompts. Typically, the pretraining corpus contains hundreds of thousands of paragraphs from sources representative of student reading, plus, for expository essays, the content of one or more textbooks in the field of the essay prompts.

2. Have a representative sample of essays scored by human readers for holistic quality and any desired analytical traits, organiza-

tional components, or aspects of knowledge. The number of prescored training essays needed varies somewhat by domain—between expository and creative essays, for example—and with the desired accuracy of the score, but generally lies between 50 and 250. One version of IEA can provide holistic scores with no human-scored training essays, but needs roughly twice as many unscored essays to achieve the same accuracy.

3. Represent every training and to-be-scored essay as a numerical vector (thus making the system indifferent to the language of the intended test-takers and the corpus for background language modeling).

4. Compute the similarity between each to-be-scored essay and every other one. Use this information, along with the scores provided by human experts, to compute a score the same as that readers would assign a to-be-scored essay, or, in the case of no pre-scored essays, to place all essays at points on a continuous quality line. Intuitively, this process may be thought of as a vicarious human judgment, one based on comparisons among a very large number of highly similar experiences. The similarity processes used by professional human raters are implied; they reach agreement on how satisfaction of a given rubric is to be achieved or a score level satisfied by reading and comparing many essays. A distinct advantage is that the system does not require a certain minimum number of essays at each of 4 or 6 scale points, as in certain other approaches—and to assign accurate scores to essays that are better or worse than any seen in training.

5. Add statistical and information-theoretic measures—some that are variants of those used in communications (coding and speech) and other pattern recognition systems, and some that are new in IEA. These measures assess the normality and level of appropriate sophistication of word choice, usage, and flow; sentence-to-sentence and sentence-to-whole coherence; redundancy and irrelevance of sentences to the whole; the variety of sentences and paragraphs in both content and expression; the syntactic and propositional complexity of sentences; plus spelling, punctuation, grammar, and other writing qualities. IEA avoids measures such as total number of words or specific trigger terms or phrases to minimize the possibility of "gaming" the system.

Because of the system can compare the totality of content and/or each aspect of the content of each essay with every other, it can detect even very clever attempts at plagiarism, as well as unusual submissions flagged for possible human attention. For example, it can flag essays that are off-topic or that contain a message to the administrator. The same capability can be applied to separate measures of quality and quantity of conceptual knowledge about multiple subtopics in an essay, regardless of whether the student essay treats them in separate passages or (appropriately) intermixed.

The system has been extended to include a wide range of applications, including writing of summaries, providing assessment of comprehension and substantive writing, and embedded assessment, tutoring, and automatic mentoring of online collaborative learning environments. It has been used in high- and low-stakes, and practice test environments for students from fourth grade to professional schools and accreditation, and widely in military training applications. Additional variants are used to align learning materials and test items with learning standards, and for matching jobs, people and instruction. For these other applications of IEA's basic capabilities, see the reference list.

Exploring Automated Essay Scoring

The formats for AES programs can be "tried out" in sample form. Some require a registration process that is relatively transparent. A public-domain Bayesian Essay Test Scoring sYstem (BETSY; see Figure 27.1) for non-commercial applications of AES (Rudner & Liang, 2002) is also available. The following link explains the system in more detail, and provides for downloading the software, help files, and demonstration data sets: edres.org/betsy.

Future Directions

It can be seen that AES technology is somewhat akin to that in the late 1980s with the potential capability of 5 MB hard disk drives. The technology worked, it had potential, but it was crude and the potential had yet to be fully realized. The two develop-

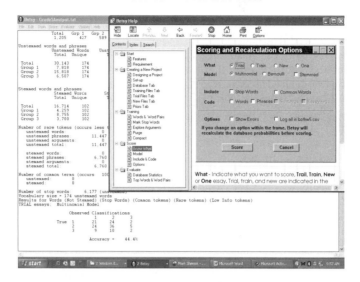

FIGURE 27.1. A screenshot of results from BETSY.

ments discussed below reflect the recent work of Burstein and Leacock, and address refinements that will help extend both the acceptability and utility of automated evaluation of essays and shorter, free-text responses.

Automated Feedback about Organizational Coherence

Among other capabilities in *Criterion*, including identification of errors in grammar, usage, and mechanics, and advice on style, the system includes an application that automatically identifies the sentence text in essays by organizational element labels: *thesis statement*, *main idea*, *supporting idea*, and *conclusion* (Burstein, Marcu, et al., 2003). Each sentence is annotated accordingly by the system. Teachers have pointed out that this is helpful feedback in that it offers students information about the organizational structure of their essay. However, as teachers correctly note, the structure might be fine, but the quality of the organizational elements might be weak. This new prototype system is an attempt to provide additional feedback that addresses the quality (coherence) of the organizational elements in the essay (see Higgins, Burstein, Marcu, & Gentile, 2004, for details about the system and evaluations).

Earlier work by Foltz, Kintsch, and Landauer (1998) and Wiemer-Hastings and Graesser (2000) developed systems that attempted to examine coherence in student writing, measured by lexical relatedness between adjacent text segments. These methods can only address local coherence, however. By considering adjacent and nonadjacent text as it relates to organizational elements, the *Criterion* system can identify a breakdown in coherence in an essay due to global aspects of organizational structure. This system uses another semantic similarity measure, called Random Indexing (Kanerva, Kristoferson, & Holst, 2000; Sahlgren, 2001).

The capability to employ Random Indexing captures the expressive quality of sentences in organizational elements related to *global coherence* (the relation between nonadjacent text) and *local essay coherence* (the relation between adjacent sentences). The dimensions of global coherence are (1) relatedness to the essay question topic (prompt), and (2) relatedness between organizational elements. Those related to local coherence are (3) intrasentential quality, and (4) sentence relatedness within an organizational segment.

The prototype system uses two approaches to classify three of the four coherence dimensions described. For the two global diensions (*relation-to-prompt* and *relation-to-thesis*), a machine-learning algorithm known as a support vector machine (Christianini & Shawe-Taylor, 2000; Vapnick, 1995) is used to model features derived from Random Indexing, and from essay-based organizational segments. A third component evaluates the technical quality of a sentence, a local coherence dimension, and it is driven by rule-based heuristics.

Essentially, the goal of the system is to be able to predict whether a sentence in an organizational element has high or low expressive quality with regard to a particular coherence dimension. For instance, sentences in the student's thesis statement may have a strong relationship to the essay topic, but may have a number of serious grammatical errors that make it hard to follow. Feedback for this student may indicate that while the sentences in the thesis statement appropriately address the topic, the same text segment is ridden with grammatical errors.

The system looks at content-based information in sentences to identify coherence between organizational elements in an essay, and how each element (sentence) relates to the essay topic and the text of other organizational elements within the essay. Based on this analysis, a student would receive feedback related to essay coherence, as it pertains to content within organizational elements in their essay. The feedback provided to students from this system advances the existing capabilities for automated essay-based discourse analysis. At the same time, it addresses an important aspect of feedback that teachers believe will be helpful in advancing students' writing abilities.

c-rater: Evaluating Free Text for Content Material

Free-response questions are designed to measure a student's understanding of specific content material, with little, if any, regard for writing skills, whether in reading comprehension, science, or history. These are usually evaluated in the context of "short-answer" responses rather than holistically scored essays, but the same technology can be applied to the latter.

The c-rater scoring engine, under development at ETS, is designed to recognize specific content in a student response. Depending on the concepts recognized, c-rater can assign full, partial, or no credit. Automated natural language processing techniques determine whether a student response contains specific information required as evidence that the concept has been learned. Other research in this area can be found in Perez, Alfonseca, and Rodriguez (2004), Penstein-Rose and Hall (2004), and Sukkarieh, Pulman, and Raikes (2004).

c-rater uses NLP techniques to determine whether a student response contains specific information required as evidence that the concept has been learned. To create a c-rater scoring model, a content expert, such as a test developer or teacher, needs to develop a scoring guide that breaks down how many score points are assigned to each of the component concepts that made up a correct answer. For example, consider a typical middle school science question:

> Describe how you would design an experiment that would investigate the importance of light to plant growth. Include the organisms required, the control and variable tested, and the method of measuring results.

For a response to receive full credit, it must contain four essential points: the need for two plants or other organisms, for a control in the light, a variable in the dark, and a way to measure the plants' growth or health.

Suppose that a question on a history quiz is "What was a result of the Third Punic War?" A model correct response might be: Rome destroyed Carthage. However, there are many ways that this answer may be expressed, as in 1–4, while 5 would receive no credit:

1. At the end of the Punic Wars, Carthage was annihilated by Rome.
2. It resulted in Rome's destruction of Carthage.
3. Carthage's destruction by the Romans was the result.
4. Carthage was invaded by the Romans, and it was destroyed.
5. Carthage destroyed Rome.

c-rater, which is designed to be a paraphrase recognizer, tries to recognize when a response is equivalent to a correct answer. As such, it recognizes a correct response when it exhibits variations that are associated with paraphrases, whether they be syntactic (1 is passive and 2–3 are nominalizations), morphological variants of a word (the verb *destroy* and the noun *destruction*), the use of a pronoun (the referent for *it* in 4), and the use of synonyms or similar words (the use of *annihilated* in place of *destroyed* in 1). In addition to these features, c-rater tries to correct for spelling errors. The recognition of the syntactic structure, morphological variation, pronoun referent, and spelling correction are fully automated. In the case of synonyms and similar words, a list of possible suggestions is generated and presented to the model builder, who selects those words that are appropriate. A detailed description of the mechanisms that drive c-rater can be found in Leacock and Chodorow (2003).

In a pilot study with the State of Indiana Commission for Higher Education and the Indiana Department of Education, c-rater models for four algebra and 19 reading comprehension questions were successfully deployed. A full description of the pilot can be found in Leacock (2004).

On average, c-rater agreed with the reader scores on cross-validation responses about 85% of the time, whereas the readers agreed with one another about 92% of the time. Kappa values, which correct for the level of agreement that is expected by chance, were also computed. The interreader kappa was .76 for c-rater–reader agreement and .88 for interreader agreement. There are several reasons for the somewhat lower c-rater performance. There are borderline responses in which, upon inspection of the c-rater "errors," it is not clear whether the c-rater score is wrong. Another reason is that humans are better than c-rater at recognizing misspelled words. For example, one question requires identifying *repetition* as a literary device. Two readers accepted *repation* as *repetition*, whereas c-rater's spelling corrector did not.

To determine how effectively a bag-of-words approach would be on this type of data, a content vector classifier (CVA) was used to score similar reading comprehension questions from an earlier Indiana pilot. When using CVA, performance dropped by 30%. We conclude that c-rater's use of predicate argument structure and similar words are responsible for its superior results.

Usually when c-rater errs, it assigns a score that is too high rather than one that is too low, thereby giving more credit than is deserved. This often occurs because a response

can contain the appropriate language even though its meaning differs from the concept required by the model. As an example, a concept that c-rater tries to identify is "it is an old house." One student wrote that "the author is telling you how old the house is," which was not credited by either reader. This becomes more problematic as a model is adjusted to accept sentence fragments as being correct answers. In this adjustment, c-rater imposes fewer requirements in order to allow fragments that nonetheless embody the elements of the model. The problem seems unavoidable, because human readers consistently accept sentence fragments—even very ungrammatical ones.

Current work on c-rater is focusing on a smarter and more flexible graphical user interface to be used for model building.

Conclusion

What can we conclude about automated essay scoring? In many ways it is like a sister technology, computerized adaptive testing (CAT). Both were developed during the 1960s, designed to make skills assessment easier, use a different approach than conventional assessment methodology to come up with a familiar score, and employ computers to achieve their ends.

There are differences between the two techniques, however. Although CAT has over 30 years of research behind it compared to AES's track record of 12 years, the latter shows greater potential to be incorporated as a set of both assessment and instructional methodologies. Its acceptance in the United States is contingent on how well it can be infused into the mainstream writing curriculum of the public school sector with teachers that have a basic understanding of how it works. Because CAT is deployed primarily for one-shot, high-stakes testing, it has the luxury of being used whether ultimate consumers understand it or not.

The future of AES is guaranteed, in part, by the increased emphasis on testing for U.S. schoolchildren. Federal mandates such as No Child Left Behind require a volume of assessments that would be nearly impossible to achieve through human ratings of writing. Because AES can be incorporated into writing instruction, it is possible to have an assessment of yearly progress without resorting to one high-stakes test in the spring. Rather, the technology keeps an accurate record of successive assessments throughout the school year. If the assessments were developed with national norms in mind, they could serve as quiet documentation of how well a child progressed during a year of writing instruction.

Acknowledgments

This work would not have been possible without the generous contributions of Elliot Inman (Measurement Incorporated), Scott Elliot (Vantage Learning), and Tom Landauer (Knowledge Analysis Technologies). We would also like to acknowledge the constructive suggestions made by the editors and by Francis DiVesta, who reviewed several drafts of this manuscript; Derrick Higgins, who put some finishing touches on it; and Yigal Attali, who helped us navigate some of the psychometric fine points of the chapter.

Note

1. All proportional measures are based on the total number of words in an essay.

References

Ajay, H. B., Tillett, P. I., & Page, E. B. (1973). *Analysis of essays by computer (AEC-II)* (No. 8-0102). Washington, DC: U.S. Department of Health, Education, and Welfare, Office of Education, National Center for Educational Research and Development.

Arbuckle, J. (1999). *Amos user's guide 4.0.* Chicago: SmallWaters.

Attali, Y. (2004, April). *Exploring the feedback and revision features of Criterion.* Paper presented at the National Council on Measurement in Education, San Diego, CA.

Attali, Y., & Burstein, J. (2004, June). *Automated essay scoring with e-rater V.2.0.* Paper presented at the Annual Meeting of the International Association for Educational Assessment, Philadelphia, PA.

Bennett, R. E., & Bejar, I. I. (1998). Validity and automated scoring: It's not only the scoring. *Educational Measurement: Issues and Practice, 17*(4), 9–17.

Breland, H. M. (1996). Word frequency and word difficulty: A comparison of counts in four corpora. *Psychological Science, 7*(2), 96–99.

Breland, H. M., Jones, R. J., & Jenkins, L. (1994). *The College Board vocabulary study* (ETS Research Report No. 94–26). Princeton, NJ: Educational Testing Service.

Burstein, J. (2003). The e-rater scoring engine: Automated essay scoring with natural language processing. In M. D. Shermis & J. Burstein (Eds.), *Automated essay scoring: A cross-disciplinary perspective* (pp. 113–122). Mahwah, NJ: Erlbaum.

Burstein, J., Chodorow, M., & Leacock, C. (2003). *Criterion: Online essay evaluation: An application for automated evaluation of test-taker essays.* Paper presented at the 15th Annual Conference on Innovative Applications of Artificial Intelligence, Acapulco, Mexico.

Burstein, J., Chodorow, M., & Leacock, C. (2004). Automated essay evaluation: The Criterion online writing service. *AI Magazine 25*(3), 27–36.

Burstein, J., Kukich, K., Wolff, S., Lu, C., Chodorow, M., Braden-Harder, L., et al. (1998, August). *Automated scoring using a hybrid feature identification technique.* Paper presented at the Annual Meeting of the Association of Computational Linguistics, Montreal, Canada.

Burstein, J., Marcu, D., & Knight, K. (2003). Finding the WRITE stuff: Automatic identification of discourse structure in test-taker essays. *Special Issues on Advances in Natural Language Processing, IEEE Intelligent Systems, 18*(1), 32–39.

Burstein, J., & Wolska, M. (2003, April). *Toward evaluation of writing style: Finding overly repetitive word use in student essays.* Paper presented at the 11th Conference of the European Chapter of the Association for Computational Linguistics, Budapest, Hungary.

Christianini, N., & Shawe-Taylor, J. (2000). *Support vector machines and other kernel-based learning methods.* Cambridge, UK: Cambridge University Press.

Cizek, G. J., & Page, B. A. (2003). The concept of reliability in the context of automated essay scoring. In M. D. Shermis & J. Burstein (Eds.), *Automated essay scoring: A cross-disciplinary perspective* (pp. 125–145). Mahwah, NJ: Erlbaum.

Elliot, S. (2003). Intellimetric: From here to validity. In M. D. Shermis & J. Burstein (Eds.), *Automated essay scoring: A cross-disciplinary perspective* (pp. 71–86). Mahwah, NJ: Erlbaum.

Foltz, P. W., Kintsch, W., & Landauer, T. K. (1998). The measurement of textual coherence with Latent Semantic Analysis. *Organizational Process, 25*(2–3), 285–307.

Higgins, D., Burstein, J., Marcu, D., & Gentile, C. (2004, May). *Evaluating multiple aspects of coherence in study essays.* Paper presented at the Annual Meeting of HLT/NAACL, Boston.

Kanerva, P., Kristoferson, J., & Holst, A. (2000). Random indexing of text samples for Latent Semantic Analysis. In L. R. Gleitman & A. K. Josh (Eds.), *Proceedings of the 22nd annual conference of the Cognitive Science Society.* Mahwah, NJ: Erlbaum.

Kawate-Mierzejewska, M. (2003, March). *e-rater software.* Paper presented at the Japanese Association for Language Teaching, Tokyo, Japan.

Keith, T. Z. (2003). Validity and automated essay scoring systems. In M. D. Shermis & J. Burstein (Eds.), *Automated essay scoring: A cross-disciplinary perspective* (pp. 147–168). Mahwah, NJ: Erlbaum.

Landauer, T. K., & Dumais, S. T. (1997). A solution to Plato's problem: The Latent Semantic Analysis theory of acquisition, induction, and representation of knowledge. *Psychological Review, 104,* 211–240.

Landauer, T. K., Laham, D., & Foltz, P. W. (1998). Learning human-like knowledge by singular value decomposition: A progress report. In M. I. Jordan, M. J. Kearns, & S. A. Solla (Eds.), *Advances in neural information processing systems* (Vol. 10, pp. 45–51). Cambridge, MA: MIT Press.

Landauer, T. K., Laham, D., & Foltz, P. W. (2003). Automated scoring and annotation of essays with the Intelligent Essay Assessor. In M. D. Shermis & J. Burstein (Eds.), *Automated essay scoring: A cross-disciplinary perspective* (pp. 87–112). Mahwah, NJ: Erlbaum.

Leacock, C. (2004). *Scoring free-responses automatically: A case study of a large-scale assessment.* Retrieved from www.ets.org/research/erater.html

Leacock, C., & Chodorow, M. (2003). C-rater: Scoring of short-answer questions. *Computers and the Humanities, 37*(4), 389–405.

Northwest Educational Research Laboratories. (1999). *6+1 traits of writing rubric.* Retrieved December 1999 from www.nwrel.org/eval/pdfs/6plus1traits.pdf

Page, E. B. (1966). The imminence of grading essays by computer. *Phi Delta Kappan, 48,* 238–243.

Page, E. B. (2003). Project Essay Grade: PEG. In M. D. Shermis & J. Burstein (Eds.), *Automated essay scoring: A cross-disciplinary perspective* (pp. 43–54). Mahwah, NJ: Erlbaum.

Page, E. B., & Petersen, N. S. (1995). The computer moves into essay grading: Updating the ancient test. *Phi Delta Kappan, 76*(7), 561–565.

Penstein-Rose, C., & Hall, B. S. (2004). *A little goes a long way: Quick authoring of semantic knowledge sources for interpretation.* Paper presented at the 2nd International Workshop on Scalable Natural Language Understanding (ScaNaLU) at HLT-NAACL, Boston.

Perez, D., Alfonseca, E., & Rodriguez, P. (2004, June). *Upper bounds of the Bleu algorithm applied to assessing student essays.* Paper presented at the 30th annual conference of the International Association for Educational Assessment (IAEA), Philadelphia.

Rudner, L. M., & Liang, T. (2002). Automated essay scoring using Bayes's theorem. *Journal of Technology, Learning and Assessment, 1*(2). Available from www.jtla.org

Sahlgren, M. (2001, August). *Vector based semantic analysis: Representing word meanings based on random labels.* Paper presented at the ESSLLI Workshop on Semantic Knowledge Acquisition and Categorisation, Helsinki, Finland.

Salton, G., Wong, A., & Yang, C.S. (1975). A vector space model for automatic indexing. *Communications of the ACM, 18*(11); 613–620.

Shermis, M. D., Burstein, J., & Bliss, L. (2004, April). *The impact of automated essay scoring on high stakes writing assessments.* Paper presented at the annual meetings of the National Council on Measurement in Education, San Diego, CA.

Shermis, M. D., Koch, C. M., Page, E. B., Keith, T., & Harrington, S. (2002). Trait ratings for automated essay grading. *Educational and Psychological Measurement, 62*(1), 5–18.

Shermis, M. D., Mzumara, H. R., Olson, J., & Harrington, S. (2001). On-line grading of student essays: PEG goes on the web at IUPUI. *Assessment and Evaluation in Higher Education, 26*(3), 247–259.

Sukkarieh, J. Z., Pulman, S. G., & Raikes, N. (2004, June). *Auto-marking 2: An update on the UCLES–Oxford University research into using computational linguistics to score short, free text responses.* Paper presented at the 30th annual conference of the International Association for Educational Assessment (IAEA), Philadelphia.

Vantage Learning. (2002). *A study of IntelliMetric™ scoring for responses written in Bahasa Malay* (No. RB-735). Newtown, PA: Author.

Vantage Learning. (n.d.). *A Preliminary study of the efficacy of IntelliMetric™ for use in scoring Hebrew assessments.* Newtown, PA: Author.

Vapnick, V. (1995). *The nature of statistical learning theory.* New York: Springer-Verlag.

Wiemer-Hastings, P., & Graesser, A. (2000). Select-a-Kibitzer: A computer tool that gives meaningful feedback on student compositions. *Interactive Learning Environments, 8*(2), 149–169.

Chapter 28

Writing Assessment
A Techno-History

Brian Huot *and* Michael Neal

In using a technological lens to examine some historical characteristics of writing assessment, we acknowledge the ideological nature of our inquiry and our choices. We realize that by choosing a technological focus, we will necessarily be addressing some issues rather than others. Our representation of writing assessment will be limited. On the other hand, seeing assessment history technologically will also help us to address current, important issues and to shed light on ways the forces shaping the history of assessment still exert power over current practices, approaches, and attitudes. Barton and Barton (1993) remind us that representations—in their case, the textual representations on maps—are necessarily political in what they do and do not communicate to the reader. The same, of course, can be said of historical representations; they draw attention to specific events, settings, people, cultures, and so forth, at the expense of other perspectives. In this vein, we acknowledge that our history of writing assessment is one representation among several others that highlight different perspectives. For example, Yancey's (1999) history of writing assessment in the 50th anniversary issue of the *Journal of the Conference on College Composition and Communication* (CCCC) highlights the history of assessment within a particular time period and in connection with a specific organization, detailing how important writing assessment has been to

the CCCC and its history. On the other hand, Williamson's (1993) history illustrates the theoretical and disciplinary evolution of writing assessment. White's (1993) historical account focuses on the dissemination of holistic scoring; battles fought, won, and lost; and the contributions of various groups and individuals to the creation of modern direct writing assessment. Our focus on technology and writing assessment history highlights not only the contribution of technological approaches to writing assessment but also acknowledges its continuing influence. We trace the tremendous strides made in the technology of writing assessment as we point out the limitations of a technological approach and advocate an adherence to theories of validity that stipulate systematic inquiry into all uses for assessment.

We begin by mapping out some important technological developments that have influenced the development, administration, and application of writing assessment for various purposes. For example, the major shift from indirect to direct writing assessment—which has recently been expanded on a national scale with writing requirements for the Standard Achievement Test (SAT) and Graduate Record Examination (GRE), for example—was made possible, in part, due to available technological developments such as holistic scoring, electronic word processing, and computerized scoring. In order to understand technological developments and their

417

continuing influence in writing assessment better, we look at some of the prevailing views about technology in American culture and attempt to examine some of the underlying assumptions that drive this growth. Ultimately, we examine some of the cultural values associated with technology and provide brief commentary about how these values play out in a technohistory of writing assessment.

By looking at the history of writing assessment from a technohistorical perspective, we can understand how ideas about technology have fueled the theories and practices associated with assessment in general and writing assessment in particular. In the spirit of historical pluralism, we would like our account to be noted, not as more or less accurate, but simply alongside other histories of writing assessment (Camp, 1993; Huot, 2002; White, 1993; Williamson, 1993; Yancey, 1999). Because we believe that technological history is a very important and neglected part of the overall picture of how writing assessment got to be where it is, we want to highlight technological narratives and counternarratives that might provide a different way of looking at not only writing assessment history but also the present and future use of various writing assessment practices.

Writing assessments can be understood as technologies by which educators collect information in order to make decisions about students, teachers, or educational units, such as programs, schools, or school districts. According to George Madaus (1993), assessment is a technology even if we do not always think of it that way:

> Granted, testing is generally not widely regarded as a *technology*, a word that usually conjures up images of major artifacts like computers, planes, televisions and telephones (Pacey, 1989). (This is how the media use the term; Ellul, 1990.) However, much of present technology is specialized arcane knowledge, hidden algorithms, and technical art; it is a complex of standardized means for attaining a predetermined end in social, economic, administrative and educational institutions (Ellul, 1990; Lowrance, 1986). Testing, embedded in our system of education with its arcane psychometric underpinnings, clearly fits this definition of technology. Testing also fits some very simple definitions of technology—the simplest being something put together for a purpose to satisfy a pressing or immediate need, or to solve a problem. (pp. 12–13)

Whether we think of multiple-choice tests of writing that contain questions on grammar and usage or editing tests used for college placement, such as COMPASS (Computer-Adapted Placement Assessment and Support Services), holistic scoring procedures, or software to machine-score student writing, all major forms of writing assessment fit Madaus's definition of technology.

Donald MacKenzie and Judy Wajcman (1999), in the introduction to their collection on the social shaping of technology, argue that technologies are more influential than human needs in shaping other technologies. Challenging the Western grand narrative of the genius inventor working in isolation, they argue that new technologies are simply inevitable: "Once the 'necessary constituent cultural elements' are present—most importantly including component technologies—there is a sense in which an invention *must* occur" (p. 8; emphasis in original). Individuals synthesize and use existing technologies in new ways for applications relevant to their context. Thus, a technological development in writing assessment, such as computerized scoring of student writing, does not emerge because of the creative genius of an individual[1]; rather, it is an inevitable development in conjunction with direct writing assessment, word processing, and other constituent computer technologies. For example, as far back as 1912, Starch and Elliott defined the problem with writing assessment as individual readers being unable to agree about scores on the same papers. Over 50 years later, in their germinal research report from 1966 that established the viability of direct writing assessment (an assessment that actually involved reading student writing) in general and holistic scoring in particular, Godshalk, Swineford, and Coffman reviewed the existing research on writing assessment and reasserted that the main problem with direct writing assessment is its reliability. Consequently, they developed and tested the use of multiple readers trained on a specific rubric and found that reliability between raters could be raised to an acceptable level. Throughout the history of writing assessment, and whether we refer to technologies such as the indirect tests of grammar usage and mechanics, the use of rubrics and rater training, or the machine scoring of student writing, we are basically referring to technological solutions to the problem of scoring consistency.

For purposes of examining the historical context of writing assessments, we briefly explore a few of the most prevalent Western assumptions about technologies, which in turn influence the ways educators approach many forms of writing assessment: (1) writing assessment as progress; (2) writing assessment as ideologically neutral; and (3) writing assessment as efficient, objective, and reliable. These representations and the assumptions they promote undergird most of the literature and practice of writing assessment over the past several decades.

Writing Assessment as Progress

Especially within Western culture, new technologies have been touted as advances, inextricably connected to the modernist grand narrative of progress (Barton, 1994; Madaus, 1994; Winner, 1985). Ellen Barton (1994) defines two prevailing discourses of technology within society:

> One is a dominant discourse characterized by an optimistic interpretation of technology's progress in American culture and by traditional views of the relations between technology, literacy, and education; the other is an antidominant discourse characterized by a skeptical interpretation of technology's integration in contemporary culture and education. (p. 56)

Barton depicts the tone of the dominant discourse of technology as similar to that of a high school history book in which each technological "advance" represents beneficial progress for individuals and society as a whole. Perhaps Barton's most intriguing argument, though, is not about the dominant discourse community but the antidominant discourse regarding technology. She claims that even the antidominant discourse—which is defined by a critique of the progressive stance by "pointing out undesirable consequences" (p. 60)—is ultimately subsumed by the dominant discourse: "The merger of antidominant into dominant here is in the shift of the domain of radical democratization squarely into pedagogy, where technology once again, is depicted as providing products and techniques assumed to be beneficial

for education" (p. 72). Even the community that adopts a critical stance to technologies by pointing out potential ways that technologies adversely act upon a population or location ultimately does so ingenuinely, buying into the same assumption of the dominant discourse community that technologies are mostly beneficial, or at least, are more beneficial than harmful. Antidominant discourse identifies potentially negative side effects of technologies, but they are most often dismissed as a mere warning.

The history of writing assessment technologies reflects both Barton's (1994) dominant and antidominant discourse. The dominant discourse of writing assessment is that new technologies necessarily are better than the old, and that the progress represented by the technology generally benefits society. In 1960, Orville Palmer of the Educational Testing Service (ETS) wrote "Sixty Years of English Testing," and in explaining why it took so long to develop effective writing assessments put the blame on English teachers and others who saw the need for actually reading students' writing to assess their ability to write: "The Board regretted the authority of a large and conservative segment of the English teaching profession which sincerely believed that the writing of essays and other free response exercises constituted the only direct means of obtaining evidence as to a student's ability to write and understand his own language" (p. 11). As Palmer's words illustrate, writing assessment literature follows form; beginning slowly to critique assessment technologies in an antidominant move, the literature is still largely accepting of the technologies even in face of the negative social and educational side effects. Nearly 20 years later, well after holistic scoring had become a viable and popular method for assessing writing (White, 1993; Yancey, 1999; and many others), Peter Cooper (1984) reviewed the writing assessment literature in a GRE Board Research Report published by ETS and contended, "From a psychometric point of view, it does appear that indirect assessment [multiple-choice tests of grammar and mechanics alone] can afford a satisfactory measure of writing skills for ranking and selection purposes" (p. 27).

As a case in point, student writing portfolios have captured the attention of writing instructors and administrators over the past two decades. The earliest accounts of writing portfolios enthusiastically embraced the new technology, espousing the connections between portfolios and current thinking in composition studies such as the process movement in writing instruction: "The portfolio itself tends to encourage students to revise because it suggests that writing occurs over time, not in a single sitting, just as the portfolio itself grows over time and cannot be created in a single sitting" (Sommers, 1982, p. 154). Other early advocates of writing portfolios argued that they were more collaborative and less teacher-centered grading systems, that they brought people together within classrooms and departments, and that they promoted more consistency with classroom pedagogy (Belanoff, 1994; Elbow & Belanoff, 1986; Murphy, 1997; Yancey, 1992). These claims, while not in dispute, represent the early dominant discourse associated with this new writing assessment technology.

The initial support for portfolio assessment by many educators is not unique. For example, Charles Cooper (1977), referring to holistic scoring, stated that this scoring system made it possible to rank all students from a particular school. Cooper's dominant discourse of technology was based upon the ability of the technology itself. He articulated no educational reason for wanting to rank students, or how this information would benefit individual students or the school itself. A similar pattern of dominant discourse can be seen with other useful writing assessment innovations historically: holistic scoring in the 1970s and 1980s (Cooper, 1977; Greenberg, Wiener, & Donovan, 1986; Myers, 1980; White, 1993), portfolios in the 1980s and early 1990s (Belanoff & Dickson, 1991; Calfee & Perfumo, 1996; Yancey, 1992), directed self-placement in the late 1990s (Royer & Gilles, 1998), and more recently, a reemergence of advocacy for computerized scoring of student writing (Page, 1994; Shermis & Burstein, 2003).

Soon after the widespread acceptance of writing technologies, the antidominant discourse followed. For example, writing portfolio scholarship in the 1990s voiced concerns about both their potential limitations and the benefits of the assessment technology (Belanoff, 1994; Callahan, 1997; Huot & Williamson, 1997; Murphy & Grant, 1996). It should be noted that these versions of technology and writing assessment can be separated chronologically with most early scholarship touting and documenting the assessments with later scholarship that provides the critique. Once the new technology is embraced on a wide scale and often uncritically, the relative warrants for using the assessment form are more tempered. Thus, scholars who were widely identified with promoting portfolios—though they had been advocating them in specific contexts for certain purposes that were often ignored by educators who were integrating them in uncritical ways—were called on to reign in the portfolio mania that had swept the country: "In truth, portfolios are not a cure-all; they are not going to magically make students better writers" (Belanoff, 1994, p. 20). But as Barton (1994) predicted, the critique surrounding the antidominant discourse was ultimately tempered in the end with a different kind of endorsement of the technology: Portfolios, if used correctly in the right context by the right people, can still produce the earlier promised benefits.

Another example of this trend in writing assessment was the initial and subsequent responses to holistic scoring. Holistic scoring initially allowed for the large-scale assessment of student writing for a variety of purposes, including student placement into writing classes that had for so long relied on indirect scores from standardized tests (Cooper, 1977; Greenberg & Witte, 1988; Odell, 1981). Holistic scoring allowed for enough reliability and efficiency to justify local expenditure at certain institutions, while providing opportunities for assessors to read student writing, usually produced in timed-writing environments. After the initial praise of the technology, of course, a second round of more critical responses appeared, arguing about the mechanical nature of calibrating readers, as well as students writing in inauthentic physical conditions under a restrictive time limitations and without the resources that many writers use on a regular basis (Williamson & Huot, 1993). In a very few cases, however, the ultimate conclusion was to move away from holistic scoring altogether. Certainly regressing to indirect writing measures was not a better option than holistic scoring (White, 1995), so holistic scoring remains the most popular form of writing assessment even for reading portfolios, though the literature and research now include a more critical approach to the technology (Huot, 2002; White, 2005). The pattern of early acceptance of a new writing assessment technology and the subsequent restricted critique can be seen in nearly all of the writing assessment in this century, from the earliest existence of standardized testing to the current discussions surrounding computerized scoring of student texts.

Writing Assessment as Ideologically Neutral

Another leading assumption about the role of technologies in Western society is that they are understood as largely neutral—or non-ideological—until they are used in a particular way (Heidegger, 1977; MacKenzie & Wajcman, 1999; Selfe, 1999; Winner, 1985). With the exception of brand new technologies—which are usually seen as necessarily beneficial to society, as we argued earlier, established technologies are more prone to appear neutral to most members of society. For example, on the surface, using holistic scoring to place students in a first-year composition class might appear less ideological to an English department that has used this method for the past decade than the computer-scored COMPASS assessment, in part, because holistic scoring is more established in that location—"It's just the way we do things." On the other hand, the adoption of a test that places students in writing courses based upon their ability to edit a random passage on a computer seems defensible purely upon a practical basis. In fact, an American College Testing (ACT) COMPASS sales representative once asked one of us if we would not rather have our faculty doing more important things than reading placement essays or portfolios. Although the adoption of any method of assessment contains ideological, theoretical, and epistemological implications, these forces can be more or less visible given local cultures and their relationship to the various technologies available and in use.

Langdon Winner, in "Do Artifacts Have Politics?" (1985), answers his title question with an articulation of the ways in which all artifacts are political:

> In controversies about technology and society, there is no idea more provocative than the notion that technical things have political qualities. At issue is the claim that the machines, structures, and systems of modern material cul-

ture can be accurately judged not only for their contributions of efficiency and productivity, not merely for their positive and negative environmental side effects, but also for the way in which they can embody specific forms of power and authority. (p. 28)

Winner contends that technological objects can be political in different ways: Some technologies can be political due to the way they were designed, created, and/or used within a particular community; other technologies are unalterably ideological in a specific way. Similarly, some writing assessments embody political qualities because of the complex educational and social systems in which they were created and operate; their ideologies are malleable depending on their use and application. Other assessment technologies, however, are inherently political in specific ways regardless of design, use, or context.

Writing assessments can be ideological in their planning, design, and development. For example, F. Allen Hanson (1993) notes the political motivation of the first known writing examination, the Chinese Civil Service Examination that dates back to between 1122 and 256 B.C. The tests were given to determine the merit of those applying for political positions, instead of the jobs being distributed by the Emperor or the ruling class based on wealth, family, or political influence. In addition, the positions were not lifelong; instead, a test had to be retaken every 3 years to retain the honored status of civil employee. While Hanson explains how testtakers subverted the testing system, the test by design and motive was political before its use. With use, however, the test became political in different ways as more motives, people, methods, and instruments were added to the assessment system. And, while the initial motivation for the first known examination was the egalitarian distribution of opportunity to the most deserving individuals, the tests were undermined by many who cheated. Similarly, testing in America was first advocated to prevent the granting of privilege and opportunity to those with connections to people in power. Huot (2002) notes that this agenda for assessment as progressive social action was subverted within existing systems of power in accordance with Michel Foucault's (1977) ideas of the way power circulates in overdetermined systems. Huot concludes that, unfortunately, "there are many good reasons why tests and testing are viewed as largely hegemonic exercises invested in re-inscribing current power relations in American Society" (2002, p. 175). Elana Shohamy (2001), in *The Power of Tests: A Critical Perspective on the Uses of Tests*, argues that "tests are used as disciplinary tools by those in authority, enticing test takers [and those who prepare them] to change their behavior along the demands to maximize their [students'] score" (p. xvi).

In addition to some technologies being ideological by design or motivation, some can be political based upon their use. And because uses differ between occasions, the ideology of some writing assessment technologies can change based on different uses. The ideological malleability is an obvious characteristic of technology, as Winner notes: "One sees the importance of technical arrangements that precede the *use* of the things in question. It is obvious that technologies can be used in ways that enhance the power, authority, and privilege of some over others" (1985, p. 32; emphasis in original). The use of writing assessment technologies certainly influences ideology. Using the student writing portfolios as an example, in 1994 the Composition Program at the University of Louisville gave students the option of being placed into a first-year writing class based upon a high school writing portfolio. Because the decision based on the same portfolio changed—in this case, it changed from assessing high school students, teachers, and school systems to providing data for student placement into a first-year writing class, the ideology of the tests changed. Because validity refers to the decisions based on the results of an assessment, a new validity argument had to be constructed to determine whether the use of these portfolios for placement was theoretically justifiable, empirically accurate, and sufficiently fair in response to any social and educational consequences resulting from the decisions (Messick, 1994). Although validity theory has for some time stipulated that each use of a test must be investigated for its validity, the trajectory of a historically technological approach to assessment has focused attention on the creation of a measure, not its use.

In addition to the different decisions based on the assessment, the politics of the portfolio assessment changed. High school writing portfolios for college placement gave the assessment a direct consequence for the students that was never present in the high school version of the portfolio. Within the Kentucky system, the high school portfolio score had few or no practical consequences for the students outside of their own self-perception as writers. Additionally, the connection (or disjuncture) between the high school portfolio score and college placement became obvious to the students. For example, a student who may have received a high rank on the portfolio within the Kentucky system might not have placed as high as he or she might have expected in the college assessment and vice versa. The purpose and use for the portfolios at the college level were different from that of the state. High school writing portfolios were used at the University of Louisville as a means of direct assessment collected outside of the context of an impromptu timed writing examination (with ACT verbal scores and impromptu essays being the existing methods for placement). The ideology of the assessment in the case of the college placement is significantly different than the state educational reform system based on its *use*. Shohamy (2001) is quick to point out that while scholarship in testing looks at tests as objects that need to be technically sound, especially in terms of validity and reliability, the real power of testing resides in its use to control the educational process.

Writing Assessment as Efficient, Objective, and Reliable

While not all technologies are said to promote it, efficiency seems to be central in the discussion of the benefits of technologies in a capitalist culture, and educational contexts and writing assessment are no exceptions (Williamson, 1994). Efficiency in academic matters mirrors the values of corporate America, and the history of writing assessment is an interesting tension between buying into and resisting efficiency and its accompanying values. Due to a variety of factors, writing assessment in the past several decades has in many ways moved toward efficient and reliable models, from standardized tests decades ago to the computer-scored papers of today.

Although the so-called drudgery of reading and responding to student writing has always been seen as a necessary and deleterious influence on composition teaching (Brereton, 1995; Connors, 1997; Crowley, 1998; Miller, 1994; and many others), as the number of students increased in American educational institutions, so did the need for efficient, objective writing assessments. As Stanley Aronowitz (2000) notes, "In 1997, the proportion of college students to the adult population had risen to 13 percent, more than four times what is was in 1941. Of a work force of some 114 million, more than 15 million people of working age were enrolled in an institution of 'higher' learning" (p. 2). In much of the literature on computerized essay scoring, authors commonly cite the time-consuming drudgery of large-scale assessment, as well as classroom assessment of student writing as rationale for the technologies: "Changes in assessment technology over the last 200 years were all geared to increasing efficiency and making the assessment system more manageable, standardized, easily administered, objective, reliable, comparable, and inexpensive as the numbers of examinees increased" (Madaus, 1993, p. 20). Once efficiency is detached from the theoretical concept of validity, it only has reliable and economic consequences. We are not saying that issues of expense and scoring consistency are unimportant in writing assessment; however, unless we consider validity, we are not adhering to the best practices available for assessing student writing in and outside the classroom.

Inherently efficient, mechanized writing assessments are often touted for their superior objectivity and reliability, since machine scoring student essays can replicate with consistency the same scores for the same paper. However, given its ability to replicate scores, just like the technohistorical application of reliability to the problem of writing assessment, machine scoring cannot by itself guarantee an educationally profitable reading for the student whose writing is so processed. The rationale for the fear and pessimism regarding technologies is partly fueled by the ability of machine technologies to work faster and longer than their human counterparts. In addition, machines are lauded for their ability to work objectively, without the "weaknesses" of subjectivity and human emotion. Writing teachers are not exempted from the list of workers that the machine will supposedly someday replace, evidenced by the many computer tech-

nologies that claim the ability to assess student writing more objectively, more consistently, and more quickly. Technologies in academic labor serve a familiar purpose, though the threat is not primarily in the replacement of human workers. Instead, instructional technologies threaten academic labor because the latter centralizes power and allows for the hiring of less expensive technicians at the expense of knowledgeable faculty (Rhoades & Slaughter, 1998). This use of assessment for efficiency is part of the application of modern management practices and principles that helped shape composition as a field (Strickland, 2001). As a result of the need to manage resources and ensure the prestige of literary education and research, a professoriate invested in the study of literature managed and subcontracted the teaching and assessing of writing at the college level, creating laborious teaching positions for those who did not hold the competitive credentials necessary for the teaching of literature.

Inherent in the lower status of writing teachers, these faculty in general, and especially part-time instructors and graduate students, are often not trusted to make educational decisions, because they are "particularly human" and prone to subjectivity in their decision-making processes. The technology of testing in this century has moved dramatically toward valuing objectivity over subjectivity in decision making, adding to the strength of the psychometric, educational assessment community: "Our tests tend to promote . . . the values of objectivity, the importance of factual knowledge and 'right' answers, and rapid visible performance. However, in doing so, they devalue subjectivity, feelings, reflection, introspection, and discernment" (Madaus, 1994, p. 80). Anne Herrington and Charles Moran (2001) reexamined the claim that computers can be better evaluators of student texts than can teachers. At a conference of Accuplacer advocates, Herrington and Moran described the buzz of excitement over computerized grading:

At the conference the Vantage spokesperson, in explaining the efficiency of [WritePlacer Plus] WPP, kept stressing "rapid, accurate scores," and concluding with this tag: "And WritePlacer rarely requires a cup of coffee." Someone in the audience added, "and it doesn't get headaches," and another, "and doesn't get tired." Another added that it would not be biased, as would be some faculty who were giving low scores in an attempt to fill up their own classes. (p. 486)

Despite the optimism of their advocates, the response of writing teachers to computerize grading reveals an impassioned rebuttal:

From our perspective, the replacement of the teacher as reader threatens not just our jobs—a real consideration—but seems likely to change our students' sense of what it means to write in school and college. More fundamentally, it defines writing as an act of formal display, not a rhetorical interaction between a writer and readers. (p. 481)

The first concern—one that is a much less convincing argument—is that of job security. If those who assess writing have no more justification for human assessment of student writing than the protection of our jobs, then perhaps we should hand over our role to computer technologies. However, Herrington and Moran's second claim—that computerized evaluation changes the rhetorical nature of writing as an act of communication—is more substantial, since it requires us to consider technology and writing assessment within their inherent ideological, theoretical, and epistemological perspectives.

Beyond Technocentric Writing Assessment

Before developing an argument for writing assessment modes that conform less to the technological assumptions presented in the previous sections, we must remark upon and acknowledge the tremendous feat accomplished by those who developed the successive technologies that eventually became the machine scoring of student writing. What began as the inability of independent readers to agree on scores for the same papers became multiple-choice tests scores that correlated to essay scores, which eventually became holistic scoring that delivered a less than perfect but statistically viable scoring consistency, which eventually became the reliable practice of machine scoring student writing. This succession of technologies developed to assess student writing reflects the inevitability that Mackenzie and Wajcman (1999) discuss in

their book about the social and inevitable process of technological development and innovation. A computer program that can produce consistency with human scores [note that actually, the software produces a score that a large number of raters would give to a student paper better than what is humanly possible for two typical raters in a holistic scoring session] ultimately solves the problem of writing assessment and reliability. An accomplishment of this sort is astounding. The opportunities for large-scale writing assessment increase exponentially when student writing can be consistently scored with minimal human effort or expense.

Depending upon who we are, what values we hold, and what uses we want to make for assessment, a technohistory of writing assessment that culminates with the reliable machine scoring of student writing can seem like a perfect technological solution to a sticky technical problem. Of course, our choice of looking at writing assessment through a specific technological lens is based upon our understanding that writing assessments more or less buy into the Western assumptions of technologies unequally. While all writing assessments are technologies, they do not uniformly adopt the same ideological positions of progress, efficiency, and the like. The current "solutions" to writing assessment are not just technological; many also tend only to address directly problems of reliability, while essentially ignoring the larger and more important issue of validity. Table 28.1 illustrates the differing assumptions that inform a technological approach to writing assessment and those approaches that focus more on the decisions being made through the assessment procedures.

While the beliefs and assumptions in Table 28.1 seem straightforward, we must understand that a technocentric approach is based upon a specific way of looking at writing assessment and its challenges, possibilities, and solutions. In other words, writing assessment developed the way it did because it was shaped by a specific understanding of its purpose and problems. For example, Donald Schon (1983), in *The Reflective Practitioner: How Professionals Think in Action*, outlines the importance of how problems get framed and knowledge gets made in a disciplinary enterprise such as the development of writing assessment:

TABLE 28.1. Differing Assumptions Regarding Writing Assessments

Technocentric reliability model	Decision-based validity model
Agreement is the most important and troublesome issue in large-scale writing assessment.	Agreement is less important to large-scale writing assessment validity than issues such as appropriateness and accuracy of the decision.
Student writing can be meaningfully categorized and labeled numerically.	Student writing should be read with educational decisions in mind rather than depersonalizing the decision with corresponding numbers.
Nonexpert raters can be trained/calibrated to agree on scores papers should receive.	Expert readers in both the subject and the local context are the best decision makers for a writing assessment.
A reliable scoring session results in a valid writing assessment.	Reliability is one of many important factors to consider in a larger argument about the degree of validity in an assessment decision.
Machine scoring is the ultimate solution to reliable writing assessments.	While machine scoring can result in impressive results in reliability, it lacks other essential qualities that would strengthen its validity.

In real-world practice, problems do not present themselves to the practitioner as given. They must be constructed from the materials of problematic situations which are puzzling, troubling and uncertain. . . . But with this emphasis on problem solving, we ignore problem setting. . . . Problem setting is a process in which interactively, we *name* the things to which we will attend and *frame* the context in which we will attend to them. (p. 40; emphasis in original)

Of course, the problem named was unreliable scoring, and it was framed within a technocentric context. The result of this "framing" was that the developmental research on writing assessment focused an inordinate amount of attention on developing better and better technologies to solve the problem of scoring consistency. This focus on reliability and its eventual conflation with validity is not new. For example, in their ETS Research Bulletin that established the efficacy of reading and scoring student writing, Godshalk et al. (1966) described the process of trying to attain interrater reliability in terms of the validity of the procedures themselves: "It looked as if the efforts to improve reading reliability had been going in the wrong direction. The solution, it seemed, was in subjecting each paper to the judgment of a number of different readers. The consensus would constitute a valid measure of writing ability, assuming of course that readers were competent" (p. 4). From the last sentence, it is clear that the creators of holistic

scoring were primarily interested in interrater reliability, and attention to the quality and/or character of the judgments being made were an afterthought.

Nonetheless, once we framed the problem of writing assessment technologically as the inability of readers to give the same scores to the same papers, we initiated a search for the technology to solve such a problem. The successive technologies we have described became inevitable, with each technological discovery driving successive technological approaches. This inevitability of the succession of technologies used to solve the technical problem of reliability even subsumed the prevailing theoretical preeminence of validity. On the other hand, if we understand that a technocentric history of writing assessment is just one approach, then we might ask how else the problems for writing assessment could be framed.

As Huot (1994) noted in the initial introduction to the journal *Assessing Writing,* the early literature on writing assessment was mostly positive, encouraging, and ultimately about documenting the viability of the direct assessment of student writing. By the early 1990s, the scholarship about writing assessment became more critical. It is within this scholarly climate that William L. Smith (1992, 1993; O'Neill, 2003) began to research the writing placement program at the University of Pittsburgh in the middle to late 1980s. Smith's research was different from the writing assessment research we have outlined. Instead of being concerned primarily with scoring reliability, Smith researched the accuracy and adequacy of the decisions being made for placement through holistic scoring. In other words, instead of focusing on reliability, "a necessary but not a sufficient condition for validity" (Cherry & Meyer, 1993, p. 110), Smith focused on validity as "an integrated evaluative judgment to support the adequacy and appropriateness of inferences and actions based on test scores and modes of assessment" (Messick, 1989, p. 5).

Smith's focus on the validity of the placement program at Pitt meant that he had to find out whether students were receiving the best possible placement. He researched a variety of factors, including the kinds of prompts, the time and environment for administering the examination, and the students who took the examination and found that none of them by themselves, or in concert, influenced the accuracy of placement decisions (O'Neill, 2003, pp. 56–57). On the other hand, once Smith turned his inquiry to the readers who read and provided scores for student writing, he began to gather very useful and important information about the decisions being made for placement at Pitt through holistic scoring. One thing Smith found was that the disagreements among raters while producing unreliable scores were reliable, so that raters disagreed on a regular, consistent basis. Since a technological approach to unreliable scoring sought not to understand how and why raters disagreed, it merely produced procedures that provided more consistency in scoring.

Once Smith knew that raters were disagreeing on a consistent basis, he began to research these differences to find out how and why teachers disagreed. The consistency of disagreement that Smith found seemed to indicate that differences in scores among his placement raters were based upon some consistent, rule-governed but different criteria raters had for placement. Eventually Smith found that rater disagreement was due to the courses individuals taught most. When Smith looked not just at individual raters but at rater sets, as he called them, he found that some raters agreed with each other at a very high rate. Raters who agreed with each other at high rates and disagreed with other raters on a consistent basis shared the experience of

teaching particular courses in the curriculum for which they were making placement decisions. Ultimately, Smith found that teachers who regularly taught a specific course were better able to make decisions for that course. Ultimately, Smith used five separate criteria to ascertain the accuracy of placement: (1) number of students moved in the beginning of a semester; (2) course grades; (3) student surveys of course appropriateness; (4) teacher survey of placement satisfaction; and (5) exit examinations or other posttests. Using these criteria, Smith concluded that his expert rater system was a more accurate and adequate method than holistic scoring for placing students at his institution.

Smith's methods structured placement procedures around the courses teachers taught. A reader who first read a student's paper had one decision to make: Does this student belong in my class? If the reader thought "yes," then the paper was given to the other reader for that specific course. If the reader thought "no," then he or she would give the paper to the reader he or she thought would be most expert for making this decision. In this way, a student was placed when two readers for a specific course thought he or she belonged there. Readers were chosen for specific courses based upon their most pervasive and recent teaching experiences. Once Smith developed his new procedures for placement, he compared results and resources of his new system with the use of holistic scoring and found that his "expert reader" procedures produced more accurate and reliable scores in less time and for less money. Not only did he find that readers were able to make decisions more quickly but there was also no need for norming sessions or the extra steps involved in summing rater scores and setting cut scores for each possible placement in the curriculum, since his readers[2] made placement decisions directly.

Smith's discovery of the consistencies in disagreements among readers framed the problem for writing assessment in a completely new way. Instead of just trying to get readers to agree, Smith looked into what made them disagree and why their disagreements were so consistent. What he found was that not all readers had the same ability to make placement decisions. Throughout the 20th century, knowledge about reading has mushroomed to support Louise Rosenblatt's (1978) contention, first voiced in the 1930s, that readers create textual representations that affect what they comprehend while reading. It is not news that people read different texts in different ways. This ability to read a text in different ways is often seen as important intellectual work, especially in literary studies (Elbow & Yancey, 1994). However, as we have rehearsed the history of writing assessment, this ability of teachers to produce different readings was the main problem in providing a viable way to assess student writing, and this "problem" with variable reading (part of the reading process) was solved through a series of related technologies that finally resulted in the ability to produce perfectly consistent readings of student writing using computer software.

It is beyond our purview in this chapter to explore all of the assumptions inherent in the expert reader procedures for placement (for a good examination of the implications of this research in writing assessment, see O'Neill, 2003), though it should be clear that these assumptions are based upon the framing of the phenomenon of readers not agreeing on scores for student writing in a very different way. Instead of fixing the disagreement problem by developing procedures such as holistic scoring, which involves rubrics and training that cause people to agree better and ultimately to create a software program that produces consistent scores, these procedures seek to embrace and harness the fact that different readers read texts in different ways. These procedures are also aimed at providing a way for teachers to make the best educational decisions (in this case, placement) rather than to produce reliable scores. We would argue that asking someone whether a paper deserves a 2 or 3 on a 4-point scale, even when that scale contains an elaborate description of various characteristics of writing, is very different than asking a teacher whether a student would most profit from being in a specific class about which the teacher is knowledgeable.

Smith's research frames the problem for writing assessment as the setting of an appropriate context within which teachers can read students' writing and make informed decisions about them. His structure focuses reading around a specific context, honoring the fact that some readers are better able

than others to make certain assessment decisions. His procedures are easily supported and explained through what we now know about reading and writing theoretically and empirically. Smith (1993) reported that without focusing on agreement at all, readers who make direct decisions about courses for which they are expert agree at a higher rate than the same raters trained to agree in holistic scoring sessions (pp. 192–196). In other words, the variation in agreement found in various studies throughout the 20th-century (see Godshalk et al., 1966, pp. 1–5) was not because teachers inherently disagreed upon writing quality or were unable to create a particular consensus of what students needed to be doing at specific junctures in writing instruction. As Smith (1992, 1993) demonstrated in his research, the problem with most of the developmental research on holistic scoring and/or direct writing assessment is that context was never an important factor. For example, in the most famous study on reliability, conducted by Diederich, French, and Carlton (1961), 55 readers read over 300 essays, and 90% of the essays received scores of 7 or more on a 9-point scoring guideline. However, these readers, who came from a variety of professions, received no context for the decisions they were making. In some ways, the research on reliability in writing assessment is a good example of the importance of context in reading and meaning making. Without context, readers cannot agree about the relative merit of specific pieces of writing and, more importantly, the decisions to be made on behalf of that writing. It seems safe to say, then, that while traditional direct writing assessment procedures are based upon a theory of scoring, of how to produce the most reliable scores for specific pieces of writing, Smith's procedures rest theoretically upon an understanding of reading and the importance of context to meaning and decision making. Within this context, not all variation in reading is bad; looking beyond a technological explanation for writing assessment, these procedures are based upon the fact that in different situations and for different purposes, different readers read different texts in different ways. Smith used the variation in reading to build procedures that are both accurate and consistent, and still variable. What is crucial in this model is the creation of a familiar and robust situation in which the reader (the teacher for a specific class) makes a decision for which he or she is expert and is supplied context based upon his or her reading of a specific student. Smith (1992, 1993) and O'Neill (2003) have both written about the difference in the kind and nature of the decision being made in which the reader considers the student and not just the writing. The context created for the reader allows him or her the opportunity to make a richer decision that considers the whole student's development as a writer, rather than just looking at a specific text according to prescribed criteria that the rater may or may not have had any say in articulating.

Conclusion

What we hope is clear in our discussion of a technocentric history of writing assessment is that the development of indirect tests of grammar, usage and mechanics; of direct tests of writing such as holistic, analytic, and primary trait scoring; and of machine scoring student writing are all based upon framing the problem for writing assessment as the inability for raters to agree on scores for the same paper and to apply technological approaches to solve this problem. We also hope we have clarified other ways to frame the problem for writing assessment, and that these other ways of understanding the difficulties and importance of rendering appropriate educational decisions for students can be based on local control, understanding, and expertise that do *not* need the application of technology to overcome local knowledge. Instead, these "local" procedures can produce reliably accurate, ethical educational decisions. Writing assessment procedures such as the expert reader model have technological features. Certain readers read specific papers, and all readers must teach the course for which they make placement decisions. Other than that, there is no technology except a teacher reading papers and making a single decision about which class best suits a particular student. Smith's procedures are supported by theories of how people read and by empirical evidence documenting the accuracy and consistency of placements decisions, satisfying the basic principles set down by Messick (1989) and

others for validity. It is also important to note here that Smith's theoretical framing of the problem and the general structure for writing assessment have been used in various locations and contexts. Susanmarie Harrington (1998) reported on procedures involving the ability of students to compose online and to have readers access and make decisions about students in an electronic environment. These researchers, and others like them, understand writing assessment to revolve around our best, most current understanding of literacy and writing theory, rather than being bound to a mechanical approach to problems of agreement. In truth, we see technological approaches such as indirect tests of writing, holistic scoring, and machine-scored essays as only one way to frame and name the problem for writing assessment. Approaches like Smith's and others that rely on local knowledge and expertise frame the problem in a different way and offer a very different solution. Figure 28.1 illustrates the separate trajectories that two different approaches to the problems of writing assessment can take in offering very different solutions.

In a perfect world, we might be content in concluding that these two very different approaches have real importance and value for those who need to make decisions about students based upon their ability to write. Unfortunately, that is not the way most technologies work. Technological innovation such as the machine scoring of student writing is not only the result reached by a handful of researchers like Ellis Page but it is also an economic product, developed and marketed on a large-scale to make a profit. Currently, ACT and SAT are marketing writing tests that allow students to compose for 25 minutes and whose scores will be generated by computer software for colleges and universities to make local, placement decisions. Students have to bear the brunt of the educational and financial costs for these new tests. What is completely lost in this new scheme is the value of other ways of framing the problem for writing assessment and the loss of a culture of committed people making decisions for the students they teach (White, in press). In addition, as we add to the national testing economy, we detract from the local economies that have been developed, supported, and sustained by a local commitment

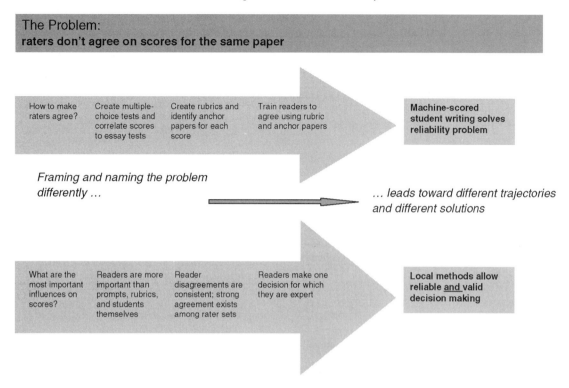

FIGURE 28.1. Framing the problem for writing assessment.

to teaching and assessing writing. The gutting of these local economies has important consequence for a continuing technological focus for writing assessment. We are not only devaluing local knowledge and expertise based upon the ability to produce perfectly consistent scores but we are also depriving local readers (often graduate students and contingent faculty) of professional development opportunities (Elbow & Belanoff, 1986; Edgington & McCarren, in preparation; White, 1993; and many others). While we are talking economy, it is important to note that the procedures developed by Smith and others, such as Richard Haswell (2001), are not monetarily unviable. For example, in an expert reader model for placement we worked on at the University of Louisville, we were able to make valid placement decisions based on the reading of student portfolios for less than $5 per person.

Finally, we hope it is clear that writing assessment developed the way it did not because that was the only way, or even the best way, but because the problem was framed technically that the approach to solving the technical problem of reliability was wholly technological. However, even as we have addressed problems with reliability, we have created a system that values scoring over decision making, consistency over local knowledge, and an economy that transfers any economic compensation for faculty labor and expertise to national companies using computer software. We believe that assessing student writing and making educational decisions based upon those assessments is not only very important to the nature of the work we do in teaching writing but it is also a very powerful statement about what we value (Broad, 2003). This is not to say that we do not value the accomplishments of those who have framed the problem for writing assessment technologically and have created the technology to score student writing with computer software. We applaud these efforts and see much value in being able to provide scores for huge populations of students. For us, the greatest potential for machine scoring student writing is as a research tool that can not only look at huge numbers of student essays but also can provide various kinds of scores depending upon the readings the software is programmed to duplicate. For example, we could examine a number of different readings available from different institutions and contexts, and answer questions about the ways writing is valued. It would be interesting to know how institutions' placement decisions compare. Of course, these purpose are different from those of the industry that paid for the development of this software and is already finding new markets and ways of generating income for its companies.

On the other hand, we call for writing teachers, writing program administrators, and other people affected by writing assessment decisions to look beyond technological approaches and to frame the problem for writing assessment as the way to produce the best decisions (validity) for students and teachers. Either through the adaptation of local methods based upon teacher expertise or with computer software, we have solved the problem of scoring consistency (reliability). It is crucial that we understand the difference between reliability-driven writing assessment and those procedures driven by a need to make the best decisions for students (validity). Understanding the history of writing assessment, and the influence of technology on that history, should allow us to make the best possible decisions for writing assessment, building on and protecting the gains we have made in writing assessment on a technological and local level.

Notes

1. Even though postmodern theories of invention explain how systemic influences replicate and perpetuate existing cultural systems and sustain their inherent unequal power relations, it is important to note that Ellis Page championed the machine scoring of student writing for nearly 40 years.
2. We use the word "rater" when referring to writing assessments that have teachers produce scores, and "readers" when teachers make direct decisions.

References

Aronowitz, S. (2000). *The knowledge factory: Dismantling the corporate university and creating true higher education.* Boston: Beacon Press.

Barton, B. F., & Barton, M. S. (1993). Ideology and the map: Toward a postmodern visual design practice. In N. R. Blyler & C. Thralls (Eds.), *Professional communication: The social perspective* (pp. 49–78). Newbury Park, CA: Sage.

Barton, E. (1994). Interpreting the discourses of technology. In C. Selfe & S. Hilligoss (Eds.), *Literacy and technology: The complications of teaching and learning with technology* (pp. 56–75). New York: Modern Language Association Press.

Belanoff, P. (1994). Portfolios and literacy: Why. In L. Black, D. Daiker, J. Sommers, & G. Stygall (Eds.), *New directions in portfolio assessment* (pp. 13–24). Portsmouth, NH: Boynton/Cook.

Belanoff, P., & Dickson, M. (Eds.). (1991). *Portfolios: Process and product.* Portsmouth, NH: Boynton/Cook.

Brereton, J. (1995). *The origins of composition studies in the American college, 1875–1925: A documentary history.* Pittsburgh: University of Pittsburgh Press.

Broad, B. (2003). *What we really value: Beyond rubrics in teaching and assessing writing.* Logan: Utah State University Press.

Calfee, R., & Perfumo, P. (Eds.). (1996). *Writing portfolios in the classroom: Policy and practice, promise and peril.* Mahwah, NJ: Erlbaum.

Callahan, S. (1997). Tests worth taking?: Using portfolios for accountability in Kentucky. *Research in the Teaching of English, 31,* 295–336.

Camp, R. (1993). Changing the model for the direct assessment of writing. In M. M. Williamson & B. Huot, (Eds.), *Validating holistic scoring for writing assessment: Theoretical and empirical foundations* (pp. 45–78). Cresskill, NJ: Hampton Press.

Cherry, R., & Meyer, P. (1993). Reliability issues in holistic assessment. In M. M. Williamson & B. Huot, (Eds.), *Validating holistic scoring for writing assessment: Theoretical and empirical foundations* (pp. 109–141). Cresskill, NJ: Hampton Press.

Connors, R. (1997). *Composition–rhetoric: Backgrounds, theory and pedagogy.* Pittsburgh: University of Pittsburgh Press.

Cooper, C. R. (1977). Holistic evaluation of writing. In C. R. Cooper, & L. Odell (Eds.), *Evaluating writing: Describing, measuring and judging* (pp. 3–32). Urbana, IL: National Council of Teachers of English.

Cooper, P. (1984). *The assessment of writing ability: A review of research* (GREEB No. 82–15). Princeton, NJ: Educational Testing Service.

Crowley, S. (1998). *Composition in the university: Historical and polemical essays.* Pittsburgh: University of Pittsburgh Press.

Diederich, P., French, J., & Carlton, S. (1961). Factors in judgment of writing quality (Research Bulletin No. 61–15). Princeton, NJ: Educational Testing Service.

Edgington, A., & Mcarren, J. (in preparation). Rater talk: Examining decision-making discourse in writing assessment for placement. In M. M. Williamson & B. Huot (Eds.) *Revising Holistic Scoring: Second Edition.* Cresskill, NJ: Hampton.

Elbow, P. & Belanoff, P. (1986). Portfolios as a substitute for proficiency examinations. *College Composition and Communication, 37,* 336–339.

Elbow, P. & Yancey, K. (1994). On the nature of holistic scoring: An inquiry composed on email. *Assessing Writing, 1,* 91–108.

Huot (Eds.), *Revising holistic scoring: A second edition.* Cresskill, NJ: Hampton.

Foucault, M. (1977). *Discipline and punish: The birth of the prison* (A. Sheridan, Trans.). New York: Pantheon.

Godshalk, F. I., Swineford, F., & Coffman, W. E. (1966). *The measurement of writing ability* (CEEB RM No. 6). Princeton, NJ: Educational Testing Service.

Greenberg, K. L., Wiener, H. S., & Donovan, R. A. (Eds.). (1986). *Writing assessment: Issues and strategies.* New York: Longman.

Greenberg, K., & Witte, S. (1988). Validity issues in direct writing assessment. *Notes from the National Testing Network in Writing, 8,* 13–14.

Hanson, F. A. (1993). The forest of pencils. In F. A. Hanson (Ed.), *Testing testing: Social consequences of the examined life* (pp. 185–221). Berkeley: University of California Press.

Harrington, S. (1998). New visions of authority in placement test rating. *WPA: Writing Program Administration, 22,* 53–84.

Haswell, R. H., & Wyche, S. (2001).Authoring an exam: Adventuring in large-scale writing assessment. In R. H. Haswell (Ed.), *Beyond outcomes: Assessment and instruction within a university writing program* (pp. 13–24). Westport, CT: Ablex.

Heidegger, M. (1977). *The question concerning technology* (W. Lovitt, Trans.). New York: Harper & Row.

Herrington, A., & Moran, C. (2001). What happens when machines read our students' writing? *College English, 63,* 480–499.

Huot, B. (1996). Toward a new theory of assessment. *College Composition and Communication, 47,* 549–566.

Huot, B. (2002). *(Re)articulating writing assessment for teaching and learning.* Logan: Utah State University Press.

Huot, B., & Williamson, M. M. (1997). Rethinking portfolios for evaluating writing: Issues of assessment and power. In K. B. Yancey & I. Weiser (Eds.), *Situating Portfolios: Four Perspectives.* Logan: Utah State University Press.

MacKenzie, D., & Wajcman, J. (Eds.). (1999). *The social shaping of technology* (2nd ed.). Buckingham, UK: Open University Press.

Madaus, G. (1993). A national testing system: Manna from above?: An historical/technological perspective. *Educational Measurement, 11,* 9–26.

Madaus, G. (1994). A technological and historical consideration of equity issues associated with proposals to change the nation's testing policy. *Harvard Educational Review, 64*(1), 76–95.

Messick, S. (1989). Meaning and values in test validation: The science and ethics of assessment. *Educational Researcher, 18*(2), 5–12.

Miller, R. (1994). Composing English studies: Toward a social history of the discipline. *College Composition and Communication, 45,* 164–179.

Murphy, S. (1997). Teachers and students: Reclaiming assessment via portfolios. In K. B. Yancey & I. Weiser (Eds.), *Situating portfolios: Four perspectives* (pp. 72–88). Logan: Utah State University Press.

Murphy, S., & Grant, B. (1996). Portfolio approaches to assessment: Breakthrough or more of the same. In E. M. White, W. D. Lutz, & S. Kamusikiri (Eds.), *Assessment of writing: Politics, policies, practices* (pp. 284–300). New York: Modern Language Association.

Myers, M. (1980). *A procedure for writing assessment and holistic scoring.* Urbana, IL: National Council of Teachers of English.

Odell, L. (1981). Defining and assessing competence in writing. In C. Cooper (Ed.) *The nature and measurement of competency in English* (pp. 95–138). Urbana, IL: National Council of Teachers of English.

O'Neill, P. (2003). Moving beyond holistic scoring through validity inquiry. *Journal of Writing Assessment, 1,* 47–65.

Page, E. (1994). Computer grading of student prose: Using modern concepts and software. *Journal of Experimental Education, 62,* 127–142.

Palmer, O. (1960). Sixty years of English testing. *College Board, 42,* 8–14.

Rhoades, G., & Slaughter, S. (1998). Academic capitalism, managed professionals, and supply-side higher education. In R. Martin (Ed.), *Chalk lines: The politics of work in the managed university* (pp. 33–68). Durham, NC: Duke University Press.

Rosenblatt, L. (1978). *The reader, the text, the poem: The transactional theory of the literary work.* Carbondale: Southern Illinois Press.

Royer, D. J., & Gilles, R. (1998). Putting assessment in its place with directed self-placement. *College Composition and Communication, 50,* 54–70.

Schon, D. (1984). *The reflective practitioner: How professionals think in action.* New York: Basic Books.

Selfe, C. L. (1999). *Technology and literacy in the twenty-first century: The importance of paying attention.* Carbondale: Southern Illinois University Press.

Shermis, M., & Burstein, J. (Eds.). (2003). *Automated essay scoring: A cross-disciplinary perspective.* Mahwah, NJ: Erlbaum.

Shohamy, E. (2001). *The power of tests: A critical perspective of the uses of language tests*. London: Longman.

Smith, W. L. (1992). The importance of teacher knowledge in college composition placement testing. In J. R. Hayes, R. E. Young, M. L. Matchett, M. McCaffrey, C. Cochran, & T. Hajduk (Eds.), *Reading empirical research studies: The rhetoric of research* (pp. 289–316). Hillsdale, NJ: Erlbaum.

Smith, W. L. (1993). Assessing the reliability and adequacy of using holistic scoring of essays as a college composition placement program technique. In M. M. Williamson & B. Huot (Eds.), *Validating holistic scoring for writing assessment: Theoretical and empirical foundations* (pp. 142–205). Cresskill, NJ: Hampton Press.

Sommers, N. (1982). Responding to student writing. *College Composition and Communication, 33,* 148–156.

Starch, D., & Elliott, E. C. (1912). Reliability of the grading of high school work in English. *School Review, 20,* 442–457.

Strickland, D. (2001). Taking dictation: The emergence of writing and the cultural contradictions of composition teaching. *College English, 63,* 457–479.

White, E. M. (1993). Holistic scoring: Past triumphs and future challenges. In M. M. Williamson & B. Huot (Eds.), *Validating holistic scoring for writing assessment: Theoretical and empirical foundations* (pp. 79–108). Cresskill, NJ: Hampton Press.

White, E. M. (1995). An apologia for the timed impromptu essay test. *College Composition and Communication, 46,* 30–45.

White, E. M. (2005). The science of writing portfolios: Phase 2. *College Composition and Communication, 56,* 581–600.

White, E. M. (in press). The misuse of writing assessment for political purposes. *Journal of Writing Assessment, 2.*

Williamson, M. M. (1993). An introduction to holistic scoring: The social, historical, and theoretical context for writing assessment. In M. M. Williamson & B. Huot (Eds.), *Validating holistic scoring for writing assessment: Theoretical and empirical foundations* (pp. 1–44). Cresskill, NJ: Hampton Press.

Williamson, M. M. (1994). The worship of efficiency: Untangling theoretical and practical considerations in writing assessment. *Assessing Writing, 1,* 147–74.

Williamson, M. M., & Huot, B. (Eds.). (1993). *Validating holistic scoring for writing assessment: Theoretical and empirical foundations*. Cresskill, NJ: Hampton Press.

Winner, L. (1985). Do artifacts have politics? In D. MacKenzie & J. Wajcman (Eds.), *The social shaping of technology* (2nd ed. pp. 28–40). Buckingham, UK: Open University Press.

Yancey, K. B. (1992). *Portfolios in the writing classroom: An introduction*. Urbana, IL: National Council of Teachers of English.

Yancey, K. B. (1999). Looking back as we look forward: Historicizing writing assessment. *College Composition and Communication, 50,* 483–503.

Chapter 29

What Does Reading Have to Tell Us about Writing?

Preliminary Questions and Methodological Challenges in Examining the Neurobiological Foundations of Writing and Writing Disabilities

Kenneth R. Pugh, Stephen J. Frost, Rebecca Sandak, Margie Gillis, Dina Moore, Annette R. Jenner, *and* W. Einar Mencl

Neuroimaging techniques have been employed with increasing frequency in recent years to examine both typical and atypical development in cognitive domains such as language, reading, memory, mathematical reasoning, attention, and executive function (Papanicolaou, Pugh, Simos, & Mencl, 2004). Research aimed at identifying the neural systems (neurocircuity) that underlie these complex cognitive functions has benefited in recent years from rapid advances in neuroimaging technologies (e.g., positron emission tomography [PET]; functional magnetic resonance imaging [fMRI]; magnetoencephalography [MEG]).

In essence, functional neuroimaging allows us to identify sets of interrelated brain regions that are engaged (activated) when the participant performs a specific cognitive task (see Papanicolaou et al., 2004, for detailed methodological discussion and contrast of different technologies). While we can assume that different cognitive functions will engage many overlapping brain regions, we also might expect domain-specific circuits, and the extant data seem to bear out this expectation. Thus, for instance, some—but not all—brain regions activated during language-processing tasks will be nonover-

lapping with regions associated with visual perception, mathematical reasoning, or memory tasks (Frackowiack, Friston, Fruth, Dolan, & Mazziotta, 1997).

In this chapter we consider the kinds of methodological and design challenges that must be met if functional neuroimaging is to be applied fruitfully to the study of composition in writing and its disorders. To date, relatively little neuroimaging research has been conducted in this complex language production domain. However, it can be reasonably assumed from the outset that writing will share with other language functions many overlapping neurobiological systems. Therefore, we begin by considering previous findings on the functional brain organization for spoken and written language perception and production. Berninger, Abbott, Abbott, Graham, and Richards (2002) have conducted extensive behavioral research on the interrelations among all of these language domains, stressing the need to determine how composition in writing and its difficulties relate to general competencies for language by ear (speech perception), mouth (speech production), eye (reading), and hand (writing). Moreover, each of these language domains is complex and hierarchically organized (Indefrey & Levelt, 2004); we have previously noted the need to develop methods and experimental designs that will allow us to isolate and examine component subprocesses in each domain (Pugh et al., 1997, 2000). For example, for any modality, we can draw meaningful distinctions between hierarchically organized sublexical, lexical, syntactic, and comprehension-related component processes. To varying degrees, each of these component processes is likely to be shared among the written and spoken language domains.

Behavioral research suggests that disorders of reading and writing are highly comorbid and may therefore share a common etiological basis (Berninger et al., 2002). Because more is known at present regarding the neurobiology of reading development and disability with respect to component process organization, as well as the neurobiological signatures of successful remediation on these processes, this literature is reviewed in some depth to provide a set of preliminary hypotheses about what might be anticipated as we begin to explore writing difficulties and their remediation. We begin however, by considering what is known about the neurobiological substrates for written versus spoken language in general.

Written Language and Its Relation to Spoken Language

Both in the history of the human species and the development of the individual child, spoken language capacity emerges prior to the secondary, derived language abilities of reading and writing. Although the cortical and subcortical organization for spoken language perception and production is viewed by many as a biological specialization, reading and writing, by contrast, are certainly not (Liberman, 1992). In contrast to spoken language communication skills, reading and writing must be explicitly taught, and significant numbers of children for whom spoken language communication skills are adequate, will fail to obtain age-appropriate reading and writing levels even with intensive training. When considered from the neurobiological perspective, the acquisition of writing skills requires the integration of visual, motor, language, and associative cortical re-

gions, which can eventually permit bidirectional mapping between the visual forms of words to already well-established spoken language representations (Price, Winterburn, Giraud, Moore, & Noppeney, 2003; Pugh et al., 2000).

Neuroimaging studies that have directly compared spoken with printed word identification have generally found largely overlapping neural networks across the left-hemisphere (LH) cortex (Carpentier et al., 2001; Chee, O'Craven, Bergida, Rosen, & Savoy, 1999; Constable et al., 2004; Howard et al., 1992; Michael, Keller, Carpenter, & Just, 2001; Shaywitz et al., 2001; Simos, Popanicolaou, & Breier, 1999). A recent study from our group is illustrative (Constable et al., 2004). Cortical regions engaged by sentence processing in the auditory versus the visual modality were mapped using fMRI. Figure 29.1A demonstrates the influence of input modality: Auditory presentation was associated with relatively higher activity at subregions within the superior temporal gyrus (STG) bilaterally, whereas printed sentences evoked heightened activity at a wider set of mostly posterior sites, including the angular gyrus, supramarginal gyrus, and the fusiform gyrus in the occipitotemporal region within the LH, along with specific loci in the inferior frontal gyrus (IFG). The intersection of these modality-dependent maps (Figure 29.1B), however, revealed many overlapping regions located primarily in the LH, including sites within the IFG, and the STG (see Figure 29.2 for a lateral view of key reading and language zones).

Thus, while reading was associated with a somewhat more broadly distributed posterior circuitry than speech processing (as anticipated by the biological specialization and naturalness argument), the two modalities also show extensive overlap in all major language zones in the LH, including the traditionally defined Broca's area in the IFG, and Wernicke's area in the STG and temporoparietal region (see Figure 29.2). Whereas printed and spoken language processing employ very different sensory level processes (i.e., vision and audition), our focus is on language; accordingly, we employed a subtraction design to control for these nonlanguage differences. The basic logic of subtraction designs is to use control or baseline tasks that share secondary operations with

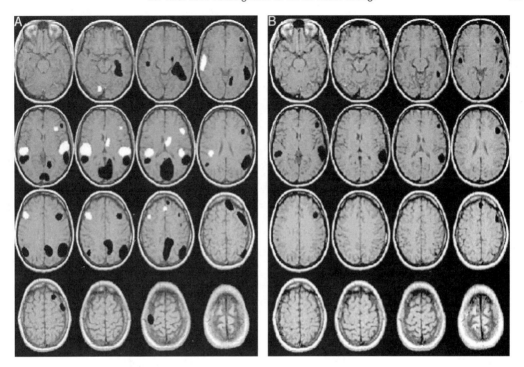

FIGURE 29.1A. In black are regions with higher activation for printed than for spoken sentences. In white are regions with higher activation for spoken than for printed sentences. Left hemisphere is shown on the right (per radiological convention).

FIGURE 29.1B. In black are regions of maximum overlap for both printed and spoken sentences. Left hemisphere is shown on the right (per radiological convention).

the task of interest (thus, for spoken sentences, we employed an auditory tone judgment control task, and for printed sentences, a visual line judgment control task to isolate language-related activation patterns). In theory, we are able to "subtract away" the brain activation due to sensory processing and are left with the brain activation due to language-specific processing. As seen in figure 29.1B, the overlap within traditional language zones appears to be the most salient feature of this type of contrast. This would certainly motivate speculation that similar patterns with respect to both overlap in traditional language zones with somewhat more diffuse activation for writing relative to speaking due to differences in biological specialization will be evident when written and spoken language production are contrasted with similar designs (controlling for differences in mode of output).

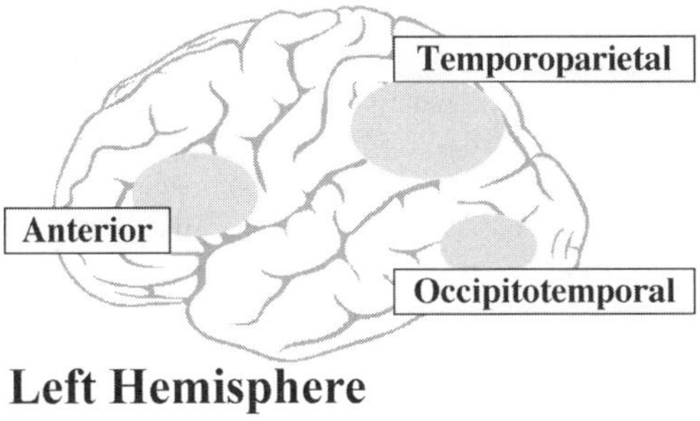

Neural Mechanisms of Language Production: Speaking and Writing

As we begin to map out the brain circuitry for language by eye, ear, mouth, and hand, in order to examine their interdependencies in struggling readers and writers (Berninger et al., 2002), we cannot point to a single experiment that has contrasted all of these pro-

Left Hemisphere

FIGURE 29.2. A schematic view of key reading and language zones.

cesses in the same subjects. To explore these complex interrelations in the absence of such studies, Indefrey and Levelt (2004) conducted a large-scale meta-analysis of 82 published neuroimaging experiments in order to identify the neurocircuitry for production of words during varied language tasks, along with the overlap between production and perception. Given the paucity of neurobiological evidence on writing and its various component processes, some consideration of the extant literature on the neurobiology of oral language production may provide some initial insights.

This meta-analysis revealed a complex taxonomy when considering both the location and relative timing of each language process, but several general patterns do emerge. First, large portions of traditionally defined language regions are activated during both spoken language perception and production tasks, including those regions discussed in the preceding section comparing spoken with printed sentence processing: bilateral STG, LH middle temporal gyrus (MTG), and LH IFG. Perhaps this evidence for highly overlapping neural networks for perception and production should not be so terribly surprising given the body of behavioral evidence suggesting that speech perception is to some degree, at least, grounded in the mechanisms of speech production (Liberman & Mattingly, 1985).

Second, while revealing tight perception–production links at the neurobiological level of analysis in broad terms, the results of the meta-analysis also suggest that hierarchically organized component processes in spoken language production are partially dissociable within these largely LH language networks. To illustrate this hierarchical organization, one that will have parallels in written language as well, consider the stream of events that need to occur if a participant is presented with pictures of objects and asked to name them aloud. This simple task should engage initially semantic–conceptual processing, followed by lexical selection (finding the word in the mental lexicon), followed by retrieval of the phonological form, and finally phonetic and articulatory planning. These operations are therefore in some sense hierarchically organized, and while they need not be strictly serial, they must logically unfold in a sequential fashion, with, for in-

stance, lexical selection necessarily preceding phonetic and articulatory planning (Levelt, Roelefs, & Meyer, 1999). The meta-analysis included studies using multiple imaging modalities, some of which yield information on spatial location of activation (e.g., PET, fMRI) and others, on the relative timing of these activations (e.g., electroencephalography [EEG], MEG). The analysis suggests that posterior temporal regions (the middle and superior temporal gyri) are active relatively early in naming tasks and likely are associated with lexical and phonological retrieval, while frontal regions, including the supplementary motor area and posterior components of the IFG and insula are activated somewhat later during the naming event and are likely associated with phonetic and articulatory planning relevant to generating the output response. While much more research is needed to gain a precise and fine-grained account of the functional anatomy of spoken language production, and while there is still ongoing debate with respect to precise timing and localization, this posterior to anterior hierarchically organized taxonomy can provide a platform for contrasting written and spoken language output. As with perception, we would anticipate that writing words will overlap speaking at brain regions associated with conceptual, lexical, and phonological processing. On the naturalness argument, we might imagine a less localized pattern for writing relative to speaking, but again, overlap at more abstract levels of processing should be the rule. Differences will no doubt emerge as we isolate later stages of processing relevant phonetic and motor output.

To date, we have few neuroimaging data on the various higher order processes involved in writing (i.e., semantic–conceptual processing, syntax, lexical selection, and phonological coding). But given the evidence discussed in the preceding sections, we might anticipate many overlapping cortical networks for writing and for speaking at more abstract conceptual and linguistic levels of analysis and, hence, the neurobiological model of speaking put forth by Indefrey and Levelt (2004) might serve as an initial framework for generating expectations about the neurocircuitry of writing. Again, in the domain of perception, both spoken and written words and sentences engage largely overlapping neural networks, with some modality-specific regions evident for prelexical input processing stages (Constable et al., 2004; see Figure 29.1).

In the domain of production, lesion studies examining patients with selective deficits in either written or oral spelling suggest that largely overlapping conceptual and lexical systems are likely to be found up to the point at which writing and speaking diverge mechanically, with neural output systems being modality-specific (Croisile et al., 1996; Del Grosso Destreri et al., 2000; Friedman, 1989; Hodges & Marshall, 1992; Miozzo & De Bastiani, 2002). Lesion studies of a relatively rare condition known as pure agraphia have implicated both the superior parietal lobule and middle frontal regions, suggesting a possible role in control of writing behavior for these regions.

A few neuroimaging studies have been conducted to date examining the neural correlates of handwriting. These studies may be thought of as beginning to reveal the neurocircuitry relevant to phonological-to-graphemic and/or graphemic-to-motor planning stages of processing during writing. In one study (Katanoda, Yoshikawa, & Sugishita, 2001), a group of Japanese participants was instructed to write the names of pictured objects, and in a second study (Menon & Desmond, 2001), a group of English speaking participants wrote sentences from dictation. Both studies converge to suggest a role for the regions previously implicated in lesion studies: the LH superior parietal lobule and LH middle to inferior frontal gyri. While the frontal regions would appear to be partially overlapping with areas implicated in speech production (Indefrey & Levelt, 2004) the involvement of the LH superior parietal lobule appears to be more specific to writing (Katanoda et al., 2001). While the tasks employed in these initial studies do not make significant demands on higher order aspects of writing behavior, such as conceptual or grammatical processing, they do suggest neural subsystems that might be crucial to the process of generating written word forms. One might speculate that if handwriting is more compromised than more general phonological and language processes in some clinical cohorts, anomalous activation patterns in these regions might be found. In any event, these studies examining handwriting now set the stage for more elaborate studies, wherein we begin to vary demands made on each of the higher order aspects of writing behavior in order to map out more fully the hierarchically organized neurocircuitry of writing. Again, given the likelihood of many shared neurobiological components with reading, listening, and speaking, studies that examine writing within a broader language context will be very important.

Much remains to be investigated in the functional brain mapping of language by eye, ear, hand, and mouth (especially for those hierarchically arranged processes that constitute composition). Nevertheless, based on our reading of the current literature, we would cautiously suggest that despite differences in input and output mechanisms associated with each of these "end organs," the brain regions associated with phonological, semantic, syntactic, and pragmatic operations should be highly overlapping and highly interrelated.

With respect to writing deficits, the literature discussed here might be taken to suggest that if an individual has core deficits in any one of these overlapping dimensions, behavioral deficits are likely to manifest similarly in both perception and production (and within production for both speaking and writing). Moreover, given these functionally and anatomically integrated networks, we would also expect complex interactions across hierarchically arranged processing functions: A deficit in one process should result in a processing bottleneck, and all language-based operations that rely on this process (and the network that underlies it) will suffer accordingly. For example, the "bottleneck hypothesis" (Perfetti, 1985), in the domain of reading, has received some support: Slow and labor-prone word identification places severe constraints on subsequent sentence processing and comprehension. We might expect to see an analog of this for writing as well (Berninger et al., 2002); if lexical, phonological, spelling, or handwriting-related networks are compromised, expressing ideas in text composition will be impeded.

As we continue to develop a more comprehensive neurobiological account of how multiple language systems are organized, we can hope to understand better why some deficits tend to co-occur (due to shared networks), while others dissociate (due to nonoverlapping networks). Such information can also help us to begin to understand subgroup and/or individual differences in cognitive profiles. Knowing that a given subgroup of children shows anomalous development of certain brain systems may allow us to predict where strengths and weaknesses in developing language skills are likely to emerge, and by extension, which skills ought to be targeted in training. In the following section, we discuss in some detail the ways in which these issues have played out in the more extensive literature on reading and reading disability. Implications for writing research are considered in each section.

Behavioral Characteristics of Reading and Writing Disability

Reading disability is characterized by the failure to develop age-appropriate reading skill despite normal intelligence and adequate opportunity for reading instruction. Significant progress has been made in understanding the cognitive and linguistic skills that must be in place to ensure adequate reading development in children (Brady & Shankweiler, 1991; Bruck, 1992; Fletcher et al., 1994; Liberman, Shankweiler, Fischer, & Carter, 1974; Rieben & Perfetti, 1991; Shankweiler et al., 1995; Stanovich & Siegel, 1994). While it has been argued that the reading difficulties experienced by some children may result from difficulties with processing speed (Wolf, Bowers, & Grieg, 1999), rapid auditory processing (Tallal, 1980), general language deficits (Scarborough & Dobrich, 1990), or visual deficits (Cornelissen & Hansen, 1998), there is growing consensus that a core difficulty in reading manifests itself as a deficiency within the language system and, in particular, a deficiency at the level of phonological analysis (e.g., Fletcher et al., 1994; Shankweiler et al., 1995; Stanovich & Siegel, 1994).

Behaviorally, deficits are most evident at the level of single-word and pseudoword reading; reading disabled (RD) performance is both slow and inaccurate relative to that of nonimpaired (NI) readers. Many lines of evidence converge on the conclusion that the word- and pseudoword-reading difficulties in RD individuals are, to a large extent, man-

ifestations of more basic deficits at the level of rapidly assembling the phonological code represented by a string of letters (Bradley & Bryant, 1983; Liberman, Shankweiler, & Liberman, 1989). In turn, at the earliest stages of literacy training, the failure to develop efficient phonological assembly skills in word and pseudoword reading appears to stem from difficulties in the development of phonological awareness.

"Phonological awareness" is defined as the metalinguistic understanding that spoken words can be decomposed into phonological primitives, which in turn can be represented by alphabetic characters (Brady & Shankweiler, 1991; Bruck, 1992; Fletcher et al., 1994; Liberman et al., 1974; Rieben & Perfetti, 1991; Shankweiler et al., 1995; Stanovich & Siegel, 1994). A large body of evidence directly relates deficits in phonological awareness to difficulties in learning to read: Phonological awareness measures predict later reading achievement (Bradley & Bryant, 1983; Stanovich, Cunningham, & Cramer, 1984; Torgesen, Morgan, & Davis, 1992); deficits in phonological awareness consistently separate RD and NI children (Fletcher et al., 1994; Stanovich & Siegel, 1994); phonological deficits persist into adulthood (Bruck, 1992; Felton, Naylor, & Wood, 1990; Shaywitz et al., 1999); and instruction in phonological awareness promotes the acquisition of reading skills (Ball & Blachman, 1991; Bradley & Bryant, 1983; Foorman, Francis, Fletcher, Schatschneider, & Mehta, 1998; Torgesen et al., 1992; Wise & Olson, 1995). For children with adequate phonological skills, the process of phonological assembly in word and pseudoword reading becomes highly automated and efficient, and, as a growing body of evidence suggests, this phonological decoding continues to serve as an important component in rapid word identification even for mature, skilled readers (Frost, 1998; Lukatela & Turvey, 1994; Van Orden, Pennington, & Stone, 1990).

Given the high incidence of comorbid reading and writing deficits, and given that input and output likely rely on many overlapping brain systems, we might anticipate that for many poor writers, problems at the phonological level of analysis might undermine development of composition skills. There is some evidence that supports this relational conjecture for many children (see Berninger et al., 2002, for a discussion). Clearly though, if for some children writing problems reside in the more abstract domain of planning and message construction, and not in the phonological coding domain, we might anticipate unique writing problems in the absence of classic reading deficits. Implications of this possible subgrouping dimension for neurobiological analyses are considered later. In the next section, we consider the known neurobiological markers of RD children and how these markers might be expected to have parallels in writing (at least for children with cross-domain deficits) as this research line proceeds.

The Cortical Reading Systems and Their Roles in Skilled Reading

Recently, functional neuroimaging techniques have been employed in the area of reading development, reading disability, and intervention (for reviews, see Pugh et al., 2000; Sarkari et al., 2002). Much research has focused on the processing of words in isolation, because this constitutes a particularly acute deficit in RD. Substantial converging evidence indicates that skilled word recognition requires the development of a highly organized cortical system that integrates processing of visualorthographic, phonological, and lexical–semantic features of words. As illustrated in Figure 29.2, this system includes two posterior subsystems in the LH: a ventral (occipitotemporal) and a dorsal (temporoparietal) system, and a third area anterior to the other two (the IFG).

The ventral system includes a left inferior occipitotemporal–fusiform area and extends anteriorly into the middle and inferior temporal gyri. Importantly, the functional specificity of this region appears to be late developing and critically related to the acquisition of reading skills (Booth et al., 2001; Shaywitz et al., 2002). Although some researchers have suggested that the occipitotemporal (OT) regions function as a presemantic visual word form area (VWFA) (Cohen et al., 2002; but see Price et al., 2003, for an alternative account), we refer to this putative VWFA more neutrally as the ventral "skill zone." More anterior foci within the ventral system extending into the middle to inferior temporal gyri appear to be semantically tuned (Fiebach,

Friederici, Mueller, & von Cramon, 2002; Simos et al., 2002; Tagamets, Novick, Chalmers, & Friedman, 2000). It should be noted that there is some disagreement in the literature about the precise localization of critical subregions comprising the ventral system (Price et al., 2003). Nevertheless, recent studies examining both timing and stimulus-type effects suggest that moving anteriorly through this ventral system, subregions respond to word and word-like stimuli in a progressively abstracted and linguistic manner (Tagamets et al., 2000; Tarkiainen, Cornelissen, & Salmelin, 2003).

The more dorsal temporoparietal system broadly includes the angular gyrus and supramarginal gyrus in the inferior parietal lobule, and the posterior aspect of the superior temporal gyrus (Wernicke's area). Among their other functions (e.g., attentionally controlled processing), areas within this system seem to be involved in mapping visual percepts of print onto the phonological and semantic structures of language (Black & Behrmann, 1994). In skilled readers, certain regions within the LH temporoparietal system (particularly the supramarginal gyrus) respond with greater activity to pseudowords than to familiar words (Price, Wise, & Frackowiak, 1996; Simos et al., 2002; Xu et al., 2001), and show sensitivity to phonological priming (Mencl et al., submitted). This finding, along with our developmental studies discussed later (Shaywitz et al., 2002), suggests that the temporoparietal system plays a role in the types of phonological analyses that are relevant to learning new material.

An anterior system centered in posterior aspects of the IFG appears to be associated with phonological recoding during reading, among other functions (e.g., phonological memory, syntactic processing); the more anterior aspects of IFG seem to play a role in semantic retrieval (Poldrack et al., 1999). The phonologically relevant components of this multifunctional system have been found to function in silent reading and in overt naming (see Fiez & Peterson, 1998, for review; Pugh et al., 1997). Like the temporoparietal system, the posterior aspect of IFG is more strongly engaged by pseudowords and low-frequency words (particularly, irregular/exception words whose pronunciations deviate from the pronunciation of the majority of similarly spelled words, e.g., *pint* vs. *mint, hint, lint, print*) than by high-frequency words (Fiebach et al., 2002; Fiez & Petersen, 1998). We have speculated that this anterior system operates in close conjunction with the temporoparietal system to decode new words during normal reading development (Pugh et al., 2000).

This initial, speculative taxonomy of three broad LH systems (dorsal, ventral, and anterior) and their computational processing roles is obviously very coarse-grained and underspecified. Indeed, each of these component systems consists of distinct subregions that most likely engage in different types of processing relevant to orthographic, phonological, and semantic integration. In order to refine our basic theoretical framework, we have recently conducted a series of experiments to obtain a more detailed understanding of the information-processing characteristics of the major LH reading-related regions. These recent word recognition experiments have examined phonological priming (Mencl et al., submitted), phonological–semantic trade-offs (Frost et al., 2005), and critical factors associated with repetition effects and repetition learning in reading (Katz et al., in press; Sandak et al., 2004a). These studies have converged on a set of findings that requires us to refine our initial taxonomy (Sandak et al., 2004b). Across these studies, identical loci in the supramarginal gyrus (within the temporoparietal system), posterior aspects of IFG (within the anterior system), and the OT "skill zone" (within the ventral system) showed (1) increased activation for pseudowords relative to words, (2) strong phonological priming effects, and (3) repetition-related reductions that were most salient in a phonologically analytic training condition during repetition learning (Sandak et al., 2004a). This pattern strongly suggests a phonological "tuning" in these subregions. By contrast, the angular gyrus (within the temporoparietal system) and the middle/inferior temporal gyri (within the ventral system) appear to have more abstract lexicosemantic functions across our recent studies (see Price, More, Humphreys, & Wise, 1997, for similar claims). Thus, we might anticipate that individual differences in core deficits will be associated with variability in the locus of dysfunction across different components of the general reading circuitry. Moreover, if deficits are localized to the subsystems that code orthographic and phonological relations in reading (particularly the temporoparietal and inferior frontal learning subsystems), we might anticipate that these deficits will manifest similarly in both reading and writing behaviors.

With respect to reading development in its early stages, of these three broad systems, reading tasks appear predominately to activate the dorsal and anterior systems in normally developing children during initial reading acquisition, while activation in the ventral system, particularly the posterior "skill zone," increases as children develop greater proficiency in word recognition. We observed that normally developing children younger than 10.5 years of age show strong engagement of dorsal and anterior systems, but limited engagement of the ventral system during reading tasks (Shaywitz et al., 2002). In contrast, children older than 10.5 years of age tend to show increased engagement of the ventral system, which in turn is associated with increasingly skilled reading. Indeed, when we used multiple regression analyses to examine the relation between both age and reading skill (measured by performance on standard reading tests) and activation level in the ventral system, the critical predictor was reading skill: The higher the reading skill level, the stronger the response in the LH ventral cortex (with several other areas showing age- and skill-related reductions). Based on these developmental findings, we have suggested (Pugh et al., 2000) that a beginning reader on a successful trajectory employs a widely distributed cortical system for print processing, including temporoparietal, frontal, and right hemisphere (RH) posterior areas. As reading skill increases, these regions play a somewhat diminished role, while LH ventral sites become more active, and presumably more central to the rapid recognition of printed (word) stimuli (for similar arguments, see Booth et al., 2001; McCandliss, Cohen, & Dehaene, 2003; Tarkiainen et al., 2003; Turkeltaub, Gareau, Flowers, Zeffiro, & Eden, 2003).

It will be quite important to employ developmental imaging designs to examine parallels and differences in neurobiological trajectories for writing behaviors such as spelling and composition. However, given the shared demands on orthographic–phonological relational learning for both reading and writing, we can at minimum predict that typical development will be associated with similar reductions in RH regions as spelling and composition skills develop. Whether a parallel to the reading skill zone in the ventral cortex would have a parallel in writing is uncertain, but again, progressively more localized processing within major LH regions might be a reasonable target state for the neurocircuitry of writing as children develop competence in this domain.

Altered Circuits in Reading Disability

There are clear functional differences between NI and RD readers with regard to activation patterns in dorsal, ventral, and anterior sites during reading tasks. A number of functional imaging studies of RD readers have indicated LH posterior functional dysfunction at both dorsal and ventral sites during phonological processing tasks (Brunswick, McCrory, Price, Frith, & Frith, 1999; Paulesu, et al, 2001; Pugh et al., 2000; Salmelin, Service, Riesila, Uutela, & Salonen, 1996; Shaywitz et al., 1998, 2002; Temple et al., 2001). This disruption is instantiated as a relative underengagement of these regions, specifically when processing linguistic stimuli (words and pseudowords) or during tasks that require explicit decoding. This functional anomaly in posterior LH regions has been observed consistently in children (Shaywitz et al., 2002) and adults (Salmelin et al., 1996; Shaywitz et al., 1998). Hypoactivation in three key dorsal and ventral sites, including the angular gyrus within the temporoparietal region and the ventral occipitotemporal skill zone, is detectable as early as the end of kindergarten in children who have not reached important milestones in learning to read (Simos et al., 2002). Moreover, this ventral disruption has been seen as a critical signature of reading disability across several languages (Paulesu et al., 2001; Salmelin et al., 1996). Given the critical role for the temporoparietal regions in learning to integrate orthography, phonology, and semantics, we might anticipate similar disruptions in writing behavior.

Many neuroimaging studies have attempted to identify specific brain regions where activation patterns differentiate between RD and NI readers (e.g., Rumsey et al., 1997; Shaywitz et al., 1998; Simos et al., 2002; Temple et al., 2001). However, in order to achieve a deeper understanding of the neurobiology of developmental dyslexia, we must also consider relations among brain regions that function cooperatively as circuits, or networks, to process information during reading; this has been referred to as an issue of functional connectivity (Friston, 1994). Evidence consistent with the notion of a breakdown in functional connectivity within the posterior reading system in RD readers has been reported by Horwitz, Rumsey, and Donohue (1998). Using activation data from the Rumsey et al. (1997) PET study, Horwitz et al. (1998) examined relations between activation levels in the LH angular gyrus and other brain sites during two reading-aloud tasks (exception word and pseudoword reading). Activations in the LH angular gyrus and occipital and temporal lobe sites exhibited strong positive correlations in NI readers, such that when activation increased in the angular gyrus, activation also increased in the occipital and temporal sites. In contrast, the correlations between these sites were weak in RD readers. This finding suggests a breakdown in functional connectivity across the major components of the LH posterior reading system.

We also examined whether the angular gyrus and other LH posterior regions were functionally connected in an examination of a large sample of adult RD and NI readers (Pugh et al., 2000). We looked at connectivity between the angular gyrus and occipital and temporal lobe sites on those tasks that systematically varied demands on phonological assembly. LH connectivity was weaker in RD readers during complex phonological tasks (word category judgment and pseudoword rhyming) (see also Horwitz et al., 1998). However, there appeared to be no dysfunction when readers performed a simple phonological judgment (a single-letter rhyme task) or complex visual–orthographic coding (a case judgment task). These results are most consistent with a specific phonological deficit hypothesis: Our data suggest that communication among these areas is disrupted only when orthographic-to-phonological assembly is required. Thus, it is not the case that functional connectivity in this system is disrupted across all types of cognitive behaviors. Moreover, we found that on the word and pseudoword reading tasks, RH counterparts or "homologues" appear to function in a compensatory manner for RD readers; correlations among these regions in the RH were strong and stable for both reading groups, with higher values in RD readers. Functional connectivity analyses can help to reveal "system-level" anomalies in clinical populations; it is critically important to include this type of analysis in neuroimaging studies as we begin to explore writing behavior. Again, a parallel with disrupted connectivity in LH posterior regions during writing and spelling tasks can be reasonably anticipated, especially for those individuals whose writing difficulties appear to reflect general language-processing deficits.

Potentially Compensatory Processing in Reading Disability

Behavioral researchers have identified a number of markers of reading impairment. Poor readers compensate for their inadequate phonological awareness and knowledge of letter–sound correspondences by overrelying on contextual cues to read individual words; their word reading errors tend to be visual or semantic rather than phonetic (see Perfetti, 1985, for a review). These behavioral markers of reading impairment may be instantiated cortically by compensatory activation of frontal and RH regions. As noted earlier, previous research by our group has shown that on tasks that explicitly require pseudoword and word reading, RD readers showed a disproportionately greater engagement of inferior frontal and prefrontal dorsolateral sites than did NI readers (Shaywitz et al., 1998, 2002; for similar findings, see also Brunswick et al., 1999; Salmelin et al., 1996). It is noteworthy that these inferior frontal regions overlap with those areas shown to be involved in syntactic processing (discussed earlier) (Caplan, Alpert, Waters, & Olivieri, 2000; Constable et al., 2004). That poor readers show heightened reliance on these regions for word identification suggests a neuroanatomical locus

for the often-reported bottleneck effect in sentence processing and text comprehension (Perfetti, 1985; Shankweiler et al., 1995).

Evidence of a second, potentially compensatory, shift—in this case, to posterior RH regions—comes from several findings. Additionally, using MEG, Sarkari et al. (2002) found an increase in the apparent engagement of the RH temporoparietal region in RD children. A more detailed examination of this trend, using hemodynamic measures, indicates that hemispheric asymmetries in posterior temporal and temporoparietal activation (particularly the middle temporal and the angular gyri) vary significantly among reading groups (Shaywitz et al., 1998): Greater RH than LH activation was observed in RD readers, but greater LH than RH activation was observed in NI readers. Rumsey et al. (1999), who examined the relationship between RH activation and reading performance in their adult RD and NI participants, found that RH temporoparietal activation was correlated with standard measures of reading performance only for RD readers (see also Shaywitz et al., 2002).

We hypothesize that the reason why RD readers tend strongly to engage inferior frontal sites is their increased reliance on covert pronunciation (articulatory recoding) in an attempt to cope with their deficient phonological analysis of the printed word. In addition, their heightened activation of the posterior RH regions, paired with their reduced activation of the LH homologue, suggests a process of word recognition that relies on letter-by-letter processing in accessing RH localized visuosemantic representations (or some other compensatory process) rather than relying on phonologically structured word recognition strategies. These differential patterns, especially the increased activation in frontal regions, might also reflect increased effort during reading; underengagement of LH posterior areas, particularly ventral sites, would not be thought to reflect this increased effort, but rather the failure to engage these areas likely precipitates any change in effort. Given the neurobiological overlap evident for speech and reading, as well as for perception and production, it would be reasonable to hypothesize similar RH shifts as potential neurobiological markers of writing disability, especially when deficits in phonological and/or lexical processing are evident for both input and output (e.g., spelling).

Neurobiological Effects of Successful Reading Remediation

Converging evidence from several recent studies supports the notion that gains in reading skill resulting from intense reading intervention are associated with a more "normalized" localization of reading processes in the brain. In a recent MEG study, eight young children with severe reading difficulties underwent a brief but intensive phonics-based remediation program (Simos et al., 2002). After intervention, the most salient change observed on a case-by-case basis was a robust increase in the engagement of the LH temporoparietal regions, accompanied by a moderate reduction in the activation of the RH temporoparietal areas. Similarly, Temple et al. (2003) used fMRI to examine the effects of an intervention (FastForword) on the cortical circuitry of a group of 8- to 12-year-old children with reading difficulties. After intervention, increases in activation of LH temporoparietal and inferior frontal sites were observed. Moreover, the LH posterior increases correlated significantly with increased reading scores. Recently, Berninger and her colleagues reported similar LH posterior change following intensive phonological and morphological training (Aylward et al., 2003).

In a recent collaborative study with Benita Blachman of Syracuse University, we conducted a longitudinal study examining three groups of young children (average age was 6.5 years at time 1) with fMRI and behavioral indices (Shaywitz et al., 2004). The three groups consisted of a treatment RD group that received 9 months of intensive, phonics-based intervention (Blachman, Rangel, Ball, Black, & McGraw, 1999) and two control groups: a typically developing group and an RD control group. Relative to RD controls, RD treatment participants showed reliable gains on reading measures (particularly on fluency-related measures; e.g., Gray Oral Reading Test rate scores). When RD groups were compared at time 2 (posttreatment), reliably greater activation increases in LH reading-related sites were seen in the treatment group. Moreover, when pre- and post-treatment activation profiles were directly contrasted for each group, it was evident that both RD treatment and typically developing controls showed reliable increases in LH reading-related sites, while RD controls did not. Prominent differences were seen in the LH IFG, and, importantly, in the LH ventral skill zone. These changes were quite similar to changes observed in the NI controls as they also learned to read, again suggesting that the phonologically analytic intervention led to patterns of activation associated with typically developing readers. Importantly, 1 year after intervention was concluded, the treatment group showed further increases in LH activation, along with further decreases in RH activation.

Thus, initial research on the neurobiological signatures of successful reading remediation are strikingly convergent: increased LH posterior response, with often-reported reductions in RH processing. Focusing on these neurobiological signatures can provide us with highly sensitive markers for those sorts of treatment programs that are likely lead to real and stable cognitive gains. Many important issues remain to be tackled as we continue to explore how treatment modifies brain circuits for reading behavior. For one, studies to date have all contrasted one specific intervention with control conditions. There will always be a subset of children who do not respond to a given intervention; presumably at least some of these children might have a different pattern of deficits than the majority of children who do respond well. It will be desirable to begin to contrast multiple approaches to intervention (within a single study) in RD cohorts who all struggle with language but may differ in the locus of the deficit. This type of study will enable us to begin to explore the issue of whether different types of interventions work better for subgroups of children with distinct neurobiological and behavioral profiles (prior to treatment).

Indeed, the interventions employed in the extant studies have all focused on phonological training to varying degrees. While a majority of children with reading difficulties do struggle at the level of phonological and lexical processing, there may be subgroups of children whose deficits lie in other domains, and for whom alternative approaches may work better. Neuroimaging techniques might give us a particularly sensitive measure to help in identifying coherent RD subgroups, and to determine which type of approach works best for a given subgroup. By examining reading and writing interventions in parallel and in contrast, we can begin to discriminate language-general from writing-specific effects of training. At present the evidence at least encourages us that the cortical circuitry in struggling readers is directly affected by targeted and intensive treatment. This suggests a high degree of plasticity in this population.

Implications for Writing Disability and Intervention

Neuroimaging studies conducted to date have identified both an altered neurocircuitry for reading in RD subjects and a critical neurobiological signature of successful intervention (at least in younger children, most of whom have deficits for phonological and lexical-level processing). This signature appears to be increased engagement of major LH reading-related circuits and reduced compensatory reliance on RH homologues. As noted, this sets up certain plausible expectations for emerging research on writing behavior, its deficits, and effects of specific, targeted interventions.

There is good evidence, at the neurobiological level of analysis, of highly overlapping circuits for core language functions (beyond the specific modality of perception or production), and there is also good evidence, at the behavioral level of analysis, of a high incidence of comorbidity between disorders of reading and writing. For children with both reading and writing deficits, the failure to develop a coherent LH circuitry for reading would lead us to expect parallel neurobiological signatures in writing. A bottleneck associated with the failure to develop fluent lexical access and spelling, for instance, might be associated with increased reliance on RH systems for phonological processing support in both reading and writing. With respect to writing intervention, successful training, focusing on these lexical and phonological skills, would be expected to allow expression of ideas from more abstract conceptual systems to flow through the LH language systems with less RH involvement (thus, a similar signature of successful intervention as in reading for children with general phonological bottleneck difficulties).

Importantly, individual or subgroup differences in the locus of core deficits would complicate this sort of expectation when we are examining writing behavior. For example, if for some children, phonological and general language processing skills are intact and fluent, and if problems instead reside in the more abstract planning and message-generation components of written composition (and possibly in comprehension during reading), expectations are more complicated. We might not observe the RH shift in language-processing regions, and might instead anticipate anomalies in function at those prefrontal regions that have been previously associated with more abstract conceptual processing dimensions (Shaywitz et al., 2001). Of course, we should also anticipate that for such individuals, difficulties will also manifest in any production-related task, whether spoken or written. If these individuals have no demonstrable challenges in the phonological domain, guidance from those reading remediation studies conducted to date might be lacking. Thus, neurobiological signatures of successful remediation are difficult to anticipate in this hypothetical situation; indeed, we will need to acquire a good deal of preliminary data on preintervention differences for those children with good phonological but poor metacognitive skills. One might speculate at the outset, though, that if deficits reside in the metacognitive domain, successful remediation at this level of analysis might not have a straightforward neurobiological signature with respect to hemispheric asymmetries for phonological processing; perhaps changes in prefrontal control-processing regions might be evident as planning and message-generation processes improve. In considering this contrast between subtypes of writing disorders with respect to the locus of the core deficit (e.g., phonological vs. metacognitive), it becomes clear that much needs to be done relative to generating normative data on reading and writing in relation to one another. With such data in hand, however, neuroimaging might begin to serve as a useful tool in making sense of why some approaches work better than others for a given set of deficits.

Task Design in Functional Neuroimaging of Writing Behavior

While it is reasonable to expect many parallels between reading and writing with respect to neurobiological markers of disability (and possibly for those changes associated with improvement through training), this expectation has yet to be put to the test. However, at present, there is evidence that standard imaging techniques and paradigms are able to demarcate the subsystems associated with writing-related behaviors such as handwriting (Katanoda et al., 2001; Menon & Desmond, 2001), and to distinguish these systems from shared language-processing systems. Much basic taxonomic research is therefore needed before clinical issues can be assessed in this domain with neuroimaging. To begin to examine the parallels between reading and writing, it will be necessary at first to conduct comprehensive neuroimaging experiments of skilled readers–writers that (1) compare activation patterns for both reading and writing (as well as speaking and listening) within a single experiment and subject, and (2) systematically vary demands on component processes (e.g., sublexical, lexical, syntactic, pragmatic tasks for both reading and writing). As noted, it is possible to make cross-modality comparisons of more abstract language-processing domains with neuroimaging design when subtractions and controls are employed to factor out gross motor and sensory differences (Constable et al., 2004). As such designs are worked out (and the extant literature already contains good examples applied to one or another domain that explicate component processes), it will then be important to contrast groups with (1) no deficits in either reading or writing, (2) deficits for both, and (3) deficits for one or the other, but not both. We must then move to subgroup comparisons by identifying subgroups whose behavioral profiles suggest different loci of deficits in reading and/or writing (with all possible subgroups compared). Such studies will provide a comprehensive foundation and go a long way toward providing coherent expectations about the neurobiological changes to be anticipated as large-scale training and intervention studies begin. Again, the lessons learned from reading suggest that neuroimaging techniques are very sensitive to detecting neurobiological changes that underlie performance improvement. We have no reason to expect a different state of affairs as we move to the production domain.

Neuroimaging may be of real utility, because it can help us compare connections from the process under investigation to others not expected through shared neural networks. Essentially, links among diverse types of difficulties might emerge as these neurobiological links are revealed; the hope for both broader and deeper theories of childhood disorders is reinforced by the emerging cognitive neuroscience approaches.

Acknowledgments

Work on this project was supported by several grants from the National Institute of Child Health and Human Development, including No. R01-HD40411 to Kenneth R. Pugh, No. P01-HD01994 to Haskins Laboratories, and No. F32-HD42391 to Rebecca Sandak. We thank Priya Pugh for her help with the manuscript.

References

Aylward, E. H., Richards, T. L., Berninger, V. W., Nagy, W. E., Field, K. M., Grimme, A. C., et al. (2003). Instructional treatment associated with changes in brain activation in children with dyslexia. *Neurology, 61,* 212-219.

Ball, E. W., & Blachman, B. A. (1991). Does phoneme awareness training in kindergarten make a difference in early word recognition and developmental spelling? *Reading Research Quarterly, 26,* 49–66.

Berninger, V. W., Abbott, R. D., Abbott, S. P., Graham, S., & Richards, T. (2002). Writing and reading: Connections between language by hand and language by eye. *Journal of Learning Disabilities, 35,* 39–56.

Blachman, B. A., Tangel, D. M., Ball, E. W., Black, R., & McGraw, C. K. (1999). Developing phonological awareness and word recognition skills: A two-year intervention with low-income, inner-city children. *Reading and Writing, 11,* 239–273.

Black, S. E., & Behrmann, M. (1994). Localization in alexia. In A. Kertesz (Ed.), *Localization and neuroimaging in neuropsychology* (pp. 331–376). New York: Academic Press.

Booth, J. R., Burman, D. D., Van Santen, F. W., Harosaki, Y., Gitelman, D. R., Parish, T. B., et al. (2001). The development of specialized brain systems in reading and oral-language. *Child Neuropsychology, 7,* 119–141.

Bradley, L., & Bryant, P. E. (1983). Categorising

sounds and learning to read—a causal connection. *Nature, 301,* 419–521.

Brady, S., & Shankweiler, D. (Eds.). (1991). *Phonological processes in literacy: A tribute to Isabelle Y. Liberman.* Hillsdale, NJ: Erlbaum.

Bruck, M. (1992). Persistence of dyslexics' phonological deficits. *Developmental Psychology, 28,* 874–886.

Brunswick, N., McCrory, E., Price C., Frith, C. D., & Frith, U. (1999). Explicit and implicit processing of words and pseudowords by adult developmental dyslexics: A search for Wernicke's *Wortschatz. Brain, 122,* 1901–1917.

Caplan, D, Alpert, N., Waters, G., & Olivieri, A. (2000). Activation of Broca's area by syntactic processing under conditions of concurrent articulation. *Human Brain Mapping, 9,* 65–71.

Carpentier, A. C., Pugh, K. R., Westerveld, M., Studholme, C., Skrinjar, O., Thompson, J. L., et al. (2001). Functional MRI of language processing: Dependence on input modality and temporal lobe epilepsy. *Epilepsia, 42,* 1241–1254.

Chee, M. W. L., O'Craven, K. M., Bergida, R., Rosen, B. R., & Savoy, R. L. (1999) Auditory and visual word processing studied with fMRI. *Human Brain Mapping, 7,* 15–28.

Cohen, L., Lehericy, S., Chochon, F., Lemer, C., Rivaud, S., & Dehaene, S. (2002). Language-specific tuning of visual cortex: Functional properties of the visual word form area. *Brain, 125,* 1054–1069.

Constable, R. T., Pugh, K. R., Berroya, E., Mencl, W. E., Westerveld, M., Ni, W., et al. (2004). Sentence complexity and input modality effects in sentence comprehension: An fMRI Study. *NeuroImage, 22,* 11–21.

Cornelissen, P. L., & Hansen, P. C. (1998). Motion detection, letter position encoding, and single word reading. *Annals of Dyslexia, 48,* 155–188.

Croisile, B., Brabant, M. J., Carmoi, T., Lepage, Y., Aimard, G., & Trillet, M. (1996). Comparison between oral and written spelling in Alzheimer's disease. *Brain and Language, 54,* 361–387.

Del Grosso Destreri, N., Farina, E., Alberoni, M., Pomati, S., Nichelli, P., & Mariani, C. (2000). Selective uppercase dysgraphia with loss of visual imagery of letter forms: A window on the organization of graphomotor patterns. *Brain and Language, 71,* 353–372.

Felton, R. H., Naylor, C. E., & Wood, F. B. (1990). Neuropsychological profile of adult dyslexics. *Brain and Language, 39,* 485–497.

Fiebach, C. J., Friederici, A. D., Mueller, K., & von Cramon, D. Y. (2002). fMRI evidence for dual routes to the mental lexicon in visual word recognition. *Journal of Cognitive Neuroscience, 14,* 11–23.

Fiez, J. A., & Petersen, S. E. (1998). Neuroimaging studies of word reading. *Proceedings of the National Academy of Sciences, 95,* 914–921.

Fletcher, J. M., Shaywitz, S. E., Shankweiler, D. P., Katz, L., Liberman, I. Y., Stuebing, K. K., et al. (1994). Cognitive profiles of reading disability: Comparisons of discrepancy and low achievement definitions. *Journal of Educational Psychology, 86,* 6–23.

Foorman, B. R., Francis, D., Fletcher, J. K., Schatschneider, C., & Mehta, P. (1998). The role of instruction in learning to reading: Preventing reading failure in at-risk children. *Journal of Educational Psychology, 90,* 37–55.

Frackowiak R. J., Friston K. K., Frith C. D., Dolan, R. J., & Mazziotta, J. C. (1997). *Human brain function.* New York: Academic Press.

Friedman, R. (1989). Written spelling agraphia. *Brain and Language, 36,* 503–517.

Friston, K. (1994). Functional and effective connectivity: A synthesis. *Human Brain Mapping, 2,* 56–78.

Frost, R. (1998). Toward a strong phonological theory of visual word recognition: True issues and false trails. *Psychological Bulletin, 123,* 71–99.

Frost, S. J., Mencl, W. E., Sandak, R., Moore, D. L., Rueckl, J. G., Katz, L., et al. (2005). An fMRI study of the trade-off between semantics and phonology in reading aloud. *NeuroReport, 16,* 621–624.

Hodges, J., & Marshall, J. (1992). Discrepant oral and written spelling after left hemisphere tumour. *Cortex, 28,* 643–656.

Horwitz, B., Rumsey, J. M., & Donohue, B. C. (1998). Functional connectivity of the angular gyrus in normal reading and dyslexia. *Proceedings of the National Academy of Sciences, 95,* 8939–8944.

Howard, D., Patterson, K., Wise, R. J., Brown, W. D., Friston, K., Weiller, C., et al. (1992). The cortical localization of the lexicons: Positron emission tomography evidence. *Brain, 115,* 1769–1782.

Indefrey, P., & Levelt, W. J. M. (2004). The spatial and temporal signatures of word production components. *Cognition, 92,* 101–144.

Katanoda, K., Yoshikawa, K., & Sugishita, M. (2001). A functional MRI study on the neural substrates for writing. *Human Brain Mapping, 13,* 34–42.

Katz, L., Lee, C. H., Tabor, W., Frost, S. J., Mencl, W. E., Sandak, R., et al. (in press). Behavioral and neurobiological effects of printed word repetition in lexical decision and naming. *Neuropsychologia.*

Klingberg, T., Hedehus, M., Temple, E., Salz, T., Gabrieli, J. D., Moseley, M. E., et al. (2000). Microstructure of temporo-parietal white matter as a basis for reading ability: Evidence from diffusion tensor magnetic resonance imaging. *Neuron, 25,* 493–500.

Levelt, W. J. M., Roelefs, A., & Meyer, A. S. (1999). A theory of lexical access in speech production. *Behavioral and Brain Sciences, 22,* 1–38.

Liberman, A. M. (1992). The relation of speech to reading and writing. In R. Frost & L. Katz (Eds.), *Orthography, phonology, morphology, and meaning* (pp. 167–178). Amsterdam: Elsevier.

Liberman, A. M., & Mattingly, I. G. (1985). The motor theory of speech perception revised. *Cognition, 21,* 1–36.

Liberman, I. Y., Shankweiler, D., Fischer, F. W., & Carter, B. (1974). Explicit syllable and phoneme segmentation in the young child. *Journal of Experimental Child Psychology, 18,* 201–212.

Liberman, I. Y., Shankweiler, D., & Liberman, A. M. (1989). The alphabetic principle and learning to read. In D. Shankweiler & I. Y. Liberman (Eds.), *Phonology and reading disability: Solving the reading puzzle* (International Academy for Research in Learning Disabilities Monograph Series, No. 6 (pp. 1–33). Ann Arbor: University of Michigan Press.

Lukatela, G., & Turvey, M. T. (1994). Visual lexical access is initially phonological: 1. Evidence from associative priming by words, homophones, and pseudohomophones. *Journal of Experimental Psychology: General, 123,* 107–128.

McCandliss, B. D., Cohen, L., & Dehaene, S. (2003). The visual word form area: Expertise for reading in the fusiform gyrus. *Trends in Cognitive Sciences, 7,* 293–299.

Mencl, W. E., Frost, S. J., Sandak, R., Lee, J. R., Jenner, A. R., Mason, S., et al. (Manuscript submitted for publication). *Effects of orthographic and phonological priming in printed word identification: An fMRI study.*

Menon, V., & Desmond, J. E. (2001). Left superior parietal cortex involvement in writing: Integrating fMRI with lesion evidence. *Cognitive Brain Research, 12,* 337–340.

Michael, E. B., Keller, T. A., Carpenter, P. A., & Just, M. A. (2001). fMRI investigation of sentence comprehension by eye and ear: Modality fingerprints on cognitive processes. *Human Brain Mapping, 13,* 239–252.

Miozzo, M., & De Bastiani, P. (2002). The organization of letter-form representations in written spelling: Evidence from acquired dysgraphia. *Brain and Language, 80,* 366–392.

Papanicolaou, A. C., Pugh, K. R., Simos, P. G., & Mencl, W. E. (2004). Functional brain imaging: An introduction to concepts and applications. In P. McCardle & V. Chhabra (Eds.), *The voice of evidence in reading research* (pp. 385–416). Baltimore: Brookes.

Paulesu, E., Demonet, J.-F., Fazio, F., McCrory, E., Chanoine, V., Brunswick, N., et al. (2001). Dyslexia: Cultural diversity and biological unity. *Science, 291,* 2165–2167.

Perfetti, C. A. (1985). *Reading ability.* New York: Oxford University Press.

Poldrack, R. A., Wagner, A. D., Prull, M. W., Desmond, J. E., Glover, G. H., & Gabrieli, J. D. (1999). Functional specialization for semantic and phonological processing in the left inferior prefrontal cortex. *NeuroImage, 10,* 15–35.

Price, C. J., More, C. J., Humphreys, G. W., & Wise, R. J. S. (1997). Segregating semantic from phonological processes during reading. *Journal of Cognitive Neuroscience, 9,* 727–733.

Price, C. J., Winterburn, D., Giraud, A. L., Moore, C. J., & Noppeney, U. (2003). Cortical localization of the visual and auditory word form areas: A reconsideration of the evidence. *Brain and Language, 86,* 272–286.

Price, C. J., Wise, R. J. S., & Frackowiak, R. S. J. (1996). Demonstrating the implicit processing of visually presented words and pseudowords. *Cerebral Cortex, 6,* 62–70.

Pugh, K. R., Mencl, W. E., Jenner, A. R., Katz, L., Frost, S. J., Lee, J. R., et al. (2000). Functional neuroimaging studies of reading and reading disability (developmental dyslexia). *Mental Retardation and Developmental Disabilities Research Reviews, 6,* 207–213.

Pugh, K. R., Shaywitz, B. A., Shaywitz, S. A., Shankweiler, D. P., Katz, L., Fletcher, J. M., et al. (1997). Predicting reading performance from neuroimaging profiles: The cerebral basis of phonological effects in printed word identification. *Journal of Experimental Psychology: Human Perception and Performance, 2,* 1–20.

Rieben, L., & Perfetti, C. A. (1991). *Learning to read: Basic research and its implications.* Hillsdale, NJ: Erlbaum.

Rumsey, J. M., Horwitz, B., Donohue, B. C., Nace, K. L., Maisog, J. M., & Andreason, P. A. (1999). Functional lesion in developmental dyslexia: Left angular gyral blood flow predicts severity. *Brain and Language, 70,* 187–204.

Rumsey, J. M., Nace, K., Donohue, B., Wise, D., Maisog, J. M., & Andreason, P. (1997). A positron emission tomographic study of impaired word recognition and phonological processing in dyslexic men. *Archives of Neurology, 54,* 562–573.

Salmelin, R., Service, E., Kiesila, P., Uutela, K., & Salonen, O. (1996). Impaired visual word processing in dyslexia revealed with magnetoencephalography. *Annals of Neurology, 40,* 157–162.

Sandak, R., Mencl, W. E., Frost, S. J., Mason, S. A., Rueckl, J. G., Katz, L., et al. (2004a). The neurobiology of adaptive learning in reading: A contrast of different training conditions. *Cognitive, Affective, and Behavioral Neuroscience, 4,* 67–88.

Sandak, R., Mencl, W. E., Frost, S. J., Mason, S. A., & Pugh, K. R. (2004b). The neurobiological basis of skilled and impaired reading: Recent findings and new directions. In R. Sandak & R. A. Poldrack (Eds.), *Scientific Studies of Reading: Special Issues on the Cognitive Neuroscience of Reading, 8,* 273–292.

Sarkari, S., Simos, P. G., Fletcher, J. M., Castillo, E. M., Breier, J. I., & Papanicolaou, A. C. (2002). The emergence and treatment of developmental reading disability: Contributions of functional brain imaging. *Seminars in Pediatric Neurology, 9*, 227–236.

Scarborough, H., & Dobrich, W. (1990). Development of children with early language delay. *Journal of Speech and Hearing Research, 33*, 70–83.

Shankweiler, D., Crain, S., Katz, L., Fowler, A. E., Liberman, A. M., Brady, S. A., et al. (1995). Cognitive profiles of reading-disabled children: Comparison of language skills in phonology, morphology and syntax. *Psychological Science, 6*, 149–156.

Shaywitz, B. A., Shaywitz, S. E., Pugh, K. R., Fulbright, R. K., Skudlarski, P., Mencl, W. E., et al. (2001). The functional neural architecture of components of attention in language processing tasks. *NeuroImage, 13*, 601–612.

Shaywitz, B. A, Shaywitz, S. E., Blachman, B., Pugh, K. R., Fulbright, R. K., Skudlarski, P., et al. (2004). Development of left occipito-temporal systems for skilled reading following a phonologically-based intervention in children. *Biological Psychiatry, 55*(9), 926–933.

Shaywitz, B. A., Shaywitz, S. E., Pugh, K. R., Mencl, W. E., Fulbright, R. K., Skudlarski, P., et al. (2002). Disruption of posterior brain systems for reading in children with developmental dyslexia. *Biological Psychiatry, 52*, 101–110.

Shaywitz, S. E., Fletcher, J. M., Holahan, J. M., Shneider, A. E., Marchione, K. E., Stuebing, K. K., et al. (1999). Persistence of dyslexia: The Connecticut Longitudinal Study at adolescence. *Pediatrics, 104*, 1351–1359.

Shaywitz, S. E., Shaywitz, B. A., Pugh, K. R., Fulbright, R. K., Constable, R. T., Mencl, W. E., et al. (1998). Functional disruption in the organization of the brain for reading in dyslexia. *Proceedings of the National Academy of Sciences, 95*, 2636–2641.

Simos, P. G., Fletcher, J. M., Bergman, E., Breier, J. I., Foorman, B. R., Castillo, E. M., et al. (2002). Dyslexia-specific brain activation profile becomes normal following successful remedial training. *Neurology, 58*, 1203–1213.

Simos, P. G., Papanicolaou, A. C., & Breier, J. I. (1999). Localization of language-specific cortex using MEG and intraoperative stimulation mapping. *Journal of Neurosurgery, 91*, 787–796.

Stanovich, K. E., Cunningham, A. E., & Cramer, B. B. (1984). Assessing phonological awareness in kindergarten children: Issues of task comparability. *Journal of Experimental Child Psychology, 38*, 175–190.

Stanovich, K. E., & Siegel, L. S. (1994). Phenotypic performance profile of children with reading disabilities: A regression-based test of the phonological-core variable-difference model. *Journal of Educational Psychology, 86*, 24–53.

Tagamets, M. A., Novick, J. M., Chalmers, M. L., & Friedman, R. B. (2000). A parametric approach of orthographic processing in the brain: An fMRI study. *Journal of Cognitive Neuroscience, 1*, 281–297.

Tallal, P. (1980). Auditory temporal perception, phonics, and reading disabilities in children. *Brain and Language, 9*, 182–198.

Tarkiainen, A., Cornelissen, P. L., & Salmelin, R. (2003). Dynamics of visual feature analysis and object-level processing in face versus letter-string perception. *Brain, 125*, 1125–1136.

Temple, E., Deutsch, G. K., Poldrack, R. A., Miller, S. L., Tallal, P., Merzenich, M. M., et al. (2003). Neural deficits in children with dyslexia ameliorated by behavioral remediation: Evidence from functional MRI. *Proceedings of the National Academy of Sciences, 100*, 2860–2865.

Temple, E., Poldrack, R. A., Salidis, J., Deutsch, G. K., Tallal, P., Merzenich, M. M., et al. (2001). Disrupted neural responses to phonological and orthographic processing in dyslexic children: an fMRI study. *Neuroreport, 12*, 299–307.

Torgesen, J. K., Morgan, S. T., & Davis, C. (1992). Effects of two types of phonological awareness training on word learning in kindergarten children. *Journal of Educational Psychology, 84*, 364–370.

Turkeltaub, P. E., Gareau, L., Flowers, D. L., Zeffiro, T. A., & Eden, G. F. (2003). Development of neural mechanisms for reading. *Nature Neuroscience, 6*, 767–773.

Van Orden, G. C., Pennington, B. F., & Stone, G. O. (1990). Word identification in reading and the promise of subsymbolic psycholinguistics. *Psychological Review, 97*, 488–522.

Wise, B. W., & Olson, R. K. (1995). Computer-based phonological awareness and reading instruction. *Annals of Dyslexia, 45*, 99–122.

Wolf, M., & Bowers, P. G. (1999). The double-deficit hypothesis for the developmental dyslexias. *Journal of Educational Psychology, 91*, 415–438.

Xu, B., Grafman, J., Gaillard, W. D., Ishii, K., Vega-Bermudez, F., Pietrini, P., et al. (2001). Conjoint and extended neural networks for the computation of speech codes: The neural basis of selective impairment in reading words and pseudowords. *Cerebral Cortex, 11*, 267–277.

Author Index

Subject Index